Whitfield's University
RHYMING
DICTIONARY

Whitfield's University
RHYMING
DICTIONARY

---

by Jane Shaw Whitfield

Edited by Frances Stillman

Thomas Y. Crowell, Publishers
Established 1834
New York

Originally published under the title
The Improved Rhyming Dictionary

APOLLO EDITION 1964

Typography by George Nehrbas

Manufactured in the United States of America
ISBN 0-8152-0080-3

80 81 82 15 14 13 12 11

Preface

RHYME is "the correspondence, in two or more words or verses, of terminal sounds beginning with an accented vowel, which, in modern English usage, must be preceded by different consonant sounds, or by a consonant in one case and none in the other." A rhyme is one of two or more words which correspond as described, and a list of rhymes is a group of such words. A rhyming dictionary, therefore, is a compendium of complete lists of rhymes, as exhaustive as it is possible to make it.

This rhyming dictionary is organized on the modern principle of giving the lists of rhymes according to the key vowel sound, and progresses from A– (ay, bay, etc.) through UZ'i-ness– (fuzziness, etc.).

The vowel sounds *A, E, I, O,* and *U* and their variations (see table of contents) are taken up in turn. Under each, the lists of rhymes are given in three sections: single or masculine rhymes, double or feminine rhymes, and triple rhymes. In each section, one proceeds in an orderly, alphabetical fashion, as, for example, from AB– (Abe, babe, etc.) through AZ– (daze, etc.), AB'i– (Abie, baby, etc.) through AZ'ing– (hazing, etc.). Due to phonetic considerations, the letter *c* is always alphabetized under *k* or *s*, its two possible sounds. The *ch* sound still stands third in alphabetical order.

In each entry, the list of rhymes is given according to number of syllables, for easier reference. One-syllable words come first, of course, then two, and so on, with each group being preceded by a figure showing the number of syllables. This will facilitate finding the right rhyme when, for .example, the poet has only one accented syllable left to fill in to complete his line. Time will be saved and the rhyme more quickly found.

When the rhyme sound is preceded by one or more syllables, in longer words, the rhymes are arranged according to the consonant directly preceding the rhyme sound —or, in other words, alphabetized backwards. This is useful because multiple rhymes thus are listed together.

In modern poetry, very frequently a kind of offbeat rhyming is used to good effect, and it is for that reason that we have included many so-called "imperfect" rhymes. These are considered to be, for the purposes of this book, words which contain the rhyme sound, but in which the sound is not accented. Such imperfect rhymes are printed in italics. Another device of modern poetry is the use of consonance, as, for example, *late, let, light, lot, lute.* Such examples of consonance may be easily found simply by looking up the corresponding section under each vowel sound.

For the sake of writers of humorous and light verse, very numerous slang and colloquial expressions have been included for the first time in such a reference book. The inclusions of foreign-language expressions commonly used in English are unusually rich, and it is hoped that they may prove useful alike to poet and verse-writer.

▼

Preface

The thesaurus-like arrangement of this dictionary makes it easier and quicker to use than the more old-fashioned, vertical-list kind of arrangement. Another advantage of this arrangement is its compactness, which makes the book far more portable than rhyming dictionaries containing much less material. Indeed, this is the most complete and inclusive, as well as the most usable, of modern rhyming dictionaries.

A Brief Guide to English Versification

IT IS easy to say what verse is: it is a written composition which uses a metrical pattern and frequently also the device of rhyme to heighten its effectiveness.

It is hard to say what poetry is. Real poetry, like beauty itself, is somehow beyond definition. Great poets have written it, but have not been able to define it.

This brief chapter on versification is about the tools of both poetry and verse—meter and rhyme.

Meter is the basic pattern of rhythm which is repeated throughout a verse. It is like the time, or repeated beat, of music.

Rhyme is the chiming of identical terminal sounds of words. It may occur regularly at the ends of lines, and within lines as well, as in many of the poems of Edgar Allan Poe. In English, rhyme is based on an accented vowel sound. This rhyme sound usually consists of accented vowel plus final consonant, and in that case is called a masculine, or one-syllable, rhyme. It may be composed of accented vowel (with or without consonant) followed by one or two unaccented syllables. A two-syllable rhyme is called a feminine rhyme, while a three-syllable rhyme has no special name.

In rhyming, there are only two rules. The rhyme sounds must be identical. And each rhyme used must vary from all the others in the consonant-sound which precedes the rhyme. Thus, va*cation* and obl*ation* are acceptable rhymes, while va*cation* and extri*cation* are not, being mere repetitions of -*cation*, instead of rhymes on -*ation*.

One out of every two or three syllables is ordinarily accented in English. In prose, the accent is allowed to fall at random, but in verse the writer arranges his language so that the accent comes at regular intervals, and the thought breaks naturally into regular lines.

As far back as we know, rhythm has been employed to make things catchy and easy to remember. Rhyme seems to have come into use a little later, but served the same purpose. The early sagas and tales of the minstrels were carried by word of mouth, and employed these devices. In the history of the world's literature, poetry came long before prose.

There are four kinds of meter in English. These are used straight, or mixed, as the occasion and the verse demands.

One unit of meter is called a foot, or a metric foot.

ENGLISH METERS

1. Iambic meter, composed of units of two syllables with the accent on the second.
    One imabic foot is called an iamb. (Pronounced eye-am′-bik, eye′-amb)
    Example: "The sea | is calm | tonight. |
                The tide | is full, | the moon | lies fair | "—Matthew Arnold
2. Trochaic meter, composed of units of two syllables with the accent on the first.
    One trochaic foot is called a trochee. (Pronounced tro-kay′-ik, tro′-kee)

Example: "On the | shores of | Gitche | Gumee |
            Of the | shining | Big Sea | Water, | "—Longfellow
3. Anapestic meter, composed of units of three syllables with the accent on the third.
    One anapestic foot is called an anapest. (Pronounced an-a-pest′-ik, an′-a-pest)
    Example: "The Assyr|ian came down | like the wolf | on the fold | "—Byron
4. Dactyllic meter, composed of units of three syllables with the accent on the first.
    One dactyllic foot is called a dactyl. (Pronounced dak-till′-ik, dak′-till)
    Example: "This is the | forest prim|eval. The | murmuring | pines and the |
              hemlocks
              Bearded with | moss and in | garments of | green, indis|tinct in the |
              twilight"—Longfellow

A convenient way to remember the kinds of meter is to memorize a little rhyme, such as:

> The iamb saunters through my book,
>   Trochees rush and tumble;
> While the anapest runs like a hurrying brook,
>   Dactyls are stately and classical.

In addition, one more kind of meter must be noted—Spondaic meter, composed of units of two syllables, both being accented. One spondaic foot is called a spondee. (Pronounced spon-day′-ik, spon′-dee)

Example: "Stop′ thief′ | "

Spondaic meter is not, properly speaking, an English meter at all, as it is impossible in English to sustain for long a meter in which every syllable is accented. However, it may occasionally be substituted for a foot in some other meter, when the effect would be heightened by it.

Scansion or scanning of verse is the analysis of its meter, and is accomplished by marking each syllable according to whether it is accented or not. Then a mark is placed between each metric foot, and it may be determined what meter predominates. When a line is out of time with the rest, it is frequently said that "it does not scan."

In addition to the kind of meter of a poem, such as iambic, it is further described according to the number of metric feet (or accents) in each line. For example, a sonnet is written in iambic pentameter, which means in five-foot iambic lines. The kinds of lines are as follows:

one-foot	monometer (mo-nah′-meh-ter)
two-foot	dimeter (di′-meh-ter)
three-foot	trimeter (tri′-meh-ter)
four-foot	tetrameter (teh-tra′-meh-ter)
five-foot	pentameter (pen-ta′-meh-ter)
six-foot	hexameter (hex-a′-meh-ter)
seven-foot	heptameter (hep-ta′-meh-ter)
eight-foot	octometer (oct-ah′-meh-ter)

Iambic pentameter is said to be the most natural English line, and it is used in most long narrative, epic, or dramatic poems in English.

Hexameters are the lines of classical poetry in Greek and Latin, as well as French and certain other modern languages. In English, the hexameter is often called an Alexandrine, and is sometimes used to give greater weight to a poem which is mainly in pentameters. Alexandrines occur regularly in certain stanza forms, such as the Spenserian stanza.

The length of the line, in verse, generally follows a pattern. Either all are the same, or else the varying lengths recur in a regular fashion. Beginning verse-writers would do well to check their poems from this point of view. For example, if a poem is written in four-line stanzas, with lines alternating between three and four feet, it is not a good idea suddenly to insert a line of five feet somewhere, nor should one substitute a four-foot line for a three-foot line in the pattern.

THE STANZA

A stanza is a division within a poem, and is composed of a group of lines, sometimes only one line; it is set off by space between it and the next stanza.

A poem may be written in set stanzas that follow a regular pattern, or the poet may divide his stanzas according to the thought content, in which case the stanza division is entirely analogous to pargaraphing in prose. These two different ways of handling the stanza may be called formal stanzas and free stanzas.

Stanzas are named according to the number of lines they contain.

couplet	two lines
triplet or tercet	three lines
quatrain	four lines
cinquain	five lines
sestet	six lines
septet	seven lines
octave	eight lines

Beyond these, one refers simply to a nine-line stanza, and so on. The length of the lines in a stanza, and the ryhme scheme, if any, are a matter of choice for the poet. Infinite variety is possible, but there are a number of fixed stanza forms which have qualities of charm and malleability, which the beginning poet would do well to practice.

The quatrain is probably the most widely used stanza form, and may be rhymed in a number of ways. The loose ballad quatrain, with the first and third lines, and second and fourth lines rhyming, or with only the second and fourth lines rhymed, is a universal favorite. The lines may be of any length, but alternating four- and three-foot lines are perhaps the most used.

To indicate a rhyme scheme, one marks the first rhyme with the letter *a*, the second *b*, and so on. For example:

> I never saw a purple cow,   (*a*)
> I never hope to see one,   (*b*)
> But I can tell you, anyhow,   (*a*)
> I'd rather see than be one.   (*b*)
> —Gelett Burgess

Thus, the rhyme scheme of the above quatrain is *a-b-a-b*.

A combination of triplets which can be very effective is called terza rima; it was originally an Italian form. This is composed of three-line stanzas with interlocking rhyme, ending with a couplet. It goes *a-b-a, b-c-b, c-d-c, d-d*—or it may go on much longer before the concluding couplet. Shelley's "Ode to the West Wind" is written in this form.

Another famous Italian stanza is the ottava rima. It contains eight lines and three rhymes, as, follows: *a-b-a-b-a-b-c-c*.

The Spenserian stanza contains nine lines, the first eight in iambic pentameter and the last line an Alexandrine. The rhyme scheme is an interlocking one, and goes: *a-b-a-b-b-c-b-c-c*.

POEMS IN FIXED FORMS

The Sonnet

The sonnet is the best-known and most widely practiced of all the fixed forms of poetry. It consists of fourteen lines in iambic pentameter, and has one of several rhyme schemes and thought divisions.

The Italian, or Petrarchan, sonnet, so called because it was first used by Petrarch, is the oldest of the sonnet forms. It is composed of an octave and a sestet, and it may be said in general that the octave states the case, while the sestet resolves it or in some way presents the main point which the poet has in mind. The rhyme scheme of this kind of sonnet is: *a-b-b-a, a-b-b-a, c-d-e, c-d-e*. Edna St. Vincent Millay wrote many beautiful sonnets in this form. Throughout English and American literature one finds it used, although the Shakespearean sonnet has been on the whole more popular. Here is a good example:

MILTON

> I pace the sounding sea-beach and behold   (*a*)
> How the voluminous billows roll and run,   (*b*)
> Upheaving and subsiding, while the sun   (*b*)
> Shines through their sheeted emerald far unrolled   (*a*)
> And the ninth wave, slow gathering fold by fold   (*a*)
> All its loose-flowing garments into one,   (*b*)
> Plunges upon the shore, and floods the dun   (*b*)
> Pale reach of sands, and changes them to gold.   (*a*)

So in majestic cadence rise and fall	*(c)*
The mighty undulations of thy song,	*(d)*
O sightless bard, England's maeonides!	*(e)*
And ever and anon, high over all	*(c)*
Uplifted, a ninth wave superb and strong,	*(d)*
Floods all the soul with its melodious seas.	*(e)*

—Henry Wadsworth Longfellow

There have been many variations on the Italian sonnet. Sometimes the break between the octave and the sestet does not mark any break in the thought. The break may come elsewhere, even in the middle of a line. The rhyme scheme may be varied. One may have *a-b-b-a, c-d-d-c; a-b-b-a, a-c-c-a;* or *a-b-b-a, c-b-b-c,* in the octave. The sestet may also be varied in many ways. Here is an example.

EVENING ON THE BEACH

It is a beauteous evening, calm and free;	*(a)*
The holy time is quiet as a nun	*(b)*
Breathless with adoration; the broad sun	*(b)*
Is sinking down in its tranquillity;	*(a)*
The gentleness of heaven is on the sea:	*(a)*
Listen! the mighty Being is awake,	*(c)*
And doth with his eternal motion make	*(c)*
A sound like thunder—everlastingly.	*(a)*
Dear child! dear girl! that walkest with me here,	*(d)*
If thou appear untouched by solemn thought	*(e)*
Thy nature is not therefore less divine:	*(f)*
Thou liest in Abraham's bosom all the year,	*(d)*
And worship'st at the Temple's inner shrine,	*(f)*
God being with thee when we know it not.	*(e)*

—William Wordsworth

The Shakespearean sonnet has probably been the most popular of all the fixed forms in English poetry. Like other sonnets, it has fourteen lines written in iambic pentameter. The rhyme scheme and divisions of thought are different from those of the Italian sonnet. It is composed of three quatrains and a final couplet, and the rhyme scheme goes: *a-b-a-b, c-d-c-d, e-f-e-f, g-g.*

As is readily seen, the rhyme scheme is easier to use because there are only two rhymes on each terminal sound throughout. The final couplet is usually the climax of the poem, stating the point in a memorable fashion.

The matter of indenting the lines of a sonnet is one of personal preference. They may be indented according to the rhyme scheme, or not indented at all.

Here is one of Shakespeare's sonnets:

SONNET 29

When, in disgrace with fortune and men's eyes,	(*a*)
I all alone beweep my outcast state,	(*b*)
And trouble deaf heaven with my bootless cries,	(*a*)
And look upon myself, and curse my fate,	(*b*)
Wishing me like to one more rich in hope,	(*c*)
Featured like him, like him with friends possessed,	(*d*)
Desiring this man's art and that man's scope,	(*c*)
With what I most enjoy contented least;	(*d*)
Yet in these thoughts myself almost despising,	(*e*)
Haply I think one thee, and then my state,	(*f*)
Like to the lark at break of day arising	(*e*)
From sullen earth, sings hymns at heaven's gate;	(*f*)
For thy sweet love remembered such wealth brings	(*g*)
That then I scorn to change my state with kings.	(*g*)

—William Shakespeare

The Triolet

This is an eight-line poem, in which the first line is repeated as the fourth line, and the first and second lines repeated as the seventh and eighth. These lines should be identical in sound, if not in meaning—that is, they may contain puns and various plays on words, if desired. However, a triolet in which the lines are repeated as a simple refrain can be very charming. The rhyme scheme—with (*R*) following the indication of lines which are repeated—is as follows: *a-b-a-a*(*R*)-*a-b-a*(*R*)-*b*(*R*). An example of a triolet which is not quite regular follows.

ROSE FEVER

Go, lovely rose!
I think you'll drive me mad.
   Kerchoo! the mischief grows—
Blow, lovely nose!
I've nothing now but woes,
And all the joys I had
   Go.—Lovely rose,
I think you'll drive me mad.

The Rondel

The rondel contains fourteen lines and two rhymes. The first and second lines form the refrain, and are repeated as the seventh and eighth, and thirteenth and fourteenth. The rhyme scheme is *a-b-b-a*, *a-b-a*(*R*)-*b*(*R*), *a-b-b-a-a*(*R*)-*b*(*R*).

A rondel of thirteen lines omits one of the last two lines, and goes exactly as above except for that omission.

The Rondelet

The rondelet, or little rondel, has seven lines, of which the first, third and seventh are the refrain, in iambic dimeter, while the other four lines are in iambic trimeter or tetrameter. The rhyme scheme is *a-b-a(R)-a-b-b-a(R)*.

The Rondeau

The rondeau contains fifteen lines in iambic tetrameter or pentameter. The fourth and the fifteenth lines are the refrain, and are composed of the first part of the first line; this refrain does not rhyme. The rhyme scheme follows: *a-a-b-b-a, a-a-b-R, a-a-b-b-a-R*.

IN AFTER DAYS

In after days when grasses high	(*a*)
O'ertop the stone where I shall lie,	(*a*)
Though ill or well the world adjust	(*b*)
My slender claim to honored dust,	(*b*)
I shall not question or reply.	(*a*)
I shall not see the morning sky;	(*a*)
I shall not hear the night-wind's sigh;	(*a*)
I shall be mute, as all men must	(*b*)
In after days!	(*R*)
But yet, now living, fain were I	(*a*)
That some one then should testify,	(*a*)
Saying—"He held his pen in trust	(*b*)
To Art, not serving shame or lust."	(*b*)
Will none?—Then let my memory die	(*a*)
In after days!	(*R*)

–Austin Dobson

The Villanelle

The villanelle is a poem in three-line stanzas in which the same two rhyme sounds are used throughout. The first and third lines of the first stanza serve as refrains, returning in alternation as the last line of each following stanza. The last stanza is a quatrain and ends with both refrain lines. The most usual length of the villanelle is six stanzas, but it may be longer or shorter if the poet so desires. The rhyme scheme is: *a-b-a, a-b-a(1), a-b-a(3)*, etc., *a-b-a(1)-a(3)*.

The Ballade

The ballade is a lyric poem containing three stanzas and an Envoy, or fourth stanza, usually half the length of the others.

There are two main forms of the ballade, that using an eight-line stanza and four-line envoy, and that using a ten-line stanza and five-line envoy.

The last line of every stanza and of the envoy is a refrain.

The eight-line ballade, strictly speaking, should be written in iambic tetrameter, while the ten-line form should be written in iambic pentameter. However, these rules are not now observed so strictly as in the original French ballades of several centuries ago.

The rhyme scheme of the eight-line stanza ballade is as follows: a-b-a-b-b-c-b-$c(R)$ for three stanzas, then b-c-b-$c(R)$ for the envoy.

The ten-line stanza ballade goes: a-b-a-b-b-c-c-d-c-$d(R)$ for three stanzas, then c-c-d-c-$d(R)$ for the envoy.

A seven-line stanza was used by Chaucer, as follows:

BALLADE OF GOOD COUNSEL

by Geoffrey Chaucer

Flee from the crowd and dwell with truthfulness,	(a)
Suffice thee with thy goods, tho' they be small;	(b)
To hoard brings hate, to climb brings giddiness,	(a)
The crowd has envy, and success blinds all;	(b)
Desire no more than to thy lot may fall,	(b)
Work well thyself to counsel others clear,	(c)
And Truth shall make thee free, there is no fear!	(cR)

(modern version by Henry van Dyke)

The Limerick

The limerick is a light-verse form containing five lines, the first, second and fifth lines having three metric feet, and the third and fourth lines two metric feet. It is rhymed a-a-b-b-a, and as written by many famed practitioners the last line is a repetition or partial repetition of the first. It is usually written in mixed iambs and anapests.

The subject of a limerick is frequently a person, but it may be anything in this wide world, or out of it. A few examples follow.

> There once was a man from Nantucket
> Who kept all his cash in a bucket;
> But his daugher, named Nan,
> Ran away with a man,
> And as for the bucket, Nantucket.

—Anonymous

An epicure, dining at Crewe,
Found quite a large mouse in his stew.
    Said the waiter, "Don't shout
    And wave it about,
Or the rest will be wanting one, too!"

—Anonymous

VERSE, BLANK VERSE, AND FREE VERSE

The expressions that head this paragraph often seem to cause confusion, and yet they are not really so difficult. Verse applies to any of the forms which have been described thus far. In fact, it may apply to anything which is written with the line-separations common to poetry. Blank verse is metrical verse which is unrhymed. Free verse is verse which is separated into lines, but has not any definable meter. It is usually cadenced, or rhythmical in a loose way. It is called "free" because it does not have any identifiable rules.

KINDS OF POETRY

Poetry and verse, like heaven, have many mansions.

There are certainly as many kinds of poetry as there are of prose, and probably more. Thus far, we have only considered the tools of writing verse, but before we close, it will be a good idea to mention briefly some of the kinds of verse which have been written in the past.

Poetry That Tells a Story

1. Epic poetry is storytelling on a vast and majestic scale. It tells not just the story of one person, but of nations and wars and great cataclysms, in which the supernatural often plays a part.

2. Narrative poetry, such as "Hiawatha" or "Evangeline," tells a long story, but is on a smaller scale than an epic. It has been very popular in the past. In recent years long narrative poems, novels in verse, have continued to appear, but have not found great popular favor.

3. The Ballad. This is short, lyrical storytelling, as old as time, and just as universal. The earliest known ballads are folk ballads, whose authors are unknown, such as "Sir Patrick Spens." "The Rime of the Ancient Mariner," by Coleridge, the "Ballad of Reading Gaol," by Oscar Wilde, the "Ballad of William Sycamore," by Stephen Vincent Benét, are some examples of ballads that might be read again by the student of verse-writing.

Poetry That Teaches a Lesson

This is so-called didactic or religious verse and may take the form of long philosophizing. On the other hand, some beautiful lyrics may fall in this category.

Poetry That Describes Something

This is called descriptive poetry, and has as its primary aim the painting of a picture. It may be quite long, or it may be in lyric form, but it usually strives to be objective.

Poetry to Be Acted Out

This is called dramatic poetry. It is found in Shakespeare's plays and in Browning's dramatic monologues, to name but a few examples.

Poetry That Expresses Feelings

This is usually called lyric poetry and comprises the greatest variety imaginable. There are many forms of lyric poetry—odes, or poems in praise of something or somebody; elegies, or poems lamenting the loss of something or somebody; epigrams, epitaphs, lullabies, or just plain lyrics, or songs.

Light or Humorous Verse

This kind of verse usually expresses feelings, too, but in such a light way that it deserves a separate category. Its object is to amuse the reader.

Occasional Verse

This may be either light or serious, and is written to suit some special occasion. It runs the gamut from Kipling's famous "Recessional" to greeting-card verse.

As usual when one talks about poetry, one has the cage without the bird. Yet one must start somewhere, if one wishes to write poetry or verse, and where else but in a discussion of technique can one learn how to go about it?

Aside from the special rules of writing verse, all the general precepts of good writing in general apply to the writing of poetry. Freshness of expression and of viewpoint are usually rewarded with success; clichés and worn-out, second-hand ideas with failure.

Above all, Socrates' old advice to "know thyself" applies to poets. "Fool, said my muse to me, look in thy heart and write!" remains as good advice as when Sir Philip Sidney wrote it.

KEY TO VERSIFICATION

METERS

NAME OF METER	ONE UNIT	NO. OF SYLLABLES	ACCENT ON	PATTERN	EXAMPLE
iambic	iamb	2	2nd	$\_\,'$	Marie
trochaic	trochee	2	1st	$'\,\_$	Dickens
anapestic	anapest	3	3rd	$\_\_\,'$	cigarette
dactyllic	dactyl	3	1st	$'\,\_\_$	Italy
spondaic	spondee	2	both	$'\,'$	stop! thief!

LINES, ACCORDING TO NUMBER OF METRIC FEET

monometer	one foot	pentameter	five feet
dimeter	two feet	hexameter	six feet
trimeter	three feet	heptameter	seven feet
tetrameter	four feet	octometer	eight feet

STANZAS

couplet	two lines	sestet	six lines
triplet or tercet	three lines	septet	seven lines
quatrain	four lines	octave	eight lines
cinquain	five lines		

FIXED FORMS*

NAME	NO. OF LINES	METER	LENGTH OF LINE	RHYME SCHEME
sonnet	14	iambic	pentameter	*abba, abba, cde, cde* or *abab, cdcd, efef, gg*
triolet	8	any	any	*abaa(R)aba(R)b(R)*
rondel	14 or 13	any	any	*abba, aba(R)b(R), abbaa(R)b(R)* same, minus last line
rondelet	7	any	any	*aba(R)abba(R)*
rondeau	15 or 12	iambic	tetrameter or pentameter	*aabba, aabR, aabbaR* *abbaabR, abbaR*
villanelle	19 (or 12, 26, etc.)	any	any	*aba, aba(1), aba(3), aba(1), aba(3), aba(1)a(3).*
ballade	28 (8-line stanza) 35 (10-line stanza)	iambic (or other) iambic (or other)	tetrameter pentameter	*ababbcbc(R)* (3 times), *bcbc(R)* *ababbccbcb(R)* (3 times), *ccdcd(R)*
limerick	5	mixed	trimeter and dimeter	*aabba*

*Note: This chart is not exhaustive. While these are the main fixed forms, others exist, as well as variations of the ones given.

How to Use This Rhyming Dictionary

1. Look for rhymes under the vowel sound of the rhyme you want. For example, if you want a rhyme for "hat," look under short *A*; for "table," look under long *A*.

2. The vowel sounds are given in alphabetical order. In case you are looking for a vowel sound which puzzles you, consult the table of contents.

3. The page head at the top of each page will tell you which rhyme sound you have before you. Within the vowel sound, there are always three sections: one-, two-, and three-syllable rhymes. Within each section, the entries are arranged alphabetically, except that the letter *c* is put with *k* or *s* according to which of its two pronunciations is used.

4. Note that within each entry the words are arranged in numbered groups, according to the number of syllables. Thus, if you need a one-syllable word to finish your line, you need look no further than the words following the numeral 1. If you need three syllables, look at the words which come after the number 3. You might also take a one- or two-syllable word for the rhyme and qualify it with an adjective, thus making up your three syllables.

5. In a few cases where regional pronunciations vary, words have been included which may not seem to be rhymes according to your pronunciation. This may be true in a few words ending in *r* in particular, for this is a sound which often modifies the pronunciation of the preceding vowel. If this is the case, do not use the word which does not rhyme for you. Remember, it rhymes for some people, and that is why it is there.

6. Cross references to entries containing additional rhymes are usually to another entry in the same section. In this case, the indication "above" or "below" is given. Otherwise, the reference is to another section and will be found by turning to the appropriate vowel sound and one-, two-, or three-syllable rhyme section.

ABBREVIATIONS USED IN THIS BOOK

Ar.	Arabic	exc.	except	loc.	local
Aram.	Aramic	F.	French	M.L.	Medieval Latin
arch.	archaic	G.	German	N.	north
coll.	colloquial	Gr.	Greek	N.L.	New Latin
D.	Dutch	Heb.	Hebrew	obs.	obsolete
dial.	dialect	Hind.	Hindustani	Pg.	Portuguese
e.g.	*exempli gratia* [L.], for example	Ir.	Ireland	Pol.	Polish
		It.	Italian	Sp.	Spanish
Eng.	England	Jap.	Japanese	Scot.	Scotland
etc.	et cetera	L.	Latin	Tag.	Tagalog

Note: "loc.," "slang," and "dial." are assumed to refer to the United States unless otherwise indicated.

Contents

Ĭ (bib)

Ō (oh)

Ŏ (awe)

ŎŌ (good)

OĬ (boy)

OŬ (how)

Ū (you)

Ŭ (tub)

A (ay)

1.

SINGLE (MASCULINE) RHYMES IN A (ay)

Primary or Secondary Accent Falls on Last
Syllable; Imperfect Rhymes Are in Italics.

A– 1. a, A, ay, aye, eh 2. Coué, roué [F.]
3. mariée [F.], à pied [F.] 4. couturier
[F.], roturier [F.], habitué [F.].

BA– 1. bay, bey 2. abbé [F.], *ambay*,
embay, Bombay, *bomb bay*, obey 3. dis-
embay, disobey, Baffin Bay, dapple bay.

DA– 1. day, dey 2. today, *heyday*, *playday*, *Mayday*, *payday*, idée [F.], *midday*,
Friday, *weekday*, undé, *Monday*, *Sunday*,
noonday, *doomsday*, *Tuesday*, Lord's Day,
Thursday, *birthday* 3. workaday, wedding day, working day, holiday, every
day, quarter day, Easter Day, yesterday,
Saturday, Wednesday, market day, judgment day, Christmas Day 4. alackaday.

FA– 1. fay, fey, fe [Sp.] 2. café, parfait,
au' fait [F.] 3. Santa Fe, coryphée, re-
chauffé [F.], pousse-café [F.].

GA– 1. gay, gai [F.] 2. *nosegay*, *margay*,
morgay 3. distingué [F.].

HA– 1. hay, hey 2. ahey.

JA– 1. j, J, jay 3. popinjay.

KA– 1. k, K, Kay, kay, cay, quai [F.]
2. decay, piqué, okay, bouquet, roquet,
croquet, tokay, parquet, *Biscay*, risqué
[F.] 3. appliqué [F.], sobriquet [F.] 4.
communiqué [F.].

LA– 1. lay, lei, blé [F.], clay, Clay, flay,
play, splay, slay, sley, sleigh 2. allay,
Malay, ailé, waylay, Calais, chalet, belay,
delay, relay, inlay, *parlay*, parler [F.],
soleil [F.], mislay, *outlay*, coulé [F.],
soufflé [F.], *morglay*, fair play, *byplay*, dis-
play, misplay, *horseplay*, *bobsleigh* 3.

Mandalay, roundelay, virelay, De Molay,
reveille, Chevrolet, underlay, interlay,
overlay, rissolé [F.], photoplay, Passion
Play etc., underplay, overplay, interplay,
pourparler [F.] 4. cabriolet, café-au-lait
[F.], au pis aller [F.], coup de soleil [F.],
cantabile.

MA– 1. Mae, May 2. lamé [F.], semé
[F.], *gourmet*, dismay 3. entremets, con-
sommé, resumé.

NA– 1. nay, né, née [both F.], neigh
2. ainé [F.], Chiné [F.], donnée [F.],
tourné [F.] 3. Hogmanay, matinee,
satiné [F.], Ciboney, dragonné [F.], rai-
sonné [F.], dejeuner [F.], cloisonné
4. estaminet [F.].

PA– 1. pay, spay 2. frappé, epée [F.],
repay, prepay, Gaspé, coupé, toupet
3. canapé [F.], overpay.

RA– 1. ray, re, rey [Sp.], bray, brae,
scray, dray, fray, gray, gré [F.], grey, pray,
pré [F.], prey, spray, tray, trey, stray
2. array, bewray, *chambray*, padre,
André, *Deirdre*, affray, defray, beret,
stingray, doré [F.], *foray*, *moray*, moiré,
soiree, repray, bespray, respray, betray,
entrée, portray, astray, estray, distrait,
outré [F.], hurray, curé [F.], purée
3. disarray, liseré, autospray, emigree,
émigré [F.], dapple gray, iron-gray, silver
gray, Honoré, Monterrey 4. jeunesse
dorée [F.].

SA– 1. say, se 2. assay, glacé [F.], *nay-
say*, passé, chassé, essay, essai [F.], blessé

1

[F.], presay, missay, lycée [F.], plissé [F.], gainsay, pensée [F.], unsay, *hearsay*, foresay, *soothsay* 3. fiancé, fiancée, déclassé [F.], divorcé [F.], divorcée [F.], repoussé [F.], retroussé [F.]; *see* also ZA-blasé etc. below.

SHA- 1. shay, chez [F.] 2. cachet, sachet, sashay, cliché, broché, crochet, cherchez [F.], touché [F.] 3. attaché, ricochet, recherché 4. papier mâché [F.], à bon marché [F.].

TA- 1. tay, the [F.], stay 2. paté [F.], été [F.], astay, *bobstay*, *backstay*, *jackstay*, *mainstay*, *forestay*, outstay, santé [F.], bonté [F.] 3. comité [F.], overstay, liberté [F.], velouté [F.] 4. légèreté, égalité, fraternité, éternité, déporté [all F.].

THA- 1. they 2. Cathay.

VA- 2. pavé [F.], nevé [F.], inveigh, convey, corvée [F.], kurvey, purvey, survey 3. reconvey, repurvey, resurvey, énervé [F.].

WA- 1. way, wey, Wei, weigh, qua, quey, sway, tway, whey 2. away, aweigh, *subway*, *hatchway*, *archway*, *headway*, *roadway*, *Broadway*, midway, *guideway*, *leeway*, reweigh, *seaway*, halfway, *gangway*, *cogway*, *byway*, *highway*, *walkway*, *railway*, *hallway*, *tramway*, *someway*, *runway*, *slipway*, *fairway*, *stairway*, *doorway*, *crossway*, *straightway*, *outway*, outweigh, *pathway*, *causeway* 3. breakaway, Rockaway, stowaway, wellaway, runaway, straightaway, getaway, caraway, castaway, cutaway, milky way, entryway, everyway, passageway, cableway, Galloway, underweigh, waterway, overweigh.

YA- 1. yea 2. denier [F.], foyer, croupier [F.], dossier [F.], métier, soigné [F.] 3. ennuyé, escalier, chevalier [all F.].

ZA- 2. blasé, visé 3. exposé 4. Champs Élysées.

ZHA- 2. congé [F.], Roget 3. dégagé [F.], agrégé, protégé, protégée, négligée.

AB- 1. Abe, babe 3. cosmolabe, astrolabe.

ACH- 1. h, H, aitch.

AD- 1. ade, aid, aide, bade, bayed, fade, hade, jade, cade, lade, laid, blade, flayed, glade, played, sleighed, slade, made, maid, neighed, paid, spade, spayed, raid, braid, brayed, grayed, grade, prayed, preyed, sprayed, trade, strayed, shade, staid, stayed, wade, weighed, suéde, wheyed 2. obeyed, gambade, forbade, brigade, baccade, decayed, alcaide, falcade, cockade, blockade, brocade, stockade, arcade, cascade, allayed, delayed, relayed, relade, relaid, inlaid, unlade, unlaid, parleyed, old-maid, handmade, *handmaid*, remade, self-made, *milkmaid*, homemade, pomade, unmade, *mermaid*, *bridesmaid*, dismayed, *nursemaid*, *housemaid*, grenade, apaid, repaid, prepaid, unpaid, postpaid, respade, croupade, parade, charade, abrade, unbraid, upbraid, afraid, aggrade, degrade, regrade, tirade, retrade, glacéed, passade, chasséd, glissade, torsade, crusade, *sunshade*, crocheted, *nightshade*, sautéed, unstaid, evade, invade, pervade, conveyed, purveyed, surveyed, reweighed, persuade 3. orangeade, renegade, lemonade, citronade, gingerade, appliquéd, barricade, cavalcade, ambuscade, escalade, defilade, enfilade, fusillade, accolade, everglade, readymade, dairymaid, undismayed, esplanade, promenade, serenade, marinade, pasquinade, dragonnade, gasconade, colonnade, cannonade, carronade, escapade, gallopade, overpaid, disarrayed, masquerade, unafraid, centigrade, retrograde, balustrade, palisade, overweighed 4. harlequinade, fanfaronade, rodomontade.

AF- 1. chafe, kef, strafe, safe, waif 2. enchafe, vouchsafe, unsafe.

AFD- 1. chafed, strafed 2. vouchsafed.

AG- 1. Hague, plague, Prague, vague 2. fainaigue.

AJ- 1. age, gage, gauge, cage, mage, page, rage, sage, stage, wage, swage 2. engage, encage, *nonage*, repage, rampage, enrage, outrage, presage, Osage, backstage, *forestage*, upstage, assuage **3.** overage, disengage.

AJD– 1. aged, gauged, caged, paged, raged, staged, waged **2.** engaged, encaged, repaged, rampaged, enraged, outraged, upstaged, assuaged **3.** disengaged.

AK– 1. ache, bake, fake, hake, haik, jake, cake, lake, flake, slake, make, snake, spake, rake, brake, break, drake, crake, traik, strake, sake, take, stake, steak, wake, quake **2.** *headache, backache, earache, heartache,* toothache, clambake, *friedcake, hoecake, nocake, shortcake, nutcake, fruitcake,* remake, opaque, *daybreak, heartbreak, outbreak, sheldrake, mandrake, muckrake, namesake, keepsake,* forsake, betake, retake, *intake, uptake,* partake, *grubstake, beefsteak,* mistake, *sweepstake,* awake, rewake, *earthquake* **3.** johnnycake, griddlecake, havercake, rattlesnake, undertake, overtake.

AKS– aches, etc., *see* **AK–** ache etc. above, plus "s" or " 's."

AKT– 1. ached, baked, faked, caked, flaked, slaked, snaked, raked, braked, traiked, staked, quaked **2.** *grubstaked,* rewaked.

AL– 1. ail, ale, bale, bail, Bel, dale, fail, gale, Gael, hale, hail, gaol, jail, kale, scale, flail, mail, male, nail, snail, pail, pale, spale, rail, brail, Braille, frail, grail, Graal, trail, sale, sail, shale, tale, tail, tael, stale, vale, vail, veil, wail, wale, quail, squail, whale, Yale **2.** *Clydesdale,* regale, inhale, exhale, percale, hallel, remail, *blackmail, hangnail,* canaille, *hobnail,* tenaille, *agnail, thumbnail,* empale, impale, *handrail, landrail, pedrail, guardrail,* derail, *taffrail, cograil,* engrail, assail, *resale, wholesale,* grisaille, *staysail, headsail,* resail, *lugsail, skysail, trysail, mainsail, topsail, foresail, spritsail,* outsail, *telltale, bobtail, broadtail,* detail, retail, entail, *pigtail, bangtail, cocktail, forktail,*

bucktail, fantail, pintail, horntail, thorntail, sheartail, curtail, *cattail, sprittail, boattail, coattail, foxtail, shavetail, dovetail,* avail, travail, prevail, enveil, bewail, *narwhale* **3.** Abigail, farthingale, nightingale, martingale, fingernail, monorail, tattletale, fairy tale, draggletail, disentail, swallowtail, scissortail, paravail, intervale.

ALD– 1. ailed, aled, baled, bailed, failed, galed, haled, gaoled, jailed, scaled, flailed, mailed, nailed, snailed, paled, railed, trailed, sailed, tailed, veiled, wailed, waled, quailed, whaled **2.** regaled, inhaled, exhaled, remailed, *blackmailed, hobnailed,* empaled, impaled, derailed, assailed, resailed, outsailed, *bobtailed, broadtailed,* detailed, retailed, entailed, *pigtailed, bangtailed, cocktailed,* curtailed, availed, travailed, prevailed, enveiled, unveiled, bewailed **3.** unregaled, farthingaled, draggletailed, disentailed, swallowtailed.

ALZ– ails etc., *see* **AL–** ail etc. above, plus "s" or " 's"; **1.** Wales **2.** Marseilles.

AM– 1. aim, dame, fame, game, hame, came, lame, blame, flame, claim, maim, name, frame, crême, same, Sejm [Pol.], shame, tame **2.** defame, became, aflame, inflame, acclaim, declaim, reclaim, proclaim, disclaim, exclaim, *quitclaim,* rename, *byname, nickname, forename, surname,* misname, *doorframe, selfsame* **3.** overcame, counterclaim.

AMD– 1. aimed, famed, gamed, lamed, blamed, flamed, claimed, maimed, named, framed, shamed, tamed **2.** defamed, inflamed, acclaimed, declaimed, reclaimed, proclaimed, disclaimed, exclaimed, renamed, *nicknamed,* misnamed, ashamed **3.** undefamed, counterclaimed.

AMZ– aims etc., *see* **AM–** aim etc. above, plus "s" or " 's"; **1.** James **2.** St. James.

AN– 1. bane, chain, Dane, deign, feign, fane, fain, gain, gaine, Jane, cane, Cain, skein, lane, lain, laine, blain, plane, plain, slain, Maine, main, mane, pain, pane, Paine, Spain, rein, reign, rain, brain, drain, grain, crane, sprain, train, strain, sane, sain, tain, stain, thane, vane, vain, vein, wane, swain, twain, zain 2. urbane, *herbbane, fleabane, wolfsbane,* rechain, enchain, unchain, *mundane,* ordain, disdain, profane, regain, chicane, again, Elaine, delaine, *chilblain, seaplane, biplane, triplane, volplane, airplane,* Champlain, explain, amain, demesne, remain, domain, romaine, ptomaine, germane, humane, chow mein, inane, cocaine, Cockaigne, campaign, champagne, champaign, arraign, Karen, terrane, terrain, *checkrein,* unrein, forane, moraine, *subdrain,* refrain, migraine, engrain, ingrain, *grosgrain, crossgrain,* detrain, entrain, restrain, distrain, constrain, insane, attain, obtain, detain, retain, maintain, contain, pertain, abstain, *bloodstain, tearstain,* distain, dustain, *cordwain, coxswain, boatswain,* sixain 3. inurbane, hurricane, sugar cane, reordain, preordain, foreordain, aquaplane, multiplane, monoplane, aeroplane, hydroplane, gyroplane, Charlemagne, inhumane, windowpane, counterpane, scatterbrain, featherbrain, subterrane, suzerain, overstrain, chevrotain, ascertain, appertain, entertain, quatorzain 4. demimondaine, legerdemain, elecampane, mediterrane.

AND– 1. chained, deigned, feigned, gained, caned, planed, pained, rained, reigned, brained, drained, grained, craned, sprained, trained, strained, stained, veined, waned 2. enchained, unchained, rechained, ordained, disdained, unfeigned, profaned, regained, arraigned, explained, remained, campaigned, unreined, engrained, ingrained, detrained, entrained, restrained, distrained, constrained, attained, detained, retained, maintained, contained, pertained, abstained, *bloodstained* 3. preordained, foreordained, featherbrained, scatterbrained, overstrained, ascertained, entertained.

ANJ– 1. change, mange, range, grange, strange 2. exchange, shortchange, arrange, derange, estrange 3. rearrange, prearrange, disarrange, interchange.

ANT– 1. faint, feint, plaint, paint, saint, taint, quaint 2. complaint, bepaint, repaint, Geraint, restraint, distraint, constraint, ensaint, attaint, acquaint.

ANTS– faints etc., *see* **ANT–** faint etc. above, plus "s" or " 's."

ANZ– banes etc., *see* **AN–** bane etc. above, plus "s" or " 's."

AP– 1. ape, chape, gape, jape, cape, scape, nape, rape, drape, grape, crape, crepe, scrape, shape, tape 2. agape, *landscape,* escape, *seascape, skyscape,* bedrape, reshape, misshape, transhape, *shipshape,* red-tape.

APS– apes etc., *see* **AP–** ape etc. above, plus "s" or " 's"; 1. traipse 3. jackanapes.

APT– 1. aped, gaped, shaped, raped, draped, scraped, taped 2. escaped, bedraped, reshaped, red-taped, untaped.

AR– 1. air, Eir, heir, eyre, e'er, bear, bare, chair, dare, fair, fare, faire [F.], hair, hare, care, scare, lair, blare, flare, flair, glare, glair, Clare, mare, mer [F.], mère [F.], n'er, snare, pair, pare, pear, père [F.], spare, rare, frère [F.], prayer, share, tear, tare, terre [F.], stair, stare, there, their, vair, ware, wear, swear, square, where, yare 2. Pierre, coheir, whene'er, where'er, howe'er, *threadbare, cudbear, bugbear, forebear,* forbear, misbear, *armchair,* bedare, outdare, affair, *Mayfair, fieldfare, welfare, warfare, horsehair, mohair,* eclair, declare, *nightmare,* grand'mère [F.], belle-mère [F.], ensnare, repair, prepare, impair, compare, grand-père [F.], beau-père [F.], despair, *confrere, corsair, plowshare,* Voltaire, parterre, outstare, trouvère [F.], aware, *hardware,* beware, *tinware, glassware, footwear,* outwear, resquare, unsquare, hiver [F.], *somewhere, nowhere,*

elsewhere, première [F.], portière [F.]
3. overbear, Camembert, rocking-chair, thoroughfare, maidenhair, mal de mer [F.], jardinière [F.], doctrinaire, debonair, billionaire, millionaire, questionnaire, disrepair, proletaire, solitaire, countervair, Delaware, unaware, earthenware, ironware, underwear, silverware, otherwhere, anywhere, everywhere, wheresoe'er, savoir faire [F.], laissez-faire [F.], vivandière [F.], fonctionnaire [F.] **4.** commissionnaire [F.], concessionnaire [F.], Finistère, Finisterre.

ARD– **1.** aired, bared, dared, fared, hared, cared, scared, laird, blared, flared, glared, shared, snared, spared, rared, stared, squared **2.** gray-haired, fair-haired etc., declared, ensnared, repaired, prepared, impaired, compared, outstared **3.** undeclared, curly-haired, golden-haired, Titian-haired, raven-haired.

ARN– **1.** bairn, cairn, tairn.

ARS– **1.** scarce, Perse [F.] **2.** commerce [F.].

ARZ– airs etc., *see* AR– air etc. above, plus "s" or "'s."

AS– **1.** ace, base, bass, chase, dace, dais, face, case, lace, place, plaice, mace, pace, space, race, brace, grace, trace, Thrace, vase **2.** abase, debase, surbase, enchase, vendace, efface, deface, reface, *boldface*, *frogface*, *blackface*, *paleface*, *catface*, outface, *cardcase*, *bookcase*, encase, *showcase*, *staircase*, *notecase*, *suitcase*, ukase, *bridelace*, anlace, enlace, *shoelace*, replace, *fireplace*, displace, misplace, *birthplace*, grimace, apace, *footpace*, outpace, erase, *tailrace*, *millrace*, embrace, *scapegrace*, disgrace, retrace, Alsace, *ambsace* **3.** contrabass, octobass, steeplechase, Boniface, platterface, baby face, angel face etc., interlace, populace, hiding place, resting place, commonplace, interspace, chariot race.

AST– **1.** baste, based, faced, haste, cased, chaste, chased, laced, placed, paste, paced, spaced, raced, braced, graced, traced, taste, waste, waist **2.** abased, lambaste, unchaste, bald-faced, bold-faced, shame-faced, two-faced etc., posthaste, encased **3.** baby-faced, dirty-faced, angel-faced double-faced, freckle-faced, interlaced, aftertaste.

AT– **1.** eight, ate, ait, bate, bait, date, fate, fête, gate, gait, hate, Kate, skate, late, plate, plait, slate, mate, pate, rate, freight, grate, great, crate, prate, trait, strait, straight, sate, state, weight, wait **2.** create, abate, debate, rebate, *crowbait*, *whitebait*, redate, predate, sedate, misdate, postdate, outdate, *floodgate*, *negate*, *seagate*, *Vulgate*, *placate*, *oblate*, sublate, elate, belate, delate, relate, deflate, inflate, conflate, sufflate, collate, breastplate, translate, playmate, cremate, checkmate, stalemate, *comate*, *shipmate*, *helpmate*, *classmate*, *messmate*, mismate, *tentmate*, enate, innate, ornate, berate, prorate, cut-rate, estate, restate, instate, misstate, await, lightweight **3.** recreate, procreate, discreate, celibate, approbate, reprobate, incubate, depredate, antedate, candidate, validate, lapidate, cuspidate, liquidate, inundate, afterdate, decaudate, denudate, nucleate, permeate, roseate, nauseate, propagate, divagate, ablegate, delegate, relegate, abnegate, segregate, aggregate, congregate, crash the gate, get the gate [both slang], obligate, profligate, fumigate, irrigate, litigate, mitigate, castigate, instigate, navigate, abrogate, subrogate, subjugate, conjugate, corrugate, fasciate, gladiate, radiate, mediate, foliate, opiate, expiate, seriate, floriate, satiate, vitiate, tertiate, aviate, obviate, deviate, desiccate, exsiccate, deprecate, imprecate, abdicate, dedicate, mendicate, judicate, delicate, triplicate, implicate, complicate, supplicate, duplicate, explicate, formicate, tunicate, fabricate, imbricate, fimbricate, lubricate, rubricate, intricate, extricate, vesicate, corticate, masticate, rusticate, relocate, allocate, collocate, dislocate, embrocate, advocate, demarcate, altercate, bifurcate, confiscate, expiscate, obfuscate, infuscate, coruscate, educate, correlate, sibilate, jubilate, depilate, pupilate, mutilate, ventilate, cancellate, flagellate, lamellate, crenellate, immolate, desolate, isolate, contemplate, copperplate, silver plate, legislate, mistranslate, ambulate, tubulate, peculate, speculate, calculate, flocculate, circulate, osculate, adulate, pendulate, undulate, nodulate, regulate, angulate, ungulate, stellulate, ululate, emulate, simulate, stimulate, formulate, cumulate, granulate, crenulate, lunulate, stipulate, populate, copulate, spherulate, insulate, consulate, decimate, animate, ultimate, intimate, optimate, estimate, consummate, dichromate, conformate, explanate, sultanate, hyphenate, alienate, arsenate, catenate, septenate, juvenate, impregnate, obsignate, designate, turbinate, vaccinate, fascinate, ordinate, marginate, machinate, echinate, declinate, pollinate, geminate, fulminate, dominate, marinate, patinate, pectinate, destinate, glutinate, bipinnate, carbonate, functionate, coronate, assonate, detonate, intonate, hibernate, quaternate, inornate, fortunate, adipate, dissipate, exculpate, syncopate, extirpate, saccharate, separate, disparate, celebrate, cerebrate, calibrate, obsecrate, desecrate, consecrate, execrate, dehydrate, liberate, lacerate, macerate, ulcerate, federate, moderate, tolerate, numerate, generate, operate, asperate, desperate, literate, integrate, emigrate, immigrate, transmigrate, aspirate, decorate, perforate, biforate, camphorate, pignorate, corporate, perorate, doctorate, overrate, penetrate, impetrate, perpetrate, arbitrate, infiltrate, concentrate, orchestrate, fenestrate, sequestrate, magistrate, registrate, capistrate, demonstrate, remonstrate, illustrate, accurate, obdurate, figurate, fulgurate, sulphurate, tellurate, suppurate, purpurate, saturate, inspissate, tête-à-tête [F.], delectate, eructate, acetate, vegetate, oscitate, meditate, agitate, digitate, cogitate, gurgitate, militate, imitate, limitate, sanitate, capitate, crepitate, palpitate, irritate, hesitate, nictitate, quantitate, gravitate, levitate, occultate, edentate, segmentate, potentate, annotate, connotate, decurtate, devastate, *intestate*, reinstate, apostate, understate, interstate, overstate, degustate, acutate, permutate, amputate, vacuate, graduate, valuate, tenuate, sinuate, adequate, antiquate, actuate, punctuate, fluctuate, fructuate, situate, excavate, aggravate, depravate, elevate, salivate, derivate, titivate, cultivate, motivate, captivate, estivate, renovate, innovate, enervate, recurvate, hundredweight, pennyweight, heavyweight, bantamweight, underweight, featherweight, paperweight, welterweight, overweight 4. elucidate, invalidate, consolidate, intimidate, accommodate, enucleate, delineate, extravagate, variegate, depreciate, appreciate, officiate, associate, dissociate, eradiate, irradiate, repudiate, collegiate, trifoliate, calumniate, ammoniate, pogoniate, marsupiate, inebriate, excoriate, depatriate, negotiate, exuviate, asphyxiate, hypothecate, syllabicate, irradicate, rededicate, revindicate, adjudicate, indelicate, multiplicate, authenticate, decorticate, domesticate, sophisticate, prognosticate, intoxicate, reciprocate, equivocate, annihilate, assimilate, nucleolate, alveolate, inviolate, interpolate, disconsolate, apostolate, capitulate, expostulate, salicylate, amalgamate, legitimate, penultimate, permanganate, hydrogenate, concatenate, rejuvenate, predesignate, vaticinate, hallucinate, inordinate, immarginate, ingeminate, inseminate, disseminate, peregrinate, indoctrinate, procrastinate, predestinate, conglutinate, exsanguinate, bicarbonate, impersonate, subalternate, emancipate, provertebrate, deliberate, reverberate, protuberate, incarcerate, eviscerate, confederate, preponderate, vociferate, exaggerate, refrigerate, accelerate, conglomerate, exonerate, remunerate, cooperate, exasperate, recuperate, commiserate, reiterate, adulterate, presbyterate, asseverate, redecorate, imperforate, invigorate, ameliorate, commemorate, evaporate, incorporate, recalcitrate, extravasate, improvisate, tergiversate, capacitate, felicitate, resuscitate, premeditate, tridigitate, inadequate, effectuate, perpetuate, accentuate, eventuate, insalivate, recaptivate **5.** baccalaureate, circumnavigate, supererogate, intermediate, unifoliate, circumstantiate, differentiate, renegotiate, quadrifoliate, excommunicate, recapitulate, insubordinate, unaffectionate, disproportionate, incompassionate, deteriorate, incommensurate, incapacitate, individuate, superannuate.

ATH– **1.** faith, wraith, staith **2.** unfaith, misfaith.

ATH– **1.** bathe, scathe, lathe, snathe, spathe, rathe, swathe **2.** unswathe.

ATHD– **1.** bathed, scathed, lathed, swathed.

ATS– eights etc., see **AT–** eight etc. above, plus "s" or "'s."

AV– **1.** Dave, gave, cave, lave, glaive, slave, nave, knave, pave, rave, brave, grave, crave, trave, save, shave, stave, wave, waive, suave **2.** forgave, behave, portglaive, enslave, repave, engrave, ingrave, deprave **3.** misbehave, autoclave, antenave, architrave.

AVD– **1.** caved, laved, slaved, paved, raved, braved, craved, saved, shaved, staved, waved, waived **2.** behaved, enslaved, repaved, unpaved, engraved, depraved **3.** misbehaved, unenslaved, unengraved.

AVZ– Dave's etc., see **AV–** Dave etc. above, plus "s" or "'s."

AZ– ayes etc., see **A–** ay etc. through **ZHA–** congé etc. above, plus "s" or "'s" (except for French plurals, where the "s" is not pronounced); **1.** baize, daze, faze, phase, gaze, haze, Hayes, laze, blaze, glaze, maze, maize, raze, raise, braise, braze, phrase, graze, craze, praise, chaise, vase **2.** bedaze, malaise, ablaze, emblaze, amaze, bemaze, *mizmaze*, rephrase, upraise, appraise, bepraise, *sideways* **3.** nowadays, Marseillaise, hollandaise, mayonnaise, lyonnaise, polonaise, paraphrase, metaphrase, reappraise, underpraise, overpraise.

AZD– **1.** dazed, fazed, gazed, hazed, lazed, blazed, glazed, raised, razed, braised, phrased, grazed, crazed, praised **2.** bedazed, emblazed, unglazed, amazed, bemazed, unraised, upraised, rephrased, unphrased, appraised, unpraised, dispraised **3.** paraphrased, reappraised, underpraised, overpraised.

AZH– **1.** beige, greige.

A (ay)

DOUBLE (FEMININE) RHYMES IN A (may'hem)

Primary or Secondary Accent Falls on Next to Last
Syllable; Imperfect Rhymes Are in Italics.

A'a– **2.** haya, Maia, Freya **3.** Isaiah **4.** Himalaya.

A'ad– **1.** naiad, sayid.

A'al– **1.** Baal. **2.** Ethbaal. **3.** defrayal, betrayal, portrayal, conveyal, purveyal, surveyal.

A'am– **2.** faham, mayhem, graham, play 'em.

A'an– **3.** Biscayan, Malayan **4.** Paraguayan, Uruguayan.

A'ans– **3.** abeyance, conveyance, purveyance, surveyance.

A'ant– **2.** mayn't **3.** abeyant.

AB'an– **2.** Laban, Leben [G.], geben [G.].

AB'er– **2.** Gheber, Ghabre, caber, labor, neighbor, saber, sabre, tabor **3.** belabor.

AB'erz– Ghebers etc., see AB'er– Gheber etc. above; **2.** jabers **3.** bejabers.

AB'e– **2.** baby, gaby, maybe **3.** *crybaby.*

AB'ez– **2.** babies, gabies, Jabes, scabies rabies, maybes **3.** *crybabies.*

AB'l– **2.** Abel, able, Babel, fable, gable, cable, label, labile, Mabel, sable, table, stable **3.** enable, unable, disable, retable, *timetable, turntable,* unstable **4.** fibblefable [dial.].

AB'ld– **2.** fabled, gabled, cabled, labeled, sabled, tabled, stabled **3.** enabled, disabled, besabled, retabled.

AB'ler– **2.** abler, fabler, cabler, labeler, sabler, tabler, stabler **3.** enabler, disabler, retabler, unstabler.

AB'lest– **2.** ablest, stablest **3.** unstablest.

AB'ling– **2.** cabling, labelling, tabling, stabling **3.** enabling, disabling, retabling.

AB'lz– Abels etc., see AB'l– Abel etc. above, plus "s" or "'s."

AB'rum– **2.** Abram, labrum, flabrum **4.** candelabrum.

AD'a– **2.** Ada, Veda **3.** cicada, armada, Pinctada **5.** Digitigrada.

A'da– **2.** heyday, Mayday, payday, playday.

AD'ans– **2.** aidance, cadence **3.** decadence.

AD'ant– **2.** aidant, cadent **3.** decadent, abradent.

AD'ed– **2.** aided, faded, jaded, bladed, gladed, spaded, raided, braided, graded, traded, shaded, waded **3.** unaided, unfaded, cockaded, blockaded, brocaded, cascaded, paraded, unbraided, upbraided, degraded, crusaded, evaded, invaded, pervaded, dissuaded, persuaded. **4.** barricaded, ambuscaded, enfiladed, doublebladed, accoladed, promenaded, serenaded, colonnaded, cannonaded, masqueraded, retrograded, unpersuaded.

AD'en– **2.** Aden, Haydn, laden, maiden **3.** menhaden, snow maiden **4.** overladen, heavy-laden.

AD'ens– **2.** cadence **3.** decadence.

AD'er– **2.** aider, fader, spader, raider, braider, grader, trader, Seder, staider, wader **3.** unbraider, upbraider, crusader, invader, dissuader, persuader **4.** barricader, promenader, serenader, masquerader.

AD′est– 2. staidest.

AD′ez– 2. Hades, Cadiz, ladies.

AD′i– 2. fady, shady, jady, cadi, lady, glady, maidy, Brady, 'fraidy, Grady, Sadie, vade **3.** O'Grady, milady, *forelady.*

AD′ing– 2. aiding, fading, lading, spading, raiding, braiding, grading, trading, shading, wading **3.** blockading, cascading, unfading, parading, unbraiding, upbraiding, degrading, crusading, evading, invading, pervading, dissuading, persuading **4.** barricading, ambuscading, serenading, cannonading, masquerading.

AD′ish– 2. jadish, staidish **3.** oldmaidish, *mermaidish.*

AD′l– 2. ladle, gradal, cradle, tradal **3.** encradle.

AD′less– 2. aidless, fadeless, bladeless, spadeless, braidless, gradeless, tradeless, shadeless **3.** paradeless, cockadeless, crusadeless.

AD′li– 2. staidly **3.** dismayedly.

AD′ling– 2. ladling, maidling, cradling **3.** encradling.

AD′ness– 2. frayedness, staidness **3.** afraidness, unstaidness.

AD′o– 2. dado, credo **3.** gambado, fumado, tornado, strappado **4.** bastinado, carbonado, desperado, camisado.

AD′os– 3. Barbados, intrados, extrados.

AD′oz– dados etc., *see* **AD′o–** dado etc. above, plus "s" or "'s."

AD′us– 2. cladus, gradus, made us etc. **3.** dismayed us etc.

A′er– 2. feyer, gayer, layer, flayer, player, slayer, mayor, payer, brayer, grayer, prayer, preyer, sprayer, strayer, stayer, weigher **3.** obeyer, waylayer, delayer, bricklayer, parleyer, outlayer, displayer, mormaor, taxpayer, forayer, hoorayer, defrayer, betrayer, portrayer, assayer, essayer, gainsayer, soothsayer, inveigher, conveyer, purveyor, surveyor.

A′est– 2. feyest, gayest, grayest, greyest **3.** assayist, *essayist*; *see* also **A′ist–** Ptolemaist etc. below.

AF′er– 2. chafer, safer, strafer, wafer **3.** cockchafer, vouchsafer.

AF′ing– 2. chafing, strafing **3.** enchafing, vouchsafing.

AG′a– 2. saga **3.** omega **4.** rutabaga, Onondaga.

AG′er– 2. plaguer, vaguer, jager.

AG′in– 2. Fagin, plaguin', regen [G.] **4.** Copenhagen.

AG′l– 2. plagal, paigle, vagal **3.** finagle.

AG′o– 2. Dago, sago **3.** Sebago, lumbago, plumbago, Diego, galago, imago, farrago, suffrago **4.** Solidago, San Diego, Archimago, galapago **6.** Tierra del Fuego.

AG′rans– 2. flagrance, fragrance, vagrance.

AG′rant– 2. flagrant, fragrant, vagrant **3.** infragrant, unfragrant.

AG′us– 2. Magus, pagus, plague us, tragus, vagus **3.** choragus **4.** archimagus.

A′i– 2. Dei [L.], clayey, Mayey, wheyey **4.** Agnus Dei [L.].

A′ij– 2. drayage, weighage.

A′ik– 2. laic **3.** Chaldaic, Judaic, trochaic, archaic, Romaic, Spondaic, Hebraic, Passaic, mosaic, prosaic, altaic, deltaic, voltaic, stanzaic **4.** Aramaic, Ptolemaic, stenopaic, algebraic, tesseraic, Pharisaic.

A′ing– 2. baying, laying, slaying, sleighing, Maying, neighing, fraying, graying, preying, praying, straying, saying, weighing **3.** obeying, decaying, croqueting, waylaying, parleying, displaying, a-Maying, dismaying, foraying, defraying, portraying, assaying, essaying, gainsaying, crocheting, conveying, surveying, reweighing **4.** disobeying, appliquéing, overpaying, disarraying, overstaying.

Ā'is– 2. dais, Lais, nais.

Ā'ish– 2. bayish, gayish, clayish, grayish, wheyish.

Ā'ist– 4. Ptolemaist, algebraist, Pharisaist; *see also* **Ā'est–** gayest etc. above.

AJ'ed– 2. aged **3.** coaged.

AJ'ent– 2. agent **3.** reagent.

AJ'er– 2. ager, gager, gauger, major, pager, sager, stager, wager, swager **3.** drum major, presager, assuager **4.** trumpet major.

AJ'est– 2. sagest.

AJ'ez– 2. ages, gages, gauges, cages, pages, rages, sages, stages, wages, swages **3.** engages, encages, impages, compages, outrages, presages **4.** disengages.

AJ'i– 2. cagey, Meiji, sagy, stagy.

AJ'ing– 2. aging, gauging, caging, paging, raging, staging, waging **3.** engaging, enraging, presaging, assuaging **4.** disengaging.

AJ'less– 2. ageless, gageless, gaugeless, cageless, pageless, stageless, wageless.

AJ'li– 2. sagely.

AJ'ment– 3. engagement, enragement, presagement, assuagement **4.** pre-engagement, disengagement.

AJ'us– 2. age us etc. **3.** ambagious, rampageous, outrageous, courageous, umbrageous, contagious, enrage us etc. **4.** advantageous, noncontagious **5.** disadvantageous.

AK'a– 2. Cheka, raca, weka, cueca **3.** Macaca, Jamaica, Kapeika, bareca **4.** abhiseka.

AK'at– 2. placate, pacate, vacate.

AK'en– 2. Aiken, bacon, Macon, shaken, taken, waken **3.** Jamaican, forsaken, unshaken, wind-shaken, untaken, mistaken, awaken, rewaken **4.** Godforsaken, unforsaken, undertaken, overtaken, reawaken.

AK'er– 2. acher, acre, baker, faker, fakir, laker, maker, nacre, raker, breaker, shaker, Shaker, taker, staker, waker, Quaker **3.** *wiseacre, matchmaker, watchmaker, bookmaker, peacemaker, dressmaker, lawmaker, shoemaker, strikebreaker, heartbreaker, lawbreaker*, forsaker, *salt-shaker*, partaker, mistaker, painstaker **4.** simulacre, mischiefmaker, Sabbathbreaker, pepper-shaker, undertaker.

AK'erd– 2. acred, nacred **3.** wiseacred.

AK'erz– achers etc., *see* **AK'er–** acher etc. above, plus "'s" or "'s."

AK'i– 2. achy, faky, caky, laky, slaky, snaky, braky, traiky, shaky, quaky **3.** headachy.

AK'ij– 2. flakage, brakeage, breakage.

AK'ing– 2. aching, baking, faking, cak̄ing, slaking, raking, braking, breaking, shaking, waking, quaking **3.** *watchmaking, bookmaking, dressmaking, heartbreaking*, forsaking, partaking, mistaking, *painstaking* **4.** merrymaking, unforsaking, unpartaking, undertaking.

AK'ish– 2. achish, snakish, rakish.

AK'less– 2. acheless, fakeless, cakeless, lakeless, slakeless, snakeless, rakeless, breakless, shakeless, takeless, stakeless, steakless, wakeless, quakeless **3.** mistakeless.

AK'man– 2. cakeman, brakeman, steakman.

AK'o– 2. Draco, Waco **3.** macaco.

AK'red– 2. sacred.

AK'rum– 2. sacrum **3.** synsacrum **4.** simulacrum.

AL'a– 2. ala, chela, gala, mala **3.** kamala, canela [Sp.], panela, osela.

AL'aks– 2. Galax, malax, Spalax.

AL'anks– 2. phalanx, Caranx.

AL'ek– 2. alec.

AL'ens– 2. valence **3.** trivalence, covalence **4.** univalence, equivalence.

AL'ent– 2. valent **3.** inhalant, exhalant, transcalant, assailant, bivalent, trivalent, surveillant   **4.** ambivalent, *equivalent*, polyvalent.

AL'er– 2. alar, baler, bailer, bailor, haler, jailer, jailor, gaoler, scalar, scaler, malar, mailer, nailer, paler, frailer, trailer, sailer, sailor, talar, tailer, tailor, Taylor, staler, wailer, squalor, whaler **3.** regaler, inhaler, exhaler, assailer, *wholesaler*, *retailer*.

AL'erz– alars etc., *see* **AL'er–** alar etc. above, plus "s" or "'s."

A'less– 2. dayless, payless, playless, rayless, prayless, preyless, wayless, swayless.

AL'est– 2. halest, palest, frailest, stalest; and verbs ending in **AL** plus -est.

AL'ful– 2. baleful, pailful, wailful.

AL'i– 2. aly, bailie, Bailey, daily, gaily, scaly, snaily, grayly, traily, taily, waily **3.** shillalah **4.** apercaillie, ukelele, counterpaly; *see* also **AL'li–** palely etc. below.

AL'if– 2. aleph, alef, bailiff, calif, caliph **3.** bumbailiff.

AL'ij– 2. bailage, scalage, sailage **3.** *retailage*, curtailage.

AL'ik– 2. Gaelic, malic, Salic.

AL'iks– 2. calix, calyx, Salix **4.** epicalyx.

AL'ing– 2. ailing, bailing, failing, hailing, jailing, scaling, mailing, paling, railing, grayling, trailing, sailing, tailing, veiling, wailing, whaling **3.** unfailing, regaling, inhaling, exhaling, *blackmailing*, impaling, *wholesaling*, detailing, retailing, entailing, curtailing, *dovetailing*, availing, prevailing, bewailing **4.** countervailing.

AL'ish– 2. palish, frailish, stalish.

AL'less– 2. aleless, bailless, failless, jailless, scaleless, maleless, mailless, nailless, trailless, sailless, tailless, veilless, whaleless.

AL'li– 2. halely, palely, frailly, stalely; *see* also **AL'i–** aly etc. above.

AL'ment– 2. ailment, bailment **3.** regalement, impalement, derailment, assailment, retailment, entailment, curtailment, availment, bewailment.

AL'o– 2. halo **3.** Canelo, canelo.

AL'ya– 5. regalia, Centralia, Australia, azalea **6.** paraphernalia; *see* also **AL'i–a–** galea, etc.

AL'yun– 3. alien **4.** regalian, Centralian, Australian, Pygmalion **5.** bacchanalian, saturnalian **6.** sesquipedalian, tatterdemalion; *see* also **AL'i–an–** alien etc.

AM'a– 2. Fama, lama, Brahma, drama, krama, squama **3.** kalema, salema, Bahama.

A'man– 2. dayman, cayman, layman, drayman **3.** *highwayman*; *see* also **AM'en–** amen etc. below.

AM'ant– 2. claimant, clamant **3.** adhamant, reclaimant.

AM'at– 2. hamate, squamate **3.** desquamate.

AMB'er– 2. chamber **3.** bedchamber **4.** antechamber

AMB'rik– 2. cambric.

AM'en– 2. amen, Haman, daimen, flamen, Bremen, stamen **3.** velamen, clinamen, foramen, duramen, examen, putamen, gravamen; *see* also **A'man–** dayman etc. above.

AM'ent– 2. ament, pament, payment, raiment **3.** allayment, repayment, defrayment, betrayment.

AM'er– 2. aimer, amor, gamer, lamer, blamer, claimer, maimer, namer, framer, shamer, tamer **3.** acclaimer, declaimer, reclaimer, proclaimer, disclaimer, exclaimer, nicknamer, testamur.

AM'est– 2. gamest, lamest, tamest; and verbs ending in **AM** plus –est.

AM'ful– 2. aimful, gameful, blameful, shameful.

AM'i– 2. Amy, gamy, Jamie, flamy, Mamie, rami, zemi.

AM'ing– 2. aiming, gaming, laming, blaming, flaming, claiming, maiming, naming, framing, shaming, taming **3.** acclaiming, declaiming, reclaiming, proclaiming, disclaiming, exclaiming, inflaming nicknaming, misnaming.

AM'ish– **2.** lamish, samish, Samish, tamish.

AM'less– **2.** aimless, fameless, gameless, blameless, claimless, flameless, nameless, frameless shameless, tameless **3.** *nicknameless.*

AM'li– **2.** gamely, lamely, namely, samely, tamely.

AM'ness– **2.** gameness, lameness, sameness, tameness.

AM'us– **2.** Amos, famous, hamus, hamous, ramus, ramous, samos, shame us etc. squamous **3.** mandamus, biramous **4.** ignoramus.

AN'a– **2.** ana, Dana, Rana, rena, scena **3.** arcana, campana **4.** Cartagena, omniana, Geoplana **5.** Americana.

AN'al– **2.** banal, manal, veinal **3.** bimanal **4.** septimanal, interveinal.

AN'an– **2.** Canaan, rainin' etc.

AND'er– **3.** remainder, attainder, detainder.

AN'er– **2.** chainer, feigner, caner, gainer, plainer, saner, seiner, stainer, vainer **3.** urbaner, ordainer, profaner, chicaner, complainer, humaner, inaner, retainer, abstainer.

A'ness– **2.** gayness, grayness, greyness; *see* also AN'ness– plainness etc. below.

AN'est– **2.** plainest, sanest, vainest **3.** urbanest, profanest, humanest, inanest; and verbs ending in AN plus –est.

AN'ful– **2.** baneful, gainful, painful **3.** disdainful, ungainful, complainful.

AN'i– **2.** cany, Janey, rainy, brainy, grainy, veiny, zany **4.** Allegheny, miscellany, castellany.

AN'ij– **2.** chainage, drainage, cranage, trainage.

AN'ing– **2.** deigning, feigning, caning, planing, paining, reigning, reining, raining, craning, training, straining, seining,

waning **3.** ordaining, disdaining, complaining, *airplaning*, campaigning, arraigning, unreining, detraining, entraining, restraining, retaining **4.** uncomplaining, aquaplaning, ascertaining, entertaining.

AN'ish– **2.** Danish, sanish, vainish **3.** urbanish.

ANJ'el– **2.** angel **3.** archangel.

ANJ'er– **2.** changer, danger, manger, ranger, stranger **3.** exchanger, endanger, arranger, deranger, *bushranger*, estranger **4.** money-changer, interchanger, rearranger, disarranger.

ANJ'est– **2.** strangest; and verbs ending in ANJ plus –est.

ANJ'ez– **2.** changes, ranges, granges **3.** exchanges, shortchanges, arranges, deranges, estranges **4.** rearranges, prearranges, interchanges, disarranges.

ANJ'i– **2.** mangy, rangy.

ANJ'ing– **2.** changing, ranging **3.** unchanging, exchanging, shortchanging, estranging **4.** interchanging, rearranging, prearranging, disarranging.

ANJ'less– **2.** changeless, mangeless, rangeless, grangeless **3.** exchangeless.

ANJ'li– **2.** Rangeley, strangely.

ANJ'ling– **2.** changeling, strangeling.

ANJ'ment– **2.** changement **3.** arrangement, derangement, estrangement **4.** rearrangement, prearrangement, disarrangement.

ANJ'ness– **2.** strangeness.

AN'less– **2.** chainless, gainless, maneless, painless, rainless, brainless, grainless, strainless, stainless, vaneless, veinless, waneless, swainless.

AN'li– **2.** fainly, plainly, mainly, sanely, vainly **3.** urbanely, profanely, ungainly, humanely, insanely **4.** inhumanely.

AN'ment– **3.** enchainment, ordainment, regainment, arraignment, attainment, detainment, retainment **4.** reordainment, ascertainment, entertainment.

AN'ness– **2.** plainness, saneness, vainness **3.** urbaneness, profaneness, humaneness, inaneness, insaneness; *see* also **A'ness–** gayness etc. above.

AN'o– **2.** Drano **3.** volcano, sereno [Sp.].

ANT'ed– **2.** fainted, feinted, painted, sainted, tainted **3.** ensainted, attainted, acquainted **4.** unacquainted.

ANT'er– **2.** fainter, feinter, painter, quainter.

ANT'est– **2.** faintest, quaintest.

ANT'i– **2.** dainty, fainty.

ANT'if– **2.** plaintiff **3.** coplaintiff.

ANT'ing– **2.** fainting, feinting, painting, sainting, tainting **3.** repainting, attainting, acquainting.

ANT'ish– **2.** faintish, saintish.

ANT'iv– **2.** plaintive **3.** complaintive, constraintive.

ANT'li– **2.** faintly, saintly, quaintly **3.** unfaintly, unsaintly.

ANT'ness– **2.** faintness, quaintness.

AN'um– **3.** Arcanum, Solanum.

AN'us– **2.** heinous, Janus, manus, veinous, pain us **3.** ananas, Silvanus **4.** decumanus.

A'o– **2.** kayo, bleo, Mayo **3.** cacao.

A'on– **2.** rayon, crayon **3.** Lycaon.

A'or– **2.** mayor **3.** mormaor, conveyor, purveyor, surveyor; *see* **A'er–** feyer etc. above.

A'os– **2.** chaos, naos, Naos, Taos **3.** pronaos **4.** epinaos.

AP'en– **2.** shapen, tapen **3.** unshapen, misshapen.

AP'er– **2.** aper, gaper, caper, paper, draper, scraper, sapor, shaper, taper, tapir, vapor **3.** nordcaper, *landscaper*, escaper, *wallpaper*, *gunpaper*, *newspaper*, *skyscraper*, redtaper.

AP'erz– apers etc., *see* **AP'er–** aper etc. above, plus "s" or "'s."

AP'i– **2.** gapy, grapy, crapy, crepy, scrapy **3.** red-tapey.

AP'ing– **2.** aping, gaping, Peiping, draping, scraping, shaping, taping **3.** escaping, *landscaping*, *skyscraping*, reshaping, misshaping, retaping.

AP'is– **2.** apis, tapis **3.** sinapis, Serapis.

AP'ish– **2.** apish, gapish, papish **3.** redtapish.

AP'ist– **2.** papist, tapist **3.** *landscapist*, escapist, red-tapist.

AP'izm– **2.** apism, papism **3.** red-tapism.

AP'l– **2.** capel, maple, papal, staple **3.** nonpapal **4.** antipapal.

AP'less– **2.** capeless, grapeless, shapeless, tapeless.

AP'let– **2.** apelet, capelet, grapelet.

AP'li– **2.** shapely **3.** unshapely, *shipshapely*.

AP'lz– **2.** maples, Naples, staples.

AP'on– **2.** capon, tape on etc.

AP'ron– **2.** apron, napron.

AR'a– **2.** Eire, Sara, Sarah, tera **3.** Madeira, caldera, Sahara, cascara, gallera.

AR'ans– **3.** forbearance, appearance **4.** unforbearance.

AR'er– **2.** airer, error, bearer, barer, darer, fairer, farer, carer, scarer, blarer, flarer, glarer, snarer, pairer, parer, sparer, rarer, sharer, tearer, terror, starer, wearer, swearer, squarer **3.** sword-bearer, talebearer, pallbearer, cupbearer, mace-bearer, outdarer, wayfarer, seafarer, declarer, ensnarer, repairer, preparer, impairer, comparer, despairer, awarer, forswearer **4.** standard-bearer, armor-bearer.

AR'erz– airers etc., *see* **AR'er–** airer etc. above, plus "s" or "'s."

AR'ess– **2.** heiress, bearess **3.** coheiress.

AR'est– **2.** barest, fairest, rarest, squarest **3.** unfairest; and verbs ending in **AR** plus -est.

AR'ez– **2.** Ares, Aries, Dares, caries, Lares, nares, paries **4.** Buenos Aires.

AR'ful– **2.** dareful, careful, prayerful **3.** uncareful, despairful.

AR'i– **2.** airy, aerie, chary, dairy, fairy, faerie, Gary, hairy, Carey, scary, lairy, blary, flary, glary, glairy, clary, Mary, nary, snary, prairie, seri, stary, vary, wary; *see* also AR'i– scarry etc.; AR'i– Barrie etc.; ER'i– berry etc. **3.** *quandary*, vagary, *rosemary*, canary, contrary, unwary **4.** syllabary, columbary, dromedary, lapidary, prebendary, legendary, secondary, nucleary, tertiary, formicary, persicary, tutelary, mammilary, capillary, ancillary, axillary, maxillary, corollary, medullary, formulary, scapulary, titulary, calamary, lachrymary, customary, millenary, parcenary, mercenary, centenary, ordinary, culinary, seminary, luminary, doctrinary, sanguinary, legionary, regionary, pulmonary, coronary, sublunary, stationary, cautionary, missionary, dictionary, functionary, pensionary, passionary, questionary, visionary, numerary, vulnerary, Tipperary, literary, honorary, temporary, arbitrary, *accessary*, necessary, emissary, commissary, janissary, adversary, dietary, proletary, planetary, monetary, secretary, military, solitary, sanitary, dignitary, sedentary, fragmentary, commentary, momentary, voluntary, tributary, salutary, reliquary, antiquary, January, February, statuary, actuary, sanctuary, sumptuary, mortuary, estuary, salivary, cassowary **5.** subsidiary, stipendiary, incendiary, pecuniary, fiduciary, apothecary, hypothecary, epistolary, vocabulary, constabulary, accustomary, bicentenary, tercentenary, imaginary, disciplinary, preliminary, veterinary, ganglionary, probationary, precautionary, discretionary, processionary, additionary, traditionary, seditionary, pe-

titionary, tuitionary, reactionary, confectionary, ablutionary, revisionary, divisionary, provisionary, itinerary, contemporary, extemporary, unnecessary, proprietary, depositary, prothonotary, contributary, residuary, obituary, tumultuary, voluptuary **6.** beneficiary, intermediary, accidentiary, adminiculary, prolegomenary, valetudinary, latitudinary, multitudinary, eleemosynary, insurrectionary, elocutionary, evolutionary, revolutionary, supernumerary **7.** consuetudinary, vicissitudinary.

AR'id– **2.** varied **3.** unvaried; *see* also AR'id– carried etc.; ER'id– berried etc.

AR'ing– **2.** airing, baring, bearing, daring, faring, haring, herring, caring, chairing, scaring, blaring, flaring, glaring, pairing, paring, sparing, sharing, tearing, staring, wearing, Waring, swearing, squaring **3.** *talebearing, seafaring*, declaring, repairing, impairing, despairing, outstaring, outwearing, outswearing, forswearing **4.** overbearing, undeclaring.

AR'is– **2.** naris **3.** Polaris' **4.** cucullaris.

AR'ish– **2.** bearish, barish, fairish, garish, cherish, rarish, squarish **3.** nightmarish **4.** debonairish.

AR'less– **2.** airless, heirless, hairless, careless, chairless, glareless, snareless, pairless, spareless, prayerless, shareless, tareless, stairless.

AR'li– **2.** barely, fairly, rarely, squarely, yarely **3.** unfairly.

AR'line– **2.** airline, hairline.

AR'man– **2.** airman, chairman.

AR'ness– **2.** bareness, fairness, spareness, rareness, thereness, squareness, whereness **3.** *threadbareness*, unfairness, awareness **4.** debonairness, unawareness.

AR'o– **2.** aero, faro, Pharaoh **3.** ranchero, cochero, vaquero, bolero, llanero, dinero, sombrero, torero [all Sp.] **4.** sudadero, matadero, hacendero, caballero,

bandolero, campanero, zapatero [all Sp.];
see also **AR'o–** arrow etc.

AR'u– 2. Meru, Nehru.

AR'um– 2. arum, garum, harem, carrom, scare 'em etc. 4. harumscarum 9.
scientia scientiarum.

AS'a– 2. Asa, mesa, presa [It.], vasa
[L.] 3. cabeza [Sp.].

AS'al– 2. basal, casal, vasal 3. oasal.

AS'eez– 2. bases 3. oases.

AS'en– 2. basin, facin' etc., hasten, Jason,
chasten, mason, sasin 3. *washbasin*, enchasten, freemason, *stonemason*; *see also*
AS'on– caisson etc. below.

AS'ens– 3. abaisance, obeisance, adjacence, complaisance, complacence, renascence, connascence 4. interjacence, uncomplaisance.

AS'ent– 2. jacent, nascent, naissant 3.
obeisant, subjacent, adjacent, complacent,
renascent, renaissant, connascent 4. circumjacent, interjacent, uncomplacent.

AS'er– 2. Acer, baser, chaser, facer, caser,
lacer, placer, macer, pacer, spacer, racer,
bracer, tracer 3. abaser, debaser, defacer, effacer, eraser, horse racer, embracer,
begracer, disgracer, retracer, encaser, belacer, enlacer, unlacer, grimacer, outpacer,
replacer, misplacer, displacer 4. steeplechaser, interlacer

AS'ez– aces, etc. *see* **AS–** ace etc. above,
plus "s" or "'s."

AS'ful– 2. spaceful, graceful 3. ungraceful, disgraceful.

ASH'a– 2. Asia, geisha 3. Acacia, Dalmatia.

ASH'al– 2. facial, glacial, spatial, racial
3. abbatial, palatial, prelatial, primatial
4. unifacial, interspatial, interracial.

ASH'an– 2. Asian 3. predacean, phocacean, cetacean, testacean, crustacean;
see also **ASH'un–** nation etc. below.

ASH'ens– 2. facients, patience, patients
3. impatience, outpatients.

ASH'ent– 2. facient, patient 3. impatient, outpatient 4. sorbefacient, rubefacient, calefacient, tumefacient, stupefacient, somnifacient, liquefacient.

ASH'un– 2. nation, ration, station 3.
cibation, libation, limbation, jobation,
probation, placation, vacation, peccation,
plication, sulcation, truncation, location,
vocation, furcation, piscation, gradation,
foundation, laudation, sudation, creation,
legation, ligation, rogation, purgation,
jugation, striation, alation, halation, ablation, oblation, sublation, elation, delation,
gelation, relation, velation, deflation, sufflation, inflation, conflation, dilation,
vallation, illation, collation, prolation,
cremation, sigmation, himation, gemmation, commation, summation, formation,
planation, adnation, enation, agnation,
signation, cognation, damnation, conation,
donation, phonation, pronation, lunation,
libration, vibration, hydration, ceration,
spheration, migration, liration, oration,
moration, nitration, titration, filtration,
curation, duration, neuration, gyration,
cessation, causation, pausation, natation,
jactation, lactation, tractation, dictation,
nictation, citation, saltation, peltation,
cantation, plantation, dentation, mentation, tentation, floatation, notation, potation, rotation, quotation, votation, captation, septation, flirtation, hortation, curtation, substation, gestation, testation,
crustation, gustation, guttation, lutation,
mutation, nutation, putation, equation,
lavation, ovation, novation, starvation,
nervation, servation, curvation, laxation,
taxation, vexation, fixation, luxation, fluxation 4. reprobation, approbation, perturbation, accubation, incubation, titubation, intubation, desiccation, exsiccation,
deprecation, imprecation, comprecation,
albication, radication, abdication, dedication, medication, predication, indication,
vindication, syndication, replication, triplication, implication, complication, application, supplication, duplication, explica-

tion, varication, fabrication, imbrication, lubrication, rubrication, lorication, extrication, vesication, mastication, rustication, toxication, allocation, collocation, dislocation, embrocation, avocation, convocation, provocation, demarcation, altercation, bifurcation, confiscation, obfuscation, coruscation, degradation, aggradation, depredation, validation, lapidation, trepidation, liquidation, emendation, commendation, inundation, retardation, denudation, desudation, transudation, trabeation, ideation, nucleation, permeation, lineation, recreation, procreation, propagation, divagation, delegation, relegation, allegation, abnegation, segregation, aggregation, congregation, obligation, fumigation, irrigation, litigation, mitigation, castigation, instigation, fustigation, elongation, prolongation, abrogation, derogation, objurgation, expurgation, subjugation, conjugation, corrugation, fasciation, radiation, mediation, ciliation, filiation, palliation, foliation, spoliation, expiation, variation, seriation, satiation, vitiation, aviation, obviation, deviation, debarkation, embarkation, demarkation, inhalation, exhalation, congelation, correlation, revelation, insufflation, sibilation, jubilation, strigilation, vigilation, depilation, compilation, ventilation, mutilation, installation, flabellation, cancellation, flagellation, lamellation, crenellation, compellation, appellation, tessellation, castellation, constellation, vacillation, oscillation, fibrillation, titillation, scintillation, distillation, instillation, decollation, percolation, violation, immolation, desolation, isolation, insolation, consolation, avolation, legislation, contemplation, tabulation, tribulation, ambulation, peculation, speculation, calculation, circulation, osculation, adulation, undulation, stridulation, modulation, nodulation, regulation, angulation, ululation, emulation, simulation, stimulation, nummulation, formulation, cumulation, granulation, crenulation,

annulation, population, stipulation, sporulation, insulation, pustulation, ovulation, defamation, acclamation, declamation, reclamation, proclamation, exclamation, desquamation, racemation, decimation, sublimation, acclimation, collimation, animation, intimation, estimation, inflammation, consummation, affirmation, confirmation, deformation, reformation, malformation, information, conformation, transformation, inhumation, exhumation, lachrymation, profanation, explanation, emanation, impanation, hyphenation, alienation, catenation, impregnation, indignation, obsignation, designation, resignation, assignation, consignation, combination, turbination, vaccination, fascination, ordination, pagination, machination, declination, reclination, inclination, pollination, lamination, gemination, semination, culmination, fulmination, commination, domination, nomination, germination, termination, vermination, lumination, rumination, supination, fibrination, destination, glutination, ruination, divination, condemnation, carbonation, condonation, coronation, personation, detonation, intonation, incarnation, hibernation, alternation, consternation, subornation, eburnation, dissipation, inculpation, exculpation, syncopation, extirpation, usurpation, occupation, nuncupation, declaration, reparation, preparation, separation, celebration, palpebration, cerebration, terebration, vertebration, calibration, adumbration, lucubration, obsecration, desecration, consecration, execration, dehydration, liberation, verberation, laceration, maceration, ulceration, carceration, federation, ponderation, moderation, toleration, numeration, generation, veneration, cineration, operation, asperation, desperation, iteration, literation, alteration, severation, integration, emigration, remigration, immigration, transmigration, admiration, aspiration, respiration, transpiration, inspiration, perspiration, suspiration, expiration, decoration, adoration, perforation, coloration, imploration, exploration, pignoration, corporation, peroration, restoration, aberration, saburration, susurration, penetration, impetration, perpetration, arbitration, infiltration, concentration, orchestration, fenestration, sequestration, registration, ministration, demonstration, remonstration, illustration, procuration, obduration, induration, figuration, fulguration, objuration, conjuration, depuration, suppuration, mensuration, maturation, saturation, trituration, suturation, condensation, compensation, dispensation, conversation, endorsation, incrassation, inspissation, succussation, decussation, dilatation, delactation, affectation, delectation, humectation, expectation, reluctation, eructation, hebetation, vegetation, habitation, dubitation, recitation, incitation, oscitation, excitation, meditation, agitation, digitation, cogitation, gurgitation, militation, imitation, limitation, sanitation, capitation, crepitation, palpitation, irritation, hesitation, visitation, nictitation, gravitation, levitation, invitation, exaltation, occultation, auscultation, consultation, exultation, decantation, recantation, incantation, implantation, transplantation, indentation, lamentation, segmentation, pigmentation, augmentation, commentation, fomentation, fermentation, frumentation, presentation, ostentation, sustentation, frequentation, confrontation, denotation, annotation, connotation, compotation, misquotation, adaptation, impartation, dissertation, dehortation, exhortation, deportation, importation, transportation, exportation, devastation, infestation, molestation, forestation, detestation, intestation, contestation, protestation, attestation, reinstation, degustation, incrustation, confutation, refutation, salutation, immutation, commutation, permutation, transmutation, deputation, reputation, amputation, imputation, computation, disputation,

graduation, valuation, adequation, actuation, punctuation, fluctuation, fructuation, situation, excavation, aggravation, depravation, elevation, salivation, derivation, deprivation, cultivation, motivation, captivation, estivation, renovation, innovation, enervation, innervation, observation, reservation, preservation, conservation, decurvation, incurvation, relaxation, annexation, prefixation, affixation, suffixation, solmization 5. disapprobation, exacerbation, hypothecation, syllabication, eradication, revindication, adjudication, albification, pacification, specification, calcification, dulcification, edification, nidification, codification, modification, deification, salification, qualification, vilification, mellification, jollification, mollification, nullification, prolification, amplification, simplification, magnification, dignification, signification, damnification, unification, aerification, clarification, verification, nigrification, glorification, petrification, thurification, purification, falsification, versification, classification, ossification, ratification, gratification, lactification, rectification, sanctification, notification, certification, fortification, mortification, testification, justification, mystification, vivification, republication, multiplication, misapplication, reduplication, quadruplication, communication, prevarication, authentication, domestication, sophistication, prognostication, intoxication, reciprocation, equivocation, retrogradation, invalidation, consolidation, intimidation, delapidation, recommendation, accomodation, enucleation, delineation, allineation, variegation, investigation, interrogation, emaciation, depreciation, appreciation, officiation, enunciation, denunciation, renunciation, annunciation, pronunciation, excruciation, eradiation, irradiation, remediation, repudiation, retaliation, conciliation, affiliation, humiliation, defoliation, exfoliation, despoliation, calumniation, colum-

niation, inebriation, excoriation, appro-
priation, expropriation, repatriation, ex-
patriation, infuriation, luxuriation, expa-
tiation, ingratiation, initiation, propitia-
tion, novitiation, substantiation, nogotia-
tion, alleviation, abbreviation, lixiviation,
exuviation, asphyxiation, disembarkation,
intercalation, interrelation, invigilation,
annihilation, assimilation, horripilation,
circumvallation, interpellation, vitriola-
tion, etiolation, interpolation, disconsola-
tion, confabulation, somnambulation, per-
ambulation, noctambulation, ejaculation,
fasciculation, vermiculation, matriculation,
reticulation, denticulation, articulation,
gesticulation, miscalculation, tubercula-
tion, emasculation, triangulation, dissimu-
lation, accumulation, manipulation, de-
population, repopulation, congratulation,
capitulation, expostulation, amalgamation
reanimation, approximation, reaffirma-
tion, misinformation, malconformation,
hydrogenation, alienation, concatenation,
rejuvenation, hallucination, subordina-
tion, preordination, coordination, imag-
ination, origination, disinclination, con-
tamination, insemination, dissemination,
elimination, recrimination, incrimination,
discrimination, abomination, predomina-
tion, denomination, renomination, pre-
nomination, determination, extermina-
tion, acumination, illumination, peregri-
nation, indoctrination, assassination, pro-
crastination, predestination, agglutina-
tion, conglutination, impersonation, an-
ticipation, participation, emancipation,
preoccupation, exhilaration, deliberation,
reverberation, incarceration, evisceration,
confederation, desideration, consideration,
preponderation, immoderation, vocifera-
tion, proliferation, exaggeration, refrigera-
tion, acceleration, deceleration, intolera-
tion, concameration, agglomeration, con-
glomeration, enumeration, renumeration,
degeneration, regeneration, incineration,
itineration, exoneration, remuneration,
co-operation, exasperation, depauperation,

recuperation, vituperation, commisera-
tion, reiteration, obliteration, alliteration,
transliteration, adulteration, asseveration,
redintegration, elaboration, collaboration,
corroboration, imperforation, invigora-
tion, amelioration, deterioration, discolor-
ation, commemoration, incorporation,
expectoration, recalcitration, administra-
tion, prefiguration, transfiguration, inau-
guration, commensuration, circumgyra-
tion, intravasation, extravasation, im-
provisation, tergiversation, interpretation,
inhabitation, capacitation, felicitation,
solicitation, resuscitation, premeditation,
exagitation, recogitation, precogitation,
regurgitation, habilitation, debilitation,
facilitation, delimitation, exploitation,
decapitation, decrepitation, precipitation,
revisitation, necessitation, ornamentation,
supplementation, sedimentation, regimen-
tation, alimentation, documentation, ar-
gumentation, instrumentation, represen-
tation, inadaptation, coadaptation, mani-
festation, deforestation, reforestation, cir-
cumnutation, evaluation, revaluation, at-
tenuation, extenuation, insinuation, con-
tinuation, effectuation, perpetration, ha-
bituation, accentuation, insalivation, re-
captivation, ostracization, hybridization,
iridization, oxidization, aggrandization,
standardization, syllogization, eulogiza-
tion, catechization, focalization, vocaliza-
tion, feudalization, vandalization, idealiza-
tion, realization, legalization, racializa-
tion, socialization, alkalization, formal-
ization, normalization, penalization, mor-
alization, centralization, neutralization,
vitalization, tantalization, totalization,
equalization, chattelization, stabilization,
mobilization, sterilization, fertilization,
utilization, tranquilization, civilization,
crystallization, verbalization, symboliza-
tion, idolization, formulization, minimi-
zation, victimization, atomization, urban-
ization, vulcanization, organization, Chris-
tianization, humanization, galvanization,
pollenization, scrutinization, solemniza-

tion, columnization, carbonization, ionization, colonization, mnemonization, harmonization, canonization, synchronization, patronization, modernization, fraternization, polarization, summarization, mercerization, mesmerization, pauperization, cauterization, pulverization, arborization, theorization, authorization, vaporization, temporization, proctorization, phosphorization, pasteurization, sulphurization, dramatization, stigmatization, magnetization, monetization, sensitization, amortization, analyzation, paralyzation 6. contraindication, decalcification, solidification, disqualification, exemplification, indemnification, saponification, personification, transmogrification, electrification, emulsification, intensification, diversification, beatification, identification, excommunication, unsophistication, interlineation, supererogation, mispronunciation, intermediation, domiciliation, reconciliation, misappropriation, transubstantiation, consubstantiation, circumstantiation, differentiation, tintinnabulation, circumambulation, recapitulation, abalienation, ratiocination, insubordination, inco-ordination, indiscrimination, predetermination, indetermination, reconsideration, inconsideration, maladministration, incapacitation, unpremeditation, prestidigitation, interdigitation, rehabilitation, experimentation, misrepresentation, individuation, discontinuation, superannuation, deoxidization, devocalization, commercialization, materialization, decimalization, nationalization, liberalization, generalization, demoralization, decentralization, naturalization, capitalization, devitalization, revitalization, immortalization, visualization, caramelization, demobilization, remobilization, monopolization, legitimization, economization, anatomization, epitomization, reorganization, inorganization, disorganization, antagonization, recolonization, familiarization, depolarization, formulariza-

tion, popularization, militarization, polymerization, characterization, deodorization, categorization, systematization, acclimatization, aromatization, alphabetization, anesthetization, arithmetization, demonetization, desensitization 7. intercommunication, intercolumniation, denationalization, denaturalization, universalization, spiritualization, Americanization 8. internationalization, individualization, intellectualization.

ASH′und– 2. rationed, stationed 3. vacationed.

ASH′unz– nations etc., *see* **ASH′un–** nation etc. above, plus "s" or "'s."

ASH′us– 2. caseous, spacious, gracious 3. sebaceous, bibacious, bulbaceous, herbaceous, edacious, predaceous, mendacious, bodacious, smordacious, audacious, safacious, fugacious, salacious, fallacious, fumacious, tenacious, pugnacious, capacious, rapacious, rampacious, feracious, veracious, ungracious, disgracious, voracious flirtatious, ʳsetaceous, rutaceous, sequacious, loquacious, vivacious, vexatious 4. efficacious, perspicacious, pervicacious, contumacious, pertinacious, incapacious, orchidaceous, corallaceous, liliaceous, scoriaceous, capillaceous, farinaceous, carbonaceous, saponaceous, camphoraceous, pulveraceous, frumentaceous, ostentatious, disputatious 5. inefficacious.

AS′i– 2. lacy, racy, Gracie, precis, Tracy 4. contumacy, Betsy-Tacy.

AS′ik– 2. basic, phasic 3. tribasic, aphasic 4. diabasic, polybasic, monophasic, carapacic, diastasic.

AS′in– 2. basin, sasin, facin' etc. 3. washbasin; *see* also **AS′on–** caisson etc. below.

AS′ing– 2. acing, basing, chasing, facing, casing, lacing, placing, pacing, spacing, racing, bracing, tracing 3. abasing, debasing, effacing, defacing, refacing, encasing, belacing, enlacing, unlacing, shoe lacing, replacing, misplacing, outpacing, horseracing, embracing, grimacing, displacing, erasing, disgracing, retracing **4.** steeplechasing, interlacing.

AS'is– 2. basis, phasis, glacis, crasis, stasis **3.** oasis.

AS'iv– 2. suasive **3.** occasive, abrasive, assuasive, dissuasive, persuasive, evasive, invasive, pervasive.

AS'less– 2. aceless, baseless, faceless, caseless, laceless, placeless, maceless, paceless, spaceless, raceless, graceless, braceless, traceless, vaseless **3.** embraceless.

AS'let– 2. lacelet, bracelet.

AS'li– 2. basely **4.** commonplacely.

AS'ment– 2. basement, casement, placement **3.** abasement, effacement, defacement, encasement, enlacement, replacement, emplacement, displacement, misplacement, embracement, retracement.

AS'o– 2. peso, say-so **3.** Congreso.

AS'on– 2. caisson, lace on, *meson*; *see* also **AS'en–** basin etc. above.

AST'ed– 2. basted, hasted, pasted, tasted, wasted, waisted **3.** unbasted, unpasted, untasted, unwasted, long-waisted, high-waisted, short-waisted.

AST'er– 2. baster, chaster, paster, taster, waster **3.** foretaster.

AST'ful– 2. tasteful, wasteful **3.** distasteful, unwasteful.

AST'i– 2. hasty, pasty, tasty **3.** unhasty, untasty.

AST'ij– 2. wastage.

AST'ing– 2. basting, hasting, pasting, tasting, wasting **3.** unbasting, untasting, foretasting, unwasting.

AST'ingz– bastings etc., *see* **AST'ing–** basting etc. above, plus "s" or "'s"; **2.** Hastings.

AST'less– 2. basteless, hasteless, pasteless, tasteless, wasteless, waistless.

AST'ri– 2. pastry.

AS'um– 3. omasum **4.** abomasum.

AT'a– 2. Eta, Beta, data, Theta, rata, strata, Zeta **3.** albata, Caudata, relata, Squamata, pro rata **4.** Vertebrata, ultimata **5.** Invertebrata, desiderata.

AT'al– 2. datal, fatal, natal, ratal, stratal, statal **3.** prenatal, postnatal, substratal.

AT'e– Ate etc., *see* **AT'i–** Ate etc. below.

AT'ed– 2. bated, baited, dated, fated, fêted, gated, gaited, hated, plated, plaited, mated, pated, rated, grated, prated, sated, stated, waited, weighted **3.** abated, debated, rebated, predated, postdated, outdated, created, ill-fated, elated, belated, related, deflated, inflated, checkmated, stalemated, cremated, berated, frustrated, instated, awaited **4.** antedated, validated, liquidated, inundated, ideated, permeated, re-created, procreated, propagated, delegated, relegated, abnegated, aggregated, segregated, obligated, fumigated, irrigated, litigated, mitigated, instigated, subjugated, corrugated, radiated, mediated, predicated, indicated, vindicated, syndicated, implicated, complicated, duplicated, supplicated, fabricated, lubricated, extricated, rusticated, advocated, altercated, confiscated, educated, unrelated, correlated, ventilated, scintillated, mutilated, percolated, contemplated, tabulated, modulated, regulated, speculated, circulated, osculated, emulated, formulated, granulated, stipulated, acclimated, animated, intimated, estimated, consummated, emanated, hyphenated, designated, terminated, ruminated, fascinated, carbonated, intonated, hibernated, addle-pated, dissipated, syncopated separated, celebrated, desecrated, consecrated, federated, moderated, tolerated, generated, venerated, operated, emigrated, perforated, decorated, underrated, penetrated, arbitrated, concentrated, demonstrated, illustrated, saturated, compensated, meditated, agitated, cogitated, imitated, palpitated, irritated, hesitated, gravitated, reinstated, amputated, graduated, situated, antiquated, actuated, punctuated, fluctuated, aggravated, elevated, cultivated, captivated, renovated **5.** elucidated, invalidated, consolidated, intimidated, dilapidated, accommodated, repudiated, retaliated, affiliated, humiliated, appropriated, emaciated, ingratiated, appreciated, depreciated, initiated, enunciated, negotiated, associated, annihilated, assimilated, matriculated, articulated, gesticulated, inoculated, accumulated, manipulated, congratulated, capitulated, approximated, subordinated, coordinated, originated, contaminated, disseminated, illuminated, opinionated, impersonated, anticipated, participated, emancipated, exaggerated, accelerated, enumerated, exonerated, remunerated, cooperated, recuperated, commiserated, reiterated, obliterated, disintegrated, elaborated, collaborated, corroborated, commemorated, evaporated, incorporated, inaugurated, premeditated, debilitated, facilitated, precipitated, necessitated, felicitated, resuscitated, orientated, evaluated, devaluated, insinuated, infatuated, accentuated **6.** circumstantiated, differentiated, recapitulated, incapacitated.

AT'en– **2.** datin' etc., straighten, straiten, Satan.

AT'ent– **2.** latent, blatant, natant, patent **3.** inflatant, dilatant.

AT'er– **2.** bater, baiter, cater, dater, gaiter, hater, skater, later, plater, slater, mater, pater, rater, crater, frater, greater, grater, prater, traitor, satyr, sater, waiter, 'tater, stater **3.** abater, debater, rebater, placater, vacatur, Decatur, elater, delater, relater, Dis pater, confrater, barrater **4.** allocatur, deleatur, imprimatur, annotater, exequatur; *see* also **AT'or–** traitor below.

AT'erz– baiters etc., *see* **AT'er–** baiter etc. above, plus "s" or "'s."

AT'est– **2.** latest, greatest; and verbs ending in **AT** plus –est.

AT'ez– **2.** vates **3.** Primates, penates, Euphrates.

AT'ful– **2.** fateful, hateful, plateful, grateful **3.** ungrateful.

ATH'er– **2.** bather, lather, swather.

ATH'ing– **2.** bathing, scathing, lathing, swathing.

ATH'os– **2.** bathos, pathos.

AT'i– **2.** Ate, eighty, Haiti, Katie, Leyte, slaty, maty, paty, weighty **4.** Jubilate, literati [both L.].

AT'im– **3.** verbatim, gradatim [L.] **4.** seriatim, literatim [both L.].

AT'ime– **2.** daytime, Maytime, playtime, pay time.

AT'ing– **2.** baiting, bating, dating, fêting, hating, skating, plating, plaiting, slating, mating, rating, grating, crating, prating, sating, waiting **3.** abating, debating, postdating, relating, inflating, awaiting **4.** antedating, emanating, reinstating, understating, overstating; and other verbs ending in **AT** plus –ing.

AT'ish– **2.** latish, slatish, straightish.

AT'iv– **2.** dative, native, stative **3.** creative, elative, prolative, dilative, frustrative **4.** approbative, reprobative, desiccative, exsiccative, deprecative, dedicative, medicative, vindicative, judicative, vellicative, replicative, implicative, complicative, duplicative, explicative, suffocative, invocative, educative, recreative, uncreative, procreative, propagative, abnegative, segregative, aggregative, irrigative, mitigative, abrogative, radiative, mediative, palliative, variative, nomenclative, ventilative, oscillative, violative, contemplative, legislative, speculative, calculative, circulative, modulative, regulative, emulative, simulative, stimulative, cumulative, animative, estimative, emanative, designative, geminative, dominative, nominative, germinative, terminative, ruminative, lacerative, federative, generative, operative, decorative, pignorative, ministrative, illustrative, suppurative, compensative, dispensative, vegetative, meditative, cogitative, qualitative, imitative, limitative, irritative, hesitative, quantitative, gravitative, facultative, innovative, punctuative 5. eradicative, adjudicative, significative, multiplicative, communicative, prognosticative, elucidative, consolidative, accommodative, investigative, depreciative, appreciative, enunciative, denunciative, renunciative, pronunciative, associative, dissociative, retaliative, conciliative, appropriative, initiative, alleviative, gesticulative, coagulative, accumulative, manipulative, congratulative, expostulative, approximative, subordinative, imaginative, originative, contaminative, disseminative, recriminative, discriminative, denominative, determinative, illuminative, opinionative, anticipative, participative, exhilarative, deliberative, confederative, desiderative, exaggerative, accelerative, enumerative, exonerative, remunerative, inoperative, co-operative, recuperative, vituperative, reiterative, alliterative, corroborative, invigorative, ameliorative, deteriorative, commemorative, evaporative, administrative, interpretative, inhabitative, necessitative, resuscitative, premeditative, authoritative, insinuative, continuative 6. insignificative, uncommunicative, excommunicative, unappreciative, recapitulative, unimaginative, unremunerative.

AT′less– 2. baitless, dateless, fateless, gateless, gaitless, hateless, mateless, ateless, freightless, grateless, traitless, sateless, stateless, weightless 3. estateless.

AT′li– 2. lately, greatly, straitly, straightly, stately 3. oblately, sedately, striately, prolately, truncately, palmately, innately, pinnately, ternately, ornately, irately, dentately, unstately, privately 4. delicately, intricately, mediately, desolately, ultimately, intimately, proximately, obstinately, passionately, biternately, triter-

nately, alternately, fortunately, separately, moderately, temperately, desperately, corporately, accurately, obdurately, insensately, decussately, adequately 5. indelicately, immediately, appropriately, inviolately, disconsolately, immaculately, legitimately, approximately, subordinately, inordinately, co-ordinately, effeminately, discriminately, determinately, impassionately, compassionately, dispassionately, affectionately, proportionately, unfortunately, importunately, deliberately, considerately, immoderately, degenerately, intemperately, illiterately, elaborately, inaccurately, commensurately, precipitately, inadequately 6. intermediately, inappropriately, unappropriately, illegitimately, insubordinately, indiscriminately, indeterminately, unaffectionately, disproportionately, inconsiderately, incommensurately.

AT′ness– 2. lateness, greatness, straightness, straitness 3. sedateness, oblateness, innateness, ornateness, irateness 5. considerateness, appropriateness.

AT′o– 2. Cato, Plato 3. abeto [Sp.], pomato, tomato, potato.

AT′or– 2. traitor 3. abator, probator, plicator, locator, piscator, mandator, laudator, creator, legator, negator, ligator, viator, elator, delator, relator, dilator, collator, translator, cremator, senator, signator, spinator, donator, vibrator, migrator, orator, barrator, narrator, curator, gyrator, pulsator, natator, tractator, spectator, dictator, punctator, potator, rotator, portator, testator, equator, levator 4. incubator, desiccator, exsiccator, deprecator, imprecator, abdicator, dedicator, predicator, indicator, vindicator, judicator, duplicator, explicator, fabricator, lubricator, rubricator, extricator, masticator, rusticator, inculcator, advocator, evocator, invocator, convocator, demarcator, confiscator, educator, depredator, liquidator, emendator, commendator, recreator, procreator, caveator, propagator, abnegator, obligator, alligator, fumigator, irrigator, litigator, mitigator, castigator, instigator, navigator, promulgator, compurgator, expurgator, subjugator, corrugator, gladiator, radiator, mediator, palliator, spoliator, expiator, vitiator, aviator, deviator, escalator, inhalator, nomenclator, revelator, depilator, ventilator, scintillator, mutilator, flagellator, vacillator, oscillator, desolator, percolator, violator, immolator, isolator, contemplator, tabulator, ambulator, speculator, calculator, inoculator, circulator, adulator, modulator, regulator, emulator, simulator, stimulator, granulator, stipulator, insulator, decimator, estimator, consummator, emanator, designator, propugnator, vaccinator, buccinator, fascinator, machinator, comminator, dominator, nominator, terminator, ruminator, divinator, cachinnator, personator, detonator, intonator, alternator, extirpator, separator, celebrator, lucubrator, desecrator, consecrator, execrator, Pantocrator, liberator, moderator, numerator, generator, venerator, operator, integrator, emigrator, immigrator, transmigrator, aspirator, respirator, inspirator, cospirator, decorator, perforator, perpetrator, arbitrator, concentrator, demonstrator, remonstrator, illustrator, instaurator, procurator, depurator, obturator, condensator, compensator, dispensator, meditator, agitator, cogitator, imitator, commentator, annotator, devastator, reinstator, commutator, amputator, valuator, elevator, cultivator, captivator, innovator, enervator, conservator, renovator, malaxator **5.** hypothecator, adjudicator, pacificator, edificator, modificator, qualificator, significator, purificator, classificator, multiplicator, communicator, prevaricator, sophisticator, prognosticator, reciprocator, equivocator, elucidator, invalidator, consolicator, intimidator, delineator, investigator, variegator, interrogator, depreciator, ap-

preciator, officiator, enunciator, annunciator, pronunciator, repudiator, conciliator, calumniator, initiator, propitiator, negotiator, alleviator, abbreviator, asphyxiator, annihilator, assimilator, *i.a*-terpellator, interpolator, perambulator, gesticulator, emasculator, coagulator, accumulator, pedipulator, manipulator, congratulator, expostulator, amalgamator, rejuvenator, originator, contaminator, disseminator, eliminator, denominator, exterminator, illuminator, peregrinator, assassinator, procrastinator, predestinator, impersonator, anticipator, participator, emancipator, deliberator, vociferator, exaggerator, refrigerator, decelerator, accelerator, enumerator, regenerator, incinerator, remunerator, vituperator, commiserator, disintegrator, elaborator, collaborator, corroborator, invigorator, incorporator, administrator, inaugurator, improvisator, tergiversator, resuscitator, habilitator, facilitator, decapitator, evacuator, extenuator, insinuator, continuator, totalizator, catalyzator **6.** excommunicator, circumnavigator, supererogator, prestidigitator.

ĀT′oz– Cato's etc., *see* **ĀT′o–** Cato etc. above, plus "s" or "'s."

ĀT′ress– **2.** traitress, waitress **3.** oratress, dictatress **4.** imitatress.

ĀT′rik– **2.** matric, phratric.

ĀT′riks– **2.** matrix, patrix **3.** fundatrix, cicatrix, quadratrix, dictatrix, testatrix **4.** mediatrix, aviatrix, indicatrix, legislatrix, osculatrix, gubernatrix, nominatrix **5.** administratrix.

ĀT′ron– **2.** matron, natron, patron **3.** salnatron.

ĀT′um– **2.** datum, stratum **3.** relatum pomatum, quadratum, erratum, substratum, testatum **4.** seriatim, petrolatum, postulatum, ultimatum, Ageratum, capitatum **5.** desideratum.

ĀT′ur– **2.** nature **3.** denature **4.** nomenclature, legislature.

AT′us– **2.** date us, latus, flatus, stratus, stratous, status **3.** beatus, hiatus, afflatus, inflatus, senatus, conatus, postnatus, quadratus **4.** apparatus, saleratus, literatus, comitatus.

AV′a– **2.** Ava, deva.

AV′al– **2.** naval, navel **3.** precaval, octaval.

AV′en– **2.** haven, raven, graven, craven, shaven **3.** engraven, unshaven.

AV′er– **2.** laver, flavor, slaver, paver, raver, braver, graver, craver, saver, savor, shaver, waver, waiver, quaver, suaver **3.** cadaver, disfavor, enslaver, Papaver, engraver, depraver, *livesaver, time saver* **4.** demiquaver, semiquaver.

AV′erd– **2.** favored, flavored, wavered, quavered **3.** ill-favored, disfavored, unflavored.

AV′est– **2.** bravest, gravest, suavest.

AV′i– **2.** ave, Davy, Devi, cavy, cavie, slavey, navy, pavy, gravy, wavy **3.** agave, peccavi **4.** Mahadevi.

AV′id– **2.** David, flavid.

AV′ing– **2.** caving, laving, paving, raving, braving, craving, saving, shaving, staving, waving, waiving **3.** behaving, enclaving, enslaving, engraving, depraving, *lifesaving, timesaving* **4.** misbehaving, unenslaving.

AV′is– **2.** Avis, Davis, clavis, mavis, pavis **4.** rara avis [L.].

AV′ish– **2.** slavish, knavish, bravish.

AV′it– **2.** davit **3.** cessavit **4.** affidavit, indicavit, devastavit.

AV′less– **2.** caveless, slaveless, graveless, waveless.

AV′li– **2.** knavely, bravely, gravely, suavely.

AV′ment– **2.** lavement, pavement **3.** enslavement, engravement, depravement.

AV′ness– **2.** braveness, graveness, suaveness.

AV′o– **2.** Pavo, bravo **3.** octavo, centavo.

AV′or– **2.** favor, flavor, savor **3.** disfavor; *see* also **AV′er–** laver.

AV′ur– **2.** gravure **4.** pyrogravure, photogravure, autogravure.

AV′yer– **2.** clavier, pavior, savior, saviour, Xavier **3.** behavior **4.** misbehavior.

AZ′el– **2.** basil, gazel, Hazel, nasal **3.** witch-hazel, appraisal, Azazel **4.** reappraisal.

AZ′en– **2.** raisin, glazen, brazen.

AZ′er– **2.** gazer, hazer, lazar, blazer, mazer, raser, raiser, razor, phraser, grazer, praiser **3.** *stargazer,* upraiser, appraiser, self-praiser, dispraiser **4.** paraphraser.

AZ′ez– baizes etc., *see* **AZ–** baize etc. above, plus "s" or "'s."

AZH′al– **2.** basial **3.** gymnasial.

AZH′an– **2.** Asian **3.** Caucasian, Eurasian, equation **4.** Australasian; *see* also **AZH′un–** rasion etc. below.

AZH′er– **2.** azure, glazier, rasure, frasier, brazier, grazier **3.** embrasure, erasure.

AZH′un– **2.** rasion, suasion **3.** occasion, abrasion, corrosion, equation, persuasion, dissuasion, evasion, invasion, pervasion; *see* also **AZH′an–** Asian etc. above.

AZ′i– **2.** daisy, gazy, lazy, jasey, lazy, glazy, sleazy, mazy, phrasy, crazy **3.** patesi **4.** lackadaisy.

AZ′ing– **2.** dazing, gazing, hazing, lazing, blazing, glazing, braising, phrasing, grazing, praising.

AZ′iz– **2.** daisies.

AZ′less– **2.** hazeless, phraseless, praiseless.

AZ′ment– **3.** amazement, appraisement **4.** reappraisement.

AZ′o– **2.** Mazo **4.** Valparaiso.

AZ′on– **2.** scazon, blazon **3.** emblazon, Malmaison **4.** diapason.

AZ′ur– **2.** azure, rasure **3.** embrasure, erasure; *see* also **AZH′er–** azure etc. above.

A (ay)

3.

TRIPLE RHYMES IN A (pay'ab-le)

Primary or Secondary Accent Falls on Second
from Last Syllable.

A'a–bl– 3. playable, payable, sayable, weighable, swayable 4. repayable, prepayable, impayable, unpayable, defrayable, portrayable, unsayable, unswayable, conveyable, surveyable 5. unportrayable, unconveyable.

AB'i–a– 3. labia, trabea, Swabia 4. Arabia.

AB'i–an– 3. Fabian, Sabian, Swabian 4. Arabian.

AB'i–ez– 2. abies, scabies, rabies.

AB'l–ness– 3. ableness, stableness 4.̈ unableness, unstableness.

AB'or–er– 3. laborer, taborer.

AB'or–ing– 3. laboring, neighboring, taboring 4. belaboring, unlaboring.

AD'a–bl– 3. gradable, tradable, shadable, wadable 4. retradable, persuadable, evadable 5. unpersuadable, undissuadable.

AD'ed–li– 3. fadedly, jadedly 4. degradedly.

AD'ed–ness– 3. fadedness, jadedness, shadedness 4. cockadedness, degradedness.

AD'i–a– 3. stadia 4. Acadia, Arcadia, Palladia.

AD'i–al– 3. radial 5. uniradial, multiradial, interstadial.

AD'i–an– 3. radian 4. Barbadian, Palladian, Acadian, Akkadian, Arcadian, nomadian, Canadian.

AD'i–ans– 3. radiance 4. irradiance.

AD'i–ant– 3. radiant, gradient 4. irradiant.

AD'i–at– 3. radiate 4. eradiate, irradiate.

AD'ing–li– 3. fadingly 4. degradingly, pervadingly.

AD'i–um– 3. radium, stadium 4. Palladium, vanadium.

AD'i–us– 3. gladius, radius 4. adradius 5. hyporadius.

A'er–at– 2. aerate.

A'et–on– 3. phaeton.

AG'ran–si– 3. flagrancy, fragrancy, vagrancy.

A'ik–al– 3. laical 4. archaical, Hebraical 5. algebraical, pharisaical 6. paradisaical.

A'it–i– 3. gaiety, laity.

AJ'a–bl– 3. gaugeable, stageable 4. assuageable, dissuageable.

AJ'i–a– 3. Hagia 4. aphagia, dysphagia, Panagia 5. polyphagia.

AJ'i–an– 3. Magian 4. pelagian, contagion 5. Brobdignagian 6. archipelagian.

AJ'i–li– 3. cagily, stagily.

AJ'us–li– 4. rampageously, outrageously, courageously, contagiously 5. advantageously 6. disadvantageously.

AJ'us–ness– 4. rampageousness, outrageousness, courageousness, contagiousness, 5. advantageousness 6. disadvantageousness.

AK'a–bl– 3. acheable, placable, slakable, pacable, breakable, shakable, takable 4. implacable, unslakable, unbreakable, unshakable, mistakable, awakable 5. undertakable, unmistakable.

AK'at–ed– 3. placated, vacated 4. unplacated, revacated.

AK'er–i– 3. bakery, fakery, snakery, rakery, Quakery 5. undertakery.

AK'er–izm– 4. fakirism, Lakerism, Shakerism, Quakerism.

AK'i–a– 3. trachea 4. Batrachia.

AK'i–al– 3. rachial, brachial, tracheal.

AK'i–an– 3. trachean 4. Noachian, batrachian, Eustachian.

AK'i–ness– 3. fakiness, shakiness, flakiness, snakiness, quakiness.

AK'we–us– 3. aqueous 4. subaqueous, terraqueous.

AL'a–bl– 3. bailable, mailable, salable, sailable 4. inhalable, exhalable, unmailable, wholesalable, unsalable, assailable, unsailable, available, retailable 5. unassailable, unavailable.

AL'i–a– 3. galea, palea, Thalia 4. Sedalia, idalia, Westphalia, regalia, Eulalia, Mammalia, Massalia, azalea, sponsalia, Psoralea, Arctalia 5. Lupercalia, paralalia, pseudolalia, echolalia, Bacchanalia, marginalia, Terminalia, Saturnalia, Antarctalia 6. Marsupialia, paraphernalia; *see* also **AL'ya–** regalia etc.

AL'i–an– 3. alien 4. Daedalian, Idalian, regalian, mammalian, Castalian 5. phantasmalian, bacchanalian, saturnalian 6. sesquipedalian, Episcopalian; *see* also **AL'yum–** alien etc.

AL'i–as– 3. alias 4. Sibelius, Ortelius.

AL'i–ness– 3. dailiness, scaliness, wailiness 4. tridailiness.

AL'i–um– 3. Galium, kalium 4. Idalium.

AL'yen–at– 4. alienate.

AL'yen–izm– 5. alienism 6. bacchanalianism 7. sesquipedalianism, Episcopalianism, universalianism.

AM'a–bl– 3. blamable, claimable, namable, framable, tamable 4. unblamable, reclaimable, unnamable, unframable, untamable.

AM'ful–ness– 3. gamefulness, blamefulness, shamefulness 4. unshamefulness.

AM'i–a– 3. lamia 5. adynamia; 6. Mesopotamia.

AM'less–ness– 3. aimlessness, famelessness, blamelessness, namelessness, shamelessness, tamelessness.

AN'a–bl– 3. gainable, chainable, planable, drainable, sprainable, trainable, strainable 4. ordainable, profanable, explainable, untrainable, restrainable, constrainable, attainable, obtainable, maintainable, sustainable 5. inexplainable, unexplainable, unobtainable, unattainable, ascertainable.

AN'a–bli– 4. explainably 5. unexplainably, unrestrainably, unattainably, unobtainably.

AN'e–a– 4. Castanea 5. succedanea, miscellanea, collectanea; *see* also **AN'i–a–** mania etc. below.

AN'e–an– 4. terranean, castanean 5. subterranean 6. Mediterranean, circumforanean, contemporanean, extemporanean; *see* also **AN'i–an–** Albanian etc. below.

AN'e–us– 4. siccaneous, araneous, terraneous, spontaneous, castaneous, cutaneous 5. succedaneous, miscellaneous, temporaneous, subterraneous, coetaneous, simultaneous, instantaneous, consentaneous, dissentaneous, subcutaneous 6. antecedaneous, contemporaneous, extemporaneous.

AN'ful–i– 3. banefully, gainfully, painfully 4. disdainfully, ungainfully.

AN'ful–ness– 3. gainfulness, painfulness 4. disdainfulness, ungainfulness.

AN′i-a– **3.** mania **4.** Albania, amania, Tasmania, Rumania, Ukrainia, Urania, Titania, Castanea **5.** succedanea, miscellanea, florimania, theomania, Gallomania, melomania, Anglomania, monomania, hydromania, pyromania, nosomania, kleptomania, dipsomania, potomania, Pomerania, Aquitania, Lithuania, Transylvania, Pennsylvania, collectanea **6.** bibliomania, decalcomania, megalomania, demonomania, Tripolitania.

AN′i-ak– **3.** maniac **5.** egomaniac, ergomaniac, Gallomaniac, Anglomaniac, monomaniac, pyromaniac, dipsomaniac, kleptomaniac **6.** bibliomaniac, curiomaniac, megalomaniac.

AN′i-al– **3.** cranial **4.** domanial, acranial, cutaneal **5.** subterraneal.

AN′i-an– **4.** Albanian, volcanian, Vulcanian, Tasmanian, Rumanian, Iranian, Ukrainian, Uranian. **5.** Pomeranian, Lithuanian, Transylvanian, Pennsylvanian; *see* also AN′e-an– terranean etc. above.

AN′i-ness– **3.** raininess, braininess, graininess, veininess.

AN′ing-li– **4.** complainingly **5.** uncomplainingly, entertainingly.

AN′i-um– **3.** cranium **4.** germanium, geranium, uranium, titanium **5.** succedaneum.

ANJ′a-bl– **3.** changeable **4.** unchangeable, exchangeable, arrangeable, derangeable **5.** interchangeable, rearrangeable.

ANJ′a-bli– **3.** changeably **4.** unchangeably, exchangeably **5.** interchangeably.

ANJ′i-ness– **3.** manginess, ranginess.

ANT′a-bl– **3.** paintable, taintable **4.** acquaintable.

ANT′i-li– **3.** daintily, saintily.

AP′a-bl– **3.** capable, papable, drapable, shapable **4.** incapable, escapable, reshapable, unshapable **5.** inescapable.

AP′a-bli– **3.** capably **4.** incapably **5.** inescapably, unescapably.

AP′er-er– **3.** caperer, naperer, paperer, taperer, vaporer.

AP′er-i– **3.** apery, apiary, japery, napery, papery, drapery, grapery, vapory.

AP′er-ing– **3.** capering, papering, tapering, vaporing.

AP′i-an– **3.** Apian **5.** Aesculapian.

AR′a-bl– **3.** arable, airable, bearable, pairable, parable, sparable, sharable, tearable, wearable, squarable, swearable **4.** unbearable, repairable, unsparable, unwearable, unsquarable.

AR′a-bli– **3.** bearably **4.** unbearably.

AR′ful-i– **3.** carefully, sparefully, prayerfully **4.** uncarefully.

AR′ful-ness– **3.** carefulness, sparefulness, prayerfulness **4.** uncarefulness.

AR′i-a– **3.** aria, area, pariah **4.** herbaria, Bulgaria, Icaria, cercaria, malaria, talaria, solaria, ranaria, dataria, cataria, wistaria, aquaria, Bavaria **5.** topiaria, urticaria, honoraria, adversaria, planetaria.

AR′i-al– **3.** aerial, areal, Ariel, ariel, narial **4.** diarial, vicarial, malarial, riparial, glossarial, bursarial, nectarial, sectarial, notarial, ovarial **5.** calendarial, commissarial, secretarial, actuarial.

AR′i-an– **3.** Arian, Aryan, Parian **4.** barbarian, gregarian, Bulgarian, vulgarian, Icarian, lunarian, riparian, librarian, agrarian, Caesarian, rosarian, nectarean, sectarian, Bavarian, ovarian **5.** millenarian, centenarian, septenarian, Sabbatarian, nonsectarian, vegetarian, proletarian, Trinitarian, Unitarian, antiquarian **6.** abecedarian, quinquagenarian, septuagenarian, octogenarian, honegenarian, disciplinarian, predestinarian, totalitarian, utilitarian, humanitarian, necessitarian, ubiquitarian, parliamentarian, sacramentarian, veterinarian, alphabetarian **7.** valetudinarian, latitudinarian, platitudinarian.

AR′i-ans– **3.** variance **4.** invariance.

AR′i-ant– **3.** variant **4.** bivariant, invariant, covariant, contrariant.

AR'i–at–   **4.** salariat   **5.** commissariat, proletariat, secretariat.

AR'i–er–   **3.** airier, charier, hairier, glarier, varier, warier.

AR'i–est–   **3.** airiest, chariest, hairiest, glariest, wariest.

AR'i–ez–   **3.** Aries, caries, paries.

AR'i–form–   **3.** aeriform, nariform, variform   **4.** scalariform.

AR'i–ness–   **3.** airiness, chariness, hairiness, glariness, wariness   **4.** contrariness   **5.** sanguinariness, temporariness, arbitrariness, solitariness, sedentariness, momentariness, voluntariness.

AR'ing–li–   **3.** daringly, blaringly, flaringly, glaringly, sparingly   **4.** forbearingly.

AR'i–ti–   **3.** rarity   **5.** debonairity.

AR'i–um–   **3.** barium   **4.** herbarium, verbarium, solarium, fumarium, ranarium, terrarium, sacrarium, rosarium, lactarium, aquarium, vivarium   **5.** columbarium, cinerarium, honorarium, cometarium, planetarium, sanitarium.

AR'i–us–   **3.** carious, scarious, various   **4.** nefarious, gregarious, precarious, Icarius, vicarious, calcareous, vagarious, hilarious, senarius, riparious, setarious, nectareous, octarius, Aquarius   **5.** septenarius, quaternarius, confessarius, Sagittarius, Januarius, Februarius, Stradivarius.

AS'a–bl–   **3.** faceable, placeable, traceable   **4.** effaceable, defaceable, replaceable, unplaceable, erasable   **5.** irreplaceable, unerasable; *see* also **AS'i–bl–** suasible etc. below.

AS'ed–ly–   **4.** shamefacedly, barefacedly.

AS'en–si–   **4.** adjacency, complacency.

ASH'al–i–   **3.** facially, glacially, racially   **5.** interracially.

ASH'i–a–   **3.** Asia   **4.** Sabbatia, acacia, solatia, Dalmatia, Alsatia, Cetacea, Crustacea.

ASH'i–al–   **3.** basial, spatial   **4.** abbatial, palatial, primatial   **5.** interspatial.

ASH'i–an–   **3.** Asian, Haitian, Thracian   **4.** Sabbatian, Dalmatian, Horatian, Alsatian, Eustachian.

ASH'i–at–   **3.** glaciate, satiate   **4.** sagaciate, emaciate, expatiate, ingratiate, insatiate.

ASH'i–ent–   *see* **ASH'ent–** facient etc.

ASH'ı–o–   **3.** ratio   **4.** locatio [L.], Horatio   **7.** Nova Constellatio.

ASH'un–al–   **3.** stational   **4.** probational, vocational, relational, translational, vibrational, gyrational, sensational, rotational, quotational, equational   **5.** incubational, recreational, congregational, conjugational, variational, convocational, educational, revelational, informational, combinational, inclinational, terminational, occupational, inspirational, condensational, compensational, gravitational, presentational, salutational, deputational, derivational, observational   **6.** interrogational, denominational, commemorational, representational.

ASH'un–er–   **3.** stationer   **4.** probationer, foundationer, oblationer   **5.** restorationer.

ASH'un–ist–   **4.** creationist, deflationist, inflationist, salvationist   **5.** convocationist, federationist, moderationist, tolerationist, emigrationist, inspirationist, restorationist, conversationist, imitationist, annotationist, innovationist, transmutationist   **6.** repudiationist, annihilationist, emancipationist, colonizationist.

ASH'un–less–   **3.** nationless, rationless, stationless   **4.** foundationless, vibrationless, temptationless   **3.** educationless, inspirationless, conversationless, imitationless; *see* also **ASH'un–** nation etc., plus –less.

ASH'us–ness–   **3.** spaciousness, graciousness   **4.** edaciousness, audaciousness, mendaciousness, sagaciousness, fugaciousness, fallaciousness, salaciousness, pugnaciousness, tenaciousness, capaciousness, rapaciousness, ungraciousness, veraciousness, voraciousness, sequaciousness, loquaciousness, vivaciousness, vexatiousness **5.** efficaciousness, contumaciousness, pertinaciousness, incapaciousness, perspicaciousness, ostentatiousness, disputatiousness.

AS'i–bl– **3.** suasible **4.** evasible, persuasible **5.** unpersuasible; *see* also AS'a–bl– faceable etc. above.

AS'i–ness– **3.** laciness, raciness.

AS'iv–ness– **4.** abrasiveness, assuasiveness, dissuasiveness, persuasiveness, evasiveness, invasiveness, pervasiveness.

AST'ful–i– **3.** tastefully, wastefully **4.** distastefully.

AST'i–li– **3.** hastily, pastily, tastily.

AT'a–bl– **3.** baitable, hatable, matable, ratable, gratable, satable, statable **4.** abatable, debatable, creatable, relatable, inflatable, dilatable, translatable, beratable **5.** unrelatable, regulatable.

AT'a–bly– **3.** ratably **5.** untranslatably.

AT'a–li– **3.** fatally **4.** prenatally.

AT'en–si– **3.** latency, patency.

AT'ful–i– **3.** fatefully, hatefully, gratefully **4.** ungratefully.

AT'ful–ness– **3.** fatefulness, hatefulness, gratefulness **4.** ungratefulness.

AT'i–ness– **3.** slatiness, weightiness.

AT'ing–li– **3.** gratingly **5.** deprecatingly, nauseatingly, mediatingly, contemplatingly, calculatingly, fascinatingly, alternatingly, penetratingly, meditatingly, irritatingly, hesitatingly, aggravatingly, captivatingly **6.** accommodatingly, interrogatingly, excruciatingly, alleviatingly, discriminatingly, premeditatingly, insinuatingly.

AT'iv–li– **3.** natively **4.** creatively **5.** predicatively, implicatively, legislatively, speculatively, emulatively, simulatively, cumulatively, germinatively, terminatively, operatively, decoratively, dubitatively,

meditatively, cogitatively, qualitatively imitatively, hesitatively, quantitatively **6.** significatively, multiplicatively, gestic ulatively, accumulatively, manipulatively imaginatively, determinatively, opinion atively, anticipatively, participatively co-operatively, vituperatively, commis eratively, reiteratively, alliteratively, cor roboratively, invigoratively, commemo ratively, administratively, interpretatively authoritatively, insinuatively **7.** incom municatively.

AT'iv–ness– **3.** nativeness **5.** penetra tiveness, imitativeness **6.** imaginative ness.

AT'ron–al– **3.** matronal, patronal.

AT'ron–ij– **3.** matronage, patronage.

AV'a–bl– **3.** lavable, savable, shavable **4** unsavable, unshavable.

AV'er–er– **3.** favorer, laverer, flavorer waverer, quaverer.

AV'er–i– **3.** Avery, slavery, knavery bravery, wavery, quavery, savory **4** unsavory **5.** antislavery.

AV'er–ing– **3.** favoring, flavoring, savor ing, wavering, quavering **4.** unwaver ing.

AV'er–us– **3.** favorous, flavorous, quaver ous, savorous **4.** papaverous.

AV'i–a– **3.** Moravia, Belgravia, Batavia Octavia **5.** Jugoslavia, Scandinavia.

AV'i–al– **3.** gavial, clavial.

AV'i–an– **3.** avian **4.** Moravian, Belgra vian, Batavian, Octavian **5.** Scand navian.

AV'i–er– **3.** clavier, wavier.

AV'ish–ness– **3.** slavishness, knavishnes

AZ'a–bl– **3.** raisable, praisable **4.** ap praisable, persuasible **5.** unpersuasible.

AZH'i–a– **3.** Asia **4.** abasia, aphasia, e gasia, aplasia, gymnasia, Eurasia, acrasi Acrasia, fantasia, astasia **5.** paraphasi hemostasia.

AZH'i–al– **3.** basial **4.** gymnasial.

AZH′i–an– 3. Asian 4. Caucasian, Eurasian 5. Australasian.

AZ′i–ness– 3. haziness, laziness, maziness, craziness.

AZ′ing–li– 3. dazingly, gazingly, blazingly 4. amazingly.

AZ′on–ing– 3. blazoning 4. emblazoning.

A (ah)

1.

SINGLE (MASCULINE) RHYMES IN A (ah)

Primary or Secondary Accent Falls on Last Syllable; Imperfect Rhymes Are in Italics.

A– **1.** ah, baa, bah, da, fa, ha, hah, la, blah [slang], ma, na, nah [both slang], pa, pas [F.], spa, rah, Ra, bra [slang], fra [It.], kra, saa, shah, ta, t'a, taa, va [F.], qua, foi [F.], moi [F.], roi [F.], froid [F.], ya, yah, ja **2.** dada, *howdah*, *lowdah*, aha, haha, raca, éclat [F.], amah, mama, sama, *grandma*, papa, *grandpa*, faux pas [F.], *Para*, hurrah, état [F.], bourgeois [F.], patois [F.], chaud-froid [F.], huzza **3.** oh and ah, alala, Panama, elema, Parana, acara, baccarat, abaca, Bogota, tiers état [F.], vive le roi [F.].

AB– **1.** ab [Heb.], squab, swab **2.** kitab, *gabgab*; *see* also **OB–** bob etc.

AD– **1.** ahed, baaed, had, wad, quad [slang] **2.** aubade [F.], ballade, roulade, pomade, charade, estrade, hurrahed, façade, glissade, metad **3.** ohed and ahed, esplanade, promenade; *see* also **OD–** odd etc.

AF– **1.** half, Kaf, calf, laugh, Graf [G.], strafe, quaff **2.** behalf, *moon calf*, *horselaugh* **3.** better half, half and half.

AFT– **1.** laughed, strafed, quaffed, waft.

AG– **1.** Dag, blague [F.], Prague; *see* also **OG–** bog etc.

AJH– **1.** raj, saj, taj **2.** coupage [F.], barrage, garage, mirage, massage, corsage, potage [F.], lavage [F.] **3.** entourage [F.], repoussage [F.], sabotage, esclavage [F.].

AK– **1.** ach [G.], lac [F.], plaque [F.] **2.** macaque, Iraq, chittak **3.** Sarawak.

AL– **1.** Baal, dal, râle [F.], kraal [D.], salle [F.], Taal, Saal [G.] **2.** Yigdal, *Heimdall*, agal, mahal, locale, *Landsmaal*, choral, chorale, morale, cheval [F.], Transvaal, étoile [F.], quetzal **3.** Taj Mahal, laical, farcical, radical, medical, codical, magical, tragical, nymphical, ethical, mythical, biblical, cyclical, helical, comical, technical, ethnical, finical, cynical, conical, apical, epical, topical, typical, centrical, vesical, whimsical, classical, musical, physical, optical, cryptical, vertical, cortical, vortical, mystical, nautical, silvical, cardial, cordial, genial, splenial, finial, hernial, aerial, ferial, serial, ambrosial, tertial, bestial, animal, minimal, lachrymal, decanal, bacchanal, tympanal, turbinal, carcinal, marginal, virginal, machinal, echinal, staminal, matinal, pectinal, retinal, inguinal, regional, torsional, missional, synchronal, seasonal, cantonal, principal, cerebral, vertebral, visceral, general, mineral, funeral, vesperal, geyseral, several, integral, admiral, anchoral, doctoral, cantoral, pastoral, mayoral, magistral, scriptural, sculptural, pastural, gestural, postural, guttural, sutural, textural, Provençal, palatal, vegetal, skeletal, orbital, digital, capital, hospital, marital, nepotal, pivotal, pedestal, gradual, casual, visual, usual, punctual, virtual, sexual, carnival, interval **4.** sporadical, unethical, encyclical, dynamical, inimical, tyrannical, dominical, ironical, electrical, eccentrical, nonclassical, antarctical, despotical, erotical, synoptical, majestical, Apocryphal, microbial, connubial, commercial, fiducial, novendial, gerundial, primordial, collegial, vestigial, conjugial, congenial, marsupial, colloquial, indigenal, phenomenal, intestinal, matutinal, adhesional, convulsional, expansional, partitional, precautional, municipal, Episcopal, preceptoral, carnivoral, continual, ventriloqual, unusual, perpetual, spiritual 5. lackadaisical, participial, entente cordiale [F.]; *see* also **AL–** Al etc.

AM– 1. âme [F.], balm, calm, malm, palm, psalm, Guam, qualm 2. embalm, madame, Baham, salaam, imam, hammam, impalm 3. Amsterdam, Rotterdam 4. ad nauseam [L.]; *see* also **OM–** bomb etc.

AMZ– balms etc., *see* **AM–** balm etc. above, plus "s" or "'s."

AN– 1. âne [F.], crâne [F.], wan, g'wan [slang], swan 2. cabane [F.], Iban, liane, macan, pecan, Iran, Koran, Bataan 3. balmacaan, Yucatan, capitan [Sp.], Turkestan, Pakistan 4. Baluchistan; *see* also **ON–** on etc.

ANCH– stanch; *see* also **ONCH–** haunch etc.

ANS– 2. séance, nuance 3. Renaissance 4. insouciance.

ANT– 1. aunt, can't, shan't, want 2. grandaunt, great-aunt 3. debutante; *see* also **ONT–** font etc.

ANTS– aunts etc., *see* **ANT–** aunt etc. above, plus "s" or "'s."

ANZ– swans etc., *see* **AN–** âne etc. above, plus "s" or "'s"; *see* also **ANZ–** bonze etc.

AP– 1. gape, swap, yahp [slang] 2. étape [F.]; *see* also **OP–** bop etc.

AR– 1. are, aar [D.], bar, dar [slang], far, gar, jar, car, char, scar, mar, gnar, gnarr, par, spar, tsar, tar, star, guar, boire [F.], foire [F.], poire [F.], Loire, gloire [F.], czar 2. debar, rebar, embar, unbar, disbar, *crossbar*, *crowbar*, sirdar, afar, Safar, segar,

cigar, bahar, ajar, evejar, nightjar, *sidecar*, *tramcar*, sircar, *forecar*, Bakar, shicar, Lascar, *Kedar*, *streetcar*, simar, canard [F.], *feldspar*, hussar, catarrh, katar, guitar, sitar, kantar, *daystar*, *lodestar*, *polestar*, *earthstar*, *evestar*, pour boire [F.], espoir [F.], savoir [F.], bazaar, bizarre 3. gangliar, foliar, caviar, jaguar, Malabar, cinnabar, centibar, Zanzibar, saddle bar, axle bar, deodar, calendar, insofar, vinegar, *Trafalgar*, railroad car etc., gyrocar, autocar, tutelar, flagellar, lamellar, tessellar, similar, tonsillar, axillar, tabular, nebular, globular, tubular, schedular, glandular, modular, Cagoulard [F.], regular, angular, singular, jugular, stellular, secular, ocular, jocular, circular, torcular, vascular, scapular, popular, spherular, insular, consular, capsular, spatular, titular, ovular, uvular, valvular, tintamarre, laminar, seminar, columnar, sublunar, registrar, commissar, avatar, scimitar, boulevard [F.], Bolivar, samovar, abatoir [F.], escritoire [F.], repertoire [F.], evening star etc. 4. Excalibar, dissimilar, somnambular, irregular, triangular, quadrangular, spectacular, vernacular, molecular, vehicular, funicular, particular, binocular, crepuscular 5. perpendicular.

ARB– 1. barb, darb [slang], garb, carb [slang], marb [slang], yarb 2. coarb, *rhubarb*.

ARCH– 1. arch, larch, march, parch, starch 2. inarch, remarch, outmarch, cornstarch 3. overarch, countermarch.

ARD– 1. bard, barred, chard, charred, fard, hard, guard, jarred, card, scarred, lard, marred, knarred, nard, pard, sparred, sard, shard, tarred, starred, yard 2. debarred, bombard, regard, *safeguard*, *lifeguard*, *blackguard*, *vanguard*, *placard*, discard, unscarred, foulard, poulard, Reynard, canard, Girard, *spikenard*, Bernard, petard, retard, bestarred, *churchyard*, back yard, *dockyard*, *steelyard*, *barnyard*, *foreyard*, front yard, *courtyard*, *graveyard* 3.

disregard, bodyguard, avant-garde [F.], interlard, boulevard **4.** camelopard.

ARF– **1.** scarf, sharf, zarf.

ARJ– **1.** barge, charge, large, marge, sparge, sarge, targe **2.** surcharge, discharge, LaFarge, enlarge **3.** countercharge, overcharge, re-enlarge.

ARK– **1.** arc, ark, bark, barque, dark, hark, cark, lark, Clark, clerk, mark, marque, nark [slang], snark [slang], park, spark, sark, shark, stark **2.** *shagbark, snakebark, shellbark,* embark, *tanbark, woodlark, skylark, titlark, landmark,* remark, *hallmark, thumbmark,* Denmark, *earmark, reichsmark, postmark, birthmark,* impark, dispark, *whitesark, aardvark,* Ozark **3.** disembark, watermark, countermark, hierarch **4.** ecclesiarch.

ARKS– arcs etc., *see* **ARK–** arc etc. above, plus "s" or "'s"; **1.** Marx.

ARKT– **1.** arced, barked, harked, carked, larked, clerked, marked, parked, sparked **2.** embarked, skylarked, remarked, thumbmarked, earmarked, postmarked, birthmarked **3.** disembarked, watermarked.

ARL– **1.** harl, jarl, carl, Carl, Karl, marl, gnarl, snarl, parle **2.** imparl **3.** Albemarle.

ARLZ– harls etc.; *see* **ARL–** harl etc. above, plus "s" or "'s"; **1.** Arles, Charles.

ARM– **1.** arm, barm, charm, farm, harm, larm, larme [F.], marm, tharm **2.** *yardarm,* rearm, inarm, *firearm,* forearm, disarm *crossarm,* gendarme [F.], alarm, schoolmarm **3.** underarm, overarm.

ARN– **1.** barn, darn, larn [slang], Marne, tarn, yarn **2.** lucarne [F.], goldarn, consarn [both slang].

ARND– **1.** darned, yarned **2.** goldarned, consarned [both slang].

ARP– **1.** harp, carp, scarp, sharp, tarp [slang], yarp [slang], zarp **2.** *syncarp,*

escarp, *cardsharp* **3.** claviharp, epicarp, pericarp, endocarp, monocarp, counterscarp.

ARS– **1.** arse, farce, garce, parse, sparse, sarse [dial.].

ARSH– **1.** harsh, marsh, warsh [slang] **2.** démarche.

ART– **1.** art, Bart, chart, dart, hart, heart, cart, carte, quarte [F.], blart [dial.], mart, smart, part, Sart, tart, start **2.** *sweetheart, faintheart, dogcart, gocart, dumpcart,* apart, depart, repart, impart, *rampart,* dispart, *forepart,* assart, astart, *redstart,* restart, upstart **3.** a la carte, counterpart, apple tart, sugar tart.

ARTH– **1.** garth, hearth **2.** fishgarth.

ARV– **1.** carve, larve, starve, varve.

ARZ– bars etc., *see* **AR–** are etc. above, plus "s" or "'s"; Lars, Mars.

AS– **2.** en masse **3.** coup de grâce [F.].

ASH– **1.** lache [F.], tache [F.], quash, squash, wash.

AT– **1.** pâte [F.], what, squat, swat, watt, boite [F.], yacht **2.** salat, berat, Duat, *kumquat* **3.** Al Sirat; *see also* **OT–** dot etc.

ATH– **1.** bath, path, rath, wrath **3.** isobath.

ATZ– squats etc., *see* **AT–** pâte [F.] etc. above, plus "s" or "'s"; **1.** batz **2.** ersatz.

AV– **1.** gav, halve, calve, slav, salve, suave **2.** Zouave **3.** Jugoslav, Yugoslav.

AVD– **1.** halved, calved, salved.

AZ– ahs etc., *see* **A–** ah etc. above, plus "s" or "'s"; **1.** vase, yahzz [slang] **2.** namaz, Shiraz, Françoise **3.** Vichyssoise.

AZH– **2.** chauffage [F.], menage, barrage, garage, mirage **3.** bavardage [F.], fuselage, persiflage, camouflage, badinage, cabotage, sabotage **4.** espionage.

A (ah)

2.

DOUBLE (FEMININE) RHYMES IN A (a'ba)

Primary or Secondary Accent Falls on Next to Last
Syllable; Imperfect Rhymes Are in Italics.

AB'a– 2. aba, baba, haba [Sp.], Caaba, Kaaba 3. casaba, aftaba 4. piassaba, Ali Baba 5. Addis Ababa.

AB'i– 2. rabi, tabi [Jap.], wabe 3. Wahabi, kohlrabi.

AB'ra– 2. abra 4. candelabra 5. abracadabra.

AD'a– 2. dada, sraddha 3. Haggada, cicada, Colada, armada, granada, Grenada, panada, contrada, Nevada, shahzada 6. Sierra Nevada.

AD'en– 2. Baden 4. Baden-Baden; *see* also **OD'en–** hodden etc.

AD'i– 2. cadi, Mahdi, wadi 3. abadi [Hind.], irade.

AD'o– 2. dado, Prado 3. Mikado, sticcado, stoccado, strappado, dorado, passado, pintado, bravado 4. avocado, desperado, Eldorado, Colorado 5. amontillado 6. incommunicado.

A'e– 2. kai, blahy [slang], tai, sai 4. kaikai.

A'ek– 2. kaik, saic.

AF'a– 2. Daffa, Jaffa, Yafa.

AF'ing– 2. laughing, strafing, quaffing.

AF'l– 2. faffle, taffle, tafel [G.], waffle.

AF'ter– 2. after, laughter.

AG'a– 2. aga, gaga [F.], glaga, Naga, saga.

AG'ar– 2. agar, laager, lager 4. agaragar.

AG'o– 2. drago 3. Iago, Chicago, sa-'ago, farrago 4. Santiago; *see* also **ARG'o–** Argo etc.

AG'wa– 2. agua, jagua, Yagua 3. Managua, piragua.

A'ha– 2. kaha, maha, taha 3. *taiaha.*

A'hu– 2. kahu, Mahu, Rahu, sahu, wahoo, Yahoo 3. Oahu.

A'ing– 2. ahing, baaing, blahing [slang] 3. blah-blahing [slang] 5. ohing and ahing.

AJ'a– 2. rajah 4. maharajah.

AJ'e– 2. haje, hagi, Bragi.

AK'a– 2. haka [Maori], Hakka, raca 3. Karaka, Osaka, pataca 4. Titicaca.

AK'as– 3. Caracas.

AK'en– 2. Aachen, Achen, baken [D.], kraken.

AK'er– 3. fiacre, polacre.

AK'i– 2. kaki, khaki, sake, saki 4. Anunnaki, sukiyaki.

AK'o– 2. hako, Chaco, mako, caco, paco, guaco, huaco 3. cheechako, fondako, guanaco 4. makomako.

AK'wa– 2. aqua 3. namaqua, anaqua.

AL'a– 2. Allah, gala, hala, kala, wallah 3. koala, impala, Marsala, Patala, owala.

AL'et– 2. wallet, swallet; *see* also **OL'et–** collet etc.

AL'i– 2. Ali, Bali, dali, gali, galee, Kali, pali, tali, Vali 3. Bengali, tahali, tamale, Somali, finale 4. Mexicali, pastorale.

AL'o– 2. calo, lalo, malo, palo, swallow, wallow 3. hog wallow; *see* also **OL'o–** follow etc.

AL'u– 2. baloo, balu.

AL'yo– 3. caballo, seraglio, intaglio.

AM'a– 2. ama, gama, jama, caama, Kama, lama, llama, mama, mamma, Rama, Brahma, drama, grama, shama, Tama 3. Bahama, pajama, pyjama 4. Alabama, Yokohama, ramarama, melodrama, monodrama, diorama, cyclorama, cosmorama, panorama, Fujiyama 5. myriorama, polyorama.

AM'an– 2. Brahman, saman, shaman, zaman 4. Parabrahman.

AM'as– Brahmas etc., see AM'a– ama etc. above, plus "s" or " 's."

AM'ba– 2. samba 3. caramba [Sp.].

AM'er– 2. calmer, Kammer [D.], palmer 3. embalmer.

AM'i– 2. balmy, jami, calmy, malmy, palmy, pahmi, qualmy, swami 3. palame, salami.

AM'ing– 2. calming, malming, palming, qualming 3. embalming, becalming, salaaming, empalming.

AM'ish– 2. calmish, qualmish.

AM'ist– 2. palmist, psalmist 3. embalmist.

AN'a– 2. Bana, kana, mana, rana, prana, tana, thana 3. nagana, Guiana, liana, gymkhana, banana, mañana [Sp.], kerana, zenana, purana, Etana, Sultana, lantana, Montana, Curtana, nirvana, iguana 4. apadana, tramontana, marijuana 5. Americana 6. cassabanana, Shakespeariana.

AND'o– 2. bando 3. tardando, calando, Orlando, Fernando, Hernando, ritando, lentando, scherzando 4. ritardando, declamando, lacrimando, recitando, allentando, rallentando.

AN'i– 2. ani, rani 4. frangipani, Maharani, Hindustani.

AN'o– 2. ano, mano, grano 3. piano, solano, soprano, gitano 4. pudiano, castellano, altiplano, bonamano, capitano, Montesano 9. mens sana in corpore sano [L.].

ANT'a– 2. danta 3. Vedanta, Infanta.

ANT'ay– 2. Dante, sante 3. andante, volante 5. pococurante.

ANT'i– 2. aunty, Dante, tanti 3. Chianti, andante, Kiranti.

A'o– 2. ao, dao, tao 3. cacao, macao, talao, Karao [Hind.], parao 4. carabao, Mindanao.

AP'a– 2. apa, capa, kapa, papa, tapa 5. anapanapa.

AP'i– 2. Hapi 3. okapi, serape.

AR'a– 2. cara, Mara, narra, Tara, vara 3. tiara, ziara, fugara, Sahara, vihara, Sakkara, kaikara, cascara, mascara, Damara, Gemara, apara, arara, chitarra 4. caracara, tantarara, Demerara, solfatara 5. Guadalajara, taratantara.

ARB'er– 2. arbor, barber, Barbour, harbor 3. enharbor.

ARB'ij– 2. garbage.

ARB'l– 2. barbel, garble, garbill, marble 3. enmarble.

ARB'lz– 2. barbels, garbles, marbles.

ARB'on– 2. charbon, carbon 4. hydrocarbon.

ARB'ord– 2. arbored, harbored, larboard, starboard.

ARCH'er– 2. archer, marcher, parcher, starcher 4. countermarcher.

ARCH'ez– arches etc., see ARCH– arch etc., plus "es" or "'s."

ARCH'i– 2. Archie, archy, larchy, starchy.

ARCH'ing– 2. arching, marching, parching, starching 3. outmarching 4. overarching, countermarching.

ARCH'ment– 2. archment, parchment 3. emparchment.

ARD'ant– 2. ardent, gardant, guardant 3. regardant, retardant.

ARD'ed– 2. farded, guarded, carded, larded, sharded 3. bombarded, safeguarded, placarded, discarded, regarded, retarded 4. disregarded, interlarded, unretarded.

ARD'el– 2. bardel, fardel, sardel, sardelle.

ARD'en– 2. Arden, garden, harden, Varden 3. tea garden, enharden 4. Dolly Varden [Dickens].

ARD'end– 2. gardened, hardened, pardoned 3. unhardened, unpardoned.

ARD'er– 2. ardor, guarder, harder, carder 3. discarder, retarder 4. disregarder.

ARD'i– 2. hardy, lardy, mardy, tardy 3. *Lombardy*, foolhardy.

ARD'ij– 2. yardage.

ARD'ik– 2. bardic 3. Lombardic, Sephardic 4. anacardic, pericardic.

ARD'ing– 2. farding, guarding, Harding, carding, larding 3. unguarding, discarding, retarding 4. disregarding.

ARD'less– 2. fardless, guardless, cardless, lardless, shardless 3. regardless, retardless.

ARD'ment– 3. bombardment, retardment.

ARD'ship– 2. guard ship, hardship.

AR'e– 2. bari, lari, pari, sari 3. safari, shikari, kanari, curare 4. Karharbari, aracari, Carbonari; *see* also AR'i– barry etc. below.

AR'er– 2. barrer, marrer, sparrer, tarrer 3. debarrer, bizarrer.

AR'fish– 2. barfish, garfish, starfish 3. cigarfish, guitarfish.

ARG'et– 2. target.

ARG'l– 2. argal, argol, gargle.

ARG'o– 2. Argo, argot, Fargo, cargo, largo, Margo, Margot, pargo, sargo 3. embargo, botargo 4. supercargo.

ARG'on– 2. argon, jargon.

ARG'u– 2. argue 3. reargue, redargue.

AR'i– 2. barry, scarry, charry, jarry, parry, sparry, tarry, starry 4. Carbonari; *see* also AR'e– bari etc. above.

AR'ik– 3. Amharic, Gemaric, tartaric.

AR'ing– 2. barring, scarring, charring, jarring, marring, parring, sparring, tar-

ring, starring 3. debarring, disbarring, bestarring.

ARJ'ent– 2. argent, margent, sergeant, Sargent 3. minargent.

ARJ'er– 2. barger, charger, larger, sparger 3. surcharger, discharger, enlarger.

ARJ'ez– 2. barges, charges, marges 3. recharges, surcharges, discharges, enlarges 4. countercharges, overcharges.

ARJ'ik– 3. pelargic, lethargic.

ARJ'in– 2. bargin', chargin', margin.

ARJ'ing– 2. barging, charging 3. discharging, enlarging 4. overcharging.

ARK'a– 2. Charca, parka, markka 3. bidarka.

ARK'al– 3. anarchal, monarchal 4. oligarchal, matriarchal, patriarchal, hierarchal.

ARK'asm– 2. sarcasm.

ARK'en– 2. barken, darken, hearken, starken 3. bedarken, endarken.

ARK'er– 2. barker, darker, harker, carker, larker, marker, markhor, parker, sparker, starker 3. embarker, skylarker.

ARK'est– 2. darkest, starkest.

ARK'et– 2. market 3. newmarket.

ARK'i– 2. arky, barky, darky, larky, Markey, sparky, starky 3. malarkey [slang] 4. oligarchy, hagiarchy, chiliarchy, matriarchy, patriarchy, hierarchy.

ARK'ik– 3. anarchic, monarchic 4. oligarchic, matriarchic, patriarchic.

ARK'ing– 2. barking, harking, carking, larking, marking, parking, sparking, sarking, starking 3. embarking, disbarking, *skylarking*, *earmarking*.

ARK'ish– 2. darkish, carkish, larkish, parkish, sparkish, starkish 3. skylarkish.

ARK'ist– 4. oligarchist, matriarchist, patriarchist, hierarchist.

ARK'l– 2. barkle, darkle, sparkle 3. besparkle.

ARK′ld– 2. barkled, darkled, carkled, sparkled 3. besparkled.

ARK′less– 2. barkless, carkless, larkless, markless, parkless, sparkless.

ARK′let– 2. parklet, sparklet.

ARK′li– 2. Barkley, Berkeley, darkly, sparkly, starkly.

ARK′ling– 2. darkling, larkling, sparkling.

ARK′ner– 3. darkener, hearkener.

ARK′ness– 2. darkness, starkness.

ARK′o– 2. Marco, charco [Sp.].

ARK′tik– 2. Arctic 3. subarctic, Nearctic, Holarctic, Antarctic 4. Palearctic.

ARK′us– 2. Barkis [Dickens], carcass, Marcus.

ARL′and– 2. garland 3. engarland.

ARL′ans– 2. parlance.

ARL′er– 2. gnarler, snarler, parlor 3. sunparlor.

ARL′es– 2. barless, carless, scarless, jarless, marless, tarless, starless, czarless 3. cigarless, catarrhless.

ARL′et– 2. carlet, scarlet, marlet, starlet, varlet; see also ARL′ot– harlot etc. below.

ARL′i– 2. barley, Charlie, Farley, marly, marli, gnarly, snarly, parley 3. bizarrely.

ARL′ik– 2. garlic, sarlyk 3. pilgarlic.

ARL′ike– 2. barlike, carlike, scarlike, tarlike, starlike, czarlike 3. cigarlike, catarrhlike.

ARL′in– 2. carlin, marlin, marline.

ARL′ing– 2. darling, carling, harling, marling, gnarling, snarling, parling, sparling, starling.

ARL′ot– 2. harlot, carlot, Charlotte; see also ARL′et– carlet etc. above.

ARL′us– 2. parlous, snarl us etc.; see also ARL′es– barless etc. above.

ARM′a– 2. dharma, karma 3. adharma.

ARM′ent– 2. garment, sarment 3. debarment, disbarment.

ARM′er– 2. armer, armor, charmer, farmer, harmer 3. disarmer, snake charmer, dirt farmer, alarmer.

ARM′ful– 2. armful, harmful, charmful 3. unharmful.

ARM′i– 2. army, barmy, farmy.

ARM′ik– 2. pharmic, ptarmic 4. polypharmic 5. alexipharmic.

ARM′in– 2. harmine, carmine, charmin′ 3. encarmine.

ARM′ing– 2. arming, charming, farming, harming 3. uncharming, forearming, alarming, disarming.

ARM′less– 2. armless, charmless, harmless 3. alarmless.

ARM′let– 2. armlet, charmlet.

ARM′ot– 2. carmot, marmot.

ARN′a– 2. arna, sarna.

ARN′al– 2. charnel, darnel, carnal 3. uncarnal.

ARN′at– 2. carnate 3. incarnate, discarnate 4. reincarnate.

ARN′el– 2. charnel, darnel.

ARN′er– 2. darner, garner, yarner.

ARN′erd– 2. Barnard, garnered.

ARN′ess– 2. farness, harness 3. reharness, unharness, bizarreness.

ARN′i– 2. barny, carney, blarney 3. Killarney.

ARN′ij– 2. carnage.

ARN′ing– 2. darning, yarning 3. goldarning, consarning [both slang].

ARN′ish– 2. garnish, tarnish, varnish.

ARN′isht– 2. garnished, tarnished, varnished 3. ungarnished, untarnished, unvarnished.

AR′o– 2. karo, claro, taro 3. denaro, cantaro, saguaro 4. carbonaro.

ARP′al– 2. carpal 4. metacarpal, intercarpal.

ARP′er– 2. harper, carper, sharper 3. cardsharper.

ARP′et– 2. carpet.

ARP′i– 2. harpy, carpy, sharpy, sharpie.

ARP′ing– 2. harping, carping, sharping 3. cardsharping.

ARS′al– 2. carcel, parcel, tarsal 4. metatarsal.

ARS′er– 2. carcer [L.], parser, sparser, Sarsar.

ARS′ez– 2. farces, parses, sarses.

ARSH′al– 2. martial, marshal, Marshall, partial 3. field marshal, impartial.

ARSH′an– 2. Martian.

ARS′li– 2. parsley, sparsely.

ARS′on– 2. arson, Carson, Larson, parson, squarson.

ARS′us– 2. tarsus 3. protarsus 4. metatarsus.

ART′a– 2. charta [L.], Sparta, cuarta 4. Magna Charta.

ART′an– 2. partan, Spartan, tartan, Tartan; see also ART′en– hearten etc. below.

ART′ay– 3. ex parte, Astarte 4. colla parte [It.].

ART′ed– 2. darted, hearted, carted, charted, smarted, parted, started 3. kindhearted, hardhearted, freehearted, weakhearted, warmhearted, downhearted, falsehearted, softhearted, lighthearted, fainthearted, stouthearted, truehearted, uncharted, outsmarted, departed, imparted, upstarted 4. stonyhearted, heavyhearted, simplehearted, singlehearted, gentlehearted, chickenhearted, brokenhearted, openhearted, lionhearted, ironhearted, tenderhearted.

ART′en– 2. barton, Barton, hearten, carton, marten, smarten, tarten 3. enhearten, dishearten 4. Tiergarten, kindergarten; see also ART′an– partan etc. above.

ART′er– 2. arter, barter, charter, darter, garter, carter, parter, martyr, smarter, tartar, tarter, starter 3. departer, imparter, bemartyr, restarter, self-starter 4. protomartyr, cream-of-tartar.

ART′erd– 2. bartered, chartered, gartered, martyred.

ART′ful– 2. artful, heartful, startful.

ART′i– 2. arty, darty, hearty, smarty, party, tarty, starty 3. McCarty, tea party, ex parte, Astarte.

ART′ing– 2. charting, darting, carting, smarting, parting, starting 3. sweethearting, departing, imparting, disparting, restarting, self-starting, upstarting.

ART′ist– 2. artist, chartist, Chartist 4. Bonapartist.

ART′l– 2. dartle, spartle, startle 4. Rosa Dartle [Dickens].

ART′less– 2. artless, dartless, cartless, chartless, heartless, smartless, partless, startless.

ART′let– 2. artlet, Bartlett, heartlet, partlet, martlet, tartlet.

ART′li– 2. smartly, partly, tartly.

ART′ling– 2. dartling, spartling, startling.

ART′ment– 3. apartment, department, impartment, compartment.

ART′ness– 2. smartness, tartness.

ART′o– 3. lagarto, esparto.

ART′on– 2. barton, Barton, carton 4. set one's heart on; see also ART′en– barton etc. above.

ART′rij– 2. cartridge, partridge.

AR′u– 2. baru, maru.

AR′um– 2. garum, larum 3. alarum.

ARV′a– 2. arva, larva.

ARV′al– 2. Arval, arval, barvel, carval, larval, marvel.

ARV′er– 2. carver, marver, starver.

AS′a– 2. casa [Sp., It., Pg., L.], pasa [Sp.], guasa.

AS′ta– 2. basta, hasta, pasta [It.].

AT′a– 2. bata, data, gata, rata 3. reata [Sp.], regatta, riata, toccata, stoccata, camata, sonata, batata, patata, cantata **4.** alpargata [Sp.], boniata, matamata, carromata, serenata **5.** enamorata, inamorata.

AT'er– **2.** mater, pater, quatre **3.** Dis Pater **4.** alma mater, Stabat Mater.

AT'i– **2.** Sati, zati **3.** piatti, coati, Amati **4.** Jubilate, Cincinnati **5.** illuminati.

AT'o– **2.** dato, datto [both Tag. & Sp.] **3.** legato, staccato, spiccato, marcato [It.], pomato, tomato, annatto, barato [Sp.], vibrato, ritratto [It.] **4.** moderato, obbligato, pizzicato, passionato [It.], disperato [It.], allentato [It.] **5.** demilegato, appassionato.

AT'ra– **2.** matra **3.** Sumatra **4.** Cleopatra.

AT'um– **2.** datum **3.** pomatum.

AV'a– **2.** Java, kava, lava, Brava, guava **3.** cassava **4.** kavakava, piassava.

AV'er– **2.** halver, calver, salver, suaver **3.** palaver.

AV'i– **2.** Ave, Kavi **3.** Mohave, Mojave, peccavi **6.** Rikki-tikki-tavi [Kipling].

AV'ing– **2.** halving, calving, salving.

AV'o– **2.** bravo **3.** octavo, centavo.

A'wa– **2.** awa, tawa **3.** Chihuahua.

A'ya– **2.** aya, Maya, raya, saya **3.** kabaya, papaya, karaya, Hawaii **4.** Surabaya.

AZ'a– **2.** plaza, maza [Sp.].

AZH'ing– **3.** barraging, garaging **4** persiflaging, camouflaging.

AZ'i– **2.** ghazi **3.** Benghazi.

A (ah)

3.

TRIPLE RHYMES IN A (art'less-ly)

Primary or Secondary Accent Falls on
Second from Last Syllable.

AB'i–la– **4.** cantabile **5.** lamentabile.

AK'i–a– **4.** Slovakia **6.** Czechoslovakia.

AM'ist–ri– **3.** palmistry, psalmistry.

ARB'er–ing– **3.** barbering, harboring.

ARD'en–ing– **3.** gardening, hardening, pardoning.

ARD'i–li– **3.** hardily, tardily **4.** foolhardily.

AR'i–ness– **3.** barriness, tarriness, starriness.

AR'i–o– **4.** scenario, Cesario **5.** impresario.

ARK'i–kal– **3.** archical **4.** hylarchical, anarchical, monarchical, tetrarchical **5.** hierarchical.

ARL'a–tan– **3.** charlatan, tarlatan.

ARM'a–bl– **3.** farmable, armable, harmable, charmable, **4.** disarmable, unfarmable, unharmable, uncharmable, alarmable.

ARM'ing–li– **3.** farmingly, harmingly, charmingly **4.** disarmingly, alarmingly.

ARN'ish–er– **3.** garnisher, tarnisher, varnisher.

ARN'ish–ing– **3.** garnishing, tarnishing, varnishing **4.** revarnishing.

ARS'en–er– **3.** larcener, parcener **4.** coparcener.

ARS'en–i– **3.** larceny **4.** coparceny.

ART'ed–li– **4.** halfheartedly, lighheartedly, faintheartedly, stoutheartedly.

ART'ed–ness– **4.** kindheartedness, hardheartedness, downheartedness, lightheartedness **5.** simpleheartedness, openheartedness, lionheartedness.

ART'er–er– **3.** barterer, charterer.

ART'er–i– **3.** artery, bartery, martyry.

ART'i–kl– **3.** article, particle.

ART'i–zan– **3.** artisan, bartizan, partisan.

ART'less–li– **3.** artlessly, heartlessly.

A (cab)

1.

SINGLE (MASCULINE) RHYMES IN A (cab)

AB– 1. ab, abb, Bab, dab, gab [coll.], cab, scab, lab, blab, slab, Mab, nab, snab [slang], rab, brab, drab, grab, crab, tab, stab 2. *Joab, confab, lablab,* Queen Mab, *eartab* 3. baobab, taxicab.

ACH– 1. batch, bach [slang], hatch, catch, latch, slatch, match, natch, snatch, patch, ratch, brach, cratch, scratch, thatch 2. *nuthatch, seecatch, potlatch,* mismatch, *tolpatch,* dispatch, *Wasatch,* attach, detach 3. overmatch.

ACHD– 1. batched, bached [slang], hatched, latched, matched, snatched, patched, scratched, thatched 2. mismatched, dispatched, attached, detached.

AD– 1. ad, add, bad, bade, dad, fad, gad, had, cad, Chad, Tchad, scad, lad, blad [Scot.], glad, clad, plaid, mad, pad, rad [dial.], brad, grad [slang], sad, shad, tad 2. readd, *Sindbad,* forbade, aubade [F.], egad, begad, *mailclad,* unclad, kneepad 3. Iliad, chiliad, myriad, Trinidad, ironclad, winter clad, heavy clad, ivy clad, reculade [F.], Leningrad, undergrad, Olympiad, little tad.

ADZ– ads 'etc., *see* **AD–** ad etc. above, plus "s" or "'s."

AF– 1. aff [Scot.], baff, chaff, daff, faff, gaff, half, calf, laugh, laff [slang], raff, Wraf, draff, graph, staff, quaff 2. *chiffchaff,* behalf, *mooncalf, horselaugh,* carafe, *riffraff,* agraffe, giraffe, *gibstaff, flagstaff, distaff, Falstaff, forestaff* 3. shandygaff, anagraph, paragraph, telegraph, melograph, phonograph, monograph, dictograph, au-

tograph, photograph, lithograph, epitaph, cenotaph, better half, quarter staff 4. mimeograph, stereograph, radiograph, cardiograph, heliograph.

AFT– 1. aft, baffed, daft, daffed, gaffed, haft, laughed, raft, draft, graft, craft, shaft, Taft, staffed, waft, quaffed 2. abaft, engraft, *witchcraft, woodcraft, seacraft, folkcraft, aircraft,* awaft 3. overdraft, handicraft, metalcraft 4. antiaircraft.

AG– 1. ag [slang], bag, dag, fag, gag, jag, cag [slang], scag, skag, lag, flag, slag, mag [coll. and slang], nag, knag, snag, rag, brag, drag, crag, scrag, sag, shag, tag, stag, vag [slang], wag, quag, swag, zag 2. *handbag, gasbag, shagrag, ragtag, wigwag, zigzag* 3. moneybag, saddlebag, demihag, scalawag, chew the rag [slang], Brobdingnag.

AGD– 1. bagged, fagged, gagged, cagged, lagged, flagged, nagged, snagged, dragged, sagged, tagged, wagged 2. betagged, *wigwagged, zigzagged.*

AJ– 1. badge, fadge, hadj, cadge, Madge.

AK– 1. back, bac, hack, jack, kak, kack, cack [all slang], lack, lac, black, clack, claque, plaque, slack, mack, mac [both slang], smack, knack, snack, pack, pac, rack, crack, track, wrack, sack, sac, sacque, shack, tac, tack, stack, Waac, wack [slang], quack, whack, thwack, yak 2. *ack-ack,* aback, *wayback, pinchback, hunchback, switchback, holdback, halfback, puffback, crookback, quillback, fullback, comeback, drawback, throwback, humpback, horseback,*

41

kiack, blackjack, flapjack, slapjack, skipjack, bootjack, muntjak, alack, shellac, *flicflac, lampblack, bootblack, knickknack,* repack, unpack, *calpac, woolpack, wisecrack,* re- track, *backtrack, racetrack,* tesack, *sicsac, woolsack,* ransack, *rucksack,* attack, *hard- tack, ticktack, thumbtack, haystack, bull- whack, Anzac* **3.** zodiac, cardiac, maniac, Pontiac, piggyback, pickaback, hucka- back, saddleback, turtleback, quarterback, leatherback, razorback, Union Jack, nat- terjack, almanac, bric-a-brac, tamarack, cul-de-sac, haversack, bivouac, paddy- whack, cattleyak **4.** tacamahac, yakkity- yak [slang].

AKS– **1.** ax, axe, backs, jacks, lax, lacks, flax, slacks, Max, max, snacks, pax, packs, tracks, Thrax, sax, sacks, tax, tacks, stacks, wax, yaks, zax **2.** *addax, pickax, poleax, greenbacks,* relax, *toadflax, climax, back- tracks,* ransacks, *haystacks,* dewax, *chaffwax, beeswax, paxwax* **3.** battle-ax, Halifax, parallax, supertax, overtax, income tax.

AKST– **1.** axed, flaxed, taxed, waxed **2.** relaxed, dewaxed **3.** supertaxed, over- taxed.

AKT– **1.** act, fact, lacked, pact, packed, racked, wracked, bract, cracked, tract, tact, tacked, quacked, whacked **2.** react, triact, coact, redact, *hunchbacked, hump- backed, confact,* enact, epact, impact, com- pact, unpacked, defract, diffract, entr'acte, *sidetracked,* ransacked, transact, intact, *contact,* exact **3.** saddle-backed, cataract, interact, counteract, overact, re-enact, retroact, cataphract, inexact **4.** matter- of-fact.

AKTS– acts etc., *see* **AKT–** act etc. above, plus "s" or "'s."

AL– **1.** Al, dalle, gal [slang], Cal, mal, pal, sal [slang], salle, shall **2.** cabal, locale, canal, corral, morale, La Salle, *aval* **3.** musicale, chaparral, pastorale, entresalle; *see* also **AL–** Baal etc.

ALD– **1.** palled **2.** caballed, corralled **3.** emerald.

ALK– **1.** alk, calk, calc, talc **3.** cata- falque.

ALKS– **1.** falx, calks, calx.

ALP– **1.** alp, scalp, palp **3.** auriscalp.

ALPS– **1.** Alps, scalps, palps **3.** auri- scalps.

ALT– **1.** alt, shalt.

ALV– **1.** salve, valve **2.** bivalve.

AM– **1.** am, bam, Cham, cham [dial.], dam, damn, gam, gamb, ham, jam, jam'b, cam, camm [slang], lam, lamb, clam, flam, slam, ma'am, pam, rhamn, ram, dram, drachm, dramme, gram, gramme, cram, pram, tram, Sam, sham, tam, swam, wham, yam, zam [slang] **2.** madame, *beldam, grandam,* Siam, *jimjam,* enjamb, *flimflam,* Assam, *tamtam, whimwham,* Khayyam **3.** Alabam', cofferdam, Abraham, Birming- ham, Nottingham, choriamb, demijambe, diaphragm, diagram, anagram, telegram, milligram, epigram, centigram, cablegram, kilogram, melogram, monogram, crypto- gram, marjoram, dithyramb, petersham, Uncle Sam **4.** ad nauseam [L.], The Great I Am **5.** parallelogram.

AMB– **1.** amb, gamb **3.** choriamb, dith- yramb.

AMD– **1.** damned, dammed, gammed, jammed, lambed, lammed [slang], clammed, flammed, slammed, rammed, crammed, shammed, whammed.

AMP– **1.** amp [slang], champ, damp, gamp, guimpe, camp, scamp, lamp, clamp, ramp, cramp, tramp, samp, tamp, stamp, vamp, yamp **2.** *chokedamp, firedamp,* decamp, encamp, *slampamp,* restamp, *backstamp,* revamp **3.** Davy lamp, safety lamp, signal lamp.

AMPS– amps etc., *see* **AMP–** amp etc. above, plus "s" or "'s."

AN– **1.** Ann, Anne, ban, Chan, Dan, dan, fan, gan [slang], khan, can, scan, clan, plan, man, pan, Pan, panne, span, ran, bran, Fran, fran [slang], gran, cran, scran, san, tan, than, van **2.** cabane, redan, sedan, Sudan, began, bahan, pecan, *oilcan, cancan, ashcan,* Milan, replan, *madman, reman, seaman, cabman, jibman, clubman, subman, tubman, headman, leadman, madman, oddman, bandman, sandman, bondman, hodman, woodman, rodman, wardman, birdman, iceman, freeman, cageman, bargeman, dirgeman, brakeman, lineman, tapeman, fireman, wireman, shoreman, horseman, Norseman, flagman, ragman, dragman, swagman, pegman, yeggman, hangman, songman, cogman, tugman, coachman, Welchman, ranchman, henchman, Frenchman, churchman, watchman, switchman, Scotchman, Dutchman, ploughman, freshman, Welshman, Bushman, Northman, packman, checkman, lockman stockman, milkman, bankman, bookman, workman, oilman, bellman, billman, millman, stillman, tollman,* Pullman, *dolman, schoolman, penman, trainman, gunman, yeoman,* Roman, *woman, capman, chapman, shipman, tipman, shopman, topman, barman, carman, spearman,* German, *Herman,* Sherman, *merman, airman,* Norman, *floorman, beadsman, headsman, leadsman, oddsman, bandsman, landsman, bondsman, woodsman, guardsman, herdsman, swordsman, tribesman, tradesman, desman, spokesman, salesman, talesman, dolesman, shoresman, statesman, dragsman, gangsman, marksman, bailsman, spoilsman, almsman, helmsman, groomsman, clansman, kinsman, townsman, oarsman, passman, messman, pressman, batsman, craftsman, draftsman, yachtsman, huntsman,* Scotsman, *sportsman, batman, meatman, boatman, pitman, footman, postman,* Truman, *crewman, bowman, cowman, showman, plowman, cayman, layman, playman, drayman, wayman, flyman,* Japan, *lapin,* sapan, *sapin, hardpan,* trepan, *sampan,* Chopin, *inspan, outspan,* Iran, outran, Bataan, rattan, *gratin, fantan,* divan **3.** Marianne, Caliban, balmacaan, barbican, rubican, indican, Anglican, Gallican, pemmican, African, Vatican, Mexican, Oppidan, harridan, orlean, joulean,

tinean, Marnean, Etnean, Kordofan, suffragan, cardigan, Michigan, mulligan, hooligan, ptarmigan, wanigan, origan, larrigan, Jonathan, astrakhan, Serbian, Lesbian, Nubian, Indian, guardian, Gordian, Lydian, saffian, ruffian, Belgian, Georgian, Pythian, Fijian, Anglian, Tullian, Julian, simian, Marnian, Appian, Caspian, Thespian, Marian, Austrian, Elysian, Tahitian, Egyptian, Servian, Latvian, Chinaman, husbandman, *policeman,* Orangeman, nobleman, middleman, rifleman, gentleman, longshoreman, signalman, Mussulman, dragoman, midshipman, alderman, fisherman, superman, waterman, peterman, slaughterman, quarterman, overman, sailorman, backwoodsman, Irishman, talisman, *frontiersman,* aircraftsman, *selectman,* merchantman, highwayman, clergyman, tallyman, liveryman, dairyman, ferryman, merryman, countryman, vestryman, marzipan, tragopan, Lutheran, veteran, Alcoran, Parmesan, courtesan, Powhatan, Yucatan, *Tibetan,* Puritan, rheotan, Turkestan, Pakistan, caravan, cordovan, Libyan, Wesleyan **4.** militiaman, jinrikiman, artilleryman, deliveryman, infantryman, catamaran, Baluchistan, Afghanistan, orangutan.

ANCH– 1. ganch, canch [slang], Blanche, blanch, flanch, ranch, branch, stanch **3.** avalanche.

AND– 1. and, band, banned, dand [slang], fanned, hand, canned, scanned, land, bland, gland, planned, manned, panned, spanned, brand, grand, strand, sand, tanned, stand **2.** *headband, neckband,* disband, *breastband, wristband,* offhand, *backhand,* unhand, *shorthand,* firsthand, *headland, midland woodland, eland, mainland, dreamland,* Greenland, *Rhineland, inland, lowland,* Lapland, *upland, moorland, grassland,* Queensland, *wasteland, northland,* demand, remand, command, expand, *firebrand, quicksand, greensand, lampstand,* withstand **3.** saraband, contraband, bellyband, *four-in-hand,* behind·

hand, secondhand, evenhand, underhand, afterhand, overhand, upper hand, samarcand, fairyland, wonderland, borderland, hinterland, fatherland, motherland, overland, reprimand, confirmand, countermand, Rio Grande, ampersand, understand 4. multiplicand, Chateaubriand, misunderstand.

ANG– 1. bang, bhang, dang [dial.], fang, gang, hang, lang [Scot. and dial.], clang, slang, pang, spang [coll.], rang, sprang, sang, tang, swang, twang, whang, vang 2. shebang, *gambang*, gobang, *holmgang*, *ingang*, *sirgang*, *outgang*, *oxgang*, *boomslang*, Penang, trepang, harangue, meringue, serang, *mustang* 3. overhang, boomerang, burrawang 4. orangoutang.

ANGD– 1. banged, danged [dial.], fanged, ganged [coll.], hanged, clanged, twanged, whanged 2. bifanged, harangued 3. boomeranged.

ANGZ– bangs etc., *see* ANG– bang etc. above, plus "s" or "'s."

ANJ– 1. banj [slang], gange, flange 2. *phalange*, *sporange*.

ANK– 1. ank [slang], bank, banc, dank, hank, lank, blank, flank, clank, plank, spank, rank, frank, Frank, franc, crank, prank, sank, shank, tank, thank, swank, yank 2. embank, point-blank, outflank, *gangplank*, disrank, outrank, *redshank*, *foreshank* 3. mountebank, riverbank, savings bank.

ANKS– banks etc., *see* ANK– bank etc. above, plus "s" or "'s"; 1. Manx, thanx [slang], Yanks 2. *Fairbanks*, *phalanx*, *longshanks* 3. bonyshanks.

ANKT– 1. banked, blanked, flanked, clanked, planked, spanked, ranked, franked, cranked, sanct, tanked, thanked, swanked, yanked 2. outflanked, outranked 3. sacrosanct, spindle-shanked.

ANS– 1. anse, chance, dance, hanse, lance, glance, manse, nance [slang], France, prance, trance, stance 2. bechance, per-

chance, mischance, seance, enhance, askance, romance, finance, expanse, entrance, *brilliance*, advance 3. *disturbance*, *impedance*, *misguidance*, *avoidance*, *ascendance*, permeance, elegance, arrogance, radiance, *allegiance*, *appliance*, variance, nonchalance, sibilance, jubilance, vigilance, ambulance, simulance, petulance, maintenance, countenance, sustenance, prévenance [F], provenance, convenance [F.], *repugnance*, ordinance, dominance, resonance, consonance, assonance, dissonance, governance, *remembrance*, *encumbrance*, sufferance, furtherance, tolerance, temperance, utterance, severance, ignorance, aberrance, penetrance, *remonstrance*, *defeasance*, *malfeasance*, *complaisance*, *obeisance*, *conversance*, *expectance*, *inductance*, *conductance*, *reluctance*, oscitance, hesitance, *repentance*, *acceptance*, circumstance, *inconstance*, *pursuance*, issuance, relevance, *clairvoyance* 4. significance, extravagance, inelegance, insouciance, irradiance, luxuriance, discountenance, appurtenance, preordinance, predominance, inconsonance, vociferance, intemperance, deliverance, recalcitrance, reconnoisance, reconnaissance, exorbitance, concomitance, precipitance, inheritance, continuance, perpetuance, irrelevance 5. insignificance, disinheritance, discontinuance.

ANST– 1. chanced, danced, lanced, glanced, pranced, tranced 2. enhanced, romanced, financed, entranced, advanced.

ANT– 1. ant, aunt, bant [slang], gant [slang], hant [slang], chant, cant, can't, scant, plant, slant, pant, rant, grant, shan't 2. enchant, decant, recant, askant, descant, gallant, replant, *eggplant*, *pieplant*, implant, transplant, supplant, aslant, courant, courante, extant, levant, bezant 3. Corybant, agacant, desiccant, exsiccant, dodecant, imprecant, albicant, radicant, abdicant, dedicant, mendicant, indicant, applicant, formicant, fabricant, lubricant, vesicant, toxicant, coruscant, confidant, permeant, recreant, procreant, miscreant, elegant, congregant, obligant, irrigant, litigant, mitigant, arrogant, elephant, oliphant, *triumphant*, sycophant, resiant, otiant, nonchalant, libelant, revelant, sibilant, jubilant, vigilant, tremolant, circulant, osculant, stridulant, undulant, ululant, stimulant, cumulant, petulant, postulant, *informant*, revenant, covenant, ordinant, culminant, dominant, consonant, assonant, dissonant, mancipant, Sacripant, celebrant, tolerant, alterant, cauterant, integrant, emigrant, immigrant, odorant, colorant, cormorant, ignorant, penetrant, registrant, ministrant, obscurant, figurant, fulgurant, hebetant, vegetant, dilettant, habitant, oscitant, militant, comitant, crepitant, irritant, hesitant, visitant, *important*, *inconstant*, debutant, menstruant, issuant, fluctuant, gallivant, innovant, cognizant 4. communicant, intoxicant, consolidant, extravagant, inelegant, depreciant, officiant, renunciant, insouciant, circumvolant, matriculant, coagulant, articulant, congratulant, impetulant, capitulant, appurtenant, discriminant, determinant, aggultinant, conglutinant, horrisonant, reverberant, protuberant, exuberant, preponderant, refrigerant, intolerant, agglomerant, itinerant, deodorant, ameliorant, decolorant, expectorant, recalcitrant, administrant, resuscitant, incogitant, regurgitant, concomitant, continuant, attenuant, irrelevant, incognizant.

ANTS– ants¨etc., *see* **ANT–** ant etc. above, plus "s" or "'s."

ANZ– Ann's etc., *see* **AN–** Ann etc. above, plus "s" or "'s"; 1. banns.

AP– 1. chap, dap, gap, hap, Jap, cap, lap, Lapp, flap, clap, slap, map, nap, knap, snap, pap, rap, wrap, crap, scrap, trap, strap, sap, tap, yap, yapp 2. *stopgap*, mayhap, *mishap*, *madcap*, *redcap*, becap, *kneecap*, recap, *skullcap*, uncap, *icecap*, *nightcap*, *whitecap*, *foolscap*, *bluecap*, cat-

lap, *dewlap*, *flyflap*, *flip-flap*, beclap, *backslap*, genapp, genappe, surnap, resnap, unsnap, enwrap, *mantrap*, entrap, *claptrap*, bestrap, *checkstrap*, *rattrap*, *winesap*, *heeltap*, lagniappe 3. handicap, overlap, thunderclap, afterclap, photomap, rattletrap.

APS– chaps etc., *see* **AP–** chap etc. above, plus "s" or "'s"; 1. apse, lapse, schnapps 2. perhaps, elapse, relapse, collapse, prolapse, synapse 3. pettichaps.

APST– 1. lapsed 2. elapsed, relapsed, collapsed.

AR– through **ARZ–**, *see* long **A** (ay): **AR–** through **ARZ–**; also broad **A** (ah): **AR–** through **ARZ–**.

AS– 1. ass, bass, fas, gas, lass, blas, glass, class, mass, pass, wrasse, brass, brasse, grass, crass, strass, sass [dial. and slang], tass, vas 2. *jackass*, rubasse, *fracas*, *Dorcas*, *Midas*, *nefas* [L.], bagasse, fougasse, alas, *Hellas*, *eyeglass*, *hourglass*, declass, reclass, outclass, amass, remass, *Lammas*, en masse, *Thomas*, *Christmas*, *pampas*, *compass*, impasse, surpass, *trespass*, *upas*, *arras*, harass, *Madras*, *Mithras*, terras, terrass, cuirass, morass, *dronkgrass*, *eelgrass*, *Kansas*, kavass, crevasse, *Texas* 3. anabasse, contrabass, octobass, pancreas, Boreas, isinglass, looking glass, galloglass, weatherglass, middle class, working class, sonderclass, underclass, upper-class, superclass, bonny lass, Nicholas, Pythias, alias, Elias, Candlemas, Michaelmas, Martinmas, Hallowmas, underpass, overpass, Khyber Pass, *encompass*, sassafras, coupde-grâce [F.], peppergrass, sparrowgrass, Alcatras, *Honduras*, demitasse, tarantass.

ASH– 1. ash, bash, dash, gash, hash, hache, cash, cache, lash, lâche [F.], flash, clash, plash, splash, slash, mash, smash, gnash, pash [dial.], rash, brash, crash, thrash, sash, stash [dial. and slang], vache 2. abash, rondache, *slapdash*, rehash, encash, *eyelash*, *backlash*, *pearlash*, *mishmash*, panache, apache, patache [F.], pistache, moustache, soutache [F.] **3.** calabash, balderdash, spatterdash, sabretache.

ASHT– 1. bashed, dashed, gashed, hashed, cashed, cached, lashed, flashed, clashed, splashed, slashed, mashed, smashed, gnashed, crashed, thrashed, sashed, stashed **2.** abashed, moustached.

ASK– 1. ask, bask, Basque, casque, cask, flask, mask, task **2.** unmask **3.** antimask.

ASP– 1. asp, gasp, hasp, clasp, rasp, grasp **2.** agasp, unhasp, enclasp, unclasp.

AST– 1. bast, dast [dial], fast, gassed, gast [slang], hast, cast, caste, last, blast, mast, massed, nast, past, passed, sassed, vast **2.** *bombast, broadcast, molecast,* recast, forecast, *dicast, downcast,* upcast, miscast, outcast, *steadfast, holdfast, handfast, breakfast,* aghast, *ballast, portlast,* outlast, outclassed, amassed, remast, *foremast, mainmast, durmast,* unmast, dismast, *gymnast, dynast,* repast, repassed, *mainpast, trispast,* surpassed, harassed, *contrast, peltast, phantast,* avast **3.** undercast, overcast, scholiast, counterblast, unsurpassed, antispast, pederast, paraphrast, metaphrast, flabbergast **4.** elegiast, bucoliast, ecclesiast, symposiast, enthusiast, iconoclast.

AT– 1. at, bat, chat, fat, gat, hat, cat, scat, skat, lat, blat, flat, plat, plait, splat, slat, mat, matte, gnat, pat, patte, spat, rat brat, drat, frat [slang], prat, sprat, sat, tat,

that, vat **2.** hereat, thereat, whereat, *brickbat, hurlbat,* begat, highhat, top hat, *woodchat, whinchat, stonechat, grasschat, chitchat, bobcat, wildcat, hellcat, polecat, tipcat, bearcat,* plakat, *muscat,* surat, cravat **3.** caveat, acrobat, flitterbat, tabby cat, kittycat, pussycat, waterchat, lariat, diplomat, pitapat, tokopat, Ararat, democrat, monocrat, bureaucrat, autocrat, plutocrat, thermostat, Rubaiyat **4.** Magnificat, aristocrat, heliostat **5.** commissariat, proletariat, secretariat.

ATCH– batch etc., *see* **ACH–** batch etc. above.

ATH– 1. bath, Gath, hath, lath, math, snath, path, rath, wrath, strath **2.** *bypath, towpath, warpath, footpath* **3.** demibath, isobath, polymath, misomath, aftermath, philomath, allopath **4.** homeopath, osteopath, physiopath.

AV– 1. bave [F.], have, halve, calve, lav [slang], Slav, salve **2.** épave [F.] **3.** Jugoslav.

AVZ– 1. halves, calves, Slavs, salves **3.** Jugoslavs.

AZ– 1. as, chaz [slang], has, jazz, razz [slang], yazz [slang] **2.** thereas, whereas **3.** razzmatazz.

AZM– 1. phasm, chasm, plasm, spasm **2.** *sarcasm, orgasm, miasm, empasm, phantasm* **3.** idiasm, schediasm, chiliasm, cataclasm, metaplasm, pseudoplasm, neoplasm, protoplasm, pleonasm **4.** enthusiasm, demoniasm, iconoclasm.

A (cab)

2.

DOUBLE (FEMININE) RHYMES IN A (gab′ber)

Primary or Secondary Accent Falls on
Next to Last Syllable: Imperfect Rhymes
Are in Italics.

AB′er– 2. dabber, gabber, jabber, blabber, clabber, slabber, nabber, grabber, stabber.

AB′erd– 2. gabbard, jabbered, scabbard, blabbered, clabbered, tabard.

AB′i– 2. abbey, Abbie, gabby, cabby, scabby, blabby, flabby, rabbi, crabby, shabby, tabby.

AB′id– 2. rabid, tabid.

AB′ij– 2. cabbage.

AB′ik– 2. rabic 3. syllabic, cannabic 4. asyllabic, bisyllabic, trisyllabic 5. polysyllabic, multisyllabic, monosyllabic.

AB′il– 2. habile; *see* also **AB′l–** babble etc. below.

AB′in– 2. cabin, dabbin' etc. 3. log cabin.

AB′ing– 2. dabbing, gabbing, jabbing, cabbing, blabbing, nabbing, slabbing, stabbing 3. confabbing 4. taxicabbing.

AB′it– 2. Babbitt, habit, rabbet, rabbit, drabbet 3. inhabit, cohabit.

AB′l– 2. babble, dabble, gabble, habile, jabble, cabble, scabble, rabble, brabble, drabble, grabble, scrabble, ˡyabble 3. bedabble, bedrabble 4. applicable, duplicable, explicable, amicable, despicable, extricable, practicable, masticable, educable, manducable, formidable, noticeable, serviceable, balanceable, marriageable, damageable, manageable, knowledgeable, challangeable, *dischargeable*, malleable, permeable, *unliveable*, propagable, refragable, segregable, obligable, irrigable, mitigable, navigable, publishable, perish-

able, amiable, expiable, variable, leviable violable, calculable, regulable, estimable, fathomable, terminable, pardonable, fashionable, pensionable, actionable, sanctionable, mentionable, questionable, poisonable, personable, governable, exculpable, separable, execrable, renderable, ponderable, preferable, offerable, sufferable, tolerable, numerable, venerable, vulnerable, temperable, superable, miserable, alterable, utterable, conquerable, severable, answerable, admirable, gibblegabble, ribble-rabble, memorable, honorable, favorable, pleasurable, measurable, exorable, censurable, mensurable, purchasable, marketable, covetable, habitable, dubitable, creditable, *forgettable*, profitable, limitable, hospitable, charitable, irritable, equitable, evitable, comfortable, valuable, *inequable*, issuable 5. eradicable, multiplicable, inapplicable, inexplicable, inextricable, impracticable, prognosticable, unnoticeable, disserviceable, unmanageable, acknowledgeable, unchallengeable, impermeable, ˡimmitigable, interrogable, distinguishable, extinguishable, enunciable, remediable, affiliable, inexpiable, invariable, imperviable, inviolable, incalculable, inoculable, coagulable, inestimable, unfathomable, inalienable, imaginable, disciplinable, contaminable, examinable, abominable, determinable, interminable, unpardonable, companionable, impassionable, impressionable, objectionable, exceptionable, proportionable, unquestionable, developable, inseparable, rememberable, considerable, imponderable, insufferable, decipherable, intolerable, innumerable, invulnerable, insuperable, unalterable, inseverable, deliverable, recoverable, discoverable, unanswerable, commemorable, dishonorable, unfavorable, immeasurable, impenetrable, incensurable, immensurable, commensurable, interpretable, inhabitable, indubitable, discreditable, hereditable, unprofitable, illimitable, inimitable, indomitable, decapitable, precipitable, inhospitable, uncharitable, inequitable, inevitable, uncomfortable, contributable, distributable, attributable, invaluable, perpetuable **6.** ineradicable, indistinguishable, inextinguishable, irremediable, inalienable, unimaginable, indeterminable, disproportionable, undevelopable, inconsiderable, undecipherable, irrecoverable, incommensurable, uninhabitable; *see* also **IB′l**– bibble etc.

AB′ler– **2.** babbler, dabbler, gabbler, cabbler, scabbler, brabbler, grabbler, scrabbler **3.** bedabbler.

AB′let– **2.** crablet, tablet.

AB′li– **2.** babbly, dabbly, drably.

AB′ling– **2.** babbling, dabbling, gabbling, scabbling, brabbling, grabbling.

AB′lish– **2.** babblish **3.** establish **4.** reestablish, disestablish.

AB′o– **2.** jabot, sabot.

AB′ot– **2.** abbot, Abbot, Cabot.

ACH′el– **2.** hatchel, ratchel, satchel.

ACH′er– **2.** batcher, hatcher, catcher, latcher, matcher, snatcher, patcher, scratcher, thatcher **3.** *dogcatcher*, *flycatcher*, dispatcher, *back-scratcher*.

ACH′et– **2.** hatchet, latchet, matchet, ratchet, brachet.

ACH′ez– **2.** batches, baches, hatches, catches, latches, Natchez, patches, matches **3.** *nuthatches*, mismatches, *crosspatches*, dispatches, attaches, detaches **4.** Kaffee Klatches.

ACH′i– **2.** catchy, matchy, machi, snatchy, patchy, scratchy **3.** seecatchie.

ACH′ing– **2.** batching, baching, hatching, catching, latching, matching, snatching, patching, scratching, thatching **3.** dispatching, rematching, mismatching, attaching, detaching, back-scratching.

ACH′less– **2.** batchless, hatchless, catchless, latchless, matchless, patchless, scratchless, thatchless **3.** dispatchless.

ACH′ment– **2.** hatchment, ratchment **3.** attachment, detachment, dispatchment.

AD′a– **2.** adda, dada, stadda.

AD′am– **2.** Adam, madam **3.** macadam.

AD′ed– **2.** added, gadded, plaided, padded, bradded **3.** readded, unadded, unpadded.

AD′en– **2.** gladden, madden, sadden **3.** engladden, Macfadden.

AD′er– **2.** adder, badder, gadder, ladder, bladder, gladder, madder, sadder **3.** stepladder.

AD′est– **2.** baddest, gladdest, maddest, saddest.

AD′i– **2.** daddy, faddy, caddy, caddie, laddie, gladdy, maddy, paddy **4.** sugar daddy, finnanhaddie.

AD′ij– **2.** adage.

AD′ik– **3.** decadic, haggadic, triadic, Helladic, nomadic, monadic, faradic, sporadic, octadic, Sotadic, dyadic, nexadic.

AD′ing– **2.** adding, gadding, padding, bradding.

AD′ish– **2.** faddish, caddish, gladdish, plaidish, maddish, radish, saddish.

AD′l– **2.** addle, paddle, raddle, straddle, saddle, staddle [dial.] **3.** skedaddle [coll.], astraddle, bestraddle, unsaddle **4.** fiddlefaddle.

AD′ld– **2.** addled, paddled, raddled, straddled, saddled, staddled [dial.] **3.** skedaddled [coll.], unsaddled **4.** fiddlefaddled.

AD′li– **2.** badly, gladly, madly, sadly.

AD'ling– 2. addling, paddling, straddling, saddling, spraddling, staddling [dial.] skedaddling, unsaddling 4. fiddle-faddling.

AD'lz– addles etc., *see* AD'l– addle etc. above, plus "s" or "'s"; 4. Thomas Traddles [Dickens].

AD'ness– 2. badness, gladness, madness, sadness.

AD'o– 2. shadow 3. foreshadow 4. Colorado, overshadow.

AD'ok– 2. baddock, haddock, paddock, shaddock.

AF'er– 2. chaffer, gaffer, Kaffir, laugher quaffer, piaffer, zaffer.

AF'i– 2. baffy, chaffy, daffy, faffy, draffy, taffy.

AF'ik– 2. maffick, graphic, traffic, Sapphic 3. seraphic, engraphic 4. diagraphic, paragraphic, telegraphic, choregraphic, calligraphic, geographic, melographic, zoographic, lithographic, orthographic, biographic, holographic, stylographic, demographic, homographic, seismographic, cosmographic, chromographic, stenographic, ethnographic, phonographic, chronographic, topographic, typographic, macrographic, micrographic, chirographic, chorographic, neurographic, pyrographic, isographic, pantographic, photographic, cryptographic, cartographic, histographic, autographic, polygraphic 5. paleographic, oleographic, ethneographic, idiographic, bibliographic, heliographic, crystallographic, dactylographic 6. autobiographic, cinematographic.

AF'ing– 2. chaffing, faffing, gaffing, laughing, staffing, quaffing 4. telegraphing, autographing, paragraphing, photographing, lithographing.

AF'l– 2. baffle, daffle [dial.], gaffle, snaffle, raffle, scraffle, yaffle.

AF'ling– 2. baffling, calfling, haffling, snaffling, raffling.

AFT'ed– 2. rafted, drafted, grafted, shafted, wafted 3. engrafted, ingrafted.

AFT'er– 2. after, dafter, laughter, rafter, drafter, draughter, grafter, wafter 3. hereafter, thereafter, whereafter 4. hereinafter, thereinafter.

AFT'i– 2. rafty, drafty, grafty, crafty, wafty.

AFT'ij– 2. draftage, draughtage, graftage, waftage.

AFT'ing– 2. hafting, rafting, drafting, draughting, grafting, shafting, wafting 3. engrafting, ingrafting.

AFT'less– 2. draftless, graftless, craftless, shaftless.

AG'a– 2. Agha, dagga, saga, quagga.

AG'ed– 2. jagged, knagged, ragged, cragged, scragged.

AG'er– 2. bagger, dagger, fagger, gagger, jagger, lagger, flagger, nagger, snagger, ragger, bragger, dragger, sagger, tagger, stagger, wagger, swagger 3. two-bagger, *wigwagger*, *zigzagger* 4. agar-agar, carpetbagger.

AG'erd– 2. haggard, laggard, blackguard, staggard, staggered, swaggered.

AG'ert– 2. braggart, staggart.

AG'i– 2. Aggie, baggie, baggy, faggy, gaggy, haggy [Scot. and dial. Eng.], jaggy, laggy, flaggy, slaggy, Maggie, naggy knaggy, snaggy, raggy, raggee, braggy, draggy, craggy, scraggy, saggy, shaggy, taggy, staggy, quaggy, waggy, swaggy.

AG'ij– 2. baggage.

AG'ing– 2. bagging, gagging, lagging, flagging, nagging, ragging, bragging, tagging, stagging 3. *zigzagging*.

AG'is– 2. haggis.

AG'ish– 2. haggish, flaggish, naggish, braggish, waggish.

AG'it– 2. agate 3. moss agate.

AG'l– 2. daggle, gaggle, haggle, draggle, straggle, waggle, waggel 3. bedraggle 4. raggle-taggle.

AG'ler– 2. daggler, gaggler, haggler, straggler, waggler 3. bedraggler.

AG'ling– 2. daggling, gaggling, haggling, raggling, draggling, straggling, waggling 3. bedraggling.

AG'ma– 2. magma 3. malagma.

AG'nat– 2. agnate, magnate, stagnate.

AG'nes– 2. Agnes, Sphagnous, magnus.

AG'net– 2. magnet, dragnet.

AG'num– 2. Sphagnum, magnum.

AG'on– 2. agon, flagon, dragon, wagon 3. pendragon, *snapdragon*.

AG'ot– 2. fagot, faggot, maggot.

AJ'ent– 2. pageant.

AJ'er– 2. agger, badger, cadger.

AJ'i– 2. hadji, cadgy 3. koradji.

AJ'ik– 2. magic, tragic 3. pelagic, choragic 4. theophagic, sarcophagic, theomagic, hemorrhagic, antitragic 5. archipelagic.

AJ'il– 2. agile, fragile.

AJ'in– 3. imagine.

AK'a– 2. bacca, lacca 3. sifaka, Malacca, alpaca.

AK'ard– 2. placard, Packard.

AK'at– 2. baccate, placate, saccate.

AK'en– 2. blacken, slacken, bracken, kraken.

AK'er– 2. backer, hacker, lacquer, blacker, clacker, slacker, smacker, knacker, packer, cracker, tracker, sacker, tacker, stacker, whacker 3. *whinchacker*, *hijacker*, shellacker, polacre, *clamcracker*, *corncracker*, *firecracker*, ransacker, *bushwhacker*.

AK'est– 2. blackest, slackest.

AK'et– 2. jacket, flacket, placket, packet, racket, rackett, bracket, sacket, tacket 3. *redjacket*, *bluejacket*.

AK'i– 2. hacky, Jacky, blackie, khaki, lackey, blacky, maki, knacky, raki, cracky, sake, tacky, quacky, wacky 3. *gimcracky* 4. Nagasaki.

AK'ij– 2. backage, package, wrackage, trackage, sackage, stackage.

AK'ing– 2. backing, lacking, blacking, clacking, smacking, packing, racking, cracking, tracking, sacking, tacking, quacking, whacking 3. shellacking, unpacking, ransacking, attacking.

AK'ish– 2. blackish, slackish, knackish, brackish, quackish.

AK'l– 2. hackle, cackle, mackle, macle, grackle, crackle, shackle, tackle, quackle 3. debacle, *piacle*, *manacle*, *pinnacle*, *barnacle*, *miracle*, *oracle*, *coracle*, *ramshackle*, unshackle, *spectacle*, *obstacle* 4. tabernacle, hibernacle.

AK'ler– 2. cackler, hackler, crackler, shackler, tackler.

AK'less– 2. backless, hackless, lackless, clackless, slackless, knackless, crackless, trackless, sackless, tackless, stackless.

AK'li– 2. cackly, blackly, slackly, crackly 3. ramshackly.

AK'ling– 2. cackling, crackling, shackling, tackling.

AK'ma– 2. chacma, drachma 4. tetradrachma.

AK'ness– 2. blackness, slackness.

AK'o– 2. jako, shako, squacco 3. tobacco, icaco, goracco.

AK'rid– 2. acrid.

AK'sen– 2. flaxen, waxen.

AK'sent– 2. accent.

AK'ser– 2. taxer, waxer 3. relaxer.

AK'ses– 2. access.

AK'sez– 2. axes, laxes, taxes, waxes 3. relaxes, dewaxes, rewaxes 4. battle-axes.

AK'shun– 2. action, faction, fraction, traction, taction 3. abaction, subaction, reaction, enaction, coaction, compaction, refraction, diffraction, infraction, contraction, protraction, attraction, abstraction, distraction, extraction, transaction, contaction, exaction 4. interaction, counteraction, rubefaction, calefaction, malefaction, putrefaction, liquefaction, satisfaction **5.** dissatisfaction, counterattraction.

AK'shus– 2. factious, fractious.

AK'si– 2. flaxy, Maxie, braxy, taxi, taxy, waxy **4.** biotaxy, zootaxy, homotaxy.

AK'sing– 2. axing, taxing, waxing **3.** relaxing, rewaxing.

AK'sis– 2. axis, praxis, taxis, staxis **3.** synaxis, syntaxis **4.** prophylaxis, parapraxis, chiropraxis, parataxis, hypotaxis, epistaxis.

AK'son– 2. axon, Jackson, klaxon, Saxon **3.** diaxon, dendraxon **4.** Anglo-Saxon.

AKT'a– 2. acta, facta.

AKT'ed– 2. acted, pacted, fracted **3.** enacted, coacted, redacted, reacted, impacted, defracted, diffracted, attracted, subtracted, detracted, retracted, contracted, protracted, abstracted, distracted, extracted, transacted, contacted, exacted **4.** retroacted, abreacted, arefacted.

AKT'er– 2. acter, actor, factor, tractor, tactor **3.** abactor, redactor, attracter, diffractor, subtracter, contracter, contractor, protracter, protractor, abstracter, extractor, exacter, exactor **4.** calefactor, malefactor, benefactor.

AKT'ful– 2. tactful **3.** distractful.

AKT'ik– 2. lactic, practic, tactic **3.** didactic, galactic, stalactic, malactic, phylactic, climactic, synactic, emphractic, syntactic, protactic **4.** parallactic, catallactic, prophylactic, chiropractic.

AKT'iks– 2. tactics **3.** didactics **4.** catallactics.

AKT'il– 2. dactyl, fractile, tractile, tactile **3.** adactyl, didactyl, syndactyl, retractile, contractile, protractile.

AKT'ing– 2. acting **3.** redacting, enacting, defracting, attracting, retracting, contracting, abstracting, distracting, transacting, exacting **4.** double-acting, counteracting, retroacting.

AKT'is– 2. practice, practise **3.** malpractice.

AKT'iv– 2. active, factive **3.** reactive, enactive, inactive, olfactive, refractive, diffractive, attractive, subtractive, detractive, retractive, contractive, protractive, abstractive, distractive, extractive **4.** radioactive, retroactive, counteractive, calefactive, benefactive, rarefactive, putrefactive, liquefactive, unattractive.

AKT'less– 2. factless, bractless, pactless, tractless, tactless **3.** *compactless, abstractless.*

AKT'li– 3. compactly, abstractly, intactly, exactly **5.** matter-of-factly.

AKT'ment– 3. enactment, impactment, extractment **4.** re-enactment.

AKT'ness– 3. compactness, intactness, exactness **4.** inexactness **5.** matter-of-factness.

AKT'o– 2. acto, facto **3.** de facto.

AKT'or– 2. actor, acter, factor, tractor, tactor **3.** enacter, diffractor, extractor, exactor **4.** benefactor; *see* also **AK'ter-** acter etc. above.

AKT'ress– 2. actress **3.** exactress **4.** malefactress, benefactress.

AKT'um– 2. actum, factum, pactum.

AKT'ur– 2. facture, fracture **3.** compacture, contracture **4.** manufacture.

AKT'us– 2. actus, cactus, tactus **4.** Ferocactus.

AL'a– 2. alla, Allah, galla, gala, calla, palla, pallah **3.** *cabala*, emgalla, Valhalla, mashallah, cavalla.

AL'ad– 2. ballad, salad.

AL'ans– 2. balance, valance **3.** unbalance **4.** counterbalance, overbalance.

AL'ant– 2. gallant, callant, talent **3.** ungallant.

AL'as– 2. balas, Dallas, Pallas.

ALB'a– 2. alba, galba **3.** xibalba.

ALB'e– 2. albe, halbe.

ALB'ert– 2. Albert, halbert.

AL'eed– 2. dallied, rallied, sallied, tallied 4. dilly-dallied, shilly-shallied.

AL'ent– 2. talent; *see* also AL'ant– gallant etc. above.

AL'er– 2. pallor, valor 3. caballer.

AL'et– 2. ballot, gallet, mallet, palate, pallet, palette, sallet, valet.

ALF'a– 2. alfa, alpha 3. alfalfa, pentalpha.

AL'i– 2. ally, bally, dally, gally, pally, rally, sally, Sallie, challie, challis, tally, valley 3. Bengali, tamale 4. dilly-dally, Mexicali, shilly-shally, hot tamale.

AL'id– 2. calid, pallid, valid 3. impallid, invalid.

AL'ik– 2. Aleck, Gallic, phallic, malic, grallic, Salic, thallic 3. cabalic, vocalic, vandalic, Uralic, medallic, metallic, italic, Tantalic, smart aleck [coll.], oxalic 4. encephalic, misogallic, intervallic.

AL'is– 2. Alice, allice, chalice, malice, palace 4. digitalis.

ALJ'e– 2. algae, Algy 3. neuralgy, nostalgy.

ALJ'ik– 2. algic 3. gastralgic, neuralgic, antalgic, nostalgic.

ALM'a– 2. Alma, halma 3. agalma.

ALM'ud– 2. almud, Talmud.

AL'o– 2. aloe, fallow, hallow, callow, mallow, sallow, shallow, tallow 3. Allhallow, unhallow, dishallow, marshmallow.

AL'on– 2. gallon, kalon, salon, talon.

AL'op– 2. galop, gallop, scallop, shallop 3. escallop.

AL'or– 2. pallor, valor 3. caballer.

AL'ot– 2. ballot; *see* also AL'et– gallet etc. above.

AL'oz– 2. aloes, gallows, hallows 3. Allhallows, dishallows, marshmallows.

ALP'in– 2. Alpine 3. subalpine, Cisalpine, transalpine.

ALP'ing– 2. scalping, palping.

ALT'o– 2. alto 3. Rialto, contralto.

AL'u– 2. value 3. evalue, devalue, revalue 4. undervalue.

AL'um– 2. alum, vallum 3. chloralum, catallum.

AL'us– 2. phallus, Gallus, callus, callous, thallus 4. aryballus.

AL'ya– 2. Alya, dahlia.

AL'yant– 2. valiant.

AL'yun– 2. scallion, pallion, stallion 3. medallion, rapscallion, battalion, Italian.

AM'a– 2. amma, chamma, Gamma, drama, Shammah, Yama 3. Digamma, pajama, pyjama, programma 4. Alabama, panorama, melodrama, monodrama, duodrama.

AM'al– 2. Hamal, mammal; *see* also AM'el– camel etc. below.

AMB'er– 2. amber, camber, clamber, sambar, tambour 3. grisamber 4. liquidamber.

AMB'ik– 3. Iambic 4. galliambic, choliambic, choriambic, Pythiambic.

AMB'ist– 2. gambist, cambist 3. iambist.

AMB'it– 2. ambit, gambit.

AMB'l– 2. amble, gamble, gambol, ramble, bramble, scramble, shamble, wamble 3. *preamble*, unscramble.

AMB'ler– 2. ambler, gambler, rambler, scrambler, shambler.

AMB'ling– 2. ambling, gambling, rambling, brambling, scrambling.

AMB'lz– 2. ambles, gambles, gambols, rambles, brambles, scrambles, shambles 3. preambles, unscrambles.

AMB'o– 2. ambo, jambeau, flambeau, crambo, sambo, Sambo, zambo.

AMB'ol– 2. gambol; *see* also AMB'l– amble etc. above.

AMB'us– 3. iambus 4. dithyrambus.

AM'ed– 3. Mohammed.

AM'el– 2. camel, Hamal, mammal, trammel 3. enamel, entrammel, untrammel.

AM'er– 2. ammer, dammer, damner, gammer, hammer, jammer, lamber, glamor, clamor, slammer, rammer, grammar, crammer, shammer, stammer, yammer 3. *sledgehammer*, exhammer, *windjammer*, enamor 4. yellowhammer.

AM'fer– 2. camphor, chamfer.

AM'i– 2. gammy, hammy, jammy, clammy, mammy, sammy, chamois, shammy, tammy 3. Miami.

AM'ij– 2. damage, ramage 3. endamage.

AM'ik– 2. amic, gamic 3. Adamic, agamic, syngamic, cinnamic, dynamic, ceramic, engrammic, balsamic, potamic, Benthamic 4. preadamic, polygamic, homogamic, monogamic, Abrahamic, dioramic, cycloramic, cosmoramic, panoramic, telegrammic, monogrammic.

AM'in– 2. amine, famine, gamin, lamin, stamin 3. prolamine, examine 4. reexamine, cross-examine.

AM'ing– 2. damming, damning, gamming, jamming, lambing, lamming [slang], flamming, clamming, slamming, ramming, cramming, shamming, whamming.

AM'is– 2. amice, chlamys, tamis 3. dynamis.

AM'ish– 2. famish, lambish, clammish, rammish 3. enfamish.

AM'let– 2. hamlet, Hamlet, camlet, samlet.

AM'ok– 2. hammock, cammock, mammock.

AM'on– 2. ammon, Ammon, gammon, mammon, salmon, shaman 3. backgammon.

AM'oth– 2. mammoth.

AMP'an– 2. jampan, sampan, tampan.

AMP'ant– 2. rampant.

AMP'as– 2. lampas, pampas.

AMP'er– 2. champer, damper, hamper, camper, scamper, clamper, pamper, pampre, ramper, tramper, tamper, stamper, vamper 3. decamper, revamper.

AMP'i– 2. dampy, crampy, vampy.

AMP'ing– 2. damping, camping, scamping, clamping, ramping, tramping, tamping, stamping, vamping 3. decamping, revamping.

AMP'ish– 2. dampish, campish, scampish, trampish, vampish.

AMP'l– 2. ample, trample, sample 3. ensample, example.

AMP'ler– 2. ampler, trampler, sampler 3. exampler.

AMP'li– 2. amply, damply.

AMP'ling– 2. sampling, trampling 3. ensampling.

AMP'ment– 3. decampment, encampment.

AMP'us– 2. campus, grampus 4. hippocampus.

AM'ut– 2. gamut, Mammut.

AMZ'el– 2. amsel, damsel.

AMZ'un– 2. damson, ramson.

AN'a– 2. ana, Ana, anna, Anna, Hannah, canna, Lana, manna 3. bandanna, Diana, Guiana, liana, banana, sultana, lantana, Montana, ruana, Havana, savanna, Savannah, hosanna, Susanna 4. Indiana, Georgiana, Pollyanna, Marianna, dulciana, Gloriana, tertiana, Susquehanna, Poinciana, Texarkana 5. Louisiana.

AN'al– 2. annal; *see* also AN'el– channel etc. below.

ANCH'er– 2. blancher, plancher, rancher, brancher, stancher.

ANCH'ez– 2. blanches, ranches, branches, stanches 4. avalanches.

ANCH'i– 2. ranchy, branchy.

ANCH'ing– 2. blanching, planching, ranching, branching, stanching.

ANCH'less– 2. ranchless, branchless, stanchless.

AND'a– 2. panda, vanda 3. Uganda, Amanda, veranda, Miranda 4. propaganda, jacaranda, memoranda, observanda.

AND'al– 2. scandal, pandal, sandal, Randall, crandall, vandal, Vandal; *see* also AND'l– dandle etc. below.

AND'ant– 2. mandant 3. demandant, commandant.

AND'ed– 2. banded, handed, candid, landed, glanded, branded, stranded, sanded 3. disbanded, red-handed, free-handed, three-handed, highhanded, back-handed, blackhanded, fullhanded, clean-handed, unhanded, forehanded, four-handed, closehanded, neat-handed, left-handed, light-handed, right-handed, shorthanded, two-handed, unlanded, demanded, remanded, commanded, expanded, unbranded 4. contrabanded, empty-handed, heavy-handed, single-handed, openhanded, evenhanded, over-handed, underhanded, reprimanded, countermanded.

AND'eed– 2. bandied, candied, brandied.

AND'er– 2. bander, dander, gander, candor, Landor, lander, blander, slander, pandar, pander, brander, grander, stander, zander 3. disbander, Leander, meander, *backhander*, left-hander, right-hander, philander, *Icelander*, *inlander*, *outlander*, demander, remander, commander, pomander, germander, Menander, expander, Isander, goosander, dittander, *bystander*, *outstander*, withstander 4. oleander, coriander, Afrikander, Newfoundlander, salamander, gerrymander, reprimander, Alexander, understander.

AND'erd– 2. pandered, slandered, standard.

AND'erz– 2. Flanders, glanders, sanders 4. oleanders, salamanders.

AND'ez– 2. Andes 3. Hernandez.

AND'i– 2. Andy, bandy, dandy, handy, candy, Mandy, pandy, randy, brandy, sandy, shandy 3. unhandy, Jim Dandy 4. sugar-candy, jack-a-dandy, spick-and spandy, Rio Grande, jaborandi 6. Yankee Doodle Dandy.

AND'ij– 2. bandage, standage.

AND'ik– 3. Icelandic 4. propagandic.

AND'ing– 2. banding, handing, landing, stranding, sanding, standing 3. disbanding, unhanding, expanding, demanding, remanding, commanding, outstanding, withstanding 4. understanding, notwithstanding 5. misunderstanding.

AND'ish– 2. blandish, brandish, grandish, standish 3. outlandish, Myles Standish.

AND'ist– 4. contrabandist, propagandist.

AND'it– 2. bandit, Pandit.

AND'l– 2. dandle, candle, scandle, handle, pandle, pandal, sandal, vandal 3. manhandle, mishandle; *see* also AND'al– scandal etc. above.

AND'ler– 2. chandler, dandler, handler, candler 3. panhandler.

AND'less– 2. bandless, handless, landless, glandless, brandless, strandless, sandless 3. demandless, commandless.

AND'li– 2. blandly, grandly.

AND'ling– 2. bandling, candling, handling, brandling 3. manhandling, mishandling.

AND'ment– 3. disbandment, remandment, commandment.

AND'ness– 2. blandness, grandness.

AND'o– 2. bandeau, landau 3. Orlando, commando, Fernando, Hernando, lentando 4. Ferdinando.

AND'on– 2. Landon, Brandon 3. abandon.

AND'ra– 2. mandra, Sandra 3. Cassandra 4. Alessandra, Alexandra.

AND'stand– 2. bandstand, handstand, grandstand.

AND'um– 2. mandom, random, tandem 3. notandum 4. memorandum, observandum, avizandum 10. de gustibus non est disputandum [L.].

ANDZ'man– 2. bandsman, landsman.

AN'eed– 2. nannied, grannied, crannied 3. benannied, begrannied, becrannied.

AN'el– 2. annal, channel, cannel, flannel, panel, scrannel, stannel 3. empanel, impanel.

AN'elz– annals, etc. *see* **AN'el–** annal etc. above, plus "s" or "'s."

AN'er– 2. banner, fanner, canner, scanner, planner, manner, manor, panner, spanner, tanner, vanner 3. japanner, trepanner.

AN'erd– 2. bannered, mannered 3. unmannered, well-mannered, ill-mannered.

AN'et– 2. gannet, Janet, cannet, planet, vannet; *see* also **AN'it–** granite etc. below.

ANG'er– 2. banger, ganger, hanger, hangar, clangor, whanger, sanger 3. haranguer 4. paper hanger.

ANG'ger– 2. anger, angor, Bangor, hangar, languor, clangor.

ANG'i– 2. bangy, fangy, clangy, slangy, tangy, twangy, whangy.

ANG'ing– 2. banging, hanging, clanging, slanging, twanging, whanging 3. haranguing 4. paper hanging, overhanging.

ANG'l– 2. angle, bangle, dangle, fangle, gangle, jangle, mangle, spangle, strangle, wrangle, tangle, wangle 3. fandangle, quadrangle, leeangle, triangle, rectangle, pentangle, septangle, sexangle, bespangle, entangle, untangle 4. jingle-jangle, interjangle, intertangle, disentangle.

ANG'ler– 2. angler, dangler, gangler, jangler, spangler, wrangler 3. entangler, untangler.

ANG'less– 2. bangless, dangless, fangless, gangless, clangless, pangless, twangless.

ANG'li– 2. bangly, dangly, gangly, jangly, spangly, tangly.

ANG'ling– 2. angling, dangling, gangling, jangling, mangling, spangling, strangling, wrangling, tangling, wangling.

ANG'man– 2. hangman, gangman.

ANG'o– 2. mango, tango 3. fandango, Cipango, contango 4. Pago Pago, Pango-pango.

ANG'ster– 2. bangster, gangster, slangster.

ANG'win– 2. anguine, sanguine 3. ensanguine, consanguine, exsanguine.

ANG'wish– 2. anguish, languish.

AN'i– 2. Annie, Danny, Fanny, canny, clanny, nanny, branny, granny, cranny 3. Aani, afghani, uncanny, tin-panny 4. frangipani.

AN'ij– 2. manage, pannage, crannage, tannage 3. mismanage.

AN'ik– 2. phanic, panic, tannic, stannic 3. neanic, paganic, organic, cyanic, mechanic, volcanic, vulcanic, Brahmanic, Germanic, tympanic, Hispanic, Iranic, tyrannic, Koranic, uranic, satanic, tetanic, Britannic, titanic, sultanic, botanic, Spartanic, galvanic 4. oceanic, diaphanic, lexiphanic, theophanic, inorganic, exorganic, cosmorganic, opianic, Messianic, porcelanic, aldermanic 5. hydrocyanic, transoceanic, Aristophanic.

AN'ing– 2. banning, fanning, canning, scanning, flanning, clanning, planning, manning, panning, spanning, tanning 3. japanning, trepanning, replanning, remanning, unmanning, outspanning.

AN'ish– 2. banish, fannish, clannish, planish, mannish, Spanish, vanish 3. evanish.

AN'ist– 2. tanist 3. picanist, sopranist 4. Alcoranist.

AN'it– 2. granite 4. pomegranate.

ANJ'ent– 2. plangent, frangent, tangent 3. refrangent, bitangent, cotangent.

ANJ'ez– 2. Ganges, flanges 3. phalanges.

ANK'a– 2. tanka 3. Bianca, barranca 4. Casablanca.

ANK'er– 2. anchor, banker, danker, hanker, canker, chancre, lanker, blanker, flanker, clanker, planker, spanker, ranker, rancor, franker, cranker, pranker, shanker, tanker, thanker, yanker 3. unanchor, up-anchor, sheet anchor, embanker, encanker, outflanker, outranker.

ANK'erd– **2.** anchored, cankered, brancard, tankard **3.** unanchored, uncankered.

ANK'est– **2.** dankest, lankest, blankest, rankest, frankest.

ANK'et– **2.** banket, blanket.

ANK'ful– **2.** prankful, tankful, thankful **3.** unthankful.

ANK'ĭ– **2.** ankee, banky, hanky, hankie, lanky, clanky, planky, cranky, pranky, tanky, swanky, Yankee **4.** hanky-panky [coll.].

ANK'ing– **2.** banking, blanking, flanking, clanking, planking, spanking, ranking, franking, cranking, tanking, thanking, yanking **3.** embanking, outflanking, unclanking, outranking.

ANK'ish– **2.** dankish, lankish, blankish, frankish, prankish.

ANK'l– **2.** ankle, hankle, rankle, crankle, tankle.

ANK'less– **2.** bankless, hankless, blankless, flankless, clankless, plankless, spankless, rankless, frankless, francless, crankless, prankless, shankless, tankless, thankless.

ANK'li– **2.** dankly, lankly, blankly, rankly, frankly.

ANK'ment– **2.** bankment **3.** embankment.

ANK'ness– **2.** dankness, lankness, blankness, rankness, frankness.

ANK'ok– **2.** Bangkok, Hancock.

ANK'or– **2.** anchor, rancor; *see* also **ANK'er–** anchor, banker etc. above.

AN'less– **2.** banless, fanless, canless, clanless, planless, manless, panless, spanless, tanless.

AN'li– **2.** manly **3.** unmanly, *statesmanly* **4.** gentlemanly.

AN'o– **2.** piano, soprano **5.** melopiano, mezzo-soprano.

AN'ok– **2.** bannock, Bannock, jannock.

AN'on– **2.** fanon, canon, cannon, Shannon **3.** Rhiannon, colcannon.

ANS'a– **2.** hansa, Hansa.

ANS'el– **2.** chancel, Handsel, handsel, cancel.

ANS'er– **2.** Anser, answer, chancer, dancer, cancer, lancer, glancer, prancer **3.** fan dancer, merganser, enhancer, romancer, entrancer, advancer **4.** hula dancer, bubble dancer, geomancer, chiromancer, necromancer.

ANS'ez– chances ·etc., *see* **ANS–** chance etc. plus "s" or "'s."

ANSH'al– **3.** ganancial, financial, substantial **4.** transubstantial, insubstantial, unsubstantial, circumstantial.

ANSH'ent– **2.** transient.

ANSH'un– **2.** scansion, mansion, panchion, stanchion **3.** expansion.

ANS'ĭ– **2.** Ancy, chancy, dancy, fancy, Nancy, prancy, Sancy **3.** mischancy, unfancy, *nomancy, romancy, vacancy, peccancy, verdancy, mordancy, infancy, brilliancy, vallancy, tenancy, stagnancy, regnancy, pregnancy, sonancy, flagrancy, fragrancy, vagrancy, errancy, blatancy, constancy, piquancy, truancy, buoyancy* **4.** mendicancy, *redundancy, accordancy, discordancy,* recreancy, termagancy, elegancy, arrogancy, sycophancy, sibilancy, petulancy, chalcomancy, sycomancy, pedomancy, podomancy, geomancy, theomancy, psychomancy, lithomancy, halomancy, belomancy, xylomancy, onomancy, capnomancy, oomancy, ceromancy, necromancy, hydromancy, aeromancy, chiromancy, aldermancy, gyromancy, pyromancy, cartomancy, lithomancy, *lieutenancy, repugnancy,* consonancy, dissonancy, *discrepancy,* occupancy, penetrancy, *incessancy, recussancy, expectancy, reluctancy,* habitancy, oscitancy, militancy, irritancy, hesitancy, exultancy, *accountancy, inconstancy,* relevancy, conservancy **5.** ornithomancy, bibliomancy, theriomancy, cephalomancy, selenomancy, icthyomancy, aleuromancy, sideromancy, hieromancy, oneiromancy, diathermancy, significancy, extravagancy, predominancy, preponderancy, recalcitrancy, inhabitancy, exorbitancy, precipitancy, irrelevancy **6.** dactyliomancy, logarithmomancy, insignificancy.

ANS'id– **2.** fancied, rancid.

ANS'ing– **2.** chancing, dancing, Lansing, glancing, prancing, trancing **3.** enhancing, romancing, financing, entrancing, advancing **4.** necromancing.

ANS'iv– **3.** enhancive, expansive, advancive **4.** inexpansive.

ANS'ment– **3.** enhancement, entrancement, advancement **4.** nonadvancement.

ANS'um– **2.** hansom, handsome, ransom, transom.

ANT'a– **2.** anta, planta, manta, Santa **3.** Vedanta, infanta, Atlanta **4.** Atalanta.

ANT'al– **2.** antal **3.** gigantal, atlantal, quadrantal, octantal **4.** consonantal; *see* also ANT'l– cantle etc. below.

ANT'e– **2.** ante, Dante **3.** andante, bacchante, chianti, durante **4.** Rosinante, Hypapante, dilettante **5.** pococurante, non obstante [L.]; *see* also ANT'i– aunty etc. below.

ANT'ed– **2.** hanted, chanted, canted, scanted, planted, slanted, panted, ranted, granted **3.** enchanted, recanted, descanted, implanted, supplanted.

ANT'er– **2.** banter, hanter, chanter, canter, cantor, scanter, planter, slanter, panter, ranter, granter, grantor **3.** enchanter, decanter, trochanter, descanter, supplanter, transplanter, instanter, levanter.

ANT'ez– **2.** Dantes **3.** atlantes **4.** Corybantes.

ANTH'er– **2.** anther, panther.

ANTH'us– **2.** canthus **3.** Dianthus, acanthous, ananthous, synanthous, monanthous, epanthous, chrysanthous **4.** polyanthus, amianthus.

ANT'i– **2.** aunty, anti, banty, chanty, scanty, slanty, panty, ranty, Santy, shanty, tanti **3.** chianti; *see* also ANT'e– ante etc. above.

ANT'ij– **2.** chantage, plantage, vantage **3.** advantage **4.** disadvantage.

ANT'ik– **2.** antic, antick, mantic, frantic **3.** pedantic, Vedantic, gigantic, Atlantic, semantic, romantic **4.** corybantic, elephantic, sycophantic, cisatlantic, transatlantic, geomantic, theomantic, chiromantic, pyromantic, necromantic, consonantic.

ANT'in– **2.** plantain **3.** *Levantine, Byzantine* **4.** elephantine, adamantine.

ANT'ing– **2.** hanting, chanting, canting, scanting, slanting, planting, panting, ranting, granting **3.** enchanting, decanting, recanting, descanting, implanting, supplanting.

ANT'ist– **2.** Kantist, Vedantist **4.** Esperantist, noncurantist, ignorantist, dilettantist.

ANT'l– **2.** cantle, mantle, mantel **3.** dismantle, immantle; *see* also ANT'al– antal etc. above.

ANT'ler– **2.** antler, mantler, pantler **3.** dismantler.

ANT'let– **2.** gantlet, cantlet, plantlet, mantelet.

ANT'li– **2.** scantly, slantly **3.** *gallantly,* aslantly.

ANT'ling– **2.** bantling, scantling, plantling, mantling **3.** dismantling.

ANT'ment– **2.** chantment **3.** enchantment **4.** disenchantment.

ANT'o– **2.** canto, manteau **3.** portmanteau, pro tanto **4.** Esperanto.

ANT'ress– **2.** chantress **3.** enchantress.

ANT'ri– **2.** chantry, gantry, pantry.

ANT'rum– 2. antrum, tantrum 3. hypantrum.

ANT'um– 2. Antum, bantam, phantom 4. adiantum.

AN'yel– 2. Daniel, Haniel, spaniel 3. Nathaniel, field spaniel, toy spaniel 4. springer spaniel, water spaniel.

AN'yun– 2. banian, banyan, fanion, canyon 3. companion.

ANZ'a– 2. stanza 3. bonanza 5. extravaganza.

ANZ'i– 2. pansy, tansy 3. chimpanzee.

AP'a– 2. cappa, Kappa, kappa.

AP'er– 2. chapper, dapper, capper, flapper, clapper, slapper, mapper, napper, knapper, wrapper, scrapper, trapper, strapper, tapper, yapper 3. didapper, *kidnapper*, entrapper, unwrapper, wiretapper, backslapper 4. handicapper, overlapper, snippersnapper, whippersnapper.

AP'et– 2. lappet, scrappet, tappet.

AP'i– 2. chappie, chappy, gappy, happy, mappy, nappy, snappy, pappy, crappie, scrappy, trappy, sappy 3. unhappy, serape.

AP'id– 2. rapid, sapid, vapid.

AP'ij– 2. lappage, scrappage, wrappage.

AP'ing– 2. chapping, dapping, gapping, capping, lapping, clapping, flapping, slapping, mapping, napping, knapping, snapping, rapping, wrapping, scrapping, trapping, strapping, tapping, yapping 3. entrapping, enwrapping 4. handicapping, overlapping.

AP'is– 2. lapis, tapis.

AP'ish– 2. gappish, knappish, snappish, yappish.

AP'ist– 2. mappist, Trappist.

AP'l– 2. apple, chapel, dapple, capple, grapple, scrapple 3. *Whitechapel, pineapple*, love apple 4. antechapel.

AP'less– 2. hapless, gapless, capless, lapless, clapless, flapless, slapless, mapless,

napless, snapless, papless, rapless, wrapless, scrapless, trapless, strapless, sapless, yapless 4. handicapless.

AP'let– 2. chaplet, taplet.

AP'ling– 2. dappling, lapling, grappling, sapling.

AP'nel– 2. grapnel, shrapnel.

AP'SH'un– 2. caption 3. recaption, elapsion, collapsion, contraption 4. usucaption.

APS'ing– 2. lapsing 3. relapsing, collapsing.

APT'er– 2. apter, chapter, captor, rapter, raptor 3. adapter, recaptor.

APT'est– 2. aptest, raptest 3. inaptest, unaptest.

APT'ist– 2. Baptist 4. Anabaptist.

APT'iv– 2. captive 3. adaptive 4. unadaptive.

APT'ur– 2. capture, rapture 3. recapture, enrapture 4. manucapture.

AR'a– 2. Eire, Clara 3. Sahara, tiara.

AR'ab– 2. Arab, scarab.

AR'ans– 2. bearance, Clarence 3. forbearance, apparence, transparence.

AR'ant– 2. arrant, parent 3. forbearant, declarant, apparent, stepparent, transparent 4. unapparent, nontransparent.

AR'as– 2. arras, barras, harass, terrace 3. debarras, embarras, embarrass 4. disembarrass.

AR'el– 2. barrel, carrell, carol, parrel 3. pork-barrel, apparel 4. disapparel.

AR'eld– 2. barreled etc., *see* AR'el– barrel etc. above plus -ed.

AR'en– 2. barren, Karen; *see* also AR'on– Aaron etc. below.

AR'ent– 2. parent 3. apparent, stepparent, transparent 4. unapparent; *see* also AR'ant– arrant etc. above.

AR'er– 2. barer, bearer, darer, farer, snarer, parer, sparer, sharer, tearer, starer, wearer, swearer, squarer 3. wayfarer, seafarer, forswearer.

AR'est– 2. barest, rarest, sparest, squarest.

AR'et– 2. garret, carat, caret, claret; *see* also **AR'ot–** garrot etc. below.

AR'i– 2. airy, ary [dial.], Barrie, Barry, berry, bury, fairy, harry, Harry, carry, Carrie, Larry, marry, nary [dial.], tarry 3. Du Barry, shooldarry, Glengarry, miscarry, remarry 4. hari-kari, intermarry, charivari; *see* also **AR'i–** scarry etc.; **ER'i–** berry etc.

AR'id– 2. arid, harried, carried, married, parried, tarried 3. Polarid, miscarried, unmarried 4. intermarried.

AR'ij– 2. carriage, marriage 3. miscarriage, disparage 4. intermarriage.

AR'ik– 2. baric 3. barbaric, Pindaric, agaric, Bulgaric, saccharic, polaric, tartaric 4. cinnabaric, centrobaric, isobaric, Balearic.

AR'ing– 2. airing, bearing, baring, daring, faring, haring, herring, caring, scaring, blaring, glaring, flaring, paring, pairing, sparing, sharing, tearing, staring, wearing, waring, swearing, squaring 3. tale bearing, seafaring, declaring, repairing, impairing, despairing, outstaring, forswearing, outwearing 4. overbearing, undeclaring.

AR'is– 2. arris, baris, Harris, Clarice, Paris 3. Polaris.

AR'ish– 2. bearish, garish, marish, parish, squarish 4. debonairish.

AR'li– 2. barely, fairly, rarely, quarely. 3. awarely 4. debonairly.

AR'ness– 2. bareness, fairness, rareness, quareness 3. awareness 4. debonairness.

AR'o– 2. arrow, barrow, farrow, faro, harrow, marrow, narrow, sparrow, yarrow 3. wheelbarrow, restharrow; *see* also **AR'o–** aero etc.

AR'on– 2. Aaron, baron, barren, Charon, Karen, Sharon.

AR'ot– 2. garrot, carrot, parrot; *see* also **AR'et–** garret etc. above.

AR'um– 2. arum, carom, harem, larum 3. alarum 4. harum-scarum.

AS'a– 2. massa 3. Hadassah, Manasseh, madrasah, oquassa 4. Missa bassa [L.].

AS'en– 2. fasten, casson 3. assassin.

AS'er– 2. gasser, hassar, placer, masser, passer 3. Macassar, amasser, surpasser, harasser 5. antimacassar.

AS'et– 2. asset, basset, facet, placet, brasset, tacet, tacit.

AS'ez– 2. asses, gases, lasses, glasses, classes, masses, passes, brasses, grasses, sasses 3. declasses, reclasses, outclasses, *eyeglasses*, *hourglasses*, molasses, amasses, surpasses, harasses, cuirasses, morasses 4. underclasses, superclasses, looking glasses, underpasses, overpasses.

ASH'en– 2. ashen; *see* **ASH'un–** ashen etc. below.

ASH'er– 2. Asher, basher, dasher, gasher, hasher, casher, lasher, clasher, flasher, splasher, slasher, masher, smasher, rasher, brasher, crasher, thrasher, stasher 3. abasher, rehasher 4. haberdasher, baggage-smasher.

ASH'ez– 2. ashes, bashes, dashes, gashes, hashes, cashes, caches, lashes, flashes, clashes, splashes, mashes, smashes, nashes, gnashes, pashes, rashes, crashes, thrashes 3. abashes, rehashes, *eyelashes*, *backlashes*, mustaches 4. spatterdashes.

ASH'i– 2. ashy, dashy, hashy, flashy, clashy, plashy, slashy, splashy, mashie, trashy.

ASH'ing– 2. bashing, dashing, hashing, cashing, caching, lashing, flashing, clashing, splashing, slashing, mashing, gnashing, crashing 3. backlashing, mishmashing 4. balderdashing.

ASH'less– 2. dashless, hashless, cashless, lashless, flashless, clashless, splashless, mashless, crashless.

ASH′un– 2. ashen, fashion, passion, ration 3. refashion, disfashion, Circassian, Parnassian, impassion, compassion, dispassion.

ASH′und– 2. fashioned, passioned, rationed 3. old fashioned, unfashioned, impassioned, unrationed 4. unimpassioned.

AS′i– 2. dassie, gassy, Cassie, lassie, glassy, classy, massy, brassie, brassy, grassy, sassy, chassis 3. morassy 4. Malagasy, Tallahassee.

AS′id– 2. acid, placid 3. subacid, antacid.

AS′ij– 2. passage, brassage.

AS′ik– 2. classic 3. Liassic, Triassic, thalassic, postclassic, boracic, thoracis, Jurassic, potassic 4. pseudoclassic, neoclassic.

AS′il– 2. facile, gracile; *see also* **AS′l–** castle etc. below.

AS′in– 3. assassin; *see also* **AS′en–** fasten etc. above.

AS′ing– 2. gassing, classing, massing 3. reclassing, amassing, surpassing, harassing 4. underclassing, underpassing, overpassing.

AS′is– 2. assis, fascis, chassis, Cassis.

AS′it– 2. tacit; *see also* **AS′et–** asset etc. above.

AS′iv– 2. massive, passive 3. impassive.

ASK′a– 3. Alaska, marasca, Nebraska 4. Athabasca, baked Alaska.

ASK′al– 2. paschal, mascle, rascal, tascal.

ASK′er– 2. asker, basker, lascar, flasker, masker, masquer, tasker 3. unmasker 4. Madagascar, antimasker.

ASK′et– 2. basket, gasket, casket, casquet, lasket, flasket, taskit 3. breadbasket.

ASK′ing– 2. asking, basking, casking, flasking, masking, tasking 3. bemasking, unmasking.

ASK′o– 2. casco, tasco 3. Tabasco, verbasco, fiasco, Belasco.

AS′l– 2. castle, tassel, wrastle, vassal 3. forecastle, Newcastle, envassal; *see also* **AS′il–** facile etc. above.

AS′man– 2. gasman, glassman, classman, passman, grassman, Tassman 4. underclassman, upperclassman.

AS′o– 2. basso, lasso, Tasso 3. Sargasso.

AS′ok– 2. hassock, cassock.

ASP′er– 2. asper, gasper, Jasper, Casper, clasper, rasper, grasper.

ASP′ing– 2. gasping, clasping, rasping, grasping 3. enclasping, unclasping.

AST′a– 2. Shasta 3. shikasta, canasta, catasta.

AST′ed– 2. fasted, lasted, blasted, masted 3. bombasted, broad-lasted, outlasted, three-masted, contrasted 4. flabbergasted.

AST′er– 2. aster, Astor, faster, gaster, caster, castor, blaster, plaster, master, pastor, vaster 3. cadaster, piaster, broadcaster, forecaster, pilaster, Stylaster, paymaster, cubmaster, taskmaster, schoolmaster, choirmaster, bushmaster, postmaster, pinaster, disaster 4. Zoroaster, alabaster, oleaster, criticaster, burgomaster, quartermaster, overmaster, poetaster.

AST′erd– 2. bastard, dastard, plastered, mastered 3. pilastered, beplastered, unmastered.

AST′est– 2. fastest, vastest.

AST′i– 2. blasty, masty, nasty, vasty 3. dynasty 4. anaplasty, dermoplasty, epinasty, hyponasty, pederasty.

AST′ik– 2. clastic, plastic, mastic, rastic, spastic, drastic 3. bombastic, dichastic, sarcastic, elastic, gelastic, scholastic, dynastic, gymnastic, monastic, tetrastich, fantastic 4. inelastic, anaclastic, cataclastic, protoplastic, pederastic, paraphrastic 5. ecclesiastic, iconoclastic, enthusiastic.

AST′iks– 2. plastics, mastics, spastics 3. elastics, gymnastics 5. Ecclesiastics.

AST′ing– 2. fasting, casting, lasting, blasting 3. bombasting, *broadcasting*, forecasting, outlasting, contrasting. **4.** flabbergasting, everlasting.

AST'li– **2.** ghastly, lastly, vastly **3.** steadfastly.

AST'ness– **2.** fastness, vastness **3.** steadfastness.

AST'ral– **2.** astral, castral **3.** subastral, cadastral.

AST'ric– **2.** gastric **3.** digastric **4.** perigastric, hypogastric.

AST'rum– **2.** castrum, plastrum **4.** alabastrum, periastrum.

AS'us– **2.** bassus, passus **3.** Parnassus.

AT'a– **2.** atta, batta **3.** regatta **4.** matamata, yerbamata, paramatta.

AT'ed– **2.** batted, chatted, fatted, hatted, blatted, flatted, platted, plaited, slatted, matted, ratted, patted, spatted, dratted, tatted, vatted **3.** high-hatted, top-hatted, cravatted **4.** caryatid.

AT'en– **2.** Aten, batten, fatten, flatten, platan, platen, patten, paten, ratten, gratten **3.** Manhattan; *see* also **AT'in–** Latin etc. below.

AT'er– **2.** attar, batter, chatter, fatter, hatter, quatre, latter, blatter, flatter, clatter, platter, splatter, matter, smatter, patter, spatter, ratter, dratter, satyr, shatter, tatter, vatter **3.** hamfatter, bespatter.

AT'ern– **2.** slattern, pattern, Saturn.

ATH'er– **2.** gather, lather, blather, slather, rather **3.** foregather, forgather.

ATH'ik– **2.** bathic, spathic **3.** agnathic, apathic, empathic **4.** philomathic, telepathic, antipathic, psychopathic, allopathic, cosmopathic, hydropathic, neuropathic **5.** homeopathic, osteopathic, idiopathic.

AT'i– **2.** batty, chatty, fatty, Hattie, catty, matty, Mattie, natty, gnatty, patty, ratty, yati **3.** chapatty **4.** Cincinnati.

AT'ik– **2.** attic, Attic, platic, static vatic **3.** Sabbatic, ecbatic, creatic, phreatic, sulphatic, emphatic, lymphatic, phosphatic, sciatic, viatic, villatic, dramatic, hematic, schematic, rheumatic, thematic, sematic, pragmatic, judgmatic, phlegmatic, smegmatic, stigmatic, dogmatic, zeugmatic, asthmatic, climatic, dalmatic, pelmatic, grammatic, commatic, gromatic, chromatic, somatic, stomatic, termatic, plasmatic, osmatic, traumatic, unstatic, pneumatic, fanatic, enatic, agnatic, un-Attic, hepatic, pancratic, Socratic, quadratic, geratic, piratic, erratic, astatic, ecstatic, aquatic, lavatic **4.** anabatic, catabatic, metabatic, acrobatic, enneatic, cuneatic, pancreatic, ischiatic, opiatic, Adriatic, mydriatic, psoriatic, muriatic, Asiatic, aviatic, fluviatic, unthematic, emblematic, problematic, kinematic, systematic, astigmatic, dilemmatic, zygomatic, diplomatic, monomatic, aromatic, achromatic, symptomatic, automatic, miasmatic, aseismatic, numismatic, porismatic, diprismatic, macrosmatic, microsmatic, onymatic, morganatic, aplanatic, Pherecratic, theocratic, ochlocratic, democratic, timocratic, gynocratic, androcratic, autocratic, plutocratic, bureaucratic, polycratic, hieratic, operatic, diastatic, anastatic, catastatic, metastatic, geostatic, hemostatic, thermostatic, apostatic, hydrostatic, aerostatic, gyrostatic, photostatic, caryatic **5.** melodramatic, anathematic, theorematic, episematic, anallagmatic, synallagmatic, diaphragmatic, apothegmatic, paradigmatic, diagrammatic, anagrammatic, chronogrammatic, cryptogrammatic, polygrammatic, idiomatic, axiomatic, undiplomatic, iconomatic, monochromatic, isochromatic, polychromatic, cataclysmatic, empyreumatic, physiocratic, arithmocratic, hierocratic, pantisocratic, aristocratic, idiostatic, heliostatic **6.** paleoclimatic, idiosyncratic **7.** parallelogrammatic.

AT'iks– **2.** attics, statics **3.** dramatics, pneumatics, quadratics **4.** aerobatics, acrobatics, kinematics, mathematics, systematics, biostatics.

AT'in– 2. Latin, matin, Patine, gratin [F.], satin 3. au gratin [F.]; *see* also AT'en– Aten etc. above.

AT'ing– 2. batting, chatting, fatting, plaiting, platting, matting, patting, spatting, ratting, dratting, pratting, tatting, vatting 3. high-hatting, cravatting 4. cotton batting.

AT'is– 2. lattice, brattice, gratis.

AT'ish– 2. battish, fattish, cattish, flattish.

AT'l– 2. battle, battel, chattel, cattle, rattle, brattle, prattle, tattle 3. Seattle, embattle 4. tittle-tattle.

AT'ler– 2. battler, rattler, prattler, tattler, Statler.

AT'less– 2. atlas, Atlas, batless, fatless, hatless, catless, flatless, matless, patless, ratless, vatless 3. cravatless.

AT'li– 2. fatly, flatly, patly, rattly.

AT'ling– 2. battling, batling, catling, fatling, Gatling, rattling, prattling, tattling.

AT'ness– 2. fatness, flatness, patness.

AT'o– 2. *chateau, gateau, plateau* 3. mulatto, tomato.

AT'rik– 2. Patrick 3. theatric, iatric 4. pediatric, psychiatric, hippiatric, physiatric.

AT'riks– 3. theatrics 4. pediatrics, cyniatrics, phoniatrics, physiatrics.

AT'um– 2. atom, stratum.

AV'a– 2. Java, lava.

AV'el– 2. gavel, cavil, ravel, gravel, travel, tavell 3. unravel.

AV'er– 2. haver, claver 3. cadaver, palaver.

AV'ern– 2. cavern, tavern.

AV'i– 2. slavey, navvy, savvy.

AV'id– 2. avid, pavid, gravid 3. impavid.

AV'ij– 2. scavage, ravage, savage.

AV'ik– 2. Slavic 3. atavic, octavic Jugoslavic.

AV'ing– 2. having, halving, calving, salving.

AV'ish– 2. lavish, ravish 3. enravish.

AZ'a– 2. Ghazze, plaza 3. piazza.

AZ'ard– 2. hazard, mazzard 3. haphazard.

AZH'er– 2. azure.

AZ'l– 2. Basil, dazzle, razzle, frazzle 3. bedazzle 4. razzle-dazzle.

AZ'ling– 2. dazzling, jazzling 3. bedazzling 4. razzle-dazzling.

AZ'ma– 2. asthma, phasma, plasma 3. chiasma, miasma, empasma, phantasma 4. bioplasma, photoplasma.

AZ'mal– 2. chasmal 3. miasmal, phantasmal 4. protoplasmal.

AZ'mik– 2. chasmic, plasmic, spasmic 3. miasmic, marasmic, phantasmic 4. bioplasmic, protoplasmic.

A (cab)

3.

TRIPLE RHYMES IN A (rab'id-ness)

Primary or Secondary Accent Falls on
Second from Last Syllable.

AB'a–bl– 2. nabbable, grabbable, tab-babble.

AB'a–sis– 4. anabasis, parabasis, catabasis, metabasis.

AB'id–ness– 3. rabidness, tabidness.

AB'i–er– 3. gabbier, scabbier, blabbier, flabbier, crabbier, shabbier.

AB'i–est– 3. gabbiest, scabbiest, blabbiest, flabbiest, crabbiest, shabbiest.

AB'i–fi– 3. labefy, tabefy 4. syllabify 5. dissyllabify.

AB'i–kal– 3. syllabical, Arabical 6. polysyllabical, monosyllabical, multi-syllabical.

AB'i–li– 3. gabbily, blabbily, scabbily, flabbily, crabbily, shabbily.

AB'i–ness– 3. gabbiness, scabbiness, blabbiness, flabbiness, slabbiness, crabbiness, shabbiness.

AB'i–net– 3. cabinet, tabinet.

AB'it–i– 3. Babbitty, rabbity.

AB'it–ing– 3. Babbitting, rabbiting 4. inhabiting, cohabiting.

AB'la–tiv– 3. ablative, babblative.

AB'l–ment– 3. babblement, dabblement, gabblement, rabblement, brabblement, scrabblement.

AB'o–la– 4. parabola, Metabola.

AB'o–rat– 4. elaborate, collaborate.

AB'u–la– 3. fabula, tabula 4. cunabula 5. incunabula.

AB'u–lar– 3. fabular, pabular, tabular 4. confabular, vocabular, conabular 5. acetabular, tintinnabular.

AB'u–lat– 3. fabulate, tabulate 4. confabulate 5. tintinnabulate.

AB'u–list– 3. fabulist 4. vocabulist 5. incunabulist, tintinnabulist.

AB'u–lum– 3. pabulum 5. incunabulum, acetabulum, tintinnabulum.

AB'u–lus– 3. fabulous, pabulous, sabulous 5. tintinnabulous.

ACH'a–bl– 3. batchable, hatchable, catchable, latchable, matchable, snatchable, patchable, scratchable, thatchable 4. unhatchable, uncatchable, rematchable, immatchable, unmatchable, unpatchable, dispatchable, attachable, detachable.

ACH'er–i– 3. hatchery, patchery.

ACH'i–ness– 3. catchiness, snatchiness, patchiness, scratchiness.

AD'a–bl– 3. addable 4. unaddable.

AD'i–kal– 3. radical 4. sporadical.

AD'ish–ness– 3. faddishness, caddishness.

AD'i–tiv– 3. additive, traditive 4. readditive.

AD'o–ing– 3. shadowing 4. foreshadowing 5. overshadowing.

AF'a–bl– 3. affable 4. inaffable, unaffable.

AF'i–a– 3. maffia, mafia, raffia, tafia 4. agraphia, asaphia.

AF'i–kal– 3. graphical 4. seraphical 5. diagraphical, paragraphical, calligraphical, lexigraphical, geographical, biographical, orthographical, cosmographical, ethnographical, telegraphical, pornographical, glossographical, topographical, typographical, photographical, cartographical, phytographical, epitaphical **6.** bibliographical, physiographical, anthropographical, lexicographical **7.** autobiographical, paleontographical.

AF'l—ment— 3. bafflement, snafflement, rafflement, scrafflement.

AFT'i—li— 3. draftily, craftily.

AFT'less—li— 3. draftlessly, graftlessly, craftlessly, shaftlessly.

AG'a—bl— 3. faggable, gaggable, flaggable, naggable, snaggable, draggable, saggable, taggable, waggable.

AG'ed—li— 3. jaggedly, raggedly, scraggedly.

AG'ed—ness— 3. jaggedness, raggedness, craggedness, scraggedness.

AG'er—er— 3. staggerer, swaggerer.

AG'er—i— 3. faggery, jaggery, raggery, staggery, waggery **4.** zigzaggery.

AG'er—ing— 3. staggering, swaggering.

AG'i—li— 3. baggily, raggily, craggily, scraggily, shaggily.

AG'i—ness— 3. bagginess, flagginess, knagginess, bragginess, cragginess, scragginess, shagginess.

AG'ish—li— 3. haggishly, braggishly, waggishly.

AG'on—ist— 3. agonist **4.** antagonist, protagonist **5.** deuteragonist.

AG'on—iz— 3. agonize **4.** antagonize.

AG'on—izm— 4. antagonism, protagonism.

AG'ot—i— 3. fagoty, faggoty, maggoty.

AJ'er—i— 4. menagerie, potagerie.

AJ'ik—al— 3. magical, tragical **5.** theomagical.

AJ'il—ness— 3. agileness, fragileness.

AJ'in—al— 3. paginal **4.** imaginal.

AJ'in—us— 4. farraginous, voraginous **5.** oleaginous, mucilaginous, cartilaginous.

AJ'u—tant— 3. adjutant **4.** coadjutant.

AK'en—ing— 3. blackening, slackening.

AK'er—el— 3. cackerel, mackerel.

AK'er—i— 3. hackery, knackery, Thackeray, quackery, Zachary **4.** hijackery, knickknackery, gimcrackery.

AK'et—ed— 3. jacketed, placketed, packeted, racketed, bracketed.

AK'et—ing— 3. jacketing, packeting, racketing, bracketing.

AK'i—ness— 3. hackiness, tackiness, wackiness **4.** gimcrackiness.

AK'ish—ness— 3. blackishness, slackishness, knackishness, brackishness, quackishness.

AK'rit—i— 3. acrity **4.** alacrity.

AK'ron—ism— 4. anachronism, metachronism.

AKS'a—bl— 3. taxable **4.** relaxable, nontaxable, untaxable.

AKSH'un—al— 3. actional, factional, pactional, fractional, tractional **4.** reactional, redactional **5.** interactional, rarefactional.

AKSH'us—ness— 3. factiousness, fractiousness.

AKS'i—al— 3. axial **4.** abaxial, biaxial, coaxial.

AKT'a—bl— 3. actable, tractable, tactable **4.** olfactable, refractable, attractable, retractable, intractable, extractable, intactable; *see* **AKT'i—bl—** olfactible etc. below.

AKT'e—al— 3. lacteal, bracteal.

AKT'ed—ness— 4. impactedness, contractedness, protractedness, abstractedness, distractedness.

AKT'er—i— 3. factory, lactary, tractory **4.** olfactory, phylactery, enactory, refractory, detractory **5.** calefactory, malefactory, benefactory, manufactory, satisfactory **6.** dissatisfactory.

AKT'i—bl— 4. olfactible, compactible, detractible, contractible, distractible; *see* **AKT'a—bl—** actable etc. above.

AKT'i—kal— 3. practical, tactical **4.** didactical, stalactical, impractical, unpractical, syntactical.

AKT′iv–ness– 3. activeness 4. defractiveness, attractiveness, detractiveness, contractiveness, protractiveness, abstractiveness, distractiveness.

AKT′or–i– factory etc., *see* AKT′er–i– factory etc. above.

AKT′or–ship– 3. actorship, factorship 4. contractorship.

AKT′u–al– 3. actual, factual, tactual 4. impactual, contractual, contactual.

AKT′ur–ing– 3. fracturing 4. refracturing 5. manufacturing.

AK′u–at– 3. acuate 4. evacuate.

AK′u–la– 3. bacula, facula, macula, Dracula 4. tentacula.

AK′u–lar– 4. piacular, vernacular, oracular, spectacular, jentacular, tentacular 5. tabernacular, supernacular.

AK′u–lat– 3. jaculate, maculate 4. ejaculate, bimaculate, immaculate 5. interjaculate.

AK′u–lum– 4. piaculum, tentaculum.

AK′u–lus– 3. baculus, sacculus 4. abaculus, miraculous, oraculous, vernaculous.

AL′ans–ing– 3. balancing 4. unbalancing 5. counterbalancing, overbalancing.

AL′ant–ed– 3. talented 4. begallanted.

AL′a–ri– 3. alary, gallery, salary, vallary 4. subalary 5. intercalary.

AL′er–ji– 3. allergy 4. *metallurgy*.

AL′et–ed– 3. balloted, valeted 4. unvaleted.

AL′i–ans– 3. dalliance, ralliance, valiance.

AL′i–at– 3. malleate, palliate, talliate 4. retaliate.

AL′ib–er– 3. caliber, calibre, calabur 4. Excalibur.

AL′id–li– 3. pallidly, validly 4. invalidly.

AL′id–ness– 3. callidness, pallidness, validness 4. impallidness, invalidness.

AL′i–er– 3. dallier, rallier, sallier, tallier.

AL′i–fi– 3. calefy, salify 4. alkalify.

AL′i–ing– 3. dallying, rallying, sallying, tallying.

AL′ik–ly– 3. Gallicly 4. vocalicly, metallicly, smart-aleckly [coll.].

AL′i–ped– 3. aliped, taliped.

AL′i–sis– 4. dialysis, analysis, paralysis, catalysis 6. psychoanalysis.

AL′i–son– 3. alison, Alison, malison.

AL′i–ti– 4. verbality, locality, vocality, rascality, pedality, modality, sodality, feudality, reality, egality, legality, regality, frugality, lethality, formality, normality, banality, venality, signality, finality, tonality, zonality, carnality, spirality, morality, spectrality, dextrality, plurality, rurality, nasality, fatality, natality, vitality, mentality, totality, mortality, brutality, duality, rivality 5. farcicality, laicality, radicality, Biblicality, comicality, technicality, finicality, clericality, whimsicality, classicality, practicality, verticality, bipedality, ideality, lineality, unreality, illegality, prodigality, conjugality, speciality, sociality, cordiality, filiality, geniality, seriality, spatiality, partiality, bestiality, triviality, joviality, informality, abnormality, feminality, criminality, nationality, rationality, personality, internality, externality, principality, liberality, generality, laterality, literality, severality, integrality, immorality, temporality, corporality, pastorality, naturality, gutturality, commensality, vegetality, hospitality, immortality, visuality, sensuality, actuality, punctuality, virtuality, mutuality, sexuality, coevality 6. inimicality, theatricality, nonsensicality, pragmaticality, impracticality, fantasticality, reciprocality, sesquipedality, ethereality, corporeality, proverbiality, connubiality, provinciality, primordiality, parochiality, congeniality, perenniality, imperiality, materiality, substantiality, prudentiality, essentiality, potentiality, sequentiality, impartiality, colloquiality, conviviality, originality, irrationality, conditionality, conventionality, devotionality, exceptionality, proportionality, tripersonality, impersonality, municipality, illiberality, ephemerality, collaterality, conjecturality, universality, orientality, fundamentality, elementality, sentimentality, instrumentality, horizontality, effectuality, unpunctuality, conceptuality, asexuality **7.** artificiality, superficiality, immateriality, territoriality, confidentiality, insubstantiality, consubstantiality, unsubstantiality, circumstantiality, consequentiality, septentrionality, unconditionality, unconventionality, constitutionality, preternaturality, individuality, ineffectuality, intellectuality **8.** exterritoriality, inconsequentiality, unconstitutionality **9.** extraterritoriality.

ALJ'i–a– 4. myalgia, gastralgia, neuralgia, dentalgia, nostalgia.

AL'o–er– 3. hallower, callower, sallower, shallower, tallower.

AL'o–est– 3. callowest, sallowest, shallowest.

AL'o–ish– 3. callowish, sallowish, shallowish, tallowish.

AL'o–ji– 4. mammalogy, analogy, paralogy, oralogy, petralogy, tetralogy, crustalogy **5.** genealogy, mineralogy, pyroballogy **6.** genethlialogy.

AL'o–jist– 4. dialogist, Decalogist, mammalogist, analogist, penalogist **5.** genealogist, mineralogist.

AL'o–jiz– 4. dialogize, analogize, penalogize, paralogize **5.** genealogize, mineralogize.

AL'o–jizm– 3. alogism **4.** dialogism, analogism, paralogism.

AL'o–ness– 2. callowness, fallowness, sallowness, shallowness.

AL'op–er– 3. galoper, galloper, scalloper **4.** escalloper.

AL'op–ing– 3. galoping, galloping, scalloping **4.** escalloping.

AL'u–at– 3. valuate **4.** devaluate, revaluate **5.** re-evaluate.

AL'us–ez– 3. phalluses, galluses, calluses.

AL'yun–ish– 3. scallionish, stallionish **4.** medallionish, rapscallionish.

AM'a–bl– 3. Amabel, flammable **4.** inflammable.

AM'a–tist– 3. dramatist, grammatist **5.** melodramatist, anagrammatist, epigrammatist, lipogrammatist **6.** hierogrammatist.

AM'a–tiv– 3. amative **4.** exclamative.

AM'a–tiz– 3. dramatize **5.** diagrammatize, anagrammatize, epigrammatize.

AMB'u–lans– 3. ambulance **4.** somnambulance.

AMB'u–lant– 3. ambulant **4.** somnambulant, noctambulant.

AMB'u–lat– 3. ambulate **4.** deambulate, somnambulate, funambulate, perambulate **5.** circumambulate.

AMB'u–list– 4. somnambulist, funambulist, noctambulist.

AM'er–a– 3. camera **4.** incamera, Pentamera.

AM'er–al– 3. cameral **4.** decameral, bicameral, hexameral, tetrameral, pentameral.

AM'er–er– 3. hammerer, clamorer, stammerer, yammerer.

AM'er–ing– 3. hammering, clamoring, stammering, yammering **4.** enamoring, beglamouring.

AM'er–on– 4. Decameron, hexameron, Heptameron.

AM'er–us– 3. amorous, glamorous, clamorous **4.** unglamorous, hexamerous, heptamerous.

AM'et–er– 4. diameter, decameter, dynameter, parameter, tetrameter, octameter, pentameter, hexameter, heptameter, voltameter.

AM'ik–al– 3. amical **4.** dynamical, balsamical.

AM'in-a– **3.** lamina, stamina **4.** for-amina.

AM'in-at– **3.** laminate, staminate **4.** foraminate, contaminate.

AM'i-ness– **3.** hamminess, jamminess, clamminess.

AM'it-i– **3.** amity **4.** calamity.

AM'on-it– **3.** Ammonite, mammonite, Shamanite.

AM'on-izm– **3.** mammonism, Shamanism.

AM'or-ing– clamoring etc., *see* AM'er-ing– hammering etc. above.

AM'or-us– amorous etc., *see* AM'er-us– amorous etc. above.

AMP'er-er– **3.** hamperer, scamperer, pamperer, tamperer.

AMP'er-ing– **3.** hampering, scampering, pampering, tampering.

AMP'i-li– **3.** crampily, vampily.

AMP'i-on– **3.** Campion, champion, lampion, tampion.

AM'u-la– **3.** ammula, mammula.

AM'u-lus– **3.** famulus, hamulus, ramulus, ramulous.

AN'a-ble– **3.** Annabel, bannable, cannable, cannibal, mannable, pannable, sanable, tannable **4.** insanable, untannable; *see* also AN'i-bal– Hannibal etc. below.

AN'ar-i– **3.** panary, granary; *see* also AN'er-i– cannery etc. below.

AND'a-ble– **3.** bandable, handable, mandible, sandable, standable **4.** demandable, commandable, unstandable **5.** reprimandable, countermandable, understandable **6.** misunderstandable.

AND'al-iz– **3.** scandalize, vandalize.

AND'ed-li– **3.** candidly **4.** highhandedly, backhandedly **5.** openhandedly, underhandedly.

AND'ed-ness– **3.** candidness **4.** highhandedness, backhandedness, lefthanded-ness **5.** openhandedness, underhanded-ness.

AND'er-er– **3.** slanderer, panderer **4.** meanderer, philanderer.

AND'er-ing– **3.** slandering, pandering **4.** meandering, philandering.

AND'er-us– **3.** slanderous, panderous.

AND'i-al– **3.** prandial **4.** postprandial **5.** anteprandial.

AND'i-er– **3.** bandier, dandier, handier, randier, sandier **4.** unhandier.

AND'i-fi– **3.** dandify, candify.

AND'i-ing– **3.** bandying, candying, randying.

AND'i-li– **3.** bandily, dandily, handily, randily, sandily **4.** unhandily.

AND'i-ness– **3.** bandiness, dandiness, handiness, randiness, sandiness **4.** unhandiness.

AND'ing-li– **4.** demandingly, commandingly, outstandingly **5.** understandingly.

AND'ing-ness– **4.** demandingness, commandingness, outstandingness **5.** understandingness.

AND'ish-ing– **3.** blandishing, brandishing.

AND'ish-ment– **3.** blandishment, brandishment.

AN'el-ing– **3.** channelling, flannelling, panelling.

AN'er-et– **3.** banneret, lanneret.

AN'er-i– **3.** cannery, panary, granary, tannery.

ANG'gling-li– **3.** anglingly, danglingly, ganglingly, janglingly, manglingly, spanglingly, stranglingly, tanglingly, wranglingly, wanglingly.

ANG'gl-som– **3.** anglesome, janglesome, wranglesome, tanglesome.

ANG'gu-lar-ï **3.** angular, slangular **4.** triangular, quadrangular, rectangular, octangular, pentangular.

ANG'gu-lat– **3.** angulate, strangulate **4.** triangulate.

ANG'i–li– **3.** bangily, clangily, slangily, tangily, twangily.

ANG'ing–li– **3.** bangingly, hangingly, clangingly, slangingly, twangingly, whangingly **4.** haranguingly.

AN'i–bal– **3.** Hannibal, cannibal; see also AN'a–bl– Annabel etc. above.

AN'i–el– **3.** Daniel, Haniel, spaniel, Saniel, **4.** Nathaniel.

AN'i–est– **3.** canniest, clanniest **4.** uncanniest.

AN'i–fi– **3.** sanify **4.** humanify.

AN'i–form– **3.** Janiform, raniform, graniform **4.** campaniform.

AN'i–kal– **3.** manacle **4.** organical, mechanical, Brahmanical, tyrannical, botanical, galvanical **5.** charlatanical, puritanical; see also AN'i–kl– panicle etc. below.

AN'i–kin– **3.** Anniekin, cannikin, manikin, pannikin.

AN'i–kl– **3.** panicle, sanicle **4.** mechanical, tyranical, botanical; see also An'i–kal– manacle etc. above.

AN'i–mat– **3.** animate **4.** reanimate, inanimate, exanimate.

AN'i–mus– **3.** animous, animus **4.** magnanimous, unanimous, multanimous **5.** pusillanimous.

AN'i–ness– **3.** canniness, clanniness.

AN'ish–ing– **3.** banishing, planishing, vanishing.

AN'ish–ment– **3.** banishment, vanishment **4.** evanishment.

AN'ist–er– **3.** banister, ganister, canister.

AN'it–i– **3.** sanity, vanity **4.** inanity, urbanity, mundanity, profanity, paganity, organity, volcanity, gigmanity, immanity, humanity, insanity **5.** inurbanity, inorganity, Christianity, inhumanity, subterranity.

ANJ'en–si– **3.** plangency, tangency.

ANJ'er–i– **3.** lingerie, singerie.

ANJ'i–a– **3.** cangia **4.** hydrangea, sporangia.

ANJ'i–bl– **3.** frangible, tangible **4.** refrangible, infrangible, intangible.

ANK'er–er– **3.** anchorer, hankerer.

ANK'er–ing– **3.** anchoring, hankering, cankering **4.** reanchoring, encankering.

ANK'er–us– **3.** cankerous **4.** cantankerbus.

ANS'i–li– **3.** chancily, fancily, prancily.

ANS'ing–li– **3.** dancingly, glancingly, prancingly, trancingly **4.** entrancingly.

ANS'it–iv– **3.** transitive **4.** intransitive.

ANS'iv–ness– **4.** expansiveness, advanciveness **5.** inexpansiveness, unexpansiveness.

ANS'om–er– **3.** handsomer, ransomer.

ANT'a–bl– **3.** plantable, grantable **4.** transplantable, ungrantable.

ANT'el–op– **3.** antelope, cantaloupe.

ANT'er–er– **3.** banterer, canterer.

ANT'er–ing– **3.** bantering, cantering.

ANTH'ro–pi– **4.** theanthropy, lycanthropy, philanthropy, psilanthropy, misanthropy, zoanthropy **5.** aphilanthropy **6.** theophilanthropy.

ANTH'ro–pist– **4.** theanthropist, philanthropist, psilanthropist, misanthropist **6.** theophilanthropist.

ANTH'ro–pizm– **4.** theanthropism, philanthropism, psilanthropism **6.** theophilanthropism.

ANT'ik–li– **3.** anticly, franticly **4.** pedanticly, giganticly, romanticly.

ANT'ik–ness– **3.** anticness, franticness **4.** pedanticness, giganticness, romanticness.

ANT'i–li– **3.** bantily, scantily, slantily, rantily.

ANT'i–ness– **3.** bantiness, scantiness, slantiness, rantiness.

ANT'ing–li– **3.** cantingly, slantingly, pantingly, rantingly **4.** enchantingly.

ANT'u–a– 3. mantua 4. Gargantua.

AN'u–al– 3. annual, manual, Manuel 4. biannual, bimanual, Immanuel 5. semi-annual.

AN'u–la– 3. cannula, ranula, granula 4. Campanula.

AN'u–lar– 3. annular, cannular, ranular, granular 4. penannular, campanular.

AN'u–lat– 3. annulate, granulate 4. campanulate.

AN'u–let– 3. annulet, granulet.

AP'a–bl– 3. mappable, snappable, strappable, tappable 4. unmappable.

AP'id–li– 3. rapidly, sapidly, vapidly.

AP'id–ness– 3. rapidness, sapidness, vapidness.

AP'i–er– 3. happier, gappier, lappier, nappier, snappier, scrappier, sappier.

AP'i–est– 3. happiest, gappiest, lappiest, nappiest, snappiest, scrappiest, sappiest 4. unhappiest.

AP'i–li– 3. happily, gappily, snappily, scrappily, sappily 4. unhappily.

AP'o–lis– 4. Annapolis, tetrapolis, pentapolis 5. Minneapolis 6. Indianapolis.

AP'tur–ing– 3. capturing, rapturing 4. recapturing, enrapturing.

AR'a–bl– 3. arable, bearable, parable, sparable, tearable, wearable 4. unbearable, declarable, repairable, unwearable 5. undeclarable, unrepairable.

AR'a–blz– 3. parables, wearables.

AR'a–gon– 3. paragon, tarragon.

AR'ant–li– 3. arrantly 4. apparently, transparently.

AR'as–ing– 3. harassing, terracing 4. embarrassing 5. disembarrassing.

AR'as–ment– 3. harassment 4. embarrassment.

AR'at–iv– 3. narrative 4. declarative, reparative, preparative, comparative.

AR'el–ing– 3. barreling, caroling 4. pork-barreling, appareling.

AR'i–at– 3. lariat 4. salariat 5. commissariat, proletariat, secretariat.

AR'i–er– 3. barrier, charier, farrier, harrier, carrier, marrier, parrier, tarrier, warier.

AR'i–fi– 3. scarify, clarify 4. saccharify.

AR'i–form– 3. nariform, variform 4. scalariform.

AR'i–ing– 3. harrying, carrying, marrying, parrying, tarrying 5. intermarrying.

AR'i–li– 3. airily, fairily; see also ER'i–li– merrily etc.

AR'in–at– 3. carinate, marinate.

AR'i–ness– 3. chariness, wariness; see also AR'i–ness– airiness etc.

AR'i–o– 4. Philario, scenario, Lothario 5. impresario.

AR'i–on– 3. carrion, clarion, Marion, Marian 4. Maid Marian.

AR'i–ot– 3. chariot 4. Iscariot.

AR'ish–li– 3. bearishly, garishly.

AR'ish–ness– 3. bearishness, garishness.

AR'is–on– 3. garrison, Harrison, parison 4. caparison, comparison.

AR'it–i– 3. charity, clarity, parity, rarity 4. barbarity, vagarity, vulgarity, uncharity, hilarity, molarity, polarity, imparity, disparity 5. solidarity, similarity, capillarity, bipolarity, exemplarity, globularity, secularity, jocularity, circularity, vascularity, muscularity, regularity, angularity, singularity, granularity, popularity, insularity, debonairity, gemmiparity, omniparity, fissiparity, multiparity, oviparity 6. familiarity, peculiarity, dissimilarity, piacularity, vernacularity, orbicularity, molecularity, particularity, irregularity, triangularity, rectangularity, unpopularity, peninsularity, ovoviparity 7. rectilinearity, curvilinearity, perpendicularity.

AR'–o–er– 3. harrower, narrower 4. wheelbarrower.

AR'o–i– 3. arrowy, marrowy, sparrowy.

AR'o–ing– **3.** arrowing, farrowing, harrowing, narrowing **4.** wheelbarrowing.

AR'o–lik– **3.** arrowlike, barrowlike, farrowlike, farolike, harrowlike, marrowlike, sparrowlike.

AR'ot–ing– **3.** garroting, parroting.

AS'a–bl– **3.** classable, passable **4.** amassable, impassable, surpassable; *see* also AS'i–bl– passible etc. below.

AS'a–bli– **3.** classably, passably **4.** unclassably, impassibly, unpassably, surpassably **5.** unsurpassably; *see* also AS'i–bli– passibly etc. below.

AS'er–at– **3.** lacerate, macerate **4.** emaserate.

AS'et–ed– **3.** faceted.

ASH'er–i– **3.** ashery, fashery, hashery, trashery, sashery **5.** haberdashery.

ASH'i–a– **3.** fascia, cassia, quassia **4.** Circassia, parnassia.

ASH'i–an– **4.** Circassian, Parnassian.

ASH'i–er– **3.** ashier, dashier, hashier, flashier, plashier, splashier, trashier.

ASH'i–est– **3.** ashiest, dashiest, hashiest, flashiest, plashiest, splashiest, trashiest.

ASH'i–ness– **3.** ashiness, flashiness, splashiness, trashiness.

ASH'un–al– **3.** national, passional, rational **4.** irrational **5.** international.

ASH'un–at– passionate etc., *see* ASH'un–it– passionate etc. below.

ASH'un–ing– **3.** fashioning, rationing **4.** refashioning, disfashioning.

ASH'un–it– **3.** passionate, fashion it **4.** impassionate, compassionate, unpassionate, dispassionate.

AS'i–bl– **3.** passible **4.** impassible, renascible, irascible; *see* also AS'a–bl– classable etc. above.

AS'i–bli– **3.** passibly **4.** impassibly, irascibly; *see* also AS'a–bli– classably etc. above.

AS'i–fi– **3.** classify, pacify **4.** reclassify.

AS'i–kl– **3.** fascicle, classical **4.** nonclassical **5.** neoclassical.

AS'i–nat– **3.** fascinate **4.** abacinate, deracinate, assassinate.

AS'i–ness– **3.** gassiness, classiness, glassiness, massiness, brassiness, grassiness.

AS'it–i– **4.** bibacity, dicacity, procacity, edacity, mendacity, mordacity, audacity, sagacity, fugacity, salacity, tenacity, pugnacity, minacity, capacity, rapacity, opacity, feracity, veracity, voracity, sequacity, loquacity, vivacity **5.** perspicacity, pervicacity, contumacity, pertinacity, saponacity, incapacity.

AS'iv–li– **3.** massively, passively **4.** impassively.

AS'iv–ness– **3.** massiveness, passiveness **4.** impassiveness.

ASP'er–at– **3.** asperate, aspirate **4.** exasperate.

ASP'ing–li– **3.** gaspingly, raspingly, graspingly.

AST'er–i– **3.** plastery, mastery **4.** dicastery, self-mastery.

AST'er–ing– **3.** plastering, mastering, pastoring **4.** beplastering **5.** overmastering, poetastering.

AST'ik–al– **4.** elastical, gymnastical, monastical, fantastical **6.** ecclesiastical, enthusiastical.

AST'ik–li– **3.** plasticly, drasticly **4.** bombasticly, sarcasticly, elasticly, scholasticly, gymnasticly, monasticly, fantasticly.

AST'i–li– **3.** ghastily, nastily.

AST'i–sizm– **4.** plasticism **5.** scholasticism, monasticism, fanaticism.

AST'ri–an– **4.** Lancastrian **5.** Zoroastrian, alabastrian.

AST'ro–fe– **4.** diastrophe, anastrophe, catastrophe **5.** epanastrophe.

AT'a–bl– **3.** atabal, battable, hattable, mattable, pattable, rattable, vattable **4.** combatable, come-at-able, get-at-able; *see* also AT'i–bl– patible etc. below.

AT′en–ing– 3. battening, fattening, flattening.

AT′er–al– 3. lateral 4. collateral 5. unilateral, quadrilateral, plurilateral.

AT′er–er– 3. batterer, chatterer, scatterer, flatterer, clatterer, splatterer, smatterer, patterer, shatterer 4. bespatterer.

AT′er–i– 3. battery, hattery, scattery, flattery, slattery, shattery, tattery.

AT′er–ing– 3. battering, chattering, scattering, flattering, clattering, smattering, pattering, spattering, shattering 4. bespattering, unflattering.

ATH′er–er– 3. gatherer, latherer, blatherer, slatherer 4. woolgatherer, ingatherer, foregatherer.

ATH′er–ing– 3. gathering, lathering, blathering, slathering 4. woolgathering, ingathering, foregathering.

ATH′e–sis– 4. diathesis, parathesis, metathesis.

ATH′ik–al– 5. philomathical 6. idiopathical.

AT′i–bl– 3. patible 4. combatable, impatible, compatible 5. incompatible, uncompatible; *see* also **AT′a–bl–** atabal etc. above.

AT′i–fi– 3. ratify, gratify, stratify 4. beatify.

AT′ik–a– 3. Attica 4. sciatica, hepatica.

AT′ik–al– 3. statical, vatical 4. abbatical, sabbatical, emphatical, dramatical, pragmatical, dogmatical, grammatical, climatical, somatical, asthmatical, Socratical, schismatical, prismatical, fanatical, erratical, piratical, ecstatical, aquatical 5. acrobatical, mathematical, emblematical, problematical, systematical, enigmatical, ungrammatical, diplomatical, automatical, symptomatical, numismatical, democratical, bureaucratical, autocratical, apostatical, hypostatical, hydrostatical 6. anagrammatical, idiomatical, axiomatical, aristocratical, unsystematical, anagrammatical, epigrammatical, axiomatical, aristo-

cratical, aerostatical 7. anidiomatical, idiosyncratical.

AT′in–at– 3. patinate 4. Palatinate, gelatinate.

AT′i–ness– 3. battiness, cattiness, chattiness, fattiness, nattiness, rattiness.

AT′in–iz– 3. Latinize, platinize 4. gelatinize.

AT′in–us– 3. Latinus, platinous 4. gelatinous.

AT′is–ing– 3. latticing, bratticing.

AT′i–sizm– 5. pragmaticism, grammaticism, fanaticism 6. Asiaticism.

AT′i–tud– 3. attitude, latitude, platitude, gratitude 4. beatitude, ingratitude.

AT′l–ment– 3. battlement, prattlement, tattlement 4. embattlement.

AT′o–mi– 3. atomy 4. anatomy 5. tesseratomy.

AT′o–mist– 3. atomist 4. anatomist.

AT′rik–al– 3. matrical 4. theatrical, iatrical 5. psychiatrical, idolatrical.

AT′ri–sid– 3. matricide, patricide, fratricide.

AT′ron–ij– 3. matronage, patronage.

AT′ron–iz– 3. matronize, patronize.

AT′ul–a– 3. scatula, spatula 4. comatula.

AT′ul–at– 3. spatulate, gratulate 4. congratulate.

AT′ur–al– 3. natural 4. unnatural 5. supernatural, preternatural.

AT′ur–at– 3. maturate, saturate 5. supersaturate.

AV′aj–er– 3. scavager, ravager, savager.

AV′aj–est– 3. savagest.

AV′aj–ing– 3. scavaging, ravaging.

AV′an–ez– 3. Havanese, Javanese.

AV′el–er– 3. caviler, raveler, traveler 4. unraveler.

AV′el–in– 3. javelin, ravelin.

AV′el–ing– 3. caviling, raveling, graveling, traveling 4. unraveling.

AV'end–er– 3. chavender, lavender.

AV'er–ij– 3. average.

AV'er–ing– 3. havering, clavering 4. palavering.

AV'er–us– 4. cadaverous, papaverous.

AV'ish–er– 3. lavisher, ravisher.

AV'ish–ing– 3. lavishing, ravishing 4. enravishing.

AV'ish–ment– 3. lavishment, ravishment, 4. enravishment.

AV'i–ti– 3. cavity, gravity, pravity, suavity 4. concavity, depravity.

AZ'ard–us– 3. hazardous.

AZ'i–a– 3. razzia.

AZ'l–ment– 3. dazzlement, frazzlement 4. bedazzlement.

E (bee)

1.

SINGLE (MASCULINE) RHYMES IN E (bee)

Primary or Secondary Accent Falls on Last Syllable; Imperfect Rhymes Are in Italics.

E– 1. e, E, ee, 'ee.

BE– 1. b, B, be, bee 2. A.B., *bawbee*, Bebe, bribee 3. honeybee, bumblebee, humblebee, scarabee, Niobe, wallaby, Barnaby, Araby, sassaby, jacoby, cenoby.

CHE– 1. chee 2. *chee-chee*, litchi, vouchee 3. debauchee.

DE– 1. d, D, dee, Dee, dit [F.] 2. D.D., M.D., Didi, deedee, Chaldee, killdee, grandee, spondee, vendee 3. C.O.D., Ph.D., chickadee, tragedy, remedy, comedy, perfidy, subsidy, tweedledee, organdy, Normandy, dispondee, arrondi [F.], Burgundy, theody, melody, psalmody, threnody, hymnody, monody, dipody, tripody, parody, prosody, rhapsody, custodee, custody, Lombardy, jeopardy, bastardy 4. fiddlededee.

FE– 1. fee, phi 2. feoffee, Fifi 4. telegraphy, geography, biography, biographee, anaglyphy, xylography, photography, catastrophe, antistrophe, apostrophe 5. paleography 6. dactyliography.

GE– 1. ghee 2. whangee 3. Portugee.

HE– 1. he 2. hehee, tehee, bohea.

JE– 1. g, G, gee 2. agee, geegee, Gigi, squeegee, pledgee, N.G., pongee, bargee, burgee 3. mortgagee, elegy, strategy, prodigy, effigy, obligee, perigee, elogy, apogee, dilogy, trilogy, dyslogy, eulogy, allergy, synergy, theurgy, telurgy, zymurgy, liturgy, refugee, syzygy 4. biology, zoology.

KE– 1. key, cay, quay, ski, skee 2. raki, croquis [F.], marquee 3. colicky, gar-

licky, panicky, finicky, hillocky, hummocky, Cherokee, master key 4. synecdoche.

LE– 1. Lee, lea, li, Leigh, flea, flee, glee, clee 2. alee, bailee, belee, peelee, pili, folie [F.] 3. Thessaly, Rosalie, Italy, Castaly, libelee, fleur-de-lis, appellee, enrollee 4. anomaly, Annabel Lee; *also all adverbs composed of adjective-plus-suffix "-ly"* (e.g. toothsomely, longingly); *also adjectives composed of noun-plus-suffix "-ly"* (e.g. brotherly, sisterly).

ME– 1. me, smee 2. ami [F.] 3. infamy, balsamy, jessamy, dittamy, alchemy, blasphemy, Ptolemy, enemy, bonhomie, confirmee.

NE– 1. nee, knee, snee 2. trainee, Beni, Chinee, donee, pawnee, Pawnee, Shawnee 3. bargainee, distrainee, designee, assignee, consignee, alienee, domine, nominee, internee, optionee, snickersnee, Tuscany, tiffany, Romany, Germany, larceny, eugeny, kitcheny, villainy, tyranny, dysphony, euphony, cushiony, oniony, felony, colony, barony, crimsony, Antony, cottony, gluttony, muttony, Saxony 4. mahogany, Epiphany, accompany, examinee, illuminee, abandonee, petitionee, Gethsemane.

PE– 1. p, P, pe, pee 2. rappee, *earthpea*, *cowpea*, wampee, topee, toupee, rupee 3. canopy, escapee, agape, calipee, recipe, epopee 4. Calliope, Penelope.

RE– 1. re, ree, bree [dial.], Brie, dree [Scot. & dial.], free, pre [slang], spree, tree, three 2. karree, Marie, in re [L.],

73

debris, broderie [F.], enfree, unfree, *care-free*, *germ-free*, *heart-free*, *dust-free*, agree, degree, puggree, machree, doree, choree, épris [F.], esprit [F.] **3.** Barbary, quandary, boundary, vagary, beggary, sangaree, stingaree, dungaree, pugaree, sugary, diary, chickaree, salary, bain-marie, summary, rapparee, library, contrary, notary, rotary, votary, rosary, Calvary, ribaldry, husbandry, bribery, robbery, treachery, archery, witchery, thundery, prudery, referee, transferee, waggery, roguery, snuggery, drudgery, forgery, bakery, trickery, mockery, rookery, raillery, gallery, flummery, mummery, scenery, finery, fernery, drapery, slippery, trumpery, foppery, popery, tracery, passerie, chancery, sorcery, nursery, battery, flattery, watery, lottery, wintery, artery, mastery, mystery, cautery, feathery, heathery, slavery, knavery, bravery, reverie, thievery, livery, shivery, silvery, equerry, misery, fancy-free, duty-free, imagery, savagery, mimicry, disagree, cavalry, chivalry, rivalry, jugglery, hostelry, revelry, jewelry, devilry, yeomanry, demonry, masonry, jamboree, theory, priory, chicory, hickory, pillory, memory, armory, honoree, vapory, factory, rectory, victory, history, savory, ivory, seigniory, doubletree, whiffletree, Christmas tree, forestry, ancestry, augury, injury, perjury, mercury, penury, potpourri, treasury, usury, century, luxury **4.** infirmary, debauchery, commandery, sculduddery, skulduggery, diablerie, artillery, tomfoolery, gendarmery, perfumery, chicanery, machinery, rotisserie, phylactery, adultery, effrontery, upholstery, delivery, recovery, discovery, corroboree, Terpsichore, extempore, compulsory, precursory, elusory, illusory, refractory, directory, perfunctory, unsavory **5.** anniversary, parliamentary, testamentary, elementary, rudimentary, complimentary, Saulte Sainte Marie, passementerie, satisfactory, contradictory, valedictory.

SE– **1.** c, C, see, sea, cee, si **2.** asea, assis, besee, lessee, précis, sycee **3.** fricassee, releasee, Tennessee, addressee, assessee, promisee, licensee, Sadducee, surfacy, legacy, fallacy, prelacy, primacy, pharmacy, Christmasy, lunacy, papacy, piracy, Holy See, euphrasy, fantasy, prophecy, courtesy, secrecy, pleurisy, marshalcy, colonelcy, minstrelsy, captaincy, surgeoncy, vacancy, peccancy, mordancy, infancy, romancy, nomancy, stagnancy, regnancy, pregnancy, sonancy, blatancy, piquancy, truancy, buoyancy, lambency, lucency, cadency, pendency, ardency, tangency, pungency, cogency, saliency, cliency, valency, nascency, latency, fluency, leprosy, abbacy, embassy, unforesee, undersea, oversea, oversee, endorsee, bankruptcy, Dubussy, jealousy, Argosy, autopsy **4.** celibacy, delicacy, intricacy, advocacy, candidacy, delegacy, supremacy, intimacy, obstinacy, federacy, literacy, magistracy, accuracy, obduracy, adequacy, intestacy, sibilancy, petulancy, consonancy, discrepancy, oscitancy, irritancy, hesitancy, accountancy, acceptancy, inconstancy, relevancy, conservancy, impudency, negligency, excellency, succulency, truculency, corpulency, flatulency, inclemency, permanency, prominency, pertinency, abstinency, competency, penitency, delinquency, idiocy **5.** inefficacy, prolificacy, indelicacy, immediacy, inebriacy, immaculacy, legitimacy, effeminacy, episcopacy, illiteracy, inaccuracy, inadequacy, irradiancy, preponderancy, recalcitrancy, irrelevancy, expediency, incipiency, equivalency, impermanency, impertinency, belligerency, incompetency, impenitency, omnipotency, constituency.

SHE– **1.** she, shee, ski **2.** hachis [F.], Vichy, *banshee*, *banshie* **3.** garnishee, rubbishy, flourishy, debauchee.

TE– **1.** t, T, tee, tea **2.** settee, titi, draftee, high tea, grantee, goatee, coatee, mestee, mustee, trustee, bootee, suttee,

Q.T. [slang] **3.** legatee, remittee, permittee, electee, inductee, guarantee, warrantee, absentee, presentee, patentee, appointee, picottee, allottee, devotee, repartee, deportee, amputee, nicety, fidgety, hatchety, witchety, crotchety, trinkety, subtlety, trumpety, snippety, russety, velvety, laity, crudity, deity, jollity, amity, dimity, enmity, comity, sanity, dignity, trinity, charity, purity, scarcity, falsity, density, sparsity, sanctity, entity, chastity, cavity, gravity, levity, brevity, laxity, spiralty, casualty, cruelty, faculty, occulty, guaranty, sovereignty, warranty, certainty, maggoty, carroty, liberty, puberty, property, poverty, dynasty, contrasty, majesty, amnesty, sacristy, deputy **4.** acerbity, cupidity, arridity, acridity, acidity, avidity, commodity, absurdity, anxiety, dedicatee, morality, fatality, mortality, brutality, equality, ability, debility, agility, facility, docility, fertility, hostility, utility, futility, civility, credulity, calamity, deformity, conformity, amenity, benignity, affinity, infinity, divinity, eternity, community, barbarity, disparity, celebrity, celerity, asperity, sincerity, austerity, dexterity, alacrity, authority, audacity, capacity, felicity, duplicity, complicity, ferocity, atrocity, adversity, diversity, annuity, fatuity, depravity, acclivity, declivity, passivity, activity, captivity, festivity, iniquity, antiquity, complexity, convexity, dishonesty **5.** actuality, affability, changeability, capability, anonymity, Christianity, consanguinity, similarity, animosity, curiosity, electricity, authenticity, elasticity, domesticity, ambiguity, assiduity, contiguity.

THE– 1. the, thee **2.** prithee **3.** apathy, empathy, sympathy, dyspathy, eupathy, timothy.

VE– 1. v, V, vee, vie [F.] **3.** vis-à-vis, joie de vie [F.], eau de vie [F.], Muscovy, anchovy.

WE– 1. wee, we, whee, puy [F.] **2.** ennui, pui [F.], etui, etwee, drawee **3.** mildewy, meadowy, shadowy, sallowy, yellowy, billowy, pillowy, willowy, arrowy, furrowy, point d'appui [F.].

YE– 1. ye **2.** payee, bouilli [F.] **3.** employee.

ZE– 1. z, Z, zee **2.** razee, fusee **3.** bourgeoisie [F.], cognizee, advisee, devisee, chimpanzee, Zuyder Zee **4.** recognizee.

EB– 1. dieb, feeb [slang], glebe, plebe, reeb [slang], grebe **2.** ephebe, tanjib, caraibe.

EBZ– diebs etc., *see* **EB–** dieb etc. above, plus "s" or "'s"; **1.** Thebes.

ECH– 1. each, beach, beech, keach, keech, leach, leech, bleach, fleech, pleach, sleech, peach, speech, reach, breach, breech, screech, preach, teach, queach **2.** appeach, impeach, outreach, beseech **3.** overreach.

ED– 1. Ede, bead, Bede, deed, feed, gied [dial.], heed, he'd, geed, keyed, lead, bleed, flead, gleed, glede [Scot.], plead, mead, meed, Mede, need, knead, snead, peed, speed, read, reed, rede, Reid, breed, brede, freed, greed, creed, screed, treed, threed, seed, cede, teed, teaed, steed, weed, Swede, tweed, yede **2.** Candide, indeed, misdeed, unfeed, *Lockheed*, unkeyed, *nosebleed*, implead, mislead, knockkneed, stampede, impede, Godspeed, jereed, reread, misread, outread, inbreed, crossbreed, enfreed, agreed, degreed, decreed, *hayseed*, reseed, *linseed*, *flaxseed*, recede, precede, secede, accede, succeed, concede, *seaweed*, *chickweed*, *milkweed*, *pokeweed*, ennuied **3.** underfeed, overfeed, interplead, millepede, centipede, interbreed, refereed, disagreed, pedigreed, filigreed, cottonseed, epicede, antecede, aniseed, retrocede, supersede, intercede, guaranteed, tumbleweed, locoweed **4.** velocipede, unpedigreed, unguaranteed.

EDZ– beads etc., *see* **ED–** Ede etc. above, plus "s" or "'s."

EF– 1. beef, chief, feoff, fief, Lif, leaf, lief, neif, reef, reif, brief, grief, sheaf, thief 2. naif, redif, enfeoff, belief, relief, *flyleaf, broadleaf,* hanif, shereef, tashrif, motif 3. handkerchief, neckerchief, unbelief, disbelief, misbelief, bas-relief, interleaf, overleaf, velvetleaf, Teneriffe 4. apéritif [F.].

EG– 1. digue [F.], league, skeeg, kleig, peag, Grieg, Teague 2. enleague, *colleague,* banig, renege, intrigue, fatigue, squeteague.

EJ– 1. liege, siege 2. besiege.

EK– 1. eke, beak, beek, cheek, Deke, deek, deak [both slang], feke [slang], geek, geke [both slang], keek [slang], leek, leak, bleak, gleek, clique, cleek, sleek, meek, sneak, pique, peak, peek, Peke, speak, reek, freak, Greek, creek, creak, shriek, streak, wreak, seek, Sikh, chic, sheik, teak, weak, week, tweak, squeak, Zeke 2. saic, caique, *halfbeak, grosbeak,* aleak, *houseleek,* oblique, silique, comique [F.], clinique [F.], technique, unique, apeak, repique, *forepeak,* forspeak, areek, perique, cacique, reseek, batik, critique, antique, bezique, physique 3. Mosambique, Martinique, demipique, fenugreek, Politique, novantique, Holy Week, yesterweek 5. Realpolitik [G.], Geopolitik.

EKS– ekes etc., *see* EK– eke etc. above, plus "s" or "'s."

EKT– 1. eked, beaked, cheeked, leaked, sneaked, peaked, peeked, piqued, cliqued, reeked, shrieked, streaked, wreaked, tweaked, squeaked 2. pink-cheeked, unpiqued, antiqued 3. eagle-beaked, apple-cheeked, rosy-cheeked.

EL– 1. eel, beal, deal, dele, feal, feel, heal, heel, jeel, jheel, jhil, keel, skeel, leal, leel, Lille, meal, mil, neele, kneel, peal, peel, speel, spiel, reel, creel, seal, seel, ceil, sheel [Scot.], teal, teil, til, steal, steel, veal, weal, weel, squeal, wheal, wheel, twille, zeal 2. abele, Mobile, redeal, ideal, ordeal, misdeal, refeel, forefeel, congeal,

clownheal, vakil, coquille, Camille, *inchmeal, cornmeal, piecemeal, oatmeal,* landmil, *fistmele,* anneal, anele, chenille, appeal, repeal, *kriegspiel, Singspiel, Festspiel* [G.], *bonspiel,* enseal, conceal, unseal, baril, datil, manteel, genteel, Bastille, castile, pastille, aiguille, *cogwheel* 3. dishabille, immobile, unideal, Guayaquil, havermeal, camomile, manchineel, cochineal, glockenspiel, difficile, goldenseal, endocoele, neurocoele, commonweal, paddle wheel, balance wheel, alguazil, cacozeal 4. locomobile, automobile.

ELD– 1. eeled, field, heeled, keeled, kneeled, peeled, spieled, sealed, shield, steeled, squealed, weald, wield, wheeled, yield 2. afield, *Sheffield, Springfield, Canfield, infield, cornfield, airfield, Garfield, Warfield, Mansfield, outfield,* congealed, annealed, aneled, appealed, repealed, *windshield,* revealed 3. battlefield, Copperfield, Chesterfield, unrepealed, unrevealed.

ELZ– eels etc., *see* EL– eel etc. above, plus "s" or "'s."

EM– 1. eme, beam, deme, deem, scheme, leam, gleam, neem, reem, ream, riem, rheme, bream, dream, fream, cream, scream, stream, seam, seem, teem, team, steam, theme, yeme 2. abeam, *moonbeam, hornbeam, sunbeam, crossbeam,* adeem, addeem, redeem, misdeem, blaspheme, regime, hakeem, agleam, supreme, extreme, *daydream,* ice-cream, escrime [F.], *millstream,* downstream, upstream, raceme, Nashim, beseem, unseam, centime, esteem 3. academe, hyporcheme, disesteem, self-esteem, anatheme.

EMD– 1. beamed, deemed, schemed, gleamed, reamed, dreamed, creamed, screamed, streamed, seamed, seemed, teemed, teamed, steamed 2. redeemed, blasphemed, daydreamed, beseemed, esteemed.

EMZ– emes etc., *see* EM– eme etc. above, plus "s" or "'s."

EN– 1. ean, e'en, been, bean, dean, dene, gean, jean, Jean, Jeanne, gene, Keene, keen, skean, lean, lien, glean, clean, spleen, mean, mien, mesne, pean, peen, breen [slang], green, screen, preen, threne, seen, scene, sheen, teen, 'steen, visne, wean, ween, queen, quean, yean 2. shebeen, gombeen, ich dien [G.], sardine, dudeen, caffeine, morphine, phosphene, Beguine, sagene, Valjean, Eugene, sakeen, nankeen, buckeen, baleen, scalene, maline, *Hellene*, colleen, Pauline, moulleen, unclean, Kathleen, bemean, demean, demesne, Benin, treneen, shoneen, alpeen, scalpeen, spalpeen, careen, marine, serene, terrene, Irene, pyrene, Dorine, toureen, shagreen, *peagreen*, *sea-green*, *gangrene*, bescreen, rescreen, unscreen, Racine, obscene, Essene, Nicene, piscine, unseen, foreseen, dasheen, machine, eighteen, lateen, ratteen, sateen, fifteen, canteen, nineteen, umpteen, thirteen, fourteen, sixteen, costean, routine, ravine, subvene, prevene, convene, May queen, atween, between, cuisine, benzine 3. Capuchin, Aberdeen, gabardine, Josephine, carrageen, polygene, photogene, supergene, palanguin, palankeen, damaskeen, Magdalene, opaline, philhellene, mousseline, crinoline, gasolene, mezzanine, Philippine, atropine, submarine, bismarine, cismarine, transmarine, candareen, nectarine, mazarine, Nazarene, tangerine, kittereen, smithereen, wolverine, tambourine, figurine, aquagreen, peregrine, mythogreen, wintergreen, evergreen, Hippocrene, damascene, Damascene, kerosene, overseen, unforeseen, velveteen, turbiteen, quarantine, Byzantine, Constantine, serpentine, seventeen, Argentine, Florentine, Celestine, guillotine, libertine, contravene, supervene, intervene, Halloween, harvest queen, gobetween, therebetween, bombazine, magazine, limousine 4. heterogene, ultramarine, aquamarine; *also many other feminine names ending in the suffix "-ine"* (e.g. Georgine, Albertine).

END– 1. eaned, beaned, fiend, keened, leaned, gleaned, cleaned, screened, weaned, weened, queened, teind, yeaned 2. archfiend, demeaned, careened 3. guillotined, contravened, intervened.

ENTH– 1. greenth, 'steenth 2. eighteenth, fifteenth, nineteenth, thirteenth, fourteenth, sixteenth 3. seventeenth.

ENZ– eans etc., *see* **EN–** ean etc. above, plus "s" or "'s."

EP– 1. cheep, cheap, deep, heap, jeep, keep, leap, leep, clepe, sleep, neap, neep, sneap, peep, reap, creep, threap, threep, seep, sepe [slang], sheep, teap, steep, weep, sweep 2. aheap, upkeep, asleep, bopeep, la grippe [F.], estrepe, upsweep 3. overleap, unasleep, oversleep, chimney sweep.

EPS– cheeps etc., *see* **EP–** cheep etc. above, plus "s" or "'s."

EPT– 1. cheeped, heaped, jeeped, leaped, neaped, peeped, reaped, seeped, steeped 3. overleaped.

ER– 1. ear, beer, bier, cheer, deer, dear, fear, sphere, gear, here, hear, jeer, skeer [dial.], leer, lear, blear, flear, clear, sclere, mere, mir, smear, near, neer, sneer, peer, pier, pear, pir, spear, rear, drear, seer, sear, sere, ser, cere, shear, sheer, tear, teer, tier, Tyr, stere, steer, vire, veer, weir, queer, year 2. *wheatear*, *killdeer*, reindeer, endear, ensphere, *headgear*, *footgear*, adhere, inhere, cohere, Mynheer, fakir, King Lear, unclear, amir, emir, emeer, premier, besmear, anear, denier, veneer, appear, compeer, outpeer, arrear, career, uprear, plancier, sincere, cashier, frontier, austere, revere, brevier, severe, *midyear*, brassiere, vizier 3. shillibeer, ginger beer, brigadier, grenadier, bombardier, commandeer, interfere, hemisphere, atmosphere, pedalier, cavalier, lavaliere, chevalier, chandelier, fusilier, chanticleer, gondolier, pistoleer, buccaneer, souvenir, jardiniere, engineer, domineer, mountaineer, mutineer, scrutineer, chiffonier, cannoneer, pioneer, auctioneer, reappear, disappear, agricere, financier, insincere, caboceer, tabasheer, privateer, targeteer, musketeer, sonneteer, profiteer, gazetteer, volunteer, persevere, yesteryear.

ERD– 1. eared, beard, cheered, feared, sphered, geared, jeered, leered, bleared, cleared, smeared, neared, sneered, peered, reared, seared, sheared, sheered, tiered, steered, veered, weird, queered **2.** uneared, lop-eared, *graybeard*, *treebeard*, *Bluebeard*, endeared, afeared, unfeared, ensphered, adhered, veneered, revered, appeared, outpeered, careered, upreared, cashiered, brassiered **3.** commandeered, interfered, engineered, domineered, mountaineered, pioneered, reappeared, disappeared, privateered, profiteered, volunteered, persevered.

ERS– 1. Bierce, fierce, pierce, tierce **2.** transpierce.

ERZ– ears etc., *see* **ER–** ear etc. above, plus "s" or "'s"; **2.** Algiers, Tangiers.

ES– 1. geese, lease, lis, lisse [F.], fleece, Nice, niece, peace, piece, grease, Greece, crease, creese, Kris, cease **2.** obese, esquisse [F.], sublease, release, valise, Felice, pelisse, police, coulisse, Bernice, apiece, *endpiece*, repiece, *neckpiece*, *timepiece*, *crosspiece*, *mouthpiece*, Clarice, cerise, decrease, recrease, increase, Lucrece, Maurice, caprice, cassis, decease, surcease, atis, métis **3.** prerelease, mantelpiece, cornerpiece, centerpiece, afterpiece, masterpiece, frontispiece, ambergris, predecease.

ESH– 1. biche [F.], fiche, leash, sneesh, riche [F.] **2.** affiche [F.], unleash, potiche [F.], schottische, schottish, pastiche, postiche **3.** nouveau riche [F.].

EST– 1. east, beast, feast, geest, least, leased, fleeced, sneest, piste, pieced, greased, creased, priest, triste [F.], ceased, teest, quest, yeast **2.** northeast, southeast, modiste, subleased, released, policed, decreased, recreased, increased, archpriest,

deceased, batiste, artiste **3.** wildebeest, hartebeest, aubergiste.

ET– 1. eat, beat, beet, cheat, cheet, feat, feet, Geat, heat, keet, skeet, scete, skete, leat, leet, bleat, fleet, gleet, cleat, pleat, sleet, meat, meet, mete, neat, peat, Pete, reit, freit, greet, Crete, treat, street, cete, seat, sheet, teat, queet, vite [F.], weet, sweet, suite, tweet, wheat **2.** *deadbeat*, *offbeat*, *drumbeat*, *upbeat*, *heartbeat*, *browbeat*, escheat, effete, defeat, reheat, munjeet, mesquite, elite, delete, deplete, replete, complete, *athlete*, *helpmeet*, *mincemeat*, *forcemeat*, *sweetmeat*, repeat, compete, terete, afreet, congreet, accrete, secrete, concrete, discreet, excrete, retreat, maltreat, entreat, estreat, mistreat, downstreet, upstreet, reseat, receipt, disseat, conceit, unseat, *broadsheet*, *clipsheet*, mansuete, unsweet, tout de suite [F.], *peetweet*, *buckwheat* **3.** overeat, parrakeet, lorikeet, incomplete, uncomplete, marguerite, Marguerite, indiscreet, county seat, mercy seat, judgment seat, balance sheet, tout de suite [F.], bittersweet.

ETH– 1. heath, Keith, 'neath, sneath, sneeth, wreath, sheath, teeth **2.** beneath, eyeteeth, bequeath **3.** underneath.

ETHE– 1. sneathe, wreathe, breathe, seethe, sheathe, teethe, quethe **2.** enwreathe, imbreathe, inbreathe, outbreathe, ensheathe, bequeath.

ETS– eats, etc., *see* **ET–** eat etc. above, plus "s" or "'s"; **1.** Keats.

EV– 1. eve, Eve, eave, beeve, cheve, deave, gieve [slang], heave, keeve, leave, lieve, cleave, cleve, cleeve, sleave, sleeve, nieve, peeve, reave, reeve, reve, breve, greave, grieve, screeve, seave, sheave, steeve, Steve, thieve, weave, we've, queeve **2.** naïve, achieve, khedive, upheave, believe, relieve, bereave, aggrieve, reprieve, retrieve, *portreeve*, deceive, receive, conceive, perceive, qui vive [F.], reweave, inweave, unweave **3.** makebelieve, unbelieve, disbelieve, interleave, semibreve, reconceive, preconceive, misconceive, apperceive, reperceive, preperceive, interweave **4.** recitative.

EVD– 1. eaved, cheved, deaved, heaved, keeved, leaved, cleaved, sleaved, sleeved, peeved, reaved, greaved, grieved, screeved, sheaved, steeved, thieved **2.** achieved, upheaved, believed, relieved, bereaved, aggrieved, reprieved, retrieved, deceived, received, conceived, perceived **3.** unbelieved, disbelieved, interleaved, reconceived, preconceived, unconceived, misconceived, apperceived, reperceived, preperceived, unperceived.

EVZ– eves etc., *see* **EV–** eve etc. above, plus "s" or "'s"; **1.** Jeeves.

EZ– E's etc., *see* **E–** E etc. through **ZE–** zee etc. above, plus "s" or "'s"; **1.** ease, bise [F.], cheese, feaze, feeze, heeze, Geez [slang], Jeez [slang], please, mease, mise, neeze, neese, sneeze, pease, pes, Spes, reese, res [L.], breeze, freeze, frieze, grease, seize, tease, these, squeeze, weeze, tweeze, wheeze **2.** unease, heartsease, nipcheese, marquise, valise, Belize, displease, demise, chemise, remise, Burmese, Chinese, appease, trapeze, cerise, enfreeze, unfreeze, imprese, assise, reseize, disseize, bêtise [F.], sottise [F.], Maltese, disease, Louise **3.** Annamese, Portuguese, Singhalese, journalese, Pericles, Damocles, Androcles, Tyrolese, Herculese, Siamese, Assamese, manganese, Japanese, Havanese, Viennese, Pekinese, Cantonese, antifreeze, indices, vortices, overseas, Genevese **4.** Atlantides, Hesperides, antipodes, parentheses, hypotheses, analyses, Xenocrates **5.** Mephistopheles.

EZH– 1. tige **2.** prestige.

E (bee)

2.

DOUBLE (FEMININE) RHYMES IN E (Le'ah)

Primary or Secondary Accent Falls on
Next to Last Syllable; Imperfect Rhymes
Are in Italics.

E'a– 2. chia, Dea, deah [slang], hia, Lea,
Leah, rhea, Rea, Rhea, Sia, Thea, via, Zea
3. Rabia, rebia, obeah, Lucia, badia,
Medea, idea, Chaldea, Judea, bahia, ohia,
Hygeia, Mammea, Crimea, Carnea, Tarpeia, Maria, Sharia, Spiraea, spirea, Ko-
rea, Althea, Hosea 4. ratafia, Eogaea,
Neogaea, Arctogaea, energeia, melopoeia,
pathopoeia, diarrhea, logorrhea, pyorrhea,
panacea, fantasia, Galatea, Dorothea 5.
Antarctogea, Ave Maria, pharmacopoeia,
peripeteia 7. onomatopoeia; see also
E'ya– Hygeia etc. below.

E'ad– 2. Pleiad 3. ideaed 4. unideaed;
see also E'id– Aeneid etc. below.

E'al– 1. feal, pheal, real 2. ideal, un-
real, correal 3. unideal, beau ideal, epi-
geal, perigeal, meningeal, laryngeal, Arcto-
gaeal, hymeneal, empyreal.

E'an– 2. lien, paean 3. Sabaean, plebei-
an, Chaldean, Andean, Pandean, Shan-
dean, Judean, Orphean, Aegean, Hygeian,
trachean, Archean, Crimean, pampean,
Korean, petrean, lyncean, Dantean, pro-
tean, Lethean, Pantheian, pantheon 4.
Maccabean, amoebean, Caribbean, Nio-
bean, Jacobean, amphigean, perigean,
phalangean, laryngean, apogean, Achillean,
Galilean, Antillean, Sophoclean, Herculean, European, Eritrean, Tennessean,
Pharisean, Sadducean, gigantean, Atlan-
tean 5. Archimedean, antipodean, terp-
sichorean, Epicurean 6. Mephistophelean.

E'ant– 4. philogeant.

E'as– Aeneas; see also E'us– Deus etc. below.

EB'a– 2. iba, peba, Reba, Seba, Sheba
3. amoeba, zareba, tiriba, Bath-sheba 4.
Jehosheba.

EB'an– 2. Sheban, Theban 3. amoeban.

EB'e– 2. Phoebe, Hebe, TB 4. heeby-
jeeby, heebee-jeebee [both slang].

EB'er– 2. Eber, Heber, weber.

EB'ez– 4. heeby-jeebies, heebee-jeebees
[both slang].

EB'ic– 3. amoebic, amebic.

EB'l– 2. feeble 3. enfeeble.

EB'o– 2. eboe, Ibo, Nebo 3. placebo,
gazebo.

EB'ra– 2. libbra, zebra.

EB'us– 2. Phoebus, glebous, rebus 3.
ephebus.

ECH'er– 2. beacher, Beecher, feature,
leacher, leecher, bleacher, peacher,
reacher, breacher, breecher, creature,
screecher, preacher, teacher 3. defeature, impeacher, beseecher.

ECH'ez– beaches, etc., see ECH– each etc.,
plus "s" or "'s."

ECH'i– 2. beachy, beechy, leachy, leechy,
litchi, bleachy, sleechy, peachy, speechy,
reachy, reechy, breachy, screechy,
preachy, teachy 3. campeachy.

ECH'ing– 2. beaching, leaching, leech-
ing, bleaching, fleeching, pleaching, peach-

80

ing, reaching, breeching, screeching, preaching, teaching **3.** impeaching, outreaching, farreaching, beseeching **4.** overreaching.

ECH'less– **2.** beachless, beechless, leachless, peechless, bleachless, sleechless, peachless, speechless, reachless, breechless, breachless, screechless, preachless, teachless.

ECH'ment– **2.** preachment **3.** appeachment, impeachment, beseechment.

ED'a– **2.** Leda, Theda, Veda, Vida, Ouida **3.** Aïda, kasida, reseda **4.** alameda **5.** olla-podrida.

ED'al– **2.** daedal, creedal.

ED'ay– **2.** bidet, D–day, fee day.

ED'ed– **2.** beaded, deeded, heeded, pleaded, needed, kneaded, reeded, seeded, ceded, weeded, tweeded **3.** unheeded, stampeded, impeded, receded, preceded, seceded, acceded, exceeded, succeeded, conceded, proceeded, unweeded **4.** anteceded, retroceded, superseded, interceded.

ED'en– **2.** Eden, reeden, Sweden.

ED'ens– **2.** credence **3.** recedence, precedence, concedence **4.** antecedence, antecedents, retrocedence, supersedence.

ED'ent– **2.** needn't, credent, cedent, sedent **3.** decedent, recedent, precedent **4.** antecedent, retrocedent, intercedent.

ED'ents– **3.** precedents **4.** antecedents.

ED'er– **2.** beader, feeder, heeder, leader, bleeder, pleader, needer, kneader, speeder, reader, cedar, ceder, cedre, seeder, weeder **3.** bandleader, ringleader, misleader, impleader, stampeder, impeder, receder, preceder, seceder, acceder, exceeder, succeeder, conceder, proceeder **4.** interpleader, superseder, interceder.

ED'ez– **2.** aedes, greedies **3.** Palamedes, Archimedes, Dolomedes.

ED'ful– **2.** deedful, heedful, needful, speedful, seedful **3.** unheedful, unneedful.

ED'i– **2.** beady, deedy, heedy, Midi,

needy, speedy, reedy, greedy, creedy, seedy, sidi, weedy, tweedy **3.** indeedy, unheedy, seaweedy **4.** orthopaedy.

ED'ik– **2.** Vedic **3.** comedic **4.** talipedic, cyclopedic, orthopedic **5.** encyclopedic.

ED'ing– **2.** beading, deeding, feeding, heeding, leading, bleeding, pleading, kneading, needing, speeding, reeding, reading, breeding, seeding, sheading, weeding **3.** unheeding, misleading, stampeding, impeding, rereading, misreading, inbreeding, cross breeding, reseeding, receding, preceding, seceding, acceding, succeeding, conceding **4.** underfeeding, overfeeding, anteceding, retroceding, superceding, interceding.

ED'l– **2.** beadle, daedal, needle, pedal, wheedle, tweedle **3.** bi-pedal, conquedle **4.** semipedal, centipedal.

ED'ler– **2.** needler, wheedler.

ED'less– **2.** beadless, Bedeless, deedless, feedless, heedless, leadless, needless, speedless, readless, breedless, greedless, creedless, seedless, steedless, weedless, tweedless.

ED'ling– **2.** needling, reedling, seedling, wheedling, tweedling.

ED'o– **2.** Ido, Lido, credo **3.** albedo, libido, Toledo, torpedo, Laredo, teredo, Bushido [Jap.].

ED'ra– **3.** exedra, cathedra **4.** ex cathedra.

ED'ral– **3.** dihedral, trihedral, cathedral **4.** decahedral, polyhedral, hemihedral.

ED'rik– **3.** diedric **4.** polyhedric, holohedric.

ED'ron– **2.** cedron **3.** dihedron, trihedron **4.** polyhedron.

ED'rus– **2.** Cedrus **4.** polyhedrous.

ED'um– **2.** Ledum, pedum, freedom, Sedum.

ED'ur– **3.** procedure **4.** supersedure.

E′er– 2. fleer, freer, seer 3. agreer, decreer, foreseer, sight-seer 4. disagreer, overseer.

E′est– 2. freest, weest.

EF′e– 2. Fifi 3. Afifi; *see also* EF′i– beefy etc. below.

EF′er– 2. beefer, chiefer, liefer, reefer, briefer.

EF′i– 2. beefy, Fifi, leafy, reefy, sheafy; *see also* EF′e– Fifi etc. above.

EF′less– 2. beefless, chiefless, leafless, reefless, briefless, griefless, sheafless, thiefless 3. beliefless, motifless.

EF′li– 2. chiefly, briefly.

EG′a– 2. Riga, Vega, ziega 3. bodega, omega.

EG′al– 2. legal, regal, gregal 3. illegal, unlegal, vice-regal; *see also* EG′l– eagle etc. below.

EG′er– 2. eager, eagre, leaguer, meager, meagre, zieger 3. beleaguer, intriguer, fatiguer 4. overeager, major leaguer, minor leaguer.

EG′ing– 2. leaguing 3. enleaguing, intriguing, fatiguing.

EG′l– 2. eagle, beagle, kleagle, teagle, veigle 3. bald eagle, sea eagle, porbeagle, espiegle, inveigle 4. double eagle, golden eagle; *see also* EG′al– legal etc. above.

EG′ler– 2. beagler 3. inveigler.

EG′o– 2. ego, grego 3. Otsego, Oswego.

EG′ress– 2. egress, negress, regress.

EG′ro– 2. Negro 4. Montenegro.

E′hi– 2. Lehigh, kneehigh.

E′hol– 2. keyhole, kneehole, frijol, frijole.

E′id– 3. Aeneid; *see also* E′ad– Pleiad etc. above.

E′ik– 2. rheic 3. caffeic, Palaeic, oleic, tropeic, choreic, caseic, proteic 4. mythopoeic 5. xanthoproteic 6. onomatopoeic.

E′ing– 2. being, feeing, geeing, skiing, fleeing, freeing, spreeing, treeing, seeing, teeing 3. well-being, nonbeing, tehee-ing, agreeing, decreeing, unseeing, foreseeing, sight-seeing 4. refereeing, disagreeing, overseeing, unforeseeing, guaranteeing.

E′ist– 2. deist, theist, zeist 3. ideist 4. Manicheist, polytheist, antitheist, monotheist.

E′it– 3. albeit, sobeit, howbeit.

E′izm– 2. deism, theism, weism 3. Parseeism, sutteeism 4. Manicheism, Phariseeism, Sadduceeism, absenteeism, polytheism, philotheism, cosmotheism, misotheism.

EJ′an– 3. collegian, Norwegian, Glaswegian; *see also* EJ′un– legion etc. below.

EJ′ans– 3. allegiance.

EJ′e– 2. Fiji, Gigi, squeegee.

EJ′er– 2. aeger [L.], Aegir, leger, sieger 3. besieger.

EJ′ik– 3. strategic 4. hemiplegic, cycloplegic 5. bibliopegic.

EJ′is– 2. aegis, egis 3. St. Regis.

EJ′un– 2. legion, region 3. collegian, Norwegian, Glaswegian.

EK′a– 2. chica, quica, sika, theca 3. Topeka, Areca, paprica, eureka, zotheca 4. Dominica, Salonika, Costa Rica, endotheca, Tanganyika 5. bibliotheca.

EK′al– 2. fecal, faecal, caecal, thecal, treacle 4. intrathecal 5. bibliothecal; *see also* EK′l– chicle etc. below.

EK′an– 3. Mahican, Mohican; *see also* EK′en– bleaken etc. below.

EK′ant– 2. piquant, precant, secant 3. cosecant 4. intersecant.

EK′ed– 2. beaked, peaked, streaked.

EK′en– 2. bleaken, sleeken, meeken, weaken 3. Mahican, Mohican; *see also* EK′on– beacon etc. below.

EK′er– 2. beaker, bleaker, Bleecker, sleeker, meeker, sneaker, peaker, peeker, speaker, reeker, creacker, krieker, shrieker, weaker, squeaker, tweaker.

EK'erz– beakers etc., *see* EK'er– beaker etc. above, plus "s" or "'s."

EK'est– 2. bleakest, sleekest, meekest, weakest.

EK'i– 2. beaky, cheeky, leaky, cliquey, sneaky, peaky, peeky, reeky, creaky, creeky, streaky, shieky, squeaky 6. veni, vidi, vici (L.).

EK'ing– 2. eking, beaking, cheeking, leaking, cliquing, sleeking, sneaking, peaking, peeking, piquing, speaking, reeking, wreaking, creaking, shrieking, streaking, seeking, squeaking, tweaking 3. bespeaking, unspeaking, self-seeking.

EK'ish– 2. bleakish, cliquish, meekish, sneakish, peakish, freakish, Greekish, weakish.

EK'l– 2. chicle, treacle 3. Ezek'l; *see* also EK'al– fecal etc. above.

EK'li– 2. bleakly, sleekly, meekly, treacly, weakly, weekly 3. obliquely, uniquely, biweekly, triweekly 4. semiweekly.

EK'ling– 2. weakling.

EK'ness– 2. bleakness, sleekness, meekness, weakness 3. obliqueness, uniqueness, antiqueness.

EK'o– 2. fico, mico, Nico, pico, pekoe 3. Tampico, matico 4. orange pekoe.

EK'ok– 2. Leacock, meacock, peacock, sea cock.

EK'on– 2. beacon, deacon 3. archdeacon; *see* also EK'en– bleaken etc. above.

EK'und– 2. fecund 3. infecund.

EK'wal– 2. equal, sequel 3. subequal, inequal, unequal, coequal.

EK'wens– 2. frequence, sequence 3. infrequence.

EK'went– 2. frequent, sequent 3. infrequent.

EL'a– 2. Bela, belah, gila, Leila, Leilah, selah, Shelah, Sheila, Stela 3. tequila, palila, sequela 4. Philomela, Venezuela.

EL'and– 2. eland, Zeeland 3. New Zealand.

ELD'ed– 2. fielded, shielded, wielded, yielded 3. unfielded, unshielded, unwielded, unyielded.

ELD'er– 2. fielder, shielder, wielder, yielder 3. infielder, outfielder, nonyielder.

ELD'i– 2. wieldy, yieldy 3. unwieldy.

ELD'ing– 2. fielding, shielding, wielding, yielding 3. enshielding, unyielding.

EL'e– 2. dele, peele, pili, stele 3. Belili 4. campanile, monostele, protostele; *see* also EL'i– eely etc. below.

EL'er– 2. eeler, dealer, feeler, healer, heeler, keeler, kneeler, pealer, peeler, spieler, reeler, sealer, seeler, stealer, stelar, velar, wheeler, squealer 3. misdealer, congealer, annealer, appealer, repealer, concealer, revealer, two-wheeler.

EL'est– 2. lealest 3. genteelest.

EL'i– 2. eely, Ealey, Ely, feally, mealy, freely, Greeley, seely, steely, squealy, wheely 3. genteelly; *see* also EL'e– dele etc. above.

EL'ij– 2. keelage, stealage, wheelage.

EL'ik– 2. velic 3. parhelic.

EL'iks– 2. Felix, helix 4. antihelix.

EL'in– 2. beeline, feline, tree line, sea line.

EL'ing– 2. eeling, Ealing, dealing, feeling, healing, heeling, keeling, kneeling, pealing, peeling, reeling, ceiling, sealing, seeling, shealing, steeling, stealing, wheeling, squealing 3. misdealing, unfeeling, congealing, Darjeeling, annealing, appealing, repealing, concealing, unsealing, revealing 4. double dealing 5. automobiling.

EL'ment– 3. congealment, repealment, concealment, revealment.

EL'ness– 2. lealness 3. genteelness.

EL'os– 2. Delos, melos, telos.

EL'um– 2. Caelum, velum.

EL'ya– 2. Delia, Lelia, Celia 3. lobelia,

Bedelia, Cordelia, Orphelia, Amelia, Camellia, Cornelia, Aurelia, Cecelia.

EL'yan– 2. Delian 3. Mendelian, chameleon, carnelian, cornelian, aurelian.

EL'yus– 2. Delius 3. Cornelius, Aurelius.

EM'a– 2. bema, chima, schema, Lima, Pima, rima, rhema, thema, Xema 3. edema, emblema, sclerema, sorema, blastema, Fatima, enthema, eczema 4. seriema, epiblema, hyporchema.

EM'al– 2. demal, hemal, lemel 3. blastemal 4. pseudohemal.

EM'an– 3. beeman, freeman, G–man, heman, leman, seaman, semen, T–man, Teman, teaman; see also EM'on– demon etc. below.

EM'ent– 3. agreement, decreement 4. disagreement.

EM'er– 2. beamer, deemer, femur, schemer, lemur, reamer, dreamer, creamer, screamer, streamer, seemer, seamer, teemer, steamer 3. redeemer, blasphemer, daydreamer, supremer, extremer.

EM'est– 3. supremest, extremest.

EM'ful– 2. beamful, schemeful, dreamful, teemful.

EM'i– 2. beamy, gleamy, Mime, Mimi, mneme, dreamy, creamy, screamy, streamy, seamy, teemy, steamy 3. daydreamy.

EM'ik– 2. phemic, hemic, semic 3. anemic, phonemic, eremic, racemic 4. polyhemic, monoschemic, octasemic, septicemic, monosemic.

EM'ing– 2. beaming, deeming, scheming, gleaming, reaming, dreaming, creaming, screaming, streaming, seeming, seaming, teeming, steaming, theming 3. redeeming, blaspheming, daydreaming, beseeming, esteeming 4. unredeeming, unbeseeming.

EM'ish– 2. beamish, squeamish.

EM'ist– 2. schemist, Rhemist 3. extremist.

EM'less– 2. beamless, schemeless, dreamless, gleamless, creamless, streamless, seamless, seemless, teemless, steamless, themeless.

EM'let– 2. beamlet, streamlet, themelet.

EM'li– 2. seemly 3. unseemly, supremely, extremely.

EM'o– 2. hemo, Nemo, primo [It.].

EM'on– 2. demon, daemon, leman, seaman, semen 3. eudemon 4. cacodemon; see also EM'an– beeman etc. above.

EM'ster– 2. deemster, seamster, teamster.

EM'us– 2. Remus 3. oremus [L.] 4. Academus, Nicodemus.

EN'a– 2. ina [Tag.], gena, Gina, keena, quina, lena, Lena, lina, Lina, Nina, crena, cena [L.], scena, Tina, vina 3. pembina, verbena, modena, hyena, Georgina, galena, Salina, Paulina, guapena, subpoena, arena, farina, marina, Marina, tsarina, czarina, Andrena, cassena, Messina, piscina, encina, catena, poltina, cantina, sestina, Christina, Faustina, flutina, Athena, Avena, novena, Rowena 4. quintadena, contadina [It.], Cartagena, melongena, marikina, Magdalena, Catalina, cantilena, semolina, Wilhelmina, philopena, ocarina, ballerina, signorina [It.], orchestrina, sonatina, cavatina, Argentina, Clementina, concertina, Celestina, aguavina.

EN'al– 2. plenal, penal, renal, venal 3. marinal, adrenal, machinal 4. duodenal.

EN'at– 2. enate, crenate.

EN'e– 2. genie, lene, mene [Aram.], Nini, visne 3. Selene, Silene, Camenae, Irene, Rossini 4. fantoccini, campanini, Hippocrene; see also EN'i– eeny etc. below.

EN'er– 2. keener, leaner, gleaner, cleaner, meaner, greener, screener, weaner, wiener 3. demeanor, serener, obscener, machiner, convener 4. misdemeanor, contravener, supervener, intervener, magaziner.

EN′est– 2. keenest, leanest, cleanest, meanest, greenest 3. serenest, obscenest.

EN′i– 2. eeny, beany, pleny, spleeny, meeny, meanie, sheeny, greeny, teeny, weeny, Queenie, sweeny, Sweeney 3. galeeny; see also EN′e– genie etc. above.

EN′id– 2. Enid, maenad.

EN′ij– 2. greenage, teenage 3. careenage.

EN′ik– 2. phenic, splenic, Menic, scenic.

EN′iks– 2. phoenix, phenix.

EN′ing– 2. eaning, beaning, deaning, keening, leaning, gleaning, cleaning, meaning, greening, screening, preening, weaning, weening, queening, yeaning 3. bemeaning, demeaning, well-meaning, unmeaning, careening, unscreening, machining, costeaning, subvening, advening, convening 4. double meaning, quarantining, intervening, supervening, overweaning.

EN′ish– 2. beanish, deanish, keenish, leanish, cleanish, spleenish, meanish, greenish, queenish.

EN′ist– 2. plenist 3. machinist, routinist 4. magazinist.

EN′li– 2. keenly, leanly, cleanly, meanly, greenly, queenly 3. serenely, obscenely.

EN′ling– 2. weanling, yeanling.

EN′ness– 2. keenness, leanness, cleanness, meanness, greenness 3. uncleanness, sereneness, obsceneness.

EN′o– 2. beano, keno, leno, mino, Nino, Reno 3. albino, bambino [It.], tondino, camino [Sp.], comino, Merino, casino 4. palombino, baldachino, maraschino, pianino, sopranino, Filipino, San Marino, peacherino, vetturino [It.], andantino, Valentino.

EN′um– 2. plenum, frenum, fraenum 4. duodenum.

EN′us– 2. Enos, genus, Venus, venous 3. scalenus, Silenus.

EN′ya– 2. piña, Niña.

EN′yal– 2. genial, menial 3. congenial 4. uncongenial; see also EN′i–al– genial etc.

EN′yens– 2. enience 3. prevenience, convenience 4. inconvenience, intervenience.

EN′yent– 2. lenient 3. convenient 4. inconvenient, intervenient.

EN′yor– 2. senior, signor, seignior 3. monsignor.

EN′yus– 2. genius 3. ingenious.

E′o– 2. Eo, Leo, Cleo, neo, Reo, Rio, trio, Theo 3. bohio [Sp.].

E′ol– 2. Creole, Sheol.

E′on– 2. eon, aeon, pheon, Leon, pleon, neon, peon, Creon 3. pantheon 4. Ponce de Leon.

EP′a– 2. Nepa, nipa, niepa, pipa, cepa.

EP′al– 2. ipil, pipal, sepal; see also EP′l– people etc. below.

EP′en– 2. cheapen, deepen, steepen 3. alipin [Tag.].

EP′er– 2. deeper, cheeper, cheaper, heaper, keeper, leaper, sleeper, Dnieper, peeper, reeper, reaper, creeper, tepor, steeper, weeper, sweeper 3. beekeeper, bookkeeper, timekeeper, innkeeper, shopkeeper, barkeeper, doorkeeper, horsekeeper, housekeeper, gatekeeper, mooncreeper.

EP′est– 2. deepest, cheapest, steepest.

EP′i– 2. cheepy, heapy, sleepy, creepy, seepy, sheepy, tepee, steepy, weepy, sweepy 5. Fra Lippo Lippi.

EP′ij– 2. seepage, sweepage.

EP′ing– 2. cheeping, cheaping, deeping, heaping, jeeping, keeping, leaping, sleeping, neaping, peeping, reaping, creeping, threaping, seeping, steeping, weeping, sweeping 3. beekeeping, safekeeping, shopkeeping, housekeeping 4. overleaping, oversleeping, oversteeping.

EP′ish– 2. cheapish, deepish, sheepish, steepish.

EP'l– 2. people, steeple, wheeple 3. re-people, empeople, unpeople, merpeople, dispeople, townspeople; *see also* EP'al–ipil etc. above.

EP'less– 2. cheepless, deepless, jeepless, keepless, leapless, sleepless, peepless, seep-less, sheepless, weepless.

EP'li– 2. cheaply, deeply, steeply.

EP'ness– 2. cheapness, deepness, steep-ness.

EP'oi– 2. sepoy, teapoy.

ER'a– 2. era, gerah, Hera, quira, lira, sclera, sera, Terah, Vera 3. Madeira, ga-lera, chimera, chimaera, lempira, Sarira, Sharira, asherah, hetaera 4. rangatira.

ER'ay– 4. Miserere.

ER'al– 2. eral, feral, scleral, spheral, ceral 3. vicegeral 4. hemispheral.

ER'ans– 2. clearance 3. adherence, in-herence, coherence, appearance, arrear-ance 4. interference, incoherence, reap-pearance, nonappearance, disappearance, perseverance.

ER'ant– 3. sederunt 4. perseverant; *see also* ER'ent– gerent etc. below.

ER'e– Erie etc., *see* ER'i– aerie etc below.

ER'ens– 3. adherence, inherence, coher-ence 4. interference, incoherence; *see also* ER'ans– clearance etc. above.

ER'ent– 2. gerent, querent 3. adherent, inherent, coherent, vicegerent 4. nonad-herent, incoherent, perseverant.

ER'er– 2. cheerer, dearer, fearer, hearer, jeerer, leerer, clearer, smearer, nearer, sneerer, peerer, spearer, rearer, teerer, steerer, veerer, queerer 3. endearer, ad-herer, coherer, besmearer, appearer, aus-terer, reverer, severer 4. interferer, overhearer, disappearer, perseverer 5. electioneerer.

ER'ess– 2. peeress, seeress.

ER'est– 2. dearest, merest, nearest, drear-est, sheerest, queerest 3. sincerest, aus-terest, severest.

ER'ez– 2. heres, Ceres, series; *see also* ER'iz– dearies etc. below.

ER'ful– 2. earful, cheerful, fearful, sneer-ful, tearful 3. uncheerful, unfearful.

ER'i– 2. aerie, eerie, Erie, beery, cheery, deary, sphery, jeery, keiri, kiri, leary, leery, bleary, smeary, sneery, peri, peery, speary, dreary, seri, teary, veery, weary, quaere [L.], query 3. uncheery, hetaery, aweary, world-weary 4. hara-kiri, over-weary, Miserere.

ER'id– 2. wearied, queried 3. unwea-ried, world-wearied, unqueried.

ER'ij– 2. clearage, peerage, pierage, steer-age 3. arrearage.

ER'ing– 2. earing, beering, dearing, Ber-ing, cheering, fearing, gearing, hearing, jeering, leering, blearing, clearing, near-ing, sneering, peering, spearing, rearing, searing, shearing, tiering, steering, veering, queering 3. endearing, adhering, inher-ing, cohering, besmearing, veneering, ap-pearing, careering, cashiering, revering 4. interfering, overhearing, engineering, domineering, mountaineering, pioneering, cannoneering, auctioneering, reappearing, disappeaering, privatering, profiteering, volunteering 5. electioneering.

ER'iz– 2. dearies, series, wearies, queries; *see also* ER'ez– heres etc. above.

ER'less– 2. earless, beerless, cheerless, dearless, deerless, fearless, gearless, jeer-less, leerless, Learless, mereless, peerless, spearless, tearless, yearless.

ER'li– 2. dearly, clearly, merely, nearly, drearly, queerly, yearly 3. sincerely, austerely, severely 4. cavalierly, insin-cerely.

ER'ling– 2. shearling, steerling, yearling.

ER'ment– 2. cerement 3. endearment.

ER'ness– 2. dearness, clearness, nearness, queerness 3. sincereness, austereness, se-vereness.

ER'o– 2. hero, Nero, Piro, cero, sero, Ciro, zero 5. lillibullero.

ERS'er– **2.** fiercer, piercer **3.** ear piercer.

ERS'ing– **2.** piercing **3.** transpiercing.

ER'us– **2.** sclerous, serous, cirrus, cirrhous.

ERZ'man– **2.** steersman **3.** frontiersman **4.** privateersman.

ES'a– **3.** camisa [Sp.], Theresa.

ES'eez– **2.** preces, praeses [L.], theses.

ES'ens– **2.** decence **3.** obeisance, indecence.

ES'ent– **2.** decent, recent **3.** obeisant, indecent, unrecent.

ES'ept– **2.** precept.

ES'er– **2.** leaser, fleecer, piecer, greaser, creaser **3.** releaser, decreaser, increaser.

ES'ez– **2.** leases, fleeces, nieces, pieces, peaces, greases, creases, ceases **3.** subleases, releases, pelisses, valises, repieces, decreases, increases, caprices **4.** mantelpieces, centerpieces, masterpieces, frontispieces.

ES'ful– **2.** peaceful **3.** unpeaceful, capriceful.

ESH'a– **3.** silesia, magnesia.

ESH'an– **2.** Decian, Grecian **3.** Silesian, Venetian, magnesian, Lutetian, Helvetian **4.** Polynesian.

ESH'ing– **2.** leashing, sneeching **3.** unleashing.

ESH'un– **3.** deletion, depletion, repletion, impletion, completion, accretion, secretion, incretion, excretion **4.** incompletion, internecion.

ESH'us– **2.** Decius, specious **3.** facetious.

ES'i– fleecy, greasy, creasy.

ES'ik– **2.** mnesic **3.** algesic, gynecic **4.** polynesic.

ES'ing– **2.** leasing, fleecing, piecing, greasing, creasing, ceasing **3.** releasing, policing, decreasing, increasing, unceasing, surceasing.

ES'is– **2.** schesis, tmesis, rhesis, [Gr.], thesis **3.** deësis [N.L.], algesis, orchesis, ochlesis, mimesis, kinesis, phonesis, phromesis, noesis [Gr.], ascesis, [N.L.], ecesis, centesis, mathesis, anthesis, esthesis **4.** exegesis, catechesis, hyporchesis, anamnesis, Anamnesis, synteresis, hysteresis, catachresis, antichresis, erotesis, anesthesis **5.** diaphoresis, perichoresis, hyperesthesis.

ES'iv– **3.** adhesive, cohesive **4.** inadhesive, monadhesive, incohesive, noncohesive.

ES'less– **2.** leaseless, fleeceless, nieceless, peaceless, pieceless, greaseless, creaseless, ceaseless **3.** valiseless, capriceless.

EST'a– **4.** buena vista [Sp.] **5.** hasta la vista [Sp.].

EST'ed– **2.** easted, beasted, feasted, yeasted.

EST'er– **2.** Easter, easter, feaster **3.** down-Easter, northeaster, southeaster.

EST'ern– [**2.** eastern **3.** northeastern, southeastern.

EST'i– **2.** beastie, bheesty, bheestie, sneesty, reasty, yeasty.

EST'ing– **2.** easting, beasting, feasting, questing, yeasting.

EST'li– **2.** beastly, priestly **3.** nonpriestly, unpriestly.

ES'us– **2.** Esus, rhesus, Rhesus, Croesus.

ET'a– **2.** eta, beta, cheetah, dita, keta, Fleta, meta, Meta, Nita, pita, Rita, Greta, creta, theta, seta, zeta **3.** pandita, Chiquita, Marquita, tablita [Sp.], mulita, Anita, planeta, Juanita, magneta, kareeta, amreeta, amrita, rasceta, partita, sortita [It.] **4.** palameta, manzanita, margarita, Señorita [Sp.], Carmencita, chirivita **5.** Isabelita.

ET'al– **2.** fetal, foetal, ketal, Setal **3.** decretal; *See* also **ET'l**– beetle etc. below.

ET'am– **2.** retem, raetam **3.** Antietam.

ET'an– **2.** Cretan, teetan; *see* also **ET'en** eaten etc. below; also **ET'on**– Eton etc. below.

ET′e– **2.** rete [L.] **3.** lanete; *ssee* alo ET′i– beety etc. below.

ET′ed– **2.** cheated, fetid, heated, bleated, fleeted, gleeted, cleated, pleated, sleeted, meated, meted, neated, greeted, treated, seated, sheeted, teated **3.** escheated, defeated, reheated, preheated, unheated, deleted, depleted, repleted, completed, unmeted, repeated, competed, accreted, secreted, concreted, excreted, retreated, maltreated, entreated, mistreated, reseated, receipted, conceited, unseated **4.** undefeated, overheated, underheated, uncompleted, unreceipted, unconceited, self-conceited.

ET′en– **2.** eaten, beaten, keten, sweeten, wheaten **3.** uneaten, worm-eaten, moth-eaten, unbeaten, browbeaten **4.** weather-beaten; *see* also ET′an– Cretan etc. above; also ET′on– Eton etc. below.

ET′ens– **2.** pretence.

ET′er– **2.** eater, beater, cheater, heater, liter, litre, bleater, fleeter, pleater, meter, metre, meeter, neater, Peter, peter, rhetor, greeter, praetor, pretor, treater, seater, teeter, sweeter **3.** beefeater, egg-eater, fogeater, frogeater, cake-eater, anteater, fire-eater, drum beater, browbeater, escheator, depleter, completer, Demeter, repeater, competer, saltpeter, propretor, retreater, entreater, reseater, receiptor, two-seater **4.** overeater, decaliter, hectoliter, centimeter, kilometer.

ET′est– **2.** fleetest, meetest, neatest, sweetest **3.** effetest, elitest, repletest, completest, discreetest **4.** honey-sweetest.

ETH′al– **2.** ethal, lethal **3.** bequeathal **4.** preterlethal.

ETH′an– **2.** Ethan **5.** Elizabethan.

ETH′e– **2.** Lethe.

ETH′en– **2.** heathen, wreathen.

ETH′er– **2.** either, neither, wreather, breather, seether, sheather **3.** enwreather, inbreather, outbreather, bequeather.

ETH′ez– **2.** Lethe's **4.** cacoëthes.

ET′i– **2.** beety, sleety, meaty, peaty, treaty, sweety, sweetie **3.** entreaty **4.** spermaceti; *see* also ET′e– rete etc. above.

ET′ij– **2.** eatage, cheatage, cleatage, metage **3.** escheatage.

ET′ik– **2.** cetic, cretic, Cretic, Rhaetic **3.** acetic.

ET′ing– **2.** eating, beating, cheating, heating, bleating, fleeting, gleeting, cleating, pleating, sleeting, meting, meeting, neating, greeting, treating, seating, sheeting **3.** browbeating, escheating, defeating, reheating, preheating, deleting, depleting, repleting, completing, repeating, competing, accreting, secreting, concreting, excreting, retreating, maltreating, ill-treating, entreating, mistreating, receipting, unseating **4.** overeating, nonrepeating, overheating, underheating.

ET′is– **2.** Metis, treatise, Thetis **4.** diabetes.

ET′ish– **2.** beetish, fetish, fetich, sweetish.

ET′ist– **3.** defeatist, decretist.

ET′iv– **3.** depletive, repletive, completive, accretive, decretive, secretive, concretive, discretive, excretive.

ET′iz– **2.** treaties, sweeties **3.** entreaties.

ET′l– **2.** beetle, betel, baetyl, fetal, wheetle **3.** decretal, acetyl **4.** chalchihuitl.

ET′li– **2.** featly, fleetly, meetly, neatly, sweetly **3.** completely, concretely, discreetly **4.** obsoletely, incompletely, indiscreetly.

ET′ment– **2.** treatment **3.** defeatment, maltreatment, ill-treatment, entreatment, mistreatment.

ET′ness– **2.** featness, fleetness, meetness, neatness, sweetness **3.** effeteness, repleteness, completeness, concreteness, discreetness, petiteness **4.** obsoleteness, incompleteness, indiscreetness.

ET′o– 2. keto, Leto, Tito, veto 3. Chiquito, mosquito, magneto, Benito, bonito, Negrito 4. angelito, sanbenito.

ET′on– 2. Eton, Eaton, seton, Teton; *see also* ET′an– Cretan etc. above; also ET′en– eaten etc. above.

ET′um– 2. fretum 3. zibetum, pinetum, decretum, floretum, rosetum, quercetum 4. arboretum, Tanacetum, salicetum, tilicetum, viticetum.

ET′ur– 2. feature, creature 3. defeature, refeature.

ET′us– 2. fetus, foetus, Cetus 3. quietus, acetous.

E′um– 2. Chiam, meum [L.], Meum 3. Te Deum [L.], odeum, trophaeum, nymphaeum, nympheum, Iseum, lyceum, bronteum, notaeum, museum 4. amoebaeum, hypogeum, mausoleum, athenaeum, atheneum, gorgoneum, coliseum, Colosseum 5. peritoneum.

E′us– 2. Deus [L.], deus [L.], free us 3. plumbeous, Zaccheus, Aeneas, choreus, gluteus 4. scarabaeus, Amadeus, corypheus.

EV′a– 2. Eva, diva, jiva, kiva, Siva, viva 3. khediva, Geneva, Yeshiva 4. Mahadeva.

EV′al– 2. eval, shrieval 3. coeval, grandeval, upheaval, longeval, primeval, retrieval, equaeval 4. medieval; *see also* EV′il– evil etc. below.

EV′ans– 2. grievance 3. achievance, aggrievance, retrievance, perceivance.

EV′en– 2. even, Stephen, Steven 3. uneven, bereaven, good even.

EV′er– 2. beaver, fever, heaver, keever, leaver, lever, liever, livre, cleaver, reaver, reever, reiver, griever, sheaver, weaver, weever 3. naïver, achiever, enfever, hay fever, spring fever, coalheaver, believer, reliever, aggriever, repriever, retriever, deceiver, receiver, conceiver, perceiver 4. jungle fever, yellow fever, cantilever, make believer, nonbeliever, unbeliever, disbeliever, misbeliever, preconceiver, misconceiver, interweaver, Danny Deever.

EV′i– 2. levee, Levy, leavy, peevey, peevy, peavey, peavy, Stevie, Suevi 4. Mahadevi.

EV′ij– 2. leavage, cleavage.

EV′il– 2. evil, weevil 3. boll weevil; *see also* EV′al– eval etc. above.

EV′ing– 2. heaving, leaving, cleaving, grieving, sheaving, steeving, thieving, weaving 3. achieving, upheaving, believing, relieving, bereaving, aggrieving, reprieving, retrieving, deceiving, receiving, conceiving, perceiving, inweaving 4. disbelieving, misbelieving, unbelieving, preconceiving, interweaving.

EV′ish– 2. peevish, thievish.

EV′less– 2. Eveless, heaveless, leaveless, sleeveless, sheaveless, weaveless.

EV′ment– 3. achievement, relievement, bereavement, retrievement.

EV′ning– 2. evening.

EV′u– 2. kivu.

EV′us– 2. nevus, grievous 3. longevous, primevous 4. ambilevous.

E′wa– 2. leeway, seaway.

E′ward– 2. leeward, seaward.

E′ya– 3. Hygeia, Tarpeia 4. energeia, Barranquilla 6. onomatopoeia; *see also* E′a– chia etc. above.

E′yan– 3. Hygeian, Tarpeian, Pantheian.

EZ′a– 2. pesa, Pisa, tiza, visa 3. Louisa.

EZ′ans– 3. defeasance, malfeasance, nonfeasance, misfeasance.

EZ′ant– 3. malfeasant.

EZ′er– 2. easer, beezer, cheeser, geezer, pleaser, sneezer, freezer, friezer, greaser, Caesar, seizer, seizor, teaser, squeezer, tweezer, wheezer 3. misfeasor, appeaser, displeaser, Sharezer, disseizor 4. Ebenezer.

EZH′a– 3. Rhodesia, magnesia, esthesia; *see also* EZH′i-a– Zambesia etc.

ĒZH'er– **2.** leisure, seizure **3.** reseizure.

ĒZH'un– **2.** lesion **3.** adhesion, inhesion, cohesion, Silesian, trapezian **4.** inadhesion, incohesion.

ĒZ'i– **2.** easy, cheesy, sleazy, sneezy, breezy, freezy, greasy, teasy, queasy **3.** Zambesi, speakeasy, pachisi, parchesi, uneasy.

ĒZ'in– **2.** seisin, seizin.

ĒZ'ing– **2.** easing, feazing, feezing, pleasing, sneezing, breezing, freezing, friezing, greasing, seizing, teasing, squeezing, wheezing **3.** unpleasing, displeasing, appeasing, reseizing.

ĒZ'ingz– **2.** feasings, greasings.

ĒZ'l– **2.** easel, mesel, teasel, weasel.

ĒZ'lz– **2.** easels, measles, weasels.

ĒZ'ment– **2.** easement **3.** appeasement.

ĒZ'on– **2.** reason, treason, season **3.** unreason, unseason.

ĒZ'us– **2.** Jesus.

E (bee)

3.

TRIPLE RHYMES IN E (see'a-ble)

E'a–bl– **3.** feeable, fleeable, freeable, treeable, seeable, skiable **4.** agreeable, decreeable, unseeable **5.** disagreeable.

E'a–bli– **4.** agreeably **5.** disagreeably.

E'al–i– **3.** leally, really **4.** ideally.

E'al–ist– **3.** realist **4.** idealist, surrealist.

E'al–iz– **3.** realise **4.** idealize.

E'al–izm– **3.** realism **4.** idealism.

E'al–ti– **3.** fealty, lealty, realty.

E'an–izm– **3.** peanism **4.** plebeianism, Sebaeanism **6.** Epicureanism.

E'az–on– **3.** liaison.

EB'ri–us– **3.** ebrious **4.** tenebrious, inebrious, funebrious.

ECH'a–bl– **3.** bleachable, reachable, preachable, teachable **4.** impeachable, unreachable, unteachable **5.** unimpeachable.

ECH'i–ness– **3.** peachiness, screechiness, preachiness.

ED'a–bl– **3.** deedable, feedable, heedable, leadable, pleadable, kneadable, readable, seedable, weedable **4.** impedible, unreadable, exceedable **5.** unexceedable, supersedable.

ED'en–si– **4.** precedency **5.** antecedency.

ED'er–ship– **3.** leadership, readership.

ED'ful–i– **3.** heedfully, needfully **4.** unheedfully, unneedfully.

ED'ful–ness– **3.** heedfulness, needfulness **4.** unheedfulness, unneedfulness.

ED'i–a– **3.** media **4.** comedia, acedia **5.** Fissipedia, cyclopedia, epicedia **6.** pharmacopedia, encyclopedia.

ED'i–al– **3.** medial, praedial **4.** admedial, remedial, immedial, comedial **5.** irremedial, intermedial, epicedial.

ED'i–an– **3.** median **4.** tragedian, symmedian, comedian **5.** cosymmedian **6.** encyclopedian.

ED'i–at– **3.** mediate **4.** immediate **5.** intermediate.

ED'i–ens– **4.** obedience, expedience, expedients, ingredients **5.** nonobedience, disobedience, inexpedience.

ED'i–ent– **4.** obedient, impedient, expedient, digredient, ingredient **5.** unobedient, disobedient, inexpedient.

ED'i–er– **3.** beadier, needier, speedier, reedier, greedier, seedier, weedier.

ED'i–est– **3.** beadiest, neediest, speediest, reediest, greediest, seediest, weediest.

ED'i–it– **3.** mediate **4.** immediate **5.** intermediate.

ED'i–li– **3.** beadily, needily, speedily, reedily, greedily, seedily, weedily.

ED'i–ness– **3.** beadiness, neediness, speediness, reediness, greediness, seediness, weediness.

ED'ing–li– **3.** heedingly, pleadingly **4.** unheedingly, misleadingly, exceedingly.

ED'i–um– **3.** medium, tedium **4.** soredium **5.** intermedium, epicedium.

ED′i–us– **3.** medius, tedious **5.** intermedius.

ED′less–ly– **3.** heedlessly, needlessly.

EF′i–ness– **3.** beefiness, leafiness.

EG′al–i– **3.** legally, regally **4.** illegally.

EG′al–ness– **3.** legalness, regalness **4.** illegalness.

EG′er–li– **3.** eagerly, meagerly **4.** uneagerly.

EG′er–ness– **3.** eagerness, meagerness **4.** uneagerness **5.** overeagerness.

E′it–i– **3.** deity, seity **4.** plebeity, tableity, velleity, omneity, aseity, gaseity, ipseity, multeity **5.** extraneity, spontaneity, femineity, personeity, corporeity **6.** simultaneity, instantaneity, momentaneity, incorporeity **7.** contemporaneity.

EJ′ens–i– **3.** regency **4.** vice-regency.

EJ′i–an– **4.** collegian, Fuegian, Norwegian.

EJ′i–um– **4.** collegium **5.** florilegium.

EJ′us–ness– **4.** egregiousness **5.** sacrilegiousness.

EK′a–bl– **3.** speakable **4.** unspeakable.

EK′i–li– **3.** beakily, cheekily, leakily, sleekily, sneakily, creakily, squeakily.

EK′i–ness– **3.** beakiness, cheekiness, leakiness, sneakiness, creakiness, squeakiness.

EK′ish–ness– **3.** cheekishness, cliquishness, sneakishness, freakishness.

EK′wen–si– **3.** frequency, sequency **4.** infrequency.

EK′wi–al– **4.** obsequial, exequial.

EL′a–bl– **3.** dealable, feelable, healable, peelable, reelable, sealable, stealable **4.** unhealable, congealable, annealable, appealable, repealable, concealable, revealable **5.** unconcealable, unrevealable.

EL′i–a– **3.** Elia, Delia, Lelia, Celia, Caelia, coelia **4.** lobelia, Bedelia, Ophelia, Amelia, Hamelia, cimelia, Cordelia, Cornelia, Karelia, Aurelia; *see* also EL′ya– Delia etc.

EL′i–an– **3.** Elian, Delian, Caelian **4.** Hegelian, carnelian, Karelian, aurelian **6.** Mephistophelean, Aristotelian.

EL′i–on– **3.** Pelion **4.** aphelion, parhelion, chameleon, anthelion **5.** perihelion.

EL′i–us– **3.** Delius, Helios **4.** Cornelius, Aurelius **5.** contumelius.

EM′a–bl– **3.** beamable, reamable, dreamable, creamable, seamable, steamable **4.** redeemable, esteemable.

EM′a–tist– schematist, thematist.

EM′er–i– **3.** dreamery, creamery.

EM′i–a– **3.** Nemea **4.** Euphemia, Bohemia, leukemia, anemia, paroemia, toxemia **5.** diarhemia, diarrhaemia.

EM′i–al– **3.** cnemial, gremial **4.** endemial, vindemial, proemial, paroemial.

EM′i–an– **4.** Bohemian **5.** academian.

EM′i–er– **3.** beamier, gleamier, dreamier, creamier, premier, steamier.

EM′i–li– **3.** beamily, gleamily, dreamily, creamily, steamily.

EM′i–ness– **3.** beaminess, gleaminess, dreaminess, creaminess, steaminess.

EM′ing–li– **3.** beamingly, gleamingly, dreamingly, seemingly **4.** beseemingly, unseemingly.

EM′i–um– **3.** premium **4.** proemium, gelsemium.

EM′i–us– **4.** abstemious.

EN′a–bl– **3.** gleanable, leanable, meanable, weanable **4.** amenable, convenable, unweanable.

EN′er–i– **3.** deanery, plenary, greenery, scenery **4.** machinery.

EN′i–a– **3.** taenia, xenia **4.** gardenia, Eugenia, Birkenia, Armenia **5.** neomenia, neurasthenia, schizophrenia.

EN′i–al– **3.** genial, splenial, menial, taenial, venial, xenial **4.** congenial, demesnial **5.** uncongenial, primigenial, homogeneal.

EN′i–an– 3. Fenian 4. Hellenian, Armenian, Cyrenian, sirenian, Athenian, parthenian, Ruthenian 5. Esselenian, neomenian.

EN′i–ens– 3. lenience 4. prevenience, convenience 5. inconvenience, intervenience.

EN′i–ent– 3. lenient 4. advenient, prevenient, convenient 5. inconvenient, supervenient, intervenient.

EN′i–er– 3. beanier, spleenier, sheenier, teenier, weenier.

EN′i–um– 3. rhenium, xenium 4. selenium, solenium, proscenium, postscenium 5. calistheneum.

EN′i–us– 3. genius, splenius 4. ingenious, arsenious 5. homogeneous, pergameneous 6. heterogeneous.

EN′yen–si– 3. leniency 4. conveniency 3. inconveniency.

EN′yent–li– 3. leniently 4. conveniently 5. inconveniently.

E′o–krat– 3. rheocrat, theocrat.

E′o–la– 4. areola, roseola, alveola, foveola.

E′o–lus– 3. Aeolus 4. malleolus, nucleolus, alveolus.

EP′i–a– 3. sepia.

EP′i–ad– 4. asclepiad, Asclepiad.

EP′i–li– 3. sleepily, creepily, weepily.

EP′i–ness– 3. sleepiness, creepiness, steepiness, weepiness.

ER′e–al– 3. cereal 4. sidereal, funereal, ethereal; see also ER′i–al– ferial etc. below.

ER′en–si– 4. adherency, inherency, coherency 5. incoherency.

ER′ful–i– 3. cheerfully, fearfully, tearfully.

ER′ful–ness– 3. cheerfulness, fearfulness, tearfulness.

ER′i–a– 3. eria, feria, Scleria 4. Iberia, Liberia, Siberia, Egeria, Nigeria, Algeria, Hesperia, bacteria, criteria, asteria, hysteria, wisteria, diphtheria 5. cafeteria, acroteria, Anthesteria, Eleutheria.

ER′i–ad– 4. anteriad, posteriad.

ER′i–al– 3. ferial, serial, cereal 4. aerial, sidereal, funereal, imperial, biserial, material, bacterial, arterial, asterial, ethereal, diphtherial 5. managerial, immaterial, monasterial, magisterial, ministerial, presbyterial.

ER′i–an– 3. Erian 4. aerian, Iberian, Liberian, Siberian, Algerian, Pierian, valerian, Cimmerian, Wagnerian, Shakespearean, Hesperian, vesperian, Spencerian, Spenserian, psalterian, trouserian 5. Luciferian, Presbyterian, philotherian, Eleutherian; see also ER′i–on– allerion etc. below.

ER′i–ens– 4. experience 5. inexperience.

ER′i–er– 3. eerier, beerier, cheerier, blearier, drearier, tearier, wearier; see also ER′i–or– inferior etc. below.

ER′i–est– 3. eeriest, beeriest, cheeriest, bleariest, dreariest, teariest, weariest.

ER′i–form– 3. spheriform, Seriform 4. viperiform.

ER′i–li– 3. eerily, beerily, cheerily, blearily, drearily, tearily, wearily.

ER′i–ness– 3. eeriness, beeriness, cheeriness, bleariness, dreariness, teariness, weariness.

ER′ing–li– 3. cheeringly, fearingly, jeeringly, peeringly 4. endearingly 5. domineeringly.

ER′i–o– 3. cheerio, serio.

ER′i–on– 4. allerion, Hyperion, criterion; see also ER′i–an– Erian etc. above.

ER′i–or– 4. inferior, superior, ulterior, anterior, interior, exterior, posterior; see also ER′i–er– eerier etc. above.

ER′i–um– 3. cerium 4. imperium, bacterium, psalterium 5. desiderium, elaterium, acroterium, magisterium.

ER′i–us– 3. Cereus, cereous, serious 4. imperious, mysterious, ethereous 5. jocoserious, deleterious.

ER′less–li– 3. beerlessly, cheerlessly, fearlessly, peerlessly.

ER′less–ness– 3. beerlessness, cheerlessness, fearlessness, peerlessness.

ES′a–bl– 3. leasable, peaceable, creasable, ceasable 4. releasable, increasable, unceasable.

ES′en–si– 3. decency, recency 4. indecency.

ES′ent–li– 3. decently, recently 4. indecently.

ESH′i–a– 4. silesia, Silesia, telesia, Helvetia 5. Polynesia, alopecia.

ESH′i–an– 3. Decian, Grecian 4. Silesian, Venetian, Lutetian, Helvetian.

ESH′i–at– 4. appreciate, depreciate.

ESH′un–al– 4. secretional, concretional.

ESH′us–ness– 3. speciousness 4. facetiousness.

ES′i–er– 3. fleecier, greasier, creasier.

ES′ing–li– 4. decreasingly, increasingly, unceasingly.

ES′it–i– 4. obesity.

ES′iv–li– 4. adhesively, inhesively, cohesively.

EST′i–ness– 3. reastiness, yeastiness.

EST′li–ness– 3. beastliness, priestliness.

ET′a–bl– 3. eatable, beatable, cheatable, heatable, treatable, seatable 4. uneatable, unbeatable, escheatable, defeatable, deletable, repeatable, entreatable 5. undefeatable, unrepeatable.

ET′ed–li– 3. heatedly 4. repeatedly.

ETH′e–an– 3. Lethean 4. Promethean.

ET′i–an– 3. Tahitian.

ET′i–ness– 3. meatiness, peatiness, sleetiness.

ET′or–i– 4. depletory, repletory, completory, secretory.

EV′a–bl– 3. cleavable, grievable 4. achievable, believable, relievable, retrievable, deceivable, receivable, conceivable, perceivable 5. unbelievable, irretrievable, undeceivable, inconceivable, imperceivable.

EV′a–bli– 4. believably, retrievably, conceivably, perceivably 5. unbelievably, irretrievably, inconceivably, imperceivably.

EV′i–at– 3. deviate 4. alleviate, abbreviate.

EV′ish–li– 3. peevishly, thievishly.

EV′ish–ness– 3. peevishness, thievishness.

EV′i–us– 3. devious, previous.

EZ′a–bl– 3. feasible, freezable, seizable, squeezable 4. defeasible, cohesible 4. appeasable 5. indefeasible, inappeasable, unappeasable.

EZH′i–a– 3. Freesia 4. Zambesia, parrhesia, ecclesia, amnesia, trapezia, esthesia 5. anesthesia; see also EZH′a– Rhodesia etc.

EZH′i–an– 4. Ephesian, trapezian, ecclesian, etesian, artesian; see also EZH′un– lesion etc.

EZ′i–a– 4. algesia, esthesia.

EZ′i–er– 3. easier, cheesier, sleazier, breezier, greasier, queasier, wheezier 4. uneasier.

EZ′i–est– 3. easiest, cheesiest, sleaziest, breeziest, greasiest, queasiest, wheeziest 4. uneasiest.

EZ′i–li– 3. easily, cheesily, sleazily, breezily, greasily, queasily, wheezily 4. uneasily.

EZ′i–ness– 3. easiness, cheesiness, sleaziness, breeziness, greasiness, wheeziness, queasiness 4. uneasiness.

EZ′ing–li– 3. pleasingly, freezingly, teasingly, wheezingly 4. displeasingly, appeasingly.

EZ′on–al– 3. seasonal 4. unseasonal.

EZ′on–er– 3. reasoner, seasoner.

EZ′on–ing– 3. reasoning, seasoning 4. unreasoning.

E (heh)

1.

SINGLE (MASCULINE) RHYMES IN E (heh)

Primary or Secondary Accent Falls on Last Syllable; Imperfect Rhymes Are in Italics.

E– 1. heh, yeh [slang].

EB– 1. ebb, deb [coll.], Deb, Geb, keb, Keb, bleb, pleb, Sleb, neb, reb, theb, web 2. zibeb [obs.], cubeb, subdeb [coll.], *blackneb, cobweb* 3. coulterneb.

EBD– 1. ebbed, kebbed, blebbed, nebbed, webbed 2. *cobwebbed.*

EBZ– 1. ebbs, debs [coll.], Debs, blebs, plebs, nebs, rebs, thebs, webs 2. cubebs, subdebs [coll.], *cobwebs.*

ECH– 1. etch, fetch, ketch, sketch, letch, fletch, cletch, retch, wretch, stretch, tech, tetch [both dial.], quetch [obs. exc. dial.], vetch 2. outstretch 3. photoetch, bitter vetch.

ECHD– 1. etched, fetched, sketched, fletched, retched, stretched, teched [dial.], quetched [obs. exc. dial.] 2. farfetched, outstretched 3. photoetched.

ED– 1. Ed, ed [slang], bed, dead, fed, ged, gedd, Ged, head, jed, ked, led, lead, bled, fled, gled [Scot.], plead, pled, sled, *Ned*, snead, t'nead [Scot.], *ped, sped, red, redd, med* [slang], *read, bred, bread, dread*, Fred, *spread*, shred, tread, thread, said, shed, ted, Ted, stead, wed, 'stead, zed 2. co-ed, abed, embed, imbed, *hotbed*, wellfed, unfed, ahead, *deadhead, redhead, roundhead, godhead*, behead, *blockhead, bulkhead, ramhead, drumhead, bonehead, towhead, drophead, spearhead, forehead, sorehead, hogshead, hothead*, bebfed, *bobsled*, mislead, pre-med [slang], *biped*, reread, misread, outread, *highbred, home-bred, inbred, lowbred, purebred, crossbred, sweetbread, shortbread, truebread*, widespread, bespread, well-spread, outspread, retread, rethread, unthread, resaid, gainsaid, unsaid, *bloodshed, bedstead, roadstead*, bestead, *homestead, farmstead*, instead, rewed, unwed 3. underfed, marblehead, bufflehead, fountainhead, dragonhead, arrowhead, loggerhead, copperhead, overhead, figurehead, aliped, taliped, cheliped, milliped, soliped, remiped, semiped, palmiped, plumiped, pinniped, uniped, serriped, cirriped, fissiped, multiped, breviped, octoped, quadruped, thoroughbred, underbred, gingerbread, underspread, overspread, *aforesaid*, watershed 4. maxilliped 6. parallelepiped; *also the past tense and past participle of regular verbs ending in "d" or "t"* (e.g. garlanded, coveted.)

EDTH– 1. breadth 2. hairbreadth, hairsbreadth.

EF– 1. f, F, ef, eff, deaf, def [slang], feoff, jeff, Jeff, clef, nef, ref [slang], chef 2. enfeoff.

EFT– 1. eft, deft, feoffed, heft, jeffed, left, cleft, klepht, reft, theft, weft, wheft 2. enfeoffed, infeft, aleft, bereft 3. unbereft.

EG– 1. egg, beg, keg, skeg, leg, cleg, Meg, sneg, peg, reg [slang], dreg, seg, teg, yegg [slang] 2. *blackleg, bowleg, proleg, foreleg*, nutmeg, unpeg, *goose egg* 3. philabeg, atabeg, filibeg, beglerbeg, Winnipeg, Silas Wegg [Dickens].

EGZ– eggs, etc., *see* **EG–** egg etc., above, plus "s" or " 's."

EJ– 1. edge, hedge, kedge, skedge, ledge, fledge, cledge, gledge [Scot.], pledge, sledge, dredge, sedge, tedge, wedge 2. unedge, allege, impledge 3. interpledge, sacrilege, privilege.

EJD– 1. edged, hedged, kedged, ledged, fledged, pledged, sledged, dredged, sedged, wedged 2. two-edged. unfledged, alleged, impledged, unpledged 3. double-edged, deckle-edged, privileged.

EK– 1. ec [slang], beck, checque, check, Czech, deck, feck, geck, heck, haec, keck, lec, leck, lech, lek, fleck, cleck, smeck [slang], neck, sneck, peck, speck, spec [slang], reck, wreck, brek, trek, sec, tec, tech, teck 2. home-ec [slang], *pinchbeck*, Quebec, recheck, bedeck, *foredeck, roughneck, wryneck, blackneck, breakneck, crookneck, swanneck,* sapek, *henpeck, flyspeck, shipwreck, parsec* 3. countercheck, bottleneck, rubberneck, leatherneck 4. bibliothec.

EKS– becks etc., *see* **EK–** beck etc. above, plus "s" or " 's"; 1. x, X, ex, faex, hex, kex, lex, flex, plex, spex, specs, rex, prex, sex, vex 2. *index, codex,* deflex, *reflex, biflex,* inflex, *diplex, triplex,* complex, *simplex,* perplex, *duplex,* annex, connex, *apex,* unsex, *vortex,* convex 3. dorsiflex, circumflex, retroflex, genuflex, contraplex, nulliplex, veniplex, multiplex, disannex.

EKST– 1. hexed, flexed, next, sexed, sext, text, vexed 2. annexed, perplexed, unsexed, pretext, context 3. genuflexed.

EKT– 1. becked, checked, decked, flecked, flect, necked, pecked, specked, recked, wrecked, trekked, sect 2. unchecked, bedecked, affect, effect, *defect,* refect, *prefect,* infect, perfect, traject, abject, subject, adject, eject, deject, reject, inject, conject, project, disject, elect, prelect, select, deflect, reflect, inflect, neglect, collect, *crooknecked,* connect, respect, inspect, *prospect,* expect, suspect, arrect, erect, di-

rect, correct, porrect, bisect, dissect, transect, detect, contect, protect 3. disaffect, misaffect, disinfect, retroject, interject, dialect, analect, re-elect, nonelect, intellect, circumflect, genuflect, recollect, reconnect, disconnect, self-respect, disrespect, circumspect, retrospect, introspect, indirect, misdirect, incorrect, resurrect, insurrect, intersect, architect.

EKTS– 1. sects 2. affects, effects, *defects* infects, perfects, trajects, subjects, adjects, ejects, dejects, rejects, injects, conjects, projects, disjects, elects, prelects, selects, deflects, reflects, inflects, neglects, collects, connects, respects, inspects, *prospects,* expects, suspects, arrects, erects, directs, corrects, porrects, bisects, dissects, transects, detects, contects, protects 3. disaffects, misaffects, disinfects, retrojects, interjects, dialects, analects, re-elects, intellects, circumflects, genuflects, recollects, reconnects, disconnects, disrespects, retrospects, introspects, misdirects, resurrects, insurrects, intersects, architects.

EL– 1. l, L, el, El, ell, bel, Bel, bell, belle, Belle, dell, fell, hell, Hel, jell, gel, kell, mel, mell, smell, Nell, knell, snell, schnell [G.], pell, spell, rel, cell, sell, shell, tell, well, dwell, swell, quell, yell, zel 2. gabelle, rebel, *dumbbell,* ¦Nobel, *harebell, corbeil, bluebell, cowbell,* rondell, *sardelle,* cordelle, befell, refel, miel [F.], pall-mall, pell-mell, Carmel, quenelle, spinel, Cornell, prunelle, noel, Noel, appel [F.], lapel, rappel [F.], repel, *scalpel,* impel, compel, propel, dispel, expel, respell, misspell, morel, nacelle, resell, ficelle, pucelle, excel, encell, Moselle, marcel, échelle [F.], *bombshell, sea shell,* unshell, *nutshell,* retell, bretelle, hotel, artel, cartel, foretell, cuartel [Sp.], unwell, farewell, indwell, gazelle 3. Annabel, Annabelle, Isabel, Jezebel, bonnibel, citadel, infidel, hirondelle, hydrogel, aguamiel [Sp.], parallel, caramel, bechamel, philomel, fontanel, fustanelle, sentinel, jargonelle, personnel, pimpernel, ritornel, mackerel, pickerel, nonpareil, aquarelle, chanterelle [F.], pipistrel, unicell, undersell, oversell, carrousel, cockleshell, bagatelle, brocatel, muscatel, Neufchâtel, immortelle, caravel, demoiselle **4.** matériel, mademoiselle.

ELB– **1.** elb, skelb.

ELCH– **1.** belch, keltch [slang], welsh, Welsh, quelch, squelch [both slang].

ELD– **1.** eld, belled, felled, geld, held, helled, jelled, keld, meld, smelled, knelled, shelled, pelled, spelled, celled, shelled, welled, weld, dwelled, swelled, quelled, yeld, yelled, fjeld **2.** rebelled, beheld, upheld, withheld, repelled, impelled, compelled, propelled, dispelled, expelled, respelled, misspelled, excelled, marcelled, unquelled **3.** unicelled, parallelled **4.** unparallelled.

ELF– **1.** elf, delf, pelf, self, shelf, Guelph **2.** *didelph*, myself, thyself, himself, oneself, herself, ourself, yourself, itself.

ELFT– **1.** delft, Delft, pelfed, selfed.

ELFTH– **1.** twelfth.

ELK– **1.** elk, whelk, yelk.

ELM– **1.** elm, helm, realm, whelm **2.** unhelm, dishelm, Anselm **3.** overwhelm.

ELP– **1.** help, kelp, skelp, whelp, swelp, yelp **2.** self-help.

ELS– **1.** else **2.** how else, where else, what else.

ELT– **1.** elt, belt, dealt, felt, gelt, kelt, Celt, Kelt, melt, smelt, knelt, pelt, spelt, celt, Celt, veld, veldt, svelte, welt, dwelt **2.** unbelt, misdealt, *homefelt*, unfelt, *heartfelt*, remelt, undwelt.

ELTH– **1.** health, stealth, wealth **3.** commonwealth.

ELV– **1.** delve, helve, shelve, twelve.

ELVD– **1.** delved, helved, shelved.

ELVZ– **1.** elves, delves, helves, selves, shelves, twelves **2.** themselves, ourselves, yourselves.

ELZ– l's, ells, etc., *see* **EL–** l etc. above, plus "s" or "'s"; **1.** Welles, Wells **2.** Lascelles **3.** Dardanelles.

EM– **1.** m, M, em, 'em, Em, Emm, Dem., fem, feme, hem, gem, kemb, chem [slang], Lem, phlegm, Flem, Clem, clem, mem, crème [F.], sem [slang], Shem, Tem, stem, them **2.** condemn, begem, ahem, in rem [L.], *semsem*, contemn, protem, *pipestem*, *Zemzem* **3.** anadem, diadem, Bethlehem, requiem, stratagem, theorem, apothegm **4.** ad hominem [L.].

EMP– **1.** hemp, kemp, Kemp, temp **2.** *kohemp*.

EMPT– **1.** empt, kempt, dreamt, tempt **2.** pre-empt, coempt, adempt, unkempt, undreamt, perempt, attempt, retempt, contempt, exempt.

EMZ– m's, ems etc., *see* **EM–** m etc. above, plus "s" or "'s"; **1.** Thames, temse.

EN– **1.** n, N, en, ben, Ben, benn, Chen, den, fen, hen, gen [slang], Jen, ken, Ken, Len, glen, men, pen, wren, sen, Shen, ten, then, wen, when, yen, Zen **2.** Big Ben, *benben*, again, *peahen*, beken, amen, seamen, horsemen, Norsemen, Bushmen, Northmen, *pigpen*, impen, *cowpen*, marraine [F.], cayenne, Cheyenne **3.** oxygen, endogen, halogen, nitrogen, cyclamen, specimen, partimen, gentlemen, aldermen, Englishmen, Darien, julienne, brevipen, fountain pen, poison pen, denizen, citizen **4.** tragedienne, comedienne, sicilienne, éolienne [F.], Tyrolienne, equestrienne, Valenciennes, Parisienne [F.].

ENCH– **1.** bench, kench, blench, flench, clench, drench, French, trench, wrench, tench, stench, wench, quench, squench **2.** unbench, disbench, unclench, bedrench, retrench, intrench **3.** monkey wrench.

END– **1.** end, bend, fend, kenned, lend, blend, blende, mend, pend, penned, spend, rend, friend, trend, send, shend, tend, vend, wend, Zend **2.** upend, rebend, *prebend*, unbend, *addend*, defend, offend, forfend, *pitchblende*, *hornblende*, amend, emend, remend commend, append, depend, *stipend*, impend, *compend*, perpend, misspend, expend, suspend, befriend, ascend, descend, *godsend*, transcend, attend, subtend, pretend, intend, contend, portend, extend, distend, ostend, Ostend **3.** dividend, subtrahend, apprehend, reprehend, comprehend, recommend, discommend, vilipend, reverend, condescend, repetend, coextend, minuend **4.** misapprehend, miscomprehend, superintend.

ENDZ– ends etc., *see* **END–** end etc. above, plus "s" or " 's."

ENG– **1.** dreng, drengh, kreng, sheng **2.** *thameng, ginseng, banteng.*

ENGTH– **1.** length, strength **2.** full length, full strength.

ENJ– **2.** *Stonehenge,* avenge, revenge.

ENK– **1.** renk.

ENS– **1.** dense, fence, hence, flense, mense [Scot. and N. of Eng.], pence, pense [obs.], Spence, cense, sense, tense, thence, vence [slang], whence **2.** condense, defense, defence, offense, herehence, immense, commence, prepense, threepence, propense, sixpence, twopence, dispense, expense, suspense, incense, nonsense, subtense, pretense, intense **3.** accidence, incidence, diffidence, confidence, subsidence, residence, dissidence, evidence, providence, impudence, recondense, self-defense, indigence, negligence, diligence, exigence, audience, prurience, excellence, prevalence, pestilence, redolence, indolence, condolence, violence, somnolence, insolence, turbulence, flocculence, succulence, truculence, fraudulence, opulence, corpulence, virulence, purulence, flatulence, lutulence, vehemence, recommence, immanence, permanence, eminence, imminence, prominence, continence, pertinence, abstinence, recompense, deference, reference, preference, difference, inference, conference, reverence, reticence, innocence, frankincense, commonsense, competence, ap-

petence, penitence, impotence, refluence, affluence, effluence, influence, confluence, subsequence, consequence, eloquence, congruence **4.** coincidence, improvidence, malevolence, preeminence, obedience, expedience, ebulience, experience, subservience, intelligence, equivalence, insomnolence,benevolence,impermanence, incontinence, impertinence, indifference, circumference, belligerence, irreverence, beneficence, magnificence, munificence, incompetence, inappetence, impenitence, omnipotence, inconsequence, incongruence, grandiloquence, magniloquence.

ENST– **1.** fenced, flensed, mensed, sensed, censed, tensed **2.** against, condensed, commenced, anenst, fornenst, dispensed, incensed **3.** evidenced, recommenced, recompensed, reverenced, influenced **4.** experienced **5.** inexperienced.

ENT– **1.** bent, dent, fent, Ghent, hent, gent, Kent, kent, lent, Lent, leant, blent, meant, pent, spent, rent, brent, Trent, sent, cent, scent, tent, stent, vent, went **2.** unbent, indent, relent, Ament, fornent, lament, dement, cement, augment, foment, ferment, torment, anent, repent, misspent, unspent, resent, present, assent, ascent, descent, present, dissent, concent, consent, docent, detent, intent, content, distent, extent, ostent, event, prevent, invent, frequent **3.** accident, occident, incident, diffident, confident, subsident, evident, provident, impudent, indigent, negligent, diligent, dirigent, corrigent, transigent, exigent, attrahent, contrahent, ambient, gradient, audient, salient, lenient, sapient, prevalent, excellent, somnolent, insolent, turbulent, flocculent, succulent, esculent, luculent, muculent, truculent, fraudulent, opulent, corpulent, querulent, virulent, purulent, flatulent, lutulent, ligament, parliament, armament, firmament, ornament, tournament, sacrament, testament, management, implement, complement, supplement, tenement, increment, excrement, cerement, banishment, garnishment, punishment, nourishment, lavishment, ravishment, pediment, sediment, condiment, rudiment, regiment, aliment, compliment, liniment, merriment, worriment, flurriment, detriment, nutriment, sentiment, revelment, devilment, government, wonderment, document, tegument, argument, monument, instrument, remanent, immanent, permanent, thereanent, eminent, imminent, prominent, continent, pertinent, abstinent, overspent, deferent, preferent, afferent, efferent, different, reverent, Millicent, reticent, innocent, competent, appetent, penitent, malcontent, affluent, effluent, refluent, subsequent, circumvent, underwent, represent **4.** coincident, improvident, intelligent, aperient, parturient, subservient, lineament, medicament, predicament, disarmament, temperament, disablement, ennoblement, bemuddlement, inveiglement, entanglement, accoutrement, acknowledgment, replenishment, admonishment, relinquishment, presentiment, bedevilment, enlightenment, abandonment, apportionment, environment, imprisonment, dismemberment, bewilderment, embitterment, beleaguerment, encompassment, embarrassment, impermanent, incontinent, impertinent, indifferent, belligerent, irreverent, Privatdocent [G.], misrepresent, beneficent, magnificent, munificent, incompetent, impenitent, omnipotent, mellifluent, inconsequent, grandiloquent, magniloquent **5.** circumambient, impoverishment, accompaniment, disillusionment.

ENTH– **1.** tenth **2.** *seventh, dozenth* **3.** eleventh.

ENTS– bents etc., *see* **ENT–** bent etc. above, plus "s" or "'s"; **2.** Coblentz.

ENZ– ens etc., *see* **EN–** n etc. above, plus "s" or "'s"; **1.** ense, gens, lens, cleanse **3.** Valenciennes.

ENZD– **1.** lensed, cleansed.

EP– **1.** chep [slang], dep [slang], hep [slang], skep, clep, slep, nep, pep, r.̣ prep [slang], strep [slang], step, steppe, yep [slang], zep [slang] **2.** *madnep, catnep, instep,* unstep, *stairstep,* misstep, *catstep, footstep* **3.** demirep, overstep.

EPT– **1.** kept, slept, pepped, crept, sept, stepped, wept, swept **2.** adept, unkept, y-clept, inept, accept, *precept, concept, percept,* discept, except, suscept, unswept **3.** preconcept, intercept **4.** biblioklept, intussuscept.

EPTH– **1.** depth.

ER– through **ERZ–**, *see* short **U** (tub): **UR–** through **URZ–**.

ES– **1.** s, S, es, ess, Bes, Bess, chess, dess, fess, fesse, 'fess, guess, Hess, jess, less, bless, mess, ness, pess, dress, cress, press, tress, stress, cess, sess, Tess, yes **2.** frondesce, confess, profess, quiesce, largesse, turgesce, noblesse, unless, kermess, finesse, caress, address, *headdress,* redress, undress, egress, regress, digress, ingress, progress, transgress, accresce, depress, repress, impress, compress, oppress, express, suppress, distress, duress, assess, obsess, success, recess, precess, princesse, *princess,* possess, comtesse [F.], tristesse [F.] **3.** SOS, incandesce, stewardess, shepherdess, acquiesce, recalesce, coalesce, opalesce, convalesce, nonetheless, luminesce, baroness, readdress, maladdress, allegress [F.], retrogress, water cress, phosphoresce, effloresce, fluoresce, recompress, overstress, reassess, repossess, prepossess, disposses, poetess, effervesce, deliquesce **4.** nevertheless, rejuvenesce, ambassadress; *also adjectives composed of noun-plus-suffix "-less"* (e.g. motionless, passionless); *also nouns composed of adjective-plus-suffix "-ness"* (e.g. tardiness, toothsomeness); *also nouns made feminine by addition of the suffix "-ess"* (e.g. stewardess, manageress).

ESH– **1.** hesh [slang], flesh, flèche, mesh,

spesh [slang], fresh, crèche, thresh, sesh [slang] 2. calèche [F.], *horseflesh*, enmesh, secesh, afresh, unfresh, refresh, rethresh.

ESK– 1. esk [slang], desk 2. burlesque, Moresque, grotesque 3. arabesque, Romanesque, barbaresque, picaresque, chivalresque, humoresque, plateresque, picturesque, scuplturesque, statuesque.

EST– 1. est, best, chest, fessed, fest, guest, guessed, hest, gest, geste, jest, lest, blest, blessed, nest, pest, rest, wrest, Brest, breast, dressed, crest, pressed, tressed, stressed, cest, cessed, test, vest, west, quest, yessed, zest 2. Trieste, infest, behest, suggest, digest, ingest, congest, beau geste [F.], celeste, Celeste, molest, unblest, funnest, impest, arrest, caressed, *headrest*, *bookrest*, unrest, *footrest*, abreast, *redbreast*, *blackbreast*, addressed, redressed, undressed, regressed, digressed, transgressed, progressed, *firecrest*, depressed, repressed, impressed, compressed, oppressed, suppressed, expressed, distressed, prestressed, assessed, alceste, obsessed, recessed, possessed, attest, obtest, detest, retest, pretest, contest, protest, divest, invest, bequest, request, inquest, Midwest, northwest, southwest 3. S O S-ed, incandesced, manifest, counterfessed, acquiesced, redigest, predigest, recalesced, coalesced, opalesced, convalesced, luminesced, Budapest, anapest, Bucharest, readdressed, interest, Everest, retrogressed, phosphoresced, effloresced, fluoresced, recompressed, uncompressed, unimpressed, raven-tressed, overstressed, reassessed, unassessed, repossessed, prepossessed, selfpossessed, unpossessed, dispossessed, palimpsest, effervesced, deliquesced 4. j'y suis, j'y reste [F.]; *also the superlative degree of all adjectives composed of adjective-plus-suffix -est* (e.g. steadiest, giddiest, windiest, shoddiest, sturdiest, dowdiest, rowdiest, darlingest, laughingest, belovedest, horridest).

ET– 1. et, bet, Chet, debt, fet, get, het, jet, ket, khet, let, Lett, blet, flet, plet, met, net, pet, ret, bret, fret, frette, pret, tret, threat, set, sett, shet [dial.], stet, vet, wet, quet, sweat, whet, yet 2. layette, abet, Tibet, barbette, cadet, vedette, bidet, indebt, Claudette, Odette, baguette, baguet, beget, forget, plaquette, coquette, coquet, croquette, casquette, ailette, alette, galette [F.], sublet, Gilette, toilette, roulette, plumette, Nanette, Jeannette, *genet*, dinette, cornet, lunette, brunette, pipette, aret, barrette, umbrette, soubrette, aigrette, *egret*, regret, curette, chevrette, beset, reset, *thickset*, *quickset*, dancette, *inset*, pincette, *onset*, *moonset*, *sunset*, *upset*, *farset*, *outset*, flechette, clochette, brochette, plushette, duet, revet, brevet, bewet, vignette, lorgnette, gazette, rosette, musette 3. Juliette, ariette, storiette, serviette, suffragette, etiquette, tourniquet, flannelette, novelette, landaulet, rigolette, quadruplet, quintuplet, epaulette, cassolette, pianette, villanette, castanet, cravenette, bobbinet, stockinet, clarinet, bassinet, martinet, Antoinette, minionette, mignonette, maisonette, saxcornet, tabaret, cigarette, Margaret, collaret, minaret, lazaret, pierrette [F.], farmerette, banneret, leatherette, interfret, vinaigrette, taboret, anisette, marmoset, overset, silhouette, minuet, pirouette, statuette.

ETH– 1. eth, Beth, death, breath, saith, Seth, teth, steth [slang] 2. Macbeth 3. shibboleth, twentieth, thirtieth, fortieth, fiftieth, sixtieth, eightieth, ninetieth 4. seventieth.

ETZ– bets etc., *see* **ET–** bet etc. above, plus "s" or "'s."

EV– 1. Bev, chev, rev, [slang].

EZ– 1. Ez, fez, mezz [slang], knez, prez [slang], says, sez, yez [both slang] 2. Juarez, cortez, Suez.

EZH– 1. beige, greige 2. manége, baDrége, cortége.

E (heh)

DOUBLE (FEMININE) RHYMES IN E (web'by)

Primary or Secondary Accent Falls on Next
to Last Syllable: Imperfect Rhymes Are in
Italics.

EB'er– 2. ebber, blebber [dial.], nebber [dial.], webber.

EB'i– 2. debby [slang], Debby, kebbie, kebby [both Scot. & N. of Eng.], blebby, nebby, webby 3. *cobwebby.*

EB'ing– 2. ebbing, kebbing, blebbing [dial.], nebbing [dial.], webbing 3. unebbing, *cobwebbing.*

EB'it– 2. debit 3. redebit.

EB'l– 2. debile, pebble, rebel, treble 3. archrebel.

EB'li– 2. pebbly, trebly.

ECH'ed– 2. wretched.

ECH'er– 2. etcher, fetcher, sketcher, lecher, fletcher, retcher, stretcher, quetcher.

ECH'i– 2. fetchy, sketchy, stretchy, techy, tetchy, vetchy.

ECH'ing– 2. etching, fetching, sketching, fletching, retching, stretching, quetching 3. outstretching.

ED'a– 2. Edda, khedda, Ledda, Nedda, Vedda.

ED'al– 2. medal, pedal 3. bipedal, tripedal 4. fissipedal, equipedal; *see* also **ED'l–** heddle etc. below.

ED'ant– 2. pedant.

ED'ed– 2. bedded, headed, leaded, sledded, redded, breaded, dreaded, shredded, threaded, tedded, wedded 3. embedded, imbedded, hardheaded, beheaded, pigheaded, longheaded, thickheaded, coolheaded, bullheaded, bareheaded, clearheaded, flat-headed, lightheaded, softheaded, hotheaded, unshredded, unthreaded, unwedded 4. puddingheaded, manyheaded, double-headed, rattleheaded, levelheaded, arrowheaded, Janus-headed, interthreaded.

ED'en– 2. deaden, leaden, redden, threaden 4. Armageddon.

ED'er– 2. edder, bedder, Cheddar, deader, header, leader, sledder, nedder, redder, dreader, spreader, shredder, threader, treader, shedder, tedder 3. embedder, beheader, unthreader, retreader, *homesteader* 4. double-header.

ED'est– 2. deadest, reddest, dreadest.

ED'ful– 2. headful, dreadful.

ED'head– 2. deadhead, redhead.

ED'i– 2. eddy, Eddie, beddy, heady, leady, neddy, ready, reddy, bready, Freddie, spready, shreddy, thready, Teddy, steady 3. already, unready, unsteady.

ED'ing– 2. bedding, heading, leading, sledding, redding, breading, dreading, spreading, shredding, treading, threading, shedding, tedding, steading, wedding 3. embedding, imbedding, beheading, bespreading, outspreading, retreading, rethreading, unthreading, *homesteading*, rewedding 4. overspreading, golden wedding.

ED'ish– 2. eddish, deadish, reddish, breadish.

ED'it– 2. edit, credit 3. subedit, reedit, accredit, discredit, miscredit.

ED'l– 2. heddle, meddle, medal, peddle, pedal, reddle, treadle 3. bepedal, tripedal 4. intermeddle.

ED'ler– 2. heddler, meddler, medlar, pedlar, peddler, treadler 4. intermeddler.

ED'less– 2. bedless, headless, leadless, sledless, redless, breadless, dreadless, shredless, treadless, threadless, shedless, tedless 3. co-edless, *bulkheadless*, *bedsteadless*, *homesteadless*.

ED'li– 2. deadly, medley, redly.

ED'line– 2. deadline, headline, breadline.

ED'ling– 2. heddling, meddling, peddling, reddling, treadling, 4. intermeddling.

ED'lok– 2. deadlock, headlock, kedlock, wedlock.

ED'na– 2. Edna, Sedna.

ED'ness– 2. deadness, redness.

ED'o– 2. eddo, meadow.

ED'on– 4. Armageddon; *see* ED'en-deaden etc. above.

ED'ward– 2. Edward, bedward.

ED'wood– 2. deadwood, redwood.

ED'zo– 2. mezzo 4. intermezzo.

EF'en– 2. effen, deafen, Strephon.

EF'er– 2. deafer, feoffor, Pfeffer [G.], heifer, kefir, zephyr 4. Hasenpfeffer [G.].

EF'ik– 2. brephic 3. malefic, benefic 4. peristrephic, isopsephic.

EF'is– 2. preface.

EFT'er– 2. defter, hefter, lefter, clefter 3. bereƒter.

EFT'est– 2. deftest, leftist, cleftest 3. bereftest.

EFT'i– 2. hefty, Kefti, Lefty.

EFT'li– 2. deftly 3. bereftly.

EFT'ness– 2. deftness, leftness, cleftness 3. bereftness.

EG'er– 2. egger, beggar, skegger, legger, pegger 3. *bootlegger*.

EG'i– 2. eggy, keggy, leggy, Peggy, dreggy, seggy.

EG'ing– 2. egging, begging, kegging, legging, pegging, segging 3. unkegging, bootlegging, unpegging.

EG'nant– 2. regnant, pregnant.

EJ'end– 2. legend.

EJ'er– 2. edger, hedger, kedger, ledger, pledger, sledger, dredger 3. alleger, repledger.

EJ'et– 2. pledget.

EJ'ez– 2. edges, hedges, kedges, ledges, fledges, cledges, pledges, sledges, dredges, sedges, tedges, wedges 3. alleges, repledges, unwedges 4. interpledges, sacrileges, privileges.

EJ'i– 2. edgy, hedgy, ledgy, fledgy, cledgy, sedgy, wedgy.

EJ'ing– 2. edging, hedging, kedging, ledging, fledging, pledging, sledging, dredging, wedging 3. enhedging, alleging, repledging, impledging.

EJ'less– 2. edgeless, hedgeless, kedgeless, ledgeless, pledgeless, sledgeless, dredgeless, sedgeless, tedgeless, wedgeless 3. privilegeless.

EJ'ment– 3. allegement.

EJ'o– 2. seggio [It.]. 3. solfeggio, arpeggio.

EK'a– 2. Écca, ekka, Mecca 3. sabeca, Rebecca.

EK'ant– 2. peccant 3. impeccant.

EK'er– 2. becker, decker, checker, chequer, gecker, flecker, necker, snecker, pecker, trekker, wrecker 3. rechecker, bedecker, exchequer, *woodpecker*, *henpecker* 4. double-decker.

EK'erd– 2. checkered, record.

EK'et– 2. becket, fecket 5. Thomas à Becket.

EK'i– 2. Becky, checky, kecky, flecky, pecky, specky, wrecky 3. shipwrecky.

EK'ij– 2. wreckage.

EK′ing– **2.** becking, decking, checking, flecking, necking, snecking, pecking, specking, recking, wrecking, trekking **3.** bedecking, *henpecking*, bewrecking, *shipwrecking*.

EK′ish– **2.** heckish, peckish, wreckish.

EK′l– **2.** deckle, heckle, Jeckyll, keckle, speckle, brekkle, freckle, Seckel, shekel **3.** bespeckle, befreckle.

EK′la– **2.** Thecla, Thekla.

EK′ld– **2.** deckled, neckled, keckled, fleckled, speckled, freckled **3.** bespeckled, befreckled.

EK′ler– **2.** heckler, freckler.

EK′less– **2.** beckless, checkless, deckless, feckless, geckless, fleckless, necklace, neckless, peckless, speckless, reckless, wreckless.

EK′li– **2.** speckly, freckly.

EK′ling– **2.** deckling, heckling, keckling, speckling, reckling, freckling.

EK′mate– **2.** checkmate, deckmate.

EK′ni– **4.** theotechny, agrotechny, pyrotechny.

EK′nik– **2.** technic **3.** pantechnic **4.** polytechnic, theotechnic, philotechnic, pyrotechnic.

EK′niks– **3.** eutechnics **4.** pyrotechnics.

EK′ning– **3.** beckoning, reckoning.

EK′nist– **4.** polytechnist, theotechnist, philotechnist, pyrotechnist.

EK′o– **2.** echo, bekko, gecko, secco **3.** re-echo.

EK′on– **2.** beckon, Becken, flecken, reckon.

EK′ond– **2.** beckoned, fleckened, reckoned, second.

EKS′a– **3.** annexa, adnexa.

EKS′al– **2.** nexal, plexal **3.** adnexal.

EKS′as– Texas; *see also* EKS′us– nexus etc. below.

EKS′er– **2.** hexer, flexor, vexer **3.** *indexer*, annexer, perplexer **4.** dorsiflexor.

EKSH′un– **2.** lection, flection, section, vection **3.** affection, defection, refection, effection, infection, confection, profection, perfection, abjection, adjection, trajection, ejection, dejection, rejection, injection, projection, election, prelection, selection, deflection, reflection, inflection, dilection, collection, bolection, complexion, connection, inspection, prospection, erection, direction, correction, resection, bisection, trisection, dissection, insection, exsection, detection, protection, evection, invection, convection, provection **4.** disaffection, reinfection, disinfection, imperfection, insubjection, interjection, dorsiflexion, circumflexion, genuflection, predilection, intellection, recollection, reconnection, disconnection, circumspection, retrospection, introspection, redirection, indirection, misdirection, insurrection, venesection, hemisection, vivisection, intersection.

EKSH′ur– **2.** flexure, plexure **3.** deflexure, inflexure, complexure **4.** contraflexure.

EKSH′us– **3.** infectious, selectious.

EKS′i– **2.** ecce, kexy, prexy, sexy **4.** cataplexy, apoplexy.

EKS–il– **2.** exile, flexile.

EKS′ing– **2.** X-ing, hexing, flexing, sexing vexing **3.** inflexing, complexing, perplexing, *duplexing*, annexing, unsexing, convexing.

EKS′is– **3.** Alexis, orexis, syntexis, cathexis **4.** catalexis, epiplexis.

EKS′li– **3.** complexly, convexly.

EKS′tant– **2.** extant, sextant.

EKS′til– **2.** sextile, textile **3.** bissextile.

EKS′us– **2.** nexus, plexus, Texas **3.** connexus, complexus **4.** solar plexus.

EKT′al– **2.** ectal, tectal **4.** dialectal.

EKT′ant– **3.** infectant, reflectant, amplectant, humectant, annectent, aspectant, respectant, expectant, suspectant **4.** disinfectant, unexpectant.

EKT'ed– 2. sected 3. affected, effected, infected, confected, perfected, objected, subjected, ejected, dejected, rejected, injected, projected, elected, selected, deflected, reflected, biflected, inflected, neglected, collected, complected, connected, respected, expected, inspected, suspected, erected, directed, corrected, bisected, dissected, detected, protected, invected 4. unaffected, disaffected, disinfected, interjected, re-elected, pre-elected, retroflected, recollected, disconnected, unexpected, unsuspected, redirected, misdirected, uncorrected, resurrected, intersected.

EKT'er– 2. hector, Hector, lector, nectar, specter, rector, sector, vector 3. affecter, effecter, effector, infector, perfecter, objector, ejector, injector, projector, elector, prelector, selector, deflector, reflector, inflector, neglecter, collector, connector, respecter, expecter, inspector, prospector, erector, director, corrector, bisector, dissector, detector, protector, bivector 4. disinfecter, interjecter, dialector, nonreflector, genuflector, disrespecter, resurrecter, vivisecter.

EKT'erd– 2. hectored, nectared, spectered, sectored.

EKT'ern– 2. lectern.

EKT'est– 3. abjectest, selectest, directest.

EKT'ful– 3. neglectful, respectful, suspectful 4. unrespectful, disrespectful.

EKT'ik– 2. hectic, pectic 3. ephectic, eclectic, synectic, orectic, syntectic 4. dialectic, analectic, catalectic, epiplectic, apoplectic, isopectic, orthotectic 5. acatalectic 6. hypercatalectic.

EKT'il– 2. sectile 3. insectile, projectile.

EKT'ing– 3. affecting, effecting, infecting, confecting, perfecting, objecting, subjecting, ejecting, dejecting, rejecting, injecting, conjecting, projecting, electing, selecting, deflecting, reflecting, inflecting, neglecting, collecting, connecting, respecting, expecting, inspecting, suspecting, erecting, directing, correcting, bisecting, dissecting, detecting, protecting 4. disinfecting, interjecting, re-electing, recollecting, disconnecting, self-respecting, unsuspecting, redirecting, misdirecting, resurrecting, intersecting, vivisecting.

EKT'iv– 3. affective, effective, defective, refective, infective, perfective, objective, subjective, ejective, rejective, conjective, projective, elective, selective, deflective, reflective, inflective, collective, connective, respective, inspective, prospective, perspective, erective, directive, corrective, detective, protective, invective 4. ineffective, imperfective, intellective, recollective, disconnective, irrespective, circumspective, retrospective, introspective.

EKT'li– 3. abjectly, selectly, suspectly, erectly, directly, correctly 4. circumspectly, indirectly, incorrectly.

EKT'ment– 3. ejectment, dejectment, rejectment, projectment.

EKT'ness– 3. abjectness, subjectness, selectness, erectness, directness, correctness 4. circumspectness, indirectness, incorrectness.

EKT'or– 2. hector, lector, rector, sector, vector; see also EKT'er– hector etc. above.

EKT'ral– 2. spectral.

EKT'ress– 2. lectress, rectress 3. electress, inspectress, directress, protectress.

EKT'rik– 3. electric 4. dielectric, anelectric 5. hydroelectric.

EKT'riks– 2. rectrix 3. directrix, bisectrix, trisectrix.

EKT'rum– 2. plectrum, spectrum 3. electrum.

EKT'ur– 2. lecture 3. confecture, subjecture, conjecture, projecture, belecture 4. architecture.

EKT'us– 2. pectous, rectus 3. praefectus, delectus, conspectus, prospectus.

EL'a– 2. Ella, Bella, Della, fella, fellah, kella, kellah, cella, sella, Stella, yella [slang] 3. glabella, tabella, rubella, umbella, padella, predella, lamella, canella, prunella, Prunella, Capella, Kapelle [G.], umbrella, corella, doncella, osella, rosella, Marcella, patella 4. Arabella, clarabella, Isabella, villanella, fustanella, tiarella, Cinderella, agacella, varicella, navicella, panatela, tarantella, fenestella.

EL'an– 3. Magellan, Atellan; *see* also **EL'en–** Helen etc. below; also **EL'on–** felon below.

EL'ant– 3. flagellant, appellant, repellent, impellent, propellent, propellant, expellent, expellant, revellent, divellent.

EL'ar– 2. cellar, sellar, stellar 3. glabellar, lamellar, patellar 4. interstellar; *see* also **EL'er–** Eller, etc. below.

EL'as– 2. Hellas, pellas 3. procellas; *see* also **EL'us–** Hellas etc. below.

EL'at– 2. pellate, prelate, cellate, stellate 3. debellate, flabellate, appellate, ocellate, patellate, constellate, scutellate 4. interpellate.

EL'ay– 2. melee, mele.

ELB'a– 2. Elba, Melba 3. peach Melba.

ELCH'er– 2. belcher, welsher, squelcher.

ELCH'ing– 2. belching, welshing, squelching.

ELD'ed– 2. gelded, melded, welded.

ELD'er– 2. elder, gelder, skelder [old slang], melder, welder.

ELD'est– 2. eldest.

ELD'ing– 2. gelding, melding, welding.

EL'een– 2. Hellene, melene.

EL'en– 2. Ellen, Helen 3. |Llewellyn; *see* also **EL'an–** Magellan etc. above; also **EL'on–** felon etc. below.

EL'ent– 3. repellent, impellent, propellent, expellent, revellent, divellent; *see* also **EL'ant–** flagellant etc. above.

EL'er– 2. Eller, beller, feller, heller, Keller [G.], smeller, kneller, speller, seller, cellar, sheller, teller, stellar, weller, dweller, queller, sweller, yeller 3. rebeller, lamellar, appellor, repeller, impeller, compeller, propeller, dispeller, expeller, exceller, foreteller, nonstellar, cave dweller 4. Rockefeller, underseller, storyteller, fortuneteller, interstellar.

EL'est– 2. swellest.

ELF'ik– 2. Delphic, Guelphic 3. didelphic 4. diadelphic, monodelphic.

ELF'in– 2. elfin, Delphin, delphine.

ELF'ish– 2. elfish, pelfish, selfish, shellfish 3. unselfish.

ELF'ri– 2. belfry, pelfry.

EL'i– 2. Elly, belly, delly, Delhi, felly, jelly, kelly, Kelly, melee, smelly, Nelly, shelly, Shelley 3. *shadbelly*, *redbelly*, *slowbelly*, *gorbelly*, *whitebelly*, *potbelly*, nice Nelly, cancelli 4. checkerbelly, vermicelli, Botticelli.

EL'id– 2. bellied, gelid, jellied 3. *slowbellied*, *gorbellied*, *potbellied*.

EL'ik– 2. bellic, fellic, skelic, melic, relic, telic 3. angelic, scalpelic, Pentelic 4. infidelic, evangelic, sapropelic, philatelic, autotelic.

EL'ing– 2. belling, Delling, felling, knelling, smelling, spelling, selling, shelling, telling, welling, dwelling, swelling, quelling, yelling 3. rebelling, repelling, impelling, compelling, propelling, dispelling, misspelling, expelling, outspelling, outselling, excelling, taletelling, foretelling, indwelling 4. parallelling, uncompelling, underselling, storytelling, fortunetelling.

EL'is– 2. Ellis, trellis.

EL'ish– 2. hellish, relish, wellish, swellish 3. embellish, disrelish.

EL'ist– 2. cellist, trellised.

EL'it– 2. prelate, sell it, tell it 3. appellate.

ELM'a– 2. Elma, pelma, Selma, Thelma, Velma.

ELM'et– 2. helmet, pelmet.

ELM′ing– 2. helming, whelming 3. unhelming, dishelming 4. overwhelming.

EL′ness– 2. fellness, wellness, swellness 3. unwellness 4. caramelness.

EL′o– 2. bellow, cello, fellow, Jello, mellow, melo [slang], yellow 3. *playfellow*, niello, prunello, morello, martello, Othello duello, scrivello 4. violoncello, punchinello, albarello, saltarello, Monticello, brocatello, Donatello.

EL′od– 2. bellowed, mellowed, yellowed 3. unmellowed.

EL′on– 2. felon, melon 3. *muskmelon, mushmelon* 4. watermelon; *see* also EL′an– Magellan etc. above and EL′en– Ellen etc. above.

EL′op– 3. develop, envelop.

EL′opd– 3. developed, enveloped 4. undeveloped, unenveloped.

EL′ot– 2. helot, zealot.

EL′oz– 2. bellows, cellos, fellows, mellows, yellows.

ELP′er– 2. helper, yelper.

ELP′ful– 2. helpful 3. self-helpful, unhelpful.

ELP′i– 2. kelpie.

ELP′ing– 2. helping, whelping, yelping.

ELP′less– 2. helpless, kelpless, whelpless, yelpless.

ELT′a– 2. delta, pelta, shelta.

ELT′ed– 2. belted, felted, melted, smelted, pelted, spelted, welted 3. unbelted, unmelted.

ELT′er– 2. belter, felter, kelter, melter, smelter, pelter, spelter, shelter, welter, swelter 4. helter-skelter.

ELTH′i– 2. healthy, stealthy, wealthy 3. unhealthy, unwealthy.

ELT′i– 2. beltie, felty, kelty.

ELT′ing– 2. belting, felting, melting, smelting, pelting, spelting, welting.

ELT′less– 2. beltless, feltless, peltless, weltless.

ELT′ri– 2. peltry, sweltry.

EL′um– 2. bellum [L.], vellum 3. labellum, flabellum, prebellum, cribellum, flagellum, sacellum 4. cerebellum, ante bellum.

EL′us– 2. Hellas, jealous, pellas, Tellus, zealous 3. tassellus, ocellus, procellas, Marcellus, vitellus, entellus 4. overzealous.

ELV′er– 2. delver, helver, shelver.

ELV′ing– 2. delving, helving, shelving.

EL′yun– 2. hellion, selion 3. rebellion.

EL′yus– 3. rebellious.

EM′a– 2. Emma, gemma, lemma, nema, stremma, stemma 3. dilemma, trilemma, maremma 4. analemma, tetralemma, neurilemma.

EM′an– 2. leman, lemman.

EMB′er– 2. ember, member 3. remember, dismember, December, September, November 4. disremember.

EMB′l– 2. tremble, semble 3. atremble, assemble, dissemble, resemble 4. reassemble.

EMB′lans– 2. semblance 3. assemblance, dissemblance, resemblance.

EMB′lant– 2. semblant 3. resemblant.

EMB′ld– 2. trembled, sembled 3. assembled, dissembled, resembled 4. reassembled, unassembled, undissembled.

EMB′lem– 2. emblem.

EMB′ler– 2. trembler, tremblor 3. assembler, dissembler, resembler.

EMB′li– 2. trembly, Wembley 3. assembly, dissembly.

EMB′lij– 3. assemblage.

EMB′lik– 2. emblic.

EMB′ling– 2. trembling, sembling 3. assembling, dissembling, resembling 4. reassembling.

EMB′ral– 2. membral 3. bimembral, trimembral, Septembral.

EMB′rans– 3. remembrance 4. unremembrance.

EM'ent– **2.** clement, Clement **3.** inclement.

EM'er– **2.** emmer, hemmer, tremor, stemmer **3.** condemner, begemmer, contemner.

EM'i– **2.** Emmy, demi-, gemmy, hemi-, jemmy, phlegmy, tremie, semi-, stemmy.

EM'ik– **2.** chemic **3.** ecdemic, pandemic, endemic, alchemic, ischemic, polemic, totemic, systemic **4.** academic, epidemic, polydemic, stratagemic, theoremic.

EM'ing– **2.** hemming, gemming, kembing, lemming, Fleming, clemming, stemming **3.** condemning, begemming, contemning.

EM'ish– **2.** blemish, Flemish, flemish.

EM'ishd– **2.** blemished, Flemished, flemished **3.** unblemished.

EM'ist– **2.** chemist **4.** biochemist.

EM'lin– **2.** gremlin, Kremlin.

EM'on– **2.** lemon.

EMP'er– **2.** semper [L.], temper **3.** attemper, untemper, distemper.

EMP'erd– **2.** tempered **3.** attempered, ill-tempered, distempered.

EMP'est– **2.** tempest.

EMP'l– **2.** Hempel, temple, stemple, stempel.

EMP'lar– **2.** templar **3.** Knight Templar, exemplar.

EMP'ra– **2.** sempre [It.].

EMP'shun– **2.** emption **3.** ademption, redemption, pre-emption, co-emption, exemption.

EMP'ted– **2.** empted, tempted **3.** adempted, pre-empted, attempted, untempted, exempted **4.** unattempted, unexempted.

EMP'ter– **2.** emptor, tempter **3.** preemptor, coemptor, unkempter, attempter.

EMP'ti– **2.** empty.

EMP'ting– **2.** empting, tempting **3.** pre-empting, attempting, exempting.

EMP'tiv– **3.** redemptive, pre-emptive.

EMP'tress– **2.** temptress **3.** redemptress.

EN'a– **2.** bena, henna, jenna, senna **3.** Gehenna, Alhenna, Siena, sienna, Vienna, antenna, duenna, Ravenna.

EN'ant– **2.** pennant, tenant **3.** lieutenant.

EN'as– **2.** menace, tenace; see also EN'is– Dennis etc. below.

EN'at– **2.** pennate **3.** tripennate, impennate, antennate **4.** latipennate.

ENCH'ant– **2.** penchant, trenchant **3.** intrenchant.

ENCH'er– **2.** bencher, blencher, flencher, clencher, wrencher, drencher, trencher, censure, quencher **3.** retrencher, intrencher.

ENCH'ing– **2.** benching, blenching, flenching, clenching, wrenching, drenching, trenching, quenching **3.** bedrenching, retrenching, unquenching.

ENCH'less– **2.** benchless, trenchless, quenchless.

ENCH'man– **2.** henchman, Frenchman.

ENCH'ment– **3.** retrenchment, entrenchment, intrenchment.

END'a– **2.** benda, denda, Brenda, Zenda **3.** addenda, credenda, agenda, legenda, delenda, commenda [L.] **4.** referenda, hacienda, corrigenda.

END'al– **2.** trendle, sendal, sendle **3.** prebendal **4.** referendal.

END'ans– **2.** tendance **3.** ascendance, descendance, attendance; see also END'ens– resplendence etc. below.

END'ant– **2.** pendant, tendant **3.** defendant, appendant, dependant, ascendant, descendant **4.** codefendant, codescendant; see also END'ent– splendent etc. below.

END'ed– **2.** ended, bended, fended, blended, mended, friended, trended, tended, vended, wended **3.** upended, defended, offended, unblended, amended, emended, commended, appended, depended, impended, expended, suspended, befriended, unfriended, ascended, descended, transcended, attended, pretended, intended, contended, portended, extended, distended **4.** undefended, apprehended, reprehended, comprehended, interblended, recommended, condescended, unattended, unintended, unextended **5.** misapprehended, miscomprehended, unrecommended, superintended.

END'ens– 3. resplendence, dependence, impendence, transcendence, intendence **4.** independence, condescendence **5.** interdependence, superintendence; *see* also **END'ans–** tendance etc. above.

END'ent– 2. splendent, pendent, tendent **3.** resplendent, transplendent, dependent, impendent, ascendent, descendent, transcendent **4.** independent, undependent, equipendent, condescendent **5.** interdependent, superintendent; *see* also **END'ant–** pendant etc. above.

END'er– 2. ender, bender, fender, gender, lender, blender, splendor, slender, mender, spender, render, trender, sender, tender, vender, vendor, wender **3.** defender, offender, engender, amender, commender, depender, expender, suspender, befriender, surrender, ascender, descender, pretender, contender **4.** apprehender, reprehender, comprehender, moneylender, interblender, recommender.

END'erz– fenders etc., *see* **END'er–** ender etc. above plus "s" or " 's."

END'i– 2. bendy, fendy, Mendi, Wendy **3.** effendi **5.** modus vivendi [L.].

END'ing– 2. ending, bending, fending, lending, blending, mending, pending, spending, rending, trending, sending, tending, vending, wending **3.** unending, upending, unbending, defending, offending, amending, commending, depending, impending, perpending, expending, misspending, suspending, befriending, heart-rending, ascending, de-

scending, transcending, attending, pretending, contending, portending, distending, extending **4.** unoffending, apprehending, reprehending, comprehending, interblending, moneylending, recommending, overspending, condescending, unpretending **5.** superintending.

END'less– 2. endless, bendless, mendless, trendless, friendless.

END'li– 2. friendly **3.** unfriendly.

END'ment– 3. amendment, commendment, befriendment, intendment.

END'o– 3. reddendo, crescendo **4.** decrescendo, diluendo [It.], innuendo **5.** diminuendo.

END'or– 2. splendor, vendor; *see* also **END'er–** ender etc. above.

END'um– 3. habendum, addendum, dedendum, reddendum, credendum, agendum, commendam, tenendum **4.** corrigendum, referendum.

END'us– 3. tremendous, stupendous.

EN'el– 2. bennel, fennel, kennel, vennel.

EN'ent– tenent; *see* also **EN'ant–** pennant etc. above.

EN'er– 2. penner, tenner, tenor, Venner **4.** countertenor.

EN'et– 2. Bennett, bennet, dennet, jennet, genet, rennet, sennet, senate, tenet.

ENG'then– 2. lengthen, strengthen.

ENG'thi– 2. lengthy, strengthy.

EN'i– 2. any, benne, beni, benny, Benny, fenny, henny, jenny, Jennie, Lenny, blenny, many, penny, wenny **3.** Kilkenny, *catchpenny, halfpenny, passpenny, sixpenny, twopenny.*

EN'ik– 2. phenic, genic, splenic, phrenic, scenic, sthenic **3.** Edenic, hyphenic, dysgenic, eugenic, lichenic, Galenic, galenic, selenic, Hellenic, irenic, *arsenic,* parthenic, asthenic **4.** metagenic, polygenic, oxygenic, authigenic, Diogenic, cacogenic, psychogenic, chromogenic, thermogenic, monogenic, nitrogenic, photogenic, pathogenic, philhellenic, Panhellenic, proselenic, paraphrenic, neurasthenic, calisthenic, Demosthenic.

EN'iks–   **3.** dysgenics, eugenics, poimenics, irenics.

EN'im–   **2.** denim.

EN'in–   **2.** Lenin, rennin, venin.

EN'ing–   **2.** denning, fenning, kenning, penning.

EN'is–   **2.** Dennis, menace, tenace, tennis, Venice.

EN'ish–   **2.** hennish, plenish, Rhenish, wennish   **3.** deplenish, replenish, displenish.

EN'it–   **2.** jennet, senate, sennit, sennet, sennight.

EN'iz–   **2.** bennies, jennies, pennies.

ENJ'er–   **3.** avenger, revenger.

ENJ'in–   **2.** engine.

ENJ'ing–   **2.** venging   **3.** avenging, revenging.

ENJ'ment–   **3.** avengement, revengement.

ENK'i–   **2.** renky [dial. Eng.].

EN'li–   **2.** Henley, cleanly   **3.** uncleanly.

EN'lik–   **2.** denlike, fenlike, henlike, penlike, wrenlike.

EN'om–   **2.** venom, mennom   **3.** envenom.

EN'on–   **2.** mennon, pennon, tenon.

ENS'al–   **2.** mensal   **3.** bimensal, commensal, forensal.

ENS'at–   **2.** sensate   **3.** condensate, compensate, insensate, intensate.

ENS'eez–   **2.** menses   **4.** Albigenses   **5.** amanuenses.

ENS'en–   **2.** ensign, densen.

ENS'er–   **2.** denser, fencer, flenser, menser [Scot. & N. of Eng.], spencer, Spencer, Spenser, censer, censor, senser, sensor, tenser, tensor   **3.** condenser, prehensor, commencer, dispenser, extensor, intenser   **4.** recompenser.

ENS'est–   **2.** densest, tensest   **3.** intensest.

ENS'ez–   **2.** fences, flenses, menses [Scot. & N. of Eng.], censes, senses, tenses   **3.** condenses, commences, dispenses, incenses   **4.** recompenses, quartertenses, influences.

ENS'forth–   **2.** henceforth, thenceforth, whenceforth.

ENS'ful–   **2.** penseful [obs. exc. dial.], senseful.

ENSH'al–   **3.** credential, rodential, prudential, agential, bigential, tangential, torrential, essential, sentential, potential, Provencial, sequential   **4.** precedential, confidential, residential, presidential, evidential, sapiential, pestilential, deferential, referential, preferential, differential, inferential, conferential, transferential, reverential, inessential, nonessential, penitential, influential, subsequential, consequential   **5.** jurisprudential, expediential, intelligential, circumferential, unreverential, irreverential, equipotential, inconsequential.

ENSH'alz–   **3.** credentials, essentials, potentials.

ENSH'ent–   **2.** sentient   **3.** assentient, presentient, dissentient, insentient, consentient.

ENSH'er–   **2.** censure.

ENSH'un–   **2.** gentian, mention, pension, tension   **3.** indention, prehension, declension, dimension, repension, propension, suspension, ascension, descension, recension, presention, dissension, accension, incension, consension, attention, obtention, detention, retention, pretension, intention, intension, contention, portention, abstention, extention, distention, ostension, obvention, subvention, prevention, invention, convention   **4.** apprehension, reprehension, comprehension, reascension, condescension, inattention, hypotension, hypertension, contravention, circumvention, supervention, intervention   **5.** inapprehension, misapprehension, incomprehension, uncondescension, nonintervention.

ENSH'unz– gentians etc., *see* ENSH'un-gentian etc. above, plus "s" or "'s."

ENSH'us– 3. tendentious, silentious, li-centious, dissentious, pretentious, senten-tious, contentious 4. conscientious, un-pretentious.

ENS'i– 2. pensy [Scot. & dial. Eng.].

ENS'il– 2. bensel [Scot. & dial. Eng.], pen-cil, pencel, pensile, sensile, tensile, stencil 3. prehensile, depencil, blue-pencil, exten-sile, utensil 4. hyperpencil.

ENS'ild– 2. pencilled, tensiled, stencilled 3. blue-pencilled, utensilled.

ENS'ing– 2. fencing, flensing, censing, mensing [Scot. & N. of Eng.], tensing 3. condensing, commencing, dispensing, in-censing, pretensing 4. recompensing, in-fluencing.

ENS'is– 5. amanuensis.

ENS'iv– 2. pensive, tensive 3. defensive, offensive, prehensive, expensive, suspen-sive, intensive, extensive, distensive, os-tensive 4. inoffensive, apprehensive, comprehensive, recompensive, inexpen-sive, condescensive, inextensive 5. inap-prehensive, incomprehensive.

ENS'less– 2. fenceless, penceless, senseless 3. defenseless, offenseless, expenseless 4. recompenseless.

ENS'li– 2. densely, tensely 3. immense-ly, propensely, intensely.

ENS'ment– 3. commencement, incense-ment.

ENS'ness– 2. denseness, tenseness 3. im-menseness, propenseness, intenseness.

ENS'um– 2. pensum, sensum.

ENS'us– 2. census 3. consensus.

ENT'a– 2. nenta, Senta 3. magenta, po-lenta, Pimenta, pimienta, cuarenta, pla-centa 4. pedimenta 5. rejectamenta, impedimenta.

ENT'ad– 2. entad, pentad 4. ectoentad.

ENT'al– 2. ental, dental, gentle, mental, rental, trental, cental 3. edental, bi-dental, tridental, postdental, ungentle, amental, fragmental, amental, segmental, tegmental, pigmental, momental, parental, percental 4. accidental, incidental, transcendental, interdental, oriental, fun-damental, ligamental, firmamental, orna-mental, tournamental, sacramental, atra-mental, testamental, elemental, comple-mental, supplemental, tenemental, recre-mental, incremental, pedimental, condi-mental, rudimental, regimental, alimental, complimental, detrimental, nutrimental, sentimental, governmental, apartmental, departmental, compartmental, documen-tal, tegumental, argumental, monumental, instrumental, continental, componental, grandparental, biparental 5. anteceden-tal, coincidental, medicamental, predica-mental, temperamental, impedimental, experimental, developmental; *see* also ENT'il– dentil etc. below.

ENT'alz– 2. rentals, trentals 4. inciden-tals, regimentals.

ENT'ans– 2. sentence 3. repentance 4. unrepentance.

ENT'ant– 3. repentant 4. unrepentant, representant.

ENT'at– 2. dentate 3. edentate, biden-tate, tridentate 4. testamentate.

ENT'ay– 3. dolente 4. presidente, tarda-mente [It.], lentamente [It.], cognoscente [It.] 5. aguardiente [Sp.] 6. dolce far niente [It.].

ENT'e– diapente; *see* also ENT'i– Henty etc. below.

ENT'ed– 2. dented, rented, scented, tent-ed, vented 3. indented, relented, la-mented, demented, cemented, augmented, fermented, tormented, repented, unrent-ed, assented, dissented, consented, un-scented, contented, frequented, pre-vented, invented 4. precedented, unin-dented, unlamented, ornamented, compli-mented, supplemented, battlemented, un-repented, represented, discontented, un-frequented, circumvented 5. unprecedented, unornamented, misrepresented, unrepresented.

ENT'en– 2. Lenten.

ENT'ens– 2. sentence 3. repentance 4. unrepentance.

ENT'er– 2. enter, denter, renter, center, tenter, venter 3. re-enter, indenter, lamenter, cementer, augmenter, commenter, fomenter, fermenter, tormenter, tormentor, repenter, assenter, absenter, decenter, recenter, precentor, dissenter, incenter, incentor, consenter, retentor, frequenter, preventer, inventor, resenter, presenter 4. unrelentor, ornamenter, supplementer, epicenter, barycenter, circumventor, representer 5. experimenter, misrepresenter; *see* also **ENT'or–** lentor etc. below.

ENT'erd– 2. entered, centered, tentered 3. re-entered, self-centered.

ENT'ez– 2. flentes [L.], twenties.

ENT'ful– 2. scentful 3. lamentful, contentful, resentful, eventful, inventful 4. unresentful, uneventful, uninventful.

ENT'i– 2. Henty, Lenty, plenty, twenty 3. Amenti, aplenty 4. diapente, cognoscenti [It.].

ENT'ij– 2. ventage 3. percentage.

ENT'ik– 3. identic, argentic, crescentic, authentic.

ENT'il– 2. dentil, dentile, lentil, centile, ventil 3. percentile; *see* also **ENT'al–** ental etc. above; also **ENT'l–** gentle etc. below.

ENT'ile– 2. gentile, centile.

ENT'in– 2. dentin, dentine, Quentin 3. Tridentine, San Quentin.

ENT'ing– 2. denting, renting, scentîng, tenting, venting 3. indenting, relenting, lamenting, cementing, augmenting, fomenting, fermenting, tormenting, repenting, accenting, assenting, absenting, dissenting, consenting, contenting, preventing, inventing, frequenting, resenting, presenting 4. unrelenting, ornamenting,

supplementing, complimenting, circumventing, representing 5. experimenting, misrepresenting.

ENT'is– 2. prentice 3. apprentice 5. non compos mentis [L.].

ENT'ist– 2. dentist, prenticed 3. apprenticed, trecentist, preventist, presentist.

ENT'iv– 3. pedentive, lamentive, assentive, incentive, attentive, detentive, retentive, adventive, preventive, presentive 4. inattentive, unretentive, circumventive, interventive.

ENT'l– 2. gentle 3. ungentle; *see* also **ENT'al–** ental etc. above; also **ENT'il–** dentil etc. above.

ENT'less– 2. bentless, dentless, Lentless, rentless, scentless, centless, tentless, ventless 3. relentless, lamentless, cementless, fermentless, tormentless, repentless, descentless, consentless, contentless, eventless, resentless.

ENT'li– 2. gently 3. ungently, intently 4. confidently, evidently, excellently, insolently, eminently, innocently, impotently.

ENT'ment– 3. relentment, contentment, resentment, presentment 4. discontentment, representment.

ENT'ness– 2. bentness, lentness, meantness, pentness, spentness 3. intentness 4. confidentness, evidentness, excellentness, insolentness.

ENT'o– 2. lento, cento 3. memento, pimento, pimiento, fomento, Sorrento, trecento 4. Sacramento, portamento, pentimento, quattrocento 6. pronunciamento.

ENT'oid– 2. dentoid.

ENT'or– 2. lentor, mentor, centaur, stentor 3. fermentor, tormentor, precentor, succentor, incentor, bucentaur, retentor 4. unrelentor, circumventor; *see* also **ENT'er–** enter etc. above.

ENT'os– 2. pentose.

ENT'ral– 2. central, ventral 3. subcentral, precentral, biventral 4. paracentral, metacentral, dorsiventral.

ENT'rans– 2. entrance, entrants 3. reentrance, re-entrants.

ENT'ri– 2. entry, gentry, sentry.

ENT'rik– 2. centric 3. acentric, eccentric, concentric 4. paracentric, metacentric, barycentric, geocentric, egocentric, homocentric 5. Saturnicentric, heliocentric, anthropocentric.

ENT'rum– 2. centrum 3. precentrum, epicentrum, pseudocentrum.

ENT'um– 2. mentum 3. amentum, ramentum, cementum, tegmentum, momentum, sarmentum, fermentum, tormentum, frumentum [L.], percentum, unguentum 4. fundamentum [L.], velamentum, sacramentum, testamentum 5. paludamentum.

ENT'ur– 2. denture, tenture, venture 3. debenture, indenture, rudenture, adventure, reventure 4. maladventure, peradventure, misadventure.

ENT'us– 3. pigmentous, momentous, sarmentous, portentous, unguentous 4. ligamentous, filamentous, immomentous pedetentous.

EN'um– 2. venom, mennom 3. envenom.

EN'vi– 2. envy.

ENZ'a– 3. cadenza 4. influenza.

ENZ'ez– 2. lenses, cleanses.

ENZ'i– 2. frenzy 3. Rienzi.

ENZ'iz– 2. frenzies, Menzies.

EP'er– 2. hepper, leper, pepper, strepor, tepor, stepper 3. high-stepper.

EP'erd– 2. jeopard, leopard, peppered, shepherd.

EP'i– 2. kepi, peppy, tepee 3. Apepi.

EP'id– 2. lepid, trepid, tepid 3. intrepid.

EP'ik– 2. epic 3. monepic 4. orthoëpic.

EP'ing– 2. pepping, stepping 3. high-stepping 4. overstepping.

EP'it– 3. decrepit.

EP'o– 2. Beppo, depot.

EP'od– 2. epode, depoted.

EP'ok– 2. epoch.

EP'on– 2. weapon.

EP'shun– 3. ereption, surreption, deception, reception, preception, exception, inception, conception, perception, susception 4. beneception, antiseption, preconception, misconception, apperception, preperception, imperception, interception 5. nociperception, introsusception, intussusception.

EP'si– 3. apepsy, dyspepsy, eupepsy 4. catalepsy, epilepsy.

EP'sis– 2. pepsis, sepsis, scepsis 3. syllepsis, prolepsis, asepsis 4. analepsis, paralepsis, metalepsis, antisepsis.

EPT'al– 2. heptal, septal.

EPT'ans– 3. acceptance, exceptance.

EPT'ant– 2. reptant 3. acceptant, exceptant.

EPT'ed– 3. accepted, excepted 4. unaccepted, unexcepted, intercepted.

EPT'er– 2. scepter, sceptre 3. adepter, receptor, preceptor, accepter, excepter, inceptor, susceptor 4. intercepter; see also EPT'or– receptor etc. below.

EPT'ik– 2. skeptic, kleptic, peptic, threptic, septic, sceptic 3. sylleptic, proleptic, apeptic, dyspeptic, eupeptic, aseptic 4. analeptic, cataleptic, metaleptic, epileptic, nympholeptic, bradypeptic, antiseptic 5. epanaleptic, acataleptic.

EPT'il– 2. reptile, septile.

EPT'ing– 3. accepting, excepting, incepting 4. intercepting.

EPT'iv– 3. acceptive, deceptive, receptive, preceptive, exceptive, inceptive, conceptive, perceptive, susceptive 4. nociceptive, autoceptive, apperceptive, imperceptive, interceptive, insusceptive **5.** intussusceptive.

EPT'li– 3. adeptly, ineptly.

EPT'ness– 3. adeptness, ineptness.

EPT'or– 3. receptor, preceptor, inceptor, susceptor **4.** beneceptor; *see* also **EPT'er–** scepter, etc. above.

EPT'um– 2. septum **3.** perceptum.

ER'a– 2. serra, terra [It.] **3.** sierra, acerra.

ER'af– 2. seraph, teraph; *see* also **ER'if–** serif etc. below.

ER'ald– 2. Gerald, herald, Herrold, perilled **3.** imperilled.

ER'and– 2. errand.

ER'ant– 2. errant **3.** aberrant.

ER'ens– 2. Terence **3.** aberrance.

ER'er– 2. error, terror.

ER'et– 2. ferret, lerret, terret, wherret; *see* also **ER'it–** merit etc. below.

ER'i– 2. berry, bury, cherry, derry, ferry, jerry, Kerry, skerry, flerry, merry, perry, serry, sherry, terry, very, wherry **3.** *bayberry, dayberry, burberry, redberry, breadberry, chokeberry, baneberry, wineberry, oneberry, Juneberry, youngberry, bogberry, dogberry, hackberry, blackberry, inkberry, pinkberry, bilberry, mulberry, cranberry, snowberry, crowberry, strawberry, squawberry, barberry, deerberry, mossberry, raspberry, catberry, dewberry, blueberry, gooseberry, chokecherry* **4.** chinaberry, guavaberry, coffeeberry, beriberi, partridgeberry, orangeberry, thimbleberry, bumbleberry, dangleberry, tangleberry, huckleberry, loganberry, rowanberry, checkerberry, winterberry, Christmasberry, lotusberry, locustberry, Pondicherry, millinery, stationery, lamasery, cemetery, presbytery, mesentery, monastery.

ER'id– 2. berried, buried, cherried, ferried, serried, wherried **3.** unburied, unserried.

ER'if– 2. serif, sheriff **4.** undersheriff; *see* also **ER'af–** seraph etc. above.

ER'ik– 2. Eric, deric, derrick, ferric, spheric, Herrick, cleric, ceric, Seric, pteric, terek, steric, queric **3.** suberic, valeric, dimeric, chimeric, Homeric, mesmeric, generic, piperic, glyceric, icteric, enteric, hysteric **4.** peripheric, helispheric, hemispheric, perispheric, atmospheric, metameric, isomeric, polymeric, neoteric, esoteric, exoteric.

ER'iks– 2. derricks, clerics **3.** hysterics **4.** esoterics.

ER'il– 2. beryl, ferrule, peril, sterile **3.** imperil, unsterile **4.** chrysoberyl.

ER'in– 2. Serin.

ER'ing– 2. erring, herring.

ER'is– 2. Eris, derris, ferris, terrace.

ER'ish– 2. cherish, perish.

ER'it– 2. merit **3.** inherit, demerit **4.** disinherit.

ER'iz– 2. berries, buries, cherries, ferries, sherries, wherries, queries.

ER'on– 2. heron.

ER'or– 2. error, terror.

ER'ul– 2. ferule, ferrule, spherule, perule.

ER'und– 2. errand, gerund.

ER'us– 2. ferrous **3.** nonferrous.

ES'a– 2. dessa, sessa, Tessa **3.** Odessa, Marpessa, Duessa **4.** dogaressa.

ES'al– 2. quezal, vessel **3.** redressal, processal; *see* also **ES'il–** decile etc. below; also **ES'l–** deasil etc. below.

ES'ant– 2. jessant **3.** confessant, caressant, depressant, incessant.

ES'ay– 2. esse [L.], essay.

ESCH'al– 2. bestial **3.** celestial, agrestial.

ESCH'un– 2. question **3.** suggestion, digestion, ingestion, congestion, requestion **4.** indigestion.

ES'ed– 2. essed, blessed.

ES'en– 2. Essen, lessen, lesson.

ES'ens— 2. essence, crescents 3. albescence, rubescence, candescence, quiescence, calescence, mollescence, tumescence, senescence, accrescence, excrescence, concrescence, nigrescence, virescence, florescence, floressence, vitrescence, putrescence, latescence, lactescence, quintessence, mutescence, frutescence, liquescence 4. erubescence, lapidescence, iridescence, viridescence, incandescence, recrudescence, acquiescence, requiescence, decalescence, coalescence, opalescence, convalescence, adolescence, obsolescence, intumescence, evanescence, juvenescence, luminescence, arborescence, phosphorescence, calorescence, efflorescence, deflorescence, inflorescence, sonorescence, fluorescence, deliquescence, effervescence 5. nonacquiescence, rejuvenescence.

ES'ent— 2. crescent 3. albescent, rubescent, candescent, quiescent, calescent, tumescent, senescent, lignescent, accrescent, decrescent, increscent, excrescent, nigrescent, virescent, florescent, horrescent, vitrescent, latescent, frutescent, liquescent, fervescent 4. erubescent, lapidescent, iridescent, viridescent, incandescent, acquiescent, coalescent, opalescent, convalescent, scintellescent, adolescent, obsolescent, luminescent, phosphorescent, efflorescent, sonorescent, fluorescent, deliquescent, effervescent 5. nonacquiescent, rejuvenescent, noneffervescent, uneffervescent.

ES'er— 2. guesser, jessur, lesser, lessor, blesser, plessor, messer, dresser, presser, cesser 3. confessor, professor, sublessor, addresser, redresser, redressor, aggressor, progressor, transgressor, depressor, represser, impresser, compressor, oppressor, suppressor, assessor, obsessor, successor, possessor 4. acquiescer, second guesser, predecessor, antecessor, intercessor, dispossessor.

ES'ez— 2. s's, S's, eses, esses, desses, fesses, 'fesses, guesses, jesses, blesses, messes, dresses, cresses, presses, tresses, stresses, sesses, cesses, yeses 3. confesses, professes, turgesces, kermesses, finenesses, caresses, addresses, redresses, undresses, regresses, digresses, progresses, transgresses, accresces, depresses, represses, impresses, compresses, oppresses, suppresses, expresses, distresses, assesses, obsesses, recesses, possesses, successes 4. SOS's, incandesces, stewardesses, shepherdesses, second guesses, acquiesces, coalesces, convalesces, luminesces, baronesses, readdresses, retrogresses, water cresses, phosphoresces, effloresces, fluoresces, recompresses, overstresses, reassesses, repossesses, prepossesses, dispossesses, poetesses, effervesces, deliquesces 5. rejuvenesces, ambassadresses.

ES'ful— 3. distressful, successful 4. nonsuccessful, unsuccessful.

ESH'al— 2. deasil, special 3. especial.

ESH'ens— 2. nescience, prescience.

ESH'er— 2. mesher, fresher, pressure, thresher, tressure 3. refresher, nonpressure.

ESH'i— 2. fleshy, meshy.

ESH'ing— 2. meshing, threshing 3. refreshing.

ESH'l— 2. deasil, special 3. especial.

ESH'less— 2. fleshless, meshless.

ESH'li— 2. fleshly, freshly 3. unfleshly, unfreshly.

ESH'ment— 3. enmeshment, refreshment.

ESH'un— 2. Hessian, freshen, cession, session 3. confession, profession, aggression, egression, regression, digression, ingression, congression, progression, transgression, depression, repression, impression, compression, oppression, expression, suppression, obsession, recession, precession, secession, accession, succession, concession, possession 4. nonaggression, retrogression, introgression, repossession, prepossession, self-possession, dispossession, retrocession, introcession, supersession, intercession, indiscretion, quarter session.

ESH'unz– Hessians etc., see ESH'un–
Hessian etc. above, plus "s" or "'s."

ESH'us– 2. precious 3. enmesh us, refresh us.

ES'i– 2. esse [L.], Essie, Bessie, Jesse, Jessie, messy, dressy, tressy, Tessie 3. in esse [L.].

ES'ij– 2. message, presage 3. expressage.

ES'il– 2. decile, cresyl, sessile, Cecil; see also ES'l– deasil etc. below; also ES'al– quezal etc. above.

ES'ing– 2. guessing, jessing, blessing, messing, pressing, stressing, yessing 3. confessing, professing, caressing, addressing, redressing, undressing, digressing, progressing, depressing, repressing, impressing, compressing, oppressing, suppressing, expressing, assessing, possessing, distressing 4. acquiescing, coalescing, convalescing, retrogressing, repossessing, prepossessing, unpossessing, dispossessing, effervescing 5. unprepossessing.

ES'iv– 2. crescive 3. caressive, redressive, aggressive, regressive, digressive, ingressive, congressive, progressive, transgressive, depressive, repressive, impressive, compressive, obsessive, recessive, accessive, excessive, successive, concessive, possessive 4. unprogressive, retrogressive, inexpressive, unexcessive.

ESK'i– 2. desky, pesky [coll.].

ESK'li– 3. blottesquely, grotesquely 4. picturesquely, statuesquely.

ESK'ness– 3. grotesqueness 4. picturesqueness, statuesqueness.

ESK'o– 2. fresco 3. tedesco [It.], alfresco, grotesco [obs.].

ESK'u– 2. fescue, rescue.

ES'l– 2. deasil, chessel, nestle, pestle, wrestle, trestle, sessile, Cecil, vessel 3. unnestle; see also ES'al– quezal etc. above; ES'il– decile etc. above.

ES'ler– 2. nestler, wrestler.

ES'ling– 2. nestling, wrestling.

ES'man– 2. pressman, yes man [slang].

ES'ment– 3. redressment, impressment, assessment.

ES'on– 2. Essen, lesson, lessen.

ES'or– 2. lessor, plessor 3. confessor, professor, aggressor, possessor; see also ES'er– guesser etc. above.

EST'a– 2. festa [It.], testa, cuesta, Vesta 3. podesta, egesta, ingesta, fiesta [Sp.], siesta, Avesta.

EST'al– 2. festal, vestal 3. agrestal.

EST'ant– 2. gestant, restant 3. contestant.

EST'ed– 2. bested, chested, jested, nested, rested, wrested, breasted, crested, tested, quested, vested, zested 3. infested, suggested, digested, ingested, congested, molested, arrested, unrested, attested, detested, protested, requested, unquested, divested, invested 4. manifested, predigested, undigested, unmolested, doublebreasted, single-breasted, pigeonb-reasted, interested 5. uninterested, disinterested.

EST'er– 2. ester, Esther, bester, Chester, fester, Hester, jester, Lester, Leicester, Nestor, nester, pester, rester, wrester, testar, tester, vester, wester, quester 3. infester, suggester, digester, molester, semester, trimester, arrester, attester, contester, protester, requester, sequester, Sylvestor, northwester, southwester 4. manifester, mid-semester.

EST'ern– 2. hestern [obs.], western, yestern [arch.] 3. midwestern, northwestern, southwestern.

EST'ez– 2. Estes, restes 3. Dermestes, Herpestes, Orestes.

EST'ful– 2. jestful, restful, questful, zestful 3. unrestful.

EST'i– 2. chesty, Feste, resty, cresty, teste, testy, westy, zesty.

EST'ik– 2. gestic 3. asbestic, majestic,

orchestic, telestic, telestich, domestic, amnestic, agrestic 4. anapestic, catachrestic.

ĔST″in– 2. destine, sestine 3. predestine, clandestine, intestine.

ĔST″ind– 2. destined 3. predestined, undestined.

ĔST″ing– 2. besting, guesting, jesting, nesting, resting, wresting, breasting, cresting, testing, vesting, westing, questing 3. infesting, suggesting, digesting, ingesting, congesting, arresting, attesting, detesting, contesting, protesting, divesting, investing, requesting 4. manifesting, interesting 5. disinteresting, uninteresting.

ĔST″is– 2. restis 3. Alcestis; see also ĔST″us– Festus etc. below.

ĔST″iv– 2. estive, festive, restive 3. infestive, suggestive, digestive, congestive, tempestive, attestive 4. manifestive.

ĔST″less– 2. guestless, jestless, restless, breastless, crestless, questless.

ĔST″ling– 2. nestling.

ĔST″ment– 2. vestment 3. arrestment, divestment, investment.

ĔST″o– 2. presto 4. manifesto.

ĔST″ral– 2. kestrel 3. orchestral, palestral, semestral, trimestral, fenestral, campestral, ancestral.

ĔST″ri– 2. vestry.

ĔST″ur– 2. gesture, vesture 3. revesture, divesture, investure.

ĔST″us– 2. Festus, restis, cestus 3. asbestos, Alcestis.

ĔT″a– 2. eta, Etta, geta, meta, Greta, stretta 3. vendetta, codetta [It.], Valetta, burletta, lametta, Minetta, Egretta, biretta, Rosetta, mozzetta 4. arietta, Henrietta, animetta [It.], operetta 5. comedietta.

ĔT″al– 2. metal, petal 3. abettal, begettal; see also ĔT″l– ettle etc. below.

ĔT″ed– 2. betted, jetted, netted, petted, retted, fretted, stetted, vetted, wetted, whetted, sweated 3. abetted, indebted,

coquetted, unfretted, regretted, brevetted, curvetted, gazetted 4. epauletted, coronetted, bayonetted, interfretted, unregretted, pirouetted.

ĔT″en– 2. Breton, threaten, whetten 3. rethreaten.

ĔT″er– 2. better, debtor, fetter, getter, letter, netter, petter, retter, fretter, wetter, sweater, whetter 3. abettor, enfetter, unfetter, begetter, go-getter, forgetter, dead letter, red-letter, black-letter, regretter, besetter, typesetter, upsetter.

ĔT″est– 2. wettest.

ĔT″ful– 2. netful, fretful 3. forgetful, regretful 4. unforgetful.

ĔTH″el– 2. Ethel, ethal, Bethel.

ĔTH″er– 2. feather, heather, leather, blether, mether, nether, tether, weather, wether, whether 3. tail feather, pinfeather, together, whitleather, comether, aweather, bellwether 4. altogether, patent leather.

ĔTH″erd– 2. feathered, heathered, leathered, tethered, weathered 3. pinfeathered, unfeathered, untethered, unweathered.

ĔT″i– 2. betty, Betty, chetty, Hetty, jetty, Letty, netty, Nettie, petty, petit, fretty, pretty, sweaty 3. confetti, spaghetti, libretti, sunsetty, Rossetti 4. spermaceti, Donizetti.

ĔT″ik– 2. Lettic, metic 3. ascetic, syndetic, algetic, Gangetic, aphetic, Japhetic, prophetic, bathetic, pathetic, synthetic, prothetic, aesthetic, poietic, ochletic, athletic, phyletic, gametic, emetic, mimetic, cometic, hermetic, seismetic, cosmetic, genetic, splenetic, phrenetic, threnetic, magnetic, kinetic, phonetic, goetic, noetic, Noetic, poetic, zoetic, herpetic, paretic, syncretic, heretic, heuretic, pyretic, Ossetic, zetetic, Helvetic, auxetic 4. alphabetic, diabetic, asyndetic, geodetic, cynegetic, exegetic, analgetic, energetic, synergetic, syzygetic, diathetic, apathetic, sympathetic, epithetic, antithetic, epenthetic, parenthetic, nomothetic, cosmothetic, hypothetic, anesthetic, rabietic, homiletic, arithmetic, Baphometic, hypnoetic, theoretic, anchoretic, diuretic, apatetic, erotetic, synartetic **5.** apologetic, antipathetic, polysynthetic, polyprothetic, hyperesthetic, cosmopoietic, monophyletic, polyphyletic, metagenetic, psychogenetic, morphogenetic, pathogenetic, homogenetic, thermogenetic, monogenetic, oogenetic, pyrogenetic, polygenetic, diamagnetic, parakinetic, telekinetic, autokinetic, dianoetic, mythopoetic, chrysopoetic, diaphoretic, antipyretic, peripatetic **6.** heterophyletic, paleogenetic, parthenogenetic, heterogenetic **7.** onomatopoetic.

ĔT′iks– **3.** athletics, Hermetics, cosmetics, magnetics, kinetics, phonetics, poetics, aesthetics **4.** cynegetics, exegetics, homiletics, theoretics, dietetics.

ĔT′ing– **2.** betting, getting, jetting, letting, bletting, netting, petting, retting, fretting, setting, wetting, sweating, whetting **3.** abetting, begetting, forgetting, coquetting, regretting, besetting, upsetting, brevetting, curvetting, gazetting **4.** unforgetting, somersetting, intersetting, minuetting **5.** mosquito netting.

ĔT′ish– **2.** fetish, fetich, Lettish, pettish, wettish **3.** coquettish.

ĔT′ist– **3.** cornettist, librettist, motettist, duettist, vignettist **4.** clarinettist.

ĔT′l– **2.** ettle [dial.], fettle, kettle, metal, mettle, nettle, petal, Gretel, settle, cetyl **3.** abettal, unmettle, resettle, unsettle **4.** centripetal **6.** Popocatepetl.

ĔT′ld– **2.** fettled, mettled, petalled, settled **3.** high mettled, unsettled **4.** double petalled.

ĔT′ler– **2.** nettler, settler.

ĔT′less– **2.** debtless, threatless.

ĔT′ling– **2.** fettling, nettling, settling **3.** unsettling.

ĔT′ment– **3.** abetment, indebtment, besetment, revetment.

ĔT′ness– **2.** setness, wetness.

ĔT′o– **2.** ghetto, stretto **3.** concetto [It.], zucchetto, stiletto, palmetto, rispetto [It.], libretto, falsetto, terzetto **4.** lazaretto, allegretto, amoretto.

ĔT′rad– **2.** retrad, tetrad.

ĔT′rik– **2.** metric **3.** dimetric, symmetric **4.** diametric, dynametric, asymmetric, pedometric, geometric, logometric ergometric, thermometric, chronometric, barometric, micrometric, hydrometric, hygrometric, isometric, photometric, autometric, tautometric **5.** trigonometric, magnetometric.

ĔT′sal– **2.** quetzal, pretzel.

ĔT′so– **2.** pezzo [It.]. **4.** intermezzo.

ĔT′work– **2.** network, fretwork.

ĔV′an– **2.** Evan, Bevan, Devon; *see* also **ĔV′en–** heaven etc. below.

ĔV′el– **2.** bevel, kevel, level, nevel, revel **3.** sea level, dishevel **4.** water level, spirit level; *see* also **ĔV′il–** devil etc. below.

ĔV′eld– **2.** bevelled, deviled, levelled, nevelled, revelled **3.** bedevilled, dishevelled.

ĔV′elz– bevels etc., *see* **ĔV′el–** bevel etc. above, plus "s" or " 's."

ĔV′en– **2.** heaven, leaven, seven, chevon, steven, sweven **3.** eleven; *see* also **ĔV′an–** Evan etc. above.

ĔV′enth– **2.** seventh **3.** eleventh.

ĔV′er– **2.** ever, lever, levir, clever, never, sever **3.** whichever, whenever, wherever, forever, whatever, however, whoever, endeavor, assever, dissever **4.** whichsoever, whensoever, whencesoever, wheresoever, whatsoever, whosoever, whosesoever, howsoever, cantilever **5.** whithersoever.

EV′i–   **2.** Evy, bevy, chevy, heavy, levee, levy, clevy, nevvy, Chevvy   **3.** topheavy, replevy.

EV′il–   **2.** devil, Neville   **3.** bedevil, daredevil, she-devil, blue devil, red devil; *see* also **EV′el**– bevel etc. above.

EV′ilz–   devils etc., *see* **EV′il**– devil etc. above, plus "s" or " 's."

EV′in–   **2.** levin   **3.** replevin.

EV′is–   **2.** chevise, clevis, brevis [L.], crevice   **3.** Ben Nevis   **7.** ars longa, vita brevis [L.].

EZ′ans–   **2.** pleasance, peasants, presence, presents   **4.** omnipresence.

EZ′ant–   **2.** pheasant, pleasant, peasant, bezant   **3.** unpleasant   **4.** omnipresent.

EZH′er–   **2.** leisure, pleasure, measure, treasure   **3.** displeasure, admeasure, remeasure, commeasure, entreasure.

EZH′erz–   **2.** pleasures, measures, treasures.

EZ′l–   **2.** bezel, bezzle   **3.** embezzle.

EZ′ler–   **3.** embezzler.

E (heh)

TRIPLE RHYMES IN E (eb'on-y)

Primary or Secondary Accent Falls on Second from Last Syllable.

EB′i–er– 2. blebbier, nebbier, webbier 4. cobwebbier.

EB′i–est– 3. blebbiest, nebbiest, webbiest 4. cobwebbiest.

EB′on–i– 3. ebony.

EB′ri–ti– 4. celebrity, tenebrity.

EB′u–lar– 3. nebular.

ECH′a–bl– 3. fetchable, sketchable, stretchable.

ECH′er–i– 3. lechery, treachery.

ECH′er–us– 3. lecherous, treacherous.

ECH′i–ness– 3. sketchiness, stretchiness, tetchiness.

ED′a–bl– dreadable; *see* also **ED′i–bl–** edible etc. below.

ED′en–ing– 3. deadening, leadening, reddening.

ED′er–al– 3. federal.

ED′i–bl– 3. edible, dreadable, credible 4. unedible, impedible, incredible.

ED′i–er– 3. headier, readier, breadier, spreadier, shreddier, threadier, steadier 4. unreadier, unsteadier.

ED′i–est– 3. headiest, readiest, breadiest, spreadiest, shreddiest, threadiest, steadiest 4. unreadiest, unsteadiest.

ED′i–ing– 3. eddying, readying, steadying.

ED′i–kant– 3. dedicant, medicant, predicant.

ED′i–kat– 3. dedicate, medicate, predicate 4. rededicate, depredicate.

ED′i–kl– 3. medical, pedicle 4. premedical.

ED′i–li– 3. readily, steadily 4. unreadily, unsteadily.

ED′i–ment– 3. pediment, sediment 4. impediment.

ED′i–ness– 3. headiness, readiness, breadiness, spreadiness, shreddiness, threadiness, steadiness 4. unreadiness, unsteadiness.

ED′it–ed– 3. edited, credited 4. re-edited, unedited, accredited, discredited, miscredited 5. unaccredited, undiscredited.

ED′it–er– 3. editor, creditor.

ED′it–i– 4. rubedity, heredity.

ED′it–ing– 3. editing, crediting 4. accrediting, discrediting, miscrediting.

ED′it–iv– 3. redditive, creditive, sedative 4. impeditive.

ED′it–or– 3. editor, creditor 4. subeditor.

ED′u–lus– 3. credulous, sedulous 4. incredulous, unsedulous.

EF′a–lus– 3. Cephalus 4. acephalus, acephalous, encephalous, Bucephalus.

EF′er–ens– 3. deference, reference, preference 4. cross-reference.

EF′er–ent– 3. efferent, deferent, referent, preferent.

EF′in–it– 3. definite 4. indefinite, undefinite.

EF′is–ens– 4. maleficence, beneficence.

EF′is–ent– 4. maleficent, beneficent.

EF′lu–ent– 3. effluent, defluent, refluent.

EG′a–bl– 3. beggable, legable, peggable.

EG′ar–i– 3. beggary, Weggery.

EG′a–si– 3. legacy.

EG′a–sus– 3. Pegasus.

EG′i–ness– 3. egginess, legginess, dregginess.

EG′nan–si– 3. regnancy, pregnancy.

EG′raf–i– 4. telegraphy, choregraphy.

EG′u–lar– 3. regular, tegular 4. irregular, unregular.

EJ′i–bl– 3. legible. 4. allegeable, illegible.

EJ′i–bli– 3. legibly 4. illegibly.

EJ′i–o– 4. solfeggio, arpeggio.

EK′a–bl– 3. checkable, peccable, secable 4. impeccable.

EK′ond–li– 3. fecundly, secondly.

EK′on–ing– 3. beckoning, reckoning 4. dead reckoning.

EK′re–ment– 3. decrement, recrement.

EKS′a–bl– 3. vexable 4. annexable; see also EKS′i–bl– flexible etc. below.

EKS′ed–li– 3. vexedly 4. perplexedly, convexedly.

EKS′el–ent– 3. excellent.

EKSH′un–al– 3. flectional, sectional 4. affectional, objectional, projectional, reflectional, inflectional, collectional, complexional, connectional, directional, correctional, resectional, bisectional, dissectional, protectional, convectional 5. interjectional, resurrectional, insurrectional, vivisectional.

EKSH′un–er– 4. confectioner, perfectioner, correctioner.

EKSH′un–ist– 4. perfectionist, projectionist, protectionist 3. resurrectionist, insurrectionist, vivisectionist 6. antiprotectionist 7 antivivisectionist.

EKS′i–bl– 3. flexible 4. deflexible, reflexible, inflexible; see also EKS′a–bl– vexable etc. above.

EKS′i–kal– 3. lexical 4. indexical, pyrexical.

EKS′i–ti– 4. complexity, perplexity, duplexity, convexity.

EKS′iv–ness– 4. reflexiveness, perplexiveness.

EKT′a–bl– 4. subjectable, objectable, rejectable, delectable, deflectable, respectable, expectable, suspectable, erectable, detectable 5. indelectable; see also EKT′i–bl– affectible etc. below.

EKT′a–bli– 4. delectably, respectably 5. undelectably, unsuspectably.

EKT′a–kl– 3. spectacle 4. bespectacle; see also EKT′i–kl– dialectical etc. below.

EKT′a–ri– 3. nectary, sectary; see also EKT′o–ri– rectory etc. below.

EKT′ed–li– 4. affectedly, subjectedly, dejectedly, reflectedly, neglectedly, collectedly, connectedly, respectedly, protectedly 5. unaffectedly, disaffectedly, recollectedly, disconnectedly, unexpectedly, unsuspectedly.

EKT′ed–ness– 4. affectedness, infectedness, abjectedness, dejectedness, subjectedness, neglectedness, suspectedness 5. unaffectedness, disaffectedness, disconnectedness, unexpectedness, unsuspectedness.

EKT′ful–i– 4. neglectfully, respectfully 5. unrespectfully, disrespectfully.

EKT′ful–ness– 4. neglectfulness, respectfulness, suspectfulness 5. disrespectfulness.

EKT′i–bl– 4. affectible, effectible, defectible, infectible, perfectible, subjectible, reflectible, connectible, suspectible, dissectible 5. unaffectible; see also EKT′a–bl– subjectable etc. above.

EKT′i–fi– 3. rectify 4. objectify, subjectify.

EKT′i–kl– **5.** dialectical, apoplectical; *see* also **EKT′a–kl–** spectacle etc. above.

EKT′ing–li– **4.** affectingly, objectingly, reflectingly.

EKT′i–tud– **3.** rectitude **4.** senectitude.

EKT′i–vist– **4.** objectivist, collectivist.

EKT′iv–li– **4.** affectively, effectively, defectively, infectively, perfectively, objectively, subjectively, projectively, electively, selectively, deflectively, reflectively, inflectively, neglectively, collectively, connectively, respectively, prospectively, perspectively, directively, correctively, protectively, invectively **5.** ineffectively, unreflectively, irreflectively, recollectively, irrespectively, retrospectively, introspectively.

EKT′iv–ness– **4.** effectiveness, defectiveness, perfectiveness, objectiveness, subjectiveness, reflectiveness, collectiveness, prospectiveness, protectiveness **5.** unobjectiveness, irreflectiveness, unreflectiveness, recollectiveness.

EKT′or–al– **3.** pectoral, rectoral, sectoral **4.** prefectoral, electoral, inspectoral, directoral, protectoral.

EKT′or–at– **3.** rectorate **4.** electorate, expectorate, directorate, protectorate.

EKT′or–i– **3.** rectory **4.** refectory, trajectory, directory, correctory, protectory **5.** interjectory; *see* also **EKT′ar–i–** nectary etc. above.

EKT′u–al– **3.** lectual **4.** effectual, prefectual **5.** ineffectual, intellectual.

EKT′ur–al– **4.** prefectural, conjectural **5.** architectural.

EKT′ur–er– **3.** lecturer **4.** conjecturer.

EK′u–lar– **3.** specular, secular **4.** trabecular, vallecular, molecular.

EK′u–lat– **3.** peculate, speculate.

EK′und–li– **3.** fecundly, secondly.

EK′u–tiv– **4.** executive, subsecutive, consecutive **5.** unconsecutive.

EL′a–bl– **3.** bellable, delible, fellable, gelable, spellable, sellable, tellable, quellable **4.** indelible, compellable, expellable, unspellable, foretellable, unquellable.

EL′a–tin– gelatin, gelatine, skeleton.

EL′a–tiv– **3.** relative **4.** appellative, compellative, irrelative, correlative.

EL′e–gat– **3.** delegate, relegate.

EL′er–i– **3.** celery, cellary, stellary.

EL′et–on– **3.** skeleton, gelatin, gelatine.

ELF′i–a– **4.** Didelphia **5.** Philadelphia, Monodelphia **6.** Polyadelphia.

ELF′i–an– **4.** didelphian **5.** Philadelphian, Christadelphian.

ELF′ish–li– **3.** elfishly, selfishly **4.** unselfishly.

ELF′ish–ness– **3.** elfishness, selfishness **4.** unselfishness.

EL′i–bl– **3.** delible **4.** indelible; *see* also **EL′a–bl–** bellable etc. above.

EL′i–ing– **3.** bellying, jellying.

EL′i–ka– **3.** Melica **4.** Angelica.

EL′i–kan– **3.** pelican, belly can, jelly can.

EL′i–kl– **3.** bellical, helical, pellicle **4.** angelical, vitellicle **5.** evangelical.

EL′ing–ly– **3.** tellingly, quellingly, wellingly **4.** compellingly.

EL′ish–ing– **3.** relishing **4.** embellishing.

EL′ish–ment– **3.** relishment **4.** embellishment.

EL′i–ti– **3.** pellety **4.** fidelity **5.** infidelity.

EL′o–er– **3.** bellower, mellower, yellower.

EL′o–est– **3.** mellowest, celloist, yellowest.

EL′o–i– **3.** mellowy, yellowy.

EL′o–ing– **3.** bellowing, mellowing, yellowing.

EL′on–i– **3.** felony, melony.

EL′op–ing– **4.** developing, enveloping **5.** undeveloping.

EL′op–ment– **4.** development, envelopment.

ĔLT′er–i– 3. smeltery, sheltery, sweltery.

ĔLT′er–ing– 3. sheltering, weltering, sweltering.

ĔLTH′i–er– 3. healthier, stealthier, wealthier.

ĔLTH′i–est– 3. healthiest, stealthiest, wealthiest.

ĔLTH′i–li– 3. healthily, stealthily, wealthily.

ĔL′u–lar– 3. cellular, stellular 4. bicellular 5. unicellular, interstellular.

ĔL′us–li– 3. jealously, zealously.

ĔL′us–ness– 3. jealousness, zealousness.

ĔM′an–e– 4. anemone, Gethsemane 5. pantanemone, Agapemone.

ĔM′as–i– 4. supremacy.

ĔM′a–tist– 4. emblematist 5. theorematist.

ĔMB′er–i– 3. embery 4. Decembery, September, Novembery.

ĔMB′er–ing– 3. membering 4. remembering, dismembering.

ĔMB′er–ish– 3. emberish 4. Septemberish, Decemberish, Novemberish.

ĔM′en–si– 3. clemency.

ĔM′er–al– 3. femerell, femoral, nemoral 4. ephemeral, trihemeral.

ĔM′er–ald– 3. emerald.

ĔM′er–i– 3. emery, gemmary, memory.

ĔM′e–sis– 3. emesis, Nemesis.

ĔM′i–kal– 3. chemical 4. endemical, alchemical, polemical 5. academical, epidemical 6. electrochemical.

ĔM′i–li– 3. Emily, gemmily.

ĔM′in–al– 3. feminal, geminal, seminal 4. bigeminal, tergeminal.

ĔM′in–at– 3. feminate, geminate 4. effeminate, ingeminate, tergeminate, disseminate, inseminate.

ĔM′in–ent– 3. eminent 4. pre-eminent 5. supereminent.

ĔMN′i–ti– 4. indemnity, solemnity.

Ĕm′o–ne– 4. anemone, Gethsemane 5. pantanemone, Agapemone.

ĔM′o–ra– 3. femora, remora 4. ephemera.

ĔM′o–ral– 3. femoral, nemoral; see also ĔM′er–al– femerell etc. above.

ĔM′o–ri– 3. emery, Emory, gemmary, memory.

ĔMP′er–er– 3. emperor, temperer.

ĔMP′er–i– 3. empery, tempery, tempore [L.] 4. extempore.

ĔMP′or–al– 3. temporal 4. atemporal, extemporal 5. supertemporal.

ĔMP′to–ri– 4. redemptory, peremptory.

ĔM′u–lent– 3. emulant, tremulant, temulent.

ĔM′u–lus– 3. emulous, tremulous.

ĔN′ar–i– 3. denary, hennery, plenary, senary 4. decennary, centenary, septennary.

ĔN′at–or– senator; see also ĔN′i–tor– genitor etc. below.

ĔND′a–bl– 3. endable, lendable, mendable 4. defendable, amendable, emendable, commendable, dependable, ascendable, descendable 5. recommendable, independable, undependable, unascendable; see also ĔND′i–bl– rendible etc. below.

ĔND′an–si– 4. appendancy, ascendancy, attendancy, intendancy; see also ĔND′en–si– splendency etc. below.

ĔND′en–si– 3. splendency, pendency, tendency 4. transcendency, resplendency, transplendency, dependency, impendency, intendency 5. independency, ambitendency, countertendency; see also ĔND′an–si– appendancy etc. above.

ĔND′er–er– 3. genderer, slenderer, renderer, tenderer 4. engenderer, surrenderer.

ĔND′er–est– 3. slenderest, tenderest.

END'er–ing–   3. gendering, rendering, tendering   4. engendering, surrendering.

END'er–li–   3. slenderly, tenderly.

END'er–ness–   3. slenderness, tenderness.

END'i–bl–   3. rendible, vendible   4. ascendible, accendible, extendible, invendible   5. comprehendible; see also **END' a–bl–** endable etc. above.

END'i–us–   4. compendious, dispendious.

END'less–li–   3. endlessly, bendlessly, mendlessly, friendlessly.

END'less–ness–   3. endlessness, bendlessness, mendlessness, friendlessness.

END'us–li–   4. tremendously, stupendously.

END'us–ness–   4. tremendousness, stupendousness.

EN'er–at–   3. generate, venerate   4. degenerate, regenerate, ingenerate, progenerate, intenerate.

EN'es–is–   3. genesis   4. regenesis, pangenesis, parenesis   5. paragenesis, catagenesis, metagenesis, epigenesis, neogenesis, psychogenesis, morphogenesis, pathogenesis, biogenesis, homogenesis, monogenesis, oogenesis, zoogenesis, pyrogenesis, ectogenesis, ontogenesis, histogenesis, polygenesis   6. osteogenesis, organogenesis, parthenogenesis, anthropogenesis, heterogenesis.

ENGTH'en–ing–   3. strengthening, lengthening.

EN'i–a–   4. millennia, quadrennia, decennia.

EN'i–al–   4. biennial, triennial, millennial, perennial, plurennial, decennial, tricennial, vicennial, sexennial, centennial, quotennial, septennial, novennial, quinquennial   5. bicentennial, tricentennial, tercentennial   6. duodecennial.

EN'i–form–   3. penniform   4. bipenniform, antenniform.

EN'i–kal–   3. scenical   4. Galenical, sirenical, arsenical   5. hygienical, ecumenical   6. catechumenical.

EN'i–ti–   3. lenity   4. amenity, serenity, terrenity, obscenity.

EN'i–tiv–   3. genitive, lenitive, splenitive   4. progenitive   5. primogenitive.

EN'i–tor–   3. genitor, senator   4. progenitor   5. primogenitor.

EN'i–tud–   3. lenitude, plenitude   4. serenitude.

EN'i–tur–   3. geniture   4. progeniture   5. primogeniture   6. ultimogeniture.

EN'i–um–   4. biennium, millenium, quadrennium, decennium, sexennium, septennium.

EN'i–zon–   3. benison, denizen, venison   4. endenizen.

ENS'a–bl–   4. condensable, dispensable   5. incondensable, indispensable; see also **ENS'i–bl–** sensible etc. below.

ENS'a–ri–   dispensary; see also **ENS'o–ri–** sensory etc. below.

ENS'a–tiv–   3. pensative, sensitive   4. condensative, compensative, dispensative, insensitive, intensative.

ENSH'a–ri–   4. sententiary   5. residentiary, penitentiary.

ENSH'i–at–   4. essentiate, licentiate, potentiate   5. differentiate.

ENSH'i–ent–   3. sentient   4. assentient, presentient, dissentient, insentient, consentient.

ENSH'u–al–   3. mensual, censual, sensual   4. trimensual, consensual.

ENSH'un–al–   3. tensional   4. dimensional, ascensional, descensional, attentional, intentional, contentional, extensional, preventional, conventional   5. unintentional, unconventional.

ENSH'un–er–   3. mentioner, pensioner   4. conventioner.

ENSH'un–ing–   3. mentioning, pensioning, tensioning.

ĔNSH'un–ist– 4. ascentionist, descentionist, recensionist, extensionist, preventionist, conventionist.

ĔNSH'us–ness– 4. licentiousness, pretentiousness, sententiousness, contentiousness 5. conscientiousness, unpretentiousness.

ĔNS'i–bl– 3. sensible, tensible 4. condensible, defensible, insensible, unsensible, distensible, ostensible 5. indefensible, apprehensible, reprehensible, comprehensible, inostensible 6. irreprehensible, incomprehensible; see also ĔNS'a–bl– condensable etc. above.

ĔNS'i–bli– 3. sensibly 4. defensibly, insensibly, ostensibly 5. reprehensibly, comprehensibly 6. incomprehensibly.

ĔNS'i–fi– 3. densify, sensify 4. intensify.

ĔNS'i–kal– 4. forensical, nonsensical.

ĔNS'i–ti– 3. density, tensity 4. condensity, immensity, propensity, attensity, intensity.

ĔNS'i–tiv– 3. sensitive 4. condensitive, insensative; see also ĔNS'a–tiv– pensative etc. above.

ĔNS'iv–li– 3. pensively 4. defensively, offensively, expensively, intensively, extensively 5. inoffensively, apprehensively, reprehensively, comprehensively, inexpensively 6. incomprehensively.

ĔNS'iv–ness– 3. pensiveness 4. offensiveness, expensiveness, intensiveness, extensiveness 5. comprehensiveness 6. incomprehensiveness.

ĔNS'less–li– 3. senselessly, tenselessly 4. defenselessly, offenselessly.

ĔNS'less–ness– 3. senselessness, tenselessness 4. defenselessness.

ĔNS'o–ri– 3. sensory 4. condensery, defensory, prehensory, dispensary, suspensory, incensory, ostensory 5. reprehensory.

ĔNT'a–bl– 3. rentable, tentable 4. lamentable, fermentable, repentable, contentable, preventable, inventable, frequentable, presentable 5. uncontentable, representable, unpresentable.

ĔNT'a–bli– 4. lamentably, preventably, presentably 5. unpreventably, unpresentably.

ĔNT'a–kl– 3. pentacle, tentacle.

ĔNT'a–li– 3. mentally 4. fragmentally, segmentally, pigmentally, momentally, parentally 5. accidentally, occidentally, incidentally, orientally, fundamentally, ornamentally, elementally, supplementally, regimentally, alimentally, complimentally, detrimentally, sentimentally, governmentally, monumentally, instrumentally, continentally 6. temperamentally, developmentally.

ĔNT'al–ist– 5. Occidentalist, transcendentalist, Orientalist, fundamentalist, sentimentalist, instrumentalist 6. experimentalist.

ĔNT'al–izm– 5. Occidentalism, transcendentalism, Orientalism, elementalism, fundamentalism, sentimentalism.

ĔNT'a–ri– 3. dentary 4. fragmentary, segmentary, pigmentary 5. filamentary, sacramentary, testamentary, elementary, complementary, supplementary, sedimentary, rudimentary, alimentary, complimentary, documentary, tegumentary 6. uncomplimentary, integumentary, emolumentary.

ĔNT'a–sis– 3. entasis.

ĔNT'a–tiv– 3. tentative 4. augmentative, fermentative, presentative, pretentative, sustentative, frequentative 5. alimentative, complimentative, argumentative, representative 6. experimentative, misrepresentative.

ĔNT'ed–li– 4. dementedly, tormentedly, contentedly 5. unlamentedly, discontentedly, unfrequentedly 6. unprecedentedly.

ENT′ed–ness– 3. scentedness 4. dementedness, fermentedness, tormentedness, contentedness, frequentedness, inventedness 5. discontentedness, unfrequentedness 6. unprecedentedness.

ENT′er–ing– 3. entering, centering 4. re-entering, self-centering.

ENT′ful–li– 4. resentfully, eventfully, inventfully 5. unresentfully, uneventfully.

ENT′ful–ness– 4. resentfulness, eventfulness, inventfulness 5. uneventfulness.

ENTH′e–sis– 4. epenthesis, parenthesis.

ENT′i–bl– 4. inventible; see also ENT′ a–bl– rentable etc. above.

ENT′i–kal– 3. dentical, denticle 4. identical, authentical, conventical, conventicle.

ENT′i–kul– 3. denticule, lenticule.

ENT′i–ment– 3. sentiment 4. presentiment.

ENT′i–nel– 3. dentinal, sentinel.

ENT′ing–li– 4. relentingly, lamentingly, augmentingly, tormentingly, repentingly, assentingly, dissentingly, consentingly 5. unrelentingly.

ENT′i–ti– 3. entity 4. identity, nonentity.

ENT′iv–li– 4. presentively, attentively, retentively, preventively, inventively.

ENT′iv–ness– 4. attentiveness, retentiveness, preventiveness, inventiveness, presentiveness 5. inattentiveness, uninventiveness.

ENT′l–ness– 3. gentleness 4. ungentleness 5. Occidentalness, transcendentalness, Orientalness, elementalness, fundamentalness, sentimentalness.

ENT′ral–i– 3. centrally, ventrally 4. subcentrally, uncentrally 5. dorsiventrally.

ENT′rik–al– 3. centrical, ventricle 4. eccentrical, concentrical.

ENT′u–al– 4. accentual, percentual, adventual, eventual, conventual.

ENT′u–at– 4. accentuate, eventuate.

ENT′us–li– 4. momentously, portentously.

ENT′us–ness– 4. momentousness, portentousness.

EN′u–at– 3. tenuate 4. attenuate, extenuate.

EN′u–us– 3. tenuous, strenuous 4. ingenuous 5. disingenuous.

EP′a–rat– 3. reparate, separate.

EP′er–us– 3. leperous, streperous 4. obstreperous.

EP′ik–al– 3. epical 5. orthoëpical.

EP′it–ant– 3. crepitant, strepitant.

EPSH′un–al– 4. exceptional, conceptional 5. unexceptional.

EPS′i–a– 4. apepsia, dyspepsia, eupepsia 5. monoblepsia.

EPT′i–bl– 4. deceptible, receptible, acceptable, perceptible, susceptible 5. imperceptible, insusceptible, unsusceptible.

EPT′i–bli– 4. perceptibly, susceptibly 5. indeceptibly, imperceptibly, unsusceptibly.

EPT′ik–al– 3. skeptical, septical 4. sylleptical, aseptical, receptacle, conceptacle 5. antiseptical.

EPT′iv–ness– 4. deceptiveness, receptiveness, perceptiveness, susceptiveness 5. imperceptiveness.

EPT′u–al– 4. preceptual, conceptual, perceptual 5. preconceptual.

ER′a–fim– 3. seraphim, teraphim.

ER′an–si– 3. errancy 4. aberrancy, inerrancy.

ER′a–pi– 3. therapy 5. theotherapy, psychotherapy, hydrotherapy, autotherapy 6. balneotherapy, radiotherapy.

ER′i–bl– 3. errable, terrible.

ER′i–dez– 4. Pierides, Hesperides.

ER′i–er– **3.** berrier, burier, ferrier, merrier, terrier.

ER′i–est– **3.** merriest.

ER′i–fi– **3.** spherify, terrify, verify.

ER′i–ing– **3.** berrying, burying, ferrying, serrying, wherrying **4.** cranberrying, strawberrying, blueberrying **5.** huckleberrying.

ER′i–ka– **3.** erica, erika **4.** America.

ER′i–kal– **3.** spherical, sphericle, clerical **4.** chimerical, Homerical, mesmerical, numerical, generical, hysterical **5.** hemispherical, atmospherical, rhinocerical, climacterical, esoterical, exoterical.

ER′i–li– **3.** merrily, verily.

ER′i–ment– **3.** merriment **4.** experiment.

ER′ish–ing– **3.** cherishing, perishing **4.** uncherishing, unperishing.

ER′it–ans– **3.** heritance **4.** inheritance **5.** disinheritance.

ER′it–ed– **3.** ferreted, merited **4.** inherited, disherited, emerited, unmerited **5.** disinherited.

ER′it–er– **3.** ferreter, meriter **4.** inheritor, coheritor.

ER′it–i– **3.** verity **4.** legerity, celerity, temerity, asperity, prosperity, sincerity, alterity, dexterity, austerity, posterity, severity **5.** insincerity, indexterity **6.** ambidexterity.

ER′it–ing– **3.** ferreting, meriting **4.** inheriting, unmeriting **5.** disinheriting.

ER′it–iv– **4.** aperitive, imperative, preteritive.

ER′o–gat– **3.** derogate **4.** interrogate **5.** supererogate.

ERJ– through ERZ–, *see* short **U** (tub): URJ′en–si through URZH′un–ist.

ES′a–bl– **3.** guessable, pressable **4.** unguessable, assessable, possessable **5.** unredressable, unassessable, unpossessable.

ES′a–ri– **4.** confessary; *see* also ES′o–ri–professory etc. below.

ES′en–si– **4.** acescency, quiescency, turgescency, excrescency, liquescency **5.** erubescency, incandescency, acquiescency, convalescency, adolescency, efflorescency, delitescency, effervescency.

ES′ful–i– **3.** blessfully, stressfully **4.** successfully, distressfully.

ES′i–bl– **4.** concrescible, redressible, transgressible, depressible, repressible, impressible, compressible, suppressible, expressible, vitrescible, putrescible, accessible, concessible **5.** irrepressible, insuppressible, unexpressible, inaccessible, unconcessible, fermentescible, effervescible **6.** ineffervescible.

ES′i–bli– **4.** expressibly, accessibly **5.** irrepressibly, inexpressibly, inaccessibly.

ES′i–kat– **3.** desiccate, vesicate, exsiccate.

ES′i–ma– **3.** decima **5.** Quadragesima, Sexagesima, Quinquagesima **6.** Septuagesima.

ES′i–mal– **3.** decimal **4.** trigesimal, vigesimal, millesimal, centesimal **5.** duodecimal, nonagesimal, quadragesimal sexagesimal **6.** septuagesimal, infinitesimal.

ES′i–mo– **5.** octodecimo, sextodecimo, duodecimo.

ES′ing–li– **3.** pressingly **4.** caressingly, depressingly, distressingly **5.** prepossessingly.

ES′i–ti– **4.** obesity, necessity.

ES′iv–li– **4.** aggressively, regressively, digressively, progressively, transgressively, depressively, repressively, impressively, oppressively, expressively, excessively, successively, possessively.

ES′iv–ness– **4.** aggressiveness, progressiveness, depressiveness, impressiveness, oppressiveness, expressiveness, excessiveness, successiveness, possessiveness.

ES′o–ri– **4.** professory, confessary, accessory, successory, concessory, possessory **5.** intercessory.

ESH'i–ens– **3.** nescience, prescience.

ESH'i–ness– **3.** fleshiness, meshiness.

ESH'un–al– **3.** sessional **4.** confessional, professional, digressional, congressional, progressional, transgressional, discretional, impressional, compressional, expressional, recessional, precessional, accessional, successional, possessional, processional **5.** retrocessional, intercessional.

ESH'un–er– **3.** sessioner **4.** secessioner, possessioner, processioner.

ESH'un–ist– **4.** confessionist, progressionist, impressionist, suppressionist, expressionist, secessionist, concessionist, successionist, processionist.

EST'a–bl– **3.** testable, **4.** detestable, intestable, contestable **5.** incontestable.

EST'a–bli– **3.** testably **4.** detestably, contestably **5.** incontestably, uncontestably.

EST'a–ment– **3.** testament, vestiment.

EST'er–ing– **3.** festering, pestering, westering **4.** sequestering.

EST'ful–i– **3.** restfully, questfully.

EST'i–al– **3.** bestial **4.** celestial, agrestial **5.** uncelestial **6.** supercelestial.

EST'i–bl– **4.** digestible, suggestible, comestible, divestible **5.** indigestible; see also EST'a–bl– testable etc. above.

EST'i–kal– **4.** majestical **5.** anapaestical, catachrestical.

EST'in–al– **3.** destinal **4.** intestinal.

EST'i–ness– **3.** restiness, testiness.

EST'ing–li– **3.** jestingly, testingly **4.** protestingly **5.** interestingly **6.** uninterestingly.

EST'iv–li– **3.** festively, restively **4.** suggestively.

EST'iv–ness– **3.** festiveness, restiveness **4.** suggestiveness.

EST'ri–al– **4.** pedestrial, bimestrial, trimestrial, terrestrial **5.** decimestrial **6.** superterrestrial.

EST'ri–an– **4.** pedestrian, palaestrian, campestrian, rupestrian, sylvestrian, equestrian.

EST'ri–us– **4.** pedestrious, terrestrious.

EST'ur–al– **3.** gestural, vestural.

EST'u–us– **4.** tempestuous, incestuous.

ET'a–bl– **3.** gettable, lettable, nettable, pettable, settable **4.** forgettable, regrettable, upsettable **5.** unforgettable, unregrettable.

ET'a–bli– **4.** regrettably **5.** unforgettably.

ET'a–lus– **3.** petalous **4.** apetalous **5.** polypetalous.

ET'er–a– **4.** et cetera.

ET'er–er– **3.** betterer, fetterer, letterer.

ET'er–ing– **3.** bettering, fettering, lettering.

ET'er–it– **3.** preterit, preterite **4.** inveterate.

ET'ful–i– **3.** fretfully **4.** forgetfully, regretfully.

ET'ful–ness– **3.** fretfulness **4.** forgetfulness, regretfulness.

ETH'er–i– **3.** feathery, heathery, leathery, tethery, weathery.

ETH'er–ing– **3.** feathering, leathering, tethering, weathering **4.** untethering.

ETH'i–kal– **3.** ethical **4.** nonethical, unethical.

ETH'less–li– **3.** deathlessly, breathlessly.

ETH'less–ness– **3.** deathlessness, breathlessness.

ET'i–kal– **4.** ascetical, prophetical, pathetical, synthetical, hermetical, cosmetical, planetical, genetical, threnetical, noetical, poetical, syncretical, heretical **5.** alphabetical, diabetical, exegetical, energetical, catechetical, apathetical, metathetical, epithetical, antithetical, parenthetical, nomothetical, hyperthetical, homiletical, arithmetical, unpoetical **6.** apologetical, antipathetical, homogenetical.

ET′i–ness– **3.** jettiness, pettiness, sweatiness.

ET′i–nu– **3.** detinue, retinue.

ET′ish–li– **3.** pettishly **4.** coquettishly.

ET′ish–ness– **3.** pettishness **4.** coquettishness.

ET′i–sizm– **4.** athleticism, phoneticism, asceticism, aestheticism.

ET′i–tiv– **3.** vetitive **4.** repetitive, competitive **5.** noncompetitive, uncompetitive.

ET′ri–fi– **3.** metrify, petrify.

ET′ri–kal– **3.** metrical **4.** symmetrical, nonmetrical, unmetrical, obstetrical **5.** diametrical, dynametrical, heptametrical, hexametrical, perimetrical, asymmetrical, pedometrical, geometrical, stichometrical, graphometrical, biometrical, thermometrical, clinometrical, chronometrical, barometrical, hydrometrical, horometrical, isometrical **6.** craniometrical, trigonometrical, electrometrical **7.** isoperimetrical.

ET′ri–ment– **3.** detriment.

EV′a–lent– **3.** prevalent **4.** unprevalent.

EV′el–er– **3.** beveler, deviler, leveler, reveler.

EV′el–ing– **3.** beveling, deviling, leveling, reveling **4.** bedeviling, disheveling.

EV′el–ment– **3.** devilment, revelment **4.** bedevilment, dishevelment.

EV′el–ri– **3.** devilry, revelry.

EV′er–ans– **3.** reverence, severance **4.** irreverence, disseverance.

EV′er–er– **3.** leverer, cleverer, severer **4.** endeavorer.

EV′er–est– **3.** Everest, cleverest.

EV′er–et– **3.** Everett, leveret.

EV′er–ij– **3.** beverage, leverage.

EV′er–ing– **3.** severing **4.** endeavoring.

EV′i–ti– **3.** levity, brevity **4.** longevity.

EV′o–lens– **4.** benevolence, malevolence **5.** unbenevolence.

EV′o–lent– **4.** benevolent, malevolent **5.** unbenevolent.

EV′o–lus– **4.** benevolous, malevolous.

EV′o–lut– **3.** evolute, devolute, revolute.

EZ′ant–ri– **3.** pheasantry, pleasantry, peasantry.

EZH′er–er– **3.** pleasurer, measurer, treasurer.

EZH′er–ing– **3.** pleasuring, measuring, treasuring.

EZ′i–dens– **3.** residents, residence, presidents **4.** vice-presidents.

EZ′i–dent– **3.** resident, president **4.** nonresident, vice-president.

EZ′i–tant– **3.** hesitant **4.** unhesitant.

EZ′o–nant– **3.** resonant **4.** unresonant.

I (eye)

1.

SINGLE (MASCULINE) RHYMES IN I (eye)

Primary or Secondary Accent Falls on Last
Syllable; Imperfect Rhymes Are in Italics.

I– **1.** i, I, ay, aye, ai, eye **2.** *redeye, frog-eye, black-eye, black eye, pink-eye, cockeye, buckeye, peepeye, fisheye, cat's-eye, oxeye* **3.** weather eye.

BI– **1.** by, bye, buy **2.** good-bye, bye-bye, *go-by, hereby, thereby, whereby,* forby, foreby **3.** by-and-by, rockaby, lullaby, hushaby, by the by, by the bye, underbuy, overbuy, alibi, passer-by, incubi.

DI– **1.** die, dye **2.** bedye, redye, undye.

FI– **1.** fie, phi **2.** defy, fie-fie [coll.] **3.** labefy, tabefy, tumefy, tepefy, stupefy, arefy, rarefy, torrefy, putrefy, pinguefy, liquefy, verbify, rubify, ladify, edify, nidify, dandify, mundify, codify, modify, deify, preachify [coll.], speechify, French-ify, churchify, mythify, qualify, steelify, vilify, jellify, mollify, nullify, amplify, simplify, duplify, ramify, mummify, hu-mify, sanify, magnify, dignify, minify, damnify, bonify, carnify, unify, torpify, typify, scarify, clarify, lubrify, micrify, spherify, verify, terrify, nigrify, horrify, glorify, petrify, nitrify, vitrify, aurify, purify, pacify, specify, calcify, classify, falsify, ossify, rectify, versify, crucify, ratify, gratify, sanctify, fructify, stultify, quantify, daintify, notify, certify, fortify, mortify, testify, justify, mystify, prettify, beautify, sanguify, vivify, satisfy, argufy [coll. & dial.], ladyfy, monkeyfy **4.** syllabify, decalcify, remodify, disqualify, exemplify, divinify, indemnify, personify, saccharify, transmogrify, electrify, ob-jectify, emulsify, beatify, identify, re-vivify, complexify **5.** diabolify.

GI– **1.** guy, Guy **2.** fall guy, wise guy [both slang].

HI– **1.** hie, high, heigh, hi [slang] **2.** knee-high, sky-high.

KI– **1.** chi, sky, Skye **2.** haikai, kai-kai, ensky, blue sky **3.** starry sky.

LI– **1.** lie, lye, cly [cant], fly, ply, sly **2.** ally, Ely, belie, rely, outlie, *dayfly, bobfly, gadfly, gallfly, jarfly, firefly, horsefly, house-fly, botfly, shoofly,* apply, reply, imply, comply, supply, unsly, July **3.** re-ally, alkaly, disally, misally, dragonfly, butterfly, reapply, misapply, multiply, re-imply, underlie, overlie, lazuli **4.** over-supply **5.** lapis lazuli.

MI– **1.** my **2.** demi, demy.

NI– **1.** nigh, nye, sny **2.** deny, well-nigh **3.** redeny, termini, *alumni.*

PI– **1.** pi, pie, spy **2.** *magpie, nanpie, mincepie, potpie,* espy, bespy **3.** humble pie, apple pie, occupy **4.** preoccupy.

RI– **1.** rye, wry, dry, fry, gri, gry [both Gypsy], cry, scry, pry, spry, try **2.** awry, adry, *roughdry, fish fry,* decry, de-scry, *outcry,* atry.

SI– **1.** sigh, scye **2.** *armscye, Versailles* **3.** prophesy.

SHI– **1.** shy **2.** unshy.

TI– **1.** tie, ty, tye, Tai, Thai, sty, stye **2.** hogtie, untie, *necktie, pigsty.*

THI–   **1.** thigh, thy.

VI–   **1.** vie   **2.** outvie.

WI–   **1.** y, Y, wye, Wye, why.

IB–   **1.** gibe, jibe, kibe, libe [slang], bribe, scribe, tribe   **2.** imbibe, ascribe, subscribe, describe, prescribe, transcribe, inscribe, conscribe, proscribe, perscribe   **3.** circumscribe, superscribe, diatribe.

IBD–   **1.** gibed, jibed, kibed, bribed   **2.** imbibed, ascribed, subscribed, described, prescribed, transcribed, inscribed, conscribed, proscribed, perscribed   **3.** circumscribed, superscribed.

IBZ–   gibes etc., *see* **IB–** gibe etc. above, plus "s" or " 's."

ID–   **1.** ide, I'd, eyed, bide, chide, died, dyed, guide, guyed, hide, Hyde, lied, Clyde, glide, slide, nide, snide, pied, spied, ride, bride, cried, scried, dried, gride, pride, pried, tried, stride, side, sighed, tide, tied, vied, wide   **2.** *red-eyed, calf-eyed, pie-eyed, black-eyed, snake-eyed, meek-eyed, pink-eyed, cock-eyed, hawk-eyed, pale-eyed, wall-eyed, owl-eyed, dull-eyed, green-eyed, pop-eyed, blear-eyed, clear-eyed, cat-eyed, soft-eyed, squint-eyed, blue-eyed, dove-eyed, lynx-eyed, ox-eyed,* abide, carbide, redyed, defied, sulphide, confide, misguide, *rawhide, cowhide, bromide,* denied, espied, arride, child bride, undried, *hydride,* deride, descried, *boride, chloride, nitride,* night ride, untried, astride, bestride, outstride, outride, aside, *wayside,* subside, *bedside, broadside,* beside, decide, *seaside,* reside, preside, offside, *lakeside, brookside, hillside,* inside, *topside, fireside, foreside, white-side,* outside, *excide, ebb tide, flood tide, high tide, low tide, neap tide,* betide, retied, *Yuletide, springtide, noon tide, Shrovetide,* divide, provide, world-wide   **3.** iodide, almond-eyed, bonafide, tumefied, tepefied, stupefied, rarefied, torrefied, putrefied, liquefied, pacified, specified, calcified, dulcified, crucified, edified, modified, deified, qualified, mollified, nullified, magnified, dignified, bonified, evri-

fied, glorified, terrified, petrified, vitrified, purified, falsified, versified, ossified, ratified, gratified, stratified, rectified, sanctified, fructified, stultified, notified, certified, fortified, mortified, testified, justified, mystified, beautified, vivified, satisfied, disulphide, eagle-eyed, goggle-eyed, evileyed, unallied, misallied, unbelied, unapplied, misapplied, multiplied, cyanide, arsenide, occupied, saccharide, fluoride, override, telluride, prophesied, Barmecide, alongside, herbicide, verbicide, regicide, fungicide, homicide, germicide, vermicide, lapicide, parricide, matricide, patricide, fratricide, countryside, vaticide, suicide, larvicide, slickenside, oceanside, mountainside, coincide, glucoside, peroxide, genocide, underside, waterside, riverside, unbetide, eventide, Whitsuntide, Hallowtide, undertide, Eastertide, Lammastide, Christmastide, subdivide, nation-wide   **4.** microbicide, tyrannicide, sororicide, uxoricide, insecticide, infanticide, giganticide, parenticide, liberticide, nematocide, decalcified, solidified, unqualified, saponified, unverified, electrified, emulsified, intensified, diversified, beatified, unsanctified, identified, revivified, dissatisfied, formaldehyde, preoccupied, unoccupied, Allhallowtide, Michaelmastide   **5.** parasiticide.

IDZ–   ides etc., *see* **ID–** ide etc. above, plus "s" or " 's";   **3.** Ironsides, sobersides.

IF–   **1.** fife, kife [slang], life, knife, rife, strife, wife   **2.** *jackknife, midwife, oldwife, goodwife, alewife, housewife, fishwife*   **3.** afterlife, bowie knife, pocket knife, puddingwife.

IJ–   **1.** Lige, 'blige   **2.** oblige   **3.** reoblige, disoblige.

IK–   **1.** Ike, bike, dike, fyke, hike [coll.], haik, Haikh, like, Mike, mike [slang], Smike, pike, pyke, spike, grike, shrike, trike [slang], strike, sike, tyke, tike, wike [obs.]   **2.** Vandyke, *hitchhike* [slang], alike, *seedlike, childlike, godlike,* belike, *lifelike,* *wifelike, flamelike, homelike, dovelike, elflike, kinglike, winglike, manlike, swanlike, queenlike, hornlike,* unlike, *apelike, earlike, starlike, warlike, airlike,* dislike, mislike, *catlike, ghostlike, deathlike, toothlike, earthlike, screwlike, rampike, turnpike* **3.** unalike, womanlike, tigerlike, Quakerlike, fatherlike, motherlike, brotherlike, sisterlike, peasantlike, ladylike, fairylike, marlinspike.

ĪKS– dikes etc., *see* **ĪK–** Ike etc. above, plus "s" or " 's."

ĪL– **1.** aisle, isle, I'll, bile, file, guile, gyle, Heil, chyle, lisle, mile, smile, Nile, pile, spile, rile, tile, stile, style, vile, wile, weil, while **2.** Kabyle, defile, *profile,* beguile, enisle, *senile,* repile, compile, unpile, resile, *exile,* ensile, *centile, gentile, reptile, septile, fertile, turnstile, hostile, futile, rutile,* revile, awhile, meanwhile, erstwhile, worthwhile, therewhile **3.** atrabile, crocodile, photofile, Francophile, rheophile, theophile, ergophile, halophile, Anglophile, Gallophile, thermophile, Sinophile, hippophile, typophile, psychrophile, Negrophile, gastrophile, pyrophile, mesophile, Russophile, Slavophile, camomile, juvenile, recompile, thermopile, domicile, reconcile, volatile, vibratile, versatile, mercantile, infantile, decastyle, pentastyle, peristyle, monostyle, polystyle, otherwhile **4.** Italophile, aelurophile, dodecastyle.

ĪLD– **1.** aisled, child, filed, mild, smiled, piled, spiled, styled, wild, whiled **2.** *grandchild, godchild,* defiled, beguiled, enisled, compiled, self-styled, reviled.

ĪLZ– aisles etc., *see* **ĪL–** aisle etc. above, plus "s" or " 's."

ĪM– **1.** I'm, chime, dime, disme, chyme, lime, clime, climb, slime, mime, rhyme, grime, crime, prime, sime, cyme, time, thyme, zyme **2.** sublime, *birdlime, quicklime, brooklime,* beslime, berhyme, begrime, *daytime, playtime, bedtime,* betime, *lifetime, springtime,* meantime, *noontime,*

sometime, mistime **3.** paradigm, maritime, pantomime, summertime, aftertime, overtime.

ĪMD– **1.** chimed, limed, climbed, mimed, rhymed, primed, timed **2.** berhymed, unrhymed, well-timed, ill-timed.

ĪMZ– chimes etc., *see* **ĪM–** chime etc. above, plus "s" or " 's"; **2.** betimes, sometimes, ofttimes **3.** oftentimes.

ĪN– **1.** eyn, eyne [both arch. & dial.], ein [G.], bine, chine, dine, dyne, fine, kine [arch. & dial.], line, spline, mine, nine, pine, spine, Rhine, brine, shrine, trine, sine, tsine, shine, tine, Tyne, stein, thine, vine, wine, swine, twine, whine **2.** *Sabine, woodbine,* combine, *carbine,* turbine, *Aldine,* indign, condign, *nundine,* define, refine, confine, trephine, porcine, aline, align, malign, *saline, headline, beeline, tapeline, fishline, carline, airline, hairline, crossline, outline, bowline,* decline, recline, incline, feline, moline, *cauline, Pauline, damine, gold mine, carmine, canine,* ranine, benign, *quinine,* repine, *Alpine,* vulpine, opine, *vespine, lupine, supine, cedrine, ferine,* enshrine, *caprine, Petrine, murrhine,* assign, design, resign, piscine, calcine, langsyne, sinsyne, consign, *cosine,* phocine, hircine, ursine, beshine, *shoeshine, moonshine, sunshine,* outshine, *equine,* divine, *ovine, bovine, cervine, corvine,* entwine **3.** cannabine, columbine, concubine, muscadine, monodyne, anodyne, hirundine, paludine, superfine, realign, alkaline, tourmaline, sepaline, opaline, disalign, petaline, hyaline, disincline, monocline, angeline, musteline, aniline, aquiline, inquiline, caballine, coralline, metalline, crystalline, suilline, sibylline, berylline, Caroline, underline, interline, figuline, Ursuline, vituline, sycamine, calamine, calcimine, undermine, countermine, asinine, leonine, pavonine, eburnine, saturnine, elapine, porcupine, catarrhine, saccharine, viperine, anserine, passerine, riverine, peregrine, sapphirine, viberrine, platyrrhine, lemurine, azurine, soricine, reconsign, undersign, countersign, monkeyshine [slang], palatine, cisplatine, anatine, infantine, Constantine, argentine, Argentine, valentine, serpentine, turpentine, Aventine, lacertine, Palestine, Celestine, Ernestine, Philistine, brandywine, interwine, Auld Lang Syne **4.** incarnadine, heterodyne, antalkaline, Evangeline, Capitoline, accipitrine, elephantine, hyacinthine, labyrinthine, aberdevine.

IND– **1.** bind, dined, find, fined, hind, kind, lined, blind, mind, pined, rynd, rind, rined, grind, signed, tined, vined, wind, twined, whined **2.** combined, unbind, *bearbind*, defined, refined, ahind, behind, mankind, unkind, aligned, maligned, unlined, declined, reclined, inclined, purblind, opined, *millrynd*, unwind, entwined **3.** undefined, unrefined, unconfined, gavelkind, womankind, humankind, realigned, disinclined, color-blind, underlined, interlined, undermined, master mind, unresigned, undersigned, countersigned, interwind, intertwined **4.** incarnadined.

INT– **1.** jint [dial.], pint **2.** ahint, behint [both Scot. & N. of Eng.], half pint.

INTS– **1.** Heintz, pints **2.** half pints.

INZ– dines etc., *see* **IN–** eyn etc. above, plus "s" or " 's."

IP– **1.** hipe, kipe, hyp [dial.], slipe [Scot. & dial.], slype, snipe, pipe, ripe, gripe, tripe, stripe, type, stipe, vipe [slang], wipe, wype, swipe **2.** *pitchpipe, windpipe, bagpipe, hornpipe, blowpipe, rareripe*, unripe, retype, *ectype, tintype, piewipe, sideswipe* **3.** guttersnipe, overripe, megatype, teletype, antitype, linotype, phototype **4.** stereotype **5.** daguerreotype.

IPS– hipes etc., *see* **IP–** hipe etc. above, plus "s" or " 's."

IPT– **1.** hiped, sliped [Scot. & dial.], sniped, piped, griped, striped, typed, stiped, wiped, swiped **2.** retyped, *sideswiped* **4.** stereotyped.

IR– **1.** ire, byre, dire, fire, hire, gyre, lyre, mire, pyre, pyr, spire, sire, shire, tire, Tyre, wire, quire, choir, squire **2.** afire, *backfire, blackfire, needfire, wildfire, hell-fire, shellfire*, bonfire, misfire, *spitfire*, rehire, admire, bemire, aspire, respire, expire, transpire, inspire, conspire, perspire, suspire, *grandsire*, desire, *gudesire, belsire*, attire, retire, envire, barbwire, rewire, unwire, acquire, require, inquire, esquire **3.** overtire; *see* also **I'er–** eyer etc.

IRD– **1.** fired, hired, mired, spired, sired, tired, wired, squired **2.** backfired, misfired, admired, bemired, aspired, respired, expired, transpired, inspired, conspired, perspired, desired, attired, retired, rewired, acquired, required, inquired **3.** overtired, uninspired.

IS– **1.** ice, bice, dice, lice, splice, slice, mice, nice, gneiss, pice, spice, speiss, rice, rais, grice, price, trice, thrice, sice, syce, vice, vise, twice **2.** suffice, resplice, *titmice*, bespice, *allspice*, reprice, precise, concise, entice, advice, device **3.** paradise, sacrifice, overnice, camphor ice, edelweiss.

IST– **1.** iced, diced, feist [loc.], Geist [G.], spliced, riced, Christ, priced **2.** uniced, Weltgeist [G.], Zeitgeist [G.], bespiced, repriced, enticed **3.** poltergeist, antichrist **4.** emparadised.

IT– **1.** ite [slang], bite, bight, dite, dight, fight, hight, height, kite, skite [dial.], light, lite [slang], blight, blite, flight, plight, slight, sleight, mite, might, smite, night, knight, snite [Scot. & dial.], spite, rite, right, write, wright, bright, fright, krait, sprite, trite, sight, site, cite, tight, tite [dial.], wight, quite, white **2.** *Sadite*, bedight, *lyddite, endite*, indict, indite, condite, *podite, cordite*, sea fight, *graphite, cockfight, bullfight, sulphite, ophite*, Ophite, turfite, fist fight, *Shiite*, alight, *halite, daylight*, red light, *floodlight*, delight, relight, *twilight, skylight, stylite*, green light, *moonlight, sunlight, go-light*, polite, *lamplight, hoplite, stoplight, marlite,* *starlite,* flashlight, *footlight, Hamite, Semite, bromite, somite, termite, Danite, Tanite, midnight,* good night, benight, beknight, ignite, *lignite, ichnite, finite, crinite, Stannite, sennight,* unknight, *Sunnite,* tonight, *bornite, fortnight,* unite, despite, aright, *barite, playwright, dendrite, bookwright, wheelwright,* downright, *shipwright,* upright, *cartwright,* outright, birthright, forthright, *plowwright, pyrite,* eyebright, affright, contrite, attrite, eyesight, accite, *calcite, felsite, insight,* incite, *townsite, foresight,* excite, *latite, ratite, partite,* airtight, requite, *Levite,* invite, *Servite,* bobwhite, snow-white, lintwhite, *quartzite* **3.** Rechabite, Moabite, Jacobite, Niobite, trilobite, cenobite, anthracite, boracite, plebiscite, extradite, expedite, recondite, incondite, troglodyte, erudite, hanifite, *t*piphyte, neophyte, lithophyte, dermophyte, zoophyte, microphyte, hydrophyte, aerophyte, mesophyte, ectophyte, entophyte, Fahrenheit, malachite, hyalite, corallite, crystallite, Ishmaelite, Israelite, proselyte, candlelight, satellite, nephelite, Carmelite, ampelite, menilite, acolyte, impolite, zoolite, chrysolite, Loyolite, kimberlite, spherulite, lazulite, Adamite, Gothamite, calamite, Elamite, Islamite, dynamite, wolframite, Hiramite, Moslemite, eremite, stalagmite, hellgrammite, Edomite, dolomite, widow's mite, vulcanite, manganite, melanite, Canaanite, sylvanite, reignite, ebonite, aconite, Mammonite, Maronite, overnight, day and night, reunite, disunite, Sybarite, Lazarite, siderite, dolerite, copyright, anchorite, Laborite, Minorite, underwrite, overwrite, azurite, lazurite, marcasite, pargasite, parasite, leucocyte, phagocyte, oversight, second sight, hematite, stalactite, magnetite, appetite, tripartite, celestite, Ballistite, muscovite **4.** meropodite, Amalekite, Ishmaelite, Israelite, Raphaelite, gastrophilite, toxophilite, monophylite, theodolite, cosmopolite, siderolite,

novaculite, ventriculite, Bethlehemite, labradorite, meteorite, Monophysite, Dyophysite.

ITH– **1.** lithe, blithe, writhe, sithe, scythe, tithe, stythe, withe.

ITHD– **1.** writhed,   scythed,   tithed, withed.

ITS– bites etc., *see* **IT–** bite etc. above, plus "s" or " 's."

IV– **1.** I've, chive, dive, five, hive, gyve, jive [slang], skive, live, clive, rive, drive, shrive, strive, thrive, shive, stive [Scot. & dial. Eng.], wive **2.** redive, *high dive, swan dive, nose dive,* ungyve, *ogive, beehive,* alive, connive, arrive, derive, deprive, contrive, revive, convive, survive **3.** overdrive.

IVD– **1.** dived, hived, gyved, skived, knived, rived, shrived, strived, thrived, shived, stived, wived **2.** long-lived, short-lived, connived, arrived, derived, deprived, contrived, revived, survived.

IVZ– chives, etc., *see* **IV–** chive, etc. above, plus "s" or " 's"; **1.** Ives **2.** St. Ives.

IZ– i's, ayes etc., *see* **I–** i etc. through **WI–** y etc. above, plus "s" or " 's"; **1.** guise, rise, prize, prise, size, sice, vise, wise **2.** sheep's eyes, *brighteyes,* disguise, demise, remise, premise, *bromize,* surmise, despise, arise, *moonrise, sunrise,* apprise, reprise, emprise, comprise, uprise, misprize, surprise, assize, resize, excise, incise, capsize, baptize, chastise, advise, devise, revise, *sidewise, endwise, edgewise, likewise, clockwise,* unwise, *nowise, crosswise* **3.** Judaize, archaize, Hebraize, hybridize, iridize, chloridize, subsidize, liquidize, oxidize, gormandize, aggrandize, iodize, melodize, psalmodize, rhapsodize, standardize, jeopardize, elegize, syllogize, eulogize, energize, catechize, empathize, sympathize, verbalize, feudalize, legalize, racialize, specialize, socialize, martialize, alkalize, penalize, signalize, journalize, papalize,

opalize, moralize, centralize, neutralize,
vitalize, tantalize, dualize, equalize, royal-
ize, obelize, angeleyes, novelize, stabilize,
sterilize, fossilize, fertilize, utilize, tran-
quilize, civilize, metallize, crystallize, sym-
bolize, idolize, fabulize, formulize, euphe-
mize, itemize, minimize, pilgrimize, vic-
timize, compromise, presurmise, urbanize,
vulcanize, paganize, mechanize, Christian-
ize, Romanize, Germanize, humanize,
galvanize, heathenize, Hellenize, recog-
nize, pollinize, feminize, Latinize, gluti-
nize, scrutinize, solemnize, tyrannize, ebon-
ize, carbonize, agonize, symphonize, eu-
phonize, unionize, lionize, fractionize,
colonize, demonize, harmonize, sermonize,
canonize, synchronize, patronize, plato-
nize, peptonize, modernize, fraternize, im-
munize, communize, syncopize, philip-
pize, barbarize, vulgarize, plagiarize, bur-
glarize, summarize, notarize, mercerize,
tenderize, etherize, mesmerize, pauperize,
cauterize, pulverize, satirize, theorize, au-
thorize, memorize, vaporize, temporize,
terrorize, proctorize, enterprise, pasteurize,
sulphurize, martyrize, emphasize, synthe-
size, ostracize, laicize, ethicize, Gothicize,
publicize, Anglicize, Gallicize, Sinicize,
classicize, criticize, synopsize, exorcise,
dramatize, pragmatize, dogmatize, mag-
netize, monetize, sensitize, narcotize,
egotize, iotize, hypnotize, amortize, depu-
tize, colloquize, zigzagwise, anywise,
corner wise, weather-wise, otherwise 4.
italicize, catholicize, politicize, domesti-
cize, deoxidize, apostrophize, theosophize,
philosophize, radicalize, provincialize,

commercialize, substantialize, potentialize,
decimalize, nationalize, rationalize, sec-
tionalize, personalize, liberalize, federalize,
generalize, demoralize, decentralize, nat-
uralize, capitalize, devitalize, immortalize,
visualize, actualize, ritualize, mutualize,
sexualize, evangelize, caramelize, solubil-
ize, diabolize, metabolize, monopolize,
macadamize, epitomize, dehumanize, re-
juvenize, antagonize, philanthropize, mis-
anthropize, plagiarize, familiarize, circu-
larize, regularize, singularize, formularize,
popularize, militarize, characterize, deo-
dorize, allegorize, categorize, extemporize,
desulphurize, panegyrize, metastasize, hy-
postasize, parenthesize, emblematize, sys-
tematize, acclimatize, democratize, apos-
tatize, alphabetize, anesthetize, demag-
netize, demonetize, desensitize, Protes-
tantize, proselytize, contrariwise 5. phe-
nomenalize, professionalize, denationalize,
irrationalize, conventionalize, imperson-
alize, denaturalize, spiritualize, Ameri-
canize, deoxygenize, platitudinize, atti-
tudinize, revolutionize, particularize,
apotheosize, anathematize, legitimatize
6. testimonialize, participialize, interna-
tionalize, institutionalize, constitution-
alize, individualize, cosmopolitanize.

ÍZD– 1. prized, sized, wised [slang] 2.
disguised, demised, surmised, despised,
apprised, comprised, surprised, incised,
capsized, baptized, chastised, advised, de-
vised, revised; *also past tense of all verbs
ending in verbal suffix "-ize"* (*see* Judaize
etc. above).

I (eye)

2.

DOUBLE (FEMININE) RHYMES IN I (li'ar)

Primary or Secondary Accent Falls on Next to Last
Syllable; Imperfect Rhymes Are in Italics.

I'a– 2. ayha, dia, pia, chria, praya, stria, via, Zia 3. Tobiah, Sophia, Thalia, Maria, latria, Uriah, messiah, Josiah, Isaiah, Keziah 4. Obadiah, Zebediah, asaphia, Hezekiah, Jeremiah, Black Maria, Zachariah, callisteia 5. hyperdulia, Hippodamia, Iphigenia.

I'ad– 2. dyad, Pleiad, naiad, dryad, triad 4. jeremiad, hamadryad.

I'adz– dyads etc., *see* **I'ad–** dyad etc. above, plus "s" or "'s"; 2. Hyads.

I'ak– 2. Dyak, kayak, guaiac 4. elegiac.

I'al– 2. dial, phial, gayal, myall, pial, spial, ryal, trial, vial, viol 3. sundial, defial, supplial, denial, genial, espial, decrial, retrial, mistrial, bass viol 4. self-denial, intrapial, interstrial.

I'am– 2. I am, lyam, Priam, Siam.

I'amb– 2. iamb 3. diiamb.

I'an– 2. Ian, Chian, Ryan, Bryan 3. thalian, genian, Orion 4. Jeremian; *see* also **I'on–** ion etc. below.

I'ans– 2. fiance [obs.], science 3. affiance, defiance, alliance, reliance, appliance, compliance, suppliance 4. misalliance, self-reliance, incompliance, noncompliance; *see* also **I'ants–** fiants etc. below.

I'ant– 2. fiant, giant, client, pliant, riant, Bryant, scient 3. affiant, defiant, reliant, appliant, repliant, compliant 4. self-reliant, uncompliant.

I'ants– fiants etc., *see* **I'ant–** fiant etc. above plus "s" or "'s."

I'ar– 2. liar, briar, friar; *see* also **I'er–** eyer etc. below.

I'as– 2. eyas, bias, Lias, drias, Trias 3. unbias, Tobias, Elias, Messias, Josias, Marrhias 4. Jeremias, Ananias; *see* also **I'us–** pious etc. below.

I'at– fiat; *see* also **I'et–** diet etc. below.

IB'al– 2. Bible, libel, scribal, tribal 4. intertribal.

IB'eks– 2. ibex, vibex.

IB'er– 2. fiber, giber, liber, Liber, briber, scriber, Tiber 3. imbiber, subscriber, describer, prescriber, transcriber, inscriber, proscriber 4. circumscriber.

IB'ing– 2. gibing, jibing, bribing, scribing 3. imbibing, ascribing, subscribing, describing, prescribing, transcribing, inscribing, conscribing, proscribing, perscribing 4. circumscribing, superscribing.

IB'l– 2. Bible, libel, scribal, tribal 3. intertribal.

IB'ol– 2. eyeball, highball, fly ball.

IB'rant– 2. vibrant.

IB'rat– 2. librate, vibrate 4. equilibrate.

IB'rid– 2. hybrid, Librid 4. polyhybrid.

ICH'us– 2. righteous 3. unrighteous 4. superrighteous, overrighteous.

ID'a– 2. Ida, Haida, Lida, cnida, Vida 3. Oneida.

ID'al– 2. bridal, tidal 3. cotidal 4. regicidal, fungicidal, homicidal, germicidal, vermicidal, parricidal, matricidal, patricidal, fratricidal, septicidal, suicidal **5.** tyrannicidal, sororicidal, insecticidal, infanticidal; *see also* **ID′l–** idle etc. below.

ID′ans– **2.** guidance **3.** abidance, misguidance, subsidence.

ID′ed– **2.** bided, chided, guided, glided, prided, sided, tided, tidied **3.** abided, confided, misguided, elided, collided, derided, decided, lopsided, one-sided, bothsided, two-sided, betided, divided, presided **4.** undecided, many-sided, coincided, subdivided, unprovided.

ID′en– **2.** Leyden, Dryden, widen **3.** rewiden; *see also* **ID′on–** guidon etc. below.

ID′ent– **2.** bident, rident, trident, strident **3.** subsident.

ID′er– **2.** eider, bider, chider, guider, hider, glider, slider, nidor, spider, rider, strider, stridor, sider, cider, wider **3.** abider, confider, misguider, backslider, derider, roughrider, outrider, decider, insider, East-sider, outsider, provider, resider, presider **4.** coincider, subdivider.

ID′est– **2.** piedest, widest.

ID′ful– **2.** prideful.

ID′i– **2.** didy, Friday, sidy, tidy, vide **3.** untidy **4.** bonafide.

ID′ij– **2.** guidage, hidage, sideage.

ID′il– **2.** idyl, idyll.

ID′ing– **2.** biding, chiding, guiding, hiding, gliding, sliding, niding, riding, priding, striding, siding, tiding **3.** abiding, confiding, misguiding, eliding, colliding, *backsliding*, deriding, subsiding, betiding, dividing, providing, residing, presiding **4.** law-abiding, coinciding, redividing, subdividing.

ID′ingz– **2.** ridings, sidings, tidings.

ID′l– **2.** idle, idol, bridle, bridal, sidle, tidal **3.** unbridle; *see also* **ID′al–** bridal etc. above.

ID′led– **2.** idled, bridled, sidled **3.** unbridled.

ID′ler– **2.** idler, bridler, sidler.

ID′less– **2.** guideless, rideless, brideless, sideless, tideless **4.** suicideless.

ID′li– **2.** idly. bridely, widely.

ID′ling– **2.** idling, bridling, sidling **3.** unbridling.

ID′ness– **2.** piedness, wideness.

ID′o– **2.** Dido, dido, Fido.

ID′on– **2.** guidon, Sidon **3.** Poseidon; *see also* **ID′en–** Leyden etc. above.

ID′or– **2.** nidor, stridor; *see also* **ID′er–** eider etc. above.

ID′rat– **2.** hydrate **3.** dehydrate **4.** carbohydrate.

ID′us– **2.** Didus, Midas, nidus.

I′ens– **2.** clients, science; *see also* **I′ans–** fiance etc. above.

I′ent– **2.** client, scient; *see also* **I′ant–** fiant etc. above.

I′er– **2.** eyer, buyer, dyer, dier, higher, liar, lier, flier, flyer, plier, plyer, slyer, nigher, spyer, wrier, briar, brier, drier, friar, fryer, frier, crier, prier, pryer, prior, spryer, trier, trior, sigher, shier, tier, vier **3.** defier, applier, implier, complier, supplier, denier, greenbrier, sweetbrier, decrier, descrier **4.** stupefier, liquefier, speechifier, edifier, modifier, deifier, vilifier, qualifier, amplifier, simplifier, nullifier, ramifier, dignifier, signifier, unifier, typifier, clarifier, terrifier, verifier, glorifier, classifier, pacifier, falsifier, versifier, crucifier, ratifier, gratifier, rectifier, sanctifier, certifier, fortifier, testifier, justifier, beautifier, satisfier, multiplier, underlier, occupier, prophesier **5.** disqualifier, exemplifier, indemnifier, personifier, calorifier, intensifier, diversifier, identifier.

I′ern– **2.** iron **3.** sadiron, gridiron, andiron, flatiron **4.** grappling iron, curling iron.

I′est– **2.** highest, slyest, nighest, wriest, driest, shyest, spryest, shiest.

I′et– **2.** diet, fiat, piet, riot, quiet **3.** inquiet, unquiet, disquiet; *see also* **I′ot–** eyot etc. below.

IF′a– 2. Haifa, typha.

IF′en– 2. hyphen, siphon, Typhon.

IF′er– 2. bifer, fifer, lifer, knifer, rifer, cipher, sypher 3. decipher.

IF′est– 2. rifest.

IF′id– 2. bifid, trifid.

IF′ing– 2. fifing, knifing, wifing.

IF′l– 2. Eiffel, rifle, trifle, stifle.

IF′ler– 2. rifler, trifler, stifler.

IF′less– 2. fifeless, lifeless, knifeless, strifeless, wifeless.

IF′li– 2. rifely, wifely 3. *housewifely*.

IF′lik– 2. lifelike, knifelike, wifelike.

IF′ling– 2. rifling, trifling, stifling.

IG′a– 2. biga, striga, saiga 3. quadriga.

IG′al– 2. pygal, zygal.

IG′at– 2. ligate, strigate.

IG′er– 2. geiger, tiger.

I′glas– 2. eyeglass, spyglass.

I′glif– 2. diglyph, triglyph 4. monotriglyph.

IG′o– 3. caligo, fuligo [L.], lentigo, vertigo 4. impetigo.

IG′rant– 2. migrant 3. transmigrant.

IG′ress– 2. tigress, Tigris.

I′i– 2. eyey, skyey, criey.

I′id– 2. sly-eyed, pie-eyed, dry-eyed.

I′ing– 2. eyeing, buying, bying, dying, dyeing, guying, hieing, skying, lying, flying, plying, pieing, piing, spying, drying, frying, crying, prying, trying, sighing, shying, tying, stying, vying 3. undying, defying, allying, belying, relying, applying, replying, implying, complying, supplying, outlying, denying, espying, decrying, descrying, outcrying, outsighing, untying, outvying 4. alibiing, stupefying, putrefying, liquefying, edifying, dandifying, modifying, deifying, preachifying [coll.], speechifying, qualifying, vilifying, mollifying, nullifying, amplifying, simplifying, ramifying, magnifying, dignifying, signifying, unifying,

typifying, clarifying, terrifying, verifying, horrifying, glorifying, petrifying, purifying, classifying, pacifying, specifying, falsifying, versifying, crucifying, ratifying, gratifying, rectifying, stultifying, notifying, certifying, fortifying, prettifying, mortifying, testifying, mystifying, justifying, beautifying, vivifying, satisfying, argufying [coll. & dial.], multiplying, occupying, prophesying 5. solidifying, disqualifying, exemplifying, humanifying, indemnifying, personifying, emulsifying, electrifying, objectifying, beatifying, identifying, revivifying, self-satisfying, unsatisfying, oversupplying, preoccupying.

I′ish– 2. slyish, dryish, shyish.

IJ′a– 3. Abijah, Elijah 4. Jehudijah.

IJ′er– 2. Niger 3. obliger.

IJ′ing– 2. obliging 4. unobliging, disobliging.

IK′a– 2. plica, mica, Micah, pica, pika, spica, Spika, styca 3. nagaika, lorica, vesica [L.] 4. balalaika, hydromica.

IK′al– 2. plical, Michal, Michael, pical 4. interplical.

IK′at– 2. plicate, spicate.

IK′en– 2. liken, lichen 3. unliken, disliken, misliken.

IK′er– 2. ichor, diker, hiker [coll.], liker, piker, spiker, striker 3. *hitchhiker* [slang], disliker.

IK′i– 2. ikey, piky, spiky, Psyche 4. phytopsyche.

IK′ik– 2. psychic 3. nonpsychic, unpsychic.

IK′ing– 2. diking, liking, piking, spiking, striking, viking 3. hitchhiking [slang], disliking, misliking.

IK′l– 2. Michael, pical, cycle, psychal 3. recycle, bicycle, tricycle 4. interplical, hemicycle, epicycle, monocycle, multicycle, motorcycle.

IK′li– 2. likely 3. belikely, unlikely.

IK'lik– 2. cyclic 3. acyclic, bicyclic, encyclic 4. polycyclic, epicyclic.

IK'ling– 2. cycling 3. bicycling 4. motorcycling.

IK'on– 2. icon.

IK'us– 2. Ficus, Picus, spicous 3. anticous, anticus [L.], posticous, posticus [L.] 4. umbilicus, Andronicus.

IL'a– 2. Ila, Hyla, Lila, pyla 3. strobila, Delilah.

IL'aks– 2. lilacs, smilax.

IL'and– 2. island, highland, Thailand 3. Rhode Island, Long Island.

IL'ar– 2. filar, pilar, stylar 3. bifilar, trifilar; see also IL'er– filer etc. below.

IL'ark– 2. phylarch, skylark.

ILD'er– 2. milder, wilder.

ILD'est– 2. mildest, wildest.

ILD'ish– 2. childish, mildish, wildish.

ILD'li– 2. mildly, riledly [coll.], wildly 3. beguiledly.

ILD'lik– 2. childlike, mild-like [dial.], riled-like [dial.], wild-like [dial.] 3. beguiled-like [dial.].

ILD'ness– 2. mildness, riledness [coll.], wildness 3. beguiledness, unwildness.

IL'e– 2. hyle 3. sedile, ancile; see also IL'i– highly etc. below.

IL'eks– 2. ilex, silex.

IL'ent– 2. silent 3. unsilent.

IL'er– 2. filer, filar, Schuyler, miler [slang], smiler, piler, pilar, Tyler, tiler, styler, stylar, viler 3. defiler, bifilar, trifilar, beguiler, compiler, reviler 4. reconciler.

IL'est– 2. vilest.

IL'et– 2. eyelet, islet, smilet, stylet.

IL'ful– 2. guileful, smileful, wileful.

IL'i– 2. highly, hyle, slyly, smily, wryly, riley [coll.], Riley, dryly, shyly, wily 3. sedile, ancile.

IL'ij– 2. mileage, smileage, silage.

IL'ing– 2. filing, smiling, piling, spiling, riling, tiling, styling, wiling, wi.'ling 3. defiling, beguiling, compiling, exiling, restyling, reviling 4. domiciling, reconciling.

IL'is– 3. Aprilis, Quintilis, Sextilis.

IL'ish– 2. stylish 3. unstylish.

IL'less– 2. guileless, smileless, styleless, wileless.

IL'ment– 3. defilement, beguilement, compilement, resilement, exilement 4. domicilement, reconcilement 5. irreconcilement.

IL'o– 2. high-low, milo, silo, Shiloh, stilo.

IL'oid– 2. styloid, xyloid.

IL'on– 2. phylon, nylon, pylon.

IL'ot– 2. Nilot, pilot 3. sky pilot.

IL'um– 2. filum [L.], phylum, hilum, pilum 3. asylum.

IL'us– 2. hilus, Nilous, Silas, stylus.

IM'a– 2. Phyma, Lima, mima, rima, tryma, sima, cyma 3. Tellima, Jemima 4. arapaima.

IM'aks– 2. Limax, climax 4. anti-climax.

IM'al– 2. rimal, primal, shtreimel 4. isocheimal, isocrymal.

IM'an– 2. pieman, shy man, Wyman.

IM'at– 2. primate, my mate, shy mate.

IM'en– 2. daimon, Hymen, limen, crimen [L.], Simon, taimen, Timon, vimen.

IM'er– 2. chimer, limer, climber, mimer, rimer, primer, timer, timor 3. sublimer, begrimer, reprimer, old-timer.

IM'est– 2. primest 3. sublimest.

IM'i– 2. limy, limey [slang], blimy, slimy, rimy, rhymy, primy, stymie, stimy, thymy 3. beslimy, old-timy.

IM'ik– 2. rhymic, thymic, zymic 3. enzymic 4. isocheimic, catathymic.

IM'ing– 2. chiming, climbing, sliming, rhyming, griming, priming, timing 3. begriming, berhyming, pump priming, two-timing [slang].

IM'ish– 2. chimish, rhymish, timish.

IM'ist– 2. rhymist, timist.

IM'it– 2. climate, time it 3. acclimate.

IM'less– 2. chimeless, dimeless, limeless, climbless, slimeless, mimeless, rhymeless, rimeless, grimeless, timeless.

IM'li– 2. primely, timely 3. sublimely, untimely.

IM'ness– 2. primeness 3. sublimeness.

IM'us– 2. rimous, primus, simous, cymous, timeous [Scot. & Ir.], thymus.

IN'a– 2. Ina, China, Dinah, Heine, Jaina, mina, myna, vina [L.] 3. Sabina, Medina, Regina, Shekinah, trichina, Salina, salina, farina, Sabrina, piscina, Lucina, glucina 4. Adelina, Angelina, Evelina, Carolina, Platyrrhina.

IN'aks– 2. pinax, Thrinax.

IN'al– 2. binal, final, spinal, rhinal, crinal, trinal, sinal, vinal 3. acclinal, declinal, synclinal, caninal, prorhinal 4. semifinal, isoclinal, periclinal, interspinal, endocrinal, matutinal 5. cerebrospinal.

IN'an– 2. Hainan, Tainan 3. Salinan.

IN'at– 2. binate, spinate, quinate.

IND'ed– 2. blinded, minded, rinded, winded 3. snow-blinded, reminded, free-minded, strong-minded, high-minded, weak-minded, like-minded, low-minded, fair-minded, light-minded 4. unreminded, carnal-minded, feeble-minded, double-minded, evil-minded, simple-minded, bloody-minded, worldly-minded, earthly-minded, even-minded, narrow-minded, sober-minded.

IND'er– 2. binder, finder, hinder, kinder, blinder, minder, grinder, winder 3. *bookbinder, spellbinder, faultfinder, pathfinder,* reminder, sidewinder, stem-winder 4. organ grinder.

IND'est– 2. kindest, blindest.

IND'ful– 2. mindful 3. remindful, unmindful.

IND'hand– 3. behindhand.

IND'ing– 2. binding, finding, blinding, minding, grinding, winding 3. rebinding, bookbinding, unbinding, reminding, unwinding.

IND'less– 2. bindless, mindless, rindless, grindless, windless.

IND'li– 2. kindly, blindly 3. unkindly, purblindly.

IND'ness– 2. kindness, blindness 3. unkindness, snow blindness 4. color blindness.

IN'er– 2. diner, finer, liner, miner, minor, piner, Shriner, signer, shiner, winer, twiner, whiner 3. combiner, definer, refiner, confiner, maligner, headliner, streamliner, recliner, incliner, outliner, benigner, repiner, supiner, assigner, resigner, consigner, diviner, entwiner, designer, resigner 4. underliner, underminer, intertwiner.

IN'ess– 2. highness, nighness, slyness, wryness, dryness, spryness, shyness.

IN'est– 2. finest 3. benignest, supinest, divinest 4. superfinest.

IN'i– 2. Heinie, liny, miny, piny, spiny, briny, tiny, viny, winy, whiny 3. sunshiny, moonshiny.

IN'ing– 2. dining, fining, lining, mining, pining, signing, shining, Vining, wining, twining, whining 3. combining, defining, refining, confining, relining, declining, reclining, inclining, outlining, repining, opining, resigning, designing, outshining, entwining 4. unconfining, underlining, interlining, undermining, countersigning, intertwining.

IN'is– 2. finis 3. Erinys.

IN'it– 2. finite, crinite.

IN'land– 2. Rhineland, Vineland.

IN'less– 2. fineless, lineless, pineless, spineless, signless, tineless, vineless, wineless.

IN'li– 2. finely 3. condignly, malignly, benignly, supinely, divinely 4. superfinely, unbenignly, saturninely, undivinely.

IN'lik– 2. binelike, finelike, linelike, pinelike, spinelike, signlike, tinelike, vinelike, winelike.

IN'ment– 3. refinement, confinement, alignment, malignment, enshrinement, assignment, designment, resignment, entwinement 4. unrefinement, realignment, interlinement, intertwinement.

IN'ness– 2. fineness 3. condignness, benignness, supineness, divineness 4. superfineness.

IN'o– 2. Aino, rhino, Taino 3. sabino, albino.

IN'um– 2. Linum, vinum [L.] 3. tablinum 4. Antirrhinum.

IN'us– 2. dinus, Linus, minus, Minos, Pinus, spinous, sinus, vinous 3. echinus, Lupinus.

I'o– 2. io, Io, Clio, trio 3. Ohio.

I'ol– 2. viol 3. bass viol; see also I'aldial etc. above.

I'on– 2. ion, lion, scion, Zion 3. Arion, Orion, Ixion, sea lion 4. dandelion; see also I'an– Ian etc. above.

I'or– 2. prior, trior; see also I'er– eyer etc. above.

I'ot– 2. eyot, piot, riot, Sciot; see also I'et– diet etc. above.

IP'a– 2. nipa, pipa, ripa, Stipa.

IP'al– 2. ripal, typal 4. archetypal; see also IP'l– stipel etc. below.

IP'ed– 2. biped, striped 6. parallelepiped.

IP'end– 2. ripened, stipend.

IP'er– 2. hyper, niper [obs.], sniper, piper, riper, griper, striper, typer, viper, wiper, swiper 3. sandpiper, bagpiper, sideswiper 4. linotyper, windshield wiper 5. stereotyper 6. daguerreotyper.

IP'est– ripest; see also IP'ist– typist etc. below.

IP'i– 2. pipy, stripy, swipy 4. polytypy, antitypy, chromotypy, phonotypy 6. daguerreotypy.

IP'ing– 2. piping, Peiping, griping, striping, typing, wiping, swiping 3. retyping, restriping, sideswiping 4. linotyping 5. electrotyping 6. daguerreotyping.

IP'ist– 2. typist, ripest 4. linotypist, phonotypist 5. electrotypist 6. daguerreotypist.

IP'l– 2. stipel 3. disciple; see also IP'alripal etc. above.

IP'less– 2. pipeless, gripeless, stripeless, typeless, wipeless, swipeless.

IP'o– 2. hypo, typo.

IP'rus– 2. Cyprus, cypress, Cypris.

IR'a– 2. Ira, eyra, beira, daira, lira, Lyra, Mira, Myra 3. hegira, Almira, almirah, palmyra, Elmira, hetaira, Elvira.

IR'al– 2. gyral, chiral, pyral, spiral, styryl 3. papyral, retiral 4. polygyral, allochiral.

IR'ant– 2. gyrant, spirant, tyrant 3. aspirant, expirant, conspirant, archtyrant; see also IR'ent– virent etc. below.

IR'at– 2. pirate 3. archpirate.

IR'ate– 2. irate, gyrate, lyrate, lirate 3. agyrate 4. circumgyrate, dextrogyrate 5. sinistrogyrate.

IR'e– 2. daire, kairi [Jap.] 3. venire 4. praemunire, Dies Irae [L.]; see also IR'i– eyrie etc. below.

IR'een– 2. Irene, kyrene, kairine, pyrene, styrene, squireen.

IR'en– 2. kairine, siren 5. lepidosiren; see also IR'on– Byron etc. below.

IR'ent– 2. virent 3. inquirent 4. sempervirent; see also IR'ant– gyrant etc. above.

IR'er– 2. direr, firer, hirer, mirer, tirer, wirer 3. admirer, bemirer, aspirer, respirer, expirer, inspirer, conspirer, perspirer, suspirer, attirer, retirer, haywirer [slang], rewirer, acquirer, requirer, enquirer, inquirer, desirer.

IR′est– 2. direst 3. *haywirest* [slang].

IR′ful– 2. ireful, direful 3. desireful.

IR′i– 2. eyrie, dairi, fiery, miry, spiry, wiry, squiry 3. expiry, perspiry, enquiry, inquiry.

IR′id– 2. irid, Lyrid, xyrid 3. mormyrid, Osiride 4. sempervirid.

IR′ik– 2. gyric 3. onciric, epeiric 4. photogyric.

IR′ing– 2. firing, hiring, miring, spiring, tiring, wiring, squiring 3. admiring, bemiring, aspiring, respiring, expiring, inspiring, conspiring, perspiring, attiring, retiring, untiring, unwiring, acquiring, requiring, inquiring, desiring 4. unaspiring, uninspiring, reacquiring, uninquiring, undesiring.

IR′is– 2. iris, Iris, Siris 3. Osiris.

IR′ish– 2. Irish, squirish.

IR′ist– 2. irised, lyrist.

IR′less– 2. tireless, wireless, squireless.

IR′li– 2. direly, squirely 3. entirely.

IR′lik– 2. byrelike, firelike, lyrelike, mirelike, pyrelike, spirelike, tirelike, wirelike, choirlike.

IR′ling– 2. hireling, squireling.

IR′ment– 3. bemirement, attirement, retirement, acquirement, requirement.

IR′ness– 2. direness 3. entireness.

IR′o– 2. gyro, Cairo, pyro, tyro 4. Autogiro.

IR′on– 2. Byron, gyron, Chiron, myron, Myron, siren 3. environ.

IR′one– 2. pyrone, Tyrone.

IR′os– 2. gyrose, virose.

IR′sum– 2. iresome, tiresome 3. desiresome.

IR′us– 2. gyrus, Pyrus, spirous, Cyrus, virus 3. Epirus, apyrous, papyrus, desirous.

IS′a– 2. beisa, Meissa.

IS′al– 2. sisal 4. paradisal; *see* also IZ′al– sizal etc. below.

IS′ens– 2. license, licence 3. dog license 4. marriage license, driver's license 5. poetic license.

IS′er– 2. icer, dicer, geyser, slicer, splicer, nicer, spicer, ricer, pricer, cicer 3. preciser, conciser, enticer 4. sacrificer 5. self-sacrificer.

IS′est– 2. nicest 3. precisest, concisest.

IS′ez– 2. ices, dices, slices, splices, spices, rices, prices, vices 3. suffices, entices, advices, devices 4. sacrifices.

IS′ful– 3. enticeful, deviceful.

IS′i– 2. icy, nisi, spicy, ricey.

IS′ing– 2. icing, dicing, slicing, splicing, spicing, pricing 3. sufficing, enticing 4. sacrificing 5. self-sacrificing.

IS′is– 2. Isis, physis, lysis, crisis, phthisis; *see* also IS′us– nisus etc. below.

IS′iv– 3. collisive, derisive, decisive, precisive, incisive, divisive 4. cicatrisive, indecisive, undivisive.

IS′less– 2. iceless, diceless, sliceless, spliceless, spiceless, riceless, priceless, viceless 3. adviceless 4. sacrificeless.

IS′li– 2. nicely 3. precisely, concisely 4. overnicely.

IS′man– 2. iceman, viseman, viceman.

IS′ment– 3. sufficement, enticement.

IS′ness– 2. niceness 3. preciseness, conciseness 4. overniceness.

IS′on– 2. bison, hyson, grison, vison.

IST′er– 2. Meister [G.], shyster [coll.] 4. Kapellmeister [G.].

IST′lik– 2. Christlike.

IST′ro– 2. maestro.

IS′us– 2. nisus, Nisus, risus [L.] 4. Dionysus; *see* also IS′is– Isis etc. above.

IT′a– 2. vita 3. baryta, Nerita 4. amalaita.

IT'al– **2.** dital, title, vital **3.** detrital, recital, entitle, mistitle, requital **4.** microphytal, parasital.

IT'ant– **3.** incitant.

IT'e– **2.** rite **3.** Venite **4.** Aphrodite, Amphitrite, arborvitae; *see also* IT'i– blighty etc. below.

IT'ed– **2.** bighted, dited, dighted, heighted, kited, lighted, blighted, plighted, slighted, knighted, nighted [rare], spited, righted, frighted, sighted, cited, sited, whited **3.** indited, indicted, alighted, delighted, relighted, unlighted, benighted, beknighted, unknighted, ignited, united, despited, affrighted, attrited, recited, excited, incited, long-sighted, farsighted, clear-sighted, nearsighted, shortsighted, requited, invited **4.** candlelighted, satellited, reunited, ununited, disunited, copyrighted, eagle-sighted, oversighted, uninvited, unrequited.

IT'em– **2.** item, bite 'em.

IT'en– **2.** heighten, chitin, chiton, lighten, brighten, frighten, triton, Triton, tighten, Titan, whiten **3.** enlighten, retighten, untighten.

IT'er– **2.** iter, biter, fighter, kiter, lighter, blighter, flighter, plighter, slighter, miter, mitre, smiter, niter, righter, writer, brighter, triter, sighter, citer, tighter, whiter **3.** *backbiter*, indicter, inditer, indictor, *bullfighter*, alighter, delighter, politer, *lamplighter*, unmiter, igniter, uniter, rewriter, *typewriter*, exciter, inviter, requiter **4.** candlelighter, impoliter, dynamiter, reuniter, copy writer, underwriter.

IT'est– **2.** lightest, slightest, rightest, brightest, tritest, tightest, whitest **3.** politest, *uprightest* **4.** impolitest.

IT'ez– **2.** nighties **3.** barytes, pyrites, sorites.

IT'ful– **2.** mightful, spiteful, rightful, frightful, sprightful **3.** delightful, despiteful, unrightful.

ITH'er– **2.** either, blither, neither, writher, tither.

ITH'est– **2.** lithest, blithest.

ITH'ful– **2.** litheful, blitheful.

ITH'ing– **2.** nithing, writhing, trithing, scything, tithing.

ITH'li– **2.** lithely, blithely.

ITH'nes– **2.** litheness, blitheness.

ITH'on– **2.** python.

ITH'sum– **2.** lithesome, blithesome.

IT'i– **2.** blighty, flighty, mighty, mity, nighty, nightie, whity **3.** almighty **4.** Aphrodite, highty-tighty; *see also* IT'e– rite etc. above.

IT'ing– **2.** biting, diting, fighting, kiting, skiting [dial.], lighting, blighting, plighting, slighting, smiting, knighting, spiting, writing, righting, frighting, citing, sighting, whiting **3.** *backbiting*, inditing, indicting, *cockfighting*, *bullfighting*, alighting, delighting, beknighting, uniting, affrighting, *handwriting*, reciting, inciting, exciting, inviting, requiting **4.** proselyting, dynamiting, reuniting, disuniting, expediting, copywriting, copyrighting, underwriting, uninviting.

IT'is– **3.** phlebitis, carditis, rachitis, nephritis, iritis, arthritis, neuritis **4.** meningitis, laryngitis, tonsillitis, dermatitis **5.** pericarditis, appendicitis, peritonitis.

IT'ish– **2.** lightish, slightish, spitish, brightish, tritish, tightish, whitish **4.** eremitish, anchoritish.

IT'iv– **3.** attritive, excitive **4.** expeditive, appetitive.

IT'l– **2.** title, vital **3.** recital, betitle, entitle, mistitle, requital; *see also* IT'al– dital etc. above.

IT'less– **2.** bightless, fightless, heightless, kiteless, lightless, miteless, mightless, nightless, knightless, spiteless, riteless, rightless, frightless, sprightless, sightless **3.** delightless **4.** proselyteless, dynamiteless, copyrightless.

IT'li– 2. lightly, slightly, nightly, knight-ly, rightly, brightly, sprightly, tritely, sightly, tightly, whitely 3. politely, *fortnightly*, uprightly, contritely, unsightly 4. eruditely, impolitely.

IT'ment– 3. indictment, affrightment, incitement, excitement, invitement.

IT'ner– 2. heightener, lightener, brightener, frightener, whitener.

IT'ness– 2. lightness, slightness, rightness, brightness, triteness, whiteness 3. politeness, uprightness 4. eruditeness, impoliteness.

IT'ning– 2. heightening, lightning, lightening, tightening, brightening, frightening, whitening 3. streak lightning, chain lightning, sheet lightning.

IT'oid– 2. cytoid.

IT'on– 2. chiton, Triton, cyton, Titan.

IT'um– 2. item, Blitum 5. ad infinitum.

IT'us– 2. litus, ritus [L.], situs, Titus 3. attritus, detritus, St. Vitus.

I'us– 2. pious, Pius, prius 3. bacchius, unpious, Darius 4. nisi prius 5. antibacchius; *see* also I'as– eyas etc. above.

IV'a– 2. iva, Iva, daiva, Siva, Saiva 3. saliva 4. conjunctiva.

IV'al– 2. nival, rival, thivel 3. ogival, archival, salival, arrival, corrival, deprival, outrival, estival, revival, survival 4. nonarrival, relatival, genitival, adjectival, conjunctival 5. imperatival.

IV'an– 2. Ivan, divan; *see* also IV'en– liven etc. below.

IV'ans– 3. connivance, arrivance, contrivance, survivance.

IV'ant– 2. trivant 3. connivant, survivant.

IV'at– 2. private 3. unprivate.

IV'en– 2. liven 3. enliven; *see* also IV'an– Ivan etc. above.

IV'er– 2. diver, fiver [slang], hiver, jiver [slang], skiver, liver, livor, sliver, river, driver, shriver, striver, thriver, stiver 3.

pearl diver, conniver, depriver, arriver, slave driver, contriver, survivor 4. deep sea diver.

IV'est– 2. livest 3. alivest.

IV'i– 2. ivy, jivy [slang], skivie [Scot.], stivy 4. poison ivy.

IV'ing– 2. diving, hiving, jiving [slang], skiving, riving, driving, striving, shriving, thriving, stiving [Scot. & dial. Eng.], wiving 3. conniving, arriving, deriving, contriving, reviving, surviving.

IV'li– 2. lively, shively 3. unlively.

IV'ment– 3. deprivement, revivement.

IV'us– 2. divus, clivus 3. salivous, acclivous, declivous, proclivous.

I'way– 2. byway, highway, skyway.

IZ'a– 2. Isa, Liza 3. Eliza, coryza.

IZ'al– 2. sizal 3. surmisal, despisal, arrhizal, apprizal, reprisal, comprisal, surprisal, incisal, capsizal, advisal, revisal 4. paradisal.

IZ'en– 2. bison, dizen, greisen 3. bedizen, horizon 4. spiegeleisen, Blut und eisen [G.].

IZ'er– 2. geyser, Kaiser, miser, riser, prizer, sizer, sizar, visor, vizor, wiser 3. disguiser, elisor, remiser, surmiser, apprizer, surpriser, assizer, incisor, excisor, capsizer, baptizer, chastiser, deviser, devisor, reviser, divisor 4. gormandizer, aggrandizer, eulogizer, catechizer, vocalizer, analyzer, paralyzer, vitalizer, moralizer, neutralizer, tantalizer, totalizer, equalizer, sterilizer, fertilizer, civilizer, symbolizer, idolizer, itemizer, atomizer, organizer, humanizer, scrutinizer, solemnizer, lionizer, colonizer, harmonizer, sermonizer, canonizer, synchronizer, patronizer, modernizer, fraternizer, mesmerizer, cauterizer, pulverizer, theorizer, temporizer, terrorizer, authorizer, enterpriser, exerciser, exorciser, magnetizer, appetizer, sympathizer, improviser, supervisor 5. apologizer, generalizer, demoralizer, monopolizer, economizer, epitomizer, deodorizer, extemporizer, nonsympathizer.

ĪZ'est– 2. wisest 3. unwisest.

ĪZ'i– 2. sizy 3. capsizy.

ĪZ'ing– 2. rising, prizing, sizing, wising 3. disguising, surmising, despising, arising, comprising, surprising, uprising, chastising 4. gormandizing, standardizing, jeopardizing, enfranchising, disfranchizing, merchandizing, eulogizing, realizing, localizing, vocalizing, penalizing, moralizing, neutralizing, specializing, tantalizing, mobilizing, sterilizing, compromising, enterprising, ostracising, publicizing, criticizing, advertising, sympathizing, improvising, supervising 5. philosophizing, materializing, demoralizing, generalizing, capitalizing, devitalizing, revitalizing, immortalizing,

monopolizing, visualizing, uncompromising, familiarizing, characterizing, italicizing, systematizing; *also all other verbs ending in "ize" plus "ing."*

ĪZ'ment– 3. franchisement, apprizement, assizement, baptizement, chastisement, advisement 4. aggrandizement, enfranchisement, disfranchisement.

ĪZ'mik– 2. seismic 3. aseismic, coseismic.

ĪZ'nes– 2. wiseness 3. unwiseness.

ĪZ'o– 3. aviso, proviso 4. Valparaiso, improviso.

ĪZ'on– 2. bison 3. horizon.

ĪZ'or– 2. visor, vizor 3. elisor, incisor, devisor, divisor 4. supervisor; *see* also **ĪZ'er–** geyser etc. above.

I (eye)

3.

TRIPLE RHYMES IN I (eye′a-ble)

I′a–bl– 3. eyeable, liable, pliable, friable, triable, viable 4. reliable, appliable, impliable, compliable, deniable 5. modifiable, qualifiable, undeniable, verifiable, classifiable, pacifiable, falsifiable, rectifiable, fortifiable, justifiable, satisfiable, unreliable, multipliable, undeniable 6. solidifiable, exemplifiable, electrifiable, diversifiable, identifiable, unjustifiable, unsatisfiable.

I′a–bli– 3. pliably 4. reliably, appliably, compliably, deniably 5. justifiably, unreliably, undeniably 6. unjustifiably, unsatisfiably.

I′a–dez– 3. Hyades, Pleiades, naiades, dryades 5. hamadryades.

I′a–gram– 3. diagram, skiagram, viagram.

I′a–kal– 3. piacle 4. dandiacal, zodiacal, heliacal, maniacal 5. prosodiacal, elegiacal, demoniacal, simoniacal 6. pyromaniacal, dipsomaniacal, kleptomaniacal, hypochondriacal, paradisiacal 7. encyclopediacal, bibliomaniacal.

I′al–lik– 3. dial-like, phial-like, trial-like, vial-like, viol-like 4. sundial-like.

I′an–si– 3. cliency, pliancy, riancy 4. compliancy.

I′ant–li– 3. pliantly 4. defiantly, reliantly, compliantly.

I′ar–i– 3. diary, briary, friary; *see* also I′er–i– fiery etc. below.

I′ar–ist– 3. diarist, Piarist.

I′ark–i– 3. diarchy, triarchy.

I′as–is– 4. psychiasis, psoriasis 5. odontiasis 6. hypochondriasis, elephantiasis.

I′at–er– 4. psychiater, archiater, hippiater.

I′at–ri– 4. podiatry, psychiatry, phoniatry, hippiatry.

I′at–rist– 4. podiatrist, psychiatrist, hippiatrist.

IB′a–bl– 3. bribable, scribable 4. ascribable, subscribable, describable, prescribable, inscribable, proscribable 5. indescribable, undescribable, circumscribable.

IB′a–bli– 4. describably 5. indescribably, undescribably.

IB′er–i– 3. bribery.

ID′a–bl– 3. guidable, hidable, ridable 4. unguidable, elidable, unridable, bestridable, decidable, dividable, providable 5. undecidable, subdividable, undividable, unprovidable.

ID′ed–li– 4. unguidedly, misguidedly, decidedly, lopsidedly 5. undecidedly, undividedly, unprovidedly.

ID′ful–li– 3. pridefully.

ID′ing–li– 3. chidingly, guidingly, hidingly, glidingly, slidingly, stridingly, sidingly 4. abidingly, confidingly, misguidingly, unhidingly, unchidingly.

I′en–si– 3. cliency, pliancy, riancy 4. compliancy.

I′er–i– 3. fiery, lyery, briery, priory; *see* also I′ar–i– diary etc. above.

145

I′et–al– 3. dietal, hyetal 4. parietal, varietal, societal 5. isohyetal.

I′et–ed– 3. dieted, rioted, quieted. 4. unquieted, disquieted.

I′et–er– 3. dieter, rioter, quieter 4. proprietor, disquieter.

I′et–est– 3. quietest 4. unquietest.

I′et–i– 3. piety 4. ubiety, dubiety, filiety, impiety, variety, ebriety, sobriety, propriety, society, satiety, anxiety 5. contrariety, inebriety, insobriety, notoriety, impropriety.

I′et–ing– 3. dieting, rioting, quieting 4. unquieting, disquieting.

I′et–ist– 3. dietist, pietist, quietist 4. varietist.

I′et–izm– 3. pietism, quietism 4. varietism.

IF′en–at– 3. hyphenate, siphonate.

IF′er–ing– 3. ciphering, syphering 4. deciphering.

IF′ling–li– 3. triflingly, stiflingly.]

I′il–at– 4. annihilate.

I′il–ist– 3. nihilist.

I′ing–li– 3. lyingly, flyingly, pryingly, sighingly, vyingly 4. defyingly 5. gratifyingly, mystifyingly, satisfyingly.

IK′a–bl– 3. likeable, spikeable 4. unlikeable, dislikeable.

IK′li–hud– 3. likelihood 4. unlikelihood.

IK′lik–al– 3. cyclical 4. bicyclical, encyclical.

IL′a–bl– 3. smilable, rilable, filable, stylable, wilable, whilable 4. defilable, beguilable 5. reconcilable 6. irreconcilable, unreconcilable.

IL′and–er– 3. islander, highlander, Thailander.

IL′er–i– 3. guilery, pilary.

IL′ful–i– 3. guilefully, wilefully 4. beguilefully.

IL′ful–ness– 3. guilefulness, wilefulness 4. beguilefulness.

IL′ing–li– 3. smilingly 4. beguilingly.

IM′er–i– 3. rhymery, primary.

IM′i–ness– 3. liminess, sliminess, riminess, griminess.

IN′a–bl– 3. finable, linable, signable 4. combinable, definable, declinable, inclinable, opinable, assignable, designable, divinable 5. undefinable, undeclinable, unassignable, undivinable.

IN′a–bli– 4. definably, assignably 5. undefinably, undeclinably, unassignably.

IN′a–li– 3. finally, spinally.

IND′er–i– 3. bindery, grindery.

IN′er–i– 3. binary, finery, finary, minery, pinery, vinery, winery, quinary, swinery 4. refinery, alpinery.

IN′i–er– 3. spinier, brinier, shinier, tinier, winier.

IN′i–est– 3. spiniest, briniest, shiniest, tiniest, winiest.

IN′les–li– 3. spinelessly, winelessly.

I′ol–a– 3. viola, Viola 4. variola.

I′ol–et– 3. triolet, striolet, violet.

I′ol–ist– 3. sciolist, violist.

I′ol–us– 3. sciolous 4. gladiolus, modiolus, variolous.

I′on–iz– 3. ionize, lionize.

I′op–i– 3. myopy 4. presbyopy, Calliope.

I′or–i– priory; see also I′ar–i– diary etc. above; and I′er–i– fiery etc. above.

I′os–en– 3. Pliocene, Miocene 4. post-Pliocene.

I′ot–er– 3. rioter, quieter.

IP′ing–li– 3. pipingly, gripingly.

IP′les–li– 3. pipelessly, gripelessly, stripelessly, typelessly.

IR′a–bl– 3. fireable, hirable 4. respirable, expirable, inspirable, transpirable, perspirable, untirable, acquirable, requirable, inquirable, desirable 5. uninspirable, undesirable.

IR′as–i– 3. piracy 4. retiracy.

IR'ful–ness– **3.** irefulness, direfulness **4.** desirefulness.

IR'ing–li– **4.** admiringly, aspiringly, conspiringly, retiringly, inquiringly, desiringly.

IR'on–i– **3.** irony, sireny.

IS'a–bl– **3.** sliceable, spiceable, riceable, priceable **4.** enticeable.

IS'er–i– **3.** spicery **4.** irrisory, derisory, incisory.

IS'i–er– **3.** icier, spicier.

IS'i–est– **3.** iciest, spiciest.

IS'i–kl– **3.** icicle, bicycle, tricycle.

IS'i–li– **3.** icily, spicily.

IS'iv–li– **4.** derivisely, decisively, incisively **5.** indecisively, undecisively.

IS'iv–ness– **4.** derisiveness, decisiveness, incisiveness **5.** undecisiveness.

IS'or–i– derisory etc., *see* IS'er–i– spicery etc. above.

IT'a–bl– **3.** lightable, writable, sightable, citable **4.** indictable, ignitable, unitable, recitable, excitable, incitable, requitable **5.** extraditable.

IT'a–bli– **4.** indictably, unitably, excitably.

IT'al–iz– **3.** vitalize **4.** devitalize, revitalize.

IT'at–iv– **3.** writative **4.** recitative, excitative, incitative, requitative.

IT'en–er– **3.** heightener, lightener, brightener, frightener, tightener, whitener **4.** enlightener.

IT'ful–i– **3.** spitefully, rightfully, frightfully, sprightfully **4.** delightfully.

ITH'som–li– **3.** lithesomely, blithesomely.

ITH'som–ness– **3.** lithesomeness, blithesomeness.

IT'i–er– **3.** flightier, mightier **4.** almightier.

IT'il–i– **3.** flightily, mightily, sprightily **4.** almightily.

IT'i–ness– **3.** flightiness, mightiness **4.** almightiness.

IT'ing–li– **3.** bitingly, blightingly, slightingly **4.** excitingly, invitingly.

IT'less–ness– **3.** nightlessness, sightlessness.

IT'li–ness– **3.** knightliness, sprightliness, sightliness **4.** unsightliness.

IV'a–bl– **3.** drivable **4.** undrivable, deprivable, derivable, contrivable, revivable **5.** unrevivable.

IV'an–si– **4.** connivancy, contrivancy, survivancy.

IV'as–i– **3.** privacy.

IV'ing–li– **3.** jivingly [slang], drivingly, strivingly, thrivingly.

IZ'a–bl– **3.** prizable, sizable **4.** demisable, surmisable, despisable, comprisable, excisable, advisable, devisable **5.** subsidizable, oxidizable, realizable, analyzable, crystallizable, utilizable, civilizable, organizable, recognizable, incognizable, exercisable, inadvisable.

IZ'a–bli– **3.** sizeably **4.** advisably **5.** inadvisably.

IZ'ed–li– **4.** surmisedly, advisedly **5.** unadvisedly, improvisedly, unprovisedly.

IZ'ing–li– **4.** despisingly, surprisingly **5.** enterprisingly, tantalizingly, scrutinizingly, agonizingly, appetizingly.

IZ'or–i– **4.** advisory, revisory, provisory **5.** supervisory.

I (bib)

1.

SINGLE (MASCULINE) RHYMES IN I (bib)

Primary or Secondary Accent Falls on Last Syllable; Imperfect Rhymes Are in Italics.

IB– 1. bib, bibb, chib, dib, fib, gib, jib, Lib, lib [slang], glib, mib [dial.], nib, snib, rib, drib, crib, sib, Tib, tib [slang], quib, squib, zib [slang] 2. Adib, ad lib [slang], renib, *midrib*.

IBD– 1. bibbed, dibbed, fibbed, jibbed, ribbed, cribbed, squibbed 3. rockribbed.

IBZ– bibs etc., *see* **IB–** bib etc. above, plus "s" or "'s"; 2. his nibs.

ICH– 1. itch, bitch, ditch, dich, fitch, hitch, skitch [slang], lich, flitch, miche, smitch [slang], niche, snitch, pitch, rich, britch [dial.], stitch, witch, quitch, switch, twitch, which 2. unhitch, enrich, restitch, *seamstitch, hemstitch, chainstitch, whipstitch, catstitch*, bewitch 3. featherstitch, czarevitch.

ICHD– 1. itched, bitched [vulgar], ditched, hitched, niched, snitched, pitched, stitched, switched, twitched 2. unhitched, enriched, restitched, bewitched 3. featherstitched.

ID– 1. id, bid, chid, did, fid, gid, hid, kid, Kidd, skid, lid, slid, mid, rid, grid, strid, Sid, Cid, quid, squid 2. rebid, forbid, outbid, undid, outdid, *bifid, trifid, eyelid*, amid, *Enid, aphid*, Madrid, *Muphrid, Astrid* 3. underbid, overbid, overdid, katydid, invalid, pyramid.

IDST– 1. didst, midst 2. amidst.

IDTH– 1. width. f

IF– 1. if, biff, diff [slang], pfiff, jiff [slang], skiff, glyph, cliff, miff [dial. & slang], sniff, piff, spiff [slang], riff, griffe, griph,

Sif, tiff, stiff, wiff [slang], quiff, whiff 2. *Saiph, midriff* 3. handkerchief, neckerchief, logogriph, hippogriff, Teneriffe, bindle stiff [slang] 4. hieroglyph.

IFS– 1. ifs, cliffs, sniffs, tiffs, whiffs, ziffs, etc.

IFT– 1. biffed, gift, lift, miffed [dial. & slang], sniffed, snift, spiffed [slang], rift, drift, shrift, thrift, sift, shift, tiffed, tift, squiffed [slang], swift, whiffed 2. relift, uplift, adrift, *spindrift, spoondrift, snowdrift, spendthrift, muckthrift*, reshift, *makeshift, gearshift* 3. chimney swift.

IFTH– 1. fifth.

IG– 1. big, bigg, dig, fig, gig, jig, skig [slang], nig, snig [slang], pig, spig [slang], rig, wrig, brig, Frigg, grig, crig, prig, sprig, trig, cig [slang], tyg, wig, swig, twig, Whig, zig 2. fishgig, fizzig, renege, bigwig, earwig 3. Mr. Big, infra dig [coll.], caprifig, whirligig, Guinea pig, thimblerig, periwig 4. thingumajig [coll.].

IGD– 1. figged, rigged, grigged, wigged, swigged, twigged, zigged 2. reneged, full-rigged, square-rigged, bewigged.

IGZ– bigs etc., *see* **IG–** big etc. above, plus "s" or "'s"; 1. Biggs, Briggs, digs [slang], Jiggs, Riggs 3. Mrs. Wiggs.

IJ– 1. fidge [dial.], midge, smidge, nidge, ridge, bridge, whidge [slang], squidge 2. enridge, abridge, *cabbage, cribbage, bondage, yardage, cordage, leafage, roofage, package, leakage, coinage, carnage, dumpage, stoppage, moorage, storage, dosage, message, sausage, usage, shortage, hostage, postage,*

148

language, selvage, drayage, voyage 3. brigandage, *appendage, impoundage,* lineage, verbiage, foliage, vassalage, *assemblage,* tutelage, mucilage, cartilage, pilgrimage, appanage, vicinage, alienage, badinage, peonage, siphonage, baronage, patronage, parsonage, personage, *equipage,* vicarage, plunderage, brokerage, cooperage, porterage, quarterage, fosterage, average, beverage, leverage, flowerage, saxifrage, anchorage, harborage, tutorage, hemorrhage, arbitrage, pasturage, surplusage, armitage, hermitage, heritage, clientage, parentage 4. espionage.

ĬJD– 1. fidged [dial.], nidged, ridged, bridged 2. unridged, abridged, unbridged 3. unabridged.

ĬK– 1. ich [G.], ick [slang], chic, chick, tchick, Dick, dick [slang & dial.], hic, hick, kick, lick, flick, click, slick, mick, nick, snick, pick, pic [slang], spick, rick, wrick, brick, Frick, crick, cric, creek [coll.], scrick [slang], prick, trick, sick, sic, tick, tic, stick, stich, thick, Vic, vic [slang], wick, quick 2. *dabchick, peachick, cowlick, nutpick, toothpick, hayrick, firebrick, landsick, seasick, homesick, brainsick, moonsick, heartsick, lovesick, knobstick, yardstick, broomstick, drumstick, chopstick, metestick,* Old Vic, *lampwick, Warwick, Brunswick* 3. Benedick, benedick, Catholic, arsenic, chivalric, choleric, limerick, turmeric, whitterick, maverick, plethoric, rhetoric, bishopric, lunatic, heretic, politic, walking stick, fiddlestick, candlestick, bailiwick, candlewick, double quick 4. allocochick, ich liebe dich [G.], kinnikinnick, archbishopric, arithmetic, impolitic 5. cosmopolitic.

ĬKS– chicks etc., *see* **ĬK–** ich [G.] etc. above, plus "s" or "'s"; 1. Bix, chix [slang], Dix, fix, mix, nix, Pnyx, pyx, pix, rix, Trix, six, Styx 2. affix, adfix, refix, prefix, infix, confix, transfix, postfix, suffix, prolix, admix, immix, commix 3. antefix, crucifix, intermix, undermix, overmix,

cicatrix, Beatrix, twenty-six 4. aviatrix, executrix.

ĬKST– 1. fixed, mixed, nixed [slang], sixte, 'twixt 2. affixed, adfixed, refixed, prefixed, infixed, confixed, transfixed, postfixed, suffixed, admixed, immixed, commixed, betwixt 3. antefixed, dorsifixed, intermixed, undermixed, overmixed.

ĬKT– 1. dict [arch.], kicked, licked, clicked, picked, Pict, bricked, tricked, strict, sicked, ticked, wicked 2. addict, *edict,* predict, delict, *relict,* afflict, inflict, conflict, depict, astrict, restrict, constrict, evict, convict, two-wicked 3. contradict, benedict, Benedict, interdict, overstrict, preconvict.

ĬL– 1. ill, bill, Bill, chill, chil, dill, fill, Phil, phil [slang], gill, hill, jill, kil, kill, kiln, skil, skill, lill, li'l [dial.], Lil, mill, mil, nil, pill, spill, rill, brill, drill, frill, grill, grille, prill, shrill, trill, thrill, sill, shil, shill, til, till, still, thill, vill, ville, will, Will, quill, squill, swill, twill 2. *playbill, waybill, redbill, handbill, broadbill, ringbill, wrybill, cockbill, hornbill, thornbill, spoonbill, waxbill, crossbill, boatbill, shortbill, bluebill, shoebill,* spadille, refill, fulfill, *scrodgill, bluegill, molehill,* downhill, uphill, *anthill,* sijill, *limekiln, treadmill, windmill,* quadrille, befrill, *footrill, headsill, groundsill,* retill, until, bestill, standstill, distill, instill, coutil, Seville, goodwill, ill will, Brazil, frazil 3. dishabille, dollar bill, razorbill, piccadill, daffodil, Francophil, Gallophil, Anglophil, demophil, Sinophil, chlorophyll, astrophil, Negrophil, chrysophyll, Celtophil, phytophil, underfill, overfill, cement mill, juvenile, puerile, imbecile, codicile, domicile, verticil, window sill, Mother Sill, volatile, vibratil, pulsatile, versatile, mercantile, infantile, reinstill, thereuntil, intertill, undertill, overtill, Faneuil, Louisville, Evansville, whippoorwill.

ĬLCH– 1. filch, milch, pilch, zilch [slang].

ILD– 1. build, billed, chilled, filled, gilled, gild, guild, killed, skilled, milled, pilled, spilled, frilled, trilled, stilled, quilled, willed 2. rebuild, rebilled, unfilled, fulfilled, begild, *wergild*, *Brunhild*, unskilled, untilled, distilled, instilled, unstilled, self-willed, strong-willed 3. unfulfilled, octogild, undistilled.

ILK– 1. ilk, bilk, milk, silk, whilk 2. sour milk, spilt milk, spun silk.

ILN– 1. kiln, Milne 2. limekiln.

ILT– 1. built, gilt, guilt, hilt, jilt, kilt, lilt, milt, spilt, silt, tilt, stilt, wilt, quilt 2. rebuilt, unspilt, atilt, uptilt 3. Vanderbilt, clipper built.

ILTS– 1. gilts, guilts, hilts, jilts, kilts, lilts, silts, tilts, stilts, wilts, quilts 3. Vanderbilts.

IM– 1. Bim, bim [slang], dim, him, hymn, gym, Jim, jim [slang], Kim, skim, limn, limb, flim [slang], glim, Clim, Klim, slim, mim, nim, Nym, rim, brim, grim, grimme, scrim, prim, trim, Sim, shim, Tim, vim, swim, whim, zimb 2. bedim, enlimn, corymb, betrim 3. cherubim, paradigm, seraphim, pseudonym, synonym, antonym, undernim, interim, hexastigm, Tiny Tim.

IMD– 1. dimmed, hymned, skimmed, limbed, slimmed, rimmed, brimmed, trimmed 2. bedimmed, untrimmed.

IMF– 1. lymph, nymph 2. wood nymph 3. endolymph, paranymph, water nymph.

IMP– 1. imp, bimp [slang], gimp, jimp, skimp, scimp, limp, blimp, mimp, pimp, grimp [slang], crimp, scrimp, primp, shrimp, simp [slang], tymp.

IMZ– Bim's etc., *see* **IM–** Bim etc. above, plus "s" or " 's."

IN– 1. in, inn, bin, been, chin, tchin, din, fin, Finn, finn [slang], gin, jinn, kin, skin, Lynn, lin, Glynn, min, Min, pin, spin, brin, grin, crin, sin, shin, tin, thin, win, twin, whin, Yin 2. herein, therein,

wherein, within, *nubbin*, *globin*, robin, *rubin*, has-been, *Cochin*, urchin, *Odin*, Baffin, Boffin, *redfin*, *threadfin*, *black fin*, elfin, *dolphin*, dauphin, bowfin, Fagin, begin, piggin, noggin, pidgin, Elgin, engine, margin, virgin, akin, Pekin, blood kin, *lambkin*, *bodkin*, *princekin*, welkin, napkin, catkin, reskin, redskin, calfskin, pigskin, sealskin, doeskin, lambskin, sharkskin, moleskin, sheepskin, bearskin, deerskin, maudlin, mafflin, *mufflin*, Franklin, collin, colin, Kremlin, drumlin, dunlin, poplin, carline, marlin, Berlin, merlin, Merlin, muslin, villain, chaplain, stamin, vermin, Lenin, lignin, tannin, rennin, lapin, repin, inchpin, pippin, unpin, tenpin, ninepin, kingpin, pushpin, hatpin, sculpin, respin, Crispin, fibrin, agrin, chagrin, corinne, caprin, dextrin, Turin, tocsin, rosin, trypsin, Tientsin, Latin, pectin, glutin, Swithin, penguin, pinguin, sequin 3. carabin, jacobin, Jacobin, colobin, paladin, amidin, morindin, *Alladin*, paraffin, Micky Finn, origin, waringin, Capuchin, absinthine, manakin, baldachin, ramekin, bodikin, birdikin, spilikin, billikin, manikin, cannikin, pannikin, bootikin, *grimalkin*, kilderkin, tigerkin, nipperkin, tigerskin, hyaline, caballine, alkaline, tourmaline, coralline, crystalline, ptyalin, Gobelin, gobelin, capelin, Zeppelin, javelin, sibylline, aniline, aquiline, bandoline, mandolin, violin, lanoline, crinoline, Caroline, tarpaulin, globulin, capulin, insulin, discipline, masculine, Ursuline, Benjamin, jessamine, vitamin, *albumin*, *illumine*, mezzanine, Fescennine, feminine, pavonine, heroine, wankapin, terrapin, chinquapin, calepin, underpin, saccharine, whipper-in, margarin, tamarin, nectarine, Sanhedrin, viperine, aspirin, anserine, peregrine, glycerin, Catherine, Lohengrin, tambourin, moccasin, *Wisconsin*, damassin, mortal sin, agatine, bulletin, Byzantine, *asbestine*, *intestine*, *Rasputin*, thick and thin, brodequin, harlequin, mannequin, lambrequin, *Algonquin*, genuine 4. hemoglobin, ragamuffin, digitalin, Evangeline, tuberculin, elaterin, alabastrine, highfalutin **5.** nitroglycerin.

INCH– **1.** inch, chinch, finch, kinch, linch, lynch, flinch, clinch, minch [slang], pinch, cinch, squinch **2.** redfinch, goldfinch, bullfinch, greenfinch, grass finch, hawfinch, unclinch, bepinch.

INCHT– **1.** inched, lynched, flinched, clinched, pinched, cinched **2.** unclinched, uncinched.

IND– **1.** binned, chinned, finned, ginned, lind, lynde, pinned, grinned, sind, scind, sinned, thinned, wind **2.** thick-skinned, thin-skinned, unskinned, abscind, rescind, exscind, whirlwind **3.** disciplined, tamarind, Amerind **4.** undisciplined.

ING– **1.** ing, Ing, Inge, bing, ching, ding, ging, hing, king, ling, fling, cling, Kling, pling [slang], Ming, ping, ring, wring, bring, dring, spring, string, sing, singh, ting, sting, thing, wing, swing, zing **2.** beking, Chungking, Nanking, *fledgeling, changeling, weakling, dukeling, stripling, Riesling, princeling*, Peiping, enring, aspring, *offspring, mainspring, latchstring, checkstring, hamstring, bowstring, shoestring, Singsing, Storting, something, nothing,* bewing, *redwing, pinwing, lapwing, waxwing, whitewing* **3.** scaffolding, rescinding, rewarding, horseshoeing, triumphing, pillaging, managing, foraging, à la king, mafficking, trafficking, dialing, rivaling, caviling, toweling, sanderling, underling, fingerling, easterling, maddening, widening, deafening, stiffening, roughening, toughening, strengthening, slackening, thickening, sickening, opening, happening, lessening, threatening, sweetening, softening, fastening, hastening, moistening, fattening, leavening, evening, rationing, pensioning, auctioning, questioning, echoing, larruping, sugaring, soldering, murdering, differing, suffering, angering, ushering, weathering, soldiering, hankering, hollering, summering, centering, sauntering, quartering, blistering, answering,

doctoring, motoring, licquoring, conjuring, murmuring, featuring, fracturing, lecturing, picturing, culturing, posturing, purchasing, ʻsolacing, menacing, latticing, financing, promising, witnessing, publishing, famishing, ravishing, fidgeting, blanketing, coveting, surfeiting, limiting, fagoting, balloting, adapting, ballasting, Odelsting, anything, everything, arguing, issuing, elbowing, swallowing, yellowing, billowing, merrywing, climaxing, lobbying, fancying, monkeying, volleying, journeying, moseying, curtseying, bullying, whinnying, copying, wearying, varying, querying, dairying, curtsying, emptying, partying, puttying, envying. **4.** mismanaging, disparaging, encouraging, discouraging, awakening, imagining, determining, occasioning, envisioning, beleaguering, continuing, mutinying **5.** administering, accompanying; *and present participle of all other verbs ad infinitum.*

INGD– **1.** dinged, pinged, ringed, stringed, tinged, winged, zinged **2.** beringed, *webwinged*, bewinged.

INJ– **1.** binge, dinge, hinge, pinge, fringe, cringe, scringe, springe, singe, tinge, swinge, twinge **2.** unhinge, impinge, infringe, *syringe*, astringe, attinge, atwinge.

INK– **1.** ink, Inc., inc [slang], chink, dink, Fink, fink [slang], gink [slang], jink, kink, skink, link, blink, clink, slink, mink, smink [slang], pink, spink, rink, brink, drink, prink, shrink, trink, sink, cinque, stink, think, wink, quink [slang], twink, zinc **2.** perjink, *iceblink*, relink, enlink, unlink, pincpinc, Sintsink, bethink, forethink, *hoodwink* **3.** bobolink, interlink, countersink, tiddlywink, jinniwink.

INKS– inks etc., *see* **INK–** ink etc. above, plus "s" or "'s"; **1.** sphinx, jinx, lynx, minx **2.** methinks **3.** criosphinx.

INKT– **1.** inked, chinked, kinked, linked, blinked, clinked, minked, pinked, rinked, prinked, tinct, winked **2.** beminked, succinct, discinct, instinct, distinct, extinct, *hoodwinked* 3. indistinct.

INS– 1. chinse, mince, rinse, prince, since, wince, quince 2. evince, convince 3. merchant prince; *see* also **INTS–** bints etc. below.

INT– 1. bint, dint, hint, lint, blint [slang], flint, glint, splint, mint, print, sprint, tint, stint, vint, quint, squint. 2. *skinflint, gunflint, capmint, spearmint, catmint,* reprint, *hoofprint,* imprint, misprint, *footprint, blueprint* 3. sodamint, calamint, peppermint, gingerprint, aquatint, monotint, mezzotint 4. septuagint.

INTH– 1. plinth 2. *Corinth* 3. terebinth, labyrinth, hyacinth, colocynth.

INTS– bints etc., *see* **INT–** bint etc. above, plus "s" or "'s"; 1. chintz.

INZ– ins etc., *see* **IN–** in etc. above, plus "s" or "'s."

IP– 1. chip, dip, fip [slang], gip, hip, gyp, jip, jipp [both slang], kip, skip, lip, blip [slang], flip, glip [slang], clip, slip, nip, snip, pip, rip, drip, grip, grippe, scrip, trip, strip, thrip, sip, ship, tip, quip, whip, yip, zip 2. redip, inclip, unclip, *harelip, cowslip, catnip,* adrip, unrip, unstrip, outstrip, sibship, *headship,* midship, *friendship, hardship, lordship wardship,* reship, *flagship, judgeship, clanship,* transship, *queenship, kinship, sonship, township, troopship, airship, heirship, worship, warship, lightship, saintship, courtship,* equip, *coachwhip, horsewhip* 3. pogonip, comradeship, amidship, stewardship, *trusteeship,* ladyship, battleship, seamanship, workmanship, penmanship, horsemanship, chairmanship, statesmanship, sportsmanship, fellowship, scholarship, membership, leadership, partnership, ownership, censorship, sponsorship, authorship 4. guardianship, partisanship, citizenship, companionship, relationship, survivorship, acquaintanceship, apprenticeship.

IPS– chips etc., *see* **IP–** chip etc. above, plus "s" or "'s"; 1. Phipps 2. ellipse, eclipse 4. Apocalypse.

IPT– 1. chipped, gipped, gypped, skipped, lipped, clipped, clipt, slipped, dripped, crypt, script, whipped 2. *harelipped, thin-lipped, stiff-lipped, red-lipped, close-lipped,* subscript, *transcript,* conscript, proscript, *postscript, horsewhipped* 3. eucalypt, antescript, superscript, manuscript 4. apocalypt.

IR– through **IRZ–**, *see* short **U** (tub): **UR–** through **URZ–**.

IS– 1. bis, Dis, diss, hiss, kiss, lis, liss, bliss, gliss [slang], miss, Chris, priss [coll.], Tris, sis, siss, this, vis, wis [arch. or obs.], quis, cuisse, Swiss 2. abyss, dehisce, amiss, remiss, dismiss, iwis, ywis [both arch.] 3. magadis, cowardice, prejudice, benefice, edifice, sacrifice, orifice, artifice, Judas kiss, chrysalis, fortalice, Salamis, Artemis, reminisce, precipice, avarice, dentifrice, verdigris, mistigris, ambergris, licorice, Beatrice, cockatrice, emphasis, synthesis, emesis, Nemesis, genesis, abatis, clematis, armistice, interstice 4. Gallipolis, acropolis, necropolis, metropolis, anabasis, metabasis, psoriasis, periphrasis, metastasis, hypostasis, antithesis, parenthesis, diaeresis, analysis, paralysis 5. fideicommiss, sui generis [L.], biogenesis, metamorphosis 6. elephantiasis, abiogenesis, adipogenesis.

ISH– 1. ish, dish, fish, gish, lish, mish [slang], pish, wish, cuish, squish, swish 2. mayfish, crayfish, redfish, goldfish, swordfish, kingfish, clingfish, stingfish, dogfish, hogfish, frogfish, blackfish, creekfish, weakfish, inkfish, sailfish, shellfish, filefish, tilefish, greenfish, queenfish, pinfish, jawfish, crawfish, sawfish, garfish, starfish, batfish, catfish, flatfish, ratfish, whitefish, jewfish, bluefish, cowfish, plowfish, anguish 3. jellyfish, killifish, candlefish, devilfish, squirrelfish, tasselfish, cuttlefish, ribbonfish, surgeonfish, cigarfish, guitarfish, amberfish, barberfish, thunderfish, niggerfish, triggerfish, silverfish, babyish, dowdyish, devilish, womanish, heathenish, yellowish, willowish, ogreish, Quakerish, feverish, cleverish.

ISK– 1. bisque, disc, disk, fisc, Fiske, lisk [dial.], pisk, risk, brisk, frisk, tisk! [coll.], whisk 2. *lutfisk*, francisc 3. odalisque, obelisk, basilisk, tamarisk, asterisk.

ISM– *see* **IZM–**.

ISP– 1. lisp, risp, crisp, wisp, whisp.

IST– 1. ist, fist, fyst, hissed, hist, gist, jist, kissed, list, missed, mist, rist, frist [slang], wrist, grist, prissed [coll.], tryst, sist, sissed, cist, cyst, schist, wist, twist, whist 2. puckfist, dehisced, agist, bekissed, unkissed, alist, enlist, bemist, unmissed, dismissed, assist, subsist, desist, resist, encyst, insist, consist, exist, persist, atwist, entwist, untwist 3. Judaist, archaist, ultraist, prosaist, Arabist, methodist, psalmodist, threnodist, monodist, synodist, parodist, rhapsodist, concordist, Talmudist, atheist, tritheist, pacifist, specifist, elegist, strategist, eulogist, liturgist, monachist, catechist, anarchist, monarchist, apathist, amethyst, cymbalist, pedalist, feudalist, racialist, specialist, socialist, martialist, formalist, annalist, analyst, catalyst, journalist, choralist, moralist, pluralist, ruralist, fatalist, vitalist, novelist, pugilist, nihilist, libellist, duellist, symbolist, Aeolist, sciolist, fabulist, querulist, dynamist, ceramist, alchemist, pessimist, optimist, ophthalmist, undismissed, lachrymist, urbanist, Urbanist, vulcanist, organist, mechanist, Shamanist, Romanist, botanist, alienist, Hellenist, reminisced, terminist, Alpinist, Latinist, Calvinist, columnist, trombonist, hedonist, unionist, visionist, actionist, factionist, fictionist, notionist, Zionist, colonist, mnemonist, mammonist, harmonist, canonist, modernist, saturnist, communist, Taoist, egoist, jingoist, banjoist, soloist, Shintoist, landscapist, syncopist, Eucharist, diarist, solarist, summarist,

glossarist, Lazarist, mesmerist, preterist, satirist, theorist, aphorist, colorist, amorist, armorist, humorist, terrorist, motorist, symmetrist, Scripturist, synthesist, pharmacist, solecist, mythicist, biblicist, publicist, classicist, physicist, exorcist, hydrocyst, colipsist, progressist, prelatist, schematist, stigmatist, dogmatist, pietist, quietist, magnetist, phonetist, syncretist, occultist, scientist, presentist, Adventist, narcotist, egotist, hypnotist, nepotist, despotist, altruist, casuist, bolshevist, archivist, passivist, activist, pre-exist, coexist, intertwist, essayist, hobbyist, lobbyist, copyist 4. mosaicist, polemicist, empiricist, romanticist, chiropodist, telegraphist, telepathist, commercialist, nominalist, nationalist, liberalist, federalist, literalist, naturalist, capitalist, Scripturalist, ritualist, revivalist, evangelist, philatelist, parabolist, hyperbolist, monopolist, legitimist, epitomist, zootomist, accompanist, hygienist, alienist, determinist, protagonist, tobacconist, religionist, opinionist, communionist, revisionist, extensionist, delusionist, illusionist, reactionist, perfectionist, obstructionist, eudaemonist, misogynist, emancipist, plagiarist, apiarist, secularist, ocularist, singularist, militarist, psychiatrist, hexametrist, pedometrist, problematist, systematist, enigmatist, diplomatist, automatist, numismatist, separatist 5. bibliopegist, industrialist, conventionalist, Universalist, transcendentalist, spiritualist, automobilist, indeterminist, revolutionist, particularist, caricaturist, experimentist, apocalyptist; *and many other agent nouns ending in the suffix "-ist."*

IT– 1. it, bit, bitt, chit, dit, ditt [both dial.], fit, phit, git [dial.], hit, jit [slang], kit, skit, lit, flit, split, slit, mit, mitt, smit, nit, knit, pit, spit, writ, rit, brit, frit, grit, sprit, sit, cit, tit, wit, whit, quit, twit, zit [slang] 2. *tidbit, titbit, forebitt*, befit, unfit, misfit, *outfit*, alit, unlit, *twilit, moonlit, sunlit*, submit, admit, emit, demit, remit, commit, omit, permit, transmit, reknit.

unknit, *cockpit, coalpit, armpit, ashpit, lickspit, turnspit, pitpit, daywrit,* outsit, tomtit, *godwit, chickwit,* outwit, acquit **3.** counterfeit, compromit, intromit, pretermit, intermit, manumit, Messerschmitt, definite, infinite, interknit, preterit, hypocrite, favorite, apposite, opposite, requisite, exquisite, perquisite, Jesuit **4.** indefinite, prerequisite, inapposite, unopposite.

ĬTH– 1. kith, lith, myth, smith, smyth, pith, frith, crith. sith **2.** *trilith, goldsmith, locksmith, tinsmith, gunsmith* **3.** megalith, neolith, monolith, acrolith, coppersmith, silversmith, Arrowsmith **4.** paleolith, anthropolith.

ĬTHE– 1. with, withe **2.** bewith, hamewith, herewith, therewith, wherewith, forthwith.

ĬTS– its etc., *see* **IT–** it etc. above, plus "s" or "'s"; **1.** Fitz, blitz, spitz, Ritz, Fritz, sitz.

ĬV– 1. chiv [slang], div [slang], give, live, fliv [slang], spiv [slang], sieve, shiv [slang] **2.** forgive, misgive, relive, outlive **3.** combative, negative, sedative, quiddative, purgative, talkative, ablative, amative, sanative, narrative, curative, causative, fixative, auditive, quietive, expletive, fugitive, primitive, dormitive, nutritive, tortitive, partitive, substantive **5.** conciliative; *and many other adjectives ending in the suffix "-ive."*

ĬVD– 1. lived, sieved **2.** relived, unlived, outlived, long-lived, short-lived **3.** negatived.

ĬZ– 1. is, biz [slang], Diz, fizz, phiz [slang], his, gizz [Scot. & N. of Eng.], Liz, riz [dial.], friz, sizz, 'tis, viz, wiz [slang], quiz, whiz, zizz **2.** Cadiz, gin fizz, befriz, requiz, gee whizz [coll.].

ĬZM– 1. ism, schism, chrism, prism **2.** abysm **3.** Judaism, archaism, Lamaism, Hebraism, ultraism, Mosaism, prosaism,

Methodism, Yankeeism, atheism, bitheism, pacifism, dandyism, Toryism, rowdyism, syllogism, eulogism, energism, synergism, liturgism, catechism, anarchism, monarchism, Baalism, cabalism, tribalism, verbalism, vandalism, feudalism, realism, legalism, regalism, frugalism, localism, vocalism, carnalism, journalism, papalism, moralism, centralism, pluralism, ruralism, racialism, socialism, fatalism, vitalism, dualism, loyalism, royalism, nihilism, pugilism, servilism, cataclysm, embolism, symbolism, idolism, botulism, euphemism, animism, pessimism, optimism, peanism, paganism, organism, Romanism, Satanism, Brahmanism, feminism, cretinism, destinism, Calvinism, Darwinism, lionism, Zionism, demonism, Mormonism, Platonism, modernism, communism, unionism, Taoism, egoism, heroism, Shintoism, barbarism, plagiarism, solarism, Quakerism, mesmerism, mannerism, pauperism, theorism, aphorism, humorism, terrorism, historism, pasteurism, ostracism, solecism, Gallicism, Biblicism, publicism, Anglicism, synicism, Sinicism, stoicism, lyricism, classicism, criticism, witticism, skepticism, mysticism, paroxysm, sabbatism, dogmatism, grammatism, pietism, quietism, magnetism, syncretism, Semitism, occultism, egotism, hypnotism, nepotism, despotism, Hinduism, altruism, untruism, atavism, Bolshevism, nativism, powwowism, Kukluxism **4.** theosophism, philosophism, cannibalism, surrealism, radicalism, rationalism, liberalism, federalism, commercialism, capitalism, teetotalism, ritualism, evangelism, catabolism, metabolism, hyperbolism, alcoholism, monopolism, somnambulism, Confucianism, Puritanism, determinism, impressionism, infusionism, plagiarism, peculiarism, militarism, allegorism, Epicurism, amateurism, Italicism, Catholicism, empiricism, grammaticism, fanaticism, phoneticism, asceticism, romanticism, neuroticism, agnosticism, astigmatism, automatism, democratism, conservatism, favoritism, patriotism, absolutism, progressivism, subjectivism, collectivism, somniloquism, ventriloquism **5.** proverbialism, imperialism, materialism, colloquialism, phenomenalism, sensationalism, professionalism, conventionalism, municipalism, universalism, controversialism, sentimentalism, instrumentalism, spiritualism, republicanism, Americanism, Mohammedanism, microorganism, multitudinism, indeterminism, restorationism, prohibitionism, exhibitionism, evolutionism, revolutionism, incendiarism, peculiarism, particularism **6.** supernaturalism, individualism, cosmopolitanism **7.** humanitarianism, parliamentarianism **8.** valetudinarianism, establishmentarianism; *and many other nouns ending in the suffix "ism."*

I (bib)

2.

DOUBLE (FEMININE) RHYMES IN I (bib'ber)

Primary or Secondary Accent Falls on Next to Last
Syllable; Imperfect Rhymes Are in Italics.

IB–ald– ribald; *see* also **IB'ld–** bibbled etc. below.

IB'er– 2. bibber, dibber, fibber, gibber, jibber, glibber, nibber, ribber, cribber, squibber 3. winebibber, ad libber [slang].

IB'est– 2. glibbest.

IB'et– 2. gibbet, libbet, ribbet, zibet 3. inhibit, prohibit, exhibit 5. flibbertigibbet.

IB'i– 2. gibby, skibby [loc.], Libby, nibby [Scot. & N. of Eng.], ribby, fribby, tibby 4. nibby-jibby, nibby-gibby.

IB'ij– 2. cribbage.

IB'ing– 2. bibbing, fibbing, jibbing, ribbing, cribbing, squibbing 3. winebibbing, ad libbing [slang].

IB'it– 3. adhibit, inhibit, prohibit, exhibit; *see* also **IB'et–** gibbet etc. above.

IB'l– 2. bibble, dibble, gibel, kibble, nibble, ribble, dribble, fribble, gribble, scribble, tribble, thribble, sibyl, cibol, quibble 3. transcribble 4. ishkabibble [slang].

IB'ld– 2. bibbled, dibbled, ribald, dribbled, scribbled, quibbled.

IB'ler– 2. bibbler, dibbler, kibbler, nibbler, dribbler, cribbler, scribbler, quibbler 3. transcribbler.

IB'let– 2. giblet, riblet, driblet, triblet.

IB'li– 2. glibly, nibbly, dribbly, scribbly, quibbly.

IB'lik– 2. Biblic, niblick 4. philobiblic.

IB'ling– 2. bibbling, dibbling, kibbling, nibbling, dribbling, fribbling, cribbling, scribbling, sibling, quibbling 3. transcribbling.

IB'on– 2. gibbon, ribbon 3. blue ribbon.

IB'onz– 2. bibbons, gibbons, Gibbons, ribbons.

IB'sen– 2. Ibsen, Gibson.

IB'ut– 2. tribute 3. attribute, retribute, contribute, distribute.

ICH'el– 2. Mitchell, switchel.

ICH'en– 2. kitchen.

ICH'er– 2. itcher, ditcher, hitcher, snitcher [slang], pitcher, richer, stitcher, switcher, twitcher 3. enricher, bewitcher.

ICH'est– 2. richest.

ICH'et– 2. fitchet, witchet, twitchet.

ICH'ez– 2. itches, bitches, ditches, hitches, flitches, niches, snitches [slang], pitches, riches, britches, breeches, stitches, witches, switches, twitches 3. enriches, bewitches.

ICH'i– 2. itchy, bitchy, fitchy, hitchy, pitchy, stitchy, witchy, switchy, twitchy.

ICH'ing– 2. itching, ditching, hitching, pitching, stitching, witching, switching, twitching 3. enriching, bewitching.

ICH'less– 2. itchless, ditchless, hitchless, pitchless, stitchless, witchless, switchless, twitchless.

ICH'li– 2. richly.

ICH'ment– 3. enrichment, bewitchment.

ID'ans– 2. biddance, riddance 3. forbiddance, good riddance.

ID′ed– 2. kidded, skidded, lidded, ridded 4. invalided, pyramided.

ID′en– 2. bidden, hidden, midden, slidden, ridden, stridden 3. unbidden, forbidden, beridden, bedridden, childridden, hagridden, plague-ridden, unthridden 4. unforbidden, kitchen midden, feverridden, overridden.

ID′er– 2. bidder, kidder, Kidder, skidder, slidder, ridder 3. rebidder, forbidder, outbidder, consider 4. overbidder, reconsider, disconsider.

ID′erd– 3. considered 4. reconsidered, ill-considered, well-considered, unconsidered.

ID′i– 2. biddy, diddy [dial.], giddy, kiddy, skiddy, middy, tiddy, widdy 3. Dinwiddie 4. chickabiddy.

ID′ik– 3. rubidic, iridic, juridic, acidic, fatidic, druidic 4. pyramidic.

ID′ing– 2. bidding, kidding, skidding, ridding 3. forbidding, outbidding 4. underbidding, overbidding, unforbidding, pyramiding.

ID′ish– 2. kiddish, Yiddish.

ID′l– 2. diddle, fiddle, middle, niddle [Scot. & Ir.], piddle, riddle, riddel, griddle, quiddle, twiddle 3. flumdiddle, condiddle, unriddle 4. flummadiddle, tarradiddle.

ID′ler– 2. diddler, fiddler, piddler, riddler, twiddler 4. tarradiddler.

ID′ling– 2. diddling, fiddling, kidling, middling, piddling, riddling, griddling twiddling.

ID′ni– 2. kidney, Sidney, Sydney.

ID′o– 2. kiddo [slang], widow.

IF′en– 2. striffen, stiffen; see also IF′in– biffin etc. below.

IF′er– 2. differ, niffer, sniffer, stiffer, squiffer [slang], whiffer.

IF′est– 2. stiffest.

IF′i– 2. iffy [slang], jiffy, Liffey, cliffy, miffy, sniffy, spiffy [slang], squiffy [slang], whiffy.

IF′ik– 2. glyphic 3. morbific, rubific, deific, algific, triglyphic, prolific, magnific, somnific, terrific, aurific, horrific, classific, pacific, Pacific, specific, sensific, ossific, lucific, mucific, lactific, pontific, vivific 4. diaglyphic, anaglyphic, geoglyphic, logogriphic, calorific, dolorific, humorific, honorific, sonorific, saporific, soporific, beatific, scientific 5. hieroglyphic 6. dactylioglyphic.

IF′iks– 3. significs, specifics 4. calorifics, colorifics 5. hieroglyphics, dermatoglyphics.

IF′in– 2. biffin, griffin, striffen, tiffin, stiffen; see also IF′on– griffon etc. below.

IF′ing– 2. biffing, miffing [dial. & slang], sniffing, spiffing, tiffing, whiffing.

IF′ish– 2. sniffish, tiffish, stiffish.

IF′l– nifle [dial.], sniffle, piffle, riffle, whiffle.

IF′ler– 2. sniffler, piffler, riffler, whiffler.

IF′li– 2. sniffly, stiffly.

IF′ling– 2. sniffling, piffling, riffling, whiffling.

IF′on– 2. griffon, chiffon.

IFT′ed– 2. gifted, lifted, rifted, drifted, sifted, shifted 3. ungifted, uplifted.

IFT′er– 2. lifter, drifter, sifter, shifter, swifter 3. uplifter, shoplifter, sceneshifter.

IFT′est– 2. swiftest.

IFT′i– 2. fifty, clifty, nifty [slang], snifty, rifty, drifty, thrifty, shifty 4. fifty-fifty.

IFT′ij– 2. driftage, siftage, shiftage.

IFT′ing– 2. gifting, lifting, snifting, rifting, drifting, sifting, shifting 3. shoplifting, uplifting, resifting, sceneshifting.

IFT′less– 2. giftless, liftless, riftless, driftless, thriftless, shiftless.

IFT′ness– 2. miffedness, swiftness.

IG′an– 2. wigan 3. balbriggan.

IG'and– 2. brigand 3. balbrigganed.

IG'er– 2. bigger, chigger, digger, gigger, jigger, ligger, nigger, snigger, rigger, rigor, prigger, sprigger, trigger, sigger, wigger, swigger, twigger, vigor 3. gold digger, gravedigger, reneger, outrigger 4. thimblerigger.

IG'erd– 2. jiggered, niggard, sniggered, triggered 3. unniggard, bejiggered.

IG'ers– chiggers etc., see IG'er– bigger etc. above, plus "s" or "'s."

IG'est– 2. biggest, triggest.

IG'i– 2. biggy, piggy, spriggy, wiggy, twiggy 4. piggy-wiggy.

IG'ing– 2. digging, gigging, jigging, rigging, trigging, wigging, swigging, twigging 3. redigging, reneging, unrigging 4. thimblerigging.

IG'ish– 2. giggish, jiggish, riggish, priggish, wiggish, Whiggish.

IG'it– 2. giggit, jigget, jiggit [both coll.], Brigit, frigate.

IG'izm– 2. priggism, wiggism, Whiggism.

IG'l– 2. giggle, higgle, jiggle, niggle, sniggle, wriggle, striggle [coll. Eng.], wiggle, swiggle [dial.], squiggle 3. *porwigle*.

IG'ler– 2. giggler, higgler, jiggler, niggler, sniggler, wriggler, wiggler, squiggler [slang].

IG'let– 2. giglet, piglet, wiglet, Whiglet.

IG'li– 2. bigly, giggly, jiggly, niggly, pigly, wiggly, wriggly, squiggly 4. Uncle Wiggly.

IG'ling– 2. giggling, higgling, jiggling, niggling, pigling, wriggling, wiggling, swiggling [dial.], squiggling.

IG'ma– 2. sigma, stigma 3. enigma, kerygma, sterigma 4. hypostigma.

IG'me– 2. pigmy, stigme.

IG'ment– 2. figment, pigment.

IG'nant– 3. indignant, malignant, benignant.

IG'net– 2. signet, cygnet.

IG'num– 2. lignum, rignum, signum, tignum.

IG'or– 2. rigor, vigor; *see* also IG'er– bigger etc. above.

IG'ot– 2. bigot, gigot, spigot, riggot, frigate.

IG'ur– 2. figure, ligure 3. refigure, prefigure, configure, disfigure, transfigure.

IJ'er– 2. ridger, bridger 3. abridger.

IJ'et– 2. fidget, midget, nidget, Bridget, digit.

IJ'i– 2. gidgee, miugy, ridgy, squidgy.

IJ'id– 2. rigid, frigid 3. unrigid, unfrigid.

IJ'il– 2. strigil, sigil, vigil.

IJ'ing– 2. fidging [dial.], nidging, ridging, bridging 3. abridging, enridging.

IJ'it– digit; *see* also IJ'et– fidget etc. above.

IJ'on– 2. smidgen, pigeon, pidgin, widgeon, wigeon 3. religion 4. irreligion, gyropigeon.

IJ'us– 3. prodigious, religious, litigious 4. irreligious, unreligious, sacrilegious 5. overreligious, unsacrilegious.

IK'a– 2. licca, sicca, ticca, tikka.

IK'ed– 2. wicked.

IK'en– 2. chicken, Rikken, stricken, sicken, thicken, quicken 4. wonder-stricken, terror-stricken, horror-stricken.

IK'enz– chickens etc., see IK'en– chicken etc. above, plus "s" or "'s"; 2. Dickens.

IK'er– 2. icker [Scot.], bicker, dicker, kicker, licker, liquor, flicker, clicker, slicker, smicker, nicker, knicker, snicker, picker, ricker, pricker, tricker, sicker, ticker, tikker, sticker, thicker, vicar, wicker, quicker 3. *bootlicker*.

IK'erz– ickers etc., see IK'er– icker etc. above, plus "s" or "'s."

IK'est– 2. slickest, sickest, thickest, quickest.

IK'et– 2. clicket, smicket, snicket, picket, spicket, cricket, pricket, siket [dial.], ticket, thicket, wicket   **3.** reticket, mid-wicket   **4.** walking ticket.

IK′ets–   **2.** pickets, rickets, crickets, tickets, wickets.

IK′i–   **2.** icky [slang], dicky, dickey, hickey, Micky, Nicky, snickey, picky, rickey, bricky, crickey [slang], pricky, tricky, tickey, sticky, Vicky, wicky   **3.** doo hickey [slang], jinriki, gin rickey.

IK′ing–   **2.** kicking, licking, flicking, clicking, slicking, nicking, snicking, picking, ricking, bricking, cricking, tricking, ticking, wicking   **3.** bootlicking, hand picking   **4.** pocket-picking.

IK′ish–   **2.** slickish, hickish [slang], pickish, prickish, trickish, sickish, stickish, thickish.

IK′l–   **2.** chicle, fickle, mickle [dial.], nickel, pickle, pikle, prickle, trickle, strickel, sickle, tickle   **3.** renickel, depickle   **4.** cupronickel, pumpernickel.

IK′ler–   **2.** fickler, pickler, prickler, strickler, tickler, stickler.

IK′let–   **2.** chiclet, tricklet.

IK′li–   **2.** slickly, prickly, trickly, sickly, tickly, stickly, thickly, quickly.

IK′ling–   **2.** chickling, pickling, prickling, trickling, tickling, stickling.

IK′lish–   **2.** pricklish, ticklish.

IK′ness–   **2.** slickness, sickness, thickness, quickness   **3.** *homesickness, heartsickness, lovesickness.*

IK′nik–   **2.** picnic, pyknic, strychnic   **4.** isopycnic.

IK′ning–   **3.** sickening, thickening, quickening.

IKS′a–   **2.** Bixa.

IKS′en–   **2.** Bixin, mixen, vixen.

IKS′er–   **2.** fixer, mixer, sixer   **3.** affixer, prefixer, transfixer, elixir   **4.** intermixer.

IKSH′a–   **2.** ricksha   **3.** jinricksha   **4.** jinrickisha.

IKSH′un–   **2.** diction, fiction, friction, striction   **3.** addiction, prediction, indic-

tion, affixion, prefixion, transfixion, suffixion, reliction, affliction, infliction, confliction, depiction, obstriction, restriction, constriction, eviction, conviction   **4.** contradiction, malediction, valediction, benediction, interdiction, jurisdiction, crucifixion, dereliction.

IKS′i–   **2.** Dixie, dixie, dixy, jixie, mixy, nixie, nixy [cant], pixy, pixie, rixy [loc., Eng.], tricksy, Trixie.

IKS′ing–   **2.** fixing, mixing   **3.** affixing, prefixing, admixing, commixing   **4.** intermixing.

IKS′it–   **2.** dixit   **4.** ipse dixit.

IKS′tur–   **2.** fixture, mixture   **3.** affixture, immixture, commixture   **4.** intermixture.

IKT′al–   **2.** rictal   **3.** edictal.

IKT′at–   **2.** dictate, nictate.

IKT′ed–   **3.** addicted, predicted, relicted, afflicted, inflicted, conflicted, depicted, restricted, constricted, evicted, convicted   **4.** contradicted, interdicted, self-inflicted, unrestricted, unconstricted.

IKT′er–   **2.** fictor, lictor, Pictor, stricter, victor   **3.** predictor, afflicter, inflicter, conflicter, depicter, depictor, constrictor, evictor, convictor   **4.** contradicter, contradictor   **5.** boa constrictor.

IKT′est–   **2.** lickedest, strictest.

IKT′i–   **5.** corpus delicti.

IKT′ik–   **2.** ictic   **3.** deictic   **4.** apodictic, endeictic.

IKT′im–   **2.** victim, kicked him.

IKT′ing–   **3.** addicting, predicting, afflicting, inflicting, conflicting, depicting, restricting, constricting, evicting, convicting   **4.** contradicting, unconflicting, unconstricting.

IKT′iv–   **2.** fictive   **3.** addictive, predictive, indictive, afflictive, inflictive, conflictive, depictive, astrictive, restrictive, constrictive, convictive   **4.** contradictive, maledictive, benedictive, apodictive, interdictive, jurisdictive, nonrestrictive.

ĬKT′or– **2.** fictor, lictor, Pictor, victor **3.** depictor, convictor **4.** interdictor **5.** boa constrictor.

ĬKT′um– **2.** dictum **3.** delictum.

ĬKT′ur– **2.** picture, stricture **3.** depicture, impicture, word picture.

ĬKT′us– **2.** ictus, rictus **3.** Invictus **4.** Benedictus, acronyctous.

ĬK′up– **2.** dikkop, hiccup, hiccough, pickup.

ĬL′a– **2.** Scylla, villa, squilla, Squilla, Zilla **3.** chincilla, cedilla, camilla, Camilla, armilla, Manila, manilla, vanilla, papilla, guerrilla, spirilla, gorilla, Priscilla, Drusilla, mantilla, scintilla, flotilla, axilla, maxilla **4.** sabadilla, granadilla, cascarilla, camarilla **5.** sarsaparilla.

ĬL′an– **2.** Villain, villein **3.** archvillain.

ĬL′ar– **2.** pillar **4.** caterpillar, camarilla; *see* also ĬL′er– iller etc. below.

ĬLB′ert– **2.** filbert, Gilbert.

ĬLCH′er– **2.** filcher, milcher, pilcher.

ĬLD′a– **2.** Hilda, tilde **3.** Brünnhilde, Matilda, Mathilda.

ĬLD′ed– **2.** builded, gilded **3.** begilded, ungilded.

ĬLD′er– **2.** builder, gilder, guilder, wilder **3.** rebuilder, shipbuilder, housebuilder, begilder, bewilder.

ĬLD′ing– **2.** building, gilding **3.** begilding, shipbuilding **4.** castle-building.

ĬLD′u– **2.** mildew, will do.

ĬL′er– **2.** iller, biller, chiller, filler, giller, hiller, killer, miller, pillar, spiller, driller, friller, griller, shriller, triller, thriller, siller, schiller, tiller, stiller, thiller, willer, quiller, swiller **3.** fulfiller, painkiller, man-killer, befriller, pralltriller, distiller, instiller **4.** killer-diller [slang], giant-killer, lady-killer [slang], caterpillar.

ĬL′est– **2.** illest, chillest, shrillest, stillest.

ĬL′et– **2.** billet, fillet, skillet, millet, pillet, rillet, drillet, trillet, willet, quillet **3.** pilwillet.

ĬL′fer– **2.** pilfer **4.** Bella Wilfer [Dickens].

ĬL′ful– **2.** skillful, willful **3.** unskillful, unwillful.

ĬL′grim– **2.** pilgrim.

ĬL′i– **2.** billy, Billie, chilly, chili, Chile, dilly, dilli, filly, gillie, hilly, lily, Millie, rilly, frilly, grilly, shrilly, thrilly, silly, Scilly, tilly, tilley, Tillie, Willie, willy, willey, quilly, twilly **4.** Piccadilly, daffodilly, piccalilli, tiger lily, water lily, willy-nilly **5.** daffydowndilly; *see* also ĬL′li– illy etc. below.

ĬL′id– **2.** gillied, lilied.

ĬL′ij– **2.** pillage, grillage, tillage, stillage, village.

ĬL′ik– **3.** idyllic, odylic, vanillic, Cyrillic, basilic, dactylic, exilic **4.** hemophilic, zoophilic, imbecilic, salicylic **5.** homodactylic.

ĬL′ing– **2.** billing, chilling, filling, killing, milling, spilling, drilling, frilling, grilling, trilling, thrilling, shilling, schilling, tilling, stilling, willing, quilling, swilling **3.** fulfilling, befrilling, distilling, instilling, unwilling **4.** unfulfilling, overwilling.

ĬL′ip– **2.** fillip, Philip.

ĬL′is– **2.** Phyllis, cilice, Willis **4.** amaryllis.

ĬL′iz– **2.** billies, dillies, fillies, gillies, lilies, sillies, Scillies, willies **3.** Achilles.

ĬLK′en– **2.** milken, silken.

ĬLK′er– **2.** bilker, milker, silker.

ĬLK′i– **2.** milky, silky, Willkie.

ĬLK′ing– **2.** bilking, milking, silking.

ĬL′li– **2.** illy, skilly, stilly, willy; *see* also ĬL′i– billy etc. above.

ĬL′man– **2.** billman, Gilman, hill man, millman, pillman, grillman, Stillman.

ĬL′ment– **3.** fulfilment, distillment, instillment.

ĬL′mi– **2.** filmy.

IL′ness– 2. illness, chillness, shrillness, stillness.

IL′o– 2. billow, kilo, pillow, willow 3. Camillo, lapillo, Negrillo 4. peccadillo, armadillo, grenadillo, tabardillo, weeping willow.

IL′ok– 2. fillock, hillock, sillock.

ILT′ed– 2. hilted, jilted, kilted, lilted, silted, tilted, stilted, wilted, quilted 3. tip-tilted, unwilted 4. crazy-quilted.

ILT′er– 2. filter, philter, jilter, kilter, milter, tilter, stilter, wilter, quilter 3. refilter, infilter.

ILT′i– 2. guilty, silty, tilty, stilty.

ILT′ing– 2. jilting, kilting, lilting, silting, tilting, stilting, wilting, quilting 3. tip-tilting, unwilting 4. crazy quilting.

IL′um– 4. aspergillum.

IL′us– 2. gryllus, villus, villous 3. camillus, capillus, lapillus, arillus, fibrillous, bacillus, favillous, pulvillus 4. aspergillus.

ILV′er– 2. silver 3. resilver, quicksilver.

IL′yans– 2. brilliance 3. non-brilliance, resilience, consilience; *see* also **IL′i–ens–** resilience etc.

IL′yant– 2. brilliant 3. unbrilliant, resilient 4. overbrilliant; *see* also **IL′i–ent–** resilient etc.

IL′yar– 3. familiar, auxiliar 4. unfamiliar 5. overfamiliar.

IL′yard– 2. billiard, milliard.

IL′yun– 2. billion, million, pillion, prillion, trillion, stillion 3. tourbillion, mandilion, modillion, vermilion, nonillion, carillon, quadrillion, decillion, octillion, centillion, quintillion, cotillion, septillion, sextillion, postilion, pavilion, civilian.

IL′yus– 2. bilious 4. atrabilious; *see* also **IL′i–us–** punctilious etc.

IM′aj– 2. image, scrimmage 3. archimage.

IM′ba– 2. simba 3. marimba.

IMB′al– 2. gimbol, cymbal, symbol, simball, timbal 4. clavicymbal.

IMB′er– 2. limber, timber, timbre 3. unlimber, retimber.

IMB′l– 2. bimbil, fimble, nimble, cymbal, simbil, symbol, simball, timball, thimble, wimble.

IMB′o– 2. kimbo, limbo 3. akimbo.

IMB′us– 2. limbus, limbous, nimbus.

IM′el– 2. Himmel [G.], heml, kümmel; *see* also **IM′l–** gimmal etc. below.

IM′er– 2. dimmer, gimmer, hymner, skimmer, limmer, glimmer, slimmer, nimmer, brimmer, grimmer, krimmer, primer, primmer, trimmer, simmer, shimmer, swimmer 3. aglimmer, asimmer, ashimmer 4. trihemimer.

IM′est– 2. dimmest, slimmest, grimmest, primmest, trimmest.

IM′i– 2. gimme [slang], jimmy, skimmy, limby, shimmy, whimmy, zimme.

IM′id– 2. imid, jimmied, shimmied, timid.

IM′ij– 2. image, scrimmage 3. arch image.

IM′ik– 2. gimmick [slang], mimic, wimick, zymic 3. alchimic, etymic 4. cherubimic, zoomimic, pantomimic, pseudonymic, homonymic, synonymic, eponymic, patronymic, metronymic, metonymic.

IM′ing– 2. dimming, skimming, limbing, blimbing, slimming, brimming, trimming, swimming 3. bedimming, retrimming.

IM′it– 2. limit.

IM′l– 2. gimmal, Himmel [G.], heml, kümmel, Friml.

IM′less– 2. hymnless, limbless, rimless, brimless, vimless, whimless.

IM′li– 2. dimly, slimly, grimly, primly, trimly.

IM′ner– 2. hymner, limner.

M'ness– **2.** dimness, slimness, grimness, primness, trimness.

M'ni– **2.** chimney **3.** lamp chimney.

MP'er– **2.** skimper, limper, crimper, scrimper, shrimper, simper, whimper.

MP'est– **2.** limpest.

IMP'i– **2.** impi, impy, skimpy, limpy, crimpy, scrimpy, shrimpi, shrimpy.

IMP'ing– **2.** imping, skimping, limping, crimping, scrimping, primping, shrimping.

IMP'ish– **2.** impish, limpish, shrimpish.

IMP'l– **2.** dimple, pimple, rimple, crimple, simple, wimple **3.** bewimple, unwimple.

IMP'ler– **2.** dimpler, rimpler, simpler, wimpler.

IMP'lest– **2.** simplest.

IMP'li– **2.** dimply, limply, pimply, simply.

IMP'ling– **2.** impling, dimpling, pimpling, rimpling, crimpling.

IMZ'i– **2.** flimsy, slimsy, mimsey, whimsey.

IMZ'on– **2.** crimson **3.** encrimson.

IN'a– **2.** binna, Mina, pinna **3.** meminna, Corinna.

IN'as– **2.** inness, pinnace **3.** Erinys.

IN'at– **2.** innate, pinnate **3.** bipinnate.

INCH'er– **2.** lyncher, flincher, clincher, pincher, cincher **4.** penny pincher [slang].

INCH'ing– **2.** inching, lynching, flinching, clinching, pinching, cinching **4.** penny-pinching [slang].

IND'a– **2.** Linda, pinda **3.** Belinda, Lucinda **4.** Ethelinda.

IND'ed– **2.** brinded, sinded, winded **3.** abscinded, rescinded, exscinded, longwinded.

IND'en– **2.** linden **5.** Unter den Linden.

IND'er– **2.** dinder, hinder, linder, flinder, pinder, Pindar, cinder, tinder, winder **3.** unhinder, rescinder.

IND'i– **2.** Lindy, pindy [dial.], Sindhi, Cindy, shindy [slang & loc.], windy **3.** Lucindy.

IND'ik– **2.** indic, Indic, syndic.

IND'l– **2.** dindle, kindle, Mindel, spindle, rindle, brindle, sindle, dwindle, swindle **3.** rekindle, enkindle.

IND'ler– **2.** kindler, swindler **3.** enkindler.

IND'ling– **2.** kindling, dwindling, swindling **3.** rekindling, enkindling.

IND'o– **2.** lindo, window **3.** show window, shopwindow.

IND'rans– **2.** hindrance.

IND'red– **2.** kindred.

IND'u– **2.** Hindu.

IND'us– **2.** Indus.

IN'en– **2.** linen **4.** Irish linen.

IN'er– **2.** inner, dinner, finner, ginner, skinner, pinner, spinner, grinner, sinner, shinner, tinner, thinner, winner, twinner **3.** beginner, breadwinner **4.** afterdinner.

IN'est– **2.** innest, thinnest.

IN'et– **2.** linnet, minute, pinnet, spinet.

IN'fant– **2.** infant.

IN'ful– **2.** skinful, sinful **3.** unsinful.

ING'er– **2.** dinger, blinger [slang], flinger, slinger, ringer, wringer, springer, stringer, singer, stinger, winger, swinger, whinger **3.** humdinger, night-winger, klipspringer, left-winger **4.** Minnesinger, Meistersinger.

ING'ger– **2.** finger, linger **3.** forefinger, malinger.

ING'gerz– **2.** fingers, lingers **4.** butterfingers.

ING'i– **2.** bingey, binghi, bingy, dingy, dinghy, flingy, clingy, pingy, ringy, springy, stringy, wingy, swingy.

ING'ing– **2.** dinging, flinging, clinging, slinging, ringing, wringing, bringing, springing, stringing, singing, stinging,

winging, swinging 3. enringing, up-
bringing, outwinging.

ING'l– 2. dingle, jingle, lingel, lingle,
mingle, pingle, cringle, pringle, tringle,
single, shingle, tingle, swingle 3. swing-
dingle, immingle, commingle, Kriss Krin-
gle, surcingle, reshingle 4. intermingle.

ING'ler– 2. jingler, mingler, pingler,
shingler, tingler 3. commingler.

ING'less– 2. kingless, pingless, ringless,
springless, stingless, wingless.

ING'let– 2. jinglet, kinglet, ringlet,
springlet, winglet.

ING'li– 2. dingly, jingly, kingly, mingly,
springly, singly, shingly, tingly.

ING'ling– 2. dingling, jingling, kingling,
mingling, Ringling, singling, shingling,
wingling, swingling 3. immingling, com-
mingling 4. intermingling.

ING'lish– 2. English, tinglish 3. non-
English.

ING'lz– dingless etc., see ING'l– dingle
etc. above, plus "s" or "'s."

ING'o– 2. bingo, dingo, jingo, lingo,
gringo, stingo 3. flamingo, eryngo.

IN'i– 2. chinny, finny, guinea, hinny, gin-
ny, jinni, Jinny, jinny, skinny, Pliny,
Minnie, Minne, ninny, pinny, spinney,
shinny, tinny, vinny, Winnie, squinny,
whinny 3. New Guinea 4. ignominy,
pickaninny, Ol' Virginny.

IN'ik– 2. dinic, finick, Finnic, clinic,
pinic, Sinic, cynic, vinic, quinic 3. Rab-
binic, Odinic, delphinic, aclinic, triclinic,
pollinic, Brahminic, encrinic, succinic,
platinic 4. Jacobinic, polyclinic, man-
darinic, narcotinic.

IN'ing– 2. inning, chinning, dinning, gin-
ning, skinning, pinning, spinning, grin-
ning, sinning, shinning, tinning, thinning,
winning 3. beginning, unpinning, bread-
winning 4. underpinning, overthinning.

IN'is– 2. pinnace 3. Erinys.

IN'ish– 2. finish, Finnish, tinnish, thin-
nish 3. refinish, diminish.

IN'ist– 4. violinist.

INJ'ens– 3. attingence, contingence, con-
tingents.

INJ'ent– 2. fingent, ringent, fringent,
stringent, tingent 3. impingent, refrin-
gent, astringent, restringent, constringent,
attingent, contingent.

INJ'er– 2. injure, hinger, ginger, fringer,
cringer, singer, tinger, swinger 3. im-
pinger, infringer.

INJ'ez– 2. binges, dinges, hinges, cringes,
scringes, fringes, singes, tinges, swinges,
twinges 3. unhinges, befringes, infringes,
impinges, constringes, perstringes.

INJ'i– 2. dingy, cringy, fringy, stingy,
twingy.

INJ'ing– 2. dingeing, hinging, cringing,
fringing, singeing, tingeing, swingeing,
twinging 3. unhinging, impinging, re-
fringing, infringing, constringing, per-
stringing.

INJ'ment– 3. unhingement, impingement,
infringement, perstringement.

INK'a– 2. Inca, Dinka, Xinca 3. Ka-
tinka, Katrinka, stotinka.

INK'er– 2. inker, skinker, linker, blinker,
clinker, slinker, pinker, drinker, prinker,
shrinker, sinker, tinker, stinker, thinker,
winker, swinker 3. enlinker, bethinker,
freethinker, hoodwinker.

INK'est– 2. pinkest.

INK'i– 2. inky, chinky, dinky, dinkey,
kinky, linky, blinky, pinky, sinky, stinky,
zincky.

INK'ij– 2. linkage, shrinkage.

INK'ing– 2. inking, chinking, kinking,
skinking, linking, blinking, clinking,
slinking, pinking, rinking, drinking,
shrinking, sinking, stinking, thinking,
winking 3. enlinking, unlinking, free-
thinking, unthinking, hoodwinking.

INK'l– 2. inkle, kinkle, wrinkle, crinkle,
sprinkle, strinkle, tinkle, winkle, winkel
3. besprinkle, unwrinkle 4. intersprin-
kle, periwinkle.

INK'ler– 2. wrinkler, sprinkler, tinkler, twinkler.

INK'li– 2. pinkly, wrinkly, crinkly, tinkly, twinkly.

INK'ling– 2. inkling, wrinkling, crinkling, sprinkling, tinkling, twinkling.

INKT'iv– 3. distinctive, extinctive, instinctive 4. indistinctive, undistinctive.

INKT'li– 3. succinctly, distinctly 4. indistinctly 5. contradistinctly.

INKT'ness– 3. succinctness, distinctness 4. indistinctness, undistinctness.

INKT'ur– 2. cincture, tincture 3. pollincture, encincture.

INK'went– 3. delinquent, relinquent.

INK'wish– 3. relinquish.

IN'land– 2. inland, Finland.

IN'less– 2. dinless, finless, ginless, kinless, skinless, pinless, sinless, tinless, winless.

IN'let– 2. inlet, tinlet.

IN'li– 2. inly, thinly, twinly 3. McKinley.

IN'ness– 2. inness, thinness.

IN'o– 2. minnow, winnow.

INS'el– 2. tinsel.

INS'ens– 2. incense 3. St. Vincent's.

INS'er– 2. mincer, rinser, wincer 3. convincer.

INS'ic– 3. intrinsic, extrinsic.

INS'ing– 2. mincing, rinsing, wincing 3. evincing, convincing 4. unconvincing.

INS'ment– 3. evincement, convincement.

INST'er– 2. minster, spinster 3. Axminster, Westminster.

INST'rel– 2. minstrel.

INT'ed– 2. dinted, hinted, flinted, glinted, splinted, minted, printed, sprinted, tinted, stinted, squinted 3. reprinted, imprinted, misprinted, footprinted, unstinted, rosetinted 4. fingerprinted, rosy tinted.

INT'er– 2. hinter, linter, splinter, minter, printer, sprinter, tinter, stinter, winter, squinter, twinter 3. imprinter, midwinter 4. mezzotinter.

INTH'in– 3. absinthin, absinthine 4. terebinthine, labyrinthine, hyacinthine.

INT'i– 2. Dinty, linty, flinty, glinty, splinty, minty, shinty, tinty, squinty 3. McGinty.

INT'ij– 2. splintage, mintage, tintage, vintage.

INT'ing– 2. dinting, hinting, glinting, splinting, minting, printing, sprinting, tinting, stinting, squinting 3. imprinting, misprinting.

INT'l– 2. lintel, pintle, scintle, quintal 3. trigintal.

INT'o– 2. pinto, Shinto 4. mezzotinto.

INT'ri– 2. vintry, wintry.

IN'u– 2. sinew 3. unsinew, continue 4. discontinue.

IN'yun– 2. minion, mignon, minyan, pinion, pignon 3. Virginian, dominion, opinion.

IP'ant– 2. flippant, trippant 3. unflippant 4. countertrippant.

IP'er– 2. chipper, dipper, kipper, skipper, lipper, flipper, clipper, slipper, nipper, snipper, ripper, dripper, gripper, tripper, stripper, sipper, shipper, tipper, whipper 3. Big Dipper, Yom Kippur, outstripper, horsewhipper 4. lady's-slipper, gallinipper.

IP'erd– 2. kippered, skippered, slippered.

IP'erz– chippers etc., see IP'er– chipper etc. above, plus "s" or " 's."

IP'est– 2. flippest.

IP'et– 2. skippet, snippet, pipit, rippet, rippit, trippet, sippet, tippet, whippet.

IP'i– 2. chippy, dippy, hippy, lippy, klippe, slippy, nippy, snippy, pippy, drippy, grippy, shippy, tippy, zippy 3. Xanthippe 4. Aganippe, Mississippi.

IP'id– 3. insipid.

IP'ij– 2. chippage, kippage, slippage, scrippage, strippage.

ĬP'ik– 2. hippic, typic 3. adipic, phil-
hippic, Philippic, atypic 4. polytypic,
stenotypic 5. electrotypic 6. daguer-
reotypic.

ĬP'in– 2. pippin.

ĬP'ing– 2. chipping, dipping, skipping,
flipping, clipping, slipping, nipping, snip-
ping, ripping, dripping, gripping, strip-
ping, sipping, shipping, tipping, quip-
ping, whipping, zipping 3. outstrip-
ping, equipping, horse whipping.

ĬP'ish– 2. hippish, hyppish, snippish,
grippish, quippish.

ĬP'it– 2. pipit, rippit; see also ĬP'et–
skippet etc. above.

ĬP'l– 2. nipple, ripple, cripple, gripple,
grippal, triple, sipple, tipple, tiple, stip-
ple 3. becripple 4. participle.

ĬP'ler– 2. rippler, crippler, strippler, tip-
pler, stippler.

ĬP'let– 2. chiplet, liplet, ripplet, triplet,
striplet, tiplet.

ĬP'li– 2. ripply, cripply, triply, stipply.

ĬP'ling– 2. chipling, Kipling, rippling,
crippling, stripling, tippling, stippling.

ĬP'ment– 2. gripment, shipment 3.
equipment, reshipment, transhipment.

ĬP'o– 2. gippo, hippo, shippo 3. filippo.

ĬP'on– 2. slip-on, Nippon.

ĬPSH'un– 2. scription 3. Egyptian,
conniption [coll.], ascription, subscrip-
tion, description, prescription, transcrip-
tion, inscription, proscription 4. cir-
cumscription, superscription.

ĬPS'i– 3. ipse [L.], gypsy, tipsy 3.
Poughkeepsie.

ĬP'sis– 2. krypsis, tripsis, stypsis 3. el-
lipsis.

ĬPST'er– 2. tipster, quipster, whipster.

ĬPT'ik– 2. diptych, glyptic, cryptic, kryp-
tic, triptych, styptic 3. ecliptic, elliptic,
syncryptic 4. diaglyptic, anaglyptic,
holocryptic, hypostyptic 5. apocalyp-
tic.

ĬPT'iv– 3. descriptive, prescriptive,
transcriptive, inscriptive, conscriptive,
proscriptive 4. circumscriptive.

ĬPT'ur– 2. scripture.

ĬP'us– 2. hippus 3. philippus 4. Epi-
hippus, Protohippus.

ĬR– through ĬRZ–, see also short U (tub):
UR'a through URZ'i.

ĬR'a– 2. Irra, lira, sirrah 4. tirralira.

ĬR'er– 2. dearer, clearer, mirror, nearer,
sneerer, peerer.

ĬR'ik– 2. lyric, pyrrhic, Pyrrhic 3. ar-
gyric, vampiric, empiric, satiric, satyric,
butyric 4. panegyric.

ĬR'il– 2. Cyril, squirrel, virile 3. un-
virile.

ĬR'ist– 2. lyrist 4. panegyrist.

ĬR'it– 2. spirit 3. dispirit, inspirit 4.
party spirit.

ĬRK– through ĬRT–, see short U (tub):
URK'a through URT'um.

ĬR'up– 2. chirrup, syrup, stirrup.

ĬR'us– 2. byrrus, cirrus, cirrous, cirrhous.

ĬS'a– 2. lyssa, Missa [L.] 3. Melissa,
Clarissa, vibrissa, Nerissa, abscissa, man-
tissa 4. paterissa.

ĬS'al– 2. missal 3. abyssal, dismissal.

ĬSCH'an– 2. Christian 3. non-Christian,
unchristian 4. anti-Christian.

ĬS'eez– 2. Pisces, sissies 3. Ulysses.

ĬS'el– 2. missel, rissel, scissel, wissel
[Scot.] 3. dickcissel; see also ĬS'l– fissile
etc. below.

ĬS'en– 2. listen, glisten, christen 3. relisten, rechristen.

ĬS'ens– 3. dehiscence 4. indehiscence,
reminiscence, obliviscence, reviviscence.

ĬS'ent– 3. dehiscent 4. indehiscent,
reminiscent, reviviscent.

ĬS'er– 2. hisser, kisser, misser, risser 3.
remisser, dismisser 4. reminiscer.

ĬS'ez– hisses etc., see ĬS– bis etc. plus
"es" or " 's"; 2. Mrs.

IS'ful– 2. blissful 3. unblissful, remissful.

ISH'a– 3. militia, Letitia 4. Aloysia.

ISH'al– 3. judicial, official, comitial, initial, solstitial 4. prejudicial, unjudicial, beneficial, edificial, sacrificial, artificial, unofficial, superficial, postcomitial, interstitial 5. extrajudicial, unbeneficial, unsuperficial.

ISH'an– 2. Priscian, Titian 3. magician, logician, technician, patrician, optician, physician, musician 4. rhetorician, politician, statistician 5. mathematician; see also **ISH'un–** fission etc. below.

ISH'ens– 3. efficience, deficience, proficience, sufficience, omniscience 4. inefficience, self-sufficience, unsufficience.

ISH'ent– 3. efficient, deficient, proficient, sufficient, objicient, volitient, omniscient 4. inefficient, self-sufficient, insufficient, unproficient.

ISH'er– 2. disher, fisher, fissure, wisher, swisher 3. kingfisher, well-wisher.

ISH'ful– 2. dishful, fishful, wishful 3. unwishful.

ISH'i– 2. fishy, Vichy, squishy, swishy.

ISH'ing– 2. dishing, fishing, wishing, swishing 3. well-wishing, ill-wishing.

ISH'na– 2. Mishna, Krishna.

ISH'op– 2. bishop 3. archbishop.

ISH'pan– 2. Ishpan, dishpan.

ISH'u– 2. issue, fichu, tissue 3. reissue.

ISH'un– 2. fission, mission, Priscian, Titian 3. ambition, addition, tradition, edition, dedition, reddition, sedition, rendition, vendition, condition, audition, perdition, magician, logician, volition, submission, admission, emission, demission, remission, commission, omission, permission, dismission, transmission, ignition, cognition, technician, munition, punition, suspicion, attrition, patrician, detrition, metrician, contrition, nutrition, petition, tactician, optician, partition, sortition, fruition, tuition, physician, transition, po-

sition, musician 4. inhibition, prohibition, exhibition, readdition, extradition, recondition, precondition, erudition, coalition, abolition, demolition, ebullition, insubmission, readmission, preadmission, intromission, intermission, manumission, mechanician, inanition, recognition, definition, admonition, premonition, ammunition, apparition, rhetorician, electrician, malnutrition, tralatition, repetition, competition, politician, statistician, superstition, intuition, acquisition, requisition, inquisition, perquisition, disquisition, apposition, deposition, preposition, imposisupposition, disposition, exposition 5. superaddition, preadmonition, mathematician, contraposition, juxtaposition, anteposition, decomposition, predisposition, indisposition.

ISH'us– 2. vicious 3. ambitious, seditious, judicious, officious, flagitious, malicious, delicious, pernicious, puniceous, propitious, auspicious, suspicious, capricious, nutritious, factitious, fictitious 4. expeditious, injudicious, unofficious, unpropitious, inauspicious, unsuspicious, avaricious, meretricious, tralatitious, repetitious, adventitious, surreptitious, supposititious 5. supposititious.

IS'i– 2. missy, nisse, prissy [coll.], sissy [coll.].

IS'ik– 2. lyssic 3. silicic, anisic, masticic.

IS'il– 2. fissile, missile, scissile; see also **IS'l–** fissile, missal etc. below.

IS'ing– 2. hissing, Gissing, kissing, missing, sissing [chiefly dial.] 3. dehiscing, dismissing 4. prejudicing, reminiscing.

IS'it– 2. licit 3. elicit, illicit, solicit, implicit, explicit 4. inexplicit.

IS'iv– 2. fissive, missive 3. submissive, admissive, emissive, remissive, omissive, commissive, promissive, permissive, dismissive, transmissive 4. unsubmissive, intermissive.

ISK'a– 3. francisca.

ISK'al– 2. discal, fiscal, friscal 4. obeliscal.

ISK'an– 2. priscan 3. Franciscan 4. San Franciscan.

ISK'er– 2. risker, brisker, frisker, whisker 3. bewhisker.

ISK'est– 2. briskest, friskest.

ISK'et– 2. biscuit, brisket, frisket, wisket 3. Sea Biscuit.

ISK'i– 2. pisky [dial.], risky, frisky, whiskey.

ISK'in– 2. griskin, siskin, whiskin.

ISK'ing– 2. risking, brisking, frisking, whisking.

ISK'it– 2. biscuit 3. Sea Biscuit; see also ISK'et– biscuit, brisket etc. above.

ISK'o– 2. Frisco, cisco 3. San Francisco.

ISK'us– 2. discus, discous, fiscus [L.], viscous 3. hibiscus, trochiscus, meniscus, lemniscus, lentiscus 4. calathiscus, abaciscus.

IS'l– 2. fissile, missal, missel, missile, missle, rissel, rissle, bristle, gristle, sistle, scissel, scissile, thistle, wissel [Scot.], whistle 3. abyssal, dismissal, epistle, dickcissel 4. cacomistle.

IS'ler– 2. bristler, whistler 3. epistler.

IS'li– 2. bristly, gristly, thistly.

IS'ling– 2. bristling, brisling, whistling.

IS'mus– 2. isthmus, Christmas.

IS'n– 2. listen, glisten, christen 3. relisten, rechristen.

IS'ness– 2. thisness 3. remissness.

IS'ning– 3. listening, glistening, christening.

ISP'er– 2. lisper, risper, crisper, whisper 3. stage whisper.

ISP'est– 2. crispest.

ISP'i– 2. crispy, wispy.

ISP'ing– 2. lisping, crisping, wisping.

ISP'ness– 2. crispness.

IST'a– 2. vista 3. ballista, genista, Baptista.

IST'al– 2. distal, crystal, cystal, vistal; see also IST'l– istle etc. below.

IST'ans– 2. distance 3. outdistance, assistance, desistance, resistance 4. equidistance, unresistance.

IST'ant– 2. distant 3. assistant, resistant 4. coassistant, equidistant, nonresistant, unresistant; see also IST'ent– subsistent etc. below.

IST'ed– 2. fisted, listed, misted, wristed, trysted, cysted, twisted 3. hardfisted, closefisted, tightfisted, two-fisted, enlisted, black-listed, white-listed, strong-wristed, thin-wristed, assisted, subsisted, desisted, resisted, encysted, insisted, consisted, existed, persisted, untwisted 4. ironfisted, unassisted, unresisted, intertwisted.

IST'em– 2. system 4. solar system, nervous system, railroad system.

IST'en– 2. pristine, Sistine 3. Philistine 4. amethystine.

IST'ens– 3. subsistence, existence, insistence, consistence, persistence 4. preexistence, nonexistence, unexistence, coexistence, inconsistence.

IST'ent– 3. subsistent, existent, insistent, consistent, persistent 4. pre-existent, nonexistent, coexistent, inconsistent; see also IST'ant– distant etc. above.

IST'er– 2. bister, bistre, lister, blister' glister, mister, sister, twister, xyster 3. agister, agistor, magister, enlister, assister, sob sister, subsister, resister, exister, insister, stepsister, persister 4. water blister, foster sister.

IST'ful– 2. listful, mistful, wistful.

IST'i– 2. listy, misty, gristy.

IST'ik– 2. distich, fistic, mystic, pistic, cystic, schistic 3. Buddhistic, deistic, theistic, sophistic, logistic, ballistic, stylistic, monistic, eristic, poristic, juristic, puristic, touristic, statistic, baptistic, artistic, linguistic 4. atheistic, pantheistic, syllogistic, eulogistic, catechistic, anarchistic, cabalistic, feudalistic, realistic, formalistic, annalistic, journalistic, moralistic, socialistic, fatalistic, vitalistic, dualistic, royalistic, pugilistic, symbolistic, euphemistic, alchemistic, pessimistic, optimistic, Romanistic, humanistic, Hellenistic, Calvanistic, agonistic, canonistic, communistic, Taoistic, egoistic, eucharistic, egotistic, hypnotistic, inartistic, altruistic, casuistic, atavistic, Jehovistic **5.** polytheistic, antiphlogistic, cannibalistic, naturalistic, capitalistic, ritualistic, evangelistic, monopolistic, antagonistic, impressionistic, anachronistic, characteristic, allegoristic, romanticistic, Anabaptistic **6.** imperialistic, materialistic, phenomenalistic, universalistic **7.** supernaturalistic, individualistic.

IST'iks– **2.** mystics **3.** sphragistics, logistics, ballistics, statistics, linguistics **4.** syllogistics, agonistics, solaristics.

IST'ing– **2.** listing, misting, gristing, trysting, twisting **3.** enlisting, assisting, subsisting, desisting, resisting, existing, insisting, consisting, persisting, entwisting, untwisting **4.** pre-existing, nonexisting, intertwisting.

IST'iv– **3.** assistive, desistive, resistive, persistive.

IST'l– **2.** istle, distal, listel, pistil, pistol, Bristol, crystal, cystal, vistal.

IST'less– **2.** listless, mistless, twistless **3.** resistless.

IST'ment– **3.** agistment, enlistment.

IST'o– **3.** Mephisto, Callisto.

IST'us– **2.** cistus, schistous, xystus **3.** anhistous, rockcistus.

IS'um– **2.** lissome **3.** Alyssum **4.** sweet alyssum **5.** fideicommissum.

IS'us– **2.** Issus, byssus, missis, missus **3.** narcissus.

IT'a– **2.** Pitta, pitta, Sitta, shittah, vitta **3.** sagitta, Mylitta.

IT'al– **2.** victual **3.** remittal, committal, transmittal, acquittal; *see* also **IT'l–** kittle etc. below.

IT'an– **2.** Britain, Briton, witan **3.** Great Britain; *see* also **IT'en–** bitten etc. below.

IT'ans– **2.** pittance, quittance **3.** admittance, remittance, omittance, permittance, transmittance, acquittance.

IT'ed– **2.** bitted, fitted, flitted, slitted, knitted, pitted, spitted, ritted, gritted, witted, quitted, twitted **3.** unbitted, befitted, refitted, unfitted, submitted, admitted, emitted, demitted, remitted, omitted, committed, transmitted, unpitted, half-witted, acquitted, quickwitted, sharp-witted, short-witted, outwitted **4.** benefited, counterfeited, unremitted, recommitted, interknitted, ready-witted, nimble-witted.

IT'en– **2.** bitten, kitten, litten, mitten, smitten, written, Britain, Briton **3.** flea-bitten fly-bitten, frost-bitten, unsmitten, Great Britain, unwritten **4.** conscience-smitten, terror-smitten, underwritten.

IT'ent– **3.** emittent, remittent **4.** unremittent, intromittent, intermittent.

IT'er– **2.** bitter, fitter, hitter, jitter [slang], skitter, litter, flitter, glitter, splitter, slitter, knitter, pitter, spitter, Ritter, fritter, gritter, critter, [dial. & coll.], sitter, titter, quitter, twitter **3.** embitter, befitter, refitter, outfitter, pinch hitter, rail splitter, submitter, admitter, emitter, remitter, omitter, committer, permitter, transmitter, outsitter, atwitter, outwitter, acquitter **4.** benefiter, counterfeiter, recommitter, manumitter, baby sitter.

IT'ern– **2.** bittern, gittern, flittern, cittern.

IT'erz– bitters etc., *see* **IT'er–** bitter etc. above, plus "s" or "'s."

IT'est– **2.** fittest, flittest.

IT'ful– **2.** fitful, witful.

ITH'er– **2.** dither, hither, blither, slither, tither, thither, wither, swither, whither, zither.

ITH'i– 2. pithy, smithy, stithy, withy 3. twigwithy.

ITH'ik– 2. lithic, mythic 3. trilithic, ornithic 4. megalithic, eolithic, neolithic, monolithic, polymythic, philornithec 5. archaeolithic, palaeolithic.

ITH'm– 2. rhythm 3. logarithm, algorithm.

ITH'mik– 2. rhythmic, 4. logarithmic, polyrhythmic.

IT'i– 2. bitty, bittie, chitty, ditty, kitty, skitty, flitty, slitty, pity, gritty, grittie, pretty, city, witty, twitty 3. ambitty, poditty, committee, self-pity.

IT'id– 2. dittied, pitied, citied 3. unpitied, uncitied.

IT'ik– 2. lytic, critic 3. rachitic, graphitic, enclitic, proclitic, politic, Hamitic, Semitic, granitic, lignitic, nephritic, pyritic, arthritic, neuritic, Levitic 4. Jacobitic, neophytic, zoophytic, dialytic, analytic, paralytic, granulitic, spherulitic, Adamitic, Islamitic, dynamitic, eremitic, stalagmitic, tympanitic, Sybaritic, Nazaritic, diacritic, hypercritic, parasitic, anthracitic, hematitic.

IT'ing– 2. bitting, chitting, fitting, hitting, skitting, flitting, splitting, slitting, knitting, pitting, spitting, gritting, sitting, witting, quitting, twitting 3. befitting, outfitting, hard-hitting, pinchhitting, hairsplitting, earsplitting, submitting, admitting, emitting, remitting, omitting, committing, permitting, transmitting, unwitting, acquitting, outwitting 4. unbefitting, benefiting.

IT'ish– 2. skittish, British.

IT'l– 2. kittle, kittel, skittle, little, spittle, brittle, grittle, tittle, victual, whittle 3. belittle, remittal, committal, transmittal, lickspittle, acquittal 4. noncommittal, nonacquittal.

IT'ler– 2. skittler, littler, brittler, tittler, victualer, whittler 3. belittler.

IT'less– 2. bitless, fitless, hitless, pitless, spitless, gritless, witless.

IT'lest– 2. littlest, brittlest.

IT'li– 2. fitly 3. unfitly.

IT'ling– 2. kitling, brittling, titling, victualing, witling, whittling, whitling.

IT'lz– kittles etc., see **IT'l–** kittle etc. above, plus "s" or "'s."

IT'ment– 2. fitment 3. refitment, remitment, commitment, acquitment 4. recommitment.

IT'ness– 2. fitness, witness 3. unfitness, eyewitness.

IT'ni– 2. jitney, witney, Whitney 3. Mt. Whitney.

IT'zi– 2. Mitzy, ritzy, Fritzy.

IV'el– 2. snivel, drivel, swivel.

IV'en– 2. given, riven, driven, shriven, striven, thriven 3. forgiven, winddriven, rain-driven, undriven, unshriven 4. unforgiven, overdriven.

IV'er– 2. giver, liver, flivver [slang], sliver, river, shiver, stiver, quiver 3. forgiver, life-giver, deliver, outliver, Spoon River 4. Indian giver.

IV'erd– 2. livered, flivvered [slang], slivered, shivered, quivered 3. delivered, pale-livered, white-livered 4. undelivered, lily-livered, pigeon-livered, yellowlivered.

IV'et– 2. rivet, grivet, privet, trivet, civet.

IV'id– 2. livid, vivid.

IV'ik– 2. civic 3. uncivic.

IV'ing– 2. giving, living, sieving 3. lawgiving, forgiving, misgiving, Thanksgiving, outliving 4. unforgiving, everliving.

IV'l– 2. snivel, rivel, drivel, frivol, shrivel, civil, swivel 3. uncivil.

IV'ling– 2. sniveling, driveling, shriveling, swiveling.

IV'ness– 3. forgiveness 4. unforgiveness.

ĬV′ot– 2. divot, pivot.

ĬZ′ard– 2. izard, gizzard, blizzard, lizard, vizard, wizard 3. lounge lizzard [slang]; *see* also **ĬZ′erd–** scissored etc. below.

ĬZ′dom– 2. wisdom.

ĬZ′en– 2. dizen, mizzen, risen, ptisan, wizen 3. bedizen, arisen.

ĬZ′er– 2. rizzar, frizzer, scissor, quizzer, whizzer, visor, vizor 3. befrizzer.

ĬZ′erd– 2. scissored, visored, vizored; *see* also **ĬZ′ard–** izard etc. above.

ĬZH′un– 2. Frisian, scission, vision 3. elision, allision, illision, collision, Parisian, derision, misprision, abscission, decision, recission, rescission, precision, incision, concision, excision, revision, prevision, provision, division, envision 4. paradisian, aphrodisian, prodelision, television, subdivision, audivision, supervision.

ĬZ′i– 2. busy, dizzy, frizzy, Lizzie, mizzy, nizy, frizzy, tizzy, quizzy.

ĬZ′ik– 2. physic, phthisic 4. paradisic, metaphysic, biophysic.

ĬZ′iks– 2. physics 4. metaphysics, geophysics, biophysics, zoophysics.

ĬZ′ing– 2. fizzing, frizzing, quizzing, whizzing 3. befrizzing.

ĬZ′it– 2. visit 3. revisit, exquisite.

ĬZ′l– 2. chisel, fizzle, mizzle, drizzle, frizzle, grizzle, sizzle, swizzle, twizzle 3. enchisel, rumswizzle.

ĬZ′ler– 2. chiseler, frizzler, grizzler.

ĬZ′li– 2. chiselly, mizzly, drizzly, frizzly, grisly, grizzly.

ĬZ′ling– 2. chiseling, fizzling, mizzling, drizzling, frizzling, grizzling, sizzling, swizzling.

ĬZ′m– ism etc., *see* **ĬZM–** ism etc.

ĬZ′mal– 2. dismal, chrismal, prismal 3. abysmal, strabismal, baptismal 4. catechismal, cataclysmal, asterismal, paroxysmal.

ĬZ′mik– 2. clysmic, trismic 4. cataclysmic, embolismic, aphorismic, algorismic.

ĬZ′mus– 2. trismus 3. strabismus, accismus.

ĬZ′n– 2. dizen, his'n [dial.], mizzen, risen, prison, wizen 3. bedizen, arisen, imprison.

ĬZ′ness– 2. business 3. nonbusiness 4. monkey business [slang].

ĬZ′um– rizzom; *see* also **ĬZM–** ism etc.

I (bib)

3.

TRIPLE RHYMES IN I (Lib'y-a)

IB'i–a– **3.** Libya, tibia **4.** amphibia.

IB'i–al– **3.** tibial, stibial.

IB'i–an– **3.** Libyan **4.** amphibian, bathybian.

IB'ing–li– **3.** bibbingly, fibbingly, jibbingly, ribbingly, cribbingly, squibbingly **4.** wine bibblingly, ad libbingly [slang].

IB'it–ed– **4.** inhibited, exhibited, prohibited **5.** uninhibited, unprohibited.

IB'it–er– **4.** inhibiter, inhibitor, exhibitor, prohibiter, prohibitor.

IB'it–ing– **4.** inhibiting, exhibiting, prohibiting.

IB'it–iv– **4.** inhibitive, exhibitive, prohibitive **5.** uninhibitive, unprohibitive.

IB'i–us– **3.** stibious **4.** amphibious, bathybius.

IB'on–lik– **3.** gibbonlike, ribbonlike.

IB'u–lar– **3.** fibular **4.** mandibular, vestibular **5.** infundibular.

IB'ut–ed– **3.** tributed **4.** attributed, contributed, distributed.

IB'ut–er– **4.** attributer, contributor, distributer, distributor.

IB'ut–iv– **4.** attributive, retributive, contributive, distributive.

ICH'er–i– **3.** fitchery, michery, stitchery, witchery **4.** bewitchery.

ICH'et–i– **3.** witchetty, twitchety.

ICH'i–ness– **3.** itchiness, hitchiness, pitchiness, switchiness, twitchiness.

ICH'ing–li– **3.** itchingly, pitchingly, witchingly, switchingly, twitchingly **4.** enrichingly, bewitchingly.

ICH'ing–ness– **3.** itchingness, pitchingness, witchingness, switchingness, twitchingness **4.** enrichingness, bewitchingness.

ICH'less–li– **3.** itchlessly, hitchlessly, pitchlessly, stitchlessly, switchlessly, twitchlessly.

ID'a–bl– **3.** biddable **4.** rebiddable, unbiddable, forbiddable.

ID'en–ness– **3.** hiddenness **4.** forbiddenness **5.** unforbiddenness.

ID'i–a– **3.** Lydia, Nydia **4.** Ophidia, Numidia, Canidia.

ID'i–al– **4.** presidial, noctidial.

ID'i–an– **3.** Gideon, Lydian, Vidian **4.** ophidian, rachidian, Euclidean, Numidian, meridian, obsidian, quotidian, Ovidian **5.** nullifidian, taxaspidean, postmeridian **6.** antemeridian.

ID'if–i– **3.** nidify **4.** solidify, humidify, lapidify, acidify, rancidify, fluidify.

ID'ik–al– **4.** veridical, juridical, druidical, causidical **5.** pyramidical.

ID'it–i– **3.** quiddity **4.** rabidity, morbidity, turbidity, rigidity, frigidity, algidity, turgidity, calidity, squalidity, validity, gelidity, solidity, stolidity, timidity, humidity, tumidity, rapidity, sapidity, vapidity, trepidity, tepidity, sipidity, limpidity, torpidity, cupidity, stupidity, aridity, hybridity, acridity, viridity, floridity, torridity, putridity, acidity, placidity, flaccidity, rancidity, viscidity, lucidity, pinguidity, fluidity, liquidity, avidity, pavidity, lividity **5.** invalidity, insolidity, intrepidity, insipidity, pellucidity, translucidity, impavidity.

ID'i–um– 3. idiom, Psidium **4.** rubidium, iridium, presidium, cecidium.

ID'i–us– 3. Phidias, hideous **4.** perfidious, lapideous, insidious, fastidious, avidious, invidious.

ID'u–al– 4. residual, dividual **5.** individual.

ID'ul–at– 3. stridulate **4.** acidulate.

ID'ul–us– 3. stridulous **4.** acidulous.

ID'u–us– 3. biduous, viduous **4.** assiduous, deciduous, residuous, dividuous **5.** unassiduous, indeciduous.

IF'an–i– 3. tiffany, Tiffany **4.** Epiphany.

IF'er–us– 4. bulbiferous, limbiferous, herbiferous, morbiferous, nubiferous, splendiferous, frondiferous, tergiferous, branchiferous, conchiferous, lethiferous, aliferous, saliferous, piliferous, velliferous, celliferous, melliferous, stelliferous, foliferous, proliferous, cauliferous, armiferous, comiferous, pomiferous, laniferous, graniferous, igniferous, ligniferous, spiniferous, omniferous, somniferous, stanniferous, penniferous, coniferous, soniferous, pruniferous, umbriferous, ceriferous, floriferous, poriferous, cupriferous, ferriferous, cirriferous, rostriferous, auriferous, thuriferous, bacciferous, calciferous, vociferous, dorsiferous, ossiferous, furciferous, luciferous, muciferous, cruciferous, lactiferous, fructiferous, setiferous, pestiferous, sanguiferous, aquiferous, valviferous, multiferous, oviferous **5.** oleiferous, umbiliferous, coralliferous, metalliferous, papilliferous, petroliferous, maculiferous, ramuliferous, granuliferous, atomiferous, luminiferous, resiniferous, antenniferous, carboniferous, nectariferous, tuberiferous, odoriferous, sudoriferous, saporiferous, boraciferous, corticiferous, calyciferous, argentiferous **6.** aluminiferous, diamondiferous.

IF'ik–al– 4. magnifical, mirifical, pacifical, specifical, lactifical, pontifical, vivifical **5.** saporifical, beatifical.

IF'ik–ant– 4. nidificant, mundificant, significant, sacrificant **5.** insignificant.

IF'ik–at– 4. nidificate, nostrificate, pontificate, certificate, pacificate.

IF'i–sens– 4. magnificence, munificence.

IF'i–sent– 4. magnificent, munificent.

IF'lu–us– 4. fellifluous, mellifluous, sanguifluous.

IF'on–i– 3. triphony **4.** polyphony, antiphony, oxyphony.

IFT'a–bl– 3. liftable, siftable, shiftable.

IFT'il–i– 3. niftily [slang], shiftily, thriftily.

IFT'i–ness– 3. niftiness [slang], shiftiness, thriftiness.

IFT'less–ness– 3. shiftlessness, thriftlessness.

IF'ug–al– 4. vermifugal, febrifugal, centrifugal.

IG'am–i– 3. bigamy, digamy, trigamy **4.** polygamy.

IG'am–ist– 3. bigamist, digamist, trigamist **4.** polygamist.

IG'am–us– 3. bigamous, digamous, trigamous **4.** polygamous.

IG'er–i– 3. piggery, priggery, wiggery, Whiggery.

IG'ish–li– 3. piggishly, priggishly, Whiggishly.

IG'mat–ist– 3. stigmatist **4.** enigmatist.

IG'mat–iz– 3. stigmatize **4.** enigmatize **5.** paradigmatize.

IG'nan–si– 4. indignancy, malignancy, benignancy.

IG'nant–li– 4. indignantly, malignantly, benignantly.

IG'ne–us– 3. igneous, ligneous, cygneous **5.** pyroligneous.

IG'ni–a– 4. insignia.

IG'ni–fi– 3. ignify, dignify, lignify, signify 4. undignify.

IG'ni–ty– 3. dignity 4. indignity, condignity, malignity, benignity.

IG'on–al– 3. trigonal 4. polygonal, ditrigonal.

IG'or–us– 3. rigorous, vigorous.

IG'raf–i– 4. tachigraphy, calligraphy, polygraphy, epigraphy, pasigraphy, stratigraphy, lexigraphy 5. pseudopigraphy.

IG'u–us– 4. ambiguous, irriguous, exiguous, contiguous.

IJ'a–bl– 3. bridgeable 4. abridgable, unbridgeable 5. unabridgable.

IJ'en–us– 4. ambigenous, indigenous, cauligenous, terrigenous, rurigenous, oxygenous 5. alkaligenous, coralligenous, nepheligenous; see also IJ'in–us– polygynous etc. below.

IJ'er–ent– 4. belligerent, refrigerant 5. hederigerent.

IJ'er–us– 4. pedigerous, armigerous, plumigerous, belligerous, piligerous, cirrigerous, discigerous, cornigerous, crucigerous, setigerous, navigerous, ovigerous.

IJ'et–i– 3. fidgety, midgety.

IJ'i–a– 3. Phrygia 4. Ogygia, fastigia 5. Cantabrigia.

IJ'i–an– 3. Phrygian, Stygian 4. Ogygian, Vestigian 5. Cantabrigian.

IJ'id–li– 3. rigidly, frigidly.

IJ'id–ness– 3. rigidness, frigidness.

IJ'in–al– 4. original 5. unoriginal.

IJ'in–us– 4. polygynous, uliginous, fuliginous, lentiginous, vertiginous, vortiginous; see also IJ'en–us– ambigenous etc. above.

IJ'i–um– 3. phrygium 4. pterygium, fastigium, syzygium.

IJ'us–li– 4. prodigiously, religiously, litigiously 5. sacrilegiously.

IJ'us–ness– 4. prodigiousness, religiousness, litigiousness 5. sacrilegiousness.

IK'a–ment– 4. medicament, predicament.

IK'ar–us– 3. Icarus, lickerous.

IK'at–iv– 3. fricative, siccative 4. abdicative, predicative, indicative, vindicative, desiccative, exsiccative.

IK'en–er– 3. thickener, quickener.

IK'en–ing– 3. sickening, thickening, quickening.

IK'er–ing– 3. bickering, dickering, flickering, smickering, snickering.

IK'er–ish– 3. lickerish, liquorish, licorice.

IK'et–er– 3. picketer, cricketer, ticketer.

IK'et–i– 3. rickety, crickety, thickety 4. pernickety, persnickety.

IK'et–ing– 3. picketing, cricketing, ticketing.

IK'i–li– 3. trickily, stickily.

IK'i–ness– 3. trickiness, stickiness.

IK'li–ness– 3. prickliness, sickliness.

IK'ol–us– 3. Nicholas 4. urbicolous, sepicolous, terricolous, agricolous, silvicolous.

IK'or–i– 3. chicory, hickory 4. Halicore, Terpsichore.

IKS'a–bl– 3. fixable, mixable 4. prefixable, unfixable, immixable, unmixable.

IKS'ed–li– 3. fixedly, mixedly.

IKSH'un–al– 3. fictional, frictional 4. convictional 5. contradictional, benedictional, jurisdictional.

IKS'it–i– 3. fixity, siccity 4. prolixity.

IKT'a–bl– 4. predictable, convictable 5. contradictable, unpredictable, unrestrictable 6. uncontradictable.

IKT'iv–li– 4. predictively, vindictively, restrictively.

IKT'iv–ness– 4. predictiveness, vindictiveness, restrictiveness.

IKT'or–i– 3. victory 4. serictery 5. contradictory, maledictory, valedictory, benedictory, interdictory 6. uncontradictory.

IK'ul–a– 4. fidicula, Canicula, reticula

IK′ul–ant– 4. matriculant, articulant.

IK′ul–ar– 3. spicular 4. orbicular, vehicular, follicular, canicular, funicular, apicular, matricular, ventricular, auricular, acicular, fascicular, vesicular, versicular, reticular, denticular, lenticular, articular, particular, clavicular 5. appendicular, perpendicular, adminicular, quinquarticular.

IK′ul–at– 3. spiculate 4. orbiculate, pediculate, forficulate, folliculate, vermiculate, paniculate, geniculate, apiculate, turriculate, matriculate, auriculate, aciculate, fasciculate, straticulate, reticulate, denticulate, monticulate, articulate, particulate, gesticulate 5. appendiculate canaliculate, immatriculate, inarticulate, multarticulate, octarticulate.

IK′ul–um– 3. spiculum 4. Janiculum, geniculum, periculum, curriculum, reticulum.

IK′ul–us– 4. ridiculous, folliculous, cauliculus, cauliculous, vermiculous, panniculus, ventriculous, vesiculus, vesiculous, meticulous.

IK′u–us– 4. transpicuous, conspicuous, perspicuous 5. inconspicuous.

IK′wit–i– 4. ubiquity, obliquity, iniquity, antiquity.

IK′wit–us– 4. ubiquitous, obliquitous, iniquitous.

ĬL′a–bl– 3. billable, fillable, killable, millable, spillable, thrillable, syllable, tillable 4. refillable, unfillable, unkillable, unspillable, unthrillable, untillable, distillable.

ĬL′aj–er– 3. pillager, villager.

ĬL′ar–i– 3. phyllary, Hilary, pillary 5. codicillary.

ĬL′er–i– 3. pillery, pillory, frillery, cilery, Sillery 4. artillery, distillery.

ĬL′et–ed– 3. billeted, filleted 4. unbilleted, unfilleted.

ĬL′et–ing– 3. billeting, filleting.

IL′ful–i– 3. skillfully, willfully 4. unskillfully, unwillfully.

IL′ful–ness– 3. skillfulness, willfulness 4. unskillfulness.

ĬL′i–a– 3. ilia, cilia 4. sedilia, familia, Emilia, similia, Cecilia 5. mirabilia, notabilia, pedophilia, hemophilia, zoophilia, adactylia 6. memorabilia.

ĬL′i–ad– 3. Iliad, Gilead, chiliad, milliad.

ĬL′i–ak– 3. iliac 5. sacroiliac, hemophiliac.

ĬL′i–al– 3. ilial, filial 4. grandfilial, familial.

ĬL′i–an– 3. Ilian, Ilion, Chilean, Gillian, Lillian 4. Virgilian, Cecilian, Sicilian, reptilian, Castilian, civilian, Brazilian 5. crocodilian, Maximilian.

ĬL′i–ar– 4. familiar, conciliar, auxiliar 5. domiciliar.

ĬL′i–at– 3. filiate, ciliate 4. affiliate, humiliate, conciliate 5. domiciliate, reconciliate.

ĬL′i–ens– 4. resilience, dissilience, transilience, consilience; see also ĬL′yans– brilliance etc.

ĬL′i–ent– 4. resilient, dissilient, transilient, consilient.

ĬL′i–est– 3. chilliest, hilliest, silliest, stilliest.

ĬL′i–fī– 3. vilify 4. stabilify, nihilify, fossilify.

ĬL′i–form– 3. filiform, phylliform, liliform, stilliform 4. papilliform.

ĬL′ik–a– 3. silica 4. basilica.

ĬL′ik–al– 3. filical, silicle 4. umbilical, basilical.

ĬL′ik–in– 3. Billiken, spilikin, spillikin 4. basilican.

ĬL′ik–um– 3. tilikum, tillicum.

ĬL′i–ness– 3. chilliness, hilliness, silliness.

ĬL′ing–li– 3. fillingly, chillingly, killingly, trillingly, thrillingly, willingly 4. unwillingly.

ĬL'it–at– 3. militate 4. habilitate, stabilitate, debilitate, nobilitate, facilitate 5. rehabilitate, imbecilitate.

ĬL'it–i– 4. ability, lability, debility, mobility, nobility, nubility, nihility, agility, fragility, humility, senility, febrility, sterility, virility, scurrility, neurility, facility, gracility, docility, tensility, tactility, ductility, gentility, motility, fertility, tortility, hostility, utility, futility, civility, servility, exility, flexility 5. bribability, probability, readability, laudability, affability, changeability, chargeability, liability, pliability, viability, placability, peccability, secability, vocability, workability, saleability, amability, flammability, namability, tenability, inability, capability, culpability, wearability, errability, curability, durability, traceability, disability, versability, ratability, tractability, suitability, notability, quotability, temptability, portability, instability, mutability, suability, solvability, movability, provability, knowability, taxability, vincibility, docibility, miscibility, edibility, credibility, vendibility, audibility, legibility, frangibility, tangibility, fallibility, gullibility, feasibility, risibility, visibility, sensibility, tensibility, passibility, possibility, plausibility, fusibility, partibility, flexibility, fluxibility, immobility, ignobility, solubility, volubility, imbecility, indocility, juvenility, prehensility, volatility, vibratility, versatility, retractility, contractility, inductility, infertility, inutility, incivility 6. describability, improbability, absorbability, implacability, impeccability, applicability, amicability, practicability, masticability, revocability, avoidability, manageability, exchangeability, malleability, permeability, ineffability, navigability, approachability, punishability, perishability, reliability, amiability, variability, insatiability, negotiability, availability, violability, calculability, redeemability, inflammability, reformability, conformability, alienability, amenability,

impregnability, attainability, mentionability, questionability, governability, incapability, impalpability, reparability, separability, comparability, ponderability, preferability, transferability, venerability, vulnerability, utterability, integrability, answerability, desirability, acquirability, adorability, meliorability, deplorability, memorability, vaporability, exorability, inerrability, penetrability, demonstrability, incurability, endurability, measurability, censurability, insurability, advisability, condensability, dispensability, reversability, impassability, relatability, dilatability, translatability, retractability, attractability, delectability, respectability, predictability, marketability, habitability, excitability, creditability, imitability, irritability, unsuitability, presentability, accountability, adaptability, acceptability, attemptability, transportability, detestability, adjustability, immutability, commutability, transmutability, imputability, computability, disputability, inscrutability, retrievability, conceivability, resolvability, removability, immovability, improvability, cognizability, invincibility, convincibility, irascibility, immiscibility, cognoscibility, reducibility, conducibility, producibility, inedibility, incredibility, inducibility, seducibility, inaudibility, illegibility, dirigibility, infrangibility, intangibility, indelibility, infallibility, defeasibility, persuasibility, divisibility, invisibility, expansibility, defensibility, insensibility, distensibility, extensibility, invincibility, responsibility, reversibility, collapsibility, impassibility, accessibility, impressibility, compressibility, expressibility, admissibility, remissibility, transmissibility, impossibility, diffusibility, infusibility, compatibility, defectibility, affectibility, effectibility, perfectibility, conductibility, destructibility, deceptibility, perceptibility, susceptibility, contemptibility, corruptibility, impartibility, convertibility, digestibility, resistibility, existibility, exhaustibility, combustibility, inflexibility, insolubility **7.** indescribability, imperturbability, communicability, impracticability, irrevocability, interchangeability, impermeability, irrefragability, irreproachability, imperishability, enunciability, justifiability, invariability, influenciability, reconcilability, assimilability, inviolability, incalculability, coagulability, irredeemability, irreformability, determinability, impressionability, irreparability, inseparability, incomparability, imponderability, innumerability, invulnerability, unutterability, undesirability, inexorability, impenetrability, indemonstrability, immeasurability, commensurability, indispensability, inexcusability, untranslatability, inhabitability, hereditability, incogitability, illimitability, inimitability, inheritability, inevitability, precipitability, insurmountability, incontestability, irrefutability, incommutability, indisputability, irretrievability, inconceivability, irresolvability, recognizability, incognizability, incognoscibility, irreducibility, incorrigibility, indefeasibility, indivisibility, indefensibility, comprehensibility, irresponsibility, irreversibility, inaccessibility, irrepressibility, incompressibility, inexpressibility, irredressibility, inadmissibility, irremissibility, incompatibility, indefectibility, imperfectibility, indestructibility, imperceptibility, incorruptibility, inconvertibility, indigestibility, irresistibility, inexhaustibility, incombustibility **8.** incommunicability, indefatigability, irreconcilability, incommensurability, hyperirritability, incomprehensibility; *and numerous other derived nouns ending in "-ility."*

IL'i–um– 3. ilium, ileum, Ilium, Lilium, Liliom, pileum, trillium **4.** beryllium, auxilium, concilium.

IL'i–us– 4. punctilious **5.** supercilious; *see also* **IL'yus–** bilious etc.

ILK'i–est– 3. milkiest, silkiest.

IL'o–i– 3. billowy, pillowy, willowy.

IL'o–ji– 3. dilogy, trilogy, sylloge **4.** palilogy, fossilogy, antilogy, festilogy.

IL'o–jiz– 3. syllogize **4.** epilogize.

IL'o–jizm– 3. syllogism **4.** amphilogism, epilogism **5.** pseudosyllogism.

IL'o–kwens– 4. blandiloquence, grandiloquence, magniloquence, somniloquence, multiloquence, stultiloquence, breviloquence.

IL'o–kwent– 4. grandiloquent, melliloquent, magniloquent, somniloquent, veriloquent, flexiloquent, dulciloquent, pauciloquent, altiloquent, sanctiloquent, multiloquent, suaviloquent.

IL'o–kwi– 4. soliloquy, dulciloquy, somniloquy, ventriloquy, pauciloquy, Centiloquy, dentiloquy, multiloquy, stultiloquy **5.** pectoriloquy.

IL'o–kwist– 4. soliloquist, somniloquist, gastriloquist, ventriloquist, dentiloquist.

IL'o–kwiz– 4. soliloquize, ventriloquize.

IL'o–kwizm– 4. somniloquism, ventriloquism, gastriloquism **5.** pectoriloquism.

IL'o–kwus– 4. grandiloquous, tardiloquous, somniloquous, ventriloquous **5.** pectoriloquous.

IL'yan–si– 3. brilliancy **4.** resiliency, transiliency.

IL'yar–i– 3. miliary **4.** auxiliary.

IM'er–i– 3. glimmery, simmery, shimmery.

IM'er–ing– 3. glimmering, simmering, shimmering.

IM'er–us– 3. dimerous, glimmerous, trimerous **4.** polymerous.

IM'et–er– 3. dimeter, trimeter, scimiter **4.** millimeter, polymeter, perimeter, altimeter, voltimeter, centimeter **5.** alkalimeter, polarimeter, calorimeter.

IM'et–ri– 3. symmetry **4.** perimetry, asymmetry, altimetry, bathymetry **5.** alkalimetry, calorimetry, polarimetry.

IM'i–an– 3. simian, Simeon 4. Endymion.

IM'ik–al– 3. mimical 4. alchymical, inimical 5. homonymical, toponymical, patronymical, metonymical.

IM'il–e– 3. simile 4. dissimile, facsimile.

IM'in–al– 3. biminal, liminal, criminal, Viminal 4. regiminal, subliminal.

IM'in–at– 3. criminate 4. eliminate, recriminate, incriminate, discriminate.

IM'in–i– 3. Bimini, jiminy, crimine, criminy [both slang] 4. postliminy 6. niminy-piminy.

IM'it–at– 3. imitate, limitate 4. delimitate.

IM'it–er– 3. limiter, scimitar, scimiter.

IM'it–i– 3. dimity, limity 4. sublimity, proximity 5. magnanimity, unanimity, sanctanimity, equanimity, pseudonymity, anonymity, synonymity 6. pusillanimity.

IMP'er–er– 3. simperer, whimperer.

IMP'er–ing– 3. simpering, whimpering.

IM'u–lant– 3. simulant, stimulant.

IM'u–lat– 3. simulate, stimulate 4. assimulate, dissimulate, restimulate.

IM'u–lus– 3. limulus, stimulus.

IN'a–kl– 3. binnacle, binocle, pinnacle.

INCH'ing–li– 3. inchingly, flinchingly, clinchingly, pinchingly, cinchingly 5. penny pinchingly [slang].

IND'er–i– 3. cindery, tindery.

IND'i–a– 3. India.»

IND'i–er– 3. windier.

IND'i–kat– 3. indicate, syndicate, vindicate.

IN'e–a– 3. linea, tinea, vinea 5. Nemertinea; see also IN'i–a– Inia etc. below.

ĬN'e–al– 3. lineal, pineal, tineal, vineal 4. gramineal, stamineal, pectineal 5. interlineal, consanguineal; see also IN'i–al– inial etc. below.

IN'e–ar– 3. linear 4. trilinear, collinear 5. rectilinear.

IN'e–ma– 3. kinema, cinema.

IN'e–us– 4. vimineous, fulmineous, sanguineous 5. testudineous, ignominious, consanguineous.

ING'er–er– 3. fingerer, lingerer 4. malingerer.

ING'er–ing– 3. fingering, lingering 4. malingering.

ING'i–ness– 3. ringiness, springiness, stringiness.

ING'ul–a– 3. lingula.

ING'ul–ar– 3. cingular, singular.

ING'ul–at– 3. lingulate, cingulate.

IN'i–a– 3. Inia, linea, tinea, vinea, zinnia 4. Sardinia, Virginia, lacinia, Lavinia 5. anodynia, pleurodynia, Abyssinia, Nemertinea.

IN'i–al– 3. inial, finial, lineal, pineal, tineal, vineal 4. dominial; see also IN'e–al– lineal etc. above.

IN'i–an– 4. Sardinian, Delphinian, Virginian, Flaminian, Justinian, Darwinian 5. Carthaginian, Carolinian, Abyssinian, Serpentinean, Palestinian, Augustinian 7. anthropophaginian.

IN'i–at– 3. lineate, miniate 4. delineate, laciniate.

IN'i–er– 3. finnier, skinnier, tinnier.

IN'i–kal– 3. finical, clinical, cynical, binocle 4. rabbinical, synclinical, Brahminical, adminicle, dominical; see also IN'a–kl– binnacle etc. above.

IN'i–kin– 3. finikin, minikin.

IN'ish–er– 3. finisher 4. diminisher.

IN'ish–ing– 3. finishing 4. refinishing, diminishing 5. undiminishing.

IN'ist–er– 3. minister, sinister 4. administer 5. ambisinister.

IN'ist–ral– 3. ministral, sinistral 5. dextrosinistral.

IN′it–i– 3. finity, trinity 4. affinity, diffinity, infinity, confinity, virginity, salinity, felinity, caninity, vicinity, Latinity 5. masculinity, femininity, asininity, peregrinity, exsanguinity, consanguinity, patavinity.

IN′it–iv– 3. finitive 4. affinitive, definitive, infinitive.

IN′it–ud– 3. finitude 4. infinitude.

IN′i–um– 3. minium 4. delphinium, virginium, illinium, perinium, actinium 5. quadricinium, tirocinium, patrocinium.

IN′i–us– 5. ignominious, consanguineous; see also IN′e–us– vimineous etc. above.

INJ′ens–i– 3. stringency 4. refringency, astringency, constringency, contingency.

INJ′il–i– 3. dingily, stingily.

INJ′i–ness– 3. dinginess, stinginess.

INK′a–bl– 3. drinkable, shrinkable, sinkable, thinkable 4. undrinkable, unshrinkable, unthinkable.

INK′i–ness– 3. inkiness, kinkiness, slinkiness, pinkiness.

INK′ing–ly– 3. slinkingly, thinkingly, winkingly 4. unthinkingly.

INK′wit–i– 4. longinquity, propinquity.

INS′i–bl– 4. evincible, invincible, convincible.

INS′ing–li– 3. mincingly 4. convincingly.

INT′er–est– 3. interest 4. disinterest.

INT′er–i– 3. splintery, printery, wintery.

INT′er–ing– 3. splintering, wintering.

INTH′i–a– 3. Cynthia 4. Carinthia.

INTH′i–an– 3. Cynthian 4. Carinthian, Corinthian, absinthian 5. hyacinthian, labyrinthian.

IN′u–at– 3. sinuate 4. insinuate, continuate.

IN′u–us– 3. sinuous 4. continuous 5. uncontinuous, discontinuous.

IP′a–bl– 3. chippable, dippable, clippable, nippable, rippable, shippable, tippable.

IP′ar–us– 3. biparous 4. ambiparous, deiparous, polyparous, primiparous, gemmiparous, vermiparous, omniparous, criniparous, uniparous, floriparous, pluriparous, fissiparous, fructiparous, multiparous, dentiparous, viviparous, oviparous, larviparous 6. ovoviviparous.

IP′ath–i– 4. somnipathy, antipathy.

IP′er–i– 3. flippery, slippery, pipery, frippery.

IP′i–ent– 4. desipient, incipient, insipient, percipient 5. apercipient.

IP′ik–al– 3. typical 4. atypical, etypical, nontypical, untypical.

IP′i–ness– 3. slippiness, nippiness, snippiness, grippiness.

IP′it–al– 4. centripetal, basipetal, bicipital, occipital, ancipital, sincipital.

IP′ol–e– 3. Tripoli 4. Gallipoli.

IP′ot–ens– 4. armipotence, ignipotence, plenipotence, omnipotence.

IP′ot–ent– 4. deipotent, bellipotent, armipotent, plenipotent, ignipotent, omnipotent, noctipotent, multipotent.

IPSH′un–al– 4. transcriptional, inscriptional, conscriptional.

IPT′er–al– 3. dipteral 4. hemipteral, peripteral.

IPT′er–us– 3. dipterous, dipteros, Dipterus, tripterous 4. peripterous.

IPT′ik–al– 3. cryptical 4. elliptical 6. apocalyptical.

IPT′iv–li– 4. descriptively, prescriptively 5. circumscriptively.

IP′ul–ar– 3. stipular 4. manipular.

IP′ul–at– 3. stipulate 4. pedipulate, manipulate, astipulate.

IR′a–si– through IR′i–us, see also short U (tub): URB′a–bl through URZH′un–ist.

IR′a–si– 4. deliracy, conspiracy.

IR′i–a– 3. Syria, Styria 4. Valkyria, Elyria, Assyria; see also ER′i–a– eria etc.

IR′i–an– 3. Syrian, Tyrian, Styrian 4. Valkyrian, Assyrian.

IR′ik–al– 3. lyrical, miracle 4. empirical, satirical, satyrical 5. panegyrical.

IR′is–ist– 3. lyricist 4. empiricist.

IR′is–izm– 3. lyricism 4. empiricism.

IR′i–um– 3. Miriam 4. delirium, imperium.

IR′i–us– 3. Sirius 4. delirious, imperious.

IS′a–bl– 3. kissable, missable 4. dismissable; *see* also **IS′i–bl–** missible etc. below.

IS′en–ing– 3. listening, glistening, christening.

ISH′al–i– 4. judicially, officially 5. prejudicially, beneficially, sacrificially, artificially, unofficially, superficially.

ISH′ar–i– 4. judiciary, justiciary 5. beneficiary.

ISH′ens–i– 4. efficiency, deficiency, proficiency, sufficiency 5. beneficiency, inefficiency, unproficiency, self-sufficiency, insufficiency.

ISH′ent–li– 4. efficiently, deficiently, proficiently, sufficiently 5. inefficiently, unproficiently, insufficiently.

ISH′i–a– 4. indicia, Alicia, Galicia, Felicia, comitia, Tunisia, asitia, Justitia 5. apositia.

ISH′i–at– 3. vitiate 4. officiate, initiate, propitiate, patriciate, novitiate.

ISH′on–al– 3. missional 4. additional, traditional, conditional, volitional, commissional, nutritional, transitional, positional, petitional, tuitional 5. exhibitional, unconditional, recognitional, depositional, prepositional, impositional, compositional, propositional, expositional, suppositional, repetitional, intuitional.

ISH′on–er– 3. missioner 4. conditioner, commissioner, parishioner, petitioner, practitioner 5. exhibitioner, coalitioner, admonitioner.

ISH′on–ing– 4. conditioning, positioning, petitioning.

ISH′on–ist– 4. traditionist 5. prohibitionist, exhibitionist, expeditionist, coali-tionist, abolitionist, requisitionist, oppositionist.

ISH′us–li– 3. viciously 4. judiciously, officiously, maliciously, deliciously, perniciously, auspiciously, suspiciously, capriciously 5. injudiciously, inauspiciously, avariciously, meretriciously, adventitiously.

ISH′us–ness– 3. viciousness 4. ambitiousness, seditiousness, judiciousness, officiousness, flagitiousness, deliciousness, pernisciousness, propitiousness, auspiciousness, suspiciousness, capriciousness, nutritiousness, fictitiousness 5. injudiciousness, inauspiciousness, avariciousness, meretriciousness, adventitiousness, superstitiousness, suppositiousness.

IS′i–bl– 3. missible, miscible, scissible 4. admissible, remissible, immiscible, omissible, permissible, transmissible 5. unremissible, unpermissible, obliviscible; *see* also **IS′a–bl–** kissable etc. above.

IS′i–bli– 4. admissibly, permissibly.

IS′i–li– 3. prissily [coll.], Sicily.

IS′im–o– 4. dolcissimo [It.], altissimo, fortissimo, prestissimo, bravissimo [It.] 5. pianissimo 6. generalissimo.

IS′in–al– 3. piscinal, vicinal 4. medicinal, fidicinal, officinal, vaticinal.

IS′i–pat– 3. dissipate 4. anticipate, participate.

IS′it–i– 4. cubicity, mendicity, pudicity, publicity, felicity, triplicity, simplicity, complicity, duplicity, conicity, unicity, tonicity, stoicity, lubricity, rubricity, sphericity, centricity, pepticity, septicity, stypticity, verticity, vorticity, plasticity, spasticity, causticity, mysticity, rusticity, toxicity 5. benedicite, immundicity, spheroidicity, impudicity, infelicity, catholicity, multiplicity, accomplicity, quadruplicity, atomicity, endemicity, atonicity, canonicity, caloricity, electricity, eccentricity, concentricity, authenticity, eupepticity, ellipticity, autopticity, elasticity, domesticity **6.** periodicity, egocentricity, inelasticity.

IS'it-ing– 4. eliciting, soliciting.

IS'it-li– 3. licitly **4.** illicitly, implicitly, explicitly.

IS'it-ness– 3. licitness **4.** illicitness, implicitness, explicitness.

IS'it-or– 4. elicitor, solicitor.

IS'it-ud– 3. spissitude **4.** solicitude, vicissitude.

IS'it-us– 4. felicitous, solicitous.

ISK'i-er– 3. riskier, friskier.

ISK'i-est– 3. riskiest, friskiest.

ISK'i-li– 3. riskily, friskily.

ISK'i-ness– 3. riskiness, friskiness.

IS'or-i– 4. admissory, remissory, dimissory, dismissory, rescissory.

IST'en-si– 3. distancy **4.** subsistency, existency, insistency, consistency, persistency **5.** pre-existency, inconsistency.

IST'ent-li– 3. distantly **4.** existently, insistently, persistently **5.** inconsistently.

IST'er-i– 3. blistery, mystery **4.** baptistery, commistery; *see* also **IST'or-i–** history etc. below.

IST'er-lik– 3. blisterlike, sisterlike.

IST'ful-i– 3. listfully, wistfully.

IST'i-bl– 4. resistible, existible **5.** irresistible, unresistible.

IST'ik-al– 3. mystical **4.** deistical, theistical, logistical, sophistical, hemistichal, papistical, eristical, patristical, juristical, puristical, statistical, artistical, linguistical **5.** atheistical, pantheistical, eulogistical, synergistical, catechistical, anarchistical, cabalistical, alchemistical, Calvinistical, canonistical, synchronistical, egoistical, eucharistical, syncretistical **6.** theosophistical, antagonistical, characteristical, hypocoristical.

IST'ik-at– 4. sophisticate, phlogisticate **5.** unsophisticate, dephlogisticate.

IST'or-i– 3. history **4.** faldistory, consistory; *see* also **IST'er-i–** blistery etc. above.

IT'a-bl– 3. fittable, hittable, knittable, pittable, quittable **4.** Mehitable, admittable, remittable, omittable, committable, permittable, transmittable **5.** unremittable, unacquittable.

IT'an-i– 3. dittany, kitteny, litany, Brittany.

IT'er-al– 3. literal **4.** presbyteral, alliteral, biliteral, triliteral.

IT'er-at– 3. iterate **4.** reiterate, presbyterate, alliterate, obliterate, transliterate.

IT'er-er– 3. bitterer, jitterer [slang], litterer, glitterer, fritterer, titterer, twitterer **4.** embitterer.

IT'er-est– 3. bitterest.

IT'er-i– 3. jittery [slang], littery, glittery, tittery, twittery.

IT'er-ing– 3. jittering [slang], littering, glittering, frittering, tittering, twittering **4.** embittering.

ITH'er-i– 3. dithery, smithery, withery.

ITH'er-ing– 3. dithering, blithering, withering.

ITH'es-is– 4. epithesis, antithesis.

ITH'i-a– 3. lithia, Pythia **4.** forsythia.

IT'i-er– 3. flittier, grittier, prettier, wittier, Whittier.

IT'i-est– 3. grittiest, prettiest, wittiest.

IT'ik-al– 3. critical **4.** political, hermitical, acritical, soritical, Levitical **5.** eremitical, stalagmitical, diacritical, hypocritical, hypercritical, parasitical, Jesuitical **6.** cosmopolitical, metropolitical, oneirocritical.

IT'il-i– 3. grittily, prettily, wittily.

IT'i-ness– 3. fittiness, flittiness, grittiness, prettiness, wittiness.

IT'ing-li– 3. fittingly, flittingly, wittingly, twittingly **4.** befittingly, unwittingly **5.** unbefittingly, unremittingly.

IT′is–izm– 3. Briticism, criticism, witticism.

IT′l–ness– 3. littleness, brittleness.

IT′u–al– 3. ritual, situal 4. habitual, obitual 5. unhabitual.

IT′ul–ar– 3. titular 4. capitular.

IV′a–bl– 3. givable, livable 4. forgivable, unlivable 5. unforgivable.

IV′al–ent– 3. bivalent, divalent, trivalent 4. polyvalent, omnivalent, univalent, multivalent, equivalent.

IV′at–iv– 3. privative 4. derivative, deprivative.

IV′el–er– 3. sniveller, driveller, civiller.

IV′er–er– 3. sliverer, shiverer, quiverer 4. deliverer.

IV′er–i– 3. livery, slivery, rivery, shivery, quivery 4. delivery.

IV′er–ing– 3. slivering, shivering, quivering 4. delivering.

IV′i–a– 3. trivia 4. Olivia, Bolivia.

IV′i–al– 3. trivial 4. oblivial, quadrivial. lixivial, convivial.

IV′i–an– 3. Vivian 4. Bolivian.

IV′id–li– 3. lividly, vividly.

IV′id–ness– 3. lividness, vividness.

IV′il–i– 3. snivelly, civilly 4. uncivilly.

IV′ing–li– 3. givingly, livingly 4. forgivingly, outgivingly.

IV′it–i– 3. privity 4. acclivity, declivity, proclivity, passivity, nativity, activity, motivity, captivity, festivity 5. impassivity, compassivity, emissivity, negativity, relativity, sensitivity, positivity, inactivity, objectivity, subjectivity, electivity, collectivity, connectivity, inductivity, conductivity, productivity, receptivity, perceptivity, susceptivity 6. correlativity, alternativity, retroactivity, reproductivity.

IV′it–us– 4. acclivitous, declivitous, proclivitous.

IV′i–um– 3. trivium 4. quadrivium, lixivium.

IV′i–us– 3. bivious 4. oblivious, lascivious, lixivious, multivious.

IV′ok–al– 4. univocal, equivocal 5. unequivocal.

IV′ol–i– 3. Rivoli, Tivoli.

IV′ol–us– 3. frivolous 4. unfrivolous.

IV′or–us– 4. herbivorous, frondiverous, amphivorous, frugivorous, mellivorous, vermivorous, panivorous, ranivorous, granivorous, lignivorous, pomivorous, omnivorous, baccivorous, piscivorous, fucivorous, mucivorous, nucivorous, ossivorous, fructivorous, sanguivorous, equivorous 5. graminivorous, insectivorous, vegetivorous, sanguinivorous.

IZ′er–i– 3. misery, quizzery.

IZH′on–al– 3. visional 4. precisional, revisional, previsional, divisional, provisional.

IZ′i–an– 3. Frisian 4. Elysian, Tunisian, Parisian, precisian 5. paradisian.

IZ′i–bl– 3. risible, visible, quizzable 4. derisible, divisible, invisible, acquisible 5. indivisible, undivisible.

IZ′i–er– 3. busier, dizzier, fizzier, frizzier.

IZ′i–est– 3. busiest, dizziest, fizziest, frizziest.

IZ′ik–al– 3. physical, phthisical, quizzical 5. paradisical, metaphysical, cataphysical, geophysical, psychophysical.

IZ′il–i– 3. busily, dizzily, frizzily.

IZ′ing–li– 3. whizzingly, quizzingly.

IZ′it–iv– 4. acquisitive, inquisitive, disquisitive.

IZ′it–or– 3. visitor 4. acquisitor, requisitor, inquisitor, disquisitor.

O (oh)

1.

SINGLE (MASCULINE) RHYMES IN O (oh)

Primary or Secondary Accent Falls on Last
Syllable; Imperfect Rhymes Are in Italics.

O– 1. o, O, oh, oe, owe, eau, eaux [both F.] 2. K. O. [coll.], kayo [slang] 3. video, rodeo, studio, Indio [Sp.], Tokyo, oleo, folio, cameo, Romeo, Borneo, Scipio, Scorpio, embryo, cheerio, vireo, histrio, nuncio 4. presidio, adagio, religio [L.], punctilio, borachio, Borachio, pistachio, portfolio 5. Montevideo, ex officio, braggadocio, oratorio, impresario.

BO– 1. bo, boh, 'bo, 'boe [both slang], beau 2. jabot, sabot, embow, *rainbow*, *oboe, hobo, crossbow* 3. saddlebow.

DO– 1. do, doe, doh, dough 2. *Dido, rondo,* rondeau, Bordeau 3. Rinaldo, cabildo [Sp.].

FO– 1. foe, Fo, faux [F.] 2. *Sappho, Morpho, bufo, buffo* [It.] 3. comme il faut [F.].

GO– 1. go 2. ago, *Margot,* forego, *sorgo, outgo* 3. touch-and-go, long ago, undergo, indigo, vertigo 5. archipelago.

HO– 1. ho, hoe, Hoh 2. mahoe, heighho, oho, *moho, roho* [Sp.], soho, *Soho,* yo-ho, *brujo* [Sp.] 3. Idaho, Navaho, Westward Ho, tallyho 4. Arapaho.

JO– 1. Jo, Joe, joe [slang] 2. banjo 3. *adagio.*

KO– 1. ko, Ko, Co., Coe, coe [loc. Eng.] 2. *unco* [Scot. & N. of Eng.], *coco, cocoa, moko* 3. medico [coll.], calico, Sinico, haricot, cantico, portico, Mexico, rococo, *albarco* 4. magnifico, energico [It.], angelico, simpatico, patetico [both It.].

LO– 1. lo, low, Lowe, blow, flow, floe, glow, slow, sloe 2. alow, tableau, bibelot, [F.], *flyblow, deathblow, pueblo,* below, hello, *inflow,* ice floe, *outflow,* aglow, *moonglow, sunglow,* pilau, kolo, matelot [F.], rouleau, hullo 3. buffalo, bungalow, counterblow, overflow, alpenglow, counterglow, furbelow, pomelo, gigolo, tremolo.

MO– 1. mo, mho, Moe, mot, mow 2. bon mot, *twelvemo, haymow* 3. alamo, dynamo, chalumeau, Eskimo, centimo, ultimo, proximo 4. dolcissimo [It.], altissimo, fortissimo, prestissimo, bravissimo [It.] 5. pianissimo 6. generalissimo.

NO– 1. no, know, snow 2. tonneau, foreknow, besnow, Gounod 3. domino.

PO– 1. Po, Poe, peau [F.], poh 2. chapeau, drapeau [F.], *depot,* shippo, cachepot [F.] 3. apropos 4. malapropos.

RO– 1. roe, row, Rowe, rho, bro [slang], fro, grow, crow, scrow, pro, trow, strow, throe, throw 2. arow, carreau [F.], *windrow, hedgerow,* ingrow, outgrow, *cockcrow, pilcrow, scarecrow,* escrow, genro, carot, de trop [F.], bestrow, rethrow, downthrow, upthrow, bureau 3. to-and-fro, Pierrot, intergrow, Chatellerault, Rotten Row, overthrow.

SO– 1. so, soh, sow, sew 2. *soso, so-so,* morceau [F.], Rousseau, trousseau, how so 3. curassow, curacao, so-and-so.

SHO– 1. show, shew, sho 2. cachot [F.], *sideshow, style show,* foreshow, *horse show* 3. picture show.

TO– 1. toe, tow, stow 2. bateau, plateau, chateau, molto [It.], manteau, coiteau [F.], couteau [F.], tiptoe, bestow, sexto 3. mistletoe, timber toe [slang], undertow, manito, portmanteau 4. incognito.

THO– 1. though 2. although.

VO– 1. Vaux, voe 3. *centaro* 4. de Marivaux.

WO– 1. woe, whoa, quo 3. quid pro quo [L.], status quo [L.] 4. status in quo [L.], in statu quo [L.].

YO– 1. yo, yo' [dial.] 2. *bagnio*, noyau, *yo-yo* 3. *imbroglio, seraglio, intaglio* 4. *latticinio*.

OB– 1. obe, aube, Job, lobe, globe, robe, probe 2. conglobe, enrobe, unrobe, disrobe.

OCH– 1. coach, loach, poach, roach, broach, brooch, croche 2. encoach, abroach, cockroach, encroach, approach, reproach 3. self-reproach.

OCHT– 1. coached, poached, broached 2. uncoached, unbroached, encroached, approached, reproached.

OD– 1. ode, ohed, owed, bode, goad, hoed, code, lode, load, blowed [slang & dial.], slowed, mode, mowed, node, spode, road, rode, rowed, crowed, strode, sowed, sewed, shoad, shode, towed, toed, toad, stowed, woad, yod 2. unowed, abode, *elbowed*, embowed, unbowed, forebode, unload, explode, commode, unmowed, *epode*, erode, corrode, bestrode, intoed, bestowed 3. overload, a la mode, incommode, discommode, antipode, pigeon-toed, episode, timber-toed [slang].

ODZ– odes etc., see **OD–** ode etc. above, plus "s" or " 's"; 1. Rhodes.

OF– 1. oaf, goaf, koph, loaf, toph 2. *breadloaf, witloof* 3. half a loaf, sugar loaf, monostrophe.

OG– 1. log, rogue, brogue, drogue, drogh, trogue, togue, vogue 2. embogue, col-
logue, pirogue, prorogue 3. disembogue, epilogue, apologue.

OJ– 1. doge, loge 2. gamboge, eloge 3. horologe.

OK– 1. oak, oke [slang], boke [slang], choke, folk, hoke [slang], joke, coak, coke, bloak, bloke [both slang], cloak, sloke, moke, moch, smoke, poke, spoke, broke, croak, stroke, soak, toque, stoke, woke, yoke, yolk 2. *seafolk, kinfolk, townsfolk,* uncloak, besmoke, bespoke, forespoke, forspoke, baroque, *sunstroke*, asoak, evoke, revoke, invoke, convoke, provoke, awoke 3. artichoke, okeydoke [slang], gentlefolk, womenfolk, counterstroke, equivoque.

OKS– oaks etc., see **OK–** oak etc. above, plus "s" or " 's"; 1. hoax, coax.

OKT– 1. choked, joked, coaked, coked, cloaked, smoked, poked, spoked, croaked, stroked, soaked, stoked, yoked 2. uncloaked, besmoked, evoked, revoked, invoked, convoked, provoked 3. counterstroked, double yolked.

OL– 1. ol, ole [dial.], ol', bole, boll, bowl, dhole, dole, foal, goal, hole, whole, jowl [dial.], coal, cole, kohl, skoal, mole, knoll, poll, pole, roll, role, droll, drole [F.], scroll, troll, stroll, soul, sole, shoal, shole, toll, stole, thole, vole 2. *Creole,* embowl, *obole*, condole, segol, *borehole, bunghole, manhole, kilnhole, peephole, pinhole, loophole, porthole,* heart-whole, *tophole,* cajole, bricole, *charcoal, Maypole, tadpole, redpole, flagpole, payroll, logroll,* parole, virole, enroll, unroll, furole, enscroll, inscroll, patrol, control, resole, halfsole, rissole [F.], ensoul, insoul, console, citole, *sestole*, pistole, extoll 3. ariole, dariole, aureole, foliole, apiole, variole, cabriole, oriole, gloriole, capriole, petiole, ostiole, vacuole, amphibole, racambole, carambole, farandole, girandole, pigeonhole, buttonhole, cubbyhole, glory hole, caracole, arvicole, septimole, carmagnole, Seminole, rantipole, metropole, barcarole.

rigmarole, escarole, fumarole, fusarole, squatarole, azarole, banderole, casserole, self-control, girasole, camisole 4. bibliopole, remote control.

OLD– 1. old, bold, bowled, bolled, fold, foaled, gold, hold, cold, coaled, scold, skoaled, mold, mould, polled, rolled, sold, soled, shoaled, told, tolled, stoled, wold 2. *blindfold*, *twofold*, *threefold* etc., *bifold*, enfold, infold, unfold, *sheepfold*, spun gold, behold, *freehold*, *stronghold*, uphold, *leasehold*, *household*, *threshold*, *foothold*, withhold, cajoled, remold, *leafmold*, paroled, controlled, half-soled, unsold, retold, untold, foretold, twice-told 3. overbold, hundredfold, thousandfold, manifold, multifold, interfold, marigold, copyhold, pigeonholed, pudding mold, bullet mold, Leopold, uncontrolled, self-controlled, undersold, oversold, sable-stoled.

OLK– 1. polk, Polk, yolk, Volk.

OLT– 1. bolt, dolt, holt, jolt, colt, molt, smolt, poult, volt 2. rebolt, eyebolt, kingbolt, wringbolt, unbolt, lavolt, revolt 3. shackle bolt, thunderbolt, millivolt, demivolt.

OLZ– Ol's, bowls etc., *see* **OL–** ol etc. above, plus "s" or "'s."

OM– 1. ohm, oam, dom, dome, foam, home, holm, haulm, heaume, comb, loam, gloam, glome, mome, Nome, gnome, pome, roam, rom, Rome, drome, chrome, tome 2. endome, afoam, befoam, megohm, *coxcomb*, aplomb, Jerome 3. semidome, catacomb, honeycomb, currycomb, evenglome, metronome, gastronome, palindrome, hippodrome, aerodrome, Ethan Frome, polychrome, monochrome, microsome, chromosome.

OMZ– ohms etc., *see* **OM–** ohm etc. above, plus "s" or "'s"; 1. Holmes, Soames.

ON– 1. own, bone, Beaune, phone, hone, Joan, cone, scone, lone, loan, blown, flown, mown, moan, known, None, pone, roan, Rhone, drone, groan, grown, crone, prone, throne, thrown, sewn, sown, shown, shone, tone, stone, zone 2. disown, *aitchbone*, *backbone*, *whalebone*, *trombone*, *jawbone*, *icebone*, *fishbone*, *wishbone*, *breastbone*, condone, alone, cologne, Cologne, full-blown, unblown, highflown, unflown, bemoan, *hormone*, unknown, foreknown, depone, repone, *corn pone*, propone, dispone, postpone, ladrone, begroan, half-grown, full-grown, ungrown, bestrown, dethrone, unthrown, unsewn, unsown, unshown, foreshown, atone, intone, fronton [Sp.], *curbstone*, *headstone*, *sandstone*, *end stone*, *grindstone*, *lodestone*, *bloodstone*, *keystone*, *freestone*, *flagstone*, *clingstone*, *hailstone*, *millstone*, *milestone*, *tilestone*, *limestone*, *brimstone*, *tombstone*, *rhinestone*, *moonstone*, *soapstone*, *whetstone*, *hearthstone*, enzone, *ozone* 3. anklebone, knucklebone, cuttlebone, megaphone, vitaphone, dictaphone, telephone, graphophone, gramophone, xylophone, microphone, saxophone, unbeknown, unforeknown, interpone, chaperone, cicerone, overgrown, semitone, baritone, monotone, undertone, overtone, cornerstone, overthrown 4. radiophone, electrophone, Eau-de-Cologne.

OND– 1. owned, boned, phoned, honed, coned, loaned, moaned, monde, droned, groaned, throned, toned, zoned 2. disowned, fine-boned, bemoaned, beau monde, haut monde [F.], postponed, dethroned, atoned, high-toned, intoned, flagstoned, enzoned, unzoned 3. telephoned, demimonde, chaperoned.

ONT– 1. don't, conte, won't.

ONZ– owns etc., *see* **ON–** own etc. above, plus "s" or "'s"; 1. Jones, nones, Nones 3. lazybones, Davy Jones.

OO–, *see* under **OO** (good) following short O (awe).

OP– 1. ope [dial. or poetic], dope, hope, cope, scope, lope, slope, mope, nope [slang or loc.], pope, rope, grope, trope, soap, tope, taupe, stope 2. elope, aslope, agrope, dragrope, towrope, soft-soap 3. telescope, periscope, seismoscope, gyroscope, microscope, horoscope, spectroscope, stethoscope, cantaloupe, antelope, envelope, interlope, protopope, philanthrope, misanthrope, isotope 4. stereoscope, kaleidoscope, dipleidoscope, polemoscope, heliotrope.

OPS– opes etc., *see* **Op–** ope etc. above, plus "s" or "'s"; 1. Stopes.

OPT– 1. oped [poetic], doped, hoped, coped, loped, sloped, moped, roped, groped, soaped 2. eloped 3. *enveloped.*

OR– through **ORZ–**, *see* also short **O** (awe): **OR–** through **ORZ–**.

OR– 1. ore, oar, o'er, bore, boar, Boer, chore, door, fore, four, gore, hoar, core, corps, score, lore, floor, more, mohr, snore, pour, pore, spore, roar, soar, sore, shore, tore, store, wore, swore, yore 2. forebore, adore, Indore, indoor, outdoor, before, therefore, wherefore, Johore, décor [F.], encore, threescore, fourscore etc., galore [coll.], *folklore, booklore,* deplore, implore, explore, ignore, *downpour,* outpour, *uproar, eyesore, heartsore, footsore,* ashore, *seashore,* inshore, foreshore, restore, *drugstore,* forswore 3. troubadour, picador, matador, Isadore, stevedore, Polydore, open door, battledore, Theodore, commodore, two-by-four, semaphore, pinafore, heretofore, albacore, terpsichore, underscore, Sagamore, sycamore, paramour, Barrymore, Baltimore, sophomore, furthermore, evermore, nevermore, Singapore, carnivore 4. hereinbefore.

ORCH– 1. scorch, porch, torch 2. front porch.

ORD– 1. oared, bored, board, doored, ford, gored, gourd, hoard, hoared, horde, cored, scored, floored, snored, poured, pored, toward, stored, sword 2. aboard, *clapboard, cupboard, switchboard, headboard, breadboard, sideboard, cardboard,*

seaboard, surfboard, springboard, blackboard, buckboard, wallboard, inboard, clapboard, outboard, adored, *two-doored, four-doored,* afford, ungored, encored, uncored, deplored, implored, explored, restored 3. shuffleboard, beaverboard, overboard, ironing board, open-doored, unexplored, unrestored.

ORJ– 1. forge, gorge, porge 2. engorge, disgorge.

ORK– 1. pork 2. *morepork,* salt pork.

ORN– 1. borne, bourn, Doorn, scorn, mourn, morn, shorn, worn, sworn 2. forborne, bemourn, unshorn, betorn, *toilworn,* outworn, unsworn, forsworn 3. unforsworn.

ORND– 1. scorned, mourned 2. unscorned, bemourned, unmourned.

ORS– 1. force, hoarse, coarse, course, source 2. enforce, inforce, perforce, recourse, discourse, resource, divorce 3. reinforce, intercourse, watercourse.

ORT– 1. fort, forte, court, mort, port, sport 2. aport, apport, rapport, deport, report, *seaport,* import, comport, *airport, carport,* purport, *passport,* disport, export, transport, support, resort 3. sally port, davenport, nonsupport 4. pianoforte.

ORTH– 1. forth, fourth 2. henceforth, thenceforth.

ORZ– oars etc., *see* **OR–** oar etc. above, plus "s" or "'s"; 2. indoors, outdoors, all fours, plus fours, Azores.

OS– 1. boce, dose, kos, close, gross, soce 2. globose, verbose, nodose, jocose, engross, morose 3. overdose, grandiose, otiose, bellicose, annulose, diagnose, adipose, comatose.

OSH– 1. Boche, cloche, sosh [slang].

OST– 1. oast, boast, dosed, ghost, host, coast, most, post, roast, grossed, toast 2. *seacoast, headmost, endmost, hindmost,* almost, *inmost, topmost, upmost, foremost, utmost,* reposte, *milepost, signpost, outpost,* engrossed 3. bottommost, easternmost, northernmost, hindermost, undermost, innermost, lowermost, uppermost, centermost, outermost, uttermost, nethermost, hithermost, furthermost, diagnosed, whipping post, hitching post, letter post.

OT– **1.** oat, boat, dote, goat, coat, cote, côte [F.], scote, bloat, float, gloat, moat, mote, smote, note, rote, wrote, groat, throat, shoat, shote, tote [coll. & slang], stoat, vote, quote **2.** *lifeboat, sailboat, showboat, houseboat, scapegoat, redcoat, turncoat, topcoat, waistcoat,* afloat, refloat, emote, demote, remote, promote, denote, *keynote,* connote, *gracenote, footnote,* capote, garrote, rewrote, *starthroat, whitethroat, cutthroat,* aptote, diptote, triptote, devote, outvote, bequote, misquote **3.** ferryboat, river boat, antidote, anecdote, table d'hote, billy goat, nanny goat, mountain goat, redingote, petticoat, overcoat, underwrote, creosote, asymptote.

OTH– **1.** oath, both, loath, sloth, wroth, growth, troth, Thoth, quoth **2.** *outgrowth,* betroth **3.** behemoth, aftergrowth, overgrowth, undergrowth.

OTH– **1.** loathe, clothe **2.** reclothe, unclothe, betroth.

OTHZ– **1.** loathes, clothes **2.** reclothes, bedclothes, betroths **3.** underclothes.

OTS– oats etc., *see* **OT–** oat etc. above, plus "s" or "'s"; **1.** Oates, Coates.

OV– **1.** dove, hove, Jove, cove, loave, clove, mauve, rove, drove, grove, Shrove, trove, strove, throve, tove [Scot.], stove, wove **2.** behove, gemauve, *mangrove,* rewove, inwove **3.** perijove, apojove, treasure-trove, interwove.

OVZ– **1.** Jove's, loaves, cloves, mauves, roves, droves, groves, troves, toves [Scot.], stoves.

OZ– **1.** owes, bows, beaux, chose, doze, does, foes, goes, hose, glows, close, clothes, Mose, nose, knows, snows, pose, spose [slang], rows, rose, brose, froze, croze, prose, pros, sows, sews, toes, tows, toze, those **2.** *rainbows, bulldoze,* enclose, unclose, foreclose, disclose, depose, repose, impose, compose, oppose, propose, dispose, expose, transpose, suppose, arose, *tuberose, tea rose, wild rose, dog rose, rockrose, primrose, moss rose,* unfroze, *tiptoes* **3.** dominoes, decompose, recompose, discompose, superpose, interpose, predispose, indispose, presuppose, damask rose, bramble rose, Irish rose, pettitoes.

OZD– **1.** dozed, hosed, closed, nosed, posed, prosed **2.** *bulldozed,* enclosed, unclosed, foreclosed, disclosed, deposed, reposed, imposed, composed, opposed, proposed, disposed, exposed, transposed, supposed **3.** decomposed, discomposed, interposed, predisposed, well-disposed, ill-disposed, indisposed, presupposed.

OZH– **1.** loge **2.** gamboge, éloge.

O (oh)

2.

DOUBLE (FEMININE) RHYMES IN O (bo'a)

Primary or Secondary Accent Falls on Next to Last
Syllable; Imperfect Rhymes Are in Italics.

O'a– **2.** boa, koa, loa, moa, Noah, noa, proa, Shoa **3.** Gilboa, jerboa, aloha, Samoa, anoa, leipoa **4.** Kanaloa, Metazoa, Anthozoa, microzoa, Hydrozoa, Sporozoa, entozoa, Protozoa.

O'ab– **2.** doab, Joab, Moab.

O'al– **3.** bestowal, restowal.

O'an– **2.** cowan, rowan **3.** eoan, Samoan, Minoan.

OB'a– **2.** koba **3.** cohoba, arroba **4.** algarroba, bona roba [arch.], Manitoba.

OB'al– **2.** lobal, global, probal **3.** microbal, Cristobal.

OB'at– **2.** lobate, globate, probate.

OB'er– **2.** rober, robur, prober, sober **3.** amobyr, enrober, disrober, October.

OB'i– **2.** obi, dobe, Gobi, goby, Kobe, globy, toby [slang], Toby **3.** adobe.

OB'ik– **2.** phobic, strobic **3.** niobic, microbic **4.** phobophobic, hydrophobic, claustrophobic, photophobic.

OB'il– **2.** mobile **3.** immobile **4.** locomobile, automobile.

OB'ing– **2.** globing, robing, probing **3.** englobing, enrobing, unrobing, disrobing.

OB'it– **2.** obit, Tobit **3.** post-obit.

OB'l– **2.** coble, noble **3.** ennoble, ignoble, unnoble.

OB'o– **2.** oboe, bobo, hobo, lobo, zobo.

OB'ra– **2.** dobra, cobra.

OB'ul– **2.** lobule, globule.

OB'us– **2.** obus, Kobus, lobus [NL.], globus, globous **3.** jacobus.

OCH'er– **2.** poacher, broacher **3.** encroacher, approacher, reproacher.

OCH'ez– **2.** coaches, loaches, poaches, roaches, broaches, brooches **3.** encoaches cockroaches, encroaches, approaches, reproaches **4.** self reproaches.

OCH'ful– **3.** reproachful **4.** unreproachful, self-reproachful.

OCH'ing– **2.** coaching, poaching, broaching **3.** encoaching, encroaching, approaching, reproaching.

OCH'ment– **3.** encroachment, approachment.

OD'a– **2.** oda, coda, Rhoda, soda, Toda **3.** pagoda, salsoda **4.** baking soda, icecream soda, Scotch and soda **5.** Chinese pagoda, whisky and soda.

OD'al– **2.** odal, modal, nodal, yodel **3.** trinodal **4.** internodal.

OD'ed– **2.** boded, goaded, coded, loaded, noded, woaded **3.** foreboded, decoded, unloaded, exploded, outmoded, corroded **4.** overloaded, incommoded, discommoded, uncorroded.

OD'el– **2.** yodel, yodle.

OD'en– **2.** Odin, boden, Woden.

OD'ent– **2.** rodent **3.** explodent, erodent, corrodent.

187

OD'er– 2. Oder, odor, boder, goader, loader, roader, woader 3. foreboder, malodor, reloader, unloader, exploder, corroder.

OD'i– 2. Godey, Cody, toady, tody, woady.

OD'ik– 2. odic 4. palinodic.

OD'ing– 2. boding, goading, coding, loading 3. foreboding, decoding, unloading, exploding, outmoding, eroding, corroding 4. overloading, discommoding.

OD'ist– 2. odist, codist, modist 4. palinodist.

OD'ler– 2. yodler, yodeler.

OD'o– 2. dodo, Jodo 3. quomodo [L.] 4. Quasimodo.

OD'ster– 2. goadster, lodestar, roadster.

OD'us– 2. modus [L.], nodus, nodous.

O'e– 2. Chloë, poe, poi, Zoe 3. evoe; *see* also O'i– bowie etc. below.

O'ed– 2. co-ed.

O'el– 2. Joel, koel, Lowell, Noel, nowel, Crowell.

O'em– 2. phloem, poem, proem 4. mythopoem, Jeroboam [slang, Eng.].

O'en– 2. Owen, Cohen, rowan.

O'er– 2. o'er, ower, Boer, goer, hoer, lower, blower, glower, slower, mower, knower, rower, grower, crower, sewer, sower, shower, tower, stower 3. foregoer, outgoer, foreknower, cockcrower, foreshower, bestower 4. overthrower.

O'erd– 2. lowered, froward, toward 3. untoward.

O'est– 2. lowest, slowest.

O'et– 2. poet.

OF'a– 2. sofa.

OF'er– 2. Ophir, gopher, gaufre, loafer, chauffeur.

OF'et– 2. tophet.

OF'i– 2. trophy, strophe, Sophie.

OG'a– 2. snoga, toga, yoga 3. Tioga, noyoga 4. Saratoga, Conestoga 5. Ticonderoga.

OG'an– 2. hogan, logan, slogan, rogan, brogan.

OG'er– 2. ogre, drogher.

OG'i– 2. bogy, bogie, dogie, fogy, fogey, logy, pogy, stogy, stogie, voguey, yogi 3. old-fogy, old-fogey 6. cedant arma togae [L.].

OG'ish– 2. roguish, voguish.

OG'l– 2. ogle, bogle, fogle, Vogel [G.], Vogul 3. aasvogel [D.].

OG'o– 2. gogo, mogo, Pogo, zogo.

OG'us– 2. bogus.

O'ha– 2. poha 3. aloha [Hawaian], aloja [Sp.].

O'he– 3. evohe!

O'ho– 2. coho, moho, mojo, Mojo, Moxo, rojo [Sp.], Soho 3. corojo.

O'i– 2. bowie, Bowie, doughy, Joey, blowy, glowy, Chloë, snowy, poe, poi, roi, rowy, showy, towy, Zoë 3. evoe!

O'ij– 2. flowage, towage, stowage.

O'ik– 2. Troic, Stoic, stoic, zoic 3. echoic, diploic, heroic, dichroic, azoic, benzoic 4. authochroic, epizoic, Eozoic, Neozoic, hylozoic, protozoic 5. Archaeozoic, Paleozoic.

O'iks– 2. Coix, stoics 3. heroics.

O'ing– 2. owing, bowing, Boeing, going, hoeing, lowing, glowing, slowing, mowing, knowing, snowing, rowing, growing, crowing, throwing, sowing, sewing, showing, towing, toeing, stowing 3. elbowing, seagoing, ingoing, foregoing, outgoing, helloing, inflowing, outflowing, foreknowing, unknowing, ingrowing, outgrowing, cockcrowing, foreshowing, tiptoeing 4. easygoing, thoroughgoing, undergoing, overthrowing.

OJ'an– 2. Trojan, yojan.

OJ'e– 2. shoji 3. agoge 4. anagoge, apapoge, epagoge, paragoge, isogoge.

OJ'ent– 2. cogent 3. incogent, uncogent.

OJ'urn– 2. sojourn.

OK'a– 2. oka, oca [Sp.], boca [Sp.], choca, phoca, coca, loka, loca, sloka, mocha, polka, trocha [Sp.], stocah 3. jocoque 4. tapioca, curiboca.

OK'al– 2. bocal, focal, phocal, local, trochal, socle, vocal, yokel 3. bifocal, collocal, bivocal 4. hyperfocal, patri-local, multivocal, equivocal.

OK'e– 2. Loki, loci, moki, troche, trochee 3. jocoqui, ditrochee; see also OK'i– oaky etc. below.

OK'en– 2. oaken, spoken, broken, soken, token 3. bespoken, freespoken, un-spoken, well-spoken, plain-spoken, soft-spoken, short-spoken, outspoken, smooth-spoken, true-spoken, unbroken, *heart-broken*, betoken, foretoken.

OK'er– 2. ochre, choker, joker, coker, cloaker, smoker, poker, roker, spoker, broker, croaker, stroker, soaker, stoker, yoker 3. *stockbroker, pawnbroker*, evok-er, revoker, invoker, convoker, provoker 4. mediocre.

OK'et– 2. oket, poke it.

OK'i– 2. oaky, choky, hokey, jokey, coky, Loki, loci, moki, smoky, poky, roky, croaky, troche, trochee, soaky, yoky, yolky 3. jocoqui, ditrochee 4. okey-dokey [slang], hokeypokey [coll.].

OK'ij– 2. chokage, cloakage, rokeage [loc.], brokage, soakage.

OK'ing– 2. choking, joking, coking, cloak-ing, smoking, poking, spoking, croaking, troching, stroking, soaking, stoking, yok-ing 3. uncloaking, evoking, revoking, invoking, provoking, unyoking.

OK'l– 2. yokel 4. okel-dokel [slang]; see also OK'al– bocal etc. above.

OK'less– ?. oakless, jokeless, cokeless, blokeless [slang], cloakless, smokeless, pokeless, spokeless, croakless, yokeless, yolkless.

OK'ment– 3. revokement, invokement, provokement.

OK'o– 2. choco, coco, cocoa, koko, Ko-Ko, loco, moko, poco [It.], poco [slang], troco, soco, toco 3. rococo, al loco [It.] 4. locofoco, moko-moko, Orinoco.

OKS'er– 2. hoaxer, coaxer.

OKS'ing– 2. hoaxing, coaxing.

OK'um– 2. oakum, hokum.

OK'us– 2. focus, hocus, locus, crocus 4. hocus-pocus.

OK'ust– 2. focussed, hocussed, locust 3. unfocussed, sweet locust.

OL'a– 2. ola, bola, bowla, gola, kola, schola, Lola, mola, Mola, Nola, sola, stola, vola [L.], Zola 3. crayola, Viola, man-dola, Angola, pimola, victrola 4. caram-bola, Pensacola, pianola, Gorgonzola 5. Savonarola.

OL'an– 2. O-lan, Dolan, Nolan, tolan; see also OL'en– solen etc. and OL'on– colon etc. below.

OL'ar– 2. bolar, molar, polar, solar, volar 4. unipolar, circumpolar, lunisolar, cir-cumsolar; see also OL'er– Olor etc. below.

OLD'ed– 2. folded, scolded, molded 3. blindfolded, enfolded, unfolded 4. mani-folded.

OLD'en– 2. olden, holden, golden 3. embolden, beholden 4. misbeholden.

OLD'er– 2. older, bolder, boulder, folder, holder, colder, scolder, molder, smolder, polder, shoulder 3. enfolder, unfolder, beholder, freeholder, landholder, up-holder, shareholder, leaseholder, house-holder, withholder, slaveholder, cold-shoulder 4. manifolder, copyholder, can-dleholder, bottleholder.

OLD'erd– 2. bouldered, shouldered 3. broad-shouldered, round-shouldered, stoop-shouldered, square-shouldered 4. narrow-shouldered.

OLD'est– 2. oldest, boldest, coldest.

OLD′i– **2.** oldy, foldy, moldy, mouldy **3.** unmoldy.

OLD′ing– **2.** folding, holding, molding, scolding **3.** enfolding, landholding, beholding, upholding, withholding, slaveholding, non-molding, unmolding **4.** interfolding, overfolding.

OLD′ish– **2.** oldish, boldish, coldish.

OLD′li– **2.** oldly, boldly, coldly **4.** manifoldly.

OLD′ment– **3.** enfoldment, infoldment, withholdment.

OLD′ness– **2.** oldness, boldness, coldness.

OL′en– **2.** solen, stolen, Stollen, swollen; *see* also **OL′an**– O-lan etc. above and **OL′on**– colon etc. below.

OL′ent– **2.** olent, dolent, volant **3.** condolent.

OL′er– **2.** Olor, bowler, bolar, dolor, coaler, koller, molar, knoller, poler, polar, poller, roller, droller, scroller, troller, stroller, soler, solar, shoaler, toller, volar **3.** condoler, cajoler, enroller, patroller, controller, comptroller, consoler, extoller **4.** piegonholer, unipolar, circumpolar, Holy Roller, lunisolar.

OL′est– **2.** drollest.

OL′ful– **2.** bowlful, doleful, soulful.

OL′i– **2.** bowly, bolly, foaly, holy, wholly, coaly, lowly, slowly, moly, knolly, rolly, drolly, scrolly, soli, solely, sholy [dial.], shoaly **3.** unholy, anole, pinole, posole **4.** roly-poly, caracoli.

OL′ing– **2.** bolling, bowling, doling, foaling, goaling, holing, coaling, poling, polling, rolling, drolling, trolling, strolling, tolling **3.** condoling, cajoling, controlling, paroling, enrolling, unrolling, patrolling, half-soling, consoling, extolling **4.** caracoling.

OL′ish– **2.** Polish, drollish, soulish.

OL′jer– **2.** soldier.

OL′ment– **3.** condolement, cajolement, enrollment, controlment.

OL′ness– **2.** wholeness, drollness, soleness.

OL′o– **2.** bolo, Bolo, Cholo, Golo, Lolo, polo, solo, stolo [L.] **3.** barolo **4.** bolobolo.

OL′on– **2.** colon, Solon, stolon **3.** eidolon **4.** semicolon; *see* also **OL′an**– O-lan etc. and **OL′en**– solen etc. above.

OL′or– **2.** Olor, dolor; *see* also **OL′er**– Olor, bowler etc. above.

OL′som– **2.** dolesome, wholesome **3.** unwholesome.

OLST′er– **2.** bolster, holster **3.** upholster.

OLT′ed– **2.** bolted, jolted, molted **3.** unbolted, revolted.

OLT′en– **2.** molten **3.** unmolten.

OLT′er– **2.** bolter, colter, jolter, molter **3.** unbolter, revolter.

OLT′ij– **2.** boltage, voltage.

OLT′ing– **2.** bolting, jolting, molting **3.** unbolting, revolting.

OLT′ish– **2.** doltish, coltish.

OL′um– **2.** solum [L.] **3.** idolum.

OL′us– **2.** bolus, dolose, dolous, dolus [L.], solus [L.] **4.** holus-bolus, gladiolus.

OM′a– **2.** coma, loma, noma, Roma, stroma, soma, stoma **3.** aboma, zygoma, aloma, Tacoma, diploma, aroma, prosoma, phytoma, rhizoma.

OM′ad– **2.** nomad.

OM′al– **2.** domal, bromal, somal, stromal.

OM′an– **2.** bowman, foeman, gnomon, Roman, showman, yeoman.

OM′en– **2.** omen, nomen [L.], gnomon, yeomen **3.** abdomen, praenomen, agnomen, cognomen.

OM′end– **2.** omened **3.** ill omened, badomened **4.** happy-omened.

OM′ent– **2.** foment, loment, moment **3.** bestowment, last moment.

OM′er– 2. omer, gomer, Gomer, homer, Homer, comber, roamer, vomer 3. *beachcomber, wool comber*, misnomer.

OM′i– 2. domy, foamy, homy, homey [both coll.], Kome, Komi, loamy 3. Naomi 4. lomi-lomi.

OM′ij– 2. ohmage, homage.

OM′ik– 2. ohmic, domic, gnomic, bromic, chromic 3. achromic, dichromic 4. hydrobromic, polychromic.

OM′ing– 2. doming, foaming, homing, coaming, combing, gloaming, roaming 3. befoaming, Wyoming, *beachcombing, wool-combing*.

OM′is– 3. Nokomis, exomis.

OM′ish– 2. domish, foamish, gnomish, Romish, tomish.

OM′less– 2. domeless, foamless, homeless, combless, loamless, gnomeless.

OM′o– 2. homo, Como, momo, chromo, duomo [It.] 3. Pokomo 4. major-domo.

OM′us– 2. domus [L.], Comus, Momus, chromous 3. prodromus, disomus 4. Major Domus.

ON′a– 2. ona, bona [L.], Bona, Dona, Gona, kona, Jonah, Mona, drona, krona, trona, zona [L.] 3. annona, Annona, ancona, Ancona, cinchona, Bellona, Bologna, Ramona, Cremona, kimono 4. Barcelona, Desdemona, Toromona, Arizona.

ON′ad– 2. monad.

ON′al– 2. phonal, chronal, thronal, tonal, zonal 3. coronal, atonal, azonal 4. polytonal, polyzonal, interzonal.

ON′ant– 2. sonant, tonant 4. supersonant, intersonant; *see* also ON′ent– opponent etc. below.

ON′at– 2. donate, phonate, pronate, zonate.

ON′e– 3. euphone, Dione, Shoshone 4. abalone, macaroni, lazzaroni, cicerone.

ON′ent– 3. opponent, deponent, component, proponent, disponent, exponent 4. interponent; *see* also ON′ant– sonant etc. above.

ON′er– 2. owner, boner, donor, phoner, loaner, moaner, droner, toner, stoner 3. condoner, bemoaner, postponer, atoner, entoner, intoner.

O′ness– 2. lowness, slowness.

ON′i– 2. bony, phony [slang], cony, pony, drony, crony, tony [vulgar], stony 3. bologna, Dione, polony, Shoshone 4. chalcedony, abalone, ceremony, alimony, agrimony, acrimony, matrimony, patrimony, parsimony, sanctimony, antimony, testimony, macaroni, lazzaroni, cicerone.

ON′ij– 2. dronage 4. chaperonage.

ON′ing– 2. owning, boning, phoning, honing, loaning, moaning, droning, groaning, throning, toning, stoning, zoning 3. disowning, condoning, bemoaning, postponing, dethroning, unthroning, atoning, intoning, enzoning 4. telephoning, chaperoning.

ON′is– 3. Adonis, Coronis.

ON′less– 2. boneless, phoneless, loanless, moanless, groanless, throneless, toneless, stoneless, zoneless 4. telephoneless, chaperoneless.

ON′li– 2. only, lonely 3. alonely, unlonely 4. one and only.

ON′ment– 3. disownment, condonement, postponement, dethronement, enthronement, atonement, intonement.

ON′ness– 2. ownness, loneness, proneness 3. unknownness.

ON′o– 2. fono, Nono 3. kimono 4. Johnny Bono.

ON′som– 2. lonesome.

ON′um– 2. bonum [L.].

ON′us– 2. onus, bonus, conus, Cronus, tonus 3. colonus.

OO′– *see* under OO (good) following short O (awe).

O′on– 2. zoon 3. polyzoon, epizoon.

OP′a– 2. opah, chopa, copa, scopa 3. Europa.

OP′al– 2. opal, copal, nopal 3. sinople 4. periople 5. Adrianↄple, Constantinople.

OP′er– 2. doper, hoper, coper, loper, sloper, moper, roper, groper, soaper, toper, stoper 3. eloper, soft-soaper 4. interloper.

OP′i– 2. dopey, Hopi, slopy, mopy, ropy, soapy.

OP′ing– 2. doping, hoping, coping, loping, sloping, moping, roping, groping, soaping, toping, stoping 3. eloping, soft-soaping 4. interloping.

OP′l– 3. sinople 4. periople 5. Adrianople, Constantinople.

OP′less– 2. hopeless, popeless, soapless.

OP′ment– 3. elopement.

OP′us– 2. opus, Propus 3. lagopous, Lagopus, Canopus, pyropus.

OR′a– through **OR′us,** *see* also short **O** (awe): **OR′a** through **OR′ward.**

OR′a– 2. ora, Ora, bora, Dora, goura, hora, Cora, kora, Korah, Lora, flora, Flora, Nora, torah, Torah 3. Eldora, Pandora, rhodora, angora, señora [Sp.], signora [It.], aurora, Masora, totora 4. Floradora, Theodora, passiflora, Passiflora.

OR′aks– 2. borax, Dorax, storax, thorax.

OR′al– 2. oral, horal, choral, loral, floral, chloral, poral, roral, thoral 3. trifloral, auroral, sororal.

OR′an– 2. Koran, toran 3. Sonoran.

OR′at– 2. orate, borate, florate, chlorate, prorate 3. deflorate, biflorate.

OR′ay– 2. foray, moire 3. signore [It.] 6. improvvisatore [It.].

ORD′ed– 2. boarded, forded, hoarded, sworded 3. afforded, unhoarded.

ORD′er– 2. boarder, forder, hoarder.

ORD′ing– 2. boarding, fording, hoarding 3. affording, unhoarding 4. beaverboarding.

OR′er– 2. borer, gorer, corer, scorer, floorer, snorer, porer, pourer, roarer, sorer, soarer, storer 3. adorer, encorer, deplorer, implorer, explorer, ignorer, outpourer, restorer.

OR′ez– 2. mores 3. Cursores, Raptores 4. Grallatores.

OR′i– 2. oary, ory, dory, gory, hoary, kori, Kore, lory, flory, glory, more, snory, pory, shory, Tory, story 3. Old Glory, vainglory, maggiore [It.], pilori, signore [It.] 4. hunky-dory [coll.], allegory, category, tautegory, amphigory, counterflory, probatory, piscatory, gradatory, predatory, mandatory, mundatory, laudatory, feudatory, sudatory, prefatory, negatory, rogatory, purgatory, nugatory, oblatory, grallatory, parlatory, amatory, crematory, fumatory, chrismatory, sanatory, signatory, crinatory, donatory, phonatory, culpatory, vibratory, migratory, oratory, curatory, juratory, gyratory, pulsatory, natatory, dictatory, citatory, saltatory, potatory, rotatory, hortatory, gestatory, gustatory, mutatory, lavatory, salvatory, deletory, suppletory, expletory, decretory, excretory, feretory, bibitory, auditory, plauditory, pellitory, olitory, dormitory, fumitory, crinitory, monitory, punitory, territory, transitory, petitory, desultory, inventory, promontory, offertory, repertory, statutory 5. phantasmagory, approbatory, reverbatory, applicatory, explicatory, vesicatory, masticatory, advocatory, revocatory, invocatory, confiscatory, episcatory, manducatory, depredatory, commandatory, amendatory, emendatory, commendatory, transudatory, obligatory, fumigatory, derogatory, objurgatory, expurgatory, depreciatory, gladiatory, radiatory, mediatory, palliatory, expiatory, revelatory, habilatory, depilatory, flagellatory, constellatory, distillatory, condolatory, consolatory, ambulatory, speculatory, circulatory, osculatory, adulatory, stridulatory, undulatory, regulatory, emulatory, simulatory, postulatory, defamatory, acclamatory, declamatory, proclamatory, exclamatory, desquamatory, sublimatory, inflammatory, affirmatory, confirmatory, reformatory, informatory, lachrymatory, explanatory, designatory, criminatory, fulminatory, comminatory, terminatory, divinatory, condemnatory, cachinnatory, inculpatory, declaratory, preparatory, lucubratory, consecratory, execratory, emigratory, immigratory, transmigratory, aspiratory, transpiratory, inspiratory, perspiratory, expiratory, laboratory, exploratory, demonstratory, remonstratory, procuratory, abjuratory, adjuratory, compulsatory, compensatory, dispensatory, accusatory, excusatory, excitatory, invitatory, auscultatory, consultatory, sussultatory, incantatory, dehortatory, exhortatory, refutatory, salutatory, observatory, preservatory, conservatory, Il Trovatore, inhibitory, prohibitory, exhibitory, recognitory, admonitory, premonitory, depository, repository, suppository, expository, competitory, retributory, contributory, executory, involutory 6. disapprobatory, significatory, purificatory, certificatory, communicatory, reciprocatory, equivocatory, elucidatory, recommendatory, delineatory, investigatory, interrogatory, enunciatory, denunciatory, pronunciatory, retaliatory, conciliatory, initiatory, propitiatory, negotiatory, alleviatory, abbreviatory, preambulatory, funambulatory, perambulatory, ejaculatory, articulatory, gesticulatory, emasculatory, manipulatory, congratulatory, expostulatory, recriminatory, incriminatory, discriminatory, exterminatory, procrastinatory, anticipatory, emancipatory, reverberatory, exaggeratory, refrigeratory, acceleratory, remuneratory, corroboratory, circumgyratory, improvisatory, circumrotatory,

extenuatory, circumlocutory, interlocutory, improvvisatore [It.] 7. supererogatory, reconciliatory.

OR'ij– 2. oarage, shorage, storage.

OR'ik– 2. boric, choric, chloric, roric, psoric 3. perchloric 4. hydrochloric.

OR'ing– 2. oaring, boring, choring, goring, coring, scoring, snoring, poring, roaring, soaring, shoring, storing 3. adoring, encoring, deploring, imploring, exploring, ignoring, outpouring, restoring.

OR'is– 2. Boris, Doris, loris 3. cantoris.

OR'ist– 2. chorist, florist.

ORJ'er– 2. forger, gorger 3. disgorger.

ORJ'ing– 2. forging, gorging 3. engorging, disgorging.

ORJ'ment– 3. engorgement, disgorgement.

OR'less– 2. oarless, oreless, boreless, doorless, goreless, whoreless, coreless, scoreless, loreless, poreless, pourless, sporeless, roarless, soreless, shoreless.

OR'ment– 3. adorement, deplorement, implorement, explorement, ignorement, restorement.

ORN'ful– 2. scornful, mournful.

ORN'ing– 2. scorning, mourning, morning 3. a-borning, unscorning, deep mourning.

OR'o– 2. oro [Sp.], Oro, boro, Boro, loro, Moro, Poro, toro 4. aposoro, torotoro.

OR'on– 2. boron, moron.

ORS'er– 2. forcer, hoarser, coarser, courser 3. enforcer, discourser, divorcer.

ORS'est– 2. hoarsest, coarsest.

ORS'ful– 2. forceful 3. resourceful 4. unresourceful.

ORSH'un– 2. portion 2. apportion, proportion 4. disproportion; *see* also ORSH'un– torsion etc.

ORSH'und– 2. portioned 3. apportioned, unportioned, proportioned 4. reapportioned, unproportioned, disproportioned.

ORS'ing— 2. forcing, coursing 3. enforcing, discoursing, divorcing 4. reinforcing.

ORS'iv— 3. enforcive, discoursive, divorcive.

ORS'less— 2. forceless, sourceless 3. discourseless, resourceless, divorceless.

ORS'li— 2. hoarsely, coarsely.

ORS'ment— 2. forcement 3. deforcement, enforcement, divorcement 4. reinforcement.

ORS'ness— 2. hoarseness, coarseness.

ORS'o— 2. dorso [ML.], corso [It.], Corso, torso.

ORT'a— 2. forte.

ORT'al— 2. portal 3. transportal.

ORT'ans— 3. comportance, transportance, supportance.

ORT'ed— 2. courted, ported, sported 3. deported, reported, imported, disported, exported, transported, supported.

ORT'ent— 2. portent.

ORT'er— 2. courter, porter, sporter 3. reporter, importer, exporter, transporter, supporter.

ORT'i— 2. forty, porty, sporty.

ORT'ing— 2. courting, sporting, Storting 3. deporting, reporting, importing, exporting, transporting, supporting.

ORT'iv— 2. sportive 3. disportive, transportive.

ORT'li— 2. courtly, portly 3. uncourtly, unportly.

ORT'ment— 3. deportment, comportment, disportment, transportment.

OR'um— 2. forum, jorum [coll.], quorum 3. decorum 4. indecorum, variorum, cockalorum, pittosporum 5. schola cantorum [L.].

OR'us— 2. Horus, chorus, porus, porous, sorous, torus, torose, torous 3. decorous, pelorus, pylorus, canorous, sonorous, imporous 4. indecorous.

OS'a— 2. dosa 3. Mendoza, mimosa, Formosa 4. Mariposa, amorosa [It.].

OS'er— 2. doser, closer, grocer, grosser 3. jocoser, engrosser, greengrocer, moroser.

OS'est— 2. closest, grossest 3. morosest.

OSH'a— 2. Scotia 3. macrotia 4. Nova Scotia.

OSH'al— 2. social 3. precocial, asocial, dissocial 4. antisocial, intersocial.

OSH'er— 2. kosher, clocher.

OSH'un— 2. ocean, Goshen, lotion, motion, notion, potion, groschen 3. Boeotian, nicotian, emotion, demotion, commotion, promotion, devotion 4. braggadocian, locomotion, self-devotion.

OSH'us— 3. precocious, nepotious, ferocious, atrocious.

OS'ij— 2. dosage.

OS'ing— 2. dosing, grossing 3. engrossing.

OS'is— 2. gnosis, ptosis 3. thrombosis, lordosis, morphosis, zygosis, psychosis, zymosis, osmosis, prognosis, hypnosis, necrosis, morosis, sorosis, neurosis 4. psittacosis, ankylosis, cyanosis, diagnosis, adiposis, hematosis 5. pediculosis, tuberculosis.

OS'iv— 3. explosive, erosive, corrosive 4. inexplosive, unexplosive.

OS'li— 2. closely, grossly 3. verbosely, jocosely, morosely 4. bellicosely.

OS'ness— 2. closeness, grossness 3. verboseness, jocoseness, moroseness.

OS'o— 2. soso, so-so, mosso [It.] 3. pomposo [It.], corozo 4. arioso, gracioso, tremoloso [It.], animoso [It.], penseroso [It.], doloroso [It.], amoroso, strepitoso [It.], maestoso [It.], virtuoso.

OST'al— 2. coastal, postal 4. intracoastal, intercoastal.

OST'ed— 2. boasted, ghosted, hosted, posted, roasted, toasted 3. enghosted.

OST'er– **2.** boaster, coaster, poster, roaster, toaster **3.** four-poster **4.** roller coaster.

OST'ij– **2.** postage.

OST'ing– **2.** boasting, ghosting, hosting, coasting, posting, roasting, toasting **3.** riposting, imposting, retoasting.

OST'li– **2.** ghostly, mostly.

OT'a– **2.** cota [Tag.], lota, lotah, Lota, flota, nota, rota, tota [Amharic], vota, quota **3.** iota, Dakota, pelota, nonquota **4.** Minnesota.

OT'al– **2.** dotal, notal, rotal, total, votal **3.** teetotal, sum total, sum-total **4.** extradotal, antidotal, anecdotal, sacerdotal.

OT'at– **2.** notate, rotate **3.** *annotate.*

OT'ed– **2.** boated, doted, coated, bloated, floated, gloated, moated, moted, noted, throated, toted [coll.], voted, quoted **3.** refloated, demoted, promoted, denoted, connoted, unnoted, red-throated, dry-throated, full-throated, deep-throated, devoted, misquoted **4.** petticoated, particoated, sugar-coated, unpromoted, ruby-throated, yellow-throated, undevoted.

OT'en– **2.** oaten, crotin, croton **3.** verboten [G.].

OT'ent– **2.** flotant, potent **3.** prepotent **4.** counterpotent.

OT'er– **2.** boater, doter, coater, scoter, bloater, floater, gloater, motor, noter, poter, roter, Soter, toter, voter, quoter **3.** demoter, remoter, promoter, bimotor, trimotor, denoter, devoter, misquoter **4.** locomotor, rotomotor.

OT'est– **2.** protest **3.** remotest.

OTH'ful– **2.** loathful, slothful, trothful.

OTH'ing– **2.** loathing, clothing, trothing **3.** betrothing.

OTH'som– **2.** loathsome.

OT'i– **2.** doty, dhoti, goaty, bloaty, floaty, throaty **3.** coyote.

OT'ij– **2.** boatage, dotage, floatage, flotage **4.** anecdotage, sacerdotage.

OT'ik– **2.** otic, photic, lotic **3.** aphotic, dysphotic, parotic.

OT'ing– **2.** boating, doting, coating, bloating, floating, gloating, noting, toting [coll.], voting, quoting **3.** demoting, promoting, denoting, connoting, devoting, misquoting **4.** sugar-coating.

OT'ish– **2.** oatish, boatish, dotish, goatish.

OT'ist– **2.** scotist, noticed, votist **3.** unnoticed **4.** anecdotist.

OT'iv– **2.** floative, motive, votive **3.** emotive, promotive, denotive **4.** locomotive **5.** electromotive.

OT'o– **2.** Oto, Otoe, photo, moto [It.], roto, toto **3.** Kioto, De Soto, in toto [L.], divoto, ex voto [L.], ex-voto **4.** Mr. Moto.

OT'um– **2.** notum, totum, quotum **3.** pronotum, teetotum, factotum.

OT'us– **2.** Otus, lotus, Notus **3.** amotus, macrotous.

OV'a– **2.** ova, Ova, nova **3.** Jehovah, korova **4.** Villanova, Casanova.

OV'al– **2.** oval **3.** suboval.

OV'en– **2.** cloven, woven **3.** uncloven, rewoven, inwoven **4.** interwoven.

OV'er– **2.** over, Dover, clover, plover, drover, shrover, stover, trover **3.** walkover, moreover, leftover.

OV'i– **2.** grovy **3.** anchovy.

OV'ing– **2.** coving, roving, shroving, stoving.

OV'um– **2.** ovum, novum **3.** protovum.

O'yo– **2.** coyo, yo-yo **3.** arroyo.

OZ'a– **2.** boza, rosa [L.], Rosa **3.** Mendoza, flindosa, Spinoza, sub rosa [L.].

OZ'al– **2.** rosal **3.** deposal, reposal, opposal, proposal, disposal, transposal, supposal **4.** interposal, presupposal, predisposal.

OZ'en– **2.** chosen, frozen **3.** unchosen, forechosen, unfrozen.

OZ'er– 2. dozer, glozer, closer, noser, poser, roser, proser 3. *bulldozer*, encloser, incloser, forecloser, discloser, deposer, reposer, imposer, composer, opposer, proposer, disposer, exposer, supposer 4. decomposer, recomposer, interposer, predisposer, presupposer 5. superimposer.

OZ'ez– 2. dozes, closes, Moses, poses, roses 4. indisposes 5. superimposes.

OZH'er– 2. osier, hosier, closure, crosier 3. enclosure, foreclosure, disclosure, reposure, composure, disposure, exposure 4. decomposure, discomposure 5. superimposure.

OZH'un– 3. icosian, applosion, implosion, explosion, ambrosian, erosion, corrosion.

OZ'i– 2. dozy, fozy, cozy, nosy, posy, rosy, prosy, tosy, tozie.

OZ'ing– 2. dozing, closing, nosing, posing, prosing 3. bulldozing, enclosing, apposing, deposing, reposing, imposing, composing, opposing, proposing, disposing, exposing, transposing 4. juxtaposing, unimposing, decomposing, recomposing, interposing, indisposing 5. superimposing.

OZ'o– 2. bozo [slang], kozo.

OZ'on– 2. ozone, slow zone.

OZ'ur– 2. closure 3. enclosure, inclosure, foreclosure, disclosure, reposure, composure, disposure, exposure 4. discomposure.

O (oh)

3.

TRIPLE RHYMES IN O (know′a-ble)

Primary or Secondary Accent Falls on
Second from Last Syllable.

O′a-bl– 3. knowable, showable, 4. un-
knowable, bestowable 5. overthrowable.

OB′i-a– 3. obeah, phobia 4. Zenobia
5. brontephobia, stasiphobia, toxiphobia,
cibophobia, phobophobia, neophobia, the-
ophobia, algophobia, ergophobia, Anglo-
phobia, ochlophobia, Gallophobia, dromo-
phobia, cremnophobia,phonophobia, hyp-
nophobia, cynophobia, zoophobia, topo-
phobia, acrophobia, androphobia, hy-
drophobia, negrophobia, claustrophobia,
pyrophobia, nosophobia, lyssophobia, bat-
ophobia, nyctophobia, sitophobia, bron-
tophobia, scotophobia, photophobia 6.
agoraphobia, batrachophobia, cardiopho-
bia, bibliophobia, hagiophobia, Germano-
phobia, astrapophobia, anthropophobia,
aelurophobia, thalassophobia, thanatopho-
bia.

OB′i-an– 4. Jacobian, cenobian, macro-
bian, microbian.

OB′il-iz– 3. mobilize 4. demobilize, re-
mobilize, immobilize.

OCH′a-bl– 3. poachable 4. approach-
able, reproachable 5. unapproachable,
irreproachable.

OD′al-er– 3. odaler, yodeler.

OD′i-ak– 3. Kodiak, nodiak, zodiac.

OD′i-al– 3. podial 4. allodial, threno-
dial, prosodial, custodial 5. palinodial,
episodial.

OD′i-an– 3. Rhodian 4. Cambodian,
Herodian, prosodian, custodian.

OD′i-on– 4. Triodion, melodion, melo-
deon, collodion 5. nickelodeon.

OD′i-um– 3. odium, podium, rhodium,
sodium 4. allodium, taxodium.

OD′i-us– 3. odious 4. melodious, com-
modious 5. unmelodious, incommodi-
ous, discommodious.

OD′or-us– 3. odorous 4. malodorous,
inodorous.

OG′i-izm– 3. bogyism, fogyism.

O′ik-al– 3. stoical. 4. heroical, unstoical
5. unheroical.

O′il-i– 3. snowily, showily.

O′ing-li– 3. flowingly, glowingly, know-
ingly 4. unknowingly.

OJ′i-a– 3. loggia 4. alogia, dyslogia 5.
apologia.

OJ′i-an– 4. gambogian 5. geologian, ne-
ologian, theologian, philologian, astrolo-
gian, mythologian 6. archaeologian.

OK′a-bl– 3. smokable, vocable 4. un-
smokable, invocable 5. uninvocable.

OK′al-i– 3. focally, locally, vocally.

OK′al-ist– 3. localist, vocalist.

OK′al-iz– 3. focalize, localize, vocalize.

OK′al-izm– 3. localism, vocalism.

OK′en-li– 3. brokenly 4. outspokenly.

OK′i-er– 3. oakier, chokier, smokier, pok-
ier, croakier, soakier, yolkier.

OK′i-ness– 3. oakiness, chokiness, smoki-
ness, pokinesss, croakiness, soakiness,
yolkiness.

OK′ing-li– 3. chokingly, jokingly, croak-
ingly, strokingly, soakingly 4. provok-
ingly.

197

OK'less–li– **3.** jokelessly, smokelessly.

OKS'ing–li– **3.** hoaxingly, coaxingly.

OK'us–ing– **3.** focusing, hocusing.

OK'us–less– **3.** focusless, hocusless, locusless, crocusless.

OL'a–bl– **3.** bowlable, goalable, holable, pollable, rollable, tollable **4.** unbowlable, ungoalable, unholable, controllable, consolable **5.** uncontrollable, unconsolable, inconsolable.

OL'a–bli– **4.** consolably, controllably **5.** uncontrollably, unconsolably, inconsolably.

OL'ar–i– **3.** bolary, molary, polary, solary; *see* also OL'er–i– drollery etc. below.

OL'ar–iz– **3.** polarize, solarize **4.** depolarize.

OLD'a–bl– **3.** foldable, scoldable, moldable **4.** unfoldable, unscoldable.

OL'er–i– **3.** drollery, bolary, molary, polary, solary **4.** cajolery **5.** rigmarolery.

OL'e–um– **3.** oleum **4.** linoleum, petroleum, crystoleum; *see* also OL'i–um– oleum, folium, etc. below.

OL'ful–ness– **3.** dolefulness, soulfulness.

OL'i–a– **4.** Mongolia, magnolia, Aetolia **5.** melancholia.

OL'i–an– **4.** Aeolian, Mongolian, simoleon [slang], Napoleon, Pactolian, Aetolian **5.** metabolian, Anatolian, Capitolian.

OL'i–at– **3.** foliate, spoliate **4.** defoliate, infoliate.

OL'i–er– **3.** holier, lowlier, Grolier **4.** unholier.

OL'i–est– **3.** holiest, lowliest **4.** unholiest.

OL'i–ness– **3.** holiness, lowliness, shoaliness **4.** unholiness.

OL'ing–li– **4.** condolingly, cajolingly, consolingly, extollingly.

OL'i–o– **3.** oleo, olio, folio, roleo **4.** portfolio.

OL'i–um– **3.** oleum, folium, scholium **4.** trifolium, linoleum, arolium, petroleum, crystoleum **5.** Capitolium.

OL'o–ist– **3.** poloist, soloist.

OLST'er–er– **3.** bolsterer **4.** upholsterer.

OM'as–i– **4.** diplomacy.

OM'at–izm– **3.** chromatism **4.** achromatism, diplomatism.

OM'i–al– **3.** nomial, tomial **4.** binomial, monomial.

OM'i–er– **3.** domier, foamier, homier, loamier.

OM'i–est– **3.** domiest, foamiest, homiest, loamiest.

OM'i–ness– **3.** dominess, foaminess, hominess, loaminess.

OM'ing–li– **3.** foamingly, homingly, gloamingly, roamingly.

OM'i–o– **3.** Romeo, Dromio.

OM'i–um– **3.** chromium, tomium **4.** encomium **5.** nosocomium.

OM'luv–ing– **3.** homeloving, chromeloving.

ON'a–bl– **3.** ownable, bonable, phonable, honable, loanable, thronable, tonable, zonable **4.** condonable, atonable **5.** unatonable.

ON'i–a– **4.** Adonia, aphonia, begonia, Ionia, bryonia, Laconia, Franconia, Slavonia, valonia, ammonia, Harmonia, pneumonia, asonia, Ausonia, Antonia **5.** Caledonia, Macedonia, Patagonia.

ON'i–al– **3.** monial **4.** colonial, demonial, harmonial, baronial **5.** ceremonial, matrimonial, patrimonial, sanctimonial, testimonial **6.** intercolonial.

ON'i–an– **4.** aeonian, Gorgonian, Ionian, chelonian, demonian, Simonian, Johnsonian, Ausonian, Shoshonean, Platonian, Etonian, Oxonian, Esthonian, Miltonian, Plutonian, favonian, pavonian, bezonian **5.** Caledonian, Patagonian, Thessalonian, Babylonian, Ciceronian, Amazonian, Macedonian, halcyonian.

ON'i–er– 3. bonier, phonier [slang], dronier, tonier [vulgar], stonier.

ON'i–est– 3. boniest, phoniest [slang], toniest [vulgar], stoniest.

ON'i–um– 4. agonium, euphonium, polonium, stramonium, ammonium, harmonium, Plutonium 5. sporogonium, pelargonium, pandemonium, testimonium.

ON'i–us– 4. euphonious, symphonious, felonious, Polonius, harmonious, erroneous, ultroneous, Antonius 5. ceremonious, querimonious, acrimonious, matrimonious, parsimonious, sanctimonious, inharmonious 6. unceremonious, unsanctimonious.

O'o–lit– 3. oolite, zoolite.

O'o–lith– 3. zoolith.

OP'i–a– 3. topia 4. myopia, Utopia 5. Ethiopia, cornucopia, presbyopia, nyctalopia.

OP'i–an– 4. Aesopian, Utopian 5. Ethiopian, cornucopian.

OP'i–ness– 3. dopiness, ropiness, soapiness.

OP'ish–ness– 3. mopishness, popishness.

OR'a–bl– 3. soarable, storable 4. adorable, deplorable, explorable, restorable.

OR'a–bli– 4. adorably, deplorably.

OR'al–i– 3. orally, florally.

OR'at–iv– 4. explorative, restorative.

OR'e–al– 3. boreal 4. arboreal, phossphoreal, marmoreal, corporeal, aequoreal 5. bicorporeal, incorporeal; *see* also **OR'i–al–** boreal etc. below.

OR'e–an– 4. roborean, marmorean, aurorean, Hectorean; *see* also **OR'i–an–** Dorian etc. below.

OR'i–a– 3. doria, scoria, Gloria, noria 4. Peoria, theoria, euphoria, dysphoria, memoria, emporia, Pretoria, Victoria, Astoria 5. Infusoria 6. phantasmagoria, Waldorf Astoria.

OR'i–al– 3. boreal 4. arboreal, phosphoreal, marmoreal, corporeal, aequoreal, Escorial, enchorial, authorial, memorial, armorial, manorial, rasorial, risorial, scansorial, censorial, sensorial, sponsorial, tonsorial, rosorial, cursorial, gressorial, fossorial, factorial, rectorial, sectorial, tectorial, vectorial, pictorial, tinctorial, doctorial, proctorial, auctorial, praetorial, cantorial, raptorial, scriptorial, sartorial, quaestorial, haustorial, sutorial, tutorial, textorial, uxorial 5. bicorporeal, incorporeal, immemorial, responsorial, insessorial, dismissorial, piscatorial, purgatorial, grallatorial, amatorial, senatorial, oratorial, curatorial, natatorial, spectatorial, dictatorial, saltatorial, gestatorial, equatorial, reptatorial, prefectorial, electorial, inspectorial, directorial, editorial, territorial, sussultorial, inventorial, preceptorial, repertorial, assertorial, consistorial 6. ambassadorial, phantasmagorial, expurgatorial, gladiatorial, mediatorial, legislatorial, gubernatorial, visitatorial, observatorial, proprietorial, exterritorial, conspiratorial, inquisitorial, executorial 7. extraterritorial.

OR'i–an– 3. Dorian 4. roborean, Gregorian, marmorean, aurorean, praetorian, Hectorean, stentorian, Nestorian, historian, Victorian 5. hyperborean, purgatorian, amatorian, senatorian, oratorian, mid-Victorian 6. salutatorian, valedictorian.

OR'i–at– 3. floriate, storiate 4. excoriate 5. professoriate.

OR'i–fi– 3. scorify, glorify, storify.

OR'i–ness– 3. goriness, hoariness, poriness 5. dilatoriness, desultoriness, peremptoriness.

OR'i–ol– 3. oriole, gloriole.

OR'i–um– 3. corium, thorium 4. ciborium, triforium, emporium, sensorium, praetorium, scriptorium, pastorium, haustorium 5. sudatorium, crematorium, fumatorium, sanatorium, moratorium, natatorium, auditorium, digitorium.

OR′i–us– **3.** scorious, Lorius, glorious **4.** laborious, arboreous, inglorious, vaingloriOUS, unglorious, uproarious, censorious, victorious, stentorious, notorious, sartorius, uxorious **5.** accessorius, meritorious, amatorious, saltatorious.

ORS′a–bl– **3.** forceable, forcible **4.** enforceable, divorceable **5.** unenforceable, undivorceable.

ORSH′un–al– **3.** portional, torsional **4.** proportional **5.** disproportional.

ORSH′un–er– **3.** portioner **4.** apportioner, proportioner, extortioner.

ORT′a–bl– **3.** courtable, portable **4.** deportable, reportable, importable, exportable, transportable, supportable **5.** insupportable.

ORT′li–ness– **3.** courtliness, portliness **4.** uncourtliness.

OR′us–li– **3.** porously **4.** decorously, sonorously.

OSH′a–bl– **3.** sociable **4.** negotiable, dissociable, unsociable.

OSH′i–a– **4.** nicotia, anotia, macrotia, microtia; *see* also OSH′a– Scotia etc.

OSH′i–an– **4.** Boeotian, nicotian **5.** braggadocian.

OSH′i–ant– **3.** otiant **4.** negotiant, dissociant.

OSH′i–at– **4.** negotiate, associate, dissociate, consociate.

OSH′un–al– **3.** motional, notional **4.** emotional, commotional, promotional, devotional **5.** unemotional, nondevotional, undevotional.

OSH′us–li– **4.** precociously, ferociously, atrociously.

OSH′us–ness– **4.** precociousness, ferociousness, atrociousness.

OS′iv–li– **4.** explosively, erosively, corrosively **5.** inexplosively.

OS′iv–ness– **4.** explosiveness, erosiveness, corrosiveness.

OST′ful–i– **3.** boastfully, ghostfully.

OST′ing–li– **3.** boastingly, coastingly, roastingly, toastingly.

OST′li–ness– **3.** ghostliness, hostliness.

OT′a–bl– **3.** floatable, notable, potable, votable, quotable **4.** unfloatable, denotable, unquotable.

OT′ab–li– **3.** notably, quotably.

OT′al–er– **3.** totaler **4.** teetotaler.

OT′al–izm– **4.** teetotalism **5.** sacerdotalism.

OT′ar–i– **3.** coterie, notary, rotary, votary.

OT′at–iv– **3.** flotative, rotative **4.** denotative, connotative.

OT′ed–li– **3.** bloatedly, notedly **4.** devotedly, sweet-throatedly.

OT′er–i– **3.** coterie, notary, rotary, votary.

OT′ing–li– **3.** dotingly, bloatingly, gloatingly, quotingly.

OT′iv–li– **3.** votively **4.** emotively.

OV′en–li– **3.** clovenly, wovenly **5.** interwovenly.

OV′i–a– **3.** fovea **4.** synovia, Monrovia.

OV′i–al– **3.** foveal, jovial **4.** unjovial, synovial.

OZ′a–bl– **4.** deposable, imposable, opposable, disposable, transposable, supposable **5.** decomposable, indisposable, untransposable.

OZ′ar–i– **3.** rosary.

OZH′er–i– **3.** osiery, hosiery.

OZH′i–a– **4.** symposia, ambrosia.

OZ′i–er– **3.** dozier, cozier, nosier, rosier, prosier.

OZ′i–est– **3.** doziest, coziest, nosiest, rosiest, prosiest.

OZ′il–i– **3.** dozily, cozily, nosily, rosily, prosily.

OZ′i–ness– **3.** doziness, foziness, coziness, nosiness, rosiness, prosiness.

Ŏ (awe)

1.

SINGLE (MASCULINE) RHYMES IN Ŏ (awe)

Primary or Secondary Accent Falls on Last
Syllable; Imperfect Rhymes Are in Italics.

O– **1.** awe, aw [slang], chaw [dial.], daw, haw, jaw, caw, scaw, law, flaw, claw, slaw, maw, naw [slang], gnaw, paw, raw, braw, draw, gra, craw, straw, saw, pshaw, taw, tau, thaw, squaw, yaw **2.** *jackdaw*, guffaw, *heehaw*, macaw, pilau, pilaw, *coleslaw*, begnaw, papaw, *pawpaw*, withdraw, hurrah, *seesaw*, foresaw **3.** overawe, overdraw, oversaw **4.** mother-in-law.

OB– **1.** ob, bob, daub, fob, gob, gaub, hob, job, kob, cob, Cobb, scob [Scot. N. of Eng. & Ir.], lob, blob, glob [slang], slob, mob, nob, knob, snob, rob, brob, throb, sob, stob, thob [slang], wob [slang], swab, quab, squab **2.** *cabob*, *nabob*, *earbob*, bedaub, *corncob*, *hoblob*, *hobnob*, carob, athrob, *nawab* **3.** thingumbob **4.** thingumabob; *see* also **AB–** squab etc.

OBZ– gobs etc., *see* **OB–** ob etc. above, plus "s" or "'s."

OCH– **1.** botch, gotch, hotch [slang], cotch, scotch, Scotch, blotch, splotch, notch, nautch, rotch, crotch, watch, swatch **2.** debauch, *hopscotch*, *hotchpotch*, *deathwatch*, *dogwatch*, outwatch.

OCHT– **1.** botched, scotched, blotched, splotched, notched, crotched, watched **2.** debauched, unwatched.

OD– **1.** odd, awed, gaud, God, hod, jawed, cod, cawed, laud, clod, Claude, plod, maud, Maude, nod, gnawed, pod, pawed, rod, broad, fraud, scrod, prod, trod, sod, sawed, shod, tod, tawed, vaude [slang], wad, quad, quod [slang], squad **2.** unawed, *tomcod*, belaud, applaud, maraud, abroad, defraud, *Nimrod*, *Penrod*, hurrahed, roughshod, unshod, *slipshod*, *tightwad*, per quod [L.] **3.** overawed, Ichabod, demigod, underjawed, goldenrod; *see* also **AD–** baaed etc.

ODZ– odds etc., *see* **OD–** odd etc. above, plus "s" or "'s."

OF– **1.** off, doff, goff, koff, cough, coff [slang], scoff, prof [slang], shroff, trough, toff [slang], quaff **2.** *runoff*, *throwoff*, *setoff*, *castoff*, *chincough*, Kharkov, Orloff, Azof **3.** philosoph **4.** bibliosoph.

OFT– **1.** oft, doffed, coughed, scoffed, loft, croft, soft, toft, quaffed **2.** aloft, hayloft.

OG– **1.** Og, bog, dog, fog, gog, Gog, hog, jog, cog, log, blog [slang], flog, clog, slog, mog [slang], smog, nog, brog, frog, grog, sogg [slang], tog, quag **2.** embog, *watchdog*, *bulldog*, *firedog*, befog, agog, *Magog*, *seahog*, *hedgehog*, *quahog*, *shearhog*, *backlog*, *putlog*, *eggnog*, *crannog*, *scuppaug*, *bullfrog*, pishaug, tautog **3.** underdog, prairie dog, megafog, pettifog, pedagogue, Gogmagog, demagogue, xenagogue, synagogue, hydragogue, mystagogue, logogogue, Decalogue, Tagalog, dialogue, trialogue, grammalogue, analogue, catalogue, theologue, melologue, homologue, Sinologue, monologue, apologue, necrologue, apologue, horologue, duologue, Dannebrog, golliwogg, polliwog; *see* also **AG–** blague etc.

OGD– 1. bogged, dogged, hogged, jogged, cogged, logged, flogged, clogged, slogged 2. embogged, befogged 3. catalogued, waterlogged.

OGZ– dogs etc., *see* **OG–** Og etc. above, plus "s" or " 's."

OJ– 1. bodge, dodge, lodge, podge, stodge 2. unlodge, dislodge, *hodgepodge* 3. horologe.

OK– 1. auk, awk, balk, bock, choc [slang], chock, chalk, doc [slang], dock, gawk, hawk, hock, Jock, jock [slang], calk, cawk, cock, lock, loch, block, flock, clock, mawk [slang], smock, knock, pock, rock, roc, frock, crock, sock, shock, talk, stalk, stock, walk, squak 2. rhebok, *klipbok, blesbok,* ad hoc [L.], *Mohawk, sparhawk, sorehawk, goshawk,* acock, *woodcock, peacock, Hancock,* Bangkok, *padlock, deadlock, wedlock, Shylock, hemlock,* unlock, *gunlock, rowlock, oarlock, forelock, Sherlock, fetlock, flintlock, wristlock,* unblock, *bedrock,* unfrock, *traprock, ticktock,* restock, unstock, *livestock, sidewalk,* outwalk 3. bontebok, tomahawk, hollyhock, poppycock, shuttlecock, weathercock, Antioch, chockablock, stumbling block, fetterlock, interlock, Little Rock, alpenstock, laughingstock, overstock 4. Vladivostok; *see also* **AK–** ach etc.

OKS– auks etc., *see* **OK–** auk etc. above, plus "s" or " 's"; 1. ox, box, fox, cox, phlox, Nox, Knox, pox, vox 2. abox, bandbox, sandbox, snuffbox, strongbox, workbox, jukebox, mailbox, pillbox, hatbox, princox, Coxcox, smallpox 3. chatterbox, paradox, philodox, homodox, orthodox, Goldilocks, equinox, chicken pox 4. heterodox, unorthodox.

OKT– 1. balked, hawked, calked, blocked, crocked, talked, stalked 2. decoct, concoct.

OL– 1. all, awl, ball, bawl, doll, fall, gall, Gaul, gol [slang], hall, haul, call, caul, loll, moll, maul, small, pall, Paul, pawl, pol, poll, spall, brawl, drawl, crawl, scrawl, sprawl, trawl, Saul, Sol, shawl, tall, stall, wall, squall, yawl 2. *eyeball, highball, blackball, pinball, snowball, fireball, baseball, football, catchall, windfall,* befall, *rainfall, downfall, snowfall, nightfall, pitfall,* Bengal, spurgall, dance hall, *birdcall,* recall, miscall, *catcall,* bemaul, appal, epaule, Nepal, bethrall, enthrall, atoll, extol, *boxstall, thumbstall,* install, forestall, withal, devall, sea wall, *stonewall, Cornwall* 3. all in all, free-for-all, basketball, Montreal, evenfall, waterfall, alcohol, overhaul, protocol, folderal, disenthrall, parasol, girasol, entresol, reinstall, fingerstall, therewithal, wherewithal, caterwaul.

OLD– 1. auld, bald, bawled, galled, called, scald, drawled, crawled, walled 2. blackballed, snowballed, recalled, uncalled, socalled, appalled, enthralled, stone-walled 3. Archibald, overhauled, unappalled, unenthralled.

OLF– 1. golf 2. Rudolph.

OLS– 1. false, halse, valse, waltz.

OLT– 1. halt, fault, gault, malt, smalt, salt, vault 2. *cobalt,* default, assault, *basalt,* envault, exalt 3. pseudosalt, somersault.

OLTS– halts etc., *see* **OLT–** halt etc. above, plus "s" or " 's."

OLV– 1. solve 2. absolve, resolve, dissolve, evolve, devolve, revolve, involve 3. circumvolve, intervolve.

OLVD– 1. solved 2. absolved, resolved, dissolved, evolved, devolved, revolved, involved 3. circumvolved, intervolved.

OM– 1. bomb, chom, chawm [both slang], dom, domn, gaum, haulm, glom [slang], plomb [slang], mom [slang], rhomb, from, prom [slang], shawm, Tom, Guam, qualm 2. Bonhomme, aplomb, coulomb, geom [slang], imaum, *pompom,* therefrom, wherefrom, *pogrom, wigwam* 3. atom bomb, axiom, hecatomb; *see also* **AM–** balm etc.

OMB– 1. rhomb, stromb.

OMP– 1. comp [slang], pomp, romp, trompe, stomp, wamp, swamp.

OMPT– 1. compt, romped, prompt, swamped.

OMZ– bombs etc., *see* **OM–** bomb etc. above, plus "s" or " 's."

ON– 1. on, awn, bon, bonne [F.], don, Don, dawn, fawn, faun, gone, John, john [slang], con, lawn, mon [Scot.], non [L.], pawn, spawn, brawn, drawn, prawn, shone, wan, swan, yon, yawn 2. hereon, thereon, whereon, *bonbon*, chiffon, begone, *bygone*, *foregone*, Yukon, salon, Ceylon, anon, impawn, upon, indrawn, undrawn, withdrawn, Tucson, baton, cretonne, Yvonne, chignon, Luzon 3. hanger-on, hangers-on, Audubon, Celadon, chelidon, myrmidon, mastodon, Corydon, pantheon, galleon, colophon, Xenophon, nonagon, tarragon, tetragon, octagon, pentagon, protagon, heptagon, martagon, hexagon, woebegone, Oregon, perigon, isogon, undergone, polygon, oxygon, gabion, Albion, demijohn, Little John, Prester John, leprechaun, Rubicon, Helicon, silicon, technicon, opticon, lexicon, gonfalon, petalon, Avalon, echelon, Babylon, Pergamon, gonfanon, organon, xoanon, tympanon, noumenon, Parthenon, hereupon, thereupon, whereupon, fanfaron, megaron, Oberon, pentacron, Omicron, balatron, anatron, orison, Alençon, cabochon, abaton, phaeton, trilithon, ornithon, halcyon, Amazon, cabezon, liaison, Barbizon 4. melodicon, basilicon, catholicon, irenicon, harmonicon, sciopticon, panopticon, lapideon, Napoleon, Anacreon, chiliagon, amphibion, Endymion, Hyperion, oblivion, alluvion, Laocoon, hyperbaton, automaton 5. acolodicon, synonymicon, stereopticon 6. etymologicon; *see* also **AN–ane** [F.] etc.

ONCH– 1. haunch, launch, paunch, craunch, staunch.

OND– 1. awned, bond, donned, dawned, fond, blond, blonde, monde, pond, spawned, frond, wand, yawned 2. seconde, abscond, despond, respond, beyond 3. vagabond, overfond, demimonde, correspond.

ONG– 1. bong, dong, gong, long, flong, pong, wrong, prong, strong, throng, song, tong, thong, wong 2. Souchong, *dingdong*, mah-jongg, Hong Kong, along, daylong, headlong, belong, lifelong, prolong, erelong, nightlong, *pingpong*, sarong, *headstrong*, *singsong*, paktong, quantong, *diphthong*, *triphthong*, payong 3. billabong, underfong, overlong, scuppernong, evensong, undersong, aftersong.

ONK– 1. gonk [slang], honk, conk, konk [both slang], conch, bronc [slang], cronk, tonk, wonk, squonk [both slang] 2. triconch 3. honky-tonk.

ONKS– honks etc., *see* **ONK–** honk etc. above, plus "s" or " 's"; Bronx.

ONS– 1. bonce, sconce, nonce 2. ensconce, response, patonce.

ONT– 1. daunt, font, gaunt, haunt, jaunt, flaunt, pont, taunt, vaunt, want, wont 2. bouffant, aflaunt, romaunt, Vermont, Dupont, avaunt 3. Hellespont; *see* also **ANT–** aunt etc.

ONZ– awns etc., *see* **ON–** on etc. above, plus "s" or " 's"; 1. bonze, fons, fauns, pons [L.], bronze, frons [L.] 2. bygones.

OP– 1. op [slang], bop [slang], chop, dop, fop, gaup, gawp [slang], hop, cop, scaup, lop, flop, plop, slop, mop, knop, pop, drop, crop, prop, strop, sop, shop, top, stop, staup, wop, wap, swap, swop [both dial. & coll.], whop [coll.], yawp 2. alop, aslop, *slipslop*, *raindrop*, *snowdrop*, *teardrop*, *dewdrop*, *eavesdrop*, outcrop, unprop, asop, *milksop*, soursop, *sweetsop*, *workshop*, *pawnshop*, *redtop*, *tiptop*, *foretop*, estop, *backstop*, *nonstop*, *shortstop* 3. soda pop, lollipop, underprop, overtop 4. flippityflop; *see* also **AP–** gape etc.

OPS– bops [slang] etc., *see* **OP–** bop etc. above, plus "s" or " 's"; **1.** Ops, copse.

OPT– **1.** opt, chopped, hopped, copped, Copt, lopped, flopped, plopped, slopped, mopped, popped, dropped, propped, sopped, stopped **2.** adopt, estopped, unstopped.

OR– through **ORZ–**, *see* also long O (oh): **OR–** through **ORZ–**.

OR– **1.** or, dor, for, cor, nor, tor, Thor, war **2.** Alcor, Côte d'Or, whyfor, abhor, décor [F.], señor [Sp.], lessor **3.** mirador, comprador, matador, cantador [Sp.] picador, Labrador, meteor, mortgagor, biophor, pastophor, Ecuador, chancellor, counselor, councillor, Eleanor, alienor, bargainor, emperor, conqueror, promisor, senator, champertor, dinosaur, semitaur, Minotaur, god of war, tug of war, man of war **4.** capeador [Sp.], toreador, conquistador, Corregidor, heliodor, excelsior, deliveror, recoveror, megalosaur, ornithosaur, ichthyosaur.

ORB– **1.** orb, sorb, Sorb **2.** inorb, absorb, resorb, disorb.

ORCH– **1.** scorch, porch, torch.

ORD– **1.** bord, dord, ford, gord [slang], cord, chord, lord, warred, ward, sward, fiord **2.** afford, abhorred, accord, *whipcord*, *landlord*, belord, milord, award, reward, *greensward* **3.** unaccord, disaccord, octachord, unichord, polychord, lyrichord, harpsichord, clavichord, overlord **4.** harmonichord, misericord.

ORF– **1.** corf, morph [slang], dwarf, swarf, wharf **3.** Dusseldorf.

ORG– **1.** orgue, org [slang], borg, morgue **3.** Swedenborg.

ORJ– **1.** forge, gorge, George, corge **2.** regorge, engorge, disgorge **3.** disengorge, overgorge.

ORK– **1.** orc, ork [slang], fork, cork, corke, torque, stork, York **2.** *pitchfork*, New York.

ORKT– **1.** forked, corked, torqued.

ORL– **1.** orle, ceorl, schorl, whorl.

ORM– **1.** dorm, form, norm, storm, warm, swarm **2.** deform, reform, inform, conform, perform, misform, transform, bestorm, *barnstorm*, rewarm, lukewarm **3.** stelliform, uniform, aeriform, floriform, cruciform, multiform, misinform, chloroform, thunderstorm **4.** trapeziform.

ORMD– **1.** formed, stormed, warmed, swarmed **2.** deformed, well-formed, illformed, informed, bestormed, *barnstormed* **3.** unreformed, well-informed, uninformed.

ORN– **1.** born, dorn, horn, corn, scorn, lorn, morn, Norn, shorn, torn, thorn, worn, sworn **2.** suborn, reborn, *freeborn*, *highborn*, inborn, unborn, *lowborn*, *first-born*, *newborn*, *trueborn*, adorn, dehorn, *staghorn*, *bighorn*, Longhorn, *pronghorn*, *foghorn*, French horn, *greenhorn*, *shorthorn*, *shoehorn*, *popcorn*, forlorn, *lovelorn*, midmorn, untorn, *buckthorn*, *hawthorn*, rewarn, forewarn **3.** readorn, unadorn, Matterhorn, barleycorn, peppercorn, yestermorn.

ORND– **1.** scorned **2.** suborned, adorned, dehorned, unwarned, forewarned.

ORP– **1.** dorp, gorp [slang], torp [slang], thorp, warp **2.** moldwarp **3.** Oglethorpe.

ORPS– **1.** corpse, warps **2.** moldwarps **3.** Oglethorpes.

ORS– **1.** gorse, horse, corse, Morse, Norse, torse **2.** endorse, sea horse, unhorse, remorse, retrorse, introrse, extrorse, dextrorse **3.** rocking horse, hobbyhorse, Charley horse, sinistrorse.

ORT– **1.** ort, bort, fort, mort, snort, sort, short, tort, wart, quart, swart, thwart **2.** abort, dehort, exhort, escort, amort, assort, resort, consort, retort, intort, contort, distort, extort, cavort, athwart.

ORTH– **1** morth, north, swarth, Jorth **2.** commorth

ORTS– orts etc., *see* **ORT–** ort etc. above, plus "s" or "'s"; **1.** quarts, quartz **2.** biquartz.

ORZ– wars etc., *see* **OR–** or etc. above, plus "s" or "'s"; **2.** quatorze **4.** Louis Quatorze.

OS– 1. os, Boss, boss, doss, fosse, joss, loss, floss, gloss, moss, ross, dross, cross, sauce, soss, toss, stoss **2.** emboss, vanfoss, kaross, across, lacrosse, recross, incross, *crisscross, christcross, ringtoss* **3.** albatross, double-cross, applesauce **4.** rhinoceros.

OSH– 1. bosh, bosch, Boche, gosh, josh, losh, slosh, posh [slang], sposh [slang], frosh [slang], sash, tosh, wash, swash, quash, squash **2.** kibosh, galosh, awash, bewash, rewash, *hogwash, eyewash, siwash, backwash, wishwash, whitewash, musquash* **3.** mackintosh.

OSK– 1. bosk, Bosc, mosque **2.** kiosk, imbosk **3.** abelmosk.

OSP– 1. hosp [slang], knosp, wasp **3.** galliwasp.

OST– 1. bossed, fossed, cost, lost, mossed, frost, crossed, wast **2.** exhaust, cabossed, embossed, imbost, accost, enmossed, defrost, *hoarfrost,* recrossed, uncrossed, *criscrossed,* betossed **3.** Pentecost, holocaust, double-crossed, anagnost, geognost **4.** bibliognost.

OT– 1. ought, aught, bought, bot [slang], bott, dot, fought, got, ghat, hot, jot, cot, caught, Scot, Scott, lot, Lot, blot, clot, plot, slot, mot, knot, not, naught, snot [slang], pot, pott, spot, rot, wrought, brought, fraught, trot, sot, sought, shot, shott, tot, taught, taut, stot, thought, watt, wot, swat, squat, what, yacht **2.** *abbot, Cabot, robot,* begot, forgot, *spigot,*

ingot, argot, Margot, ergot, eyot, ryot, riot, Sciot, cocotte, plumcot, mascot, wainscot, dovecot, allot, shallot, Helot, zealot, pilot, simblot, diglot, billot, tillot, complot, onslaught, culotte, motmot, cannot, dreadnought, unknot, topknot, slipknot, love knot, whatnot, repot, teapot, crackpot, skilpot, trampot, despot, tosspot, fleshpot, sunspot, garrot, garrote, parrot, inwrought, unwrought, unfraught, hilltrot, distraut, besot, besought, resought, bloodshot, foreshot, slingshot, buckshot, gunshot, snapshot, hipshot, upshot, earshot, grapeshot, bowshot, potshot, untaught, methought, forethought, gavotte, kumquat, loquat, asquat **3.** unforgot, haricot, apricot, persicot, peridot, larigot, idiot, galiot, chariot, heriot, patriot, cheviot, cachalot, Lancelot, ocelot, pentaglot, heptaglot, hexaglot, polyglot, matalotte, counterplot, sans-culotte, bergamot, guillemot, Huguenot, Argonaut, Juggernaut, flowerpot, coffeepot, galipot, talipot, tommyrot, underwrought, overwrought, overshot, Hottentot, afterthought, aforethought, aliquot **4.** forget-me-not, Iscariot **5.** witenagemot.

OTH– 1. auth [slang], doth, Goth, cloth, moth, broth, froth, troth, swath **2.** *breechcloth, broadcloth, sackcloth, oilcloth, loincloth,* betroth **3.** Visigoth, Ostrogoth, saddlecloth, behemoth.

OTS– dots etc., *see* **OT–** ought etc. above, plus "s" or "'s."

OV– 1. of **2.** hereof, thereof, whereof.

OZ– 1. awes etc., *see* **O–** awe etc. above, plus "s" or "'s"; **1.** oz [slang], Oz, Boz, gauze, hawse, cause, clause, pause, vase, was, 'twas, yaws **2.** because, applause **3.** Santa Claus.

OZM– 3. macrocosm, microcosm, loxocosm

O (awe)

2.

DOUBLE (FEMININE) RHYMES IN O (daub'er)

OB'er– 2. dauber, jobber, cobber, lobber, blobber, slobber, knobber, snobber, robber, throbber, sobber, wabber, swabber 3. bedauber, beslobber 5. Mr. Micawber [Dickens].

OB'ern– 2. auburn.

OB'i– 2. bobby, dauby, dobby, gobby, hobby, cobby, scobby, lobby, mobby, nobby, knobby, snobby, wabby, squabby.

OB'in– 2. bobbin, dobbin, robbin, robin 3. round robin.

OB'ing– 2. bobbing, daubing, jobbing, cobbing, lobbing, mobbing, snobbing, robbing, throbbing, sobbing, swabbing 3. hobnobbing.

OB'ish– 2. bobbish, lobbish, mobbish, snobbish, squabbish.

OB'l– 2. bauble, gobble, hobble, cobble, nobble, wobble, squabble.

OB'ler– 2. gobbler, hobbler, cobbler, nobbler, wobbler, squabbler 4. turkey gobbler, cherry cobbler.

OB'let– 2. goblet, squablet.

OB'li– 2. obley, hobbly, cobbly, wobbly, squabbly.

OB'lin– 2. goblin 3. hobgoblin.

OB'ling– 2. gobbling, hobbling, cobbling, snobling, wobbling, squabbling.

OBST'er– 2. daubster, lobster.

OB'ul– 2. lobule, globule.

OCH'er– 2. botcher, notcher, splotcher, watcher, swatcher 3. debaucher, topnotcher, hopscotcher.

OCH'i– 2. botchy, Scotchy, blotchy, splotchy, notchy, crotchy.

OCH'ing– 2. botching, scotching, blotching, splotching, notching, watching 3. debauching, hopscotching.

OD'al– 2. caudal 3. acaudal, subcaudal, bicaudal; see also OD'l– dawdle etc. below.

OD'ed– 2. lauded, plodded, nodded, podded, prodded, sodded, wadded 3. belauded, applauded, marauded, defrauded.

OD'en– 2. hodden, broaden, trodden, sodden 3. introdden, downtrodden, untrodden.

OD'er– 2. odder, dodder, fodder, nodder, lauder, plodder, broader, prodder, sawder, solder 3. Cape Codder, belauder, applauder, marauder, defrauder.

OD'ern– 2. modern 3. unmodern 4. ultramodern.

OD'ess– 2. bodice, goddess 4. demigoddess.

OD'est– 2. oddest, modest, broadest 3. immodest, unmodest 4. supermodest.

OD'i– 2. body, bawdy, dawdy, gaudy, hoddy, cloddy, noddy, poddy, soddy, shoddy, toddy, wadi, waddy, squaddy 3. embody, somebody, nobody, cum laude 4. anybody, antibody, everybody, busybody, disembody, hoddy-doddy [dial.], coddy-moddy 5. magna cum laude, summa cum laude.

OD'id– 2. bodied, toddied, waddied 3. embodied, unbodied 4. ablebodied, unembodied.

OD'ik– 2. odic 3. geodic, iodic, melodic, spasmodic, anodic, threnodic, synodic, epodic, rhapsodic, methodic 4. periodic, unmelodic, hellanodic, episodic, kinesodic.

OD'ing– 2. codding, lauding, plodding, nodding, podding, prodding, wadding 3. belauding, applauding, marauding, defrauding.

OD'is– 2. bodice, goddess.

OD'ish– 2. oddish, gaudish, cloddish, poddish.

OD'it– 2. audit, plaudit.

OD'l– 2. dawdle, coddle, caudle, caudal, model, noddle, toddle, waddle, swaddle, twaddle 3. acaudal, subcaudal, remodel 4. mollycoddle.

OD'ler– 2. dawdler, coddler, toddler, waddler, swaddler, twaddler 4. mollycoddler.

OD'li– 2. oddly, godly, waddly, twaddly 3. ungodly.

OD'lin– 2. codlin, maudlin.

OD'ling– 2. dawdling, godling, codling, coddling, modeling, toddling, waddling, swaddling, twaddling 4. mollycoddling.

OD'ri– 2. Audrey, bawdry, tawdry.

O'er– 2. gnawer, pawer, rawer, drawer, sawer, tawer 4. overdrawer.

O'est– 2. rawest.

OF'e– 2. coffee, toffee, toffy.

OF'er– 2. offer, doffer, goffer, coffer, cougher, scoffer, proffer.

OF'et– 2. prophet, profit, soffit 3. archprophet 4. weather prophet.

OF'ik– 2. ophic, trophic, strophic 4. hypertrophic, catastrophic, antistrophic, apostrophic, theosophic, philosophic 5. unphilosophic.

OF'in– 2. dauphin, coffin 3. encoffin.

OF'ing– 2. offing, doffing, coughing, scoffing.

OF'is– 2. office 3. post office, War Office 5. employment office.

OF'ish– 2. offish, spoffish, crawfish, sawfish, squawfish 3. standoffish.

OF'it– 2. prophet, profit, soffit.

OF'l– 2. offal, coffle, waffle; see also O'ful– awful etc. below.

OF'n– 2. often, soften.

OF'ner– 2. oftener, softener.

OFT'er– 2. ofter, lofter, crofter, softer.

OFT'est– 2. oftest, softest.

OFT'i– 2. lofty, softy 3. toplofty.

O'ful– 2. awful, lawful 3. unlawful; see also OF'l– offal etc. above.

OG'a– 2. gogga.

OG'an– 2. goggan, moggan 3. toboggan 4. pogamoggan.

OG'er– 2. auger, augur, dogger, hogger, jogger, cogger, logger, flogger, clogger, slogger, togger 3. befogger, whole-hogger 4. pettifogger.

OG'i– 2. boggy, doggy, foggy, joggy, loggy, cloggy, moggy, smoggy, poggy, froggy, groggy.

OG'in– 2. loggin, noggin.

OG'ing– 2. bogging, dogging, fogging, hogging, jogging, cogging, logging, flogging, clogging, slogging, frogging 3. befogging, prologuing 4. cataloguing, epiloguing.

OG'ish– 2. doggish, hoggish, froggish.

OG'l– 2. boggle, goggle, joggle, coggle, toggle 3. boondoggle [slang].

OG'ler– 2. boggler, goggler, joggler.

OG'let– 2. boglet, loglet, froglet.

OG'ling– 2. boggling, goggling, joggling 3. boondoggling [slang].

OG'ust– 2. August 3. mid-August.

O'i– 2. jawy, flawy, strawy, thawy, yawy.

O'ing– 2. awing, chawing [inelegant or dial.], hawing, jawing, cawing, flawing, gnawing, pawing, drawing, sawing, pshawing, tawing, thawing, yawing **3.** guffawing, heehawing, outlawing, withdrawing, hurrahing, seesawing **4.** overawing, overdrawing.

ŎJ′er– 2. bodger, dodger, codger, lodger, Roger **3.** corndodger, dislodger.

ŎJ′ez– dodges etc., *see* **ŎJ–** dodge etc., plus "s" or " 's."

ŎJ′i– 2. dodgy, podgy, stodgy **4.** pedagogy, demagogy.

ŎJ′ik– 2. logic **3.** choplogic, eulogic, agogic **4.** pedagogic, psychagogic, demagogic, anagogic, hypnagogic, epagogic, paragogic, isagogic, mystagogic, dialogic, catalogic, metalogic, geologic, neologic, psychologic, pathologic, ethologic, mythologic, biologic, philologic, homologic, cosmologic, penologic, ethnologic, chronologic, hypnologic, zoologic, acrologic, necrologic, micrologic, hydrologic, agrologic, astrologic, ontologic, tautologic, cytologic, phytologic, histologic **5.** mineralogic, lexicologic, toxicologic, archaeologic, sociologic, hagiologic, physiologic, entomologic, etymologic, anthropologic, **6.** meteorologic.

ŎJ′iks– 4. pedagogics, anagogics, theologics.

ŎJ′ing– 2. dodging, lodging **3.** unlodging, dislodging.

ŎK′a– 2. bocca, rocca [It.].

ŎK′er– 2. balker, chalker, docker, gawker, hawker, calker, cocker, locker, blocker, clocker, mocker, smocker, knocker, rocker, soeker, soccer, shocker, talker, stalker, stocker, walker, squawker **3.** jayhawker, jaywalker, sleepwalker, streetwalker, nightwalker **4.** Knickerbocker, tomahawker.

ŎK′et– 2. docket, cocket, locket, pocket, rocket, brocket, crocket, krocket, sprocket, socket **3.** pickpocket, impocket, unpocket, hip pocket, air pocket, vest pocket, watch pocket, skyrocket.

ŎK′i– 2. balky, chalky, gawky, hawky,

hockey, jockey, cocky, locky, lochy, blocky, flocky, pocky, pawky, rocky, crocky, talky, talkie, stocky, stalky, squawky **3.** field hockey, ice hockey, disk jockey [slang], horsejockey, Milwaukee **4.** walkie-talkie.

ŎK′ij– 2. dockage, lockage, soccage.

ŎK′ing– 2. balking, chalking, docking, gawking, hawking, hocking, calking, cocking, locking, blocking, flocking, clocking, mocking, smocking, knocking, rocking, crocking, socking, shocking, talking, stocking, stalking, walking, squawking **3.** jayhawking, unlocking, unblocking, bluestocking, jaywalking.

ŎK′ish– 2. balkish, chalkish, gawkish, hawkish, cockish, mawkish, mockish, stockish **3.** peacockish.

ŎK′l– 2. hockle, cockle, strockle, socle.

ŎK′let– 2. cocklet, rocklet, stocklet.

ŎK′ling– 2. cockling, flockling, rockling.

ŎK′ni– 2. cockney, Procne.

ŎK′o– 2. jocko, socko [slang], yocco **3.** sirocco, Morocco.

ŎKS′a– 2. coxa, moxa, noxa, toxa.

ŎKS′al– 2. coxal, noxal **4.** paradoxal.

ŎKS′en– 2. oxen, cockswain.

ŎKS′er– 2. oxer, boxer **4.** paradoxer, philodoxer.

ŎKSH′al– 3. trinoctial **4.** equinoctial.

ŎKSH′un– 2. auction, coction **3.** decoction, recoction, concoction.

ŎKSH′us– 2. noxious **3.** obnoxious, innoxious.

ŎKS′i– 2. boxy, doxy, foxy, poxy, roxy, proxy **3.** Biloxi **4.** paradoxy, cacodoxy, orthodoxy **5.** heterodoxy.

ŎKS′ik– 2. toxic **4.** streptococcic, antitoxic.

ŎKS′in– 2. toxin, tocsin **4.** antitoxin.

ŎKS′ing– 2. boxing, foxing **4.** shadowboxing.

OKT′iv– 2. octave 3. decoctive, concoctive.

OKT′or– 2. auctor, doctor, proctor 3. concoctor.

OKT′rin– 2. doctrine.

OK′us– 2. Daucus, caucus, lochus, floccus, Glaucus, glaucous, raucous 4. pneumococcus, streptococcus 5. staphylococcus.

OL′a– 2. aula, olla, holla, Paula 3. corolla, chuckwalla 4. Guatemala.

OL′ar– 2. dollar, collar, scholar, sollar; see also OL′er– bawler etc. below.

OL′ard– 2. bollard, collard, collared, pollard, scholard, scholared.

OLD′er– 2. alder, balder, Balder, scalder.

OLD′est– 2. baldest.

OLD′ing– 2. balding, scalding, Spaulding.

OL′ej– 2. college, knowledge 3. acknowledge, foreknowledge.

OL′en– 2. fallen, pollen, Stollen [G.] 3. downfallen, crestfallen.

OL′er– 2. bawler, dollar, faller, hauler, holler, caller, collar, choller, choler, scholar, loller, mauler, smaller, brawler, drawler, crawler, scrawler, sprawler, trawler, sollar, taller, staller, squaller, squalor 3. hog caller, enthraller, extoller, forestaller, potwaller 4. overhauler, dorsicollar, caterwauler.

OL′erd– 2. bollard, collared, collard, dollared, hollered, pollard, scholared.

O′less– 2. awless, aweless, jawless, lawless, flawless, clawless.

OL′est– 2. smallest, tallest.

OL′et– 2. collet, wallet, swallet 3. LaFollette.

OL′fin– 2. dolphin.

OL′i– 2. dolly, folly, golly, holly, jolly, collie, Molly, molle, Polly, poly [slang], rolley, rawly, drawly, crawly, scrawly, sprawly, trolley, squally, volley 3. *loblolly* 4. melancholy.

OL′id– 2. olid, jollied, collied, solid, stolid, squalid, volleyed 4. semisolid.

OL′ij– 2. haulage, college, knowledge, stallage 3. acknowledge, foreknowledge.

OL′ik– 2. aulic, Gaulic, rollick, frolic 3, embolic, symbolic, carbolic, bucolic, hydraulic, petrolic, systolic 4. diabolic, metabolic, hyperbolic, alcoholic, vitriolic, melancholic, diastolic, epistolic, apostolic 5. bibliopolic.

OL′in– 2. colin, collin 3. tarpaulin 4. hemicollin.

OL′ing– 2. balling, bawling, falling, galling, hauling, calling, lolling, mauling, palling, Pawling, brawling, drawling, crawling, scrawling, trawling, thralling, stalling, walling, squalling 3. blackballing, snowballing, befalling, recalling, miscalling, appalling, enthralling, extolling, installing, forestalling 4. overhauling, unenthralling, caterwauling.

OL′is– 2. follis, caulis, solace, Wallace 3. Cornwallis 4. torticollis.

OL′ish– 2. dollish, Gaulish, smallish, polish, tallish, squallish 3. abolish, demolish.

OL′ive– 2. olive 3. green olive, ripe olive.

OL′ment– 3. appallment, epaulement, enthrallment, installment.

OL′ness– 2. allness, smallness, tallness.

OL′o– 2. follow, hollo, hollow, Rollo, wallow, swallow 3. Apollo; see also AL′ocalo etc.

OL′op– 2. dollop, jollop, collop, scallop, lollop, trollop, wallop [dial, coll. & slang] 3. escalop.

OLS′er– 2. falser, waltzer.

OLT′ed– 2. faulted, halted, malted, salted, vaulted 3. defaulted, assaulted, exalted.

OLT′er– 2. alter, altar, falter, halter, malter, smalter, palter, salter, psalter, vaulter, Walter 3. defaulter, unhalter, Gibraltar, assaulter, exalter.

OLT′ern– 2. altern, saltern 3. subaltern.

OLT′i– 2. faulty, malty, salty, vaulty, volti [It.].

OLT′ij– 2. faultage, maltage, vaultage.

OLT′ik– 2. Baltic 3. cobaltic, basaltic 4. peristaltic.

OLT′ing– 2. faulting, halting, malting, salting, vaulting 3. defaulting, assaulting, exalting.

OLT′less– 2. faultless, haltless, maltless, saltless 3. defaultless, assaultless.

OL′um– 2. column, solemn.

OLV′ent– 2. solvent 3. absolvent, resolvent, dissolvent, insolvent, evolvent.

OLV′er– 2. solver 3. absolver, resolver, dissolver, evolver, revolver, involver.

OLV′ing– 2. solving 3. absolving, resolving, dissolving, evolving, devolving, revolving, involving 4. undissolving, unrevolving.

OLV′ment– 3. evolvement, devolvement, involvement.

OM′a– 2. comma, cauma, momma, trauma.

OM′as– 2. Thomas, promise 4. doubting Thomas.

OMB′a– 2. domba, tromba 3. zambomba, calomba.

OMB′at– 2. combat, wombat.

OMB′er– 2. omber, ombre, Scomber, somber.

OMB′i– 2. Dombey, zombie 4. Abercrombie.

OMB′l– 2. comble, wamble 3. ensemble.

OM′et– 2. comet, domett, grommet 3. Mahomet.

OM′i– 2. mommy, pommy, tommy, Tommy.

OM′ij– 2. homage, pommage.

OM′ik– 2. comic, nomic, dromic, promic 3. encomic, dinomic, syndromic, achromic, dichromic, atomic, entomic, phantomic, dystomic, Suomic 4. tragicomic, quasi-

comic, pathognomic, pyrognomic, economic, agronomic, chironomic, metronomic, astronomic, gastronomic, isonomic, autonomic, plutonomic, taxonomic, theobromic, hydrobromic, paradromic, palindromic, orthodromic, exodromic, loxodromic, monochromic, bathochromic, xanthochromic, polychromic, diatomic, triatomic, dermatomic, anatomic, monatomic, pentatomic, heptatomic, hexatomic, epitomic, microtomic, orthotomic 5. seriocomic, physiognomic, Deuteronomic, tesseratomic, heroicomic.

OM′iks– 2. comics 4. bionomics, economics, agronomics.

OM′ing– 2. bombing, gloming, glauming [both slang].

OM′is– 2. promise, Thomas 4. doubting Thomas.

OMP′i– 2. Pompey, rompy, swampy.

OMP′ish– 2. rompish, swampish.

OMP′us– 2. pompous 3. unpompous 4. catawampus.

ON′a– 2. donna, fauna 3. madonna 4. belladonna, prima donna, avifauna, piscifauna.

ON′ald– 2. Donald, Ronald.

OND′a– 2. fonda [Sp.], honda, nonda. 3. Golconda 4. anaconda.

OND′e– 2. spondee 3. dispondee.

OND′ed– 2. bonded 3. unbonded, absconded, responded 4. corresponded.

OND′ens– 3. abscondence, despondence, respondence 4. correspondence.

OND′ent– 2. frondent 3. despondent, respondent 4. co-respondent, correspondent.

OND′er– 2. bonder, fonder, condor, launder, blonder, ponder, wander, squander, yonder 3. absconder, responder 4. corresponder.

OND′est– 2. fondest, blondest.

OND′ij– 2. bondage, frondage 4. vagabondage.

OND'ing– 2. bonding 3. absconding, responding 4. vagabonding, corresponding.

OND'l– 2. fondle, rondle, rondel.

OND'li– 2. fondly, blondly 4. overfondly, overblondly.

OND'ness– 2. fondness, blondness.

OND'o– 2. hondo, rondo, tondo [It.].

ON'e– 2. Pawnee, Shawnee, Swanee; see also ON'i– awny etc. below.

ON'er– 2. awner, honor, fawner, conner, pawner, spawner, wanner, yawner 3. dishonor, aleconner.

ON'erd– 2. honored 3. time-honored, unhonored, dishonored.

ON'est– 2. honest, wannest, non est [L.] 3. dishonest.

ON'et– 2. bonnet, sonnet 3. sunbonnet, bluebonnet.

ONG'a– 2. bonga [Tag.], donga, conga, tonga, Tonga, wonga 3. Batonga 4. wonga-wonga.

ONG'er– 2. conger, longer, wronger, stronger, thronger 3. prolonger.

ONG'est– 2. longest, strongest.

ONG'ful– 2. longful, wrongful, throngful, songful.

ONG'i– 2. thongy 3. sing-songy.

ONG'ing– 2. longing, wronging, thronging 3. ding-donging, belonging, prolonging.

ONG'ish– 2. longish, wrongish, prongish, strongish.

ONG'li– 2. longly, wrongly, strongly.

ON'i– 2. awny, bonny, fawny, Johnny, Connie, lawny, Lonnie, pawny, Ronnie, scrawny, prawny, tawny, swanny, yawny 3. gyronny 5. mulligatawny; see also ON'e– Pawnee etc. above.

ON'ik– 2. phonic, conic, clonic, nonic, chronic, tonic 3. carbonic, bubonic, aconic, laconic, draconic, iconic, zirconic, Adonic, hedonic, sardonic, paeonic, agonic, trigonic, jargonic, aphonic, siphonic, symphonic, euphonic, typhonic, Pyrrhonic, benthonic, pythonic, Brythonic, Ionic, cyclonic, colonic, demonic, mnemonic, pulmonic, gnomonic, harmonic, sermonic, pneumonic, canonic, zoonic, Japonic, Aaronic, Neronic, ironic, Byronic, masonic, parsonic, atonic, Platonic, subtonic, tectonic, Metonic, pretonic, Miltonic, syntonic, protonic, Teutonic, plutonic, Slavonic, acronyc, ozonic 4. Pharaonic, polyconic, chalcedonic, algedonic, chelidonic, pantheonic, geogonic, theogonic, cosmogonic, polygonic, megaphonic, diaphonic, telephonic, antiphonic, cacophonic, xylophonic, microphonic, polyphonic, baryphonic, histrionic, cinnamonic, eudaemonic, hegemonic, Solomonic, philharmonic, anharmonic, enharmonic, etymonic, geoponic, electronic, supersonic, diatonic, hematonic, Housatonic, pentatonic, heptatonic, orthotonic, monotonic, neurotonic, isotonic, hypertonic, intertonic, polytonic, embryonic 5. chameleonic, Napoleonic, architectonic, electrotonic, Neoplatonic, geotectonic.

ON'iks– 2. onyx 3. hedonics, sardonyx, mnemonics, harmonics 4. chalcedonyx, histrionics, geoponics.

ON'ing– 2. awning, dawning, donning, fawning, conning, pawning, spawning, yawning.

ON'is– 3. Adonis.

ON'ish– 2. donnish, monish, tonnish, wannish 3. admonish, premonish, astonish.

ONK'er– 2. honker, conquer, conker 3. reconquer.

ONK'i– 2. donkey, conky.

ONK'ing– 2. honking, conking [slang].

ONK'us– 2. rhonchus, bronchus.

ON'li– 2. wanly.

ONS'al– 2. consul, sponsal, tonsil 3. proconsul, responsal.

ONS'er– 2. sponsor, tonsor 4. chirotonsor.

ONSH′us– 2. conscious, Pontius 3. sub-
conscious, self-conscious, unconscious.

ONS′iv– 3. responsive 4. irresponsive,
unresponsive, corresponsive.

ONST′er– 2. monster.

ONS′trans– 2. monstrance 3. demon-
strance, remonstrance.

ONS′trant– 3. demonstrant, remonstrant,
Premonstrant.

ONS′trus– 2. monstrous.

ONS′ul– 2. consul, sponsal, tonsil 3.
proconsul, vice-consul, responsal.

ONT′al– 2. ontal, fontal, pontal 3. ge-
rontal 4. horizontal.

ONT′an– 2. montane 3. tramontane,
submontane, cismontane, transmontane
4. ultramontane.

ONT′ed– 2. daunted, fonted, haunted,
flaunted, taunted, vaunted, wanted, wonted 3. undaunted, unwanted, unwonted.

ONT′er– 2. daunter, gaunter, haunter,
flaunter, saunter, taunter, vaunter, wanter
5. tessaraconter.

ONT′est– 2. gauntest.

ONT′i– 2. haunty, jaunty, flaunty,
vaunty.

ONT′ij– 2. pontage, vauntage, wantage.

ONT′ik– 2. pontic, quantic 3. odontic,
gerontic 4. mastodontic, uniquantic.

ONT′in– 2. pontine, Pontine 3. dra-
contine, cispontine, transpontine 4. Hel-
lespontine.

ONT′ing– 2. daunting, haunting, jaunt-
ing, flaunting, taunting, vaunting, wanting, wonting.

ONT′less– 2. dauntless, fontless, haunt-
less, tauntless, vauntless, wantless, wont-
less.

ONT′o– 2. conto, pronto, Tonto 3. To-
ronto.

ONZ′i– 2. bronzy.

ONZ′o– 3. Alphonso, Alonzo.

OP′er– 2. chopper, hopper, copper, scaup-
er, lopper, mopper, pauper, popper, drop-
per, cropper, proper, propper, stropper,
sopper, shopper, topper, stopper, swapper
[dial. & coll.], whopper [coll.] 3. clod-
hopper, grasshopper, eavesdropper, improp-
er, tiptopper 4. window shopper.

OP′et– 2. moppet, poppet.

OP′i– 2. choppy, hoppy, copy, loppy,
floppy, sloppy, moppy, poppy, droppy,
croppy, soppy, shoppy 3. recopy, jolop-
py, jalopy [both slang].

OP′ij– 2. proppage, stoppage.

OP′ik– 2. scopic, tropic, topic 3. acopic,
syncopic, Cyclopic, diplopic, canopic,
Sinopic, hydropic, anthropic, atropic, Ae-
sopic, prosopic, atopic, ectopic, metopic,
entopic, syntopic, myopic 4. telescopic,
periscopic, geoscopic, rheoscopic, ortho-
scopic, thermoscopic, lychnoscopic, apo-
scopic, acroscopic, macroscopic, micro-
scopic, hydroscopic, aeroscopic, hygro-
scopic, poroscopic, spectroscopic, gyro-
scopic, pantoscopic, photoscopic, autoscop-
ic, polyscopic, Ethiopic, nyctalopic, lycan-
thropic, theanthropic, philanthropic, mis-
anthropic, diatropic, ametropic, nycti-
tropic, isentropic, geotropic, rheotropic,
orthotropic, allotropic, monotropic, apo-
tropic, hydrotropic, aerotropic, neuro-
tropic, isotropic, autotropic, exotropic,
polytropic, isotopic, polytopic, presbyop-
ic, polyopic 5. kaleidoscopic, hagioscop-
ic, helioscopic, deuteroscopic, fluoroscopic,
electroscopic, hemeralopic, paleanthropic,
heliotropic, dexiotropic, heterotopic.

OP′ing– 2. chopping, hopping, copping,
lopping, flopping, plopping, slopping,
mopping, popping, dropping, cropping,
propping, stropping, sopping, shopping,
topping, stopping, swapping [dial. & coll.],
whopping [coll.] 3. clodhopping, eaves-
dropping, estopping, clip-clopping 4.
overtopping.

OP′ish– 2. foppish, shoppish.

OP′l– **2.** hopple, copple, popple, thropple, topple, stopple **3.** estoppel.

OP′ling– **2.** fopling, toppling, stoppling.

OP′shun– **2.** option **3.** adoption **4.** re-adoption.

OP′si– **2.** copsy, Mopsy, dropsy, Topsy.

OP′sis– **3.** synopsis **4.** thanatopsis.

OPT′ed– **2.** opted **3.** co-opted, adopted **4.** unadopted.

OPT′er– **2.** opter **3.** adopter, diopter, orthopter **4.** helicopter, phenicopter.

OPT′ik– **2.** optic, Coptic **3.** synoptic, autoptic, orthoptic.

OPT′ing– **2.** opting **3.** adopting.

OPT′iv– **2.** optive **3.** co-optive, adoptive.

OR′a– **2.** orra, aura, gora, gorah, Laura, sorra **3.** Andorra, begorra [dial. Ir.], Camorra, Gomorrah.

OR′al– **2.** aural, oral, horral, coral, laurel, moral, sorrel, quarrel **3.** amoral, Balmoral, immoral, unmoral, binaural.

OR′anj– **2.** orange **3.** mock orange **4.** navel orange, Osage orange.

ORB′el– **2.** orbell, corbeil, corbel, warble.

ORB′ent– **3.** absorbent, resorbent **4.** nonabsorbent, unabsorbent.

ORB′ing– **2.** orbing **3.** absorbing, resorbing.

ORB′l– **2.** corbel, warble.

ORCH′er– **2.** scorcher, torcher, torture.

ORCH′erd– **2.** orchard, tortured.

ORCH′ing– **2.** scorching, torching.

ORD′al– **2.** chordal **3.** concordal.

ORD′an– **2.** Jordan, warden.

ORD′ans– **3.** accordance, concordance, discordance.

ORD′ant– **2.** mordant **3.** accordant, concordant, discordant **4.** disaccordant.

ORD′ed– **2.** corded, chorded, lorded, sordid, warded, swarded **3.** accorded, recorded, belorded, unlorded, awarded, rewarded **4.** unrecorded, unrewarded.

ORD′er– **2.** order, border, corder, warder **3.** reorder, disorder, emborder, accorder, recorder, awarder, rewarder **4.** money order.

ORD′erd– **2.** ordered, bordered **3.** well-ordered, unordered, disordered, unbordered.

ORD′ij– **2.** cordage, wardage.

ORD′ing– **2.** cording, chording, lording, warding **3.** according, recording, belording, awarding, rewarding; *see* also **ORD′-ing**– boarding etc.

ORD′on– **2.** Gordon, Jordan, cordon, warden.

OR′el– **2.** laurel, saurel, sorrel, quarrel; *see* also **OR′al**– aural etc. above.

OR′en– **2.** foreign, sporran, warren.

OR′ens– **2.** Lawrence, Florence **3.** abhorrence, St. Lawrence.

OR′ent– **2.** horrent, torrent, warrant **3.** abhorrent, death warrant, search warrant.

OR′er– **2.** horror, warrer **3.** abhorrer.

OR′est– **2.** forest **3.** afforest, deforest, reforest, disforest.

OR′fan– **2.** orphan **3.** half-orphan.

ORF′i– **4.** metamorphy, geomorphy, zoo-morphy.

ORF′ik– **2.** Orphic, morphic **3.** amorphic, dimorphic, trimorphic **4.** metamorphic, endomorphic, pseudomorphic, geomorphic, theomorphic, monomorphic, zoomorphic, theromorphic, tauromorphic, isomorphic, pantomorphic, automorphic, exomorphic, polymorphic **5.** ophiomorphic, theriomorphic, heteromorphic, deuteromorphic **6.** ephemeromorphic.

ORF′ing– **2.** dwarfing, wharfing.

ORF′it– **2.** forfeit **3.** reforfeit.

ORF′izm– **2.** Orphism, morphism **4.** metamorphism, monomorphism, zoomorphism.

ORF′us– **3.** amorphous, dimorphous, trimorphous **4.** paramorphous, metamorphoŭs, polymorphous **5.** ophiomorphous, anthropomorphous.

ORG'an– **2.** organ, Gorgon, Morgan, morgan, morgen **3.** idorgan, biorgan **4.** Demogorgon.

ORG'ij– **2.** mortgage.

OR'i– **2.** corrie, scaurie, Laurie, lorry, sorry, saury, quarry **4.** Annie Laurie.

OR'id– **2.** horrid, florid, torrid, Taurid **3.** Centaurid.

OR'ij– **2.** borage, forage, porridge.

OR'ik– **2.** auric, goric, choric, chloric, tauric, toric, Yorick **3.** sudoric, theoric, phosphoric, enchoric, caloric, pyloric, rhetoric, historic, plethoric **4.** meteoric, semaphoric, cataphoric, metaphoric, allegoric, paregoric, oratoric, androtauric, prehistoric **5.** phantasmagoric; *see* also **OR'ik–** boric etc.

OR'ing– **2.** warring **3.** abhorring.

OR'is– **2.** orris, Doris, Horace, morris; *see* also **OR'us–** Caurus etc. below.

OR'ist– **2.** chorist, florist.

ORJ'er– **2.** forger, gorger.

ORJ'i– **2.** orgy, Georgie, porgy, storge **4.** Georgy Porgy.

ORJ'us– **2.** gorgeous **3.** ungorgeous.

ORK'a– **2.** Orca **3.** Majorca, Minorca.

ORK'er– **2.** forker, corker, porker, Yorker **3.** New Yorker.

ORK'i– **2.** forky, corky.

ORK'id– **2.** orchid.

ORK'ing– **2.** forking, Dorking, corking **3.** uncorking.

ORK'us– **2.** Orcus, Dorcas, orchis.

ORM'al– **2.** formal, cormel, normal **3.** informal, unformal, abnormal, unnormal, transnormal **4.** uniformal, supernormal.

ORM'an– **2.** Mormon, Norman.

ORM'ans– **2.** dormance **3.** conformance, performance.

ORM'ant– **2.** dormant, formant **3.** undormant, informant, conformant, performant.

ORM'er– **2.** ormer, dormer, former, stormer, warmer, swarmer **3.** deformer, reformer, informer, conformer, performer, transformer, barnstormer, chair warmer **4.** misinformer, nonconformer.

ORM'est– **2.** warmest.

ORM'i– **2.** dormy, forme, horme, stormy, swarmy.

ORM'ing– **2.** forming, storming, warming, swarming **3.** deforming, reforming, informing, conforming, performing, transforming, bestorming, barnstorming, housewarming **4.** misinforming, unconforming, nonconforming.

ORM'ist– **3.** reformist, conformist **4.** nonconformist, unconformist.

ORM'less– **2.** formless, stormless.

ORM'li– **2.** warmly **4.** uniformly.

ORM'us– **2.** Ormus, cormus, cormous **3.** abnormous, enormous.

ORN'a– **2.** Lorna **3.** cromorna.

ORN'er– **2.** horner, corner, scorner, warner **3.** suborner, adorner, forewarner **4.** chimney corner, catercorner, cattycorner, kittycorner **5.** Little Jack Horner, puss in the corner.

ORN'i– **2.** horny, corny, scorny, thorny.

ORN'ing– **2.** horning, corning, scorning, morning, warning **3.** suborning, a-borning, adorning, dehorning, good morning, forewarning.

ORN'is– **2.** ornis, cornice **3.** Dinornis, Notornis **4.** Ichthyornis.

ORN'ish– **2.** hornish, Cornish, Plornish [Dickens], warnish [Scot.].

ORN'less– **2.** hornless, cornless, scornless, thornless.

ORN'ment– **3.** adornment **4.** unadornment.

OR'o– **2.** borrow, morrow, sorrow **3.** tomorrow, good morrow.

ORP′er– 2. scorper, torpor, warper.

ORS′al– 2. dorsal, morsal 3. dextrorsal 4. sinistrorsal.

ORS′el– 2. morsel, norsel, torsel, torcel 3. ensorcell.

ORS′er– 2. horser 3. endorser.

ORS′ful– 2. forceful 3. remorseful, resourceful.

ORSH′un– 2. torsion 3. abortion, consortion, detorsion, retortion, intorsion, contortion, extortion; *see also* **ORSH′un–** portion etc.

ORSH′us– 2. tortious 3. extortious.

ORS′iv– 2. torsive 3. contorsive, extorsive.

ORS′o– 2. dorso [ML.], corso [It.], torso.

ORT′a– 2. torta, Torte [G.] 3. aorta 4. sesquiquarta.

ORT′al– 2. mortal, sortal, chortle 3. aortal, immortal.

ORT′ans– 2. portance 3. importance 4. unimportance.

ORT′ed– 2. snorted, sorted, warted, thwarted 3. aborted, exhorted, escorted, assorted, resorted, consorted, unsorted, detorted, retorted, contorted, distorted, extorted, cavorted, resorted.

ORT′eks– 2. cortex, vortex.

ORT′en– 2. chorten, shorten 3. foreshorten.

ORT′er– 2. mortar, snorter, sorter, shorter, quarter, swarter, thwarter 3. dehorter, exhorter, escorter, hindquarter, forequarter, assorter, resorter, consorter, retorter, contorter, distorter, extorter.

ORT′est– 2. shortest, swartest.

ORT′i– 2. forty, snorty, sortie, Shorty, Torte [G.], warty, swarty.

ORT′ij– 2. shortage.

ŎRT′ing– 2. snorting, sorting, Storting, thwarting 3. aborting, exhorting, escorting, consorting, retorting, contorting, distorting, extorting, cavorting, resorting.

ORT′is– 2. fortis, mortise, tortoise.

ORT′iv– 2. ortive, tortive 3. abortive, retortive, contortive, distortive, extortive.

ORT′l– 2. chortle; *see also* **ORT′al–** mortal etc. above.

ORT′ment– 2. sortment 3. assortment, consortment.

ORT′un– 2. fortune 3. misfortune, importune.

OR′us– 2. Caurus, Laurus, Taurus 3. thesaurus 4. Brontosaurus, Labrosaurus, Hadrosaurus, Mixosaurus 5. Megalosaurus, Ichthyosaurus, Atlantosaurus, ceratosaurus; *see also* **OR′is–** orris etc. above.

OR′ward– 2. forward, norward 3. henceforward, thenceforward, straightforward.

OS′a– 2. Ossa, ossa [L.], fossa, glossa.

OS′al– 2. ossal, dossal, glossal 3. colossal 4. hypoglossal; *see also* **OS′il–** docile etc. and **OS′l–** jostle etc. below.

OS′er– 2. bosser, Chaucer, dosser, josser, glosser, rosser, crosser, saucer, tosser 3. embosser 4. cup-and-saucer.

OS′et– 2. bosset, faucet, cosset, Nauset, posset.

OSH′er– 2. bosher, josher, cosher, washer, swasher, squasher 3. *whitewasher*.

OSH′i– 2. boshy, sloshy, toshy, washy, swashy, squashy 4. wishy-washy.

OSH′ing– 2. joshing, sloshing, washing, swashing, squashing 3. dishwashing.

OSH′un– 2. caution 3. incaution, precaution.

OS′i– 2. bossy, flossy, Flossie, glossy, mossy, posse, drossy, saucy, tossy.

OS′ij– 2. fossage, gaussage, sausage.

OS′ik– 2. fossick, glossic 3. molossic, banausic.

OS′il– 2. docile, dossil, fossil 3. indocile; *see also* **OS′l–** jostle etc. below; **OS′al–** ossal etc. above.

OS′ing– 2. bossing, dossing, glossing, mossing, crossing, tossing 3. embossing, grade crossing 4. railroad crossing.

OS′ip– 2. gossip.

OS′l– 2. jostle, throstle, tossel, wassail 3. apostle; *see* also OS′al– ossal etc. and OS′il– docile etc. above.

OS′ler– 2. ostler, hostler, jostler.

OS′li– 2. crossly.

OS′om– 2. blossom, possum 3. reblossom, opossum.

OSP′er– 2. prosper.

OSP′i– 2. waspy.

OST′a– 2. costa, Hosta 3. subcosta.

OST′al– 2. costal 4. Pentecostal, infracostal, supracostal, intercostal.

OST′ed– 2. frosted 3. exhausted, accosted, defrosted.

OST′el– 2. hostel, rostel.

OST′er– 2. Auster, foster, coster, Gloucester, roster, froster, zoster 3. exhauster, accoster, impostor 4. pentecoster, paternoster, Pater Noster.

OST′i– 2. frosty.

OST′ij– 2. hostage.

OST′ik– 2. caustic, gnostic 3. encaustic, agnostic, prognostic, acrostic 4. diacaustic, catacaustic, diagnostic, geognostic, paracrostic, pentacrostic.

OST′il– 2. hostile, postil.

OST′ing– 2. costing, frosting 3. exhausting, accosting.

OST′iv– 2. costive 3. exhaustive 4. inexhaustive, unexhaustive.

OST′ral– 2. austral, costrel, claustral, nostril, rostral 4. longirostral.

OST′rat– 2. rostrate, prostrate.

OST′rum– 2. haustrum, nostrum, rostrum.

OST′ur– 2. posture 3. imposture.

OS′um– 2. blossom, possum 3. emblossom, opossum 4. Geoglossum.

OS′us– 3. colossus, molossus.

OT′a– 2. cotta, pottah, chrotta 3. Carlotta 4. terra cotta, Epicauta, Argonauta.

OT′al– 2. glottal 4. epiglottal; *see* also OT′l– bottle etc. below.

OT′ed– 2. dotted, jotted, lotted, blotted, clotted, plotted, slotted, knotted, potted, spotted, rotted, trotted, sotted, shotted, squatted 3. wainscotted, allotted, unknotted, unspotted, garroted 4. juggernauted.

OT′en– 2. gotten, rotten, shotten, tauten 3. begotten, ill-gotten, ungotten, forgotten, misgotten 4. misbegotten, unforgotten; *see* also OT′on– cotton etc. below.

OT′er– 2. otter, daughter, dotter, hotter, jotter, cauter, cotter, blotter, clotter, plotter, slaughter, knotter, potter, spotter, rotter, trotter, shotter, water, squatter, swatter, yachter 3. granddaughter, complotter, unknotter, garrotter, globetrotter, bogtrotter, breakwater, limewater, firewater.

OT′est– 2. hottest.

OT′ful– 2. plotful, potful, thoughtful 3. unthoughtful.

OTH′am– 2. Gotham, Jotham.

OTH′er– 2. author, bother, fother, pother, rather, frother, swather.

OTH′ful– 2. slothful, wrathful.

OTH′i– 2. bothy, mothy, frothy, swathy.

OTH′ik– 2. Gothic, Sothic 4. Visigothic, Suigothic, Ostrogothic.

OTH′ing– 2. frothing, trothing 3. betrothing.

OT′i– 2. dotty, haughty, blotty, clotty, naughty, knotty, potty, spotty, shotty, totty, squatty, yachty.

OT′id– 3. carotid, parotid.

OT′ij– 2. cottage, clottage, plottage, pottage, wattage, squattage.

OT′ik– 2. otic, glottic, nautic 3. chaotic, thrombotic, sybotic, helcotic, narcotic, zygotic, argotic, dichotic, psychotic, morphotic, orthotic, xanthotic, biotic, meiotic, diglottic, Nilotic, psilotic, culottic, demotic, thermotic, seismotic, osmotic, zymotic, henotic, kenotic, binotic, pyknotic, monotic, hypnotic, zootic, nepotic, despotic, parotic, acrotic, necrotic, dicrotic, hydrotic, erotic, cerotic, sclerotic, xerotic, porotic, pyrotic, neurotic, entotic, aptotic, exotic, quixotic, loxotic, myotic, rhizotic **4.** anecdotic, alloeotic, indigotic, symbiotic, idiotic, semeiotic, periotic, patriotic, epiglottic, polyglottic, endosmotic, exosmotic, enzymotic, melanotic, cyanotic, Argonautic, aeronautic, agrypnotic, escharotic, anacrotic, catacrotic, monocrotic, polycrotic, oneirotic, ichthyotic **5.** catabiotic, amphibiotic, antibiotic, halobiotic, macrobiotic, Iscariotic, neurohypnotic, epizootic, rhinocerotic.

OT'ĭks– **2.** nautics **3.** biotics, demotics, thermotics **4.** aeronautics.

OT'ĭng– **2.** dotting, hotting, jotting, blotting, clotting, plotting, knotting, potting, spotting, rotting, trotting, swatting, squatting, yachting **3.** allotting, unknotting, garroting, globe-trotting, besotting **4.** juggernauting.

OT'ĭs– **2.** glottis **4.** epiglottis, hypoglottis.

OT'ĭsh– **2.** hottish, Scottish, sottish, schottische, squattish.

OT'l– **2.** bottle, dottle, glottal, mottle, pottle, rotl, crottle, throttle, tottle, wattle, twattle **3.** bluebottle **4.** acocotl, axolotl, epiglottal.

OT'ler– **2.** bottler, mottler, throttler, twattler.

OT'less– **2.** dotless, cotless, blotless, plotless, knotless, potless, spotless, rotless, totless, thoughtless.

OT'lĭ– **2.** hotly, motley, tautly.

OT'lĭng– **2.** bottling, mottling, throttling, wattling, twattling.

OT'ment– **2.** squatment **3.** allotment, besotment.

OT'o– **2.** Otto, lotto, blotto [slang], motto, potto, grotto, sotto [It.] **3.** ridotto, fagotto [It.], risotto [It.].

OT'on– **2.** cotton, Lawton, frotton, Groton **3.** guncotton; *see* also **OT'en-** gotten etc. above.

OT'um– **2.** autumn, bottom.

OV'el– **2.** hovel, novel, grovel.

OV'er– **2.** hover, suaver.

OV'erb– **2.** proverb.

O'yer– **2.** lawyer, sawyer **3.** top sawyer.

OZ'al– **2.** causal, pausal, clausal; *see* also **OZ'l–** nozzle etc. below.

OZ'er– **2.** hawser, causer, pauser.

OZ'ez– **2.** gauzes, causes, clauses, pauses, vases **3.** becauses, applauses.

OZ'ĭ– **2.** gauzy, causey, lawzy [dial.].

OZ'ĭng– **2.** causing, clausing, pausing.

OZ'ĭt– **2.** closet, posit **3.** deposit, reposit, composite **4.** juxtaposit, oviposit, decomposite, incomposite, interposit.

OZ'ĭv– **2.** plausive **3.** applausive **4.** unapplausive.

OZ'l– **2.** nozzle, snozzle, sozzle; *see* also **OZ'al–** causal etc. above.

OZ'mĭk– **2.** osmic, cosmic **3.** aosmic **4.** neocosmic, macrocosmic, microcosmic.

OZ'mos– **2.** cosmos **4.** macrocosmos, microcosmos.

O (awe)

3.

TRIPLE RHYMES IN O (prob'a-ble)

OB'a-bl– 3. daubable, robbable, probable 4. improbable.

OB'er-i– 3. bobbery, daubery, jobbery, clobbery, slobbery, snobbery, robbery, strawberry.

OB'er-ing– 3. clobbering, slobbering.

OB'ul-ar– 3. lobular, globular.

OD'a-bl– 3. laudable, plaudable 4. applaudable.

OD'er-er– 3. dodderer, fodderer, solderer.

OD'er-i– 3. doddery, gaudery.

OD'er-ing– 3. doddering, foddering, soldering.

OD'i-fi– 3. codify, modify.

OD'i-ing– 3. bodying 4. embodying, disbodying 5. disembodying.

OD'ik-al– 3. codical, nodical 4. spasmodical, synodical, monodical, prosodical, rhapsodical, methodical 5. periodical, episodical.

OD'i-ness– 3. bawdiness, gaudiness.

OD'it-er– 3. auditor, plauditor.

OD'it-i– 3. oddity, quoddity 4. commodity 5. incommodity, discommodity.

OD'ul-ant– 3. modulant, fraudulent.

OD'ul-ar– 3. modular, nodular.

OF'ag-a– 4. Sarcophaga, Zoophaga.

OF'ag-al– 4. sarcophagal, esophagal.

OF'ag-an– 4. zoophagan, saprophagan.

OF'ag-us– 4. geophagous, theophagous, sarcophagus, sarcophagous, zoophagous, hippophagous, androphagous, necrophagous, esophagus, saprophagous 5. ichthyophagous.

OF'aj-i– 4. theophagy, sarcophagy, hippophagy, phytophagy, pantophagy 5. ichthyophagy, anthropophagy.

OF'aj-ist– 4. geophagist, omophagist, hippophagist, pantophagist 5. ichthyophagist, galactophagist.

OF'el-ez– 5. Mephistopheles.

OF'er-er– 3. offerer, cofferer, profferer.

OF'er-ing– 3. offering, goffering, coffering, proffering 4. thank offering, peace offering 5. freewill offering.

OF'ik-al– 3. trophical, sophical 5. theosophical, philosophical.

OF'il-us– 4. Theophilus, sarcophilous, Sarcophilus, xylophilous, saprophilous, zoophilous 5. acidophilus, heliophilous.

OF'on-i– 4. theophany, cacophony, homophony, photophony, Christophany, tautophony, orthophony.

OF'or-us– 4. zoophorus, phyllophorous, pyrophorous, pyrophorus 5. galactophorous.

OF'ul-i– 3. awfully, lawfully 4. unlawfully.

OF'ul-ness– 3. awfulness, lawfulness 4. unlawfulness.

OG'am-i– 4. endogamy, monogamy, misogamy, exogamy 5. deuterogamy.

OG'am-ist– 4. monogamist, cryptogamist, misogamist 5. deuterogamist.

OG′am–us– **4.** endogamous, homogamous, monogamous, idogamous, exogamous **5.** heterogamous.

OG′at–iv– **4.** derogative, prerogative **5.** interrogative.

OG′er–el– **3.** doggerel, hoggerel.

OG′er–i– **3.** froggery, groggery, toggery **5.** pettifoggery.

OG′nom–i– **4.** pathognomy **5.** craniognomy, physiognomy.

OG′on–i– **4.** geogony, theogony, mahogany, homogony, cosmogony, monogony, zoogony, mythogony **5.** bibliogony, physiogony, heroogony, heterogony.

OG′raf–er– **4.** logographer, lithographer, orthographer, biographer, demographer, mimographer, nomographer, cosmographer, sphenographer, stenographer, hymnographer, chronographer, zoographer, topographer, typographer, chirographer, chorographer, glossographer, photographer, cartographer, cryptographer, doxographer, mythographer **5.** lexicographer, celidographer, choreographer, selenographer, bibliographer **6.** autobiographer.

OG′raf–i– **4.** cacography, chalcography, zincography, macrography, micrography, phycography, geography, logography, psychography, morphography, ethography, lithography, anthography, orthography, mythography, biography, haplography, stylography, xylography, demography, psalmography, mimography homography, nomography, cosmography, planography, scenography, sphenography, stenography, zenography, technography, ichnography, ethnography, hymnography, phonography, chronography, pornography, zoography, lipography, topography, typography, micrography, hydrography, cerography, pterography, chirography, orography, horography, chorography, petrography, neurography, pyrography, isography, nosography, hypsography, glossography, ontography, scotography, photography, glyptography, cryp-

tography, cartography, histography, autography, phytography, myography **5.** pharmacography, lexicography, celidography, archaeography, palaeography, ideography, stereography, osteography, radiography, cardiography, semeiography, hagiography, heliography, ophiography, bibliography, physiography, hyalography, metallography, crystallography, sigillography, selenography, iconography, anthropography, siderography, hierography, heterography, papyrography, thalassography, sematography, pneumatography, thanatography, skeletography, cometography, hyetography, odontography, ichthyography **6.** zoogeography, pythogeography, chromolithography, autobiography, dactyliography, historiography, ecclesiography, oceanography, Christianography, cinematography, phantasmatography, numismatography, chromophotography.

OG′raf–ist– **4.** biographist, stenographist, phonographist, monographist, zoographist, topographist, chirographist, photographist, orthographist **5.** metallographist, selenographist, siderographist.

OG′ur–al– **3.** augural **4.** inaugural.

OJ′en–ez– **4.** Diogenes, protogenes.

OJ′en–i– **3.** progeny **4.** biogeny, homogeny, nomogeny, monogeny, ethnogeny, oögeny, misogyny, zoogeny, autogeny, pathogeny **5.** embryogeny, anthropogeny.

OJ′en–ist– **4.** biogenist, philogynist, monogenist, misogynist **5.** abiogenist, heterogenist.

OJ′en–us– **4.** endogenous, biogenous, primogenous, homogenous, thermogenous, hypogenous, hydrogenous, pyrogenous, nitrogenous, exogenous, lithogenous.

OJ′ik–al– **3.** logical **4.** alogical, illogical, unlogical **5.** anagogical, synagogical, apagogical, dialogical, analogical, symbological, geological, theological, neological, psychological, pathological, anthological, ethnological, mythological, biological, homological, cosmological, zymological, technological, penological, technological, ichnological, chronological, zoological, tropological, necrological, micrological, typological, metrological, astrological, neurological, glossological, nosological, histological, tautological, cytological, doxological **6.** genealogical, toxicological, archaeological, ideological, sociological, bibliological, physiological, etymological, entomological, terminological, anthropological, climatological, embryological, Egyptological **7.** bacteriological, ecclesiological, meteorological, palaeontological.

ŎJ'in–i– **4.** philogyny, monogyny, misogyny; *see* also ŎJ'en–i– progeny etc. above.

ŎJ'in–ist– **4.** biogenist, philogynist, monogenist, misogynist.

ŎJ'it–at– **3.** cogitate **4.** recogitate, precogitate, excogitate.

OK'at–iv– **3.** locative, talkative, vocative **4.** untalkative, invocative, provocative.

OK'er–i– **3.** mockery, rockery, crockery.

OK'il–i– **3.** chalkily, gawkily, cockily, pawkily, stockily.

OK'i–ness– **3.** chalkiness, gawkiness, cockiness, rockiness, talkiness, stockiness.

OK'ing–li– **3.** mockingly, shockingly, squawkingly.

OK'ras–i– **4.** landocracy, theocracy, theocrasy, neocrasy, ptochocracy, ochlocracy, doulocracy, democracy, timocracy, nomocracy, cosmocracy, technocracy, ethnocracy, monocracy, androcracy, isocracy, chrysocracy, stratocracy, plantocracy, autocracy, plutocracy, bureaucracy **5.** gynaecocracy, idiocrasy, hagiocracy, physiocracy, arithmocracy, millionocracy, hierocracy, pantisocracy, thalassocracy, ergatocracy, gerontocracy, despotocracy, aristocracy.

OK'rat–ist– **4.** theocratist, democratist, bureaucratist.

OK'rat–izm– **3.** Socratism **4.** democratism, bureaucratism.

OKS'ik–al– **3.** toxical **5.** paradoxical, orthodoxical.

OKS'im–al– **3.** proximal **4.** approximal.

OK'ul–ar– **3.** ocular, jocular, locular, ₎vocular **4.** binocular, monocular.

OK'ul–at– **3.** oculate, flocculate **4.** inoculate, binoculate.

OK'ul–us– **3.** oculus, loculus **4.** monoculus.

OK'ut–or– **4.** oblocutor, collocutor, prolocutor **5.** interlocutor.

OL'a–bl– **3.** callable **4.** recallable, enthrallable.

OL'at–er– **4.** idolater, pyrolater, artolater **5.** bibliolater, heliolater, Mariolater, iconolater.

OL'a–tri– **4.** symbolatry, mobolatry, idolatry, lordolatry, litholatry, theolatry, cosmolatry, onolatry, monolatry, zoolatry, topolatry, necrolatry, pyrolatry, Christolatry, plutolatry **5.** archaeolatry, hygeiolatry, gynaeolatry, hagiolatry, orphiolatry, bibliolatry, heliolatry, geniolatry, Mariolatry, patriolatry, physiolatry, angelolatry, symbololatry, uranolatry, Parthenolatry, iconolatry, demonolatry, anthropolatry, arborolatry, grammatolatry, thaumatolatry, ichthyolatry **6.** ecclesiolatry.

OL'at–rus– **4.** idolatrous, zoolatrous **5.** heliolatrous, bibliolatrous.

OL'id–li– **3.** solidly, stolidly, squalidly.

OL'if–i– **3.** jollify, mollify, qualify **4.** idolify, disqualify.

OL'i–form– **3.** colliform, cauliform **4.** emboliform.

OL'i–ing– **3.** dollying, follying, jollying.

OL'ik–al– **4.** symbolical, catholical **5.** diabolical, parabolical, hyperbolical, apostolical **6.** bibliopolical.

OL'ik–l–   3. follicle, caulicle.

OL'ik–som–   3. rollicksome, frolicsome.

OL'ing–li–   3. drawlingly, crawlingly   4. appallingly, enthrallingly.

OL'ish–er–   3. polisher   4. abolisher, demolisher.

OL'ish–ing–   3. polishing   4. abolishing, demolishing, repolishing.

OL'is–i–   3. policy   4. impolicy.

OL'is–is–   4. biolysis, hemolysis, hydrolysis, neurolysis, autolysis, histolysis.

OL'it–i–   3. jollity, polity, quality   4. equality, frivolity   5. isopolity, interpolity, inequality, coequality.

OL'it–iks–   3. politics   5. geopolitics, cosmopolitics.

OL'o–er–   3. follower, hollower, wallower, swallower.

OL'og–us–   4. homologous, isologous, tautologous   5. heterologous.

OL'o–ing–   3. following, hollowing, wallowing, swallowing.

OL'oj–er–   4. geologer, theologer, philologer, mythologer, phrenologer, acknowledger, phonologer, chronologer, horologer, astrologer   5. physiologer, etymologer.

OL'oj–i–   3. ology   4. naology, symbology, cacology, ecology, oncology, tocology, sarcology, muscology, phycology, mycology, pedology, tidology, odology, podology, pseudology, geology, rheology, theology, neology, algology, ergology, trichology, conchology, ptochology, archology, euchology, psychology, graphology, nephology, trophology, morphology, pathology, ethology, lithology, mythology, anthology, orthology, biology, philology, typhlology, haplology, hylology, xylology, sphygmology, gemmology, homology, nomology, gnomology, pomology, thermology, desmology, chresmology, seismology, cosmology, pneumology, zymology, phenology, menology, penology, phrenology, technology, ichnology, aph-

nology, ethnology, kinology, Sinology, limnology, hymnology, phonology, monology, chronology, tonology, hypnology, runology, cynology, oology, noology, zoology, apology, tropology, topology, hippology, carpology, typology, barology, pharology, ambrology, timbrology, ombrology, macrology, necrology, micrology, dendrology, hydrology, therology, pterology, agrology, hygrology, arthrology, chirology, orology, horology, chorology, latrology, patrology, metrology, petrology, astrology, gastrology, neurology, pyrology, misology, dosology, nosology, posology, threpsology, gypology, glossology, chrysology, battology, cetology, ctetology, dittology, cytology, phytology, sitology, planktology, pantology, ontology, otology, photology, glottology, cryptology, typtology, cartology, pestology, histology, Christology, tautology, plutology, taxology, sexology, doxology, auxology, myology, bryology   5. amphibology, malacology, pharmacology, gynecology, lexicology, toxicology, monadology, acidology, pteridology, dicaeology, archaeology, atheology, palaeology, ideology, pantheology, speleology, teleology, areology, thereology, phraseology, osteology, edaphology, agathology, ornithology, abiology, sociology, radiology, cardiology, semeiology, hagiology, ophiology, sophiology, caliology, bibliology, heliology, mommiology, craniology, koniology, agriology, gnosiology, physiology, etiology, axiology, praxiology, angelology, dactylology, potamology, anemology, ophthalmology, docimology, paromology, atomology, entomology, orismology, etymology, mechanology, volcanology, organology, campanology, uranology, lichenology, selenology, asthenology, arachnology, carcinology, criminology, terminology, eccrinology, actinology, iconology, pogonology, demonology, gnomonology, synchronology, Hibernology, maternology, immunology, heroology, antapology, anthropology, hierology, ponerology, heterology, enterology, oneirology, iatrology, electrology, acyrology, papyrology, martyrology, parisology, piscatology, eschatology, haematology, rhematology, sematology, agmatology, climatology, thremmatology, stomatology, dermatology, thermatology, thaumatology, pneumatology, kymatology, thanatology, geratology, teratology, olfactology, esthetology, hyetology, melittology, semantology, odontology, deontology, neontology, erotology, Egyptology, heortology, aristology, agrostology, ichthyology, embryology 6. metamorphology, geomorphology, psychopathology, neuropathology, theomythology, amphibiology, microbiology, stoichiology, dactyliology, paroemiology, bacteriology, soteriology, heresiology, hamartiology, diabolology, epistemology, phenomenology, paleethnology, meteorology, universology, emblematology, philematology, systematology, onomatology, numismatology, toreumatology, dialectology, paleontology 7. paleopsychology, idiopsychology.

OL'oj–ist– 4. geologist, neologist, theologist, echologist, conchologist, psychologist, morphologist, pathologist, lithologist, anthologist, mythologist, biologist, philologist, mimologist, palmologist, homologist, pomologist, seismologist, cosmologist, zymologist, phrenologist, technologist, ethnologist, Sinologist, hymnologist, phonologist, monologist, chronologist, hypnologist, oologist, noologist, zoologist, apologist, necrologist, dendrologist, hydrologist, horologist, petrologist, astrologist, chirologist, neurologist, glossologist, nosologist, gypsologist, battologist, ontologist, otologist, photologist, histologist, tautologist, phytologist, bryologist, myologist 5. pharmacologist, anthocologist, lexicologist, toxicologist, archaeologist, ideologist, teleologist, phraseologist, ornithologist, sociologist, hagiologist, craniologist, physiologist, ophthalmologist, etymologist, arachnologist, dem-

onologist, anthropologist, hierologist, oneirologist, dermatologist, herpetologist, neontologist, Egyptologist, melittologist, ichthyologist, embryologist 6. paroemiologist, bacteriologist, ecclesiologist, meteorologist, numismatologist, dialectologist, paleontologist.

OL'oj–iz– 4. geologize, neologize, theologize, philologize, homologize, monologize, apologize, astrologize, doxologize, battologize, mythologize 5. sociologize, entomologize, etymologize.

OL'op–er– 3. scalloper, walloper [dial., coll. & slang].

OLT'er–er– 3. alterer, falterer, palterer, psalterer.

OLT'er–i– 3. saltery, psaltery.

OLT'er–ing– 3. altering, faltering, paltering 4. unaltering, unfaltering.

OLT'i–est– 3. faultiest, maltiest, saltiest.

OLT'i–ness– 3. faultiness, maltiness, saltiness.

OL'ub–li– 3. solubly, volubly 4. insolubly 5. indissolubly.

OLV'a–bl– 3. solvable 4. absolvable, resolvable, insolvable, unsolvable, dissolvable 5. unresolvable, indissolvable.

OLV'en–si– 3. solvency 4. insolvency, revolvency.

OM'ak–i– 3. naumachy 4. theomachy, logomachy, sciomachy, psychomachy, monomachy, tauromachy, pyromachy, duomachy 5. iconomachy, centauromachy, gigantomachy 6. alectryomachy.

OM'ath–i– 4. philomathy, chrestomathy.

OM'en–a– 4. phenomena 5. prolegomena 6. antilegomena, paralipomena.

OM'et–er– 4. tribometer, oncometer, pedometer, speedometer, ondometer, udometer, geometer, rehometer, ergometer, tachometer, graphometer, bathometer, stethometer, cyclometer, kilometer, sillometer, bolometer, stylometer, pulmometer, chromometer, tromometer, thermometer, seismometer, osmometer, atmometer, cymometer, zymometer, planometer, manometer, pychometer, clinometer, vinometer, phonometer, monometer, chronometer, sonometer, tonometer, oometer, tropometer, hippometer, barometer, vibrometer, ombrometer, macrometer, micrometer, dendrometer, hydrometer, spherometer, hygrometer, psychrometer, chirometer, spirometer, orometer, horometer, spectrometer, nitrometer, astrometer, pyrometer, gasometer, pulsometer, drosometer, hypsometer, passometer, lactometer, stactometer, hectometer, altometer, pantometer, photometer, comptometer, haptometer, leptometer, optometer, cyrtometer, cryometer   **5.** tacheometer, oleometer, areometer, stereometer, heliometer, craniometer, variometer, fluviometer, pluviometer, oscillometer, scintillometer, dynamometer, anemometer, arithmometer, galvanometer, salinometer, declinometer, inclinometer, actinometer, harmonometer, micronometer, respirometer, electrometer, opisometer, thallasometer, climatometer, chromatometer, pneumatometer, thanatometer, olfactometer, refractometer, magnetometer, piezometer, horizometer **6.** diaphanometer, sphygmomanometer.

OM'et–ri–   **3.** maumetry   **4.** geometry, rheometry, Mahometry, stichometry, pyschometry, morphometry, orthometry, biometry, cyclometry, colometry, thermometry, pneumometry, planometry, phonometry, chronometry, tonometry, typometry, barometry, micrometry, hydrometry, gygrometry, horometry, chorometry, astrometry, pyrometry, gasometry, isometry, hypsometry, photometry, autometry   **5.** areometry, stereometry, osteometry, cardiometry, stoichiometry, craniometry, anemometry, uranometry, galvanometry, trigonometry, ozonometry, anthropometry, electrometry, piezometry **6.** historiometry.

OM'ik–al–   **3.** domical, comical   **4.** atomical, phantomical   **5.** tragicomical, economical, agronomical, metronomical, astronomical, anatomical, zootomical   **6.** uneconomical.

OM'in–al–   **3.** nominal   **4.** abdominal, adnominal, praenominal, cognominal, pronominal, surnominal.

OM'in–ans–   **3.** dominance, prominence **4.** predominance.

OM'in–ant–   **3.** dominant, prominent   **4.** subdominant, predominant   **5.** superdominant.

OM'in–at–   **3.** dominate, comminate, nominate   **4.** abominate, predominate, denominate, renominate, prenominate, innominate.

OM'in–i–   **3.** dominie, hominy, Romany **5.** Chickahominy.

OM'in–us–   **3.** ominous, dominus   **4.** abdominous, binominous.

OMN'i–a–   **3.** omnia   **4.** insomnia.

OM'un–ist–   **3.** communist   **4.** noncommunist   **5.** anticommunist.

OND'en–si–   **4.** despondency   **5.** correspondency.

OND'er–er–   **3.** launderer, ponderer, wanderer, squanderer.

OND'er–ing–   **3.** laundering, pondering, wandering, squandering.

OND'er–us–   **3.** ponderous   **4.** preponderous   **5.** equiponderous.

ON'i–er–   **3.** bonnier, tawnier, brawnier, scrawnier.

ON'i–est–   **3.** bonniest, tawniest, brawniest, scrawniest.

ON'if–i–   **3.** bonify   **4.** saponify, personify, ozonify.

ON'ik–a–   **3.** Monica   **4.** harmonica, japonica, Veronica.

ON'ik–al–   **3.** conical, chronicle, tonical **4.** euphonical, iconical, mnemonical, harmonical, canonical, ironical, synchronical, thrasonical   **5.** cosmogonical, histrionical, diaphonical, tautophonical, geoponical.

ON'im–i– 3. onymy **4.** homonymy, synonymy, eponymy, toponymy, patronymy, metronymy, metonymy; *see* also **ON'om–i–** morphonomy etc. below.

ON'im–ist– 4. synonymist, eponymist; *see* also **ON'om–ist–** economist etc. below.

ON'im–us– 3. onymous **4.** anonymous, pseudonymous, eponymous, homonymous, synonymous, paronymous, autonymous **5.** heteronymous.

ON'ing–li– 3. fawningly, yawningly.

ON'ish–ing– 3. monishing **4.** admonishing, premonishing, astonishing.

ON'ish–ment– 4. admonishment, premonishment, astonishment.

ON'is–izm– 4. sardonicism, laconicism, teutonicism **5.** histrionicism.

ON'it–or– 3. monitor **4.** admonitor, premonitor.

ON'o–graf– 3. phonograph, monograph, tonograph, chronograph.

ON'o–gram– 3. monogram, chronogram, tonogram.

ON'om–er– 4. astronomer, gastronomer.

ON'om–i– 4. morphonomy, economy, agronomy, astronomy, gastronomy, isonomy, taxonomy, nosonomy, autonomy **5.** dactylonomy, anthroponomy, Deuteronomy; *see* also **ON'im–i–** onymy etc. above.

ON'om–ist– 4. economist, synonymist, eponymist, agronomist, gastronomist, autonomist, plutonomist.

ON'om–iz– 4. economize, astronomize, gastronomize, autonomize.

ONS'ul–ar– 3. consular **4.** nonconsular, proconsular, vice-consular.

ONT'ing–li– 3. dauntingly, hauntingly, tauntingly, vauntingly, wantingly.

OP'ath–i– 4. theopathy, psychopathy, allopathy, somnopathy, hydropathy, neuropathy, autopathy **5.** homoeopathy, osteopathy, deuteropathy.

OP'ath–ist– 4. psychopathist, allopathist, hylopathist, somnopathist, hydropathist, neuropathist **5.** homoeopathist, osteopathist.

OP'er–i– 3. foppery, coppery **4.** zoopery.

OP'i–er– 3. choppier, copier, floppier, sloppier, soppier.

OP'i–est– 3. choppiest, hoppiest, floppiest, sloppiest, soppiest.

OP'i–ist– 3. copyist.

OP'ik–al– 3. tropical, topical **4.** subtropical **5.** microscopical, philanthropical, misanthropical.

OP'i–ness– 3. choppiness, floppiness, sloppiness, soppiness.

OP'ol–is– 3. propolis **4.** cosmopolis, acropolis, necropolis, metropolis **5.** Heliopolis.

OP'ol–ist– 4. monopolist **5.** bibliopolist, pharmacopolist.

OP'ol–it– 4. cosmopolite, metropolite.

OPT'ik–al– 3. optical **4.** autoptical.

OPT'im–ist– 3. optimist.

OP'ul–us– 3. opulus, populous **4.** unpopulous.

OR'ak–l– 3. oracle, coracle; *see* also **OR'ik–al–** oracle etc. below.

OR'al–i– 3. morally **4.** immorally, unmorally.

OR'al–ist– 3. coralist, moralist.

ORD'er–ing– 3. ordering, bordering **4.** reordering, embordering.

ORD'er–li– 3. orderly **4.** unorderly, disorderly.

ORD'i–al– 3. cordial **4.** primordial, exordial.

ORD'i–an– 3. Gordian **4.** accordion, Edwardian.

ORD'in–al– 3. ordinal **4.** biordinal, diordinal.

ORD'in–at– 3. ordinate **4.** subordinate, inordinate, co-ordinate, foreordinate **5.** insubordinate, in-co-ordinate, un-co-ordinate.

OR'e–at–   3. aureate, laureate   5. baccalaureate, poet laureate.

OR'gan–iz–   3. organize, gorgonize   4. reorganize, disorganize.

OR'i–an–   3. saurian, taurian   4. centaurian   5. dinosaurian, morosaurian.

OR'id–er–   3. corridor.

OR'id–li–   3. horridly, floridly, torridly.

OR'i–er–   3. sorrier, warrior, quarrier.

OR'if–i–   3. aurify, horrify, torrefy   4. calorify, historify.

OR'i–form–   3. floriform, moriform, poriform   4. arboriform, vaporiform.

OR'ik–al–   3. oracle, coracle   4. rhetorical, historical   5. meteorical, anaphorical, metaphorical, allegorical, categorical, tautegorical, oratorical.

OR'it–i–   4. priority, majority, minority, sonority, sorority, authority   5. meliority, seniority, juniority   6. inferiority, superiority, deteriority, anteriority, interiority, exteriority, posteriority.

ORM'a–bl–   3. formable, warmable, stormable   4. informable, conformable, performable, transformable, unwarmable.

ORM'al–iz–   3. formalize, normalize   4. informalize.

ORM'at–iv–   3. dormitive, formative   4. afformative, deformative, reformative, informative, transformative.

ORM'it–i–   4. deformity, conformity, abnormity, enormity   5. uniformity, multiformity, nonconformity, inconformity, unconformity.

OR'o–er–   3. borrower, sorrower.

OR'o–ing–   3. borrowing, morrowing, sorrowing.

ORS'a–bl–   3. forcible   4. endorsable, enforceable, divorceable.

ORSH'un–al–   3. torsional   4. abortional, contortional, distortional.

ORSH'un–ist–   4. contortionist, extortionist.

ORT'a–bl–   3. sortable   4. unsortable, distortable;   see also ORT'a–bl– courtable etc.

ORT'at–tiv–   3. hortative   4. dehortative, exhortative.

ORT'if–i–   3. fortify, mortify   4. defortify, refortify.

ORT'ik–al–   3. cortical, vortical.

ORT'un–it–   3. fortunate   4. unfortunate, misfortunate, importunate.

OS'for–us–   3. Bosphorus, phosphorus, phosphorous.

OS'i–bl–   3. possible   4. impossible, compossible, unpossible.

OS'i–er–   3. bossier, flossier, glossier, mossier, saucier.

OS'i–est–   3. bossiest, flossiest, glossiest, mossiest, sauciest.

OS'i–ness–   3. bossiness, glossiness, mossiness, sauciness.

OS'it–i–   3. docity, paucity, raucity   4. gibbosity, globosity, verbosity, precocity, jocosity, hircosity, viscosity, muscosity, mucosity, nodosity, fungosity, regosity, velocity, pilosity, callosity, villosity, gulosity, rimosity, fumosity, venosity, spinosity, vinosity, pomposity, ferocity, serosity, porosity, atrocity, neurocity, aquosity, nivosity   5. bellicosity, varicosity, vitreosity, dubiosity, graciosity, speciosity, preciosity, grandiosity, seriosity, curiosity, furiosity, vitiosity, otiosity, fabulosity, sabulosity, nebulosity, rugulosity, scrupulosity, animosity, arenosity, luminosity, glutinosity, tenebrosity, tuberosity, ponderosity, generosity, vaporosity, reciprocity, unctuosity, fructuosity, virtuosity, tortuosity, flexuosity   6. religiosity, ridiculosity, meticulosity, fuliginosity, voluminosity, vociferosity, anfractuosity, infructuosity, impetuosity   7. impecuniosity.

OSK'op–i–   3. nauscopy   4. stethoscopy, necroscopy, microscopy, horoscopy, brontoscopy, spectroscopy, gastroscopy, autoscopy, cryoscopy **5.** stereoscopy, ornithoscopy, radioscopy, cranioscopy, dactyloscopy, ophthalmoscopy, lecanoscopy, organoscopy, uranoscopy, retinoscopy, ceraunoscopy, metoposcopy, hieroscopy, deuteroscopy, fluoroscopy **6.** meteoroscopy.

OSK′op–ist– **4.** microscopist, stethoscopist, misoscopist **5.** stereoscopist, metoposcopist, oneiroscopist, ornithoscopist.

OS′of–er– **4.** theosopher, philosopher, psilosopher, misosopher.

OS′of–i– **4.** gymnosophy, theosophy, philosophy, psilosophy, misosophy.

OS′of–ist– **4.** gymnosophist, theosophist, philosophist, chirosophist, misosophist.

OS′of–iz– **4.** theosophize, philosophize.

OST′ik–al– **4.** agnostical, acrostical.

OST′is–izm– **3.** Gnosticism **4.** agnosticism, acrosticism.

OST′rof–e– **4.** monostrophe, apostrophe.

OT′an–i– **3.** botany, cottony **4.** monotony.

OT′er–er– **3.** slaughterer, totterer, waterer.

OT′er–i– **3.** cautery, lottery, pottery, tottery, watery.

OT′er–ing– **3.** slaughtering, tottering, watering.

OTH′es–is– **3.** prothesis **4.** apothesis, hypothesis.

OT′i–er– **3.** haughtier, naughtier, squattier.

OT′i–est– **3.** haughtiest, naughtiest, squattiest.

OT′ik–al– **3.** nautical **4.** biotical, despotical, erotical, exotical **5.** anecdotical, idiotical.

OT′il–i– **3.** dottily, haughtily, naughtily, spottily, squattily.

OT′il–us– **3.** nautilus.

OT′i–ness– **3.** dottiness, haughtiness, naughtiness, knottiness, spottiness, squattiness.

OT′is–izm– **4.** eroticism, neuroticism, exoticism.

OT′om–i– **3.** scotomy **4.** strabotomy, phlebotomy, dichotomy, trichotomy, cyclotomy, helotomy, aplotomy, tenotomy, zootomy, apotome, microtomy, nephrotomy, neurotomy, autotomy, phytotomy, loxotomy **5.** tracheotomy, stereotomy, osteotomy, cardiotomy, herniotomy, pogonotomy, anthropotomy, laparotomy, Caesarotomy, enterotomy, ichthyotomy, Ichthyotomi.

OT′on–i– **4.** homotony, monotony, chirotony.

OV′el–er– **3.** hoveler, groveler.

OV′el–ing– **3.** hoveling, groveling.

OZ′a–bl– **3.** causable, plausible **4.** implausible, unplausible.

OZ′it–iv– **3.** causative, positive **4.** appositive, depositive, prepositive, compositive, expositive, transpositive, suppositive.

OZ′it–or– **4.** depositor, repositor, compositor, expositor, transpositor.

OZ′it–um– **4.** depositum, suppositum.

OO (good)

1.

SINGLE (MASCULINE) RHYMES IN OO (good)

Primary or Secondary Accent Falls on Last Syllable; Imperfect Rhymes Are in Italics.

OOD– 1. good, hood, could, should, stood, wood, would 2. *manhood*, unhood, *monkshood*, *knighthood*, withstood, *scrubwood*, *beechwood*, *deadwood*, *wildwood*, *dogwood*, *cordwood*, *plywood*, *wormwood*, *gumwood*, *teakwood*, *greenwood*, *firewood*, *rosewood*, *driftwood* 3. babyhood, hardihood, likelihood, livelihood, womanhood, maidenhood, widowhood, sisterhood, spinsterhood, fatherhood, motherhood, brotherhood, parenthood, understood, sandalwood, satinwood, cottonwood, underwood 4. misunderstood.

OOF– 1. oof, phoof [both slang], woof.

OOK– 1. book, hook, cook, cuck [dial.], look, lug, lugh, hook, snook, rook, brook, crook, shook, took, zook [slang] 2. *cookbook*, sambuk, fonduk, unhook, *fishhook*, *outlook*, Chinook, forsook, ursuk, betook, partook, mistook 3. pocketbook, tenterhook, overlook, inglenook, undertook, overtook.

OOL– 1. Ull, bull, full, pull, Pul, rull, shul, wool 2. *bulbul*, *dreadful*, *handful*, *bodeful*, *gleeful*, half-full, *guileful*, *baneful*, *tuneful*, *useful*, *houseful*, *rueful*, *eyeful*, *wrongful*, *watchful*, *bashful*, *wishful*, *loathful*, *wrathful*, *healthful*, *slothful*, *mirthful*, *mouthful*, *sackful*, *bookful*, *forkful*, *soulful*, *brimful*, *roomful*, *manful*, *sinful*, *helpful*, *cupful*, *carful*, *chanceful*, *glassful*, *hatful*, *boatful*, *doubtful*, *tactful*, *artful*, *hurtful*, *boastful*, *joyful*, *wirepull* [coll.], *lamb's-wool* 3. semibull, chrysobull, tableful, thimbleful, purposeful, meaningful, stomachful, fanciful, merciful, pitiful, plentiful, bountiful, barrelful, shovelful, teaspoonful, worshipful, teacupful, wonderful, tumblerful, masterful, platterful, colorful, overfull, powerful, prayerful, pocketful, bucketful, sorrowful, bellyful [vulgar].

OOLF– 1. wolf 2. *aardwolf*, *werewolf* 3. demiwolf.

OOM– 1. room, broom, groom, whom 2. *bedroom*, *tearoom*, *cookroom* *cloakroom*, *ballroom*, *greenroom*, *gunroom*, *spare room*, *wareroom*, *barroom*, *storeroom*, *classroom*, *stateroom*, *coatroom*, *courtroom*, *East room*, *bathroom*, *mushroom*, whisk broom, *bridegroom* 3. coffeeroom, anteroom, sitting room. elbowroom; *see also* **UM–** boom etc.

OOS– 1. puss 2. *couscous*, sour puss [slang].

OOSH– 1. bush, cush, push 2. *peabush*, *shadbush*, *spicebush*, *smokebush*, *twinebush*, *sloebush*, *forebush*, *horsebush*, *lotebush*, *dogbush*, *buckbush*, *gallbush*, *pearlbush*, *ambush*, *pinbush*, *hempbush*, *kinksbush*, *goatbush*, *saltbush*, *squawbush*, *jewbush*, *snowbush*, *maybush*, *rosebush*, *kiddush* 3. coffeebush, hobblebush, bramblebush, needlebush, brittlebush, flannelbush, buttonbush, sugarbush, soldierbush, pepperbush, fetterbush.

OOT– 1. foot, put, soot 2. afoot, *webfoot*, *lobefoot*, *clubfoot*, *padfoot*, *spadefoot*, *three-foot*, *Blackfoot*, *foalfoot*, *fanfoot*, *crowfoot*, *barefoot*, *forefoot*, *four-foot*, *twofoot*, *crossfoot*, *plotfoot*, *coltsfoot*, *six-foot* 3. pussyfoot, tenderfoot, underfoot.

OO (good)

2.

DOUBLE (FEMININE) RHYMES IN OO (hood'ed)

Primary or Secondary Accent Falls on Next to Last Syllable; Imperfect Rhymes Are in Italics.

OOD'ed– 2. hooded, wooded 3. unhooded, unwooded, red-wooded, thick-wooded, well-wooded, dense-wooded, soft-wooded, copsewooded.

OOD'en– 2. wooden.

OOD'i– 2. hoodie, goody, woody 4. goody-goody.

OOD'ing– 2. gooding, hooding, pudding.

OOG'ar– 2. booger [dial.], sugar 3. loaf sugar, cane sugar, spun sugar, brown sugar, beet sugar 4. maple sugar.

OOG'i– 2. boogey, luggie 4. boogey-woogey [slang].

OOK'ed– 2. hooked, crooked.

OOK'er– 2. booker, hooker, cooker, looker, snooker, rooker, stooker 3. onlooker 4. overlooker.

OOK'i– 2. booky, bookie, hooky, cooky, rooky, brooky, stookie.

OOK'ing– 2. booking, hooking, cooking, looking, rooking, brooking, crooking 3. rebooking, unhooking, good-looking, onlooking 4. overlooking.

OOK'ish– 2. bookish, hookish, cookish, rookish.

OOK'let– 2. booklet, nooklet, brooklet.

OOL'en– 2. pullen, woolen.

OOL'er– 2. buller, fuller, puller 3. wire-puller [coll.].

OOL'est– 2. fullest.

OOL'et– 2. bullet, pullet.

OOL'i– 2. bully, fully, mulley, pulley, woolly.

OOL'ing– 2. bulling, pulling 3. wire-pulling [coll.].

OOL'ish– 2. bullish, fullish, woollish.

OOM'an– 2. woman 3. horsewoman, washwoman 4. gentlewoman.

OOSH'er– 2. busher, pusher 3. penpusher 4. pedal-pusher.

OOSH'un– 2. cushion 3. recushion.

OOS'i– 2. pussy.

OOST'er– 2. Worcester.

OOT'ed– 2. footed, sooted 3. splayfooted, web-footed, clubfooted, big-footed, wing-footed, dog-footed, duck-footed, lame-footed, one-footed, barefooted, four-footed, sure-footed, catfooted, flat-footed, left-footed, swift-footed, light-footed, right-footed, claw-footed, two-footed 4. nimble-footed, cloven-footed, slender-footed, feather-footed, pussyfooted.

OOT'er– 2. footer, putter 3. webfooter, four-footer, six-footer 4. pussyfooter.

OOT'i– 2. footy, sooty.

OOT'ing– 2. footing, putting, sooting 4. pussyfooting.

OOZ'i– 2. woozy [slang].

OO (good)

3.

TRIPLE RHYMES IN OO (wood′i-ness)

Primary or Secondary Accent Falls on
Second from Last Syllable.

OOD′i–ness– **3.** goodiness, woodiness.

OOK′ed–ness– **3.** hookedness, crookedness.

OOK′er–i– **3.** bookery, cookery, nookery, rookery.

OOK′ish–li– **3.** bookishly, cookishly.

OOK′ish–ness– **3.** bookishness.

OOL′i–ness– **3.** wooliness.

OOL′ish–ness– **3.** bullishness.

OOM′an–li– **3.** womanly **4.** unwomanly **5.** gentlewomanly.

OOT′ed–ness– **4.** flat-footedness.

OOT′i–ness– **3.** snootiness, sootiness.

OI (boy)

1.

SINGLE (MASCULINE) RHYMES IN OI (boy)

Primary or Secondary Accent Falls on Last Syllable; Imperfect Rhymes Are in Italics.

OI– **1.** oy, oye [both Scot.], boy, buoy, foy, goy, goi, joy, coy, koi, loy, cloy, moy, Roy, troy, Troy, soy, toy **2.** *playboy, highboy, callboy, schoolboy, tomboy, doughboy, lowboy, messboy, bat boy, postboy, cowboy,* pakchoi, ahoy, *kill-joy,* enjoy, montjoy, decoy, alloy, deploy, employ, annoy, *viceroy,* destroy, travois, travoy, savoy, Savoy, convoy **3.** stableboy, altar boy, overjoy, hoi polloi [Gr.], Illinois, corduroy, Iroquois **4.** hobbledehoy, avoirdupois, padausoy.

OID– **1.** buoyed, joyed, Lloyd, Floyd, cloyed, sloyd, Freud, toyed, void **2.** rebuoyed, unbuoyed, *rhomboid, stromboid, globoid, cuboid,* enjoyed, decoyed, *sarcoid, discoid, muscoid, mycoid, gadoid, lambdoid, algoid, tringoid, spongoid, fungoid, conchoid, trochoid, scaphoid, xiphoid, lymphoid, typhoid,* alloyed, *haloid,* deployed, employed, *maskoid, squaloid, tabloid, cycloid, veloid, styloid, diploid, sigmoid, comoid, prismoid,* annoyed, *nanoid, sphenoid, glenoid, ctenoid, spinoid, crinoid, conoid, lunoid, cynoid, ooid, zooid, trappoid, vespoid, laroid, fibroid, android, dendroid, chondroid, spheroid, theroid, pteroid, Negroid, congroid, ochroid, nephroid, toroid, cuproid, astroid,* destroyed, avoid, devoid, *neuroid, thyroid, ursoid, deltoid, lentoid, mastoid, lithoid, ovoid, equoid, corvoid, hyoid, myoid, rhizoid* **3.** scaraboid, overjoyed, pinacoid, coracoid, helicoid, toxicoid, *didelphoid,* ornithoid, ophioid, cardioid, histioid, cephaloid, omphaloid, alkaloid, unalloyed, sepaloid, opaloid, petaloid, hyaloid, hypsiloid, reptiloid, coralloid, metalloid, crystalloid, mongoloid, unemployed, misemployed, cuculoid, celluloid, condyloid, dactyloid, entomoid, balanoid, melanoid, drepanoid, tetanoid, adenoid, solenoid, catenoid, *arachnoid,* echinoid, cyprinoid, platinoid, belonoid, salmonoid, coronoid, anthropoid, saccharoid, xanthocroid, cylindroid, amberoid, diphtheroid, antheroid, aneroid, bacteroid, asteroid, hysteroid, lemuroid, ankyroid, ellipsoid, prismatoid, rheumatoid, thanatoid, teratoid, planetoid, herpetoid, granitoid, *odontoid,* lacertoid, obovoid, ichthyoid, trapezoid **4.** pyramidoid, encephaloid, *epicycloid, varicelloid,* marioloid, tentaculoid, tuberculoid, albumenoid, gelatinoid, *tetrahedroid, octahedroid, polyhedroid, salamandroid,* rhinoceroid, hemispheroid, Melanochroid, meteoroid, *parathyroid* **5.** pachydermatoid.

OIF– **1.** coif, quoif.

OIK– **1.** hoick, yoick.

OIKS– **1.** hoicks, yoicks.

OIL– **1.** oil, boil, Boyle, Doyle, foil, goyle, goil [slang], coil, Coyle, moil, moyle, noil, poil, spoil, roil, broil, stroil, soil, toil, voile **2.** enoil, aboil, *gumboil, parboil, gargoyle,* accoil, recoil, uncoil, *trefoil, tinfoil,* despoil, *turmoil,* embroil, *subsoil, topsoil,* etoile, entoil, estoile **3.** multifoil, quaterfoil, counterfoil, disembroil, overtoil.

OILD– **1.** oiled, boiled, foiled, coiled,

moiled, spoiled, roiled, broiled, soiled, toiled 2. unoiled, unboiled, hard-boiled, soft-boiled, parboiled, recoiled, uncoiled, despoiled, embroiled 3. multifoiled, disembroiled, unembroiled, overtoiled.

OILZ– oils etc., *see* **OIL–** oil etc. above, plus "s" or "'s."

OIN– 1. foin, join, coin, coign, quoin, loin, groin 2. sainfoin, sagoin, adjoin, subjoin, rejoin, sejoin, enjoin, conjoin, disjoin, misjoin, recoin, eloign, purloin, sirloin, Des Moines, almoign, essoin 3. surrejoin, interjoin, tenderloin, frankalmoign.

OIND– 1. joined, coined, loined, poind 2. adjoined, rejoined, enjoined, uncoined, purloined, strong-loined.

OINT– 1. oint, joint, point 2. unjoint, disjoint, *bluejoint*, anoint, appoint, *standpoint*, repoint, pour point, *pourpoint*, *blue-point*, *viewpoint* 3. reappoint, disappoint, needle-point, counterpoint, cover-point.

OIS– 1. choice, Joyce, Royce, voice 2. rejoice, Rolls Royce, *invoice* 3. second choice.

OIST– 1. foist, hoist, joist, moist, voiced 2. rejoiced, revoiced, invoiced, unvoiced, *loud-voiced*, *low-voiced*, *weak-voiced*, *clear-voiced*, *harsh-voiced*, *sweet-voiced*, *soft-voiced*, *faint-voiced* 3. dreamy-voiced, empty-voiced, feeble-voiced, hollow-voiced, silver-voiced, trumpet-voiced 4. clarion-voiced.

OIT– 1. doit, skoit [slang], moit, droit, toit, quoit 2. dacoit, exploit, adroit, Detroit, Introit 3. maladroit.

OIZ– boys etc. *see* **OI–** boy etc. above, plus "s" or "'s"; 1. noise, poise, froise [dial.] 3. Illinois, erminois, centipoise, equipoise, counterpoise, Iroquois 4. avoirdupois.

OI (boy)

2.

DOUBLE (FEMININE) RHYMES IN OI (joy'ful)

Primary or Secondary Accent Falls on Next to
Last Syllable; Imperfect Rhymes Are in Italics.

OI'al– **2.** loyal, royal **3.** unloyal, disloyal, viceroyal, unroyal, sur-royal **4.** pennyroyal, chapel royal.

OI'ans– **2.** buoyance, joyance **3.** flamboyance, annoyance, chatoyance, prevoyance, clairvoyance.

OI'ant– **2.** buoyant **3.** flamboyant, unbuoyant, chatoyant, prevoyant, clairvoyant.

OID'al– **3.** ooidal, zooidal, rhomboidal, cuboidal, typhoidal, discoidal, colloidal, cycloidal, sigmoidal, spheroidal, ovoidal **4.** anthropoidal, asteroidal, saccharoidal **5.** paraboloidal, hemispheroidal, elephantoidal, meteoroidal.

OID'ans– **2.** voidance **3.** avoidance **4.** reavoidance.

OID'er– **2.** moider, broider, voider **3.** embroider, avoider.

OID'ik– **3.** diploidic, spheroidic.

OI'er– **2.** oyer, Boyer, foyer, coyer, toyer **3.** enjoyer, decoyer, deployer, employer, annoyer, destroyer **4.** self-employer, self-destroyer.

OI'est– **2.** coyest.

OI'ful– **2.** joyful **3.** unjoyful **4.** overjoyful.

OI'ij– **2.** buoyage, voyage **3.** alloyage.

OI'ing– **2.** buoying, joying, coying, cloying, ploying, toying **3.** enjoying, decoying, deploying, employing, annoying, destroying, envoying, convoying.

OI'ish– **2.** boyish, coyish, toyish.

OIL'er– **2.** oiler, boiler, foiler, coiler, moiler, spoiler, broiler, soiler, toiler **3.** recoiler, uncoiler, despoiler, embroiler.

OIL'i– **2.** oily, doily, coyly, noily, roily.

OIL'ing– **2.** oiling, boiling, foiling, coiling, moiling, spoiling, roiling, broiling, soiling, toiling **3.** recoiling, despoiling, embroiling.

OIL'ment– **3.** despoilment, embroilment, entoilment.

OIL'som– **2.** roilsome, toilsome.

OIM'ent– **2.** cloyment, ployment **3.** enjoyment, deployment, employment **4.** unemployment.

OIND'er– **2.** joinder, poinder **3.** rejoinder, misjoinder **4.** surrejoinder.

OIN'er– **2.** joiner, coiner **3.** rejoiner, enjoiner, conjoiner, purloiner.

OI'ness– **2.** coyness.

OIN'ij– **2.** coinage.

OIN'ing– **2.** foining, joining, coining, groining, quoining **3.** adjoining, rejoining, enjoining, disjoining, purloining.

OINT'ed– **2.** jointed, pointed **3.** unjointed, conjointed, disjointed, anointed, appointed, unpointed **4.** unanointed, disappointed.

OINT'er– **2.** jointer, pointer **3.** unjointer, disjointer, anointer, appointer, appointor **4.** disappointer.

OINT'ing– **2.** jointing, pointing **3.** disjointing, anointing, appointing **4.** disappointing.

OINT'less– 2. jointless, pointless.

OINT'ment– 2. ointment 3. disjoint-ment, anointment, appointment 4. re-appointment, disappointment.

OIS'er– 2. choicer 3. rejoicer.

OIS'ing– 2. voicing 3. rejoicing, invoic-ing 4. unrejoicing.

OIS'less– 2. choiceless, voiceless 3. re-joiceless, invoiceless.

OI'som– 2. noisome, cloysome, toysome.

OIST'er– 2. oyster, foister, hoister, clois-ter, moister, roister 3. encloister.

OIST'ing– 2. foisting, hoisting, joisting.

OIT'ed– 2. doited, quoited 3. exploited 4. unexploited.

OIT'er– 2. goiter, loiter, quoiter 3. ex-ploiter, adroiter 4. reconnoiter.

OIT'i– 3. dacoity 4. hoity-toity.

OI'us– 2. joyous 3. annoyous.

OIZ'ez– 2. noises, poises.

OIZ'on– 2. foison, poison 3. empoison.

OI (boy)

TRIPLE RHYMES IN OI (loy'al-ty)

Primary or Secondary Accent Falls on
Second from Last Syllable.

OI'a–bl– **3.** buoyable **4.** enjoyable, employable **5.** unenjoyable.

OI'al–i– **3.** loyally, royally **4.** disloyally, unroyally.

OI'al–ist– **3.** loyalist, royalist.

OI'al–ti– **3.** loyalty, royalty **4.** unloyalty, disloyalty, viceroyalty.

OI'an–si– **3.** buoyancy **4.** flamboyancy, chatoyancy, clairvoyancy.

OI'ant–li– **3.** buoyantly **4.** flamboyantly, clairvoyantly.

OID'a–bl– **3.** voidable **4.** avoidable **5.** unavoidable.

OI'ing–li– **3.** cloyingly, toyingly **4.** annoyingly.

OI'ing–ness– **3.** cloyingness **4.** annoyingness.

OI'ish–ness– **3.** boyishness, toyishness.

OIL'ing–ly– **3.** boilingly, spoilingly, soilingly, toilingly **4.** recoilingly.

OIN'a–bl– **3.** joinable, coinable **4.** unjoinable, disjoinable.

OINT'ed–li– **3.** jointedly, pointedly **4.** disjointedly.

OI'som–li– **3.** noisomely, cloysomely, toysomely.

OIST'er–ing– **3.** cloistering, roistering **4.** uncloistering.

OIST'er–us– **3.** boisterous, roisterous.

OIT'er–er– **3.** loiterer **5.** reconnoiterer.

OIT'er–ing– **3.** loitering **5.** reconnoitering.

OIZ'on–ing– **3.** poisoning **4.** empoisoning.

OU (how)

1.

SINGLE (MASCULINE) RHYMES IN OU (how)

Primary or Secondary Accent Falls on Last Syllable; Imperfect Rhymes Are in Italics.

OU– **1.** ow, bow, bough, chow, dhow, how, gow, ghow [both slang], Howe, jhow, cow, scow, plow, slough, mow, now, pow [slang], row, brow, frau, prow, sow, tau, thou, vow, wow **2.** miaow, Foochow, Soochow, *chowchow*, endow, *hoosegow* [slang], somehow, allow, *snowplow*, *haymow*, enow, erenow, *eyebrow*, *highbrow*, *kowtow*, avow, bowwow, *powwow* **3.** disendow, anyhow, reallow, disallow, reavow, disavow.

OUCH– **1.** ouch, couch, slouch, pouch, grouch, crouch, vouch **2.** avouch **3.** Scaramouch.

OUD– **1.** bowed, foud, cowed, dowd, loud, cloud, plowed, crowd, scrowd [slang], proud, shroud, stroud, vowed, wowed **2.** unbowed, endowed, aloud, allowed, becloud, encloud, replowed, unplowed, beshroud, enshroud, unshroud, avowed, bowwowed **3.** overcloud, overcrowd, unavowed, disavowed.

OUF– **1.** ouf, ouphe.

OUJ– **1.** gouge, scrouge.

OUL– **1.** owl, dowl, fowl, foul, howl, jowl, cowl, cowle, scowl, growl, prowl, yowl **2.** screech owl, afoul, befoul, *peafowl*, *seafowl*, encowl **3.** guinea fowl, waterfowl.

OULD– **1.** owled, fouled, howled, cowled, scowled, growled **2.** befouled, uncowled.

OUN– **1.** down, gown, clown, noun, brown, drown, frown, crown, town **2.** adown, *rubdown*, *touchdown*, *shakedown*, *comedown*, *moondown*, *sundown*, godown, *lowdown*, *showdown*, *nightgown*, renown, *pronoun*, embrown, nutbrown, uncrown, discrown, downtown, uptown, *Charlestown* **3.** upside-down, hand-me-down, tumbledown, eider-down.

OUND– **1.** bound, downed, found, hound, gowned, clowned, mound, pound, round, browned, drowned, frowned, ground, crowned, sound, wound **2.** abound, *hidebound*, rebound, *spellbound*, inbound, *icebound*, *eastbound*, *westbound*, outbound, *northbound*, *southbound*, redound, refound, dumbfound, confound, profound, *greyhound*, *bloodhound*, *wolfhound*, *horehound*, *foxhound*, renowned, impound, compound, propound, expound, around, aground, *background*, uncrowned, surround, resound, unsound, astound, resound **3.** unrenowned, triple-crowned, vantage ground, middle ground, pleasure ground, underground **4.** superabound, merry-go-round, burying ground.

OUNDZ– **1.** bounds, hounds, pounds, rounds, grounds, sounds, wounds, zounds.

OUNJ– **1.** lounge, scrounge.

OUNS– **1.** ounce, bounce, jounce, flounce, pounce, rounce, trounce **2.** announce, enounce, denounce, renounce, pronounce **3.** mispronounce.

OUNT– **1.** fount, count, mount **2.** account, recount, discount, miscount, *viscount*, amount, remount, surmount, dismount **3.** paramount, catamount, tantamount.

OUR– 1. our, hour, gaur, scour, lour, flour, sour 2. bescour, besour, devour.

OUS– 1. bouse, chouse, douse, gauss, house, louse, blouse, mouse, nous, grouse, souse 2. *clubhouse, madhouse, guardhouse, birdhouse, doghouse, workhouse, warehouse, storehouse, poorhouse, lighthouse, penthouse, outhouse, hothouse, dormouse, titmouse* 3. countinghouse, customhouse, summerhouse, slaughterhouse, chapter house, porterhouse, Mickey Mouse, flittermouse.

OUST– 1. oust, doused, bloused, roust, groused, soused.

OUT– 1. out, bout, doubt, gout, scout, lout, flout, clout, snout, pout, spout, rout, kraut, drought, grout, Prout, sprout, trout, shout, tout, stout 2. *hangout* [slang], *dugout, tryout, blackout, knockout, walkout, lookout, hereout, thereout, whereout, shutout,* without, throughout, about, redoubt, misdoubt, boy scout,

eelpout, bespout, *downspout,* derout, devout 3. in-and-out, out-and-out, gadabout, roundabout, hereabout, thereabout, whereabout, knockabout, whirlabout, runabout, stirabout, rightabout, roustabout, waterspout, sauerkraut, undevout.

OUTH– 1. mouth, drouth, south 2. *hardmouth, frogmouth, snakemouth, flutemouth* 3. chiselmouth, cottonmouth.

OUTHD– 2. loudmouthed, bigmouthed, closemouthed.

OUTS– outs etc., *see* OUT– out etc. above, plus "s" or " 's."

OUZ– bows etc., *see* OU– ow etc. above, plus "s" or " 's"; 1. bouse, dowse, house, blouse, mouse, spouse, rouse, browse, drowse, souse, touse 2. rehouse, espouse, arouse, carouse.

OUZD– 1. housed, bloused, browsed, drowsed, soused 2. espoused, aroused, caroused.

OU (how)

2.

DOUBLE (FEMININE) RHYMES IN OU (a-vow'al)

Primary or Secondary Accent Falls on Next to Last Syllable; Imperfect Rhymes Are in Italics.

OU'al– 2. cowal 3. avowal 4. disavowal; *see* also OU'el– bowel etc. below.

OU'an– 2. gowan, rowan, rowen.

OU'ans– 3. allowance, avowance 4. disallowance, disavowance.

OU'ard– 2. Howard, coward.

OUCH'er– 2. coucher, sloucher, poucher, groucher, croucher, voucher 3. avoucher.

OUCH'i– 2. slouchy, pouchy, grouchy.

OUCH'ing– 2. couching, slouching, pouching, grouching, crouching, vouching 3. avouching.

OUCH'o– 2. Gaucho.

OUD'ed– 2. clouded, crowded, shrouded 3. beclouded, unclouded, enshrouded, unshrouded 4. unbeclouded, overclouded, overcrowded.

OUD'er– 2. chowder, louder, powder, crowder, prouder 3. clam chowder, gunpowder, face powder 4. baking powder.

OUD'est– 2. loudest, proudest.

OUD'i– 2. dowdy, Goudy, howdie, howdy, cloudy, rowdy, shroudy 3. pandowdy, cum laude 5. magna cum laude, summa cum laude.

OUD'ing– 2. clouding, crowding, shrouding 3. beclouding, enshrouding 4. overclouding, overcrowding.

OUD'ish– 2. loudish, proudish.

OUD'li– 2. loudly, proudly.

OU'el– 2. bowel, dowel, howel, nowel, Powell, rowel, trowel, towel, vowel 3. embowel, avowal 4. disembowel, disavowal, semivowel.

OU'en– 2. gowan, rowen, rowan.

OU'er– 2. bower, dower, cower, lower, flower, glower, plower, plougher, power, rower, shower, tower, vower 3. embower, endower, allower, beflower, deflower, lidflower, windflower, bloodflower, globeflower, fameflower, shoeflower, grapeflower, coneflower, horseflower, tongueflower, safflower, blackflower, snailflower, gallflower, wallflower, fanflower, swanflower, enflower, twinflower, moonflower, unflower, sunflower, cornflower, lampflower, mistflower, dayflower, Mayflower, empower, horse power, manpower, watchtower, church tower, avower 4. cauliflower, coralflower, passionflower, cuckooflower, tulipflower, honeyflower, gillyflower, Julyflower, candlepower, underpower, overpower, water power, overtower, disavower.

OU'es– 2. prowess.

OU'i– 2. dowie, cowy, yowie [slang], zowie [slang].

OU'ing– 2. bowing, cowing, ploughing, plowing, rowing, vowing 3. allowing, avowing 4. disallowing, disavowing.

OUL'er– 2. fouler, fowler, howler, scowler, growler, prowler, yowler.

OUL'est– 2. foulest.

OUL'et– 2. owlet, howlet, rowlet.

OUL'i– 2. owly, Rowley, growly.

OUL'ing– 2. fouling, fowling, howling, cowling, scowling, growling, prowling.

OUL'ish– 2. owlish, foulish.

OU'ment– 3. endowment, allowment, avowment 4. disavowment.

OUND'ed– 2. bounded, founded, hounded, mounded, pounded, rounded, grounded, sounded, wounded 3. abounded, rebounded, unbounded, redounded, dumfounded, confounded, well-founded, illfounded, unfounded, impounded, compounded, propounded, expounded, surrounded, ungrounded, astounded, resounded 5. superabounded.

OUND'er– 2. bounder, founder, flounder, pounder, rounder, sounder 3. rebounder, dumfounder, confounder, profounder, impounder, compounder, propounder, expounder, surrounder, resounder.

OUND'est– 2. roundest, soundest 3. profoundest.

OUND'i– 2. houndy, woundy.

OUND'ij– 2. poundage, groundage, soundage 3. impoundage.

OUND'ing– 2. bounding, founding, hounding, pounding, rounding, grounding, sounding, wounding 3. abounding, rebounding, unbounding, redounding, dumfounding, confounding, impounding, compounding, propounding, expounding, resounding, loud-sounding, well-sounding, deep-sounding, clear-sounding, highsounding, surrounding, resounding 4. evil-sounding 5. superabounding.

OUND'ingz– 2. groundings, soundings 3. surroundings.

OUND'less– 2. boundless, groundless, soundless.

OUND'li– 2. roundly, soundly 3. profoundly, unsoundly.

OUND'ling– 2. foundling, groundling.

OUND'ness– 2. roundness, soundness 3. profoundness, unsoundness.

OUND'rel– 2. scoundrel 3. archscoundrel.

OUND'ri– 2. foundry 4. iron foundry.

OUN'er– 2. browner, drowner, frowner, crowner 3. uptowner.

OUN'est– 2. brownest.

OUN'-i– 2. downy, brownie, browny, frowny, towny.

OUN'ing– 2. downing, gowning, clowning, browning, Browning, drowning, frowning, crowning 3. encrowning, uncrowning, discrowning.

OUN'ish– 2. clownish, brownish, frownish, townish.

OUNJ'er– 2. lounger, scrounger.

OUNJ'ing– 2. lounging, scrounging.

OUN'less– 2. downless, gownless, frownless, crownless.

OUNS'er– 2. bouncer, flouncer, pouncer, trouncer 3. announcer, denouncer, renouncer, pronouncer.

OUNS'ez– 2. ounces, bounces, flounces, pounces, trounces 3. announces, denounces, pronounces.

OUNS'il– 2. council, counsel 3. recounsel.

OUNS'ing– 2. bouncing, flouncing, pouncing, trouncing 3. announcing, denouncing, renouncing, pronouncing 4. mispronouncing.

OUNS'ment– 3. announcement, enouncement, denouncement, renouncement, pronouncement 4. mispronouncement.

OUNT'ed– 2. counted, mounted 3. accounted, recounted, uncounted, discounted, miscounted, amounted, remounted, surmounted, dismounted.

OUNT'er– 2. counter, mounter 3. accounter, encounter, discounter, remounter, surmounter 4. re-encounter.

OUNT'ess– 2. countess 3. viscountess.

OUNT'i– 2. bounty, county, mounty 3. viscounty.

OUNT'in– **2.** fountain, mountain **4.** catamountain.

OUNT'ing– **2.** counting, mounting **3.** accounting, discounting, miscounting, amounting, surmounting, dismounting.

OUN'ward– **2.** downward, townward.

OUR'er– **2.** scourer, sourer **3.** devourer.

OUR'est– **2.** dourest, sourest.

OUR'i– **2.** houri, dowry, cowrie, floury, flowery **3.** avowry.

OUR'ing– **2.** scouring, flouring, souring **3.** beflouring, devouring.

OUR'li– **2.** hourly, dourly, sourly **3.** half-hourly.

OUR'ness– **2.** dourness, sourness.

OUS'er– **2.** douser, mouser, souser.

OUS'ez– **2.** douses, louses, blouses, spouses, souses.

OUS'i– **2.** blousy, mousey, spousy.

OUS'ing– **2.** dousing, blousing, mousing, sousing.

OUST'er– **2.** ouster, jouster, rouster.

OUST'ing– **2.** ousting, rousting.

OUT'ed– **2.** doubted, gouted, scouted, flouted, clouted, pouted, spouted, routed, sprouted, shouted, touted **3.** undoubted, misdoubted, derouted, unsprouted.

OUT'er– **2.** outer, doubter, douter, jowter, scouter, louter, flouter, clouter, pouter, spouter, router, sprouter, trouter, shouter, touter, stouter **3.** devouter **4.** in-and-outer, down-and-outer.

OUT'est– **2.** stoutest **3.** devoutest.

OUTH'i– **2.** mouthy, drouthy.

OUTH'ing– **2.** mouthing, southing **3.** bemouthing.

OUT'i– **2.** doughty, gouty, louty, snouty, pouty, spouty, droughty, grouty, trouty.

OUT'ing– **2.** outing, doubting, scouting, flouting, clouting, pouting, spouting, routing, grouting, sprouting, shouting, touting **3.** undoubting, bespouting, derouting, rerouting, resprouting.

OUT'ish– **2.** outish, loutish, stoutish.

OUT'let– **2.** outlet, troutlet.

OUT'li– **2.** stoutly **3.** devoutly **4.** undevoutly.

OUT'ness– **2.** outness, stoutness **3.** devoutness.

OU'wou– **2.** bowwow, powwow, wou-wou.

OUZ'al– **2.** housal, spousal **3.** espousal, arousal, carousal; *see* also OUZ'l– ouzel etc. below.

OUZ'er– **2.** dowser, mouser, Mauser, schnauzer, rouser, browser, trouser, Towser **3.** Tannhauser, espouser, arouser, carouser.

OUZ'ez– **2.** houses, blouses, spouses, rouses, browses **3.** espouses, arouses, carouses.

OUZ'i– **2.** bousy, housy, lousy, blowsy, mousy, drowzy, frowzy, grousy.

OUZ'ij– **2.** housage, spousage **3.** espousage.

OUZ'ing– **2.** dowzing, housing, blowzing, mousing, rousing, browsing, drowsing **3.** espousing, arousing, carousing.

OUZ'l– **2.** ouzel, housal, housel, mousle, spousal, tousle **3.** espousal, carousal.

OU (how)

3.

TRIPLE RHYMES IN OU (al-low'a-ble)

OU'a–bl– 4. endowable, allowable, avow-able 5. unallowable, disallowable, un-avowable, disavowable.

OU'a–bli– 4. allowably, avowably 5. un-allowably, unavowably.

OUD'ed–ness– 3. cloudedness, crowded-ness 4. uncloudedness 5. overcrowded-ness.

OUD'il–i– 3. dowdily, cloudily, rowdily.

OUD'i–ness– 3. dowdiness, cloudiness, rowdiness.

OU'er–er– 3. flowerer, glowerer, showerer.

OU'er–i– 3. bowery, Bowery, dowery, lowery, flowery, glowery, showery, tow-ery.

OU'er–ing– 3. dowering, cowering, lower-ing, flowering, glowering, showering, tow-ering 4. deflowering, empowering 5. overpowering, overtowering.

OU'er–less– 3. dowerless, flowerless, pow-erless.

OUL'er–i– 3. owlery, fowlery.

OUND'a–bl– 3. groundable, soundable 4. confoundable, impoundable, com-poundable, astoundable.

OUND'ed–li– 3. roundedly 4. unbound-edly, dumfoundedly, confoundedly 5. unconfoundedly.

OUND'ed–ness– 3. roundedness 4. un-boundedness, dumfoundedness, confound-edness, unfoundedness, ungroundedness.

OUND'ing–li– 4. aboundingly, confound-ingly, astoundingly.

OUND'less–li– 3. boundlessly, ground-lessly, soundlessly.

OUND'less–ness– 3. boundlessness, groundlessness, soundlessness.

OUNT'a–bl– 3. countable, mountable 4. accountable, discountable, uncountable, surmountable 5. unaccountable, insur-mountable, unsurmountable.

OUNT'a–bli– 4. accountably 5. unac-countably, insurmountably, unsurmount-ably.

OUT'i–ness– 3. doughtiness, goutiness, spoutiness, droughtiness.

OUZ'il–i– 3. drowsily, frowsily.

OUZ'i–ness– 3. lousiness, drowziness, frowziness.

OUZ'ing–li– 3. rousingly 4. carous-ingly.

U (you)

1.

SINGLE (MASCULINE) RHYMES IN U (you)

Primary or Secondary Accent Falls on Last
Syllable; Imperfect Rhymes Are in Italics.

U– 1. u, U, ewe, yew, you 2. bayou 3.
w, W, double-u.

BU– 1. boo 2. Abou, abu, aboo, *baboo*,
babu, taboo, tabu, yabu, yaboo, debut,
bamboo, imbue, *zebu* 3. bugaboo, peek-
aboo, marabou, caribou.

CHU– 1. chew 2. kachoo, *choo-choo*
[slang], kerchoo, eschew 3. catechu.

DU– 1. do, due, dew 2. ado, adieu, sub-
due, bedew, redo, skiddoo [slang], *mildew*,
chandoo, chandu, endew, endue, rendu
[F.], vendue, indue, *Hindu*, undo, perdu,
perdue, Purdue, fordo, foredo, misdo,
outdo, *hoodoo*, to-do, *voodoo* 3. billet-
doux, derring-do, how-dy-do [coll.],
honeydew, residue, underdo, overdo,
overdue, well-to-do.

FU– 1. fu, fou [Scot. & dial. Eng.], fou
[F.], few, feu, phew, phoo 2. mafoo,
mafu, phoo-phoo, *curfew* 3. feverfew.

GU– 1. goo, gout [F.] 2. ragout [F.],
burgoo, burgout, googoo.

HU– 1. hoo, who, Hu, hue, hew, Hugh
2. ahu, *wahoo*, *Yahoo*, boohoo, yoohoo
3. ballyhoo [slang], Elihu.

JU– 1. Jew 2. *baju* [Malay], *bijou*, *juju*
3. acajou, kinkajou, sapajou.

KU– 1. coo, coup, q, Q, cue, queue, skew
2. *aku*, *baku*, *cuckoo*, *coo-coo* [slang],
askew 3. barbecue.

LU– 1. loo, Lu, Lou, lieu, blue, blew,
flu, flue, flew, glue, clue, clew, slue, slew
2. halloo, sky-blue, true-blue, *igloo*,

unglue, *tolu*, *curlew*, *purlieu*, *Lulu*, *Sulu*,
Zulu 3. ululu 4. hullabaloo.

MU– 1. moo, mu, mew, smeu, smew 2.
emu, *immew*, *limu*, *umu*.

NU– 1. new, knew, nu, Nu, gnu, nous
[F.] 2. anew, *Danu*, canoe, renew, *venue*,
fire-new, foreknew 3. ingénue, entre
nous [F.], avenue, revenue, parvenu,
hoochinoo, detinue, retinue 4. Tippe-
canoe.

PU– 1. pu, pugh, pew, pooh, poo [Scot.
& dial. Eng.], spew 2. *napoo*, shampoo,
rompu, pooh-pooh.

RU– 1. rue, roux [F.], brew, bruh [Malay],
drew, grew, grue [dial.], crew, cru [F.],
screw, sprew, sprue, true, strew, shrew,
through, threw 2. karroo, imbrue, with-
drew, Peru, *froufrou*, accrue, *corkscrew*,
thumbscrew, unscrew, untrue, bestrew,
construe 3. kangaroo, buckaroo, gil-
laroo, wallaroo, wanderoo, potoroo, re-
construe, misconstrue, overstrew, over-
threw.

SU– 1. sue, Sue, sou, Sioux, Soo 2. the
Soo, ensue, pursue 3. aperçu [F.], Dai-
butsu.

SHU– 1. shoo, shoe 2. cachou, cashoo,
cashew, *fichu*, *snowshoe*, *horseshoe* 3.
overshoe.

TU– 1. to, too, two, tu [L.], stew 2.
battue, tattoo, *Bantu*, *Gentoo*, *lean-to*,
unto, hereto, thereto, whereto, *set-to*,
surtout, virtu 3. cockatoo, *in situ* [L.]

rumtytoo, Timbuktu, hereunto, thereunto, whereunto, *impromptu*, passe partout, hitherto, thitherto, whitherto **4.** intransitu [L.].

VU– 1. view, vous [F.] **2.** review, revue, *preview*, *kivu*, *purview* **3.** rendezvous, interview.

WU– 1. woo, Wu, whoo, whew.

YU– 1. you, ewe, yew **2.** bayou **3.** I. O. U.

ZU– 1. zoo, Zu **2.** kazoo, razoo, cousu [F.], zoozoo **4.** Kalamazoo.

UB– 1. boob [slang], doob, jube, cube, Rube, rube [slang], tube **2.** jujube **3.** inner tube.

UCH– 1. ooch, hooch, cooch, mooch, mouch, smooch, smouch, pooch [all slang], brooch.

UD– 1. booed, chewed, dude, food, feud, hued, Jude, cued, queued, lewd, looed, blued, flued, flewed, glued, slued, slewed, mood, mooed, nude, snood, rude, rued, rood, brood, brewed, crude, screwed, prude, trued, shrewd, shood, shooed, stewed, thewed, viewed, wooed **2.** tabooed, imbued, eschewed, miscued, unglued, allude, elude, delude, prelude, illude, collude, postlude, preclude, seclude, include, conclude, occlude, exclude, almud, subnude, denude, renewed, shampooed, abrood, imbrued, accrued, unscrewed, obtrude, subtrude, detrude, retrude, intrude, protrude, construed, extrude, resued, pursued, etude, reviewed, previewed, unwooed, exude, transude **3.** reimbued, unimbued, unsubdued, interlude, unrenewed, misconstrued, unpursued, hebetude, quietude, desuetude, mansuetude, consuetude, habitude, longitude, solitude, amplitude, lenitude, plenitude, magnitude, omnitude, torpitude, turpitude, nigritude, lassitude, crassitude, spissitude, latitude, rectitude, sanctitude, altitude, multitude, lentitude, aptitude, promptitude, certitude, fortitude, pingui-

tude, servitude, gravitude **4.** inquietude disquietude, solicitude, similitude, definitude, decrepitude, vicissitude, exactitude.

UDZ– 1. dudes, foods, feuds, Jude's, moods, nudes, snoods, roods, broods, prudes **3.** interludes, solitudes, latitudes, altitudes, multitudes.

UF– 1. oof, boof, goof [all slang], hoof, loof, poof, pouf, spoof [slang], roof, proof, woof **2.** shadoof, behoof, aloof, reroof, reproof *foolproof*, *fireproof*, disproof, Tartufe **3.** cloven hoof, gable roof, bulletproof, waterproof.

UFT– 1. hoofed, spoofed [slang], roofed, woofed **3.** cloven-hoofed, bulletproofed, waterproofed.

UG– 1. boog [slang], fugue, fougue, goog [slang], toug.

UJ– 1. huge, smoodge, rouge, Scrooge, scrouge, stooge [slang], vouge **3.** subterfuge, vermifuge, febrifuge.

UK– 1. uke [slang], duke, douc, gook [slang], juke, cuke [slang], Luke, fluke, snook, puke, spook, sook, stook, yeuk, yewk, yuk, yuke **2.** rebuke, chibouk, bambuk, caoutchouc, archduke, beduke, Chinook, charuk, peruke **3.** octateuch, Pentateuch, Heptateuch, Hexateuch **4.** bashi-bazook.

UL– 1. buhl, fool, ghoul, gool [dial.], cool, school, mewl, mool, mule, pool, pule, spool, rule, drool, tool, tulle, stool, Yule **2.** *jambool*, *jambul*, befool, *whirlpool*, slide rule, misrule, pasul, *toadstool*, *footstool* **3.** vestibule, Istambul, April-fool, molecule, ridicule, vermicule, reticule, Sunday school, swimming pool, wading pool, Liverpool, overrule.

ULZ– fools etc., *see* **UL–** buhl etc. above, plus "s" or "'s"; **1.** gules, Jules.

UM– 1. boom, doom, doum, fume, ghoom, coom, coomb, loom, bloom, flume, gloom, plume, neume, spume, room, rheum, broom, brume, brougham, groom, grume,

soum, tomb, womb, whom, zoom 2. pre-
doom, foredoom, *perfume*, legume, in-
hume, exhume, illume, *heirloom*, embloom,
begloom, engloom, beplume, deplume,
displume, simoom, *bedroom*, *tearoom*,
cloakroom, *ballroom*, *barrom*, *storeroom*,
stateroom, *courtroom*, *mushroom*, *bridegroom*, assume, subsume, consume, en-
tomb, *costume*, resume, presume 3.
anteroom, reading room, dining room,
drawing room, dressing room, living
room, elbowroom, reassume, hecatomb,
disentomb.

UMD– 1. doomed, loomed, bloomed,
plumed, spumed, zoomed 2. exhumed
3. unassumed.

UMF– 1. pomph, foomph [both slang].

UMZ– booms etc., *see* **UM–** boom etc.
above, plus "s" or "'s."

UN– 1. boon, Boone, doon, dune, foon
[slang], goon [slang], hewn, June, coon,
loon, lune, moon, noon, spoon, rune,
croon, prune, strewn, soon, tune, toon,
woon, wun, swoon 2. baboon, bridoon,
typhoon, buffoon, lagoon, dragoon, Ran-
goon, Calhoun, unhewn, jejune, cacoon,
lacune, racoon, tycoon, cocoon, balloon,
galloon, shalloon, walloon, doubloon, im-
mune, simoon, commune, midnoon, fore-
noon, lampoon, tampoon, harpoon, impugn,
oppugn, expugn, teaspoon, maroon, gam-
broon, gadroon, spadroon, quadroon, se-
roon, patroon, poltroon, quintroon, be-
strewn, bassoon, monsoon, gossoon, at-
tune, platoon, ratoon, spittoon, altun,
entune, pontoon, spontoon, cartoon, fes-
toon, aswoon 3. rigadoon, barracoon,
pantaloon, honeymoon, harvest moon, af-
ternoon, tablespoon, macaroon, picaroon,
octoroon, overstrewn, oversoon, coque-
toon, musketoon, importune, opportune,
picayune 4. intercommune, vinegarroon,
inopportune.

UND– 1. mooned, spooned, runed,
crooned, tuned, wound, swooned 2.
Mahound, impugned, attuned, festooned.

UNZ– boons etc., *see* **UN–** boon etc. above,
plus "s" or "'s."

UP– 1. boop [slang], dupe, Goop, hoop,
jupe, coop, coup, scoop, loop, bloop
[slang], cloop, sloop, noop [Scot. & dial.
Eng.], snoop, poop, roup, drupe, droop,
group, croup, scroop, troop, troupe, soup,
supe [slang], stoop, stoep, stupe, stoup,
swoop, whoop 2. recoup, saloop, adroop,
aggroup 3. cock-a-hoop, Guadalupe,
nincompoop, liripoop, loop-the-loop.

UPT– 1. duped, hooped, couped, cooped,
scooped, looped, snooped, drooped,
grouped, trouped, stooped, swooped,
whooped 2. recouped, regrouped.

UR– 1. boor, dour, cure, lure, mure, moor,
pure, poor, spoor, sure, tour, your, jour
[F.] 2. endure, perdure, coiffure, bahur,
nahoor, abjure, adjure, injure, conjure,
secure, liqueur, procure, obscure, allure,
velure, colure, amour, unmoor, demure,
immure, *tenure*, inure, impure, assure,
cocksure, ensure, insure, unsure, Ashur,
brochure, mature, *detour*, *contour*, gravure,
huzoor, causeur 3. perendure, sinecure,
insecure, pedicure, manicure, epicure,
chevelure, condylure, blackamoor, bela-
mour, Kohinoor, connoisseur, reassure,
reinsure, coinsure, cynosure, ligature,
tablature, amateur, premature, immature,
climature, armature, signature, curvature,
comfiture, forfeiture, garniture, furniture,
portraiture, sepulture, garmenture, aper-
ture, overture, coverture, voyageur,
abat-jour 4. miniature, judicature, tem-
perature, literature, expenditure, dis-
comfiture, divestiture, investiture, autogravure, photogravure, rotogravure.

URD– 1. gourde, cured, moored, toured
2. secured, obscured, endured, insured
3. unsecured, reassured, self-assured, un-
assured, immatured, uninsured.

URS– 1. bourse.

URZ– boors etc., *see* **UR–** boor etc. above,
plus "s" or "'s."

US– 1. use, Duce, deuce, douce, goose, juice, luce, loose, sluice, moose, meuse, mousse, noose, pouce, puce, Bruce, cruse, spruce, truce, trousse, Zeus 2. abuse, caboose, traduce, educe, deduce, reduce, seduce, induce, conduce, produce, diffuse, profuse, *mongoose*, verjuice, excuse, unloose, recluse, occluse, vamoose [slang], burnoose, papoose, abstruse, disuse, misuse, obtuse, retuse, pertuse 3. calaboose, reproduce, introduce, Syracuse, catapuce, charlotte russe 4. superinduce, hypotenuse.

USH– 1. bouche, mouche, smush [dial.], ruche, whoosh 2. bonne bouche [F.], barouche, farouche [F.], cartouche 3. Scaramouch, gobe-mouche [F.].

UST– 1. boost, deuced, joust, loosed, noosed, roost, spruced 2. deduced, unloosed, vamoosed.

UT– 1. Ute, Butte, boot, beaut [slang], hoot, jute, coot, cute, scute, scoot, loot, lute, flute, cloot, plute [slang], sluit, moot, mute, smoot, newt, snoot, route, root, bruit, brute, fruit, soot, suit, chute, shoot, toot, tute 2. refute, confute, argute, cahoot [slang], Paiute, acute, galoot [slang], salute, dilute, pollute, volute, immute, commute, permute, transmute, Canute, minute, cornute, depute, repute, impute, compute, dispute, Rajput, imbrute, cheroot, enroot, en route, *breadfruit, grapefruit, starfruit,* recruit, nasute, dissuit, *lawsuit,* hirsute, pursuit, *offshoot, outshoot,* surtout, astute 3. marabout, attribute, retribute, subacute, persecute, execute, baldicoot, bandicoot, absolute, resolute, dissolute, obvolute, evolute, involute, convolute, Malemute, comminute, disrepute, arrowroot, orrisroot, demisuit, parachute, overshoot, substitute, destitute, institute, constitute 4. electrocute, irresolute.

UTH– 1. booth, couth, sleuth, ruth, Ruth, sooth, tooth, youth 2. uncouth, Duluth, thuluth, vermouth, untruth, forsooth 3. polling booth, voting booth.

UTHE– 1. smooth, soothe 2. besmooth, resoothe.

UTS– boots etc., *see* **UT–** Ute etc. above, plus "s" or "'s."

UV– 1. move, groove, prove, you've 2. behoove, amove, remove, ingroove, approve, reprove, improve, disprove 3. reapprove, disapprove.

UVD– 1. moved, grooved, proved 2. behooved, ungrooved, approved, unproved 3. unremoved, unimproved.

UZ– 1. ooze, use, booze, boos, choose, chews, dues, fuze, fuse, guze, Hughes, Jews, coos, skuse [dial. & coll.], lose, blues, flews, flues, clues, mews, muse, meuse, news, gnus, snooze [coll.] ruse, bruise, brews, Druse, cruise, crews, cruse, trews, strews, sues, twos, stews, shoes, shoos, woos, whose, zoos 2. abuse, taboos, imbues, effuse, refuse, refuze, diffuse, infuse, confuse, perfuse, transfuse, suffuse, accuse, excuse, amuse, bemuse, canoes, shampoos, debruise, peruse, *corkscrews,* chartreuse, masseuse, misuse, danseuse, *horseshoes,* tattoos, Bantus, contuse, enthuse, kazoos 3. disabuse, circumfuse, interfuse, avenues, Vera Cruz, Santa Cruz.

UZD– 1. oozed, used, fused, snoozed, bruised, cruised 2. ill-used, unused, enthused 3. disabused, self-accused.

UZH– 1. rouge 3. Bruges, vouge.

U (you)

2.

DOUBLE (FEMININE) RHYMES IN U (du'al)

Primary or Secondary Accent Falls on Next to Last
Syllable; Imperfect Rhymes Are in Italics.

U'a– 2. skua 3. ulua, atua 4. punalua
10. Apologia pro Vita Sua [L.].

U'al– 2. dual 3. eschewal, subdual, renewal, pursual, reviewal.

U'an– 2. duan, Siouan, Chouan.

U'ans– 2. nuance 3. eschewance, renewance, pursuance.

U'ant– 2. fluent, truant, suant 3. perfluent, pursuant.

U'ard– 2. Seward, steward.

UB'a– 2. juba, Cuba, kuba, Luba, Nuba, subah, tsuba, tuba 3. Baluba, saxtuba.

UB'al– 2. Jubal, tubal.

UB'er– 2. goober, cuber, Khubur, suber, tuber, tubar.

UB'i– 2. booby, looby, ruby.

UB'ij– 2. cubage, tubage.

UB'ik– 2. cubic 3. cherubic.

UB'ing– 2. cubing, tubing.

UB'l– 2. Jubal, ruble, tubal.

UB'let– 2. cubelet, tubelet.

UB'rik– 2. lubric, rubric.

UCH'er– 2. blucher, moocher [slang], smoocher [slang].

UCH'i– 2. smoochy [slang] 3. Il Duce [It.], penuchi 4. hootchy-kootchy [slang].

UD'a– 2. Buddha, Judah, Nuda 3. picuda, Bermuda 4. barracuda.

UD'al– 2. udal, feudal 3. paludal.

UD'ed– 2. snooded, brooded 3. alluded, eluded, deluded, colluded, precluded, se-
cluded, included, concluded, occluded, excluded, denuded, intruded, protruded, extruded, exuded, transuded 4. undeluded, unterluded, unprotruded.

UD'ens– 2. prudence 3. imprudence 4. jurisprudence.

UD'ent– 2. prudent, student 3. concludent, occludent, imprudent, protrudent 4. jurisprudent.

UD'er– 2. lewder, nuder, ruder, brooder, cruder, shrewder, sudor, Tudor 3. eluder, deluder, includer, concluder, excluder, denuder, intruder, protruder.

UD'est– 2. lewdest, nudest, rudest, crudest, shrewdest.

UD'i– 2. boodie, feudy, moody, broody 3. almude.

UD'ik– 2. Sudic 3. paludic.

UD'ing– 2. brooding 3. abrooding, alluding, eluding, deluding, precluding, including, concluding, occluding, excluding, denuding, intruding, protruding, exuding.

UD'ish– 2. dudish, moodish, nudish, prudish, shrewdish.

UD'ist– 2. Buddhist, feudist, nudist, prudist.

UD'l– 2. boodle, doodle, [coll., dial & slang], coodle, noodle, nuddle [dial.], poodle, roodle, soodle 3. caboodle [slang], flapdoodle [coll.]. 4. Yankee-Doodle.

UD'li– 2. lewdly, nudely, rudely, crudely, prudely, shrewdly, soodly.

UD′lz– boodles etc., *see* **UD′l–** boodle etc. above, plus "s" or " 's"; **2.** oodles [slang].

UD′ness– **2.** lewdness, nudeness, rudeness, crudeness, shrewdness.

UD′o– **2.** scudo, pseudo **3.** barbudo, picudo, escudo, testudo **4.** consuetudo [L.].

UD′or– **2.** sudor, Tudor.

UD′u– **2.** hoodoo, pudu, to-do, voodoo.

U′e– **2.** gooey [slang], hui, hooey [slang], cooee, blooey, bluey [both slang], fluey [rare], flooey [slang], gluey, tui; *see* also **U′i–** buoy etc. below.

U′el– **2.** duel, fuel, jewel, newel, Reuel, gruel, cruel, crewel, shewel, tewel **3.** bejewel.

U′ent– **2.** fluent **3.** confluent, perfluent.

U′er– **2.** ewer, chewer, doer, fewer, hewer, cooer, skewer, bluer, gluer, newer, ruer, brewer, screwer, truer, sewer, suer, shoer, tewer, stewer, viewer, wooer **3.** eschewer, wrongdoer, subduer, undoer, misdoer, outdoer, canoer, renewer, shampooer, bestrewer, ensuer, pursuer, horseshoer, tattooer, reviewer **4.** evildoer, overdoer, interviewer.

U′erd– **2.** skewered, sewered, steward.

U′est– **2.** fewest, bluest, gluest, newest, truest.

U′et– **2.** chewet, Jewett, bluet, cruet, suet **3.** revuette.

UF′a– **2.** buffa [It.], chufa, gufa, goofa, goofah, luffa, loofah, stufa [It.] **4.** catalufa.

UF′er– **2.** goofer, hoofer, spoofer [all slang], roofer **3.** aloofer.

UF′i– **2.** oofy, goofy, spoofy [all slang], roofy, woofy.

UF′ing– **2.** hoofing, spoofing [both slang], roofing, woofing **4.** bulletproofing, waterproofing, weatherproofing.

UF′less– **2.** roofless, proofless **3.** reproofless.

UF′us– **2.** rufus, Rufus, rufous.

UG′a– **2.** fuga [It.], muga, ruga **3.** beluga, Cayuga **4.** Chattanooga.

UG′al– **2.** bugle, fugle, fugal, jugal, frugal **3.** infrugal, unfrugal **4.** febrifugal, vermifugal.

UG′i– **2.** bugi, boogie, boogey [both slang], luggie, rugae **4.** boogey–woogey [slang].

UG′l– **2.** bugle, fugle.

UG′ler– **2.** bugler, fugler.

UG′li– **2.** bugly.

UG′o– **2.** Hugo **3.** colugo, besugo [Sp.].

UG′us– **2.** rugous.

U′i– **2.** bowie, buoy, chewy, dewy, phooey [slang], gooey, hooey [both slang], cooee, Louis, louey [slang], bluey, blooey [both slang], fluey [rare], flooey [slang], gluey, screwy, tui, stewy, thewy, viewy **3.** *mildewy*, St. Louis, chop suey.

U′id– **2.** fluid, druid.

U′ij– **2.** brewage, sewage **3.** reviewage.

U′ik– **2.** Buick **3.** toluic.

U′in– **2.** ruin, bruin, sewen **3.** aruin.

U′ing– **2.** booing, chewing, doing, hewing, cooing, cuing, blueing, gluing, mooing, ruing, brewing, trueing, strewing, suing, shoeing, stewing, viewing, wooing **3.** eschewing, subduing, wrongdoing, undoing, misdoing, outdoing, boohooing, rescuing, miscuing, canoeing, renewing, shampooing, accruing, construing, ensuing, horseshoeing, tattooing, reviewing, previewing **4.** evil-doing, overdoing, barbecuing, misconstruing, interviewing.

U′is– **2.** Lewis, Louis, brewis **3.** St. Louis.

U′ish– **2.** Jewish, bluish, gluish, newish, truish, shrewish **3.** reviewish.

U′ist– **2.** cueist **3.** canoeist, revuist.

UJ′er– **2.** huger.

UJ′i– **2.** fuji, Fuji **3.** Mt. Fuji.

UK′a– **2.** Uca, nucha, yuca **3.** cambuca, palooka [slang], festuca, fistuca, bazooka.

ŪK'al– 2. ducal, coucal, nucal, nuchal 3. archducal 4. noctilucal, Pentateuchal.

ŪK'er– 2. euchre, lucre, fluker, snooker 3. rebuker 4. involucre.

ŪK'i– 2. fluky, snooky, spooky, rouky, sooky, Sukey.

ŪK'us– 2. fucus, fucous, leucous, mucus, mucous 3. caducous 4. noctilucous.

UL'a– 2. ula, boola [slang], Beulah, gula, Gula, goolah, hula, Lula, moola [slang], Zula 3. bamboula 4. hula-hula.

UL'er– 2. cooler, mewler, puler, pooler, spooler, ruler, drooler, tooler 4. ridiculer.

UL'ess– 2. dewless, fooless, flueless, clueless, pewless, screwless, viewless 3. reviewless.

UL'est– 2. coolest, foolest.

UL'i– 2. booly, booley, duly, Dooley, coolie, coulee, coolly, bluely, newly, pooly, drooly, tule, Thule, truly 3. patchouli, unduly, unruly, untruly 5. iconoduly.

UL'ij– 2. Coolidge, schoolage.

UL'ing– 2. fooling, cooling, schooling, puling, pooling, spooling, ruling, drooling, tooling, stooling 3. befooling, misruling 4. overruling.

UL'ip– 2. julep, tulip 3. mint julep.

UL'ish– 2. foolish, ghoulish, coolish, schoolish, mulish, pulish 3. pound-foolish, tomfoolish.

UL'u– 2. ulu, hulu, Lulu, Tulu, Zulu 4. Honolulu.

UM'a– 2. duma, pneuma, puma, Yuma 3. mazuma [slang] 4. Montezuma.

UM'al– 2. brumal, tombal.

UM'an– 2. human, Newman, crewman, Truman 3. inhuman, nonhuman, unhuman 4. ultrahuman, superhuman, preterhuman; see also **UM'en–** rumen etc. below.

UM'en– 2. rumen 3. albumen, albumin, hegumen, legumen, legumin, acumen, il-

lumine, bitumen 4. catechumen; see also **UM'an–** human etc. above.

UM'ent– 3. imbuement, eschewment, subduement, induement, renewment, imbruement, accruement.

UM'er– 2. boomer, doomer, fumer, humor, bloomer, plumer, roomer, rumor, groomer, tumor 3. perfumer, ill-humor, illumer, assumer, consumer, entomber, costumer, resumer, presumer.

UM'erd– 2. humored, rumored 3. good-humored, bad-humored, ill-humored.

UM'i– 2. boomy, fumy, bloomy, gloomy, plumy, spumy, rheumy, roomy, broomy, groomy 3. perfumy.

UM'id– 2. fumid, humid, tumid.

UM'ij– 2. doomage, fumage, plumage, roomage.

UM'ik– 2. humic, cumic, tombic 3. costumic.

UM'in– 3. albumin, legumin, relumine, illumine; see also **UM'en–** rumen etc. above.

UM'ing– 2. booming, dooming, fuming, looming, blooming, glooming, pluming, spuming, rooming, brooming, tombing, zooming 3. predooming, perfuming, inhuming, exhuming, illuming, assuming, resuming, presuming, consuming, entombing 4. unassuming, unpresuming, disentombing.

UM'less– 2. doomless, fumeless, bloomless, plumeless, roomless, groomless, tombless.

UM'let– 2. boomlet, plumelet, roomlet, groomlet, tomblet.

UM'or– 2. humor, rumor, tumor; see also **UM'er–** boomer etc. above.

UM'us– 2. dumous, fumous, humus, humous, plumous, spumous, brumous, grumous 3. posthumous.

UN'a– 2. Una, luna, puna, Poonah, tuna 3. lacuna, vicuna, Peruna, Fortuna.

UN'al– 2. dunal 3. tribunal, lagoonal, lacunal, communal.

UN'ar– 2. lunar 3. lacunar, sublunar, translunar 4. semilunar, plenilunar, novilunar, interlunar, cassumunar.

UND'ed– 2. wounded 3. unwounded.

UN'er– 2. schooner, mooner, spooner, runer, crooner, pruner, sooner, tuner, swooner 3. ballooner, communer, lampooner, impugner, oppugner, harpooner, marooner, attuner 4. importuner.

U'ness– 2. fewness, blueness, newness, trueness.

UN'est– 2. soonest.

UN'ful– 2. spoonful, tuneful 3. balloonful, teaspoonful, untuneful.

UN'i– 2. duny, luny, loony, Cluny, moony, puny, puisne, spoony, tuny, swoony 3. festoony.

UN'ik– 2. Munich, Punic, runic, tunic.

UN'ing– 2. mooning, nooning, spooning, crooning, pruning, swooning 3. ballooning, communing, lampooning, impugning, oppugning, harpooning, attuning, retuning.

UN'is– 2. Eunice, funis, Tunis.

UN'ish– 2. moonish 3. buffoonish, balloonish, poltroonish.

UN'ism– 2. buffoonism, poltroonism 4. opportunism.

UN'ist– 3. balloonist, lampoonist, harpoonist, bassoonist, cartoonist 4. opportunist.

UN'it– 2. unit 3. Anunit.

UN'less– 2. boonless, moonless, spoonless, runeless, tuneless.

UN'o– 2. uno [Sp.], Juno, Juneau, Bruno.

UN'um– 2. unum [L.] 3. jejunum 6. e pluribus unum [L.].

UN'us– 2. Prunus 3. fortunous, Portunus.

UN'yun– 2. union 3. trade-union, reunion, nonunion, disunion, communion 4. labor-union, excommunion 5. intercommunion.

UP'a– 2. pupa, rupa, supa, stupa 3. macupa [Tag.], arupa, ketupa 4. kamarupa.

UP'e– 2. rupee, whoopee [slang] 4. Guadalupe; see also UP'i– kewpie etc. below.

UP'er– 2. duper, hooper, cooper, scooper, looper, snooper, grouper, trooper, trouper, super, stooper, stupor, swooper 3. recouper, mosstrooper 4. loop-the-looper.

UP'i– 2. kewpie, loopy, rupee, droopy, croupy, soupy, whoopee [slang].

UP'id– 2. Cupid, Lupid, stupid.

UP'in– 2. lupine.

UP'ing– 2. duping, hooping, cooping, scooping, looping, snooping, drooping, grouping, trooping, stooping, swooping, whooping 3. recouping, regrouping.

UP'l– 2. duple, cupel, pupal, pupil, drupel, scruple 3. subduple, quadruple, octuple, centuple, quintuple, septuple, sextuple.

UP'let– 2. duplet, looplet, drupelet 3. *quadruplet, octuplet, quintuplet, septuplet, sextuplet.*

UP'ment– 2. groupment 3. recoupment, aggroupment, regroupment.

UP'on– 2. coupon, jupon, yupon.

UP'us– 2. lupus, lupous.

UR'a– 2. cura [Sp.], lura, pleura, Mura, sura, surah 3. ahura, asura, caesura, flexura, datura, Keturah, vettura [It.], bravura 4. tambaroora, velatura, angostura 5. appoggiatura, coloratura, fioritura [It.].

UR'al– 2. Ural, dural, jural, lural, mural, neural, pleural, plural, rural, crural, sural 3. subdural, procural, tellural, adneural, hypural, bicrural, caesural 4. sinecural, intramural, extramural, antemural, intermural, interneural, commissural.

UR'ans– 2. durance 2. endurance, perdurance, procurance, allurance, assurance, insurance 4. reassurance, reinsurance.

UR′ant– 2. durant, jurant 3. endurant, obscurant, assurant, insurant.

UR′at– 2. curate, jurat, surat.

UR′er– 2. furor, juror, curer, lurer, moorer, purer, poorer, surer, tourer 3. endurer, adjurer, grand juror, obscurer, securer, procurer, allurer, demurer, inurer, impurer, assurer, ensurer, insurer, maturer 4. reassurer, reinsurer, immaturer.

UR′est– 2. purest, poorest, surest 3. obscurest, securest, demurest, impurest.

UR′i– 2. ewry, fury, Curie, houri, Jewry, jury, fleury, moory, Drury 3. grand jury, Missouri 4. counterfleury.

UR′id– 2. lurid.

UR′ij– 2. moorage, murage.

UR′ik– 2. pleuric, neuric 3. sulphuric, mercuric, telluric, caesuric 4. dolichuric.

UR′im– 2. Urim, Purim.

UR′ing– 2. during, juring, curing, luring, mooring, spooring, touring 3. enduring, adjuring, abjuring, securing, procuring, obscuring, alluring, unmooring, inuring, assuring, ensuring, insuring, maturing 4. reassuring, reinsuring.

UR′ish– 2. boorish, Moorish, poorish 3. maturish 4. amateurish.

UR′ist– 2. jurist, purist, tourist 4. manicurist 5. caricaturist.

UR′li– 2. dourly, poorly, purely, surely 3. securely, obscurely, demurely, impurely, maturely 4. prematurely, immaturely.

UR′ment– 3. abjurement, conjurement, securement, procurement, obscurement, allurement, immurement, inurement 4. reassurement, reinsurement.

UR′ness– 2. poorness, pureness, sureness 3. secureness, obscureness, demureness, impureness, cocksureness, matureness 4. insecureness, immatureness.

UR′o– 2. Uro, bureau 3. maduro 5. chiaroscuro.

UR′or– 2. furor, juror 3. adjuror, grand juror; see also **UR′er–** furor etc. above.

UR′us– 2. urus, Eurus 3. anurous, Honduras, macrurous, Arcturus 4. dolichurus.

US′a– 2. Sousa, tuza 3. Medusa, empusa 4. Arethusa, Tuscaloosa, babirusa.

US′al– 3. medusal, occlusal 5. hypotenusal.

US′ens– 2. lucence, nuisance 3. translucence 4. noctilucence.

US′ent– 2. lucent 3. adducent, traducent, abducent, reducent, conducent, producent, translucent 4. noctilucent, interlucent.

US′er– 2. looser, sluicer, nooser, sprucer 3. adducer, traducer, deducer, reducer, seducer, inducer, conducer, producer 4. reproducer, introducer.

US′est– 2. loosest, sprucest 3. profusest, abstrusest.

US′ez– uses etc., see **US–** use etc. plus "s" or " 's."

US′ful– 2. useful, juiceful 3. unuseful.

USH′a– 2. fuchsia, Lucia 3. Jerusha.

USH′al– 3. crucial 3. fiducial, minutial.

USH′an– 2. Lucian 3. Confucian, Aleutian 4. Lilliputian, Rosecrucian.

USH′un– 3. locution, ablution, pollution, dilution, solution, volution 4. attribution, retribution, distribution, contribution, execution, prosecution, persecution, elocution, absolution, dissolution, evolution, revolution, involution, convolution, resolution, immolution, diminution, comminution, substitution, destitution, restitution, institution, constitution 5. redistribution, ventrilocution, circumlocution, interlocution, electrocution, irresolution, circumvolution.

USH′us– 2. Lucius 3. astucious.

US′i– 2. goosy, juicy, Lucy, sluicy, moosey 3. Debussy.

US'id– 2. deuced, lucid, mucid 3. pellucid, translucid.

US'ij– 2. usage 3. disusage, misusage, abusage.

US'ik– 2. fucic, glucic, mucic 3. ageusic 4. anacusic, parageusic.

US'ing– 2. loosing, sprucing 3. adducing, traducing, educing, deducing, reducing, seducing, inducing, conducing, producing, unloosing 4. reproducing, introducing.

US'is– 3. prosneusis 4. therapeusis, anacrusis.

US'iv– 3. abusive, deducive, seducive, inducive, conducive, diffusive, confusive, transfusive, elusive, delusive, illusive, collusive, reclusive, seclusive, inclusive, conclusive, exclusive, obtrusive, intrusive, contusive 4. inconducive, inconclusive, unobtrusive.

US'less– 2. useless, juiceless.

US'li– 2. loosely 3. diffusely, profusely, abstrusely, obtusely.

US'ment– 3. traducement, deducement, reducement, seducement, inducement, producement 5. superinducement.

US'ness– 2. looseness, spruceness 3. diffuseness, profuseness, recluseness, abstruseness, obtuseness.

US'o– 2. trousseau, whoso 3. Caruso 5. Robinson Crusoe.

US'om– 2. gruesome, twosome.

UST'ed– 2. boosted, roosted.

UST'er– 2. booster, footer [Ir.], jouster, rooster, brewster, Brewster.

UT'a– 2. muta, tutta [It.] 3. macuta, aluta, battuta [It.], Matuta 4. barracouta 5. Mater Matuta.

UT'al– 2. brutal 3. refutal, recruital.

UT'ant– 2. mutant, nutant 3. commutant, disputant.

UT'at– 2. mutate, nutate, scutate.

UT'e– 2. bootee, putti [It.], tutti 4. tutti-frutti.

UT'ed– 2. booted, hooted, scooted, luted, looted, fluted, mooted, muted, rooted, bruited, fruited, sooted, suited, chuted, tooted 3. unbooted, refuted, confuted, saluted, diluted, polluted, immuted, commuted, transmuted, cornuted, deputed, reputed, imputed, computed, disputed, unrooted, uprooted, recruited, unsuited, voluted 4. executed, prosecuted, persecuted, undiluted, unpolluted, comminuted, undisputed, substituted, restituted, instituted, constituted, obvoluted, evoluted, revoluted, involuted, convoluted 5. electrocuted.

UT'en– 2. gluten 4. highfaluten [coll.].

UT'er– 2. booter, fouter, hooter, cooter, cuter, luter, looter, fluter, mooter, muter, neuter, pewter, rooter, router, fruiter, suitor, chuter, shooter, tooter, tutor 3. freebooter, confuter, accoutre, acuter, diluter, commuter, transmuter, minuter, imputer, computer, disputer, uprooter, recruiter, peashooter, beanshooter, sharpshooter, protutor, astuter.

UT'est– 2. cutest, mutest 3. acutest, minutest, astutest.

UTH'er– 2. Luther, smoother, soother 3. uncouther.

UTH'est– 2. smoothest.

UTH'ful– 2. ruthful, truthful, toothful, youthful 3. untruthful.

UTH'less– 2. ruthless, truthless, soothless, toothless, youthless.

UTH'ness– 2. smoothness, soothness 3. uncouthness.

UTH'som– 2. toothsome, youthsome.

UT'i– 2. booty, bootee, beauty, duty, cootie, cutie [both slang], looty, fluty, smooty, snooty, putti [It.], rooty, fruity, sooty, tutti 3. freebooty, agouti 4. tutti-frutti.

UT'ij– 2. mutage, scutage, rootage, fruitage.

UT′ik– 3. scorbutic, toreutic 4. herme-
neutic, therapeutic, pharmaceutic, dia-
zeutic.

UT′il– 2. utile, futile, sutile 3. inutile,
unfutile; *see* also UT′l– utile etc. below.

UT′in– 2. cutin, glutin 3. Rasputin 4.
highfalutin [coll.].

UT′ing– 2. booting, hooting, scooting,
looting, fluting, mooting, muting, root-
ing, fruiting, suiting, shooting, tooting
3. freebooting, refuting, confuting, dilut-
ing, polluting, saluting, commuting,
transmuting, deputing, imputing, com-
puting, disputing, uprooting, recruiting
4. executing, prosecuting, persecuting,
highfaluting [coll.], comminuting, sub-
stituting, instituting, constituting, con-
voluting.

UT′ish– 2. brutish, sootish.

UT′ist– 2. lutist, flutist, fruitist 3. com-
putist 4. absolutist, hermeneutist, ther-
apeutist, pharmaceutist, parachutist.

UT′iv– 2. fruitive 4. coadjutive, resolu-
tive, evolutive, persecutive, substitutive,
restitutive, constitutive, convolutive.

UT′l– 2. utile, futile, footle, rootle, brutal,
sutile, tootle 3. inutle, refutal, recruital.

UT′less– 2. bootless, rootless, fruitless 3.
reputeless.

UT′let– 2. rootlet, fruitlet.

UT′li– 2. cutely, mutely, brutely 3.
acutely, minutely, astutely 4. abso-
lutely, resolutely, dissolutely, convolute-
ly.

UT′ment– 3. confutement, imbrutement,
recruitment.

UT′ness– 2. cuteness, muteness, brute-
ness 3. acuteness, minuteness, hirsute-
ness, astuteness 4. absoluteness, dissolute-
ness.

UT′o– 2. Pluto, scruto, tutto [It.] 3.
tenuto [It.] 4. assoluto [It.], risoluto
[It.], sostenuto.

UT′or– 2. suitor, sutor, tutor 3. protutor 4. executor, prosecutor, persecu-
tor; *see* also UT′er– booter etc. above.

UT′um– 2. scutum, sputum 3. verutum
[L.].

UT′ur– 2. future, puture, suture.

UT′us– 2. Plutus, Brutus 3. arbutus,
scorbutus, computus.

U′um– 2. tuum.

UV′al– 3. removal, approval, reproval,
disproval 4. disapproval.

UV′en– 2. hooven, proven 3. unproven,
disproven.

UV′er– 2. Hoover, louver, Louvre, mover,
groover, prover 3. Vancouver, remover,
maneuver, approver, reprover, improver,
disprover 4. disapprover.

UV′erd– 2. louvered 3. maneuvered.

UV′i– 2. movie, groovy.

UV′ing– 2. moving, grooving, proving
3. removing, unmoving, approving, re-
proving, improving, disproving 4. dis-
approving.

UV′less– 2. moveless, grooveless.

UV′ment– 2. movement 3. approve-
ment, improvement, disprovement.

U′ya– 2. huia 4. alleluia, hallelujah.

U′yant– 2. buoyant 3. unbuoyant.

UZ′a– 2. Musa, tuza 4. Arethusa 5.
lallapalooza [slang].

UZ′al– 2. musal 3. refusal, perusal.

UZ′ans– 2. usance 3. misusance, recu-
sance.

UZ′ant– 3. accusant, recusant.

UZ′er– 2. oozer, user, boozer, chooser,
fuser, loser, muser, snoozer, bruiser,
cruiser 3. abuser, refuser, diffuser, in-
fuser, confuser, transfuser, suffuser, ac-
cuser, excuser, palouser, amuser, peruser.

UZ′ez– 2. uses, oozes, boozes, chooses,
fuses, loses, muses, snoozes, bruises,
cruses, cruises 3. misuses, abuses, re-
fuses, diffuses, infuses, confuses, trans-

fuses, suffuses, accuses, excuses, amuses, bemuses, peruses, masseuses, danseuses, contuses.

UZH'i– 2. bougie, rougy.

UZH'un– 2. fusion, trusion 3. effusion, diffusion, infusion, profusion, transfusion, suffusion, allusion, elusion, delusion, illusion, collusion, reclusion, preclusion, seclusion, inclusion, conclusion, occlusion, exclusion, obtrusion, detrusion, retrusion, intrusion, protrusion, extrusion, contusion, Malthusian 4. circumfusion, interfusion, disillusion.

UZ'i– 2. oozy, ǀboozy [coll.], choosy, choosey [both slang], newsy [coll.], snoozy [coll.], drusy, woozy [slang].

UZ'ik– 2. music.

UZ'ing– 2. oozing, boozing [coll.], choosing, fusing, losing, musing, snoozing [coll.], bruising, cruising 3. misusing, abusing, refusing, diffusing, infusing, confusing, transfusing, suffusing, accusing, excusing, amusing, bemusing, perusing, contusing 4. unaccusing, self-accusing, unamusing, interfusing.

UZ'iv– 3. accusive, amusive 4. unamusive.

UZ'l– 2. ouzel, foozle 3. bamboozle [coll.], refusal, perusal.

UZ'ler– 2. foozler 3. bamboozler [coll.].

UZ'ment– 3. accusement, amusement.

U (you)

3.

TRIPLE RHYMES IN U (do′a-ble)

Primary or Secondary Accent falls
on Second from Last Syllable.

U′a–bl– 3. doable, suable, stewable, viewable 4. undoable, subduable, renewable, construable, pursuable, reviewable, unviewable 5. unrenewable, unreviewable.

U′ant–li– 3. fluently, truantly 4. confluently, pursuantly.

UB′er–ans– 4. protuberance, exuberance.

UB′er–ant– 4. protuberant, exuberant 5. unexuberant.

UB′er–us– 3. suberous, tuberous 4. protuberous.

UB′i–a– 3. nubia, Nubia, rubia 5. rabirubia.

UB′i–al– 4. connubial.

UB′i–an– 3. Nubian 4. Danubian.

UB′ik–l– 3. cubicle, cubical 4. cherubical.

UB′it–us– 3. cubitus 4. accubitus, decubitus, concubitous, concubitus.

UB′i–us– 3. dubious, rubious.

UB′ri–kat– 3. lubricate, rubricate.

UB′ri–us– 4. lugubrious, salubrious 5. insalubrious.

UB′ul–us– 3. tubulous.

UD′a–bl– 4. alludable, deludable, precludable, includable, concludable, protrudable 5. unincludable, unconcludable.

UD′er–i– 3. prudery.

UD′in–al– 4. paludinal, testudinal 5. longitudinal, attitudinal, altitudinal, aptitudinal.

UD′i–ness– 3. moodiness, broodiness.

UD′in–us– 4. paludinous, testudinous 5. latitudinous, platitudinous, multitudinous, fortitudinous 6. solicitudinous, vicissitudinous.

UD′i–o– 3. studio 4. preludio.

UD′it–i– 3. nudity, rudity, crudity.

UD′i–um– 3. studium 4. preludium, postludium.

UD′i–us– 3. studious 4. preludious, unstudious.

U′el–er– 3. dueler, fueler, jeweler, grueler, crueler.

U′el–est– 3. cruelest, crewelist.

U′el–i– 3. cruelly.

U′el–ing– 3. dueling, fueling, grueling 4. refueling, bejeweling.

U′er–i– 3. ewery, brewery.

U′i–ness– 3. dewiness, glueyness, screwiness.

U′in–us– 3. ruinous, bruinous, pruinous.

U′it–i– 3. cruety, suety 4. acuity, vacuity, circuity, annuity, strenuity, tenuity, congruity, fatuity, gratuity, fortuity 5. assiduity, ambiguity, exiguity, contiguity, conspicuity, perspicuity, promiscuity, superfluity, ingenuity, continuity, innocuity, incongruity, perpetuity 6. incontinuity, discontinuity.

U′it–iv– 3. fruitive, tuitive 4. intuitive 5. unintuitive.

U′it–us– 4. fatuitous, gratuitous, pituitous, circuitous, fortuitous.

UJ′il–ist– 3. pugilist.

UJ'it–iv– **3.** fugitive.

UK'ar–ist– **3.** Eucharist.

UK'er–i– **3.** dukery, spookery **4.** caducary.

UK'ul–ent– **3.** luculent, muculent.

UL'e–an– **3.** joulean, Julian **4.** Herculean, cerulean.

UL'i–a– **3.** Julia, thulia **4.** abulia **5.** parabulia, hyperbulia.

UL'ish–li– **3.** foolishly, ghoulishly, mulishly.

UL'ish–ness– **3.** foolishness, ghoulishness, mulishness.

UL'it–i– **4.** credulity, sedulity, garrulity **5.** incredulity.

UL'i–um– **3.** thulium **4.** nebulium, peculium.

UM'a–bl– **4.** assumable, resumable, presumable, consumable **5.** unassumable, unpresumable, inconsumable, unconsumable.

UM'a–bli– **4.** presumably **5.** inconsumably.

UM'an–li– **3.** humanly **4.** inhumanly, unhumanly **5.** superhumanly.

UM'e–fi– **3.** humefy, tumefy.

UM'en–al– **3.** noumenal **5.** catechumenal; *see* also **UM'in–al–** luminal etc. below.

UM'er–al– **3.** humeral, numeral.

UM'er–i– **3.** plumery, bloomery **4.** perfumery, costumery.

UM'er–us– **3.** humerus, humorous, numerous, rumorous **4.** innumerous, unhumorous.

UM'in–a– **3.** lumina, numina, Rumina **4.** alumina.

UM'in–al– **3.** luminal, noumenal, ruminal **4.** cacuminal, voluminal **5.** catechumenal.

UM'in–ant– **3.** luminant, ruminant **4.** illuminant, nonruminant.

UM'in–at– **3.** luminate, ruminate **4.** acuminate, cacuminate, illuminate, ferruminate.

UM'i–ness– **3.** gloominess, spuminess, roominess.

UM'in–us– **3.** luminous, numinous **4.** albuminous, leguminous, acuminous, aluminous, voluminous, bituminous.

UM'ul–at– **3.** cumulate, tumulate **4.** accumulate **5.** reaccumulate.

UM'ul–us– **3.** cumulus, tumulus.

UN'a–bl– **3.** tunable **4.** impugnable, expugnable, untunable.

UN'er–i– **3.** lunary **4.** buffoonery, cocoonery, sublunary, poltroonery **5.** pantaloonery.

UN'i–form– **3.** uniform, funiform, cuniform, luniform.

UN'ik–ant– **4.** communicant **5.** excommunicant.

UN'ik–at– **3.** tunicate **4.** communicate **5.** excommunicate **6.** intercommunicate.

UN'it–i– **3.** unity, munity **4.** triunity, jejunity, immunity, community, impunity **5.** importunity, opportunity **6.** intercommunity, inopportunity.

UN'it–iv– **3.** unitive, punitive **4.** communitive.

UN'i–us– **4.** pecunious **5.** impecunious.

UN'yun–ist– **3.** unionist **4.** Reunionist, nonunionist, communionist.

UP'a–bl– **3.** dupable **4.** undupable, recoupable.

UP'er–at– **4.** recuperate, vituperate.

UP'er–i– **3.** dupery, coopery.

UP'er–ij– **3.** cooperage.

UP'i–al– **3.** rupial, troopial, troupial **4.** marsupial.

UP'i–er– **3.** loopier, droopier, croupier, soupier.

UP'i–est– **3.** loopiest, droopiest, soupiest.

UP'ul–us– **3.** lupulus, scrupulous **4.** unscrupulous.

UR'a–bl– **3.** durable, curable **4.** endurable, securable, incurable, procurable, assurable, insurable **5.** unsecurable, uninsurable.

UR′a–bli– 3. durably, curably 4. endurably, incurably 5. unendurably.

UR′al–i– 3. plurally, murally, rurally.

UR′al–ist– 3. pluralist, muralist, ruralist.

UR′al–izm– 3. pluralism, ruralism.

UR′at–iv– 3. durative, curative 4. indurative, depurative, maturative.

UR′et–i– 3. surety 4. cocksurety, unsurety.

UR′i–a– 3. curia [L.] 4. Manchuria, decuria, Lemuria, Etruria 5. glycosuria.

UR′i–al– 3. urial, curial, Muriel 4. figurial, augurial, mercurial, purpureal, centurial.

UR′i–an– 3. durian 4. Manchurian, tellurian, lemurian, Etrurian, Missourian, centurian, Arthurian.

UR′i–ant– 4. luxuriant.

UR′i–at– 3. muriate 4. infuriate, luxuriate, centuriate.

UR′i–ent– 3. prurient 4. esurient, luxuriant, scripturient, parturient.

UR′if–i– 3. purify, thurify.

UR′ing–li– 4. enduringly, alluringly, assuringly.

UR′i–o– 3. durio, curio, Thurio.

UR′it–i– 3. purity, surety 4. security, obscurity, demurity, impurity, cocksurety, maturity, futurity 5. insecurity, prematurity, immaturity.

UR′i–us– 3. furious, curious, spurious 4. sulphureous, injurious, perjurious, incurious, uncurious, penurious, luxurious, usurious 5. unpenurious.

US′a–bl– 4. unloosable, produceable 5. unproduceable.

US′ed–li– 3. deucedly, lucidly, mucidly 4. inducedly, pellucidly.

USH′i–a– 3. fuchsia, Lucia 4. minutia.

USH′i–al– 3. crucial 4. fiducial.

USH′i–an– 4. caducean, Confucian.

USH′un–al– 5. elocutional, evolutional, substitutional, institutional, constitutional 6. circumlocutional.

USH′un–er– 5. executioner, resolutioner, revolutioner.

USH′un–ist– 5. executionist, elocutionist, resolutionist, evolutionist, revolutionist, constitutionist.

US′en–si– 3. lucency 4. translucency.

US′i–bl– 3. crucible 4. adducible, traducible, educible, deducible, reducible, seducible, inducible, conducible, producible 5. irreducible, unreducible, unproducible.

US′id–li– 3. deucedly, lucidly, mucidly 4. inducedly, pellucidly.

US′if–er– 3. Lucifer, crucifer.

US′i–form– 3. luciform, nuciform, cruciform.

US′iv–li– 4. abusively, effusively, diffusively, allusively, elusively, delusively, illusively, conclusively, collusively, obtrusively, intrusively, protrusively 5. inconclusively, inobtrusively, unintrusively.

US′iv–ness– 4. abusiveness, effusiveness, diffusiveness, allusiveness, elusiveness, delusiveness, illusiveness, conclusiveness, exclusiveness, obtrusiveness, intrusiveness, protrusiveness 5. inconclusiveness, inobtrusiveness.

US′or–i– 3. lusory 4. elusory, delusory, prelusory, illusory, reclusory, conclusory, exclusory, collusory, prolusory, extrusory.

UT′a–bl– 3. lootable, mootable, mutable, scrutable, suitable 4. refutable, confutable, commutable, permutable, transmutable, computable, disputable, inscrutable, unsuitable 5. irrefutable, unrefutable, unconfutable, executable, prosecutable, incommutable, uncommutable, incomputable, undisputable.

UT′a–bli– 3. mutably, suitably 4. immutably, permutably, transmutably, inscrutably, unsuitably.

UT′at–iv– 3. mutative, putative, sputative 4. refutative, confutative, commutative, transmutative, imputative, reputative, disputative, sternutative **5.** uncommutative.

UT′e–al– 3. luteal, gluteal, puteal.

UT′ed–li– 3. mutedly **4.** reputedly.

UT′er–i– 3. bootery, pewtery, rootery, fruitery **3.** freebootery.

UT′e–us– 3. beauteous, duteous, luteous, gluteus.

UTH′ful–i– 3. ruthfully, truthfully, youthfully.

UTH′ful–ness– 3. ruthfulness, truthfulness, youthfulness.

UTH′les–li– 3. ruthlessly, truthlessly, youthlessly.

UTH′les–ness– 3. ruthlessness, truthlessness, youthlessness.

UT′i–fi– 3. beautify, brutify.

UT′i–ful– 3. dutiful, beautiful **4.** undutiful, unbeautiful.

UT′ik–al– 3. cuticle **4.** scorbutical, latreutical **5.** hermeneutical, therapeutical, pharmaceutical.

UT′i–ness– 3. snootiness, fruitiness, sootiness.

UT′in–i– 3. mutiny, scrutiny.

UT′in–us– 3. glutinous, mutinous, scrutinous **4.** velutinous, unmutinous.

UT′iv–li– 5. substitutively, constitutively.

UT′u–al– 3. mutual **4.** immutual, commutual, nonmutual, unmutual.

UV′a–bl– 3. movable, provable **4.** removable, immovable, approvable, improv-

able, reprovable **5.** irremovable, unapprovable, irreprovable, unimprovable.

UV′i–al– 3. uveal, fluvial, pluvial **4.** alluvial, effluvial, diluvial, colluvial, exuvial **5.** postdiluvial **6.** antediluvial.

UV′i–an– 4. alluvian, diluvian, Peruvian, Vesuvian **5.** postdiluvian **6.** antediluvian.

UV′ing–li– 3. movingly **4.** approvingly, reprovingly **5.** unapprovingly.

UV′i–um– 4. alluvium, eluvium, effluvium, diluvium, impluvium, compluvium.

UV′i–us– 3. pluvious, Pluvius **4.** Vesuvius **6.** Jupiter Pluvius.

UZ′a–bl– 3. usable, choosable, losable **4.** unusable, abusable, confusable, accusable, excusable, amusable, perusable **5.** unaccusable, inexcusable, unamusable.

UZ′a–bli– 4. excusably **5.** inexcusably, unexcusably.

UZ′at–iv– 4. accusative, recusative.

UZH′un–al– 3. fusional **4.** confusional, delusional, illusional, conclusional, intrusional.

UZH′ur–i– 3. usury.

UZ′i–bl– 3. fusible **4.** diffusible, infusible, transfusible, protrusible.

UZ′ik–al– 3. musical **4.** nonmusical, unmusical.

UZ′i–ness– 3. ooziness, booziness [coll.], chooziness [slang], newsiness [coll.], snooziness [coll.], wooziness [slang].

OO (full)

SEE OO (good), FOLLOWING O (awe).

U (tub)

1.

SINGLE (MASCULINE) RHYMES IN U (tub)

Primary or Secondary Accent Falls on Last Syllable; Imperfect Rhymes Are in Italics.

UB– 1. bub, chub, dub, hub, cub, blub, flub [coll.], club, slub, nub, knub, snub, pub [slang], rub, drub, grub, scrub, shrub, sub, tub, stub 2. hubbub, flubdub [slang], subshrub 3. sillabub, Beelzebub, rub-a-dub.

UBD– 1. dubbed, hubbed, cubbed, clubbed, snubbed, rubbed, drubbed, grubbed, scrubbed, shrubbed, subbed [slang], tubbed, stubbed.

UBZ– dubs etc., see UB– bub etc. above, plus "s" or " 's"; 3. mulligrubs [slang].

UCH– 1. Dutch, hutch, cutch, scutch, clutch, much, mutch, smutch, rutch, crutch, such, touch 2. nonesuch, retouch 3. insomuch, overmuch, inasmuch, forasmuch.

UCHD– 1. clutched, smutched, rutched, crutched, touched 2. retouched, untouched.

UD– 1. bud, dud, cud, scud, Lud, blood, flood, mud, pud [coll.], spud, rud, sud, sudd, shud, stud, thud 2. rosebud, bestud.

UDZ– buds etc., see UD– bud etc. above, plus "s" or " 's."

UF– 1. buff, chuff, chough, duff, fuf [Scot. & N. of Eng.], guff [Scot. & slang] huff, cuff, scuff, luff, bluff, fluff, clough pluff [dial.], slough, sluff [dial.], muff nuf, nuff [both slang], snuff, puff, ruff rough, gruff, scruff, sough, suff [dial.] tough, tuff, stuff, whuff 2. rebuff, Mac duff, handcuff, enough, cream puff, dan druff, crossruff 3. counterbuff, fisticuff powder puff, overstuff.

UFS– buffs etc., see UF– buff etc. above plus "s" or " 's."

UFT– 1. buffed, chuffed, cuffed, bluffed. sloughed, snuffed, puffed, tuft, stuffed 2 handcuffed, unstuffed 3. candytuft overstuffed.

UG– 1. ugh, bug, chug, dug, hug, jug lug, glug, plug, slug, mug, smug, pug spug [Scot. & dial. Eng.], rug, drug shrug, trug, tug, thug, vug 2. humbug firebug 3. ladybug, tumblebug, doodle bug, bunnyhug.

UGZ– bugs etc., see UG– ugh etc. above plus "s" or " 's."

UJ– 1. budge, fudge, judge, sludge smudge, nudge, pudge [coll.], drudg grudge, trudge 2. adjudge, prejudge, forejudge, misjudge, begrudge.

UJD– 1. budged, fudged, judged, sludged, smudged, nudged, drudged, grudged, trudged 2. adjudged, self-judged, well-judged, ill-judged, forejudged, misjudged, begrudged.

UK– 1. buck, chuck, duck, cuck [obs.], luck, gluck, cluck, pluck, muck, knuck [coll.], Puck, ruck, truck, struck, suck, shuck, tuck, stuck 2. *springbuck, prongbuck, roebuck, sawbuck, woodchuck,* lame duck, *potluck,* dumb cluck [slang], amuck, Canuck, *awestruck, moonstruck, sun-struck* 3. waterbuck, Donald Duck, chuck-a-luck, panic-struck, thunderstruck, wonder-struck, horror-struck, nip and tuck.

UKS– bucks etc., see UK– buck etc. above, plus "s" or " 's"; 1. ducks, dux, lux, flux, mux [dial.], crux, tux [slang].

UKST– 1. fluxed 2. effluxed, refluxed.

UKT– 1. bucked, chucked, duct, ducked, trucked, sucked, shucked, tucked 2. abduct, educt, deduct, induct, conduct, obduct, reluct, unplucked, eruct, instruct, construct 3. viaduct, aqueduct, fumiduct, circumduct, misconduct, usufruct, reconstruct.

UL– 1. dull, gull, hull, cull, scull, skull, lull, mull, trull, sull [dial.], stull, wull [dial.] 2. *seagull,* Mogul, ahull, dehull, école [F.], bricole, *numskull,* [coll.], annul 3. disannul.

ULB– 1. bulb 3. pseudobulb.

ULCH– 1. gulch, cultch, culch, mulch.

ULD– 1. dulled, gulled, hulled, culled, sculled, skulled, lulled, mulled 2. thick-skulled, dehulled, black-hulled, annulled.

ULF– 1. gulf 2. engulf.

ULJ– 1. bulge 2. indulge, effulge, promulge, divulge 3. reindulge 4. overindulge.

ULJD– 1. bulged 2. indulged, promulged, divulged 3. undivulged 4. overindulged.

ULK– 1. bulk, hulk, skulk, mulk, sulk.

ULKT– 1. bulked, hulked, skulked, mulct, sulked.

ULM– 1. culm, stulm.

ULP– 1. gulp, culp [slang], sculp, pulp.

ULPT– 1. gulped, pulped 2. soft-pulped 3. golden-pulped.

ULS– 1. bulse, dulse, dulce, mulse, pulse 2. repulse, impulse, expulse, avulse, revulse, convulse.

ULSD– 1. pulsed 2. repulsed, avulsed, revulsed, convulsed.

ULT– 1. cult 2. adult, incult, occult, penult, insult, consult, result, exult 3. subadult, catapult 4. antepenult.

ULZ– dulls etc., see UL– dull etc. above, plus "s" or " 's."

UM– 1. um, homme [F.], bum, chum, dumb, gum, hum, come, scum, Lum, glum, plum, plumb, slum, mum, numb, snum, rum, rhumb, drum, grum, crumb, scrum, strum, thrum, some, sum, tum, stum, thumb, swum, yum 2. *serfdom, kingdom, dogdom, dukedom, earldom, dumdum, begum,* Bonhomme, become, succumb, unplumb, benumb, *humdrum, threesome, wholesome, lonesome, awesome, toothsome, gruesome, twosome, tum-tum, yum-yum,* Yum-Yum 3. tweedledum, Christendom, martyrdom, fee-faw-fum, overcome, misbecome, colchicum, unicum, capsicum, solidum, oppidum, orpheum, horreum, labium, stibium, cambium, calcium, stadium, studium, ischium, silphium, lithium, cadmium, hafnium, opium, Arctium, vitium, otium, cingulum, septulum, sertulum, crembalum, sugarplum, symbolum, pabulum, pendulum, minimum, quadrimum, optimum, maximum, labdanum, laudanum, platinum, labarum, cerebrum, kettledrum, panjandrum, conundrum, theorum, drearisome, wearisome, frolicsome, gamblesome, troublesome, meddlesome, quarrelsome, burdensome, cumbersome, bothersome, venturesome, debitum, placitum, cognitum, compitum, vacuum, menstruum, mutuum   **4.** fee fi fo fum, ceruleum, castoreum, columbium, aerobium, exordium, sporangium, Eryngium, absinthium, agonium, euphonium, polonium, stramonium, ammonium, harmonium, opprobrium, delirium, tellurium, martyrium, gymnasium, potassium, Elysium, sestertium, consortium, nasturtium, caputium, deliquium, viaticum, chrysanthemum, molybdenum, aluminum, ad libitum, accubitum, acquisitum   **5.** periosteum, equilibrium, polyandrium, hypochondrium, epigastrium, sacerdotium.

UMD– **1.** gummed, plumbed, numbed, drummed, crumbed, strummed, thumbed **2.** ungummed.

UMF– **1.** umph, humph, grumph [Scot.] **2.** *triumph.*

UMP– **1.** ump [slang], bump, chump, dump, gump, hump, jump, lump, flump, glump [slang], clump, plump, slump, mump, pump, rump, frump, grump, crump, trump, sump, tump, stump, thump, wump [slang]. **2.** high jump, bethump, *mugwump* **3.** overtrump.

UMPS– bumps etc., *see* **UMP–** bump etc. above, plus "s" or " 's."

UMZ– chums etc. *see* **UM–** um etc. above plus "s" or " 's"; **1.** Thrums **2.** *breekums, doldrums.*

UN– **1.** un [coll. & dial.], bun, done, dun, Dunn, fun, gun, Hun, hon [slang], none, nun, pun, spun, run, sun, son, sunn, shun, tun, ton, stun, one, won **2.** well-done, ill-done, undone, foredone, outdone, begun, homespun, forerun, unrun, outrun, grandson, Whitsun, unwon **3.** clarendon, overdone, underdone, unbegun, Sally Lunn, overrun, Tennyson, atchison, Atkinson, Sheraton, Wellington, skimmington, Orpington, anyone, everyone, number one.

UNCH– **1.** bunch, hunch, lunch, clunch [dial.], munch, nunch [dial.], punch,

runch, brunch [coll.], crunch, scrunch, squnch.

UND– **1.** Bund, dunned, fund, mund, punned, sunned, shunned, stunned **2.** refund, unsunned, rotund **3.** moribund, cummerbund, verecund, rubicund, Rosamond, obrotund, orotund.

UNG– **1.** bung, hung, lung, flung, clung, slung, pung, rung, wrung, sprung, strung, sung, tongue, stung, swung, young **2.** *geebung,* unhung, among, highstrung, hamstrung, unsung, betongue, *shantung, oxtongue* **3.** underhung, overhung, underslung, hereamong, thereamong, overstrung, mother tongue.

UNGD– **1.** bunged, tongued **2.** blacktongued, bell-tongued, thick-tongued, sharp-tongued **3.** iron-lunged, leatherlunged, honey-tongued, silver-tongued, many-tongued, double-tongued, trumpettongued.

UNJ– **1.** lunge, longe, blunge, plunge, sponge **2.** expunge **3.** muskellunge.

UNK– **1.** unk, unc [both slang], bunk, chunk, dunk, funk, hunk, junk, skunk, lunk [slang], blunk [slang], clunk [Scot. & dial.], plunk, slunk, monk, nunc, punk, spunk, drunk, trunk, sunk, tunk [dial.], stunk **2.** Mauch Chunk, quidnunc, undrunk, tree trunk, unsunk.

UNKST– **1.** 'mongst **2.** amongst.

UNKT– **1.** bunked, junked, skunked, trunked **2.** defunct, injunct, conjunct, disjunct.

UNS– **1.** once, bunce [slang], dunce.

UNT– **1.** bunt, hunt, lunt, blunt, punt, runt, brunt, front, grunt, shunt, stunt, wont, wun't [dial.] **2.** *staghunt,* fox hunt, affront, *bifront,* confront, *forefront* **3.** exeunt.

UNTH– **1.** month **2.** *twelvemonth.*

UNZ– buns etc., *see* **UN–** bun etc. above, plus "s" or " 's."

UP– **1.** up, dup [dial.], cup, scup, pup, sup, tup, yup [slang] **2.** *windup,* hard

up, *roundup*, *make-up*, *breakup*, *hiccough*,
hiccup, *pickup*, *lockup*, *sunup*, *ripup*, *tipup*,
tossup, *getup*, *letup*, *setup* **3.** up-and-up,
loving cup, buttercup, stirrip cup.

ŬPT– 1. upped, cupped, supped, tupped
2. abrupt, erupt, corrupt, disrupt **3.**
interrupt, incorrupt, uncorrupt.

ŬR– 1. err, er, 'er, Er, Ur, burr, birr,
churr, chirr, fer [dial.], fir, fur, her, cur,
coeur, blur, slur, myrrh, smur, knur, per,
purr, spur, sir, sur, shirr, stir, were, whir
2. nightchurr, befur, defer, prefer, infer,
confer, chauffeur, furfur, transfer, recur,
incur, concur, occur, liqueur, demur,
larkspur, hotspur, masseur, farceur [F.],
susurr, deter, inter, hauteur, astir, Pasteur,
bestir, restir, aver, rever **3.** cocklebur,
butterbur, calaber, shillaber, massacre,
sepulchre, calendar, calender, islander,
lavender, provender, Lucifer, crucifer,
Jennifer, conifer, dapifer, rotifer, aquifer,
pillager, villager, manager, tanager ,onager,
forager, vintager, cottager, ravager, voy-
ager, voyageur [F.], dowager, integer,
armiger, claviger, breviger, hardanger,
challenger, passenger, messenger, scaven-
ger, harbinger, derringer, porringer, chron-
opher, publisher, polisher, punisher, cher-
isher, nourisher, Britisher, vanquisher,
rapier, copier, odaler, victualer, chronicler,
chiseler, traveler, leveler, hoveler, shoveler, wassailer, labeler, yodeler, quarreler,
jeweler, gossamer, dulcimer, lorimer,
customer, costumer, parcener, gardener,
hardener, lengthener, strengthener, weak-
ener, wakener, quickener, cheapener,
deepener, sharpener, loosener, lessener,
threatener, sweetener, shortener, fastener,
hastener, chastener, listener, moistener,
evener, scrivener, cozener, bargainer,
almoner, commoner, summoner, coroner,
ironer, reasoner, seasoner, poisoner, pris-
oner, northerner, southerner, easterner,
westerner, sojourner, stuccoer, diaper,
hanaper, worshiper, caliper, juniper,
gossiper, galloper, walloper, jabberer,

slumberer, numberer, sorcerer, slanderer,
panderer, murderer, pilferer, chamferer,
wagerer, staggerer, swaggerer, weatherer,
furtherer, cornerer, naperer, scamperer,
whimperer, whisperer, caterer, loiterer,
shelterer, saunterer, barterer, plasterer,
pesterer, roisterer, fosterer, blusterer,
answerer, laborer, clamorer, conjurer,
murmurer, usurer, venturer, lecturer,
capturer, torturer, connoisseur, purchaser,
silencer, licenser, trespasser, canvasser,
harnesser, accoucheur, amateur, marketer,
bucketer, arbiter, forfeiter, surfeiter,
scimiter, chapiter, Jupiter, warranter,
disinter, frankfurter, winchester, Roches-
ter, harvester, sophister, sinister, presbyter
sandiver, caliver, gilliver, Gulliver, Oliver,
miniver, Andover, Passover, journeyer
4. Ambassadeur, ambassador, restaura-
teur, artificer, admonisher, relinquisher,
astronomer, tobogganner, coparcener, en-
livener, developer, enveloper, embroi-
derer, encounterer, upholsterer, deliverer,
maneuverer, conjecturer, adventurer, Ac-
cipiter.

ŬRB– 1. herb, gerb, curb, blurb [coll.],
Serb, verb **2.** *potherb*, *suburb*, superb,
perturb, disturb, *adverb*, reverb.

ŬRBD– 1. curbed, verbed **2.** uncurbed,
disturbed, perturbed **3.** imperturbed,
unperturbed, undisturbed.

ŬRCH– 1. birch, church, lurch, smirch,
perch, search **2.** besmirch, research.

ŬRD– 1. urd, erred, bird, burred, Byrd,
furred, gird, heard, herd, curd, Kurd,
blurred, slurred, purred, spurred, surd,
shirred, turd, stirred, third, word, whirred
2. *songbird*, *blackbird*, *halberd*, *snowbird*,
bluebird, *lovebird*, befurred, inferred, con-
ferred, begird, engird, ungird, unheard,
gooseherd, recurred, occurred, demurred,
absurd, interred, averred, Cape Verde,
wayward, *watchword*, *leeward*, reword,
seaward, *homeward*, *inward*, *onward*, *downward*, *upward*, *foreword*, *forward* **3.**
mockingbird, hummingbird, ladybird,

undergird, overheard, reoccurred, disinterred, afterward, sepulchred.

URDZ– birds etc., *see* **URD–** urd etc. above, plus "s" or " 's."

URF– 1. kerf, scurf, perf [slang], serf, surf, turf 3. hippocerf.

URG– 1. erg, berg, burg, bourg 2. exergue, *Goldberg, iceberg, Strasbourg, Pittsburgh* 3. Heidelberg, Brandenburg.

URJ– 1. urge, dirge, scourge, splurge, merge, purge, spurge, serge, surge, verge 2. submerge, emerge, immerge, asperge, resurge, deterge, absterge, diverge, converge 3. demiurge, dramaturge, thaumaturge.

URK– 1. irk, burke, Burke, dirk, girk [slang], jerk, jerque, kirk, lurk, clerk, murk, smirk, perk, cirque, shirk, Turk, stirk, work, quirk, yerk 2. *hauberk,* Dunkerque, berserk, *patchwork, woodwork, bridgework, clockwork, bulwark, guesswork, network, fretwork* 3. handiwork, fancywork, needlework, openwork, overwork, latticework.

URKS– irks etc., *see* **URK–** irk etc. above, plus "s" or " 's."

URL– 1. earl, erl [dial.], burl, birl, churl, furl, girl, gurl, herl, hurl, curl, skirl, merle, knurl, pearl, perle, purl, thirl, querl, swirl, twirl, whirl, whorl 2. unfurl, becurl, uncurl, impearl 4. mother-of-pearl.

URLD– 1. burled, furled, hurled, curled, skirled, pearled, purled, world, swirled, twirled, whirled 2. unfurled, impearled, old-world 3. underworld.

URM– 1. berm, derm, firm, germ, sperm, term, therm, worm, squirm 2. affirm, infirm, confirm, *Landsturm, silkworm, bookworm, glowworm, earthworm* 3. pachyderm, reaffirm, disaffirm, isotherm, angleworm.

URMD– 1. firmed, germed, termed, wormed, squirmed 2. confirmed 3. reaffirmed, unconfirmed.

URN– 1. earn, urn, erne, burn, Berne, churn, dern [dial.], durn [dial.], fern, herne, kern, learn, pirn, spurn, tern, turn, stern, quern, yearn 2. inurn, *sunburn, heartburn, cedarn,* adjourn, sojourn, epergne, discern, concern, lucerne, Lucerne, attorn, *Saturn,* eterne, return, *nocturne,* inturn, interne, sauterne, upturn, *quartern,* astern, *eastern, cistern,* extern, *sextern, leathern, northern* 3. unconcern, sempitern, taciturn, overturn.

URND– 1. earned, urned, burned, churned, learned, spurned, turned, sterned, yearned 2. hard-earned, wellearned, unearned, sunburned, adjourned, sojourned, discerned, concerned, returned, interned, upturned 3. unconcerned, overturned.

URNZ– earns etc., *see* **URN–** earn etc. above, plus "s" or " 's."

URP– 1. urp [slang], burp [slang], chirp, lerp, slurp [dial.], purp, turp, terp, twerp, twirp [all slang] 2. discerp, usurp, *Antwerp.*

URPS– burps [slang], chirps, slurps [dial.], stirps 2. discerps, usurps.

URPT– 1. burped [slang], chirped, slurped [dial.] 2. excerpt, discerped, usurped.

URS– 1. Erse, birse, burse, cherce [dial.], hearse, curse, nurse, purse, terce, terse, verse, worse 2. imburse, disburse, rehearse, accurse, precurse, amerce, submerse, immerse, coerce, asperse, disperse, sesterce, averse, traverse, obverse, subverse, adverse, reverse, diverse, perverse, inverse, converse, transverse 3. reimburse, intersperse, universe.

URST– 1. erst, burst, first, Hearst, cursed, nursed, pursed, thirst, versed, verst, worst wurst 2. *sunburst, outburst,* rehearsed, accursed, emersed, immersed, dispersed, athirst, traversed, conversed, unversed 3. reimbursed, unrehearsed, interspersed, untraversed, liverwurst.

URT– 1. Bert, dirt, girt, hurt, curt, skirt, blurt, flirt, nert [slang], pert, spurt, cert [slang], syrt, shirt, vert, wort, quirt, squirt 2. begirt, *seagirt*, engirt, ungirt, unhurt, alert, inert, *expert*, assert, concert, exert, exsert, insert, *redshirt*, *Black Shirt*, avert, obvert, subvert, advert, evert, revert, divert, invert, convert, overt, pervert, transvert, dessert, *madwort*, *ragwort*, *figwort*, *steepwort* 3. Adelbert, Ethelbert, Camembert, malapert, inexpert, preconcert, disconcert, intersert, undershirt, ambivert, retrovert, introvert, controvert, extrovert, pennywort, liverwort, motherwort.

URTH– 1. earth, berth, birth, dearth, firth, mirth, Perth, worth 2. inearth, unearth, rebirth, unworth 3. underearth, pennyworth, money's worth.

URV– 1. curve, nerve, serve, verve, swerve 2. recurve, *incurve*, *outcurve*, innerve, unnerve, observe, subserve, deserve, reserve, preserve, disserve, conserve 3. unreserve.

URVD– 1. curved, served, swerved 2. unnerved, reserved, preserved, conserved 3. undeserved, well-deserved, well-preserved, unpreserved, unconserved.

URVZ– curves etc., see **URV–** curve etc. above, plus "s" or " 's."

URZ– errs etc., see **UR–** err etc. above, plus "s" or " 's"; 1. furze.

US– 1. us, bus, buss, chuss [slang], fuss, guss, cuss [coll.], plus, muss, pus, Russ, Grus, truss, Sus, stuss, thus 2. percuss, discuss, excuss, khuskhus, succuss, nonplus, surplus, untruss 3. harquebus, omnibus, blunderbuss, dubious, tedious, hideous, aqueous, igneous, carneous, corneous, impious, repercuss, overplus, nucleus, copious, nacreous, cupreous, vitreous, gaseous, osseous, nauseous, lacteous, piteous, plenteous, bounteous, courteous, beauteous, luteous, niveous, envious, pluvious, scandalous, libelous, cautelous, scurrilous, marvelous, frivolous, bibulous, flocculous, calculous, calculus,

surculous, surculus, nodulous, scrofulous, cellulous, cumulous, cumulus, granulous, querulous, garrulous, infamous, bigamous, blasphemous, venomous, enormous, amanous, bimanous, membranous, larcenous, ravenous, villainous, mountainous, acinous, acinus, hircinous, criminous, resijous, cretinous, sanguinous, ruinous, tyrannous, poisonous, consonous, gluttonous, dipnoous, dichroous, platypus, octopus, barbarous, nectarous, Tartarus, ludicrous, slumberous, tuberous, ulcerous, cancerous, ponderous, thunderous, dangerous, cankerous, humerus, onerous, viperous, Hesperus, prosperous, slaughterous, apterous, dexterous, pulverous, chivalrous, rancorous, nidorous, phosphorous, Phosphorus, valorous, dolorous, timorous, humorous, susurrus, susurrous, sinistrous, verdurous, fulgurous, sulphurous, murmurous, venturous, rapturous, torturous, Pegasus, covetous, halitus, halitous, aditus, fremitus, spiritous, transitus, riotous, vacuous, arduous, sensuous, fatuous, unctuous, fructuous, spiritous, sumptuous, tortuous, mischievous, atavus, flexuous 4. caduceus, polyphagous, analogous, homologous, amphibious, ingenious, calumnious, symphonious, uproarious, opprobrious, Leviticus, noctambulous, monoculous, tuberculous, unscrupulous, edentulous, didynamous, tridynamous, diaphanous, epiphanous, ferruginous, foraminous, contaminous, trigeminous, gelatinous, polygynous, polygenous, ephemerous, polymerous, obstreperous, tetrapterous, preposterous, adventurous, edematous, velocitous, calamitous, precipitous, necessitous, innocuous, promiscuous, circumfluous, superfluous, impetuous, tumultuous, presumptuous, voluptuous, incestuous, tempestuous 5. heterologous, ignominious.

USH– 1. ush [slang], gush, hush, cush, lush, blush, flush, plush, slush, mush, rush, brush, crush, thrush, tush 2. agush, ablush, aflush, reflush, *bulrush*, *onrush*, *outrush*, *tarbrush* 3. underbrush.

USK– 1. busk, dusk, fusc, husk, cusk, musk, rusk, brusque, tusk 2. embusk, adusk, subfusc, dehusk, *mollusk.*

USP– 1. cusp.

UST– 1. bust, dust, dost, fust, fussed, gust, just, cussed, lust, plussed, mussed, rust, crust, trussed, trust, thrust 2. combust, robust, adust, *gold-dust,* bedust, *stardust, august,* disgust, adjust, unjust, discussed, nonplussed, unmussed, encrust, betrust, entrust, untrussed, distrust, mistrust 3. unrobust, readjust, coadjust, undiscussed.

UT– 1. ut, but, butt, phut, gut, hut, jut, cut, scut, glut, slut, mut, mutt, smut, nut, putt, rut, strut, shut, tut, what 2. abut, rebut, *hagbut, catgut,* *woodcut,* recut, uncut, *haircut,* clear-cut, *crosscut,* besmut, *peanut, chestnut, walnut, doughnut, burnut, beechnut,* astrut, reshut, somewhat 3. surrebut, scuttle butt, halibut, betel nut, hazelnut, butternut, coconut, occiput, Lilliput.

UTH– 1. doth 2. bismuth 3. azimuth.

UV– 1. dove, guv, gov [both slang], love, glove, shove 2. above, truelove, reglove, unglove, *foxglove* 3. turtledove, ladylove.

UVD– 1. loved, gloved, shoved 2. beloved, ungloved 3. unbeloved.

UZ– 1. Uz, buzz, does, fuzz, guz, huzz, coz 2. abuzz, *humbuzz,* chauffeuse [F.], masseuse 3. dear me suz [slang].

UZD– 1. buzzed, fuzzed.

U (tub)

2.

DOUBLE (FEMININE) RHYMES IN U (rub'ber)

Primary or Secondary Accent Falls on Next to
Last Syllable; Imperfect Rhymes Are in Italics.

UB'er– 2. dubber, hubber, lubber, blubber, clubber, slubber, snubber, rubber, drubber, grubber, scrubber, tubber, stubber 3. *landlubber* 4. moneygrubber 5. India-rubber.

UB'erd– 2. Hubbard, blubbered, cupboard, rubbered 4. Mother Hubbard.

UB'i– 2. bubby, chubby, fubby [coll. Eng.], hubby, cubby, clubby, slubby, nubby, knubby, rubby, grubby, scrubby, shrubby, tubby, stubby.

UB'ing– 2. dubbing, hubbing, cubbing, blubbing, clubbing, nubbing, snubbing, rubbing, drubbing, grubbing, scrubbing, subbing [slang], tubbing, stubbing.

UB'ish– 2. cubbish, clubbish, snubbish, rubbish, grubbish, shrubbish, tubbish.

UB'l– 2. bubble, double, hubble, nubble, rubble, trouble, stubble 3. redouble 4. hubble-bubble.

UB'ld– 2. bubbled, doubled, troubled, stubbled 3. redoubled, untroubled.

UB'ler– 2. bubbler, doubler, troubler.

UB'let– 2. doublet, knublet, shrublet, tublet.

UB'li– 2. bubbly, doubly, hubbly, knubbly, nubbly, rubbly, drubbly [dial.], strubbly, stubbly.

UB'lik– 2. public 3. republic, nonpublic, unpublic.

UB'ling– 2. bubbling, doubling, nubbling, troubling 3. redoubling, untroubling.

UB'lish– 2. publish 3. republish.

UCH'er– 2. Dutcher, scutcher, clutcher, smutcher, toucher 3. retoucher.

UCH'ess– 2. duchess, Dutchess 3. archduchess, grand duchess.

UCH'ez– 2. hutches, scutches, clutches, smutches, rutches, crutches, touches 3. retouches.

UCH'i– 2. duchy, clutchy, smutchy, touchy 3. archduchy, grand duchy.

UCH'ing– 2. scutching, clutching, smutching, rutching, crutching, touching 3. retouching.

UCH'on– 2. scutcheon 3. McCutcheon, escutcheon 4. inescutcheon.

UD'ed– 2. budded, scudded, blooded, flooded, mudded, spudded, studded, thudded 3. unbudded, bestudded.

UD'er– 2. udder, dudder, scudder, flooder, mudder, rudder, sudder, shudder.

UD'i– 2. buddy, cuddy, scuddy, bloody, muddy, puddee, puddy, ruddy, study 3. *soapsuddy* 4. understudy, overstudy.

UD'id– 2. bloodied, muddied, ruddied, studied 3. unstudied 4. overstudied.

UD'ij– 2. buddage, floodage.

UD'ing– 2. budding, scudding, flooding, studding, thudding.

UD'l– 2. buddle, fuddle, huddle, cuddle, scuddle [Scot.], muddle, nuddle [dial.], puddle, ruddle, studdle 3. befuddle, bemuddle.

UD'ld– 2. fuddled, huddled, cuddled, scuddled [Scot.], muddled, puddled, studdled [dial.] 3. befuddled, bemuddled.

264

UD′ler– 2. huddler, cuddler, muddler, puddler 3. befuddler.

UD′let– 2. budlet, floodlet.

UD′li– 2. Dudley, cuddly, puddly.

UD′ling– 2. fuddling, huddling, cuddling, scuddling [Scot.], muddling, puddling, studdling [dial.] 3. befuddling, bemuddling.

UD′son– 2. Hudson, Judson.

UD′zi– 2. sudsy 3. soapsudsy.

UF′en– 2. roughen, toughen.

UF′er– 2. buffer, chuffer, duffer, guffer [Scot.], huffer, cuffer, scuffer, luffer, bluffer, fluffer, pluffer [Scot. & N. of Eng.], slougher, muffer, snuffer, puffer, ruffer, rougher, gruffer, suffer, tougher, stuffer.

UF′est– 2. bluffest, roughest, gruffest, toughest.

UF′et– 2. buffet, fuffit [Scot.], muffet, tuffet 3. Miss Muffet.

UF′i– 2. buffy, fuffy [dial.], guffy [slang], huffy, cuffy, bluffy, fluffy, pluffy [dial.], sloughy, snuffy, puffy, ruffy, roughie, stuffy 4. ruffy-tuffy.

UF′in– 2. buffin, guffin [dial. & slang], cuffin, muffin, puffin 3. mumruffin 4. ragamuffin.

UF′ing– 2. buffing, chuffing, duffing, huffing, cuffing, luffing, bluffing, fluffing, sloughing, muffing, puffing, roughing, ruffing, soughing, stuffing.

UF′ish– 2. huffish, snuffish, roughish, gruffish, toughish.

UF′l– 2. buffle, duffel, fuffle [Scot.], scuffle, muffle, snuffle, ruffle, truffle, shuffle, whuffle 3. bemuffle, reshuffle 4. double shuffle.

UF′ler– 2. scuffler, muffler, snuffler, ruffler, shuffler.

UF′li– 2. bluffly, scuffly, muffly, snuffly, ruffly, roughly, gruffly, toughly.

UF′ling– 2. scuffling, muffling, snuffling, ruffling, shuffling 3. bemuffling, unruffling.

UF′lz– 2. snuffles, ruffles, truffles.

UF′ness– 2. bluffness, roughness, gruffness, toughness.

UFT′i– 2. mufti, tufty.

UG′ed– 2. rugged.

UG′er– 2. bugger, chugger, hugger, lugger, luggar, plugger, slugger, mugger, smugger, snugger, pugger, rugger, drugger, shrugger, tugger 4. huggermugger.

UG′est– 2. smuggest, snuggest, druggist.

UG′et– 2. mugget, nugget, drugget.

UG′i– 2. buggy, fuggy, luggie, pluggy, sluggy, muggy, puggi, puggy, druggy.

UG′ij– 2. luggage.

UG′ing– 2. chugging, hugging, jugging, lugging, glugging, plugging, slugging, mugging, rugging, drugging, shrugging, tugging.

UG′ish– 2. sluggish, muggish, smuggish, snuggish, puggish.

UG′l– 2. guggle, juggle, smuggle, snuggle, puggle, struggle.

UG′ler– 2. juggler, smuggler, snuggler, struggler.

UG′li– 2. ugly, guggly, juggly, smugly, snugly, struggly 3. plug-ugly [slang]

UG′ling– 2. guggling, juggling, smuggling, snuggling, struggling.

UG′nant– 3. repugnant, oppugnant 4. unrepugnant.

UG′ness– 2. smugness, snugness.

UJ′el– 2. cudgel.

UJ′er– 2. budger, fudger, judger, sludger, smudger, nudger, drudger, grudger, trudger 3. adjudger, rejudger, prejudger, misjudger, forejudger, begrudger.

UJ′et– 2. budget.

UJ′ez– 2. budges, fudges, judges, sludges, smudges, nudges, drudges, grudges, trudges 3. adjudges, prejudges, misjudges, begrudges.

UJ′i– 2. fudgy, sludgy, pudgy, smudgy.

UJ'ing– 2. budging, fudging, judging, sludging, smudging, nudging, drudging, grudging, trudging 3. adjudging, prejudging, misjudging, begrudging.

UJ'ment– 2. judgment 3. adjudgment, misjudgment.

UJ'on– 2. dudgeon, gudgeon, bludgeon 3. curmudgeon.

UK'a– 2. bucca, pucka, pukka, yucca 3. felucca.

UK'er– 2. bucker, chucker, chukker, ducker, clucker, plucker, mucker, pucker, trucker, sucker, succor, shucker, tucker 3. seersucker.

UK'et– 2. bucket, mucket, tucket 3. Nantucket, Pawtucket.

UK'i– 2. bucky, buckie, ducky, lucky, plucky, mucky, tucky 3. unlucky, Kentucky.

UK'ij– 2. pluckage, truckage, suckage.

UK'ing– 2. bucking, chucking, ducking, clucking, plucking, mucking, trucking, sucking, shucking, tucking.

UK'ish– 2. buckish, puckish.

UK'l– 2. buckle, chuckle, huckle, muckle, knuckle, truckle, suckle, yukkel 3. unbuckle, parbuckle 4. honeysuckle.

UK'ld– 2. buckled, chuckled, cuckold, knuckled, truckled, suckled 3. unbuckled.

UK'ler– 2. buckler, chuckler, knuckler, truckler, suckler 3. swashbuckler.

UK'less– 2. buckless, duckless, luckless, suckless.

UK'ling– 2. buckling, chuckling, duckling, knuckling, truckling, suckling 4. ugly duckling.

UK'or– succor; *see* also **UK'er–** bucker etc. above.

UKS'ez– 2. fluxes, cruxes 3. effluxes, refluxes.

UKSH'un– 2. duction, fluxion, ruction, suction 3. traduction, abduction, obduction, subduction, eduction, deduction, reduction, seduction, induction, conduction, production, affluxion, defluxion, influxion, obstruction, substruction, destruction, instruction, construction 4. nonconduction, reproduction, introduction, manuduction, self-destruction, reconstruction, misconstruction 5. superinduction, overproduction.

UKS'i– 2. mucksy, puxy, druxy 3. Biloxi.

UKS'om– 2. buxom.

UKT'ans– 3. inductance, conductance, reluctance.

UKT'ant– 3. reluctant 4. unreluctant.

UKT'ed– 2. fructed 3. abducted, deducted, inducted, conducted, obstructed, instructed, constructed 4. unobstructed, misconstructed.

UKT'er– 2. ductor 3. abductor, eductor, inductor, conductor, productor, obstructor, destructor, instructor, constructor 4. nonconductor, introductor, manuductor, reconstructor.

UKT'il– 2. ductile 3. inductile, productile.

UKT'ing– 3. abducting, deducting, inducting, conducting, obstructing, instructing, constructing 4. nonconducting, misconducting, reconstructing.

UKT'iv– 3. adductive, traductive, deductive, reductive, seductive, inductive, conductive, productive, obstructive, destructive, instructive, constructive 4. reproductive, introductive, manuductive, self-destructive, reconstructive.

UKT'or– ductor etc., *see* **UKT'er–** ductor etc. above.

UKT'ress– 3. seductress, conductress, instructress 4. introductress.

UKT'ur– 2. structure 3. substructure, constructure 4. superstructure.

UK'us– 2. ruckus, succus.

UL'a– 2. bulla, mullah, nullah, sulla, Sulla, 3. medulla, cuculla, ampulla 4. nulla-nulla.

UL'en–   2. mullein, mullen, sullen, Sullan.

UL'er–   2. duller, huller, color, culler, sculler, luller, mullar, muller, cruller 3. medullar, recolor, tricolor, discolor, miscolor, annuller, ampullar   4. technicolor, versicolor, multicolor, water-color.

UL'erd–   2. dullard, colored   3. recolored, discolored, rose-colored, flesh-colored, fresh-colored, wine-colored   4. multicolored.

UL'est–   2. dullest.

UL'et–   2. gullet, cullet, mullet   3. surmullet.

ULF'er–   2. sulphur.

ULG'ar–   2. Bulgar, fulgor, vulgar.

ULG'at–   2. vulgate, Vulgate   3. promulgate, divulgate.

UL'i–   2. dully, gully, hully, cully, skully, sully, Tully.

UL'id–   2. gullied, sullied   3. unsullied.

UL'ij–   2. ullage, cullage, sullage.

UL'in–   2. mullein, sullen   3. Cuchullin.

UL'ing–   2. dulling, gulling, hulling, culling, lulling, mulling, sculling   3. dehulling, annuling.

UL'is–   2. dullis   3. portcullis.

UL'ish–   2. dullish, gullish.

ULJ'ens–   3. indulgence, effulgence, refulgence, divulgence   4. self-indulgence.

ULJ'ent–   2. fulgent   3. indulgent, effulgent, refulgent, emulgent   4. self-indulgent, interfulgent.

ULJ'er–   2. bulger   3. indulger, promulger, divulger.

ULJ'ing–   2. bulging   3. indulging, effulging, promulging, divulging.

ULJ'ment–   3. indulgement, divulgement.

ULK'at–   2. sulcate   3. inculcate, trisulcate.

ULK'er–   2. bulker, skulker, sulker.

ULK'i–   2. bulky, hulky, sulky.

ULK'ing–   2. bulking, hulking, skulking, sulking.

UL'ment–   3. annulment.

UL'ness–   2. dullness.

ULP'at–   2. culpate   3. inculpate, disculpate, exculpate.

ULP'er–   2. gulper, pulper.

ULP'i–   2. gulpy, pulpy.

ULP'tor–   2. sculptor.

ULS'er–   2. ulcer   3. repulser, expulser.

ULS'et–   2. dulcet.

ULSH'un–   2. pulsion   3. emulsion, demulsion, appulsion, repulsion, impulsion, compulsion, propulsion, expulsion, evulsion, revulsion, divulsion, convulsion.

ULS'ing–   2. pulsing   3. repulsing, expulsing, convulsing.

ULS'iv–   2. pulsive   3. emulsive, appulsive, repulsive, impulsive, compulsive, propulsive, expulsive, revulsive, divulsive, convulsive.

ULST'er–   2. ulster, hulster.

ULT'an–   2. sultan.

ULT'ant–   3. insultant, consultant, resultant, exultant.

ULT'ed–   3. occulted, insulted, consulted, resulted, exulted.

ULT'er–   3. occulter, insulter, consulter, consultor, exulter.

ULT'ing–   3. occulting, insulting, consulting, resulting, exulting.

ULT'iv–   3. consultive, resultive.

ULT'ness–   3. occultness, adultness.

ULT'ra–   2. ultra.

ULT'ri–   2. sultry.

ULT'ur–   2. culture, multure, vulture   4. vegeculture, apiculture, pomiculture, sericulture, floriculture, agriculture, pisciculture, viticulture, horticulture, aviculture, sylviculture, boviculture.

ULV'er–   2. culver, hulver.

UL'yun–   2. scullion, mullion, rullion   3. slumgullion.

UM'a–   2. summa [L.].

UMB'a– 2. dumba, jumba, rumba [Sp.]. 3. calumba, Columba.

UMB'el– 2. umbel, dumbbell.

UMB'ent– 3. accumbent, decumbent, recumbent, incumbent, procumbent, succumbent 5. superincumbent.

UMB'er– 2. umber, cumber, lumbar, lumber, slumber, number 3. encumber, renumber, outnumber 4. disencumber, unencumber, overnumber.

UMB'l– 2. umbel, bumble, fumble, humble, jumble, scumble, mumble, rumble, drumble, grumble, crumble, tumble, stumble 3. bejumble 4. overtumble.

UMB'ler– 2. bumbler, fumbler, humbler, jumbler, mumbler, rumbler, drumbler, grumbler, crumbler, tumbler, stumbler.

UMB'lest– 2. humblest.

UMB'li– 2. bumbly, fumbly, humbly, jumbly, mumbly, rumbly, grumbly, crumbly, tumbly, stumbly.

UMB'ling– 2. bumbling, fumbling, humbling, jumbling, scumbling, mumbling, rumbling, grumbling, crumbling, tumbling, stumbling 3. bejumbling 4. overtumbling.

UMB'o– 2. umbo, gumbo, Jumbo 3. columbo 4. Mumbo Jumbo, mumbo jumbo.

UMB'ra– 2. umbra 3. penumbra.

UMB'ral– 2. umbral 3. adumbral, penumbral.

UMB'rus– 2. umbrous, cumbrous, slumbrous 3. penumbrous.

UM'el– 2. hummel, pummel, pommel, trummel [loc.] 3. bepummel.

UM'er– 2. dumber, gummer, hummer, comer, cummer, scummer, glummer, plumber, slummer, mummer, number, rummer, drummer, strummer, thrummer, summer, thumber 3. incomer, newcomer, latecomer, succumber, midsummer.

UM'est– 2. dumbest, glummest, mummest, numbest.

UM'et– 2. plummet, grummet, summit.

UM'fant– 3. triumphant 4. untriumphant.

UM'i– 2. chummy [coll.], dummy, gummy, glummy, plummy, slummy, mummy, rummy, crumby, crummie, thrummy, tummy, thumby, yummy [slang] 3. gin rummy.

UM'ij– 2. chummage, plumbage, rummage, scrummage, summage 3. rerummage.

UM'ing– 2. bumming, chumming, gumming, humming, coming, scumming, plumbing, plumming, slumming, numbing, drumming, crumbing, strumming, thrumming, summing, thumbing 3. becoming, *incoming, oncoming, forthcoming*, succumbing, benumbing 4. unbecoming, overcoming.

UM'is– 2. pumice, pummice, pomace.

UM'it– 2. plummet, grummet, summit 3. consummate.

UM'li– 2. dumbly, comely, glumly, plumbly, mumly, numbly, rumly 3. uncomely 4. troublesomely, cumbersomely.

UM'nal– 3. columnal, autumnal.

UM'ness– 2. dumbness, glumness, plumbness, numbness.

UM'ok– 2. hummock, drummock, stomach.

UM'oks–? 2. hummocks, lummox, flommox [slang], glommox [dial.], stomachs.

UMP'er– 2. bumper, dumper, jumper, lumper, plumper, pumper, trumper, stumper, thumper 3. broad jumper, high jumper.

UMP'est– 2. plumpest.

UMP'et– 2. crumpet, trumpet, strumpet.

UMP'i– 2. bumpy, chumpy, dumpy, humpy, jumpy, lumpy, clumpy, plumpy, slumpy, frumpy, grumpy, crumpy, stumpy, thumpy.

UMP'ij– 2. pumpage, stumpage.

UMP′ing– 2. bumping, dumping, humping, jumping, lumping, clumping, plumping, slumping, mumping, pumping, trumping, stumping, thumping 3. highjumping 4. hurdle-jumping.

UMP′ish– 2. bumpish, chumpish, dumpish, humpish, jumpish, lumpish, plumpish, mumpish, frumpish, grumpish.

UMP′kin– 2. bumpkin, lumpkin, pumpkin 4. Tony Lumpkin.

UMP′l– 2. rumple, crumple.

UMP′ling– 2. dumpling, rumpling, crumpling 3. uncrumpling.

UMP′shun– 2. gumption 3. assumption, subsumption, resumption, presumption, consumption.

UMP′shus– 2. bumptious, gumptious, scrumptious.

UMPT′iv– 3. assumptive, subsumptive, consumptive, resumptive, presumptive.

UMP′us– 2. compass, rumpus 3. encompass 4. gyrocompass.

UM′uks– 2. lummox, flummox [slang], glommox [dial.], stomachs.

UM′zi– 2. clumsy.

UNCH′er– 2. buncher, huncher, luncher, muncher, puncher, bruncher, cruncher, scruncher 3. *cowpuncher.*

UNCH′ez– 2. bunches, hunches, lunches, munches, punches, brunches, crunches, scrunches.

UNCH′i– 2. bunchy, hunchy, punchy, crunchy, scrunchy.

UNCH′ing– 2. bunching, hunching, lunching, munching, punching, crunching, scrunching.

UNCH′on– 2. luncheon, nuncheon, sconcheon, puncheon, bruncheon, truncheon.

UND′a– 3. rotunda.

UND′an– 2. mundane 4. inframundane, intramundane, extramundane, ultramundane, antemundane, supermundane, intermundane.

UND′ans– 3. abundance, redundance 5. superabundance, overabundance.

UND′ant– 3. abundant, redundant 5. superabundant.

UND′ed– 2. funded 3. refunded, retunded, rotunded.

UND′er– 2. under, dunder, funder, plunder, sunder, thunder, wonder 3. down under, hereunder, thereunder, refunder, asunder, dissunder, rotunder, enthunder.

UND′i– 2. undy, bundy, fundi, Fundy, gundy, gundi, Monday, Sunday 3. Whitsunday 4. salmagundi.

UND′ing– 2. funding 3. refunding.

UND′l– 2. bundle, mundle [dial.], rundle, trundle 3. unbundle.

UND′ld– 2. bundled, trundled 3. unbundled.

UND′ler– 2. bundler, trundler.

UND′let– 2. bundlet, rundlet.

UND′ling– 2. bundling, trundling 3. unbundling.

UND′o– 3. secundo [L.]. 5. basso profundo.

UND′rus– 2. thundrous, wondrous.

UND′um– 3. secundum [L.], corundum 4. carborundum.

UND′us– 2. fundus.

UN′el– 2. funnel, gunnel, gunwale, runnel, trunnel, tunnel.

UN′er– 2. dunner, gunner, cunner, punner, runner, shunner, tonner, stunner 3. rumrunner, gunrunner, forerunner 4. thousand-tonner, overrunner.

UNG′er– 2. hunger, monger, younger 3. warmonger, newsmonger, fishmonger, witmonger 4. ironmonger, fashionmonger, scandalmonger, gossipmonger, costermonger.

UNG′l– 2. bungle, jungle.

UNG′li– 2. bungly, jungly.

UNG′us– 2. fungus 3. mundungus.

UN'i– 2. bunny, dunny, funny, gunny, honey, money, punny, runny, sunny, sonny, tunny.

UN'id– 2. honeyed, moneyed.

UN'ij– 2. dunnage, gunnage, punnage, tonnage.

UN'ing– 2. dunning, funning, gunning, cunning, punning, running, sunning, shunning, tunning, stunning 3. rumrunning, gunrunning, outrunning 4. overrunning.

UN'ish– 2. bunnish, Hunnish, nunnish, punish, punnish.

UNJ'ent– 2. pungent.

UNJ'er– 2. lunger, blunger, plunger, sponger 3. expunger.

UNJ'ez– 2. lunges, plunges, sponges 3. expunges.

UNJ'i– 2. plungy, spongy.

UNJ'ing– 2. lunging, plunging, sponging 3. expunging.

UNJ'un– 2. dungeon 3. Melungeon.

UNK'ard– 2. Dunkard, drunkard.

UNK'en– 2. sunken, drunken, shrunken 3. unsunken, unshrunken.

UNK'er– 2. bunker, dunker, funker, hunker, junker, flunker, punker 3. mossbunker.

UNK'et– 2. junket, tunket [dial.].

UNK'i– 2. chunky, funky, hunky, junky, skunky, flunky, flunkey, punky, punkie, spunky, monkey.

UNK'ish– 2. monkish, punkish, skunkish.

UNK'l– 2. uncle, truncal 3. carbuncle, peduncle, homuncle, caruncle.

UNK'o– 2. bunco, junco.

UNK'shun– 2. unction, function, junction, punction 3. inunction, defunction, adjunction, rejunction, injunction, conjunction, disjunction, compunction, expunction 4. interjunction, interpunction.

UNK'shus– 2. unctious 3. rambunctious, compunctious.

UNKT'iv– 3. abjunctive, adjunctive, subjunctive, conjunctive, disjunctive, compunctive.

UNKT'ur– 2. juncture, puncture 3. conjuncture.

UNK'um– 2. bunkum, Buncombe.

UN'less– 2. punless, runless, sunless, sonless.

UN'let– 2. punlet, runlet, tonlet.

UNSH'al– 2. uncial 3. quinuncial, pronuncial 4. internuncial.

UNST'er– 2. gunster, punster.

UNT'al– 2. puntal, frontal 3. confrontal 4. contrapuntal; see also UNT'l– gruntle etc. below.

UNT'ed– 2. bunted, hunted, blunted, punted, runted, fronted, grunted, shunted stunted, wonted 3. affronted, bifronted, confronted, unwonted.

UNT'er– 2. bunter, hunter, blunter, punter, fronter, grunter, shunter, stunter 3. head-hunter, affronter, confronter 4. fortune hunter.

UNT'est– 2. bluntest.

UNT'i– 2. punty, runty, stunty.

UNT'ij– 2. frontage.

UNT'ing– 2. bunting, hunting, punting, fronting, grunting, shunting, stunting 3. head-hunting, affronting, confronting 4. fortune-hunting.

UNT'l– 2. gruntle 3. disgruntle; see also UNT'al– puntal etc. above.

UNT'ness– 2. bluntness, stuntness.

UNT'o– 2. junto, punto.

UNT'ri– 2. country 3. God's country.

UN'yun– 2. onion, bunion, Bunyan, Runyon, trunnion.

UP'er– 2. upper, cupper, kupper, scupper, crupper, supper.

UP'et– 2. scuppet, puppet.

UP'i– 2. guppy, cuppy, puppy 3. hiccoughy, hiccupy.

UP′ing– 2. cupping, supping, tupping 3. *hiccoughing, hiccuping.*

UP′ish– 2. uppish, cuppish.

UP′l– 2. couple, supple 3. recouple, uncouple, unsupple.

UP′ler– 2. coupler, suppler 3. uncoupler.

UP′lest– 2. supplest.

UP′let– 2. cuplet, couplet 3. *quadruplet, quintuplet.*

UP′shal– 2. nuptial 3. postnuptial 4. antenuptial, internuptial.

UP′shun– 2. ruption 3. abruption, eruption, irruption, corruption, disruption 4. interruption, incorruption 5. uninterruption.

UPT′ed– 3. irrupted, corrupted, disrupted 4. interrupted, uncorrupted, undisrupted 5. uninterrupted.

UPT′er– 3. abrupter, corrupter, disrupter 4. interrupter.

UPT′est– 3. abruptest, corruptest.

UPT′ing– 3. erupting, corrupting, disrupting 4. interrupting.

UPT′iv– 2. ruptive 3. eruptive, irruptive, corruptive, disruptive 4. interruptive, incorruptive.

UPT′li– 3. abruptly, corruptly 4. incorruptly.

UPT′ness– 3. abruptness, corruptness 4. incorruptness.

UPT′ur– 2. rupture 3. disrupture.

UR′a– 2. gurrah 3. goburra 4. korumburra.

UR′al– 3. deferral, referral, demurral.

UR′ant– 2. currant 3. demurrant, susurrant; *see* also UR′ent– current etc. below.

URB′al– 2. herbal, verbal 3. biverbal.

URB′an– 2. urban, Bourbon, turban 3. suburban 4. interruban.

URB′ans– 3. disturbance.

URB′er– 2. Berber, curber, blurber 3. superber, perturber, disturber.

URB′est– 3. superbest.

URB′i– 2. derby, herby, blurby, verby 3. Iturbi.

URB′id– 2. herbid, turbid.

URB′ing– 2. curbing, herbing, blurbing, verbing 3. perturbing, disturbing.

URB′ish– 2. furbish 3. refurbish.

URB′it– 2. turbit, sherbet 3. concurbit.

URB′ot– 2. burbot, turbot.

URCH′ant– 2. merchant.

URCH′en– 2. urchin, birchen.

URCH′er– 2. bircher, lurcher, smircher, nurture, percher, searcher 3. besmircher, researcher.

URCH′ez– 2. birches, churches, lurches, smirches, perches, searches 3. besmirches, researches.

URCH′i– 2. churchy, lurchy, smirchy.

URCH′if– 2. kerchief 3. *neckerchief, handkerchief.*

URCH′in– 2. urchin, birchen.

URCH′ing– 2. birching, churching, lurching, smirching, perching, searching 3. besmirching, researching.

URD′ed– 2. girded, herded, curded, worded 3. begirded, engirded, reworded, misworded.

URD′en– 2. burden, guerdon 3. reburden, disburden 4. overburden.

URD′er– 2. girder, herder, murder 3. absurder, sheepherder.

URD′est– 3. absurdest.

URD′i– 2. birdie, curdy, purdy, sturdy, wordy 4. hurdy-gurdy.

URD′ing– 2. girding, herding, wording 3. begirding, engirding, rewording, miswording.

URD′l– 2. girdle, hurdle, curdle 3. begirdle, engirdle.

URD′li– 2. curdly, thirdly 3. absurdly.

UR′el– 2. burrel, squirrel.

UR′ens– 3. transference, recurrence, incurrence, concurrence, occurrence, deterrence 4. nonconcurrence, intercurrence.

UR′ent– **2.** current, currant **3.** decurrent, recurrent, concurrent, percurrent, crosscurrent, demurrant, susurrant, deterrent **4.** undercurrent, intercurrent.

UR′er– **2.** blurrer, purrer, spurrer, stirrer **3.** deferrer, preferrer, conferrer, transferrer, transferor, concurrer, demurrer, interrer, bestirrer, averrer.

UR′et– **2.** turret.

URF′i– **2.** scurfy, murphy, surfy, turfy.

URF′it– **2.** surfeit.

URG′al– **2.** ergal, tergal, virgal.

URG′er– **2.** burgher **3.** *hamburger.*

URG′l– **2.** ergal, burgle, gurgle, tergal, virgal.

URG′lar– **2.** burglar, gurgler.

URG′o– **2.** ergo [L.], Virgo **3.** a tergo [L.].

URG′us– **2.** Fergus **4.** demiurgus, thaumaturgus, Thaumaturgus.

UR′i– **2.** burry, durrie, firry, furry, gurry, hurry, curry, scurry, lurry, blurry, flurry, slurry, murrey, murry, purry, spurry, surrey, worry, whirry **4.** hurry-scurry.

UR′id– **2.** hurried, curried, scurried, flurried, worried **3.** unhurried, unworried.

UR′ij– **2.** courage, stirrage **3.** encourage, discourage, demurrage.

UR′ing– **2.** erring, burring, churring, furring, blurring, slurring, purring, spurring, shirring, stirring, whirring **3.** unerring, deferring, referring, preferring, inferring, conferring, transferring, recurring, incurring, concurring, occurring, demurring, deterring, interring, bestirring, averring **4.** disinterring.

UR′ish– **2.** burrish, currish, flourish, nourish.

UR′iz– **2.** hurries, curries, scurries, flurries, worries **3.** snow flurries.

URJ′ens– **2.** mergence, vergence **3.** submergence, emergence, resurgence, insurgence, detergence, divergence, convergence.

URJ′ent– **2.** urgent, surgent, vergent **3.** emergent, assurgent, resurgent, insurgent, detergent, abstergent, divergent, convergent.

URJ′er– **2.** urger, berger, dirger, scourger, splurger, merger, purger, perjure, verger, verdure.

URJ′ez– **2.** urges, dirges, scourges, splurges, merges, purges, verges **3.** emerges, asperges, converges.

URJ′i– **2.** clergy, surgy **4.** metallurgy, dramaturgy, thaumaturgy.

URJ′id– **2.** turgid **3.** energid, unturgid.

URJ′ik– **3.** theurgic, energic, chirurgic, liturgic **4.** demiurgic, metallurgic, dramaturgic, thaumaturgic.

URJ′in– **2.** virgin.

URJ′ing– **2.** urging, dirging, scourging, splurging, merging, purging, surging, verging **3.** submerging, emerging, immerging, deterging, diverging, converging.

URJ′ist– **4.** metallurgist, dramaturgist, thaumaturgist.

URJ′ment– **3.** submergement, divergement, convergement.

URJ′on– **2.** burgeon, surgeon, sturgeon.

URK′a– **2.** furca, circa **3.** amurca, mazurka.

URK′al– **2.** furcal, cercal **3.** novercal **4.** homocercal **5.** heterocercal.

URK′er– **2.** burker, jerker, jerquer, kirker, lurker, smirker, perker, shirker, worker **3.** nonworker, *guessworker* **4.** wonder-worker.

URK′i– **2.** jerky, lurky, murky, smirky, perky, shirky, turkey, quirky.

URK′in– **2.** firkin, gherkin, jerkin, perkin.

URK′ing– **2.** irking, jerking, lurking, clerking, smirking, perking, shirking, working, quirking **3.** hard-working, non-working **4.** wonder-working.

URK′ish– **2.** jerkish, clerkish, perkish, Turkish, quirkish.

URK'it– 2. circuit.

URK'l– 2. cercle, circle, turkle 3. encircle, excircle, novercal 4. semicircle, homocercal.

URK'li– 2. Berkeley, clerkly, circly.

URK'ling– 2. circling 3. recircling, encircling 4. semicircling.

URK'som– 2. irksome, murksome, worksome, quirksome.

URK'us– 2. cercus, circus, Quercus.

URL'er– 2. birler, burler, furler, hurler, curler, pearler, purler, twirler, whirler.

URL'et– 2. burlet, pearlet, spurlet.

URL'i– 2. early, burly, churly, girly, girlie, gurly, hurly, curly, murly, knurly, pearly, pirlie [Scot.], surly, Shirley, swirly, twirly, whirly 4. hurly-burly.

URL'in– 2. merlin, murlin, purlin.

URL'ing– 2. birling, furling, herling, hurling, skirling, knurling, pearling, purling, sperling, sterling, thirling, swirling, twirling, whirling.

URL'ish– 2. churlish, girlish, pearlish.

URL'oin– 2. purloin, sirloin.

URL'u– 2. curlew, purlieu.

URM'a– 2. Irma, Burma, derma, syrma, Syrma 4. pachyderma, terra firma.

URM'al– 2. dermal, thermal 3. synthermal 4. pachydermal, epidermal, taxidermal, hypodermal, hydrothermal, isothermal.

URM'an– 2. Burman, firman, Herman, German, germon, merman, Sherman, termen, termon.

URM'ans– 3. affirmance, confirmance 4. disaffirmance.

URM'ent– 2. ferment 3. affirmant, deferment, referment, preferment, determent, interment, averment 4. disinterment.

URM'er– 2. firmer, murmur, termer, termor, wormer, squirmer 3. affirmer, infirmer, confirmer, bemurmur.

URM'est– 2. firmest 3. infirmest.

URM'ez– 2. Hermes, kermes.

URM'i– 2. germy, spermy, wormy 4. taxidermy, diathermy.

URM'ik– 2. dermic, thermic 3. endermic 4. pachydermic, epidermic, taxicermic, diathermic, geothermic.

URM'in– 2. ermine, termin, vermin 3. determine 4. redetermine.

URM'ind– 2. ermined 3. determined 4. redetermined, undetermined.

URM'ing– 2. firming, germing, terming, worming, squirming 3. affirming, confirming.

URM'is– 2. dermis, kermis 4. epidermis, endodermis, exodermis.

URM'ish– 2. skirmish, wormish.

URM'it– 2. hermit, permit.

URM'li– 2. firmly, termly 3. infirmly, unfirmly.

URM'os– 2. hirmos, spermous, thermos.

URM'un– 2. Berman, Herman, German, germen, germon, Sherman, termen, termon.

URN'a– 2. Smyrna, sterna 3. taberna 4. parapherna.

URN'al– 2. urnal, journal, colonel, kernel, sternal, vernal 3. diurnal, hibernal, infernal, supernal, lucernal, maternal, paternal, fraternal, eternal, nocturnal, internal, external, hesternal, cavernal 4. paraphernal, coeternal, diuternal, sempiternal, hodiernal.

URN'ant– 2. vernant 3. alternant, secernent.

URN'at– 2. ternate 3. biternate, quaternate, cothurnate.

URN'ed– 2. learned 3. unlearned.

URN'el– 2. colonel, kernel; see also URN'al– urnal etc. above.

URN'er– 2. earner, burner, churner, learner, pirner, spurner, turner, sterner, yearner 3. adjourner, sojourner, returner, discorner.

URN'est– 2. earnest, Ernest, sternest.

URN'i– 2. burny, ferny, journey, pirnie, tourney 3. enurny, attorney.

URN'ing– 2. earning, urning, burning, derning [dial.], churning, learning, spurning, turning, yearning 3. inurning, adjourning, sojourning, *booklearning*, discerning, concerning, returning, interning, upturning 4. undiscerning, overturning,

URN'is– 2. furnace.

URN'ish– 2. burnish, furnish 3. reburnish, refurnish.

URN'ment– 3. adjournment, sojournment, secernment, discernment, concernment, attornment, internment.

URN'ness– 2. ternness, sternness 3. asternness 4. taciturnness.

URN'o– 3. inferno, Salerno.

URN'um– 2. sternum 3. laburnum, Viburnum, alburnum.

URN'us– 3. cothurnus, Avernus.

UR'o– 2. burro, burrow, borough, furrow, thorough 3. unthorough 4. interborough.

URP'er– 2. burper, chirper 3. hyperper, usurper.

URP'ing– 2. burping [slang], chirping, slurping [dial.] 3. usurping.

URP'l– 2. purple 3. empurple.

URS'a– 2. Ursa, bursa, Byrsa, djersa 3. vice versa.

URS'al– 2. ursal, bursal, cursal 3. rehearsal, bicursal, succursal, dispersal, reversal, transversal 4. interspersal, quaquaversal, universal, partiversal; *see* also URS'l– birsle etc. below.

URS'ant– 2. versant 3. aversant, conversant.

URS'ed– 2. cursed 3. accursed.

URS'er– 2. bursar, curser, cursor, mercer, nurser, purser, terser, verser, versor, worser 3. coercer, disburser, rehearser, accurser, precursor, amercer, disperser,

traverser, reverser, converser 4. reimburser, intersperser.

URS'et– 2. tercet, verset.

URS'ez– 2. hearses, curses, nurses, purses, verses 3. coerces, disburses, rehearses, accurses, precurses, amerces, submerses, immerses, disperses, traverses, reverses, converses 4. reimburses, intersperses, universes.

URSH'al– 2. tertial 3. commercial 4. uncommercial, sesquitertial, controversial.

URSH'an– 2. Persian, tertian 3. Cistercian, lacertian 4. sesquitertian; *see* also URSH'un– mersion etc. below.

URSH'un– 2. mersion, tersion, version 3. coercion, recursion, incursion, excursion, submersion, emersion, immersion, aspersion, dispersion, assertion, desertion, exsertion, insertion, concertion, abstersion, aversion, obversion, subversion, eversion, reversion, diversion, inversion, conversion, perversion 4. interspersion, disconcertion, introversion, retroversion 5. animadversion; *see* also URSH'an– Persian etc. above; URZH'un– version etc. below.

URS'i– 2. mercy, nursy, Percy, pursy, Circe 3. gramercy, Luperci 4. controversy.

URS'ing– 2. cursing, nursing, pursing, versing 3. coercing, disbursing, rehearsing, accursing, immersing, dispersing, traversing, reversing, conversing, transversing 4. reimbursing.

URS'iv– 2. cursive 3. coercive, decursive, recursive, precursive, incursive, discursive, excursive, immersive, aspersive, dispersive, detersive, abstersive, aversive, subversive, eversive, inversive, conversive, perversive, transversive 4. introversive, extroversive.

URS'l– 2. birsle, hirsel, nursle, tercel; *see* also URS'al– ursal etc. above.

URS'let– 2. purslet, verselet.

URS'li– 2. tersely 3. aversely, obversely, adversely, reversely, diversely, inversely, conversely, perversely, transversely.

URS'ling– 2. nurseling, verseling.

URS'ment– 3. imbursement, disbursement, amercement 4. reimbursement.

URS'ness– 2. terseness 3. averseness, adverseness, perverseness.

URS'o– 2. verso 3. concurso, reverso.

URS'on– 2. urson, person.

URST'ed– 2. bursted, thirsted, worsted.

URST'er– 2. burster, thirster.

URST'i– 2. thirsty 3. bloodthirsty, unthirsty.

URST'ing– 2. bursting, thirsting, worsting.

URST'ling– 2. firstling, Hearstling.

URS'us– 2. Ursus, cursus, thyrsus, Thyrsis, versus 3. concursus, excursus, Melursus, adversus [L.], conversus, transversus.

URT'a– 2. Berta, Goethe, serta 3. Alberta, Elberta, Lacerta 4. Ethelberta.

URT'al– 2. curtal 3. consertal.

URT'an– 2. curtain, certain 3. encurtain, uncertain 4. overcurtain, overcertain.

URT'ed– 2. skirted, blurted, flirted, spurted, shirted, squirted, verted 3. alerted, asserted, exerted, inserted, concerted, blackshirted, averted, reverted, diverted, inverted, converted, perverted 4. preconcerted, disconcerted, interserted, undiverted, introverted, extroverted, unperverted.

URT'ens– 3. advertence 4. inadvertence.

URT'ent– 3. advertent 4. inadvertent.

URT'er– 2. hurter, skirter, flirter, curter, perter, spurter, squirter 3. *frank furter*, asserter, inserter, averter, reverter, inverter, converter, perverter 4. preconcerter, disconcerter 5. animadverter.

URT'est– 2. curtest, pertest.

URT'ez– 2. certes, thirties.

URTH'a– 2. bertha, Bertha, Hertha.

URTH'en– 2. earthen, burthen.

URTH'i– 2. earthy, birthy, worthy 3. *seaworthy*, unworthy, *noteworthy*, *trustworthy*, *praiseworthy*.

URTH'less– 2. earthless, birthless, mirthless, worthless.

URTH'li– 2. earthly 3. unearthly.

URT'i– 2. cherty, cherte, dirty, Gertie, flirty, certie, certy [both Scot. & N. of Eng.], thirty.

URT'in– 2. curtain, certain 3. encurtain, uncertain 4. overcurtain, overcertain; *see* also URT'on– burton etc. below.

URT'ing– 2. hurting, skirting, blurting, flirting, spurting, shirting, squirting 3. alerting, deserting, exerting, inserting, concerting, averting, subverting, reverting, diverting, inverting, converting, perverting 4. preconcerting, disconcerting, interserting, retroverting, introverting, extroverting.

URT'iv– 2. furtive 3. assertive, exertive, insertive, revertive, divertive, invertive, convertive 4. self-assertive, introvertive, extrovertive.

URT'l– 2. fertile, hurtle, kirtle, myrtle, Myrtle, spurtle, turtle, whortle 3. infertile.

URT'less– 2. hurtless, skirtless, shirtless.

URT'li– 2. curtly, pertly 3. inertly, alertly, *expertly* 4. *inexpertly*.

URT'ness– 2. curtness, pertness 3. inertness, alertness, *expertness*.

URT'on– 2. burton, Burton, Merton 4. Gammer Gurton; *see* also URT'an– curtain etc. above.

URT'um– 2. furtum [L.], sertum 3. assertum.

UR'us– 2. byrrus, churrus 3. susurrus, susurrous.

URV'a– 2. urva 3. conferva, Minerva.

URV'al– 2. nerval, serval, vervel 3. acerval, conferval, adnerval, minerval.

URV'ans– 3. observance 4. inobservance, nonobservance, unobservance.

URV'ant– 2. fervent, curvant, servant 3. recurvant, observant, maidservant, conservant 4. inobservant, unobservant.

URV'ate– 2. curvate 3. recurvate, incurvate, tricurvate, acervate, trinervate.

URV'er– 2. fervor, nerver, server, swerver 3. unnerver, observer, deserver, reserver, preserver, observer, conserver 4. life preserver.

URV'i– 2. nervy, curvy, scurvy 4. topsy-turvy.

URV'id– 2. fervid 3. perfervid 4. topsy-turvied.

URV'il– 2. chervil, servile, vervel.

URV'ing– 2. Irving, curving, nerving, serving, swerving 3. unnerving, observing, reserving, preserving, conserving, unswerving 4. unobserving, undeserving, unconserving.

URV'is– 2. service 3. reservice, self-service, disservice, sea service, tea service.

URV'less– 2. curveless, nerveless, serveless, verveless, swerveless 3. deserveless, reserveless, preserveless.

URV'us– 2. curvous, nervous 3. confervous, recurvous, unnervous.

URZH'un– 2. version 3. recursion, incursion, discursion, excursion, submersion, immersion, aspersion, dispersion, aversion, subversion, reversion, diversion, inversion, conversion, perversion 5. animadversion.

URZ'i– 2. furzy, jersey, kersey, Mersey.

USCH'un– 2. fustian 3. combustion, inustion.

US'el– 2. mussel, Russel, trussell; see also US'l– bustle etc. below.

US'er– 2. busser, fusser, cusser, musser, trusser 3. discusser, nonplusser.

US'et– 2. gusset, russet.

US'ez– 2. busses, fusses, cusses [coll.], plus-ses, musses, trusses 3. discusses, nonplusses, untrusses.

USH'a– 2. Russia, Prussia.

USH'er– 2. usher, gusher, husher, lusher, blusher, flusher, plusher, rusher, brusher, crusher, shusher 3. fourflusher.

USH'est– 2. lushest, flushest, plushest.

USH'ez– 2. gushes, hushes, blushes, flushes, plushes, mushes, rushes, brushes, crushes, thrushes, tushes 3. four-flushes.

USH'i– 2. gushy, lushy, blushy, plushy, slushy, rushy, brushy, thrushy.

USH'ing– 2. gushing, hushing, mushing, blushing, flushing, rushing, brushing, crushing 3. unblushing, four-flushing, onrushing.

USH'un– 2. Russian, Prussian 3. recussion, incussion, concussion, percussion, discussion, succussion 4. repercussion.

US'i– 2. fussy, Gussie, hussy, mussy 4. overfussy.

US'ing– 2. bussing, fussing, cussing [coll.], mussing, trussing 3. discussing, nonplussing, untrussing.

US'iv– 2. jussive, tussive 3. concussive, percussive, discussive, successive 4. repercussive.

USK'an– 2. dusken, Tuscan 3. molluscan, Etruscan.

USK'er– 2. husker, tusker 3. cornhusker.

USK'et– 2. busket, musket.

USK'i– 2. dusky, husky, musky, tusky.

USK'in– 2. buskin, ruskin, Ruskin.

USK'ing– 2. dusking, husking, tusking 3. cornhusking.

USK'ul– 3. majuscule, minuscule, crepuscule, opuscule.

US'l– 2. bustle, duscle, hustle, justle, mussel, muscle, rustle, Russell, trussell, tussal, tussle 3. arbuscle, crepuscle, opuscle, corpuscle.

US'ler– 2. bustler, hustler, rustler, tussler.

US'li– 2. muscly, rustly, thusly.

US'ling– 2. bustling, hustling, muscling, rustling, tussling.

US'lz– 2. bustles, hustles, muscles, rustles, Brussels, tussles.

UST'a– 2. crusta 3. Augusta.

UST'ard– 2. bustard, custard, mustard; *see* also UST'erd– bustard, lustered etc. below.

UST'e– 2. fustee, fustie, mustee.

UST'ed– 2. busted, dusted, lusted, rusted, crusted, trusted 3. combusted, bedusted, disgusted, adjusted, encrusted, entrusted, distrusted, mistrusted 4. maladjusted.

UST'er– 2. buster, duster, juster, Custer, luster, bluster, fluster, cluster, muster, rustre, truster, thruster 3. robuster, trust buster, adjuster, adjustor, lackluster, distruster, mistruster 4. filibuster, readjuster, coadjuster.

UST'erd– 2. bustard, custard, lustered, blustered, flustered, clustered, mustered, mustard, rustred 3. beflustered, unclustered.

UST'est– 2. justest 3. robustest.

UST'ful– 2. gustful, lustful, trustful, thrustful 3. disgustful, untrustful, distrustful, mistrustful 4. overtrustful.

UST'i– 2. busty, dusty, fusty, gusty, lusty, musty, rusty, crusty, trusty.

UST'ik– 2. bustic, fustic, rustic 4. anacrustic.

UST'ing– 2. busting, dusting, husting, lusting, rusting, crusting, trusting, thrusting 3. bedusting, disgusting, adjusting, encrusting, entrusting, distrusting, mistrusting 4. readjusting, maladjusting, coadjusting, self-adjusting.

UST'is– 2. justice, Custis 3. injustice.

UST'iv– 3. combustive, adjustive.

UST'li– 2. justly 3. robustly, augustly, unjustly.

UST'ment– 3. adjustment, encrustment, entrustment 4. readjustment, maladjustment.

UST'ness– 2. justness 3. robustness, augustness, unjustness.

UST'ral– 2. lustral 3. lacustral, palustral.

UST'rat– 2. frustrate 3. illustrate.

UST'rum– 2. lustrum, flustrum.

UST'rus– 2. lustrous, blustrous 3. lacklustrous.

UST'um– 2. custom 3. accustom 4. reaccustom.

UST'us– 2. Justus 3. Augustus.

UT'a– 2. gutta 3. Calcutta.

UT'al– 3. abuttal, rebuttal 4. surrebuttal; *see* also UT'l– buttle etc. below.

UT'e– 2. puttee, ruttee, suttee.

UT'ed– 2. butted, gutted, jutted, smutted, nutted, rutted, strutted 3. abutted, rebutted 4. unrebutted.

UT'er– 2. utter, butter, cutter, scutter, flutter, glutter, clutter, splutter, mutter, nutter, putter, sputter, rutter, strutter, shutter, stutter 3. abutter, rebutter, woodcutter, stonecutter, meatcutter 4. bread-and-butter, peanut butter, surrebutter.

UT'erd– 2. uttered, buttered, fluttered, muttered, sputtered, shuttered, stuttered 3. unuttered, well-buttered, unfluttered.

UTH'er– 2. other, mother, smother, brother, tother 3. *grandmother*, another.

UTH'ern– 2. southern.

UT'i– 2. butty, gutty, jutty, cutty, scutty, smutty, nutty, putty, puttee, rutty.

UT'ing– 2. butting, gutting, jutting, cutting, glutting, smutting, nutting, putting, rutting, strutting, shutting 3. abutting, rebutting, woodcutting, stonecutting, crosscutting.

UT'ish– 2. sluttish, nuttish, ruttish.

UT'l– 2. buttle, guttle, cuttle, scuttle, ruttle, subtle, suttle, shuttle 3. abuttal, rebuttal, unsubtle 4. surrebuttal.

UT'ler– 2. butler, cutler, cuttler, scuttler, ruttler, subtler, sutler.

UT'let– 2. cutlet.

UT'li– 2. subtly 3. unsubtly.

UT'ling– 2. buttling, gutling [dial.], guttling, scuttling.

UT'ment– 2. butment 3. abutment, rebutment.

UT'on– 2. button, glutton, mutton 3. *bluebutton* 5. bachelor-button.

UV'ed– 3. beloved.

UV'el– 2. hovel, scovel, shovel.

UV'en– 2. oven, sloven.

UV'er– 2. hover, lover, glover, plover, cover, shover 3. windhover, recover, uncover, discover, self-lover 4. undercover, rediscover.

UV'i– 2. covey, lovey 4. lovey-dovey.

UV'ing– 2. loving, gloving, shoving 3. unloving, ungloving, self-loving.

UV'li– 2. lovely 3. unlovely.

UZ'ard– 2. buzzard, huzzard.

UZ'en– 2. dozen, cozen, cousin.

UZ'er– 2. buzzer, nuzzer.

UZ'ez– 2. buzzes, fuzzes, muzzes.

UZ'i– 2. buzzy, fuzzy, hussy, huzzy, muzzy 4. fuzzy-guzzy, fuzzy-wuzzy.

UZ'ing– 2. buzzing, fuzzing, muzzing.

UZ'l– 2. buzzle, guzzle, muzzle, nuzzle, puzzle 3. bemuzzle, unmuzzle, bepuzzle 4. crossword puzzle, jigsaw puzzle, Chinese puzzle.

UZ'ler– 2. guzzler, muzzler, puzzler.

UZ'lin– 2. muslin,

UZ'ling– 2. guzzling, muzzling, nuzzling, puzzling 3. bemuzzling, unmuzzling, bepuzzling.

UZ'n– 2. dozen, cozen, cousin.

U (tub)

3.

TRIPLE RHYMES IN U (tub′ba-ble)

Primary or Secondary Accent Falls on
Second from Last Syllable.

UB′a–bl– 3. clubbable, scrubbable, tubbable.

UB′er–er– 3. blubberer, slubberer, rubberer.

UR′er–i– 3. blubbery, rubbery, scrubbery, shrubbery.

UB′i–er– 3. chubbier, grubbier, scrubbier, shrubbier, tubbier, stubbier.

UB′il–i– 3. chubbily, grubbily, scrubbily, tubbily, stubbily.

UB′i–ness– 3. chubbiness, grubbiness, scrubbiness, shrubbiness, tubbiness, stubbiness.

UB′lik–an– 3. publican 4. republican.

UB′lish–er– 3. publisher 4. republisher.

UD′er–i– 3. duddery, shuddery, studdery.

UD′i–er– 3. bloodier, muddier, ruddier, studier.

UD′i–est– 3. bloodiest, muddiest, ruddiest.

UD′il–i– 3. bloodily, muddily, ruddily.

UD′i–ness– 3. bloodiness, muddiness, ruddiness.

UF′a–bl– 3. buffable, bluffable, ruffable 4. rebuffable, unruffable 5. unrebuffable.

UF′i–er– 3. huffier, fluffier, snuffier, puffier, stuffier.

UF′il–i– 3. huffily, fluffily, snuffily, puffily, stuffily.

UF′i–ness– 3. huffiness, fluffiness, snuffiness, puffiness, stuffiness.

UF′ing–li– 3. buffingly, huffingly, bluffingly, fluffingly, snuffingly, puffingly, stuffingly 4. rebuffingly 5. unrebuffingly.

UG′a–bl– 3. huggable, pluggable.

UG′er–i– 3. snuggery, pugaree, druggery, thuggery.

UG′i–ness– 3. bugginess, slugginess, mugginess, pugginess.

UJ′a–bl– 3. judgeable 4. adjudgeable.

UJ′er–i– 3. drudgery, grudgery.

UJ′i–ness– 3. smudginess.

UK′er–ing– 3. puckering, succoring.

UK′i–ness– 3. luckiness, pluckiness, muckiness 4. unluckiness.

UK′shun–al– 3. fluxional, suctional 4. inductional, reductional, conductional, productional, destructional, instructional, constructional.

UK′shun–ist– 3. fluxionist 4. productionist, obstructionist, destructionist, constructionist 5. reconstructionist.

UKT′i–bl– 4. deductible, conductible, productible, destructible, instructible, constructible 5. undeductible, indestructible, uninstructible.

UKT′iv–li– 4. deductively, seductively, inductively, productively, obstructively, destructively, instructively, constructively 5. unproductively.

UKT′iv–ness– 4. seductiveness, productiveness, destructiveness, instructiveness, constructiveness 5. unproductiveness, reconstructiveness.

279

UKT'or–i– 4. deductory, inductory, conductory 5. reproductory, introductory, manuductory.

UK'ul–ens– 3. truculence, succulence.

UK'ul–ent– 3. truculent, succulent.

UL'er–i– 3. gullery, colory, skullery, scullery 4. medullary.

ULK'i–ness– 3. bulkiness, sulkiness.

UL'min–ant– 3. fulminant, culminant.

UL'min–at– 3. fulminate, culminate.

ULS'if–i– 3. dulcify 4. emulsify.

ULS'iv–li– 4. repulsively, impulsively, compulsively, revulsively, convulsively.

ULS'iv–ness– 4. repulsiveness, impulsiveness, compulsiveness, revulsiveness, convulsiveness.

ULS'or–i– 4. compulsory, expulsory 5. uncompulsory.

ULT'a–bl– 4. insultable, consultable 5. uninsultable, unconsultable.

ULT'im–it– 3. ultimate 4. penultimate 6. antepenultimate.

ULT'ing–li– 4. insultingly, exultingly.

ULT'ur–al– 3. cultural 5. agricultural, floricultural, horticultural.

ULT'ur–ist– 3. culturist 5. apiculturist, agriculturist, floriculturist, horticulturist.

UM'aj–er– 3. rummager, scrummager.

UM'ar–i– 3. nummary, summary; see also UM'er–i– chummery etc. below.

UM'ar–ist– 3. summarist.

UMB'ens–i– 3. cumbency 4. decumbency, recumbency, incumbency.

UMB'er–er– 3. cumberer, lumberer, slumberer, numberer 4. encumberer.

UMB'er–i– 3. slumbery.

UMB'er–ing– 3. cumbering, lumbering, slumbering, numbering 4. encumbering, unslumbering, outnumbering.

UMB'er–som– 3. cumbersome, slumbersome, numbersome.

UMB'er–us– 3. slumberous, numberous 4. unslumberous.

UMB'ling–li– 3. rumblingly, tumblingly, stumblingly.

UM'er–i– 3. chummery, flummery, plumbery, nummary, mummery, summary, summery.

UM'er–ing– 3. summering.

UM'ing–li– 3. hummingly, numbingly 4. becomingly, benumbingly 5. unbecomingly.

UMP'i–ness– 3. dumpiness, humpiness, jumpiness, frumpiness, grumpiness, stumpiness.

UMP'ish–ness– 3. dumpishness, lumpishness, mumpishness, frumpishness, grumpishness.

UMP'shus–li– 3. bumptiously, scrumptiously.

UMP'shus–ness– 3. bumptiousness, scrumptiousness 4. assumptiousness.

UMPT'iv–li– 4. assumptively, resumptively, presumptively, consumptively.

UMPT'u–us– 3. sumptuous 4. presumptuous, unsumptuous.

UN'a–bl– 3. punnable, runnable, shunnable.

UNCH'a–bl– 3. punchable, crunchable.

UND'a–bl– 3. fundable 4. refundable.

UND'ant–li– 4. abundantly, redundantly 6. superabundantly.

UND'er–er– 3. blunderer, plunderer, sunderer, thunderer, wonderer.

UND'er–ing– 3. blundering, plundering, sundering, thundering, wondering.

UND'er–us– 3. plunderous, thunderous.

UND'it–i– 4. profundity, fecundity, jocundity, immundity, obtundity, rotundity 5. moribundity, rubicundity, orotundity.

UN'er–i– 3. gunnery, nunnery.

UNG'ar–i– 3. Hungary.

UNG'er–ing– 3. hungering, mongering 4. wordmongering, warmongering, newsmongering 5. scandalmongering, ironmongering.

UN'il–i– 3. funnily, sunnily 4. unfunnily.

UNK'shun–al– 3. unctional, functional, junctional 4. conjunctional.

UNKT'iv–li– 4. adjunctively, subjunctively, conjunctively, disjunctively.

UNK'u–lar– 3. uncular 4. carbuncular, peduncular, caruncular, avuncular.

UNT'ed–li– 3. huntedly, stuntedly, wontedly 4. affrontedly, unwontedly.

UNT'ed–ness– 3. huntedness, bluntedness, stuntedness, wontedness 4. affrontedness, unwontedness.

UNT'i–ness– 3. puntiness, runtiness, stuntiness.

UNT'ing–li– 3. buntingly, huntingly, gruntingly, stuntingly.

UP'le–ment– 3. supplement.

UPT'iv–li– 4. corruptively, disruptively 5. interruptively.

URB'a–bl– 3. curbable 4. uncurbable, perturbable 5. imperturbable, indisturbable, undisturbable.

URB'al–ist– 3. herbalist, verbalist.

URB'i–al– 4. suburbial, adverbial, proverbial.

URD'er–er– 3. murderer, verderer.

URD'il–i– 3. sturdily, wordily.

URD'i–ness– 3. curdiness, sturdiness, wordiness.

URD'it–i– 4. absurdity.

UR'ens–i– 3. currency 4. recurrency, concurrency.

UR'ent–li– 3. currently 4. recurrently, concurrently.

UR'id–li– 3. hurriedly, flurriedly, worriedly.

UR'i–er– 3. burrier, furrier, hurrier, currier, courier, scurrier, purrier, worrier.

UR'i–ing– 3. burying, hurrying, flurrying, currying, scurrying, worrying.

UR'i–ment– 3. flurriment, worriment.

UR'ish–ing– 3. flourishing, nourishing 4. unflourishing, unnourishing.

URJ'en–si– 3. urgency, vergency 4. emergency, assurgency, insurgency, detergency, divergency, convergency.

URJ'er–i– 3. perjury, purgery, surgery, vergery 4. chirurgery.

URJ'ik–al– 3. surgical 4. theurgical, energical, liturgical 5. demiurgical, metallurgical, thaumaturgical.

URK'il–i– 3. jerkily, perkily, murkily.

URK'ul–ar– 3. furcular, circular 4. tubercular, opercular 5. semicircular.

URK'ul–at– 3. circulate 4. tuberculate, operculate, recirculate.

URK'ul–um– 3. furculum 4. tuberculum, operculum.

URK'ul–us– 3. circulus, surculus, surculous 4. tuberculous.

URL'a–bl– 3. furlable 4. unfurlable.

URL'i–er– 3. earlier, burlier, churlier, curlier, pearlier, surlier.

URL'i–est– 3. earliest, burliest, churliest, curliest, pearliest, surliest.

URL'i–ness– 3. earliness, burliness, curliness, pearliness, surliness.

URL'ish–ness– 3. churlishness, girlishness.

URM'an–i– 3. Germany, verminy.

URM'ar–i– 4. infirmary.

URM'at–iv– 4. affirmative, confirmative.

URM'in–al– 3. germinal, terminal 4. adterminal, conterminal.

URM'in–ant– 3. germinant, terminant 4. determinant, interminant, conterminant.

URM'in–at– 3. germinate, terminate 4. determinate, interminate, exterminate 5. predeterminate, indeterminate.

URM'in–us– 3. terminus, verminous 4. coterminous.

URM'it–i– 4. infirmity, confirmity.

URM'it–ij– 3. hermitage.

URN'a–bl– 3. burnable, learnable, turnable 4. unburnable, unlearnable, returnable 5. unreturnable, overturnable; *see* also URN'i–bl– discernible etc. below.

URN'al–i– 3. vernally 4. infernally, eternally, externally.

URN'al–ist– 3. journalist 4. eternalist, externalist.

URN'al–iz– 3. journalize 4. infernalize, eternalize, externalize.

URN'al–izm– 3. journalism 4. infernalism, eternalism, externalism.

URN'ed–li– 3. learnedly 4. unlearnedly, concernedly 5. unconcernedly.

URN'er–i– 3. fernery, ternery, turnery.

URN'i–a– 3. hernia 4. Hibernia, Calpurnia, Saturnia, evernia.

URN'i–an– 4. eburnean, Hibernian, Falernian, Saturnian.

URN'i–bl– 4. discernible 5. indiscernible; *see* also URN'a–bl– burnable etc. above.

URN'ish–er– 3. burnisher, furnisher 4. refurnisher.

URN'ish–ing– 3. burnishing, furnishing 4. refurnishing.

URN'it–i– 4. modernity, maternity, fraternity, eternity, alternity 5. sempiternity, taciturnity, diuturnity.

URN'it–ur– 3. furniture, cerniture.

UR'o–er– 3. burrower, furrower.

URP'en–tin– 3. serpentine, turpentine.

URP'i–li– 3. burpily [slang], chirpily, slurpily [dial.].

URP'i–ness– 3. burpiness [slang], chirpiness, slurpiness [dial.].

URS'a–bl– 4. amerceable, traversable, reversable, inversable, conversable; *see* also URS'i–bl– coercible etc. below.

URS'ar–i– 3. bursary 5. anniversary; *see* also URS'or–i– cursory, etc. below.

URS'er–i– 3. cursory, nursery 4. precursory, discursory, aspersory.

URSH'i–a– 3. tertia 4. inertia 5. sesquitertia.

URSH'i–an– 3. Persian, tertian 4. lacertian, Cistercian 5. sesquitertian.

URS'i–bl– 4. coercible, submersible, immersible, reversible, conversible 5. incoercible, introversible; *see* also URS'a–bl– amerceable etc. above.

URS'i–form– 3. ursiform, bursiform, furciform, versiform 4. diversiform.

URS'it–i– 4. adversity, diversity, perversity 5. university.

URS'iv–li– 4. decursively, discursively, excursively, aspersively, dispersively, detersively.

URS'iv–ness– 4. coerciveness, discursiveness, excursiveness, detersiveness.

URS'on–al– 3. personal 4. tripersonal, impersonal 5. unipersonal.

URS'or–i– 3. cursory 4. precursory, discursory, aspersory; *see* also URS'ar–i– bursary etc. above.

URT'en–si– 4. advertency 5. inadvertency.

URT'es–i– 3. courtesy 4. discourtesy.

URTH'i–li– 3. worthily 4. unworthily.

URTH'less–ness– 3. mirthlessness, worthlessness.

URT'i–bl– 4. insertable, avertible, subvertible, revertible, divertible, invertible, convertible, pervertible 5. inconvertible, controvertible.

URT'in–ent– 3. pertinent 4. impertinent, unpertinent.

URT'is–ment– 4. advertisement, divertisement.

URV'a–bl– 3. servable 4. observable, reservable, preservable, conservable.

URV'at–iv– 3. curvative 4. observative, reservative, preservative, conservative.

URV'ed–li– 3. fervidly 4. observedly, deservedly, reservedly 5. undeservedly, unreservedly.

URV′ens-i– **3.** fervency **4.** observancy, conservancy.

URV′il-i– **3.** nervily, swervily **5.** topsy-turvily.

URV′it-i– **3.** curvity **4.** recurvity, incurvity.

URZH′un-al– **3.** versional **4.** excursional, reversional, conversional.

URZH′un-ist– **3.** versionist **4.** excursionist, immersionist, aversionist, reversionist, conversionist.

US′a-bl– **3.** mussable **4.** discussable **5.** undiscussable.

USH′a-bl– **3.** hushable, flushable, brushable, crushable **4.** unhushable, uncrushable.

USH′il-i– **3.** gushily, mushily.

USH′i-ness– **3.** gushiness, mushiness.

USH′ing-li– **3.** gushingly, blushingly, rushingly, crushingly.

USK′il-i– **3.** duskily, huskily, muskily.

USK′i-ness– **3.** duskiness, huskiness, muskiness.

USK′ul-ar– **3.** muscular **4.** majuscular, bimuscular, nonmuscular, unmuscular, minuscular, crepuscular, opuscular, corpuscular.

USK′ul-us– **3.** musculus **4.** crepusculous, corpusculous.

UST′a-bl– **3.** rustable, trustable **4.** adjustable **5.** readjustable, inadjustable; *see* also UST′i-bl– combustible etc. below.

UST′er-er– **3.** blusterer, flusterer, musterer.

UST′er-i– **3.** blustery, flustery, clustery.

UST′er-ing– **3.** blustering, flustering, clustering, mustering.

UST′ful-i– **3.** gustfully, lustfully, trustfully **4.** disgustfully, distrustfully, mistrustfully.

UST′i-bl– **4.** combustible **5.** incombustible, noncombustible, uncombustible; *see* also UST′a-bl– rustable etc. above.

UST′i-er– **3.** dustier, fustier, gustier, lustier, mustier, rustier, crustier, trustier.

UST′i-est– **3.** dustiest, fustiest, gustiest, lustiest, mustiest, rustiest, crustiest, trustiest.

UST′il-i– **3.** dustily, fustily, gustily, lustily, mustily, rustily, crustily, trustily.

UST′i-ness– **3.** dustiness, fustiness, gustiness, lustiness, mustiness, rustiness, crustiness, trustiness.

UST′ri-us– **4.** industrious, illustrious.

UT′er-er– **3.** utterer, butterer, flutterer, splutterer, mutterer, putterer, sputterer, stutterer.

UT′er-i– **3.** buttery, guttery, fluttery, spluttery, muttery, puttery, sputtery, stuttery.

UT′er-ing– **3.** uttering, buttering, guttering, fluttering, spluttering, muttering, puttering, sputtering, shuttering, stuttering.

UTH′er-er– **3.** motherer, smotherer.

UTH′er-ing– **3.** mothering, smothering, brothering, southering.

UTH′er-li– **3.** motherly, brotherly, southerly **4.** unmotherly, unbrotherly.

UT′ing-li– **3.** juttingly, cuttingly, struttingly.

UT′ler-i– **3.** butlery, cutlery, sutlery.

UT′on-i– **3.** buttony, gluttony, muttony.

UV′a-bl– **3.** lovable, shovable **4.** unlovable.

UV′el-er– **3.** hoveler, shoveler.

UV′er-er– **3.** hoverer, coverer **4.** recoverer, uncoverer, discoverer.

UV′er-i– **3.** plovery **4.** recovery, discovery.

UV′er-ing– **3.** hovering, covering **4.** recovering, uncovering, discovering.

UZ′i-li– **3.** fuzzily, muzzily, wuzzily [slang].

UZ′i-ness– **3.** fuzziness, hussiness, muzziness, wuzziness [slang].

bandolero, campanero, zapatero [all Sp.]; *see* also **AR'o–** arrow etc.

AR'u– 2. Meru, Nehru.

AR'um– 2. arum, garum, harem, carrom, scare 'em etc. 4. harumscarum 9. scientia scientiarum.

AS'a– 2. Asa, mesa, presa [It.], vasa [L.] 3. cabeza [Sp.].

AS'al– 2. basal, casal, vasal 3. oasal.

AS'eez– 2. bases 3. oases.

AS'en– 2. basin, facin' etc., hasten, Jason, chasten, mason, sasin 3. *washbasin*, enchasten, freemason, *stonemason*; *see* also **AS'on–** caisson etc. below.

AS'ens– 3. abaisance, obeisance, adjacence, complaisance, complacence, renascence, connascence 4. interjacence, uncomplaisance.

AS'ent– 2. jacent, nascent, naissant 3. obeisant, subjacent, adjacent, complacent, renascent, renaissant, connascent 4. circumjacent, interjacent, uncomplacent.

AS'er– 2. Acer, baser, chaser, facer, caser, lacer, placer, macer, pacer, spacer, racer, bracer, tracer 3. abaser, debaser, defacer, effacer, eraser, horse racer, embracer, begracer, disgracer, retracer, encaser, belacer, enlacer, unlacer, grimacer, outpacer, replacer, misplacer, displacer 4. steeplechaser, interlacer

AS'ez– aces, etc. *see* **AS–** ace etc. above, plus "s" or "'s."

AS'ful– 2. spaceful, graceful 3. ungraceful, disgraceful.

ASH'a– 2. Asia, geisha 3. Acacia, Dalmatia.

ASH'al– 2. facial, glacial, spatial, racial 3. abbatial, palatial, prelatial, primatial 4. unifacial, interspatial, interracial.

ASH'an– 2. Asian 3. predacean, phocacean, cetacean, testacean, crustacean; *see* also **ASH'un–** nation etc. below.

ASH'ens– 2. facients, patience, patients 3. impatience, outpatients.

ASH'ent– 2. facient, patient 3. impatient, outpatient 4. sorbefacient, rubefacient, calefacient, tumefacient, stupefacient, somnifacient, liquefacient.

ASH'un– 2. nation, ration, station 3. cibation, libation, limbation, jobation, probation, placation, vacation, peccation, plication, sulcation, truncation, location, vocation, furcation, piscation, gradation, foundation, laudation, sudation, creation, legation, ligation, rogation, purgation, jugation, striation, alation, halation, ablation, oblation, sublation, elation, delation, gelation, relation, velation, deflation, sufflation, inflation, conflation, dilation, vallation, illation, collation, prolation, cremation, sigmation, himation, gemmation, commation, summation, formation, planation, adnation, enation, agnation, signation, cognation, damnation, conation, donation, phonation, pronation, lunation, libration, vibration, hydration, ceration, spheration, migration, liration, oration, moration, nitration, titration, filtration, curation, duration, neuration, gyration, cessation, causation, pausation, natation, jactation, lactation, tractation, dictation, nictation, citation, saltation, peltation, cantation, plantation, dentation, mentation, tentation, floatation, notation, potation, rotation, quotation, votation, captation, septation, flirtation, hortation, curtation, substation, gestation, testation, crustation, gustation, guttation, lutation, mutation, nutation, putation, equation, lavation, ovation, novation, starvation, nervation, servation, curvation, laxation, taxation, vexation, fixation, luxation, fluxation 4. reprobation, approbation, perturbation, accubation, incubation, titubation, intubation, desiccation, exsiccation, deprecation, imprecation, comprecation, albication, radication, abdication, dedication, medication, predication, indication, vindication, syndication, replication, triplication, implication, complication, application, supplication, duplication, explica-

APOLLO EDITIONS

Thomas Y. Crowell, Publishers
Established 1834
10 E. 53rd St., New York, N.Y. 10022

ISBN: 0-8152-0080-3

cover design by Rupert Finegold